The Urban Underclass

THE
URBAN
UNDERCLASS

CHRISTOPHER JENCKS
PAUL E. PETERSON
EDITORS

THE BROOKINGS INSTITUTION
WASHINGTON, D.C.

Library of Congress Cataloging-in-Publication Data

The Urban underclass / Christopher Jencks and Paul E. Peterson,
editors.
    p.   cm.
   Includes bibliographical references and index.
   ISBN 0-8157-4606-7 (cloth)
   ISBN 0-8157-4605-9 (pbk.)
    1. Urban poor—United States.   2. Afro-Americans—Economic
conditions.   3. Afro-Americans—Social conditions.   4. Inner
cities—United States.   5. Urban policy—United States.
6. United States—Race relations.   I. Jencks, Christopher.
II. Peterson, Paul E.
HV4045.U73   1990
305.5'69'0973091732—dc20   90-23619
                                                              CIP

9   8   7   6   5

Preface

CONVENTIONAL WISDOM tells us that the United States *is* witnessing a significant growth in the size of its urban underclass. Many believe that the percentage of the population persistently poor is large and rapidly increasing, that more and more unmarried teenage girls are bearing children, and that welfare rolls are exploding. It is frequently alleged that crime is on the increase, young people are dropping out of school in record numbers, and higher percentages of the population are withdrawing from the labor force. The poor are also said to be increasingly isolated in ghettos at the cores of our metropolitan areas.

Yet none of these propositions is true. The essays on the urban underclass in this book try to separate the truth about poverty, social dislocation, and changes in American family life from the myths that have become part of contemporary folklore. They show that the most important problem—the rise in the percentage of children living in poverty—is due to the increasing number of female-headed households and the decline in the earnings of young men. They demonstrate that the main issue is not so much a growth in the size of the underclass as the persistence of poverty decades after the country thought it had addressed the problem. And they point out that the paradox of poverty in a wealthy nation will continue until society makes greater efforts to provide all citizens with improved educational and economic opportunities as well as adequate income maintenance in times of need.

These essays were initially presented at a conference held at Northwestern University in October 1989 that was sponsored by the Social Science Research Council's Committee for Research on the Urban Underclass and Northwestern University's Center for Urban Affairs and Policy Research. We especially wish to thank Martha Gephart, Robert Pearson, and Raquel Rivera, senior staff members of the Committee for Research on the Urban Underclass, who helped plan the conference, identify presenters, discussants, and other participants, obtain written comments from discussants, and prepare the volume. We also wish to thank Hervey Juris, then acting director of the center, who initiated the idea of a conference and took responsibility for the logistical arrangements at Northwestern University. The discussants at the conference were J. Lawrence Aber, Mary Jo Bane, Rebecca Blank, Barry Bluestone, John Bound, Philippe Bourgois, Anthony Bryk, Sheldon Danziger, David Elwood, Edward Gramlich, Mark Hughes, Sara McLanahan, Ruth Massinga, John Ogbu, Isabel Sawhill, and Linda Williams.

James Schneider and Nancy Davidson edited the book, Todd Quinn verified the manuscript, Eje Wray assisted in the physical preparation of the manuscript, and Max Franke compiled the index.

Financial assistance for the conference was made available by the Rockefeller Foundation, the Ford Foundation, and Northwestern University's Center for Urban Affairs and Policy Research. Additional financial assistance to the editors was provided by the Joseph B. Grossman Fund of the Center for American Political Studies at Harvard University.

The views expressed in this book are those of the authors and should not be ascribed to the people or organizations whose assistance is acknowledged above, to any agency that funded research reported here, or to the trustees, officers, or staff members of the Brookings Institution.

CHRISTOPHER JENCKS
March 1991   PAUL E. PETERSON

Contents

TABLES

Paul E. Peterson

Christopher Jencks

FIGURES

Part One ─────────────────────────────────
Thinking about the Underclass

The Urban Underclass and the Poverty Paradox

PAUL E. PETERSON

THE URBAN UNDERCLASS is at once a characterization of a fragment of American society, a statement about the interconnections among diverse social problems, and an attempt to theorize about the paradox of poverty in an affluent society. The term is powerful because it calls attention to the conjunction between the characters of individuals and the impersonal forces of the larger social and political order. "Class" is the least interesting half of the word. Although it implies a relationship between one social group and another, the terms of that relationship are left undefined until combined with the familiar word "under." This transformation of a preposition into an adjective has none of the sturdiness of "working," the banality of "middle," or the remoteness of "upper." Instead "under" suggests the lowly, passive, and submissive, yet at the same time the disreputable, dangerous, disruptive, dark, evil, and even hellish. And apart from these personal attributes, it suggests subjection, subordination, and deprivation. All these meanings are perhaps best brought together in Richard Wagner's *The Ring of the Nibelung.* Wotan goes under the earth to wrest the ring from the malicious Alberich, who had used it to enslave a vile and debased subhuman population.

Because of these diverse meanings, underclass is a word that can be used by conservatives, liberals, and radicals alike. It is a fitting term for conservatives who wish to identify those people who are unable to care for themselves or their families or are prone to antisocial behavior. But underclass, like lumpen proletariat, is also a suitable concept for those who, like Karl Marx, want to identify a group shaped and dominated by a society's economic and political forces but who have no productive role. And underclass is acceptable to some liberals who somewhat ambiguously refuse to choose between these contrasting images but who nonetheless wish to distinguish between the mainstream of working-class and middle-class America and those who seem separate from or marginal to that society. But, above all, the concept has been called back into the so-

3

cial science lexicon because it offers an explanation for the paradox of poverty in an otherwise affluent society that seems to have made strenuous efforts to eradicate this problem.

Two recent analyses of the urban underclass, Charles Murray's *Losing Ground* (1984) and William Wilson's *The Truly Disadvantaged* (1987), have generated the most vigorous research effort on the poverty paradox since the proliferation of urban studies spawned by the civil rights movement during the 1960s. Indeed, this renaissance of social science investigation into the connection between the urban underclass and the paradox of poverty in the late 1980s is, on the whole, simply a picking up of the intellectual pieces that were left scattered in the early 1970s by the acrimonious debate over the existence and nature of the culture of poverty, Daniel Moynihan's study of *The Negro Family* issued by the Labor Department, and the Nixon administration's family assistance plan.[1] The objectivity of research, the effect on scholarship of the racial background of social science investigators, and the hidden agendas of protagonists in the debates all became a matter of considerable disputation. Amidst this turmoil, college students and younger scholars turned their attention elsewhere, foundation and government agencies reoriented their research priorities, and universities closed down their urban studies programs.

The research and analysis reported in this volume is just one sign among many that at least for the moment the urban studies tide has begun to flow back in. Motivated by an effort to test some of the many hypotheses set forth in Wilson's book, it brings together research by sociologists, economists, political scientists, and policy analysts that allows us to make some empirically based assessments of the validity of various claims about the origins and significance of the urban underclass. The collection is hardly definitive, for research on this topic is today vigorous enough that new insights and findings are emerging with a rapidity quite unthinkable in the recent past. We offer these essays instead as a signpost, a marker of the understanding of the connection between the urban underclass and the poverty paradox reached in the waning years of the twentieth century.

The Paradox of Continuing Poverty

When Lyndon Johnson declared the War on Poverty in 1964, he had good reason to believe that the federal government could succeed in ridding itself of the paradox of widespread poverty in the world's wealthiest

1. Office of Policy Planning and Research (1965). On the controversy, see Rainwater and Yancey (1967).

country. The poverty rate in the United States had been declining steadily since 1940 even without any self-declared government effort to address it. In 1940 some 34 percent of the population was living in poverty; by 1960 this had decreased to 15 percent and by 1970 to 11 percent. Among black Americans the decrease had been even steeper: from 71 to 32 percent. Among Hispanics the rate fell from 55 to 23 percent.[2]

The specific battle plan drawn up by the Johnson administration for the War on Poverty failed to match the rhetorical artillery the president employed. The effort was little more than a call for citizen participation combined with a hodgepodge of hastily designed educational, job training, and neighborhood service programs that had little internal coherence and only limited financial backing. It was more important as a vehicle for involving blacks and other minorities in local political processes than as a mechanism for redistributing wealth. When the Office of Economic Opportunity, the high command for the official poverty war, was finally disbanded in the early 1970s, few noticed the difference.[3]

But a focus on the conduct of the official War on Poverty is misleading. If the war effort is understood instead as the sum total of Great Society programs enacted and enhanced during the Johnson and Nixon administrations, then the transformation of a broad range of social welfare programs in the late 1960s and early 1970s can, in comparison with previous government efforts, truly be declared a full-scale war. The elderly, for whom the poverty risk in 1960 was higher than one in three, obtained easy access to low-cost medical services and greatly improved retirement benefits. Cash assistance to the blind, deaf, and disabled was increased, funded more completely by the federal government, and indexed to changes in the cost of living. Eligibility restrictions were relaxed on aid given to needy families with dependent children, and food stamps and medical assistance were added as supplements to the cash assistance these families received. Special education programs for the disadvantaged and the handicapped were enacted. Head Start was provided to very young children, and job training programs were offered to those entering the labor market. The amount and variety of housing subsidies available to qualifying families also increased.

The most conservative way of estimating the growth of these programs

2. Smith (1988), p. 143. Smith's measure of poverty is not quite the same as the measure of poverty used by the Bureau of the Census. It is a measure that instead weights absolute and relative definitions of poverty equally. Absolute measures of poverty would show a steeper downward trend before 1960.

3. On the politics of the war on poverty, see Sundquist (1968), pp. 111–54; Moynihan (1969); and Peterson and Greenstone (1977).

is to consider the percentage of the nation's gross national product used to fund them. This estimate controls not only for inflation but also for any change in the size of the economy that occurs as a function of growth in the size of the labor force or improved economic productivity. By this conservative measure the nation doubled its social welfare effort in the fifteen years between 1965 and 1980, increasing the share of GNP allocated to social security, welfare assistance, medical services, and food stamps from 5 to 10 percent.[4] Nor did the conservative climate and fiscal crises of the 1980s cut deeply into the size and scope of these programs. As Robert Greenstein points out in this book, the Reagan administration's effort to cut back the welfare state was frequently checked by strong congressional supporters of existing programs. Thus it might be said that as a result of its war on poverty, the nation now seems finally committed to meeting the biblical requirement that a tenth of income be set aside for those in need.

This war on poverty did not fail in any absolute sense. Although the poverty rate no longer continued to decline, it remained fairly stable at the level it had reached in the late 1960s. Among whites the official rate leveled off at about one-eighth of the population; among blacks the proportion poor remained about one-third.[5] The poverty rate among older Americans continued to decline. Whereas one-quarter of those aged sixty-five or older had an income below the poverty line in 1970, only one-eighth did in 1987. Social security programs had been extended to include virtually all workers, benefit levels had been increased and indexed at a new, higher level, and medicare insured against most poverty-inducing illnesses. For this group at least, the effort to eradicate poverty had been a resounding success.

Yet in recent years there has been a gnawing sense that poverty, instead of disappearing, has become worse. Not only has the poverty rate for the population as a whole stabilized at around 13 percent, but the risk of becoming poor has increased in disconcerting ways. First, the official poverty rate among Hispanics increased from 28 to 39 percent between 1972 and 1987. It is not clear, however, how much of this apparent change actually occurred. The Bureau of the Census broadened its definition of Hispanic during this period, making comparisons over time suspect. In addition, it is not clear whether any increases that have occurred have been caused by changes that have taken place within the states. Both

4. Peterson and Rom (1988), p. 217.
5. For whites it was 9.9 percent in 1970, 10.2 percent in 1980, and 10.5 percent in 1987; for blacks the percentages were 33.5, 32.5, and 33.1.

TABLE 1. Households with Incomes below the Poverty Line, Selected Years, 1960–87

Percent

Year	Central city	Suburb	Nonmetropolitan
1960	13.7	9.6	28.2
1970	9.8	5.3	14.8
1980	14.0	6.5	12.1
1987	15.4	6.5	13.8

SOURCES: Bureau of the Census (1972), table 3; (1982), p. 445; and (1989), table 17.

the legal and illegal immigration of many low-income Latinos from Mexico, Puerto Rico, the Caribbean, Central America, and South America may have contributed to the increased rate. However, increases in Hispanic poverty before 1980 were as large among longer-term residents as among recent immigrants.[6] Whether that remained the case in the 1980s, when the number of immigrants increased sharply, is not yet clear. It is thus not certain to what extent the poverty rate has increased among Hispanics who are not recent immigrants to the United States.

Young families have also experienced a steadily increasing chance of being poor. Although the poverty rate among the elderly was cut by one-half between 1970 and 1986, the probability that a child under the age of eighteen would be living in a poor family increased from 15 to 20 percent.

The heightened risk of poverty has shifted from people in rural areas to those living in central cities. In 1960 about 28 percent of the rural households were poor, as compared with 14 percent in the nation's central cities and 10 percent in the suburbs. By 1987 the rate in rural America had fallen to 14 percent, while in the central cities it had climbed sharply from its low of 10 percent in 1970 to 15 percent (table 1). This change, it should be stressed, was not the result of any movement in the overall population from rural America to the central cities. In fact, the percentage of the nation's nonpoor population living in central cities was smaller in the late 1980s than in 1960.

Finally, the poor today are living in female-headed families more often than ever before. Whereas 25 percent of the poor were living in female-headed families in 1960, by 1980 about 35 percent were, and by 1987 perhaps 40 percent were. That female-headed families were somewhat more likely to be poor in 1987 than they were in 1970 (an increase from

6. National Council of La Raza (1989).

50 to 55 percent) provides part of the explanation. But more important was the increase in the percentage of all families that were headed by women. As Christopher Jencks points out in his essay in this volume, the percentage of female-headed families has increased rapidly among all racial and occupational groups. Between 1970 and 1987 the percentage among whites increased from 8 to 13 percent and among blacks from 28 to 42 percent.

In short, the poverty paradox continues even after a major increase in the government's commitment to the welfare state. And not only has the overall poverty rate refused to fall in the 1970s and 1980s in the way that it had in earlier decades, but the risk of poverty grew greater among Hispanics, children, residents of urban areas, and those living in female-headed families (itself a growing percentage of the population).

Nor is it just the recent trends in poverty rates that are disconcerting. The poverty paradox is even more apparent when the United States is compared with other industrial societies. With the U.S. government's official measure of poverty as a standard, comparative data were collected for eight industrial countries—Australia, Canada, Norway, Sweden, Switzerland, the United Kingdom, the United States, and West Germany—for 1979–82. Australia had a slightly higher poverty rate than the United States, while the United Kingdom's rate was 1 percentage point less. But the average poverty rate in the other countries was 5 points lower. The differences were even more dramatic when the rates of children in poverty were calculated: the United States scored higher (that is, worse) than did any other country. Its rate was only slightly higher than Australia's, but it was more than 6 percentage points higher than the rate in the United Kingdom and 10 percentage points higher than the average of the other five countries. Only among the elderly did the poverty rate in the United States not appear exceptional; it ranked fourth after the United Kingdom, Australia, and Norway, and was only slightly higher than the rate in West Germany. In other words, cross-national comparisons reinforce the impression one obtains by examining changes in the incidence of poverty within the United States over time. The poverty rate in this affluent society seems exceptionally high, and young people are especially at risk.[7]

7. Smeeding, Torrey, and Rein (1988), pp. 96–97. International comparisons of poverty levels are not easily made. I report here the indicators of absolute, not relative, poverty. If relative measures were used, the United States would look even worse.

The Underclass-Poverty Connection

The relationship between this poverty paradox and the urban under-class has been a subject of considerable debate. Many poor people are clearly not members of any underclass. The elderly poor, widows, or-phans, the severely sick and disabled, and the simply unlucky can find themselves suddenly plunged into poverty without warning. Similarly, many people who engage in activities said to be characteristic of the un-derclass are hardly poor. Indeed, some of the most celebrated instances of an underclass style of life—laziness, unreliability, unrestrained attach-ment to fancy clothes and high fashion, episodic romantic attachments, drug addiction and alcohol abuse—are to be found among the very rich.

Indeed, for some analysts the poverty paradox is only one manifesta-tion of a much more general deterioration in American society and cul-ture. The major problem is the way in which a spreading underclass culture is undermining the country's productive capacity, family life, so-cial integration, and, ultimately, its political stability.[8] Other analysts see virtually no relationship between the poverty paradox and the existence of an urban underclass. Often they object to using the word underclass, and if they accept the concept, they argue that an underclass, to the extent that one exists, is small, heterogeneous, and not growing. They argue that it constitutes no more than a minor portion of the low-income popula-tion, and that overall poverty levels have little to do with the activities of this segment of the population.[9]

From these varying views on the urban underclass, one can differen-tiate four quite separate explanations for the poverty paradox: the in-complete extension of the welfare state, the culture of poverty, the perverse incentives provided by welfare assistance, and the disproportionate ef-fects of changes in the international economy on the core areas of cities. Each explanation implicitly or explicitly addresses the way in which the urban underclass has contributed to a poverty paradox, and each offers policy recommendations designed to resolve that paradox.

8. On these themes, see Mead (1986); Bloom (1987); and Murray (1988). Earlier ver-sions of these themes can be found in Durkheim (1951); Bell (1963); Kornhauser (1959); and Riesman (1953).

9. Various estimates of the size of the underclass population have emphasized that it is much smaller than the poverty population taken as a whole. See Ricketts and Sawhill (1988); Reischauer (1987); and Adams, Duncan, and Rodgers (1988).

An Inadequate Welfare State

The standard interpretation, at least in liberal intellectual circles, is that the United States has always been an inegalitarian society in which the myth of equal opportunity has obscured a reality of submerged class conflict, racial discrimination, and tolerance of economic inequality. Compared with European societies, the United States has never had a strong labor movement, a vigorous socialist party, or a coherent set of national bureaucratic institutions that could administer an integrated welfare state.[10] Americans have instead relied on great natural resources, a decentralized governmental system, a large internal private market, and dynamic economic growth to resolve their social tensions. Extremes of wealth and poverty have emerged side by side, and although some efforts to ameliorate these extremes developed in the wake of the Great Depression of the 1930s and the civil disorders of the 1960s, the country is too committed to individual liberty, too suspicious of big government, and too divided by race and ethnicity to redistribute wealth in such a way as to meet the needs of the poor adequately.

Although the United States made greater progress toward creating a welfare state during the Great Society years than at any other time in its history, the argument continues, the result is still a patchwork of programs and institutions that fails to provide for the needs of the poor in a comprehensive manner. The most elaborate and expensive of Great Society innovations were the elaboration of the social security program and the institution of medicare, both of which addressed the economic and social needs of the elderly. Not surprisingly, it is precisely this group for which the appellation poverty paradox seems no longer appropriate. As Theda Skocpol points out in her paper, social innovation was much more modest for other demographic groups. Although the "deserving" poor— the blind, deaf, and disabled—were placed within a new, nationally funded program that materially improved their welfare, the government was still reluctant to address the needs of the "undeserving" poor—those who many people thought could and should earn a living for themselves. Aid to families with dependent children remained a program administered by the states. When the federal government supplemented this cash assistance with food stamps, the cash assistance provided by state gov-

10. Skowronek (1982); Shefter (1978); Lipset (1977); Hartz (1955); and Weir, Orloff, and Skocpol (1988).

ernments declined, leaving poor families no better off than they had been.[11] "Undeserving" men and women in households without dependent children were eligible only for state general assistance programs, which varied greatly from one part of the country to the next and in most places provided only the most token assistance. The amount of this assistance also declined in value when federally funded food stamps became available.[12] Admittedly, medicaid helped reduce the extreme disparity in medical services between the middle class and the poor, but housing subsidies reached only a small minority, and increased educational services were too marginal and too fragmented to have much effect.

For the most part the liberal view attributes the poverty paradox to the inadequate development of the welfare state rather than to any changes in society or to specific characteristics of an urban underclass. But there is one strand of thinking within the liberal tradition that at least has implications for understanding the urban class phenomenon—the discussion of social rights and citizenship that has evolved out of the writings of the British social theorist, T. H. Marshall. From this perspective, the United States has a larger, more threatening underclass than most European countries because it has done so little to incorporate marginal groups into the social and political mainstream. The United States has a dual economy, a social world divided along racial and ethnic lines, and large numbers of people who are politically apathetic and uninvolved. Any society that does not treat all its citizens as valued members of the political community encourages marginal citizens to think of themselves as political outsiders who share in neither the benefits nor the responsibilities of the social and political community. If an underclass exists, it is because the state has created a group of outcasts that are denied their social and political rights.

There are at least three major pieces of evidence that support the liberal view: the welfare state in the United States is much less uniform and comprehensive than it is in many European countries; the elderly have done much better in the past two decades than have other social groups; and the changes in public policy wrought by the Great Society have been less significant than has often been claimed. But if these pieces of evidence support the liberal interpretation, another points in another direction. Poverty in the United States had been declining steadily between 1940

11. Peterson and Rom (1990).
12. Rossi (1989), pp. 190–94.

and 1960, two decades in which the welfare state expanded hardly at all. Yet when the welfare state expanded in the 1970s, progress toward eliminating poverty came to a halt. What is more, poverty increased among young families and inner-city residents.

The Culture of Poverty

The cultural explanation, perhaps the classic statement of the relationship between the underclass and the poverty paradox, holds that the style of life to which the urban poor has become attached is self-perpetuating. Street life in the ghetto is exhilarating—at least in the short run. In a world where jobs are dull, arduous, or difficult to obtain and hold, it is more fun to hang out, make love, listen to and tell exaggerated stories of love and danger, plan parties and escapades, and exhibit one's latest purchases or conquests. Gangs provide young people thrills, protection, mutual support, friendship, prestige, and enough income to allow them to buy fashionable clothes, alcohol, and drugs. When men cannot earn enough to support their families adequately, they avoid enduring relationships with their female companions. Women respond by becoming self-reliant, domineering, and mutually supportive. But without an adult male figure in the household, they are unable to protect their children from the alluring street life that promises short-term excitement, if not much hope for a prosperous future.[13]

There is little consensus on the origins of the culture of poverty in American society. Some theorists have attributed it to the inequalities of economic power in the larger society, others to processes of urbanization that undermined the mutual interdependence of family members characteristic of traditional societies. John Ogbu has recently used an imaginative reconstruction of the cultural thesis to account for the contrasting experiences of various ethnic groups in American society.[14] Those groups—American blacks being the extreme case—who were compelled to come to or were forcefully incorporated into the United States and, once there, were subjected to poverty, discrimination, and slavery, constructed for themselves a conflictual understanding of the country's social and political institutions. Members of these forcefully incorporated groups explained personal disappointments and affronts as the product

13. This summary of the anthropological descriptions of the culture of poverty draws on Hannerz (1969); Lewis (1961, 1966); Liebow (1967); and Rainwater (1970).
14. Ogbu (1978, 1988).

of broad social forces—class dominance, racial prejudice and discrimination, cultural exclusiveness—over which they, as individuals, had little control. It was hopeless to fight the system; instead, one might as well rip off and enjoy as big a piece of it as one could. As New Yorkers would say, "Take a bite of the Big Apple." But this explanation of their experiences, Ogbu suggests, would often become self-fulfilling—both for the individual minority member and the group as a whole. The more one rejects the system, the less one is willing to study or work and the more one is rejected by the societal mainstream.

Voluntary immigrants to America experienced many of the same disappointments, affronts, and rejections, but when they compared their experience in the United States with their experience in their homeland, they found opportunity much greater in the United States. They thus explained their limited success as a function of their own shortcomings, and they believed that if their children acquired the advantages of language and education they could succeed in the new world. These voluntary immigrants worked hard, told their children to take advantage of the opportunities available to them, and, once again, often found their prophecy self-fulfilling.

Whatever the causes of ghetto social practices, anthropological studies of the culture of poverty continue to provide troubling accounts of urban underclass life. In this volume Elijah Anderson shows the processes by which teenage girls decide to keep their babies to term and raise them, the joys a young child brings to a single parent, and the sorrows and troubles that later emerge. In the subsequent essay, David Greenstone discusses the ways in which these commitments to street life can be understood both as a rational response to immediate circumstances and as a product of a distinctive cultural milieu. He then suggests, along lines similar to those developed by Ogbu, that only by reducing the distance and conflict between mainstream institutions and ghetto culture can policymakers find the mechanisms for transforming it.

If the emphasis on a cultural milieu helps explain immediate choices in poor urban neighborhoods, it is by itself too static a concept to be a satisfactory explanation for the poverty paradox. Indeed, many of those who describe the culture of poverty locate its origins in social relationships in the wider society, whether these be characterized in terms of class conflict, racial discrimination, cultural distance, or social dislocation. At its best, the explanation warns against expecting rapid change in urban neighborhoods in response to broader economic and political change. At its worst it blames the victims for their problems. In all cases, it is most satisfying when linked to other, more structural interpretations.

Perverse Government Incentives

The third interpretation of the relationship between the underclass and poverty, propounded most compellingly by Charles Murray, identifies the Great Society programs as the most important structural factor affecting inner-city culture. While accepting the description of ghetto life elaborated by cultural anthropologists, Murray claims that members of the urban underclass, far from being irrationally bound by a cultural milieu that is as self-debilitating as it is unchangeable, are quite rational in the way they live their lives. He attributes the increase in male unemployment and female-headed households not to a spreading underclass culture but, ironically enough, to the Great Society programs that were expected to eliminate the poverty paradox.[15] Murray argues that the increasing size and availability of cash assistance, disability insurance, food stamps, medicaid insurance, housing subsidies, and other government aids to the poor inadvertently created a new set of incentives for marginal members of American society. It was no longer necessary to work in order to survive; indeed, full-time employment in an unpleasant, entry-level position at times yielded less after-tax, take-home pay than the income one could receive in benefits from a multiplicity of government programs. And marriage could be economically painful. The old shibboleth that two could live more cheaply than one no longer held. Instead, a single woman with children could receive more from the government than from the earnings of her potential husband. It was better—and more fun—for both if they lived apart; she could share her welfare check with him, and he could earn through episodic or part-time employment enough to sustain an adventurous street life. The result was an increase in the poverty rate in the later years of the 1970s.

Murray's explanation resonated well with the political climate of the early 1980s. Americans were suspicious of big government, the welfare state, and the political demands made by minority spokespersons. Murray's analysis blamed government for the rising percentages of children born out of wedlock, the rising percentages of unemployed young males, the seemingly pervasive crime, drugs, and violence in cities, and the con-

15. Murray (1984). I am using Murray's argument as shorthand for a broader literature advancing a similar line of interpretation. See Mead (1986); Glazer (1988); Banfield (1969); Lenkowsky (1986); and Anderson (1978).

tinuing sharp racial tensions in American life. If most Americans were unwilling to dismantle the welfare state altogether, they certainly accepted limits on its further expansion.

Murray's critique has nonetheless been subjected to relentless criticism.[16] Some have argued that the work ethic is deeply ingrained in all parts of American society and that the dignity that comes from an earned income is something most people strongly prefer to welfare assistance. They have pointed out that most studies show little, if any, effect of welfare assistance on willingness to work. Neither do they show much effect of welfare benefit levels on the incidence of out-of-wedlock births.[17] Others have argued that inasmuch as cash assistance to welfare recipients was diminishing in terms of real dollars throughout the 1970s, it was peculiar for Murray to argue that increases in these benefits could be causing poverty to increase. As Greg Duncan and Saul Hoffman show in their paper in this volume, the income loss to a young woman who has a child out of wedlock or does not finish high school has actually increased in recent years. Still others have taken issue with his finding that the poverty rate was in fact increasing, noting that the apparent increases could be accounted for by errors in the way changes in the cost of living were being measured.

In defending his interpretation against these criticisms, Murray has pointed out that whatever the measurement problems are, it is certainly clear that the poverty paradox is not withering away. He has argued, moreover, that efforts to discredit his analysis are based on studies that focus on small variations in welfare policy from one state to another. More important than minor variations, he has claimed, is the major national increase in the level of welfare provided in the late 1960s as well as the greater ease with which the poor could receive it. If cash assistance diminished after 1975, the loss has been offset by the food stamp program, medicaid, housing assistance, and other benefit programs.[18]

The Inner City in a Changing Economy

It was in this context that a fourth interpretation of the poverty paradox was developed by William Julius Wilson. In a series of essays that resulted in *The Truly Disadvantaged*, he developed an explanation for

16. See Danziger and Gottschalk (1985); and Ellwood and Summers (1986).

17. McLanahan, Garfinkel, and Watson (1988); Ellwood and Bane (1985); Moore (1980); but see Plotnick (1989).

18. Murray (1985, 1986).

continuing poverty that accepted the accuracy of anthropological studies of the urban underclass but explained its existence not as the result of government handouts, but as the social by-product of a changing economy whose uneven impact was leaving inner cities with extraordinarily high levels of unemployment.

Wilson's thesis contains the following propositions:

—In the face of increasing competition from foreign countries, the United States has been moving from a unionized, oligopolistic, manufacturing economy to a more competitive, less unionized, service economy in which hourly earnings are falling while skill requirements are rising.

—These changes are having a disproportionate effect on urban minorities because the loss of manufacturing jobs has been greatest within large cities, and most of the new, high-technology service industries are locating in smaller cities or on the fringes of the metropolitan area. Urban minorities do not have ready access to the new jobs because the jobs are difficult to reach and educational requirements are high.

—As a result, the percentage of urban, working-age minority men who are employed in stable, reasonably well paid jobs has fallen dramatically.

—Without a decent job, men are undesirable marriage partners, and the number of female-headed households has as a result increased rapidly.

—These changes have been aggravated by the increasing social isolation of the inner-city poor caused by the outward migration of middle-class whites and blacks, who are moving to suburbs in pursuit of jobs, better houses, and more effective schools.

—Thus there are growing concentrations of low-income minorities in the inner cities, within which dysfunctional social behavior becomes contagious. Lacking middle-class adult role models, local places of employment, adequate public services, or community institutions that support traditional family values, these core areas become breeding places for sexual promiscuity, crime, violence, drug addiction, and alcohol abuse. It is here that one finds the people who are properly called the urban underclass, because they are isolated from the mainstream social, occupational, and political institutions of the society.

—To counteract these trends, Wilson advocates policies that will guarantee a full-employment economy; federal policies that provide unemployment insurance, family allowances, and other social services to all citizens; greater race and class desegregation within metropolitan areas; and revitalization of community institutions in the urban core.

The Studies Reported Here

The research and analyses presented in this volume reflect and respond to these diverse explanations for the continuing paradox of poverty. Although implicit and explicit references are made to all four interpretations, the one given the most attention is Wilson's theory of the way the changing U.S. economy has affected those living within the inner cities. The findings reported here and in other recent studies allow us to expand and qualify Wilson's hypotheses in a number of ways.

First, as Wilson hypothesized, it is becoming increasingly evident that changes in the U.S. economy are affecting the economic well-being of young black men. The annual earnings of young men between the ages of twenty-five and twenty-nine declined by 20 percent between 1973 and 1986. Among blacks the decline was 28 percent. Among those without a high school education the decline was 36 percent.[19] These changes are a function of decreases in both male employment and the hourly earnings paid to young men.

It is unlikely that the cause of this dramatic change in the earnings received by young, less educated minority men is simply that they are no longer as willing and able to work as before. For one thing, the decline in the earnings received by all young men suggests that something more than individual initiative is at issue. And as Marta Tienda and Haya Stier show, most working-age adults in the poorest neighborhoods of Chicago either are working, are seeking work, or say that they would work if they could find a job. Of course, reporting a willingness to work in a survey is different from actually bearing the heavy work, discomforts, and annoyances that typically accompany what is euphemistically called an entry-level position. But as Joleen Kirschenman and Kathryn Neckerman document, many employers hiring people for low-paid positions use racial background, minority status, place of residence, and such other indicators of social class as personal appearance, speech patterns, and family references as cues for predicting job performance.

Yet neither the use of racial cues by employers nor the unpredictability of the work habits of young inner-city men kept unemployment rates from falling dramatically in Boston when the area enjoyed a prolonged economic boom. As Richard Freeman shows, the rates fell faster in the core areas of Boston than they did in the metropolitan area as a whole. And Paul Osterman finds that the poverty rate in these core areas of Bos-

19. Sum, Fogg, and Taggart (1988), pp. 43, B-2.

ton also fell much below the national average. Similarly, black unemployment decreases at a much faster rate than white unemployment when the national economy is in the boom phase of the business cycle. For example, when the white unemployment rate fell by 4 percentage points between 1983 and 1988, the black unemployment rate fell by nearly 7 points.

The findings on the economic behavior of urban firms and inner-city residents in these papers thus complement one another. Young, poorly educated minority men are the last to be hired, but when the economic situation creates a labor shortage, employers will hire workers from core areas of the city. The corollary, of course, is that minorities are also the first to be fired when the business cycle turns downward. When white unemployment levels climbed 4 points between 1977 and 1983, black rates rose by 8 points.

These sharp short-term fluctuations in the demand for minority workers provide a clue for understanding the decline during the past two decades in the employment rates and national average hourly earnings among young, poorly educated minority men. Very likely, the decline is the result not of changes in the quality of the labor supplied by these people but of the increased competition they face in the labor market. This competition has come from various sources. Foreign workers have become more direct competitors with workers in the United States as international trade flows have increased and companies have the option of expanding operations either in the United States or overseas. Wage levels in developing countries are much lower than those in the United States, dampening the price business is willing to pay American workers. Other sources of increased competition have been internal to the United States: the rising number of legal and illegal immigrants, the increasing percentage of women participating in the labor force, and the particularly large size of the age cohort entering the labor market in the late 1970s and early 1980s. Ascertaining the exact impact of these internal sources of competition is complicated because the new workers also became new consumers who increase the demand for goods and services. But among all three groups the supply of entry-level workers increased more rapidly than the supply of more skilled, better educated, and more experienced workers. Under these circumstances the competition for beginning positions was particularly intense, depressing earnings and opportunities at the lower end of the occupational spectrum.

Had productivity rates increased as rapidly in the 1970s and 1980s as they did in the 1950s and 1960s, the increase in the labor supply might have been easier to absorb without an adverse effect on unemployment rates and worker earnings. As it was, the impact of the larger labor supply was felt keenly by young men. Women made gains because they were remaining in the labor market longer and because their relative position had been so inferior. Older workers were protected by seniority privileges and union agreements designed when labor competition was less intense. The most highly skilled workers enjoyed strong demand for their services because the economy was growing fastest in the technologically sophisticated sectors. The losers were young, poorly educated minority men.

This change in their earnings prospects may well have affected the marriage prospects of inner-city minority men. Unemployment rates are always lower for married than for unmarried men, whether because married men feel they need to work or because working men are more likely to marry.[20] Although it is probably a little of both, the weight to be attributed to each cause is not easily ascertained. Robert Mare and Christopher Winship nonetheless show that the decline in male earnings is the most important identifiable factor adversely affecting marriage rates.

But although the changing earning prospects of young men compromise their marriageability, one should not attempt to explain the increase in the percentage of female-headed households from this development alone. Mare and Winship show that the effects of employment on marriage are only one part of the story. And as Christopher Jencks points out, the increase in female-headed households in the past twenty years is occurring among blacks, whites, and Hispanics, among the middle class as well as the poor. Divorce, single-parent families, and out-of-wedlock births are becoming more or less accepted practices in many parts of the United States. The trend leaves too many children with impaired financial support, inadequate adult supervision and instruction, compromised security, fewer alternatives for establishing intergenerational relationships, and fewer adult role models. The most powerful force contributing to the formation of the urban underclass, perversely enough, may be the changing values of mainstream American society, in which the virtues of family stability, mutual support, and religiously based commitment to the marriage vow no longer command the deference they once did.

But however unfortunate some of its consequences, the trend is understandable. Women are becoming more self-sufficient. And the institution of the family seems less necessary because it is being supplemented or

20. In 1989 the unemployment rate among married men was less than 3.5 percent at a time when overall unemployment rates were above 5 percent. "Married and Jobless" (figure), *Wall Street Journal*, April 27, 1990, p. A1.

replaced by schools, day care centers, social security, health insurance, and the numerous other social services of modern society. Jencks ruminates that the only place a strong two-parent family may be critically important is the inner city, where the family is necessary to offset the powerful allure of the street. But however one assesses this change in American society, one must acknowledge that the socioeconomic forces shaping family life are not limited to the worsening economic position of young men.

Not only is the changing economic and social structure of the United States affecting the urban underclass, but the concentration of poor within the nation's inner cities may also contribute to the problem. Both Jonathan Crane and Susan Mayer provide new data to show that living in a community or attending a school with disproportionate numbers of poor people or minorities increases the chance that an adolescent will drop out or have a child out of wedlock. In both studies this finding holds even after the young person's family background is taken into account. Nor are the ill effects of poverty concentrations limited to teenage years. James Rosenbaum and Susan Popkin show that when poor women move to the suburbs, their job opportunities are better. Because these results reflect the experience of poor families who had little choice in whether they were assigned to inner-city or suburban public housing, the finding that where you live affects your economic opportunities is particularly striking.

But if concentrations of poverty have a detectable economic consequence, the political consequences are less clear. Jeffrey Berry, Kent Portney, and Ken Thomson find that living in a poor neighborhood has little effect on a person's political attitudes and behavior. Poor people living in poor neighborhoods are no more cynical or distrustful or likely to withdraw from the political process than poor people living in middle-class neighborhoods.

Whatever the consequences of concentrated poverty, there is little evidence that the poor are any more isolated than they have been in the past. Reynolds Farley's analysis of population changes in metropolitan areas between 1970 and 1980 shows that there has been virtually no change in the degree of income segregation within either the black or the white community in most of them. (There was a slight decrease in the degree of racial segregation.) Other studies have shown that in some large cities—Chicago, New York, Philadelphia, Detroit, and a few others in the Northeast—the proportion of poor people who live in neighborhoods that are extremely poor has increased. This seems to result, however, mainly from a general increase in poverty levels in these metropolitan areas rather than from any changes in the extent to which residents are segregating themselves by income.[21]

These results do not in any way diminish the seriousness of the problem of an urban underclass, but they suggest that one should be careful in making claims about the extent to which the situation is growing worse. On the contrary, Christopher Jencks shows that according to a number of indicators the underclass is shrinking. A higher percentage of the minority population is receiving high school diplomas, a smaller percentage of teenagers is having babies out of wedlock, both blacks and whites are experiencing fewer crimes committed against them, and the use of drugs is declining. Perhaps it is not so much that the situation is deteriorating as that Americans' social expectations are rising.

In the concluding essay William Julius Wilson dismisses some of these data as irrelevant to the theory he developed in *The Truly Disadvantaged*. In an important clarification of his theory, Wilson now states that the cause of the urban underclass is the simultaneous presence of economic marginality and extreme social isolation. Poverty within the inner city is debilitating when it is intensely concentrated, a condition particularly prevalent within large cities. Changes in an indicator of class segregation, such as the one used in this volume by Reynolds Farley, do not capture changes in the size of the underclass because they do not capture the extent to which extreme isolation is increasing.[22] To bolster his argument, Wilson points out that the numbers of poor people living in extremely poor neighborhoods—those in which 40 percent or more of the population are poor—increased between 1970 and 1980. The upward trend is especially evident in the largest American cities.

It is precisely the living and working conditions in these extremely isolated neighborhoods that require understanding and analysis, Wilson argues. Tests of the theory in other settings are beside the point. When Berry, Portney, and Thomson did not find significant political differences between the poor living in poor and nonpoor neighborhoods, it was because they were neither studying the largest cities of the industrial belt

21. It may be, however, that poverty became more concentrated after 1980; it will be possible to ascertain this once the 1990 census data are released.

22. Wilson suggests that the degree of isolation among those already socially isolated may increase without any change in the degree of isolation of the median poor person. All the change is occurring among people below the median. Because Farley examined changes only in the median, he missed the changes occurring at the bottom extreme of the distribution. In my view, this is possible but unlikely.

nor limiting their analysis to extremely impoverished neighborhoods.[23] Jonathan Crane's study is much more persuasive to Wilson, because Crane shows that neighborhood effects on dropping out of high school and experiencing an out-of-wedlock birth are especially powerful when poverty levels escalate above a critical threshold.

Studies that use national samples and examine overall trends (including the essays in this volume by Jencks and by Mare and Winship) are rejected by Wilson as atheoretical, inappropriate efforts to look at an urban underclass defined as economically marginal and extremely isolated socially. If theory is to guide future research, that research must focus its attention on inner-city poverty in the largest cities. To highlight his now even greater emphasis on the conjunction of economic and extreme social factors, Wilson suggests that it may be more appropriate to speak of the ghetto poor rather than the urban underclass. The new term makes clear exactly whom Wilson is speaking about—and, perhaps more important, whom he is not speaking about.

There can be little doubt that Wilson has strengthened his theory by narrowing its focus to those neighborhoods in which poverty is particularly concentrated. Once stated in these terms, the theory is not inconsistent with most, if not all, of the findings reported in the essays that follow. Most of the studies reported here can be rejected as not an adequate test because they cast their research net more widely; only Crane's and Anderson's work (both of which support Wilson's argument) examine the consequences of living in extreme poverty.

Yet there are costs as well as gains to narrowing the explanatory focus this way. At best the reformulated theory applies to only a small portion of the poverty population. Only little more than 1 percent of the U.S. population in 1980 lived in metropolitan census tracts in which the population was more than 40 percent poor. The percentage of poor people who lived in such neighborhoods was less than 9 percent; 21 percent of poor blacks and 16 percent of poor Hispanics lived in such neighborhoods. Nor does the reformulated theory account for changes that occurred in the 1970s. The increase in the ghettoization of poor black people living in metropolitan areas was only 1 percent and that of His-

23. Wilson's methodological criticism of Berry, Portney, and Thomson reveals the way in which his ideas are evolving, for in his own study of a sample of Chicago parents, he included all those living in neighborhoods in which poverty levels were 20 percent or more (see the essay by Tienda and Stier in this volume). It would seem that Wilson would now want to focus any analysis on more extremely isolated neighborhoods.

panics decreased by 5 percent.[24] The extent to which ghettoization is occurring varies dramatically among regions. According to the essay in this volume by Paul Jargowsky and Mary Jo Bane, the percentages of poor people living in these isolated communities fell in the South and West while increasing in the Northeast and Midwest. Most of the increases in the population living in extremely poor neighborhoods between 1970 and 1980 occurred in just five cities—New York, Chicago, Philadelphia, Newark, and Detroit. Such increases seem to be strongly correlated with increases in the overall level of poverty in a specific metropolitan area. Very little, if any, can be attributed to increasing class segregation within the black community. Unless the 1990 census reveals that poverty became much more concentrated in the 1980s than it did in the 1970s, a theory in which increasing class segregation and extreme social isolation play a central role will have limited ability to explain contemporary processes of social change.

Wilson's theory originally promised to provide an explanation for the poverty paradox—the perpetuation of poverty in the 1970s and 1980s when many had expected it would gradually diminish. In its more circumscribed form, the theory may still tell us important things about a very visible, politically significant portion of the population—blacks living in the largest central cities of the rustbelt. As Wilson points out, it is here that racial tensions are the greatest and where the images that help shape national discourse are most readily retrieved. But even if his theory, as clarified, helps account for the behavior of a politically salient segment of the population, it makes only a modest contribution to our understanding of the poverty paradox.

Any theory that promises to explain the connection between the poverty paradox and the urban underclass must apply more widely than just to places where poverty is extremely concentrated. Such a theory, it seems to me, needs to focus on three facets of contemporary life that Wilson and others have identified as critical—the increasing numbers of female-

24. The reader may wonder how these figures can be consistent with the fact that the number of poor people living in extremely poor neighborhoods increased by 30 percent. The answer is twofold. First, because poverty was moving from rural to urban areas, the numbers of poor living in extremely poor urban neighborhoods was rising right along with the number of poor living in less poor neighborhoods. In other words, it was not so much ghettoization that was occurring as a shift in poverty from rural to urban America (see table 1). Second, inasmuch as only a small percentage of the poor lived in such neighborhoods in 1970, a large percentage increase between 1970 and 1980 still changed by only a small amount the overall percentage of the metropolitan poor that was socially isolated.

-headed households, the declining earnings and labor force participation of young men from minority backgrounds, and the shift in poverty from rural areas to central cities (not the shift within metropolitan areas from neighborhoods that are less poor to ones that are more poor). Wilson's original formulation has stimulated debate and research because it identified connections among these three phenomena. But except perhaps under the extreme conditions that Wilson now hypothesizes, these factors may not be as closely linked as his theory has implied. The sources for the changes in the economic opportunities for young black men are not just the decline in the number of jobs within the manufacturing sector. The rise in the percentage of female-headed households is not caused just by the changing employment opportunities of young men. The shift of poverty from rural to urban settings is not simply the result of the decentralization of industry and commerce. The problem is more complex, more difficult to disentangle, and less susceptible to any one solution.

If there is no single, simple explanation, certain policy conclusions can nonetheless be drawn from the four interpretations I have summarized. Wilson is correct in emphasizing that unless the United States remains strong, growing, and economically competitive, nothing is likely to reduce the poverty rate significantly. But the experience of the 1980s shows that a steadily growing economy will not by itself eliminate the poverty paradox. In addition, as liberal theorists point out, the income transfer system needs to be restructured so that government responds to the needs of working-age adults and families in as humane a way as it does to the needs of the elderly. As both Theda Skocpol and Robert Greenstein suggest, this will require a much more centralized, comprehensive, and integrated welfare system than the nation currently has.

Adopting such a policy does not entail the rejection of Charles Murray's argument that our present welfare system discourages participation in the mainstream economy. There is something wrong about a health care system that provides assistance to the nonworking indigent but will not help those in low-paid jobs whose employers do not provide health insurance. There is also something wrong about a system in which the movement from welfare to work must be abrupt and expensive. An integrated, comprehensive national welfare policy could provide a more flexible public response to those who move in and out of low-skilled, low-paid employment.

Finally, the United States needs a much more flexible and adaptable educational system in the core areas of cities, a system that can enhance the country's human capital, strengthen the institutional position of the family, and reduce the alienation between minority youth and the mainstream institutions of society. The current expensive, bureaucratically controlled, hierarchical, rule-bound, stratified, gang-infested system of urban education needs to be drastically changed. We need to redesign our urban school systems to give families more choice and more control, provide harbors for young people seeking to escape the neighborhood peer culture, and create a learning environment that respects the culture of the low-income, minority community. If the civil rights movement wants to shed its middle-class bias and address the critical problems of the poor that became of increasing concern to Martin Luther King, it should make educational choice for urban residents and an integrated welfare system its most important concerns.

References

Adams, Terry K., Greg J. Duncan, and Willard L. Rodgers. 1988. "The Persistence of Poverty." In *Quiet Riots: Race and Poverty in the United States*, edited by Fred R. Harris and Roger W. Wilkins. Pantheon.

Anderson, Martin. 1978. *Welfare: The Political Economy of Welfare Reform in the United States*. Stanford: Hoover Institution Press.

Banfield, Edward C. 1969. "Welfare: A Crisis without 'Solutions.'" *Public Interest* 16 (Summer), pp. 89–101.

Bell, Daniel, ed. 1963. *The Radical Right: The New American Right, Expanded and Updated*. Garden City, N.Y.: Doubleday.

Bloom, Allan. 1987. *The Closing of the American Mind: How Higher Education Has Failed Democracy and Impoverished the Souls of Today's Students*. Simon and Schuster.

Bureau of the Census, 1972. "Characteristics of the Low Income Population, 1971." Series P-60, no. 86. Department of Commerce.

———. 1982. *Statistical Abstract of the United States: 1982–83*. Department of Commerce.

———. 1989. "Poverty in the United States, 1987." Series P-60, no. 163. Department of Commerce.

Danziger, Sheldon, and Peter Gottschalk. 1985. "The Poverty of *Losing Ground*." *Challenge* 28 (May–June), pp. 32–38.

Durkheim, Emile. 1951. *Suicide: A Study in Sociology*. Glencoe, Ill.: Free Press.

Ellwood, David T., and Mary Jo Bane. 1985. "The Impact of AFDC on Family Structure and Living Arrangements." In *Research in Labor Economics* 7, edited by Ronald G. Ehrenberg. Greenwich, Conn.: JAI Press, pp. 137–207.

Ellwood, David T., and Lawrence H. Summers. 1986. "Is Welfare Really the Problem?" *Public Interest* 83 (Spring), pp. 57–78.

Glazer, Nathan. 1988. *The Limits of Social Policy*. Harvard University Press.

Hannerz, Ulf. 1969. *Soulside: Inquiries into Ghetto Culture and Community*. Columbia University Press.

Hartz, Louis. 1955. *The Liberal Tradition in America: An Interpretation of American Political Thought since the Revolution.* Harcourt Brace.

Kornhauser, William. 1959. *The Politics of Mass Society.* Glencoe, Ill.: Free Press.

Lenkowsky, Leslie. 1986. *Politics, Economics, and Welfare Reform: The Failure of the Negative Income Tax in Britain and the United States.* Washington: American Enterprise Institute for Public Policy Research.

Lewis, Oscar. 1961. *The Children of Sanchez: Autobiography of a Mexican Family.* Random House.

———. 1966. *La Vida: A Puerto Rican Family in the Culture of Poverty—San Juan and New York.* Random House.

Liebow, Elliot. 1967. *Tally's Corner: A Study of Negro Streetcorner Men.* Boston: Little, Brown.

Lipset, Seymour Martin. 1977. "Why No Socialism in the United States?" In *Sources of Contemporary Radicalism,* edited by Seweryn Bialer and Sophia Sluzar. Boulder, Colo.: Westview Press.

McLanahan, Sara, Irwin Garfinkel, and Dorothy Watson. 1988. "Family Structure, Poverty, and the Underclass." In *Urban Change and Poverty,* edited by Michael G. H. McGeary and Laurence E. Lynn, Jr. Washington: National Academy Press.

Mead, Lawrence M. 1986. *Beyond Entitlement: The Social Obligations of Citizenship.* Free Press.

Moore, Kristin. 1980. *Policy Determinants of Teenage Childbearing.* Washington: Urban Institute.

Moynihan, Daniel P. 1969. *Maximum Feasible Misunderstanding: Community Action in the War on Poverty.* Free Press.

Murray, Charles A. 1984. *Losing Ground: American Social Policy, 1950–80.* Basic Books.

———. 1985. "Have the Poor Been 'Losing Ground'?" *Political Science Quarterly* 100 (Fall), pp. 427–45.

———. 1986. "No, Welfare Isn't Really the Problem." *Public Interest* 84 (Summer), pp. 3–11.

———. 1987. *In Pursuit of Happiness and Good Government.* Simon and Schuster.

National Council of La Raza. 1989. *Hispanic Poverty: How Much Does Immigration Explain?* Proceedings from the National Council of La Raza's Poverty Project Roundtable. Washington.

Office of Policy Planning and Research. 1965. *The Negro Family: The Case for National Action.* Washington: Department of Labor.

Ogbu, John U. 1978. *Minority Education and Caste: The American System in Cross-Cultural Perspective.* Academic Press.

———. 1988. "Diversity and Equity in Public Education: Community Forces and Minority School Adjustment and Performance." In *Policies for America's Public Schools: Teachers, Equity, and Indicators,* edited by Ron Haskins and Duncan MacRae. Norwood, N.J.: Ablex Publishing.

Peterson, Paul E., and J. David Greenstone. 1977. "Racial Change and Citizen

Participation: The Mobilization of Low-Income Communities through Community Action." In *A Decade of Federal Antipoverty Programs: Achievements, Failures, and Lessons,* edited by Robert H. Haveman. Academic Press.

Peterson, Paul E., and Mark Rom. 1988. "Lower Taxes, More Spending, and Budget Deficits." In *The Reagan Legacy: Promise and Performance,* edited by Charles O. Jones. Chatham, N.J.: Chatham House.

———. 1990. *Welfare Magnets: A New Case for a National Standard.* Brookings.

Plotnick, Robert D. 1989. "Welfare and Out-of-Wedlock Childbearing: Evidence from the 1980s." Paper prepared for the Conference on the Urban Underclass, Northwestern University.

Rainwater, Lee. 1970. *Behind Ghetto Walls: Black Families in a Federal Slum.* Chicago: Aldine Press.

Rainwater, Lee, and William L. Yancey. 1967. *The Moynihan Report and the Politics of Controversy.* MIT Press.

Reischauer, Robert D. 1987. "The Size and Characteristics of the Underclass." Paper prepared for the Research Conference of the American Public Policy and Management Association.

Ricketts, Erol R., and Isabel V. Sawhill. 1988. "Defining and Measuring the Underclass." *Journal of Policy Analysis and Management* 7 (Winter), pp. 316–25.

Riesman, David. 1953. *The Lonely Crowd: A Study of the Changing American Character.* Garden City, N.Y.: Doubleday.

Rossi, Peter H. 1989. *Down and Out in America: The Origins of Homelessness.* University of Chicago Press.

Shefter, Martin. 1978. "Party Bureaucracy and Political Change in the United States." In *Political Parties: Development and Decay,* edited by Louis Maisel and Joseph Cooper. Beverly Hills: Sage.

Skowronek, Stephen. 1982. *Building a New American State: The Expansion of National Administrative Capacities, 1877–1920.* Cambridge University Press.

Smeeding, Timothy, Barbara Boyle Torrey, and Martin Rein. 1988. "Patterns of Income and Poverty: The Economic Status of Children and the Elderly in Eight Countries." In *The Vulnerable,* edited by John L. Palmer, Timothy Smeeding, and Barbara Boyle Torrey. Washington: Urban Institute.

Smith, James P. 1988. "Poverty and the Family." In *Divided Opportunities: Minorities, Poverty, and Social Policy,* edited by Gary D. Sandefur and Marta Tienda. Plenum.

Sum, Andrew, Neal Fogg, and Robert Taggart. 1988. "Withered Dreams: The Decline in the Economic Fortunes of Young, Non-College Educated Male Adults and Their Families." Paper prepared for the William T. Grant Foundation Commission on Family, Work, and Citizenship.

Sundquist, James L. 1968. *Politics and Policy: The Eisenhower, Kennedy, and Johnson Years.* Brookings.

Weir, Margaret, Ann Shola Orloff, and Theda Skocpol, eds. 1988. *The Politics of Social Policy in the United States.* Princeton University Press.

Wilson, William Julius. 1987. *The Truly Disadvantaged: The Inner City, the Underclass, and Public Policy.* University of Chicago Press.

Is the American Underclass Growing?

CHRISTOPHER JENCKS

Late in 1981 Ken Auletta published three articles in the *New Yorker* on what he called the American underclass.[1] Auletta was not the first to use the term, but he was largely responsible for making it part of middle-class America's working vocabulary.[2] Six years later William Julius Wilson published *The Truly Disadvantaged*, the first book to present systematic evidence that the underclass was growing and the first to propose plausible hypotheses about why this was happening.

Since the term "underclass" is relatively new, most people assume that the phenomenon it describes must also be new. Yet what we now call the underclass bears a striking resemblance to what sociologists used to call the lower class. Both are characterized by high levels of joblessness, illiteracy, illegitimacy, violence, and despair. Ethnographic accounts of lower-class life in the 1960s, such as *Tally's Corner* or *Soulside,* describe lives that seem to me very similar in all these respects to the lives described in more recent writing on the underclass.[3]

If the American class structure is changing, as Wilson and others believe, the change is not that a completely new class has come into existence but that the old lower class has grown larger and perhaps more isolated from mainstream society. In my judgment these changes are not large enough to justify substituting the term underclass for the term lower class. But since almost everyone else now talks about the underclass rather than the lower class, I will do the same.

To determine whether the underclass is growing, one needs to define it. There is widespread agreement that "underclass" is an antonym for

I am indebted to Mary Corcoran, Sheldon Danziger, Jane Mansbridge, Susan Mayer, Paul Peterson, and Elizabeth Uhr for helpful comments on earlier versions of this essay, and to the Center for Urban Affairs and Policy Research, the Russell Sage Foundation, the Sloan Foundation, and the Ford Foundation for support while working on these issues.

1. The original articles were published November 16, 23, and 30, 1981. They are available in book form in Auletta (1982).

2. For a history of the term, see Aponte (1988).

3. See Liebow (1967); and Hannerz (1969).

"middle class," or perhaps more broadly for "mainstream" (a term that has come to subsume both the middle class and working class). But this kind of consensus does not take us very far, because Americans have never agreed on what it meant to be middle class or working class. Thus, it is just as hard to answer the question, "Is the middle class growing?" as to answer the question, "Is the underclass growing?"

The ambiguity of phrases like middle class and underclass derives from the fact that Americans use a multitude of different criteria to rank one another, including how much income people have, where they get it, whether they have mastered the cultural skills we value, and whether they conform to our ideals about social behavior. Because we all use different criteria to rank one another, we end up assigning different people to the social elite, to the middle class, and to the underclass. If you rank people primarily according to how much income they have while I rank people according to where they get their money, for example, we will put different people in the underclass. Likewise, if you think the underclass is composed of men who mug their neighbors or women who have babies out of wedlock, while I think of the underclass as composed of people who lack the social and cultural skills required to deal with mainstream American institutions, we will often disagree about whether specific individuals belong to the underclass or not.

In this chapter I consider four ranking schemes, each of which implies a different definition of the underclass.

Income level. Some social scientists equate membership in the underclass with persistent poverty. In everyday usage, however, the underclass does not include the elderly poor, the working poor, or others who are poor through no fault of their own. The underclass includes only those families whose poverty is attributable to a violation of one or more widely shared social norms, such as the family head's failure to work regularly or marry before having children. I will call this group the "impoverished underclass" (or sometimes just the "undeserving poor").

Income sources. Sociologists have traditionally assigned people to classes primarily on the basis of where they got their money rather than how much money they had. In their view the upper class got its income from capital, the middle and working classes got their money from regular jobs (or job-related pensions), and the lower class got its money from irregular work, crime, public assistance, and handouts. I will call this last group the "jobless underclass."

Cultural skills. Many Americans assign people to classes primarily on the basis of how they talk, how much they know, and how they deal with other people. From this perspective the middle class is composed of people who think, talk, and act like those who manage America's major institutions. The underclass is composed of people who lack the basic skills required to deal with these institutions. For lack of a better term I will call this group the "educational underclass."

Moral norms. Americans also talk a lot about middle-class "values," and some social critics use the term underclass to describe people who seem indifferent to these values. Three middle-class values (or as I would prefer to say, ideals) are especially salient in discussions of this kind:

—Working-age men should have a steady job. Those who violate this norm constitute the jobless underclass.

—Women should postpone childbearing until they are married. Those who violate this norm constitute what I will call the "reproductive under-class."

—Everyone should refrain from violence. Those who violate this norm constitute what I will call the "violent underclass."

Whether the underclass is growing depends on which of these ranking schemes one adopts.

Many Americans also think of the underclass as almost exclusively nonwhite. This perception may be partly due to racism, but it derives primarily from our habit of equating people's class position with their address. In most of the ranking schemes described above, the underclass includes considerably more whites than nonwhites. But the underclass constitutes only a small fraction of the white population, and American neighborhoods are only moderately segregated along economic lines. As a result, underclass whites are seldom a majority in any neighborhood. This means that if you equate membership in the underclass with living in an underclass neighborhood, not many whites will qualify.[4]

Nonwhites are far more likely than whites to have underclass characteristics, and they almost always live in racially segregated neighborhoods. Because the underclass constitutes a relatively large fraction of the nonwhite population, it is a majority or near majority in some nonwhite neighborhoods. Those who equate membership in the underclass with living in an underclass neighborhood therefore see the underclass as nonwhite.[5]

4. See Mincey (1988). The city with the largest concentration of such white underclass neighborhoods seems to be Columbus, Ohio, which attracts many immigrants from West Virginia, eastern Kentucky, and eastern Tennessee, which are the heartland of white poverty in America.

5. Wilson's (1987) definition of the underclass, while formally color-blind, also implies that it is largely nonwhite. He sees the underclass as having two crucial features: chronic

I have not incorporated either race or geographic isolation into my definitions of the underclass, but I will ask whether each definition implies that the underclass has become blacker or more geographically isolated over time. The data available for answering these questions are far from ideal. With regard to geographic isolation, the only trend data are from 1969–70 to 1979–80, and even those data are not all one might wish. With regard to race, there are a lot of data on blacks but very little on racially distinctive Latinos.

Most Latinos are a mix of black and white or native American and white, and they have traditionally used racial categories that treat race as a continuum rather than a set of sharp dichotomies. In the United States, however, the Census Bureau merely asks people whether they are black, white, native American, Asian, or "other." This schema does not work well for Latinos, nearly half of whom describe themselves as "other." [6] Furthermore, neither the Census Bureau nor any other survey organization reports data broken down by race on Latinos. Thus while I will be able to say whether each of my definitions implies that the underclass is getting blacker, I will not be able to say whether it is getting browner.

The Impoverished Underclass

Many early discussions of the underclass treated the term as a synonym for the persistently poor.[7] By the late 1980s, however, a consensus had developed that the underclass was a subset of the poor and that it included only those families and individuals whose poverty was somehow attributable to their behavior. The underclass had, in other words,

---

joblessness and social isolation. He then equates social isolation with living in a neighborhood where most residents are lower class. As a result, members of the lower class are seldom part of his underclass unless they are nonwhite.

6. The great majority of Latinos now living in the United States came here from Mexico. Most probably they have both European and native American ancestors. Many Puerto Ricans, in contrast, are of mixed European and African ancestry. When the 1980 census asked respondents to classify each member of their household as white, black, native American, Asian, or "other," non-Hispanics almost all used one of the first four categories. Only a little over half of all Hispanics used these four categories, and almost all of these said they were white. Most of the rest classified themselves as "other." I have not been able to find any data on whether Hispanics who say they are white differ in appearance or ancestry from those who say they are "other."

7. The first such study, which predated Auletta's popularization of the term, was Levy (1977). For a more recent study that equates membership in the underclass with persistent poverty, see Ruggles and Marton (1986).

become a synonym for those whom an earlier generation called the "un-deserving" poor.

To see whether the impoverished underclass is growing, I proceed in three steps. First, I look at changes in the prevalence of short-term poverty. Second, I look at changes in the proportion of the short-term poor who are likely to be poor for a long period. Third, I look at changes in the proportion of the poor who behave in ways that most Americans consider blameworthy.

Changes in the Overall Poverty Rate

The federal government classifies people as poor if their reported (or in some cases imputed) family income for the previous calendar year was less than the official poverty line. This line, which varies with family size and the age of family members, was created in 1965 and was supposedly tied to the cost of a nutritionally adequate diet.[8] In practice, however, it is best understood as a line that happened to divide the poorest fifth of Americans from the richest four-fifths in 1963.[9] The line has been adjusted every year to take account of changes in the consumer price index. It has not been adjusted to take account of changes in what more affluent families can afford to buy, so it embodies an absolute rather than a relative standard.[10]

Table 1 shows changes between 1959 and 1988 in three different measures of the prevalence of poverty. Row 1 shows the official poverty rate, published every year by the Census Bureau. This rate has two well-known flaws: it uses a faulty price index to adjust the poverty line for inflation, and it ignores noncash benefits. Because of these flaws, it understates the decrease in poverty over the past generation.

Row 2 shows how the official rate changes when we use a better measure of inflation.[11] While using a better inflation index makes poverty

8. Orshansky (1965).

9. For evidence that there is no sharp break in the prevalence of material hardship near the poverty line, see Mayer and Jencks (1989).

10. For evidence that the poverty line does not, in fact, represent a constant level of material well-being, see Jencks and Mayer (forthcoming).

11. The official rate adjusts the poverty threshold for inflation using the consumer price index for urban consumers (CPI-U). Before 1983 the CPI-U exaggerated the rate of inflation because of the way it treated the costs of home ownership. The rates in table 3 adjust for inflation using the CPI-U-X1, which estimates changes in housing costs from changes in rents. Because the CPI-U and CPI-U-X1 both use 1967 as their benchmark year, the CPI-U-X1 yields higher poverty rates than the CPI-U before 1967, the same rate in 1967, and lower rates after 1967.

TABLE 1. Poverty Rates and Characteristics of the Poor,
Selected Years, 1959–88

Percent unless otherwise specified

Item	1959	1967	1974	1981	1988
Poverty rate					
Thresholds adjusted using CPI-U	22.4	14.2	11.2	14.0	13.1
Thresholds adjusted using CPI-U-X1	23.2	14.2	10.5	12.2	11.6
Thresholds adjusted using CPI-U-X1 and income adjusted for recipient value of noncash benefits	23.1	14.0	9.7	10.8	10.5
Composition of the poverty population					
Percent black	25.1	30.5	30.7	30.0	30.6
Percent of poor families with children headed by women	28.0	39.5	57.2	54.8	63.7
Per capita income (1988 dollars)	...	7,939	10,029	11,016	13,123
Unemployment Rate	5.3	3.7	5.5	7.5	5.4

(handwritten marginalia: "accumulation", "unemploy.", "rate", "not being paid much?")

SOURCES: Row 1. Bureau of the Census, "Money Income and Poverty Status in the United States: 1988," *Current Population Reports,* series P-60, no. 166 (Department of Commerce, 1989), table 18.

Row 2. *Current Population Reports,* series P-60, no. 166, table F-2, for 1974, 1981, and 1988, and table 18 for 1967. The CPI-U-X1 is not available for 1959, but since it rose at almost the same rate between 1967 and 1988 as the fixed-weight price index for personal consumption expenditures in the national income and product accounts, I assumed that the same was true from 1959 to 1967. On this assumption the old CPI overstates inflation between 1959 and 1967 by 2.7 percent. I therefore assumed that substituting the CPI-U-X1 for the CPI should raise the 1959 poverty thresholds by about $1 - 1/1.027 = 2.63$ percent.

The CPI overstated inflation between 1967 and 1988 by 10.0 percent. This error raised the estimated 1988 poverty rate from 11.6 to 13.1 percent. I therefore assumed that each 1 percent increase in the poverty threshold increased the poverty population by $(.131/.116 - 1)/.10 = 1.29$ percent. It follows that raising the 1959 poverty thresholds by 2.63 percent should raise the poverty population by $(1.29)(2.63) = 3.4$ percent. Since the 1959 poverty rate using the CPI was 22.4 percent, I assumed that using the CPI-U-X1 would have raised it to $(22.4)(1.034) = 23.2$ percent.

Row 3. Bureau of the Census, "Estimates of Poverty, Including the Value of Noncash Benefits: 1987," Technical paper 58 (Department of Commerce, 1988), table 1, shows the effect of adding the "recipient value" of food and housing benefits to respondents' incomes in 1979 through 1987. This adjustment lowered the official poverty rate by 1.7 points in 1979, 1.6 points in 1980, 1.4 points in 1981, 1.3 points in 1982, and 1.2 or 1.1 points from 1983 through 1987. The size of the reduction was not proportional to the base rate. I therefore assumed that taking account of noncash benefits would lower poverty rates based on the CPI-X-1 by 1.4 points in 1981 and 1.1 points in 1988.

Bureau of the Census, *Statistical Abstract of the United States: 1979,* 100th ed. (Department of Commerce, 1979), table 522, and *1988,* 108th ed., table 553, show that governmental expenditure, on food and housing programs roughly doubled in real value between 1974 and 1980, so I assumed that their effect on the size of the poverty population also doubled. This implied that they reduced the poverty rate by .8 points in 1974. Analogous reasoning suggested a reduction of about .2 points in 1967.

Rows 4 and 5. *Statistical Abstract of the United States: 1988,* tables 18 and F-2. The estimates for 1967–88 are for those who fall below thresholds based on the CPI-U-X1. The estimates for 1959 are for those who fall below thresholds based on the CPI-U.

Row 6. *Current Population Reports,* Series P-60, no. 166, table F-15. These estimates are adjusted for inflation using the CPI-U-X1.

Row 7. *Economic Report of the President* (1989), table B-39.

decline somewhat more over time, the basic story is the same as when we use the official rate. Economic growth cut the poverty rate from 23.2 percent in 1959 to 10.5 percent in 1974. After 1974 progress stopped. The poverty rate was 1 point higher in 1988 than in 1974, even though the labor market was about equally tight in both years.[12]

Row 3 adjusts the estimates in row 2 for the growth of noncash government benefits. The adjustment tries to assign to food stamps and government housing subsidies the monetary value recipients would assign them. It does not assign a cash value to medicaid or medicare, because these programs have not allowed poor families to reduce their medical expenditures. Unlike food stamps and housing subsidies, therefore, medicare and medicaid have not allowed the poor to spend more on other goods and services.[13] Medicare and medicaid have, however, greatly increased poor people's access to medical services. Readers should keep this in mind when assessing the poverty counts in row 3.

While the official poverty series shows no overall progress between 1967 and 1981, the revised series in row 3 shows that poverty dropped by nearly one-third during this period. All three series agree, however, in showing minimal progress since 1981. All three also show somewhat more poverty in 1988 than in 1974.

Real per capita income rose 31 percent between 1974 and 1988 (see row 6), so we cannot blame the increase in poverty after 1974 on economic stagnation. Unemployment was also slightly lower in 1988 than in 1974, so we cannot blame slack labor markets. Poverty persisted because both earnings and per capita family income became more unequal.[14] The reasons why inequality increased are controversial and poorly understood. Indeed, the hypothesis that America has a growing underclass

12. The choice of years in table 1 was dictated by the availability of data. At the time this paper was written, counts using the CPI-U-X1 were available for only 1974 through 1988. To extend the CPI-U-X1 series back in time, I exploited the fact that 1967 was the benchmark year for the CPI-U-X1, making poverty rates using the CPI-U-X1 and CPI-U the same in that year.

13. Before the advent of medicare and medicaid in 1965, the poor seldom bought health insurance. In many cases they got free care; in other cases they did without care. In 1960–61 the Labor Department's Consumer Expenditure Survey (CES) shows that families with total expenditures below the poverty line spent 7.2 percent of their money on medical care. This figure fell to 6.6 percent in 1972–73 and remained constant from 1972–73 to 1984–85. (All these estimates are based on tabulations by Larry Radbill using the original CES interview surveys for the relevant years. They all exclude nonprescription drugs.)

14. For a detailed analysis of the changing distribution of earnings, see Juhn, Murphy, and Pierce (1989). On trends in per capita family income, see Danziger (1988), table 2.

appeals to many people precisely because it purports to explain this puzzle.[15]

Is Poverty More Persistent?

The next question is whether the proportion of the short-term poor who remain poor over a prolonged period has been constant. One simple way to address this question is to ask whether annual turnover in the poverty population has increased or decreased. Terry Adams, Greg Duncan, and Willard Rodgers have calculated the proportion of urban families who were poor one year but not the next from 1969 through 1983.[16] They found no clear trend during the 1970s: about a third of the urban families that were poor in one year escaped poverty the following year, although many undoubtedly fell back into poverty in some subsequent year. Poverty became more persistent between 1979 and 1983, but that may have been because the overall poverty rate rose by a third during these years. The increasing persistence of urban poverty in the early 1980s was also partially offset by a decline in the persistence of rural poverty.

Duncan and Rogers also examined changes in the proportion of women age 25 to 44 living in families whose mean money income over a six-year interval fell below the poverty line.[17] The proportion of black women with children who were long-term poor rose from 16.5 percent in 1967–72 to 24.2 percent in 1980–85.[18] Among white women with children, the proportion hardly changed, rising only from 2.2 percent in 1967–72 to 2.4 percent in 1980–85. The deteriorating situation of black mothers was a by-product of growing inequality, not declining mean income. Inequality grew because fewer black mothers were married.

The available evidence suggests, in short, that poverty was somewhat

15. See Paul Peterson's paper in this volume.

16. Adams, Duncan, and Rodgers (1988), figure 5.2.

17. Duncan and Rodgers (1989). The data come from the Panel Study of Income Dynamics.

18. The sampling error of the difference between 1967–72 and 1980–85 appears to be about 3 percentage points, so the 95 percent confidence interval for the 8 point change cited in the text runs from 2 to 14 points. There are not enough nonmothers of either race to draw any conclusions about their poverty rates, but it is striking that among the 69 black women age 25 to 44 who were not living with a child, the long-term poverty rate appears to have been zero. Duncan and Rodgers (1989) use the CPI-U to estimate trends in persistent poverty, and their calculations ignore the cash value of food stamps. Correcting these problems would presumably make the trend less dramatic and might make it statistically insignificant.

more persistent in the early 1980s than in the 1970s. Whether this trend continued in the late 1980s remains uncertain.

The Inheritance of Poverty

When social critics talk about persistent poverty, they often mean poverty that persists from one generation to the next rather than just from one year to the next. As we shall see, the influence of white parents' educational attainment on their children's attainment has not changed significantly in recent times, while the influence of black parents' attainment on their children's attainment has declined, but I have not been able to locate any data on changes in the inheritance of either poverty or chronic joblessness.

Many people believe that poverty is becoming more hereditary because they think it is increasingly confined to blacks. Table 1 does not support this view. Blacks constituted 31 percent of the poor in 1967, and they still constituted 31 percent of the poor in 1988.[19] Black poverty has become more urban, which makes it more visible to opinion leaders. But moving the black poor from rural to urban areas is not likely to have made their poverty more hereditary.

The Undeserving Poor

Poverty may be a necessary condition for inclusion in the underclass, but few observers think it sufficient. The term caught on because it focused attention on those who were poor because they violated mainstream rules of behavior. There are at least four socially acceptable reasons for being poor: old age, physical disability, school enrollment, and low hourly wages (at least so long as one works steadily). Table 2 shows how the proportion of those who were poor for each of these reasons changed between 1968 and 1987.[20]

19. Since blacks' share of the total population rose from 11.0 percent in 1967 to 12.3 percent in 1988, the fact that they constituted a constant fraction of the poverty population implies that racial disparities in poverty rates narrowed slightly. Blacks also constituted a slightly smaller fraction of all poor children in 1988 than in 1974, but this was because more poor children were Hispanic.

20. Because table 2 uses the official poverty thresholds, it understates the decrease in poverty between 1968 and 1987. The demographic characteristics of the poor do not change much when the threshold is lowered by 5 or 10 percent, however, so the characteristics of the poor would not change much if the CPI-U-X1 were substituted for the CPI-U and noncash benefits were included.

TABLE 2. Characteristics of Individuals and Family Heads Who
Were Poor, 1968, 1987

Characteristics	1968	1987
Percent of poor who were:		
Over 65	39.0	21.5
Under 65, disabled	11.8	13.9
Under 65, able-bodied, in school	6.7	7.8
Under 65, able-bodied, not in school, and		
Worked all year	16.7	10.7
Worked part year	13.6	24.3
Did not work	12.3	21.8
Total[a]	100.0	100.0
Percent of all individuals and family heads who were:[b]		
Poor	15.2	14.5
Poor able-bodied nonstudents under 65		
who worked less than 48 weeks	3.9	6.7
Poor disabled nonstudents under 65 who		
worked less than 48 weeks	5.7	8.7
Poor nonstudents under 65 who did		
not work at all during the year	3.7	5.2

SOURCE: Tabulations by Sheldon Danziger, using the March 1969 and 1988 Current Population Survey tapes. Estimates cover unrelated individuals (individuals who live in a household that does not include anyone related to them by blood, marriage, or adoption) and heads of families (two or more related individuals living in the same household). Families are not weighted by size. Danziger used poverty thresholds based on the CPI-U and did not adjust for the value of noncash benefits. He also found 310,000 more poor families and unrelated individuals in 1987 than the Census Bureau found, but this has almost no effect on his results.

a. Totals may not add to number shown because of rounding.

b. I took the total number of family heads and unrelated individuals in 1969 and 1988 from *Current Population Reports*, series P-60, no. 166, tables 18 and 20.

The elderly accounted for a much smaller fraction of all poverty in 1987 than in 1968. So did family heads who worked throughout the year. As a result, only 54 percent of poor families and individuals had socially acceptable reasons for being poor in 1987, compared with 74 percent in 1968. This change inevitably reduced public sympathy for the poor.

If one excludes the elderly, the disabled, students, and family heads who work year-round, one is left with a group that most Americans regard as undeserving: men and women who "should" work regularly, but do not, and who are poor as a result. In 1968, 3.9 percent of all poor families and individuals fell into this group. By 1987, 6.7 percent fell into it. This definition of the undeserving poor is problematic in at least two respects, however. First, some of the disabled are undeserving by conventional standards. Second, poor family heads who work fewer than 48 weeks a year are not always undeserving by conventional standards.

At first glance the disabled seem to be prime examples of people who are poor through no fault of their own. On closer inspection, however, their moral status turns out to be rather complicated. Some are, of course, disabled by illness or accidents over which they had no control. But many have been disabled by alcohol or drug-related problems. This is precisely the group many Americans have in mind when they talk about the underclass. In addition, a significant fraction of the disabled suffer from mental disorders of various kinds, and while some observers think such problems beyond an individual's power to control, others reject this view.

Defining everyone whose disability derives from alcohol, drugs, or mental illness as undeserving would obviously increase the proportion of the poor so classified. But table 2 shows that even if we reclassify *all* the disabled poor as undeserving, this group still grew from 5.7 to 8.7 percent of all family heads and individuals between 1968 and 1987.

Counting all able-bodied family heads and individuals who worked fewer than 48 weeks in a year as undeserving also poses problems. Some family heads and individuals work fewer than 48 weeks for reasons over which they have no control, and some end up poor as a result. Counting everyone who works fewer than 48 weeks as undeserving therefore exaggerates the size of the underclass. The unemployment rate for married men averaged 3.9 percent in 1987, compared with only 1.6 percent in 1968. This fact strongly suggests that family heads had more trouble finding steady work in 1987 than in 1968. Counting every poor head who worked fewer than 48 weeks as undeserving is therefore likely to exaggerate the size of the impoverished underclass more in 1987 than in 1968. Any family head who looked for work throughout either of these years could have earned something, however. And table 2 shows that even if we restrict our definition of the undeserving poor to those who did no work whatsoever, the group was larger in 1987 than in 1968.

One reason poor family heads were less likely to work in 1987 than in 1968 was that they were less likely to be men. Only a little over half of all single mothers work in an average month, and even fewer work year-round. A generation ago many Americans thought single mothers were morally obligated to stay home with their children. But those who took this position still thought that most single mothers had brought their poverty on themselves, since most of them had either had babies out of wedlock or were divorced. Only poor widows qualified as deserving, and most of them were elderly. Today, Americans are somewhat more fatalistic about divorce, which many regard as an accident nobody can prevent. But we are also convinced that divorced mothers ought to work. As a result, most Americans still regard poor single mothers who do not work as undeserving.

No matter how we count the undeserving poor, therefore, it seems clear that a growing fraction of the population is poor because they have violated rules that most Americans regard as reasonable. Thus if the impoverished underclass includes everyone who is poor because they violated some widely accepted social norm, it is bigger today than it was in the late 1960s.

The Jobless Male Underclass

Men without regular jobs populate every journalistic and scholarly description of lower-class life. Indeed, American sociologists have traditionally seen chronic male joblessness as a defining characteristic of the lower class, and many writers now define the underclass in the same way. Ken Auletta's book on the underclass, for example, focused on twenty-two men and women who were enrolled in a job training program for the "hard core" unemployed. William Wilson has also defined the underclass as a group "outside the mainstream of the American occupational system." [21]

Yet while many writers see chronic joblessness as a necessary condition for membership in the underclass, few see it as sufficient. A computer engineer who makes a fortune, sells his company, and never works again is not a member of the underclass, even if he spends most of his time in an alcoholic stupor. Nor is a disabled construction worker with good disability benefits and a working wife part of the underclass. It is the combination of chronic joblessness and inadequate income that makes a man part of the underclass.

The best way to measure chronic joblessness would probably be to ask working-age adults how many months they had worked in, say, the past five years. Since nobody collects data of this kind, I will use four less satisfactory indicators, all derived from the Census Bureau's monthly Current Population Survey (CPS).

Nonparticipation. If individuals have no job when the CPS surveys their household and have not looked for a job within the past four weeks, the federal government classifies them as not in the labor force. I refer to such individuals as "nonparticipants."

Unemployment. If individuals have no job but have looked for one within the past four weeks, the federal government includes them in the labor force and classifies them as unemployed.

Current joblessness. Many jobless individuals look for work in some

21. Auletta (1982); and Wilson (1987), p. 8. See also Van Haitsma (1989).

months but not others. Officially, therefore, they move back and forth between unemployment and nonparticipation. The overall rate of joblessness (the sum of the unemployment rate and the nonparticipation rate) may therefore tell more than either rate alone.[22]

Long-term joblessness. Some men normally have a steady job but occasionally lose it for some reason and are unemployed until they find another job. These men are not part of the jobless underclass. But very few of them are jobless for long periods. If a man has no job whatever for an entire calendar year, he may work again the following year, but he is unlikely to work at a steady job. I will call men who do not work for an entire year the "long-term jobless."

My analysis of trends in joblessness proceeds in two stages. First, I show that no matter how we measure it, joblessness has increased over the past generation among prime-age men. Then, I look at the extent to which these jobless men are poor and show that a growing proportion are not.

Changes in Joblessness among Mature Men

Figure 1 shows trends since 1948 in nonparticipation and unemployment among men 25 to 54 years old. The difference between the two measures is striking. The unemployment rate is dominated by the business cycle, while the nonparticipation rate is almost insensitive to the business cycle. The unemployment rate shows no long-term trend before 1970, whereas the nonparticipation rate began to climb in the late 1950s and continued to climb throughout the 1960s, even though unemployment was falling. Despite these differences, however, both the nonparticipation rate and the unemployment rate at the peak of the business cycle have risen steadily since 1970. As a result, overall joblessness has been higher at the peak of each business cycle than at the peak of the previous cycle.

22. The labor force participation rate (P) is $N_p / (N_n + N_p)$, where N_p is the number of participants and N_n is the number of nonparticipants. The official unemployment rate (U) is equal to $N_u / (N_p)$, where N_u is the number of men who are unemployed. This means that the official unemployment and nonparticipation rates are not additive. To make them additive, one must multiply the official unemployment rate by the participation rate. To avoid this difficulty, the unemployment rates I report in this section (including those in figure 1) are equal to $N_u / (N_n + N_p)$. Elsewhere, where additivity is not relevant, I use the official rate. For men, the difference is very small.

FIGURE 1. Unemployment, Nonparticipation in Labor Market, and Jobless Rates, Men 25 to 54 Years Old, 1948–88

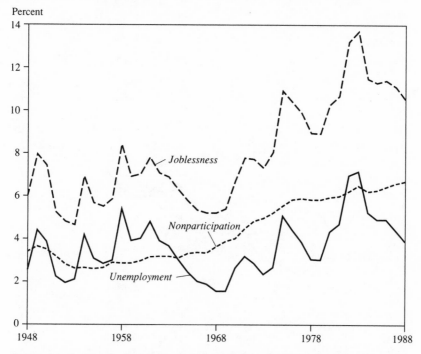

SOURCE: Annual averages for the civilian noninstitutional population derived from Current Population Survey; see Bureau of Labor Statistics, *Handbook of Labor Statistics* (Department of Commerce, 1989), tables 5 and 28. Estimates are unweighted means of rates for men age 25 to 34, 35 to 44, and 45 to 54.

We do not know how many of the men who are jobless in a given month are chronically jobless, but the fraction is certainly high. Kim Clark and Lawrence Summers reported, for example, that unemployment among men over the age of 20 averaged 3.8 percent in 1974 (a relatively good year). Eliminating men who were unemployed fewer than 15 weeks reduced the rate only to 2.8 percent.[23] Spells of unemployment have been getting longer, so chronic joblessness probably accounts for an even larger fraction of all unemployment today than in 1974.[24] Chronic job-

23. Estimated from Clark and Summers (1979), table 4. Allowing for movement between unemployment and nonparticipation, spells of nonemployment lasting 14 weeks or fewer only accounted for about a sixth of all joblessness.
    24. Sider (1985).

FIGURE 2. Men Who Did Not Work during the Year, by Age, 1959–87

Percent

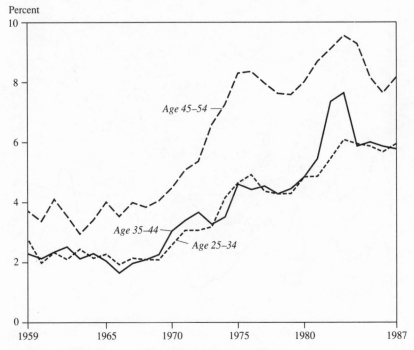

SOURCE: Bureau of Labor Statistics, *Handbook of Labor Statistics*, table 48.

lessness is even more common among those who are not looking for work in a given month (the nonparticipants) than among those who are.

Every March the CPS asks whether each member of its sample worked for pay at any time during the previous year. Except in very bad years, almost any 25- to 54-year-old man who looked for work throughout the year could have earned something. Therefore, if we set aside recession years, we can assume that men who did no paid work at all were either physically or mentally unable to work or else did not want the kinds of work that were available. (Whether they would have worked if better jobs had been available is obviously hard to determine.)

Figure 2 suggests that trends in long-term joblessness among 25- to 54-year-olds are similar to trends in nonparticipation. The business cycle has more effect on long-term joblessness than on nonparticipation, but not much more. The underlying rate of long-term joblessness among men age 25 to 54 shows no clear trend during the 1960s but rises steadily during both the 1970s and 1980s.

Because long-term joblessness began rising about 1970, some have blamed the increase on the baby boom generation's allergy to work. But figure 2 shows that long-term joblessness increased for all age groups after 1970, not just for those born after 1945. It also shows that long-term joblessness kept rising during the 1980s, despite widespread repudiation of the "hippie" values that attracted young adults in the 1960s.

The rise in long-term male joblessness during the 1970s also coincided with legislative and administrative changes that made it easier to get disability benefits. These changes presumably encouraged some chronically jobless workers to leave the labor force entirely. But since less than half of all prime-age nonparticipants collect disability benefits, other factors must also have been encouraging men to leave the labor force.[25]

The deinstitutionalization of the mentally ill also began in the early 1970s. The CPS does not survey inmates of institutions, so official estimates of the nonparticipation rate do not include inmates. But when inmates move into regular households, the CPS begins to count them. Since only a minority get jobs, the official nonparticipation rate is likely to have risen as a result.

Many other factors may also have contributed to the rise of male joblessness. International competition seems to have reduced the number of unskilled and semiskilled jobs that paid enough to support a family, and some men prefer no job to a poorly paid job. The civil rights revolution of the 1960s probably made blacks, in particular, less willing to accept "dead-end" jobs. Declining rates of marriage and rising rates of divorce also reduced the social pressure on some men to work, since they did not live with anyone who depended on their earnings. Among those who were still married, increases in wives' earning power probably made it easier to "retire" when no suitable job was available.

The Effects of Race

The Bureau of Labor Statistics does not publish estimates of long-term joblessness broken down by race, but table 3 shows estimates derived

25. See Parsons (1980), as well as the exchange between Parsons (1984) and Robert Haveman and Barbara Wolfe (1984). It is not clear how many beneficiaries would work if they did not get benefits, but John Bound (1989) has shown that few rejected applicants return to the labor force. This finding casts doubt on Parsons's argument that nonbeneficiaries are often marginal workers who have stopped working in order to demonstrate that they are disabled and hence eligible for benefits.

TABLE 3. Percentage of Men Age 25 to 54 Who Were Jobless, by Race and Economic Status, Selected Years, 1959–87

Status	Census[a]			CPS[b]				
	1959	1969	1979	1964	1968	1974	1979	1986
No job during calendar year								
Whites								
Noninmates	2.4	3.1	4.7	2.3	2.3	3.4	3.8	4.6
Poor	1.4	1.3	1.5	1.0	.9	1.1	1.1	1.7
Nonpoor	1.0	1.8	3.2	1.3	1.4	2.3	2.7	2.9
Inmates	0.9	0.6	0.6	...	...	...	...	...
Total	3.3	3.7	5.3	...	...	...	...	...
Blacks								
Noninmates	5.8	8.5	14.1	4.9	4.7	11.6	10.4	13.6
Poor	4.3	5.3	6.6	3.7	2.6	6.2	5.0	6.9
Nonpoor	1.5	3.2	7.5	1.2	2.1	5.4	5.4	6.7
Inmates	2.4	2.5	2.3	...	...	...	...	...
Total	8.2	11.0	16.4	...	...	...	...	...
	1960	1970	1980	1965	1969	1975	1980	1987
No job during survey week								
Whites								
Noninmates	6.4	6.4	9.1	5.7	4.4	10.0	8.8	10.2
Poor	2.4	1.8	1.8	1.7	1.1	1.7	1.7	2.5
Nonpoor	3.9	4.8	7.3	4.0	3.3	8.3	7.1	7.7
Inmates	1.2	0.9	0.8	...	...	...	...	...
Total	7.6	7.3	9.9	...	...	...	...	...
Blacks								
Noninmates	13.4	14.8	20.5	13.6	9.9	23.4	19.4	22.2
Poor	8.0	7.1	7.0	7.5	4.0	8.1	6.7	8.8
Nonpoor	5.5	7.7	13.5	6.1	5.9	15.3	12.7	13.4
Inmates	3.5	3.6	3.6	...	...	...	...	...
Total	16.9	18.4	24.1	...	...	...	...	...

SOURCES: Census estimates are from 1/1,000 public use samples. CPS estimates are from the annual March survey. The 1979 poverty counts are based on the official 1979 poverty thresholds. Census poverty counts for 1959 and 1969 used the fixed-weight price index for personal consumption expenditures (PCE) from the National Income and Product Accounts to adjust the 1979 poverty thresholds for price changes. CPS poverty counts for 1968, 1974, and 1986 used the CPI-U-X1 to adjust the 1979 poverty thresholds for price changes. The CPS count for 1964 used an estimate of the CPI-U-X1 for 1964 based on the relationship between the CPI-U-X1 and the CPI-U from 1967 to 1979. The difference between the PCE and CPI-U-X1 indices is trivial. Poverty status is for the year shown at the top of the column, even when joblessness is measured the following March or April. The components of the jobless population may not add to totals because of rounding.

a. Includes members of the armed forces and inmates of institutions. Excludes students living in dormitories.

b. Excludes members of the armed forces, inmates of institutions, and individuals who said they were not working because they were enrolled in school.

FIGURE 3. Jobless Men Age 25 to 54, by Race, 1954–88

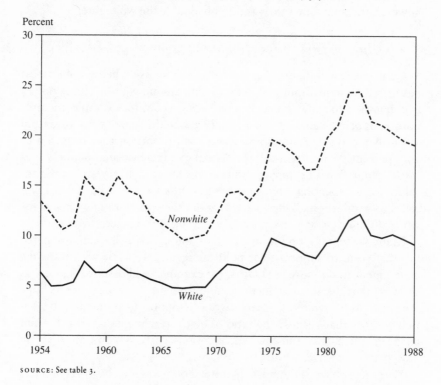

SOURCE: See table 3.

from census and CPS data. In 1959 about 8 percent of prime-age black men did not work at all, compared with about 3 percent of prime-age white men. By 1979 more than 16 percent of black men did not work at all, compared with about 5 percent of white men. The CPS shows lower rates of long-term joblessness than the census, but it too shows that long-term joblessness increased between 1964 and 1986.[26]

Figure 3 shows racial differences in the proportions of white and non-white men who were jobless at the time of the monthly CPS survey. It shows no underlying trend in joblessness among either whites or non-whites until 1970. After 1970 the underlying level of joblessness began to

26. The CPS estimates in table 3 are lower than those in figure 2 because the CPS samples used in table 3 exclude men who were not working at the time of the survey because they were enrolled in school. The census samples, in contrast, exclude everyone who said he was enrolled in school at the time of the survey, regardless of whether he was working.

climb for both groups. Regardless of whether joblessness was high or low, however, the nonwhite rate was roughly double the white rate.   ✗

Absolute versus Proportional Changes

Confronted with figure 3, a reader is likely to ask whether joblessness has increased more among nonwhites than among whites. This is not an easy question to answer. Between 1968 and 1988, for example, the proportion of prime-age white men with no job in the survey week rose from 4.8 to 9.1 percent. Among nonwhites the proportion rose from 9.9 to 19.1 percent. What I will call the "absolute" increase among nonwhites (19.1 − 9.9 = 9.2 percentage points) was thus much larger than the absolute increase among whites (9.1 − 4.8 = 4.3 points). But what I will call the "proportional" increase was about the same for nonwhites as for whites (9.2/9.9 = 93 percent as against 4.3/4.8 = 90 percent).

Many writers respond to this kind of ambiguity by looking for statistics that seem to support their political agenda. Liberals who want the government to do more for blacks, for example, will describe figure 3 as showing that the absolute increase in joblessness has been twice as large for blacks as for whites. Conservatives who oppose government intervention will say that because the ratio of black to white joblessness has not changed much, governmental interventions such as affirmative action have been ineffective.

When a problem is diminishing instead of increasing, however, liberals and conservatives often change statistical hats. In 1970, for example, the black infant mortality rate was twice the white rate. By the mid-1980s both rates had been cut in half.[27] Liberals who wanted the government to spend more on medical care for the poor argued that existing efforts were inadequate because the black rate was still twice the white rate. Conservatives argued that since the black rate had fallen faster than the white rate without the proposed programs, they were unnecessary.

To move beyond such political rhetoric, we need to recognize that different kinds of comparisons answer different questions. Consider the following questions about race and joblessness.

Has rising joblessness hurt blacks more than whites? The answer to this question depends on the absolute change for each group. A 10 point increase in joblessness hurts a group more than a 5 point change, regardless of whether the group's initial rate was 5 percent or 50 percent. Be-

27. Bureau of the Census, *Statistical Abstract of the United States: 1989*, 109th ed. (Department of Commerce, 1989), table 113.

cause blacks had a higher rate of joblessness than whites in the late 1960s, doubling both rates hurt blacks more than whites. Likewise, since blacks had a higher infant mortality rate than whites in the late 1960s, halving both rates helped blacks more than whites.

How are the changes likely to have influenced public perceptions of the jobless? America's black population is growing faster than its white population, but not much faster. This means that if the proportional increase in joblessness is greater among whites than among blacks, the jobless population will become whiter. If the proportional increase is greater among blacks, the jobless population will become blacker. The changing complexion of the jobless may, in turn, influence whether the problem is blamed on macroeconomic policy, shiftlessness, or other factors.

Do the observed changes indicate that race exerts more or less effect than in the past? While this is a common question, we cannot answer it unless we make it more precise. We must specify, "More influence compared with what?" If joblessness doubles for both blacks and whites, the absolute effect of race has clearly doubled. But to know whether race has become more important compared with other factors that influence joblessness, we must ask whether race explains more or less of the overall variation in joblessness. We cannot answer this question by comparing either absolute or proportional changes.[28]

This paper examines problems that are widely seen as causing material and emotional hardship. I therefore emphasize absolute changes in the incidence of these problems, regardless of whether I compare blacks with whites, college graduates with high school dropouts, or residents of rich and poor neighborhoods. But since proportional changes indicate how the social composition of the underclass is changing, I will sometimes discuss them as well.[29]

28. To know whether race has become more or less important relative to the past, one needs to know whether its unstandardized coefficient in a dummy variable regression has changed. To know whether race has become more or less important relative to other factors that influence joblessness, one needs to know whether its standardized coefficient has changed. Because the standard deviation of a dichotomous dependent variable is a nonlinear function of the mean, doubling the rate of joblessness for both blacks and whites does not double the standard deviation. Doubling the rate of joblessness for all groups therefore changes both the standardized coefficient and the percentage of the total variance explained by race.

29. Most quantitative social scientists now analyze dichotomous outcomes such as joblessness using log-linear models, which assume that two groups have changed by the same amount when the logged odds $(lnp/[1-p])$ change by the same amount. Log-linear models have many attractive statistical properties, but equal changes in the logged odds of a given outcome almost never imply equal changes in any real world phenomenon. A log-linear

Chronic Joblessness and Poverty

Almost everyone agrees that joblessness alone is not sufficient to make a man a member of the underclass. It is the combination of joblessness and poverty that defines the jobless underclass. This does not necessarily mean that we should exclude from the underclass every chronically jobless man whose family has an income above the poverty line. If a permanently jobless man has no income of his own, lives with his parents or a sibling, and escapes poverty only because *their* income is above the poverty line, we might want to include him in the jobless underclass. Likewise, if a man lives alone, works episodically, and earns just enough to stay above the official poverty line ($6,155 for a single man in 1988), we might want to include him in the underclass. As a first approximation, however, excluding those who are not poor from the underclass surely makes more sense than including them.

To see whether the jobless poor have grown more numerous, table 3 divides chronically jobless men into three groups: inmates of institutions, noninmates with family incomes below the poverty line, and noninmates with family incomes above the poverty line. (For this purpose, the term "family" includes individuals who do not live with relatives.) This breakdown dramatizes two surprising facts.

—Joblessness is by no means synonymous with poverty. If we set aside inmates of institutions (whose family income is unknown), more than

---

regression coefficient is meaningless unless the base rate for the group to which it applies is known. Comparing log-linear coefficients for groups with different base rates is like comparing standardized regression coefficients for groups with different variances. In both cases the results are likely to be misleading.

Suppose, for example, that joblessness is initially 5 percent among whites and 50 percent among blacks. Then suppose that the logged odds of being jobless rise by 0.75 for both groups. A little algebra shows that this would mean joblessness had reached 10 percent among whites and 68 percent among blacks. In what substantive sense might one say that these changes were the same? The jobless population would be whiter at time 2 than at time 1, because the proportional increase would be 100 percent for whites compared with only 36 percent for blacks. Yet blacks would have suffered more than whites, because the absolute increase would be 18 points for blacks compared with 5 points for whites.

None of this means social scientists should not use log-linear models. It just means that they should not draw substantive conclusions from such models until they estimate the effect of a given variable on the actual probability that individuals with different characteristics will experience different outcomes. When an investigator fails to do this, readers must do it for themselves. When they do, they will often find that they disagree with the substantive conclusions of authors who failed to do it.

half of all prime-age jobless men now live in families with incomes above the poverty line.

—The big increase in joblessness has been among men whose families are not poor. By some measures, the jobless underclass did not grow at all between 1959 and 1979. It did grow between 1979 and 1986, but that may have been partly because some parts of the country had not fully recovered from the 1980–83 recession.

The proportion of men 25 to 54 years old living in institutions did not change much between 1960 and 1980. Changes in the size of the jobless underclass therefore depend largely on changes in the number of noninmates who were both chronically jobless and poor.

Regardless of whether we include everyone who was jobless at the time of the CPS or only those who were jobless throughout the previous year, the proportion of prime-age men who were both jobless and poor increased between 1979–80 and 1986–87. Among whites, the absolute increase was less than 1 percentage point, but the proportional increase was large (on the order of half). Among blacks, the absolute increase was about 2 percentage points, but the proportional increase was smaller (about a third).[30]

The underclass story is, however, supposed to describe longer-term changes in the American class structure. At a minimum, the underclass is supposed to have grown during the 1970s as well as during the 1980s. Table 3 tells an ambiguous story about the 1970s. If everyone who was both poor and jobless at the time of the census is included in the jobless underclass, the census suggests that it was about the same size in 1980 as in 1970. This is true both among blacks and among whites.[31] If the jobless underclass includes only the hard core who did not work at all during the calendar year and were also poor, the jobless underclass grew from 5.3 percent of all prime-age black men in 1969 to 6.6 percent in 1979 and from 1.3 to 1.5 percent of all prime-age white men.

William Wilson's version of the underclass story also suggests that its growth was a by-product of macroeconomic problems that began around 1970 and that its elimination depends on restoring the more favorable conditions that prevailed in the 1960s. To test this hypothesis, we need to

30. I was not able to make comparable tabulations for 1988 and 1989 before this paper went to press, so I cannot say how much the tightening of the labor market in 1988 and 1989 reduced the estimated size of the jobless underclass.

31. The census and CPS are not strictly comparable to one another, so readers should not compare census estimates for one year with CPS estimates for another.

ask whether the jobless underclass shrank during the 1960s. If we include everyone who was poor and jobless at time of the census, the black underclass did shrink during the 1960s. But if we include only the hard core group that did not work for the entire calendar year, the black underclass grew during the 1960s as well as the 1970s.

Why should conclusions about whether the black underclass grew be so sensitive to the way in which we define chronic joblessness? The answer is that poverty decreased dramatically among irregularly employed black men between 1960 and 1980. It did not decrease nearly as fast among black men who did no work at all (data not shown).

If we use table 3 to estimate the poverty rate among jobless men, we can see that the economic cost of joblessness declined appreciably during the 1960s and 1970s, especially for blacks. The CPS data suggest that the poverty rate among the prime-age white males who did no work for an entire year fell from 43 percent in 1964 to 29 percent in 1979, before climbing back to 37 percent in 1986. Among prime-age black men who did no work, the poverty rate fell from 76 percent in 1964 to 48 percent in 1979 and then climbed to 51 percent in 1986. Poverty rates among men who were jobless at the time of the survey show the same trend.

We do not know precisely how jobless men escape from poverty, but their growing ability to do so was surely linked to the fact that other people's incomes were rising. Affluent nations can afford to provide a more generous safety net for men who do not work, and so can affluent families. When real earnings rose, as they did in the 1960s, real unemployment benefits also rose, keeping more jobless men out of poverty. In addition, disability benefits became more widely available, keeping some of the long-term jobless out of poverty. Perhaps equally important, families who took in jobless male relatives were less likely to be poor. When jobless men moved in with their parents, as they often do, their parents were less likely to be poor, so the men were also less likely to be poor. When older jobless men moved in with their children or siblings, the same logic applied. Perhaps most important, working wives were earning more, so their jobless husbands were less likely to be poor.

When the economic cost of joblessness declines, we expect some chronically jobless men to leave the labor force. The puzzle is not why such men stop working but why everyone else gets so upset when this happens. Judging by what the men were paid, employers never thought their services worth much. Their departure from the labor force cannot, therefore, have reduced the nation's economic output significantly. Nonetheless, their idleness makes almost everyone who works angry. Indeed, the spread of idleness among prime-age men is one of the main reasons why the affluent now feel less moral obligation to the poor than they felt in the 1960s or early 1970s.

Neighborhoods and Joblessness

Most theories about the underclass assume that chronic joblessness has increased more in poor inner-city neighborhoods than elsewhere. Published evidence on this point is surprisingly difficult to find, but an unpublished paper by Mark Hughes suggests that geographic differences followed much the same pattern as racial differences, at least during the 1970s. The proportional increase in joblessness was roughly the same in good and bad neighborhoods, so the absolute increase was much greater in bad neighborhoods.[32]

The Census Bureau divides metropolitan areas into tracts with 2,000 to 8,000 residents. For each tract the bureau reports the percentage of men older than 16 who worked fewer than 26 weeks during the year before the census. I will call this the rate of protracted joblessness. Hughes looked at changes in the geographic distribution of protracted joblessness in eight metropolitan areas: Atlanta, Chicago, Cincinnati, Cleveland, Detroit, Louisville, Newark, and Paterson. Averaging across all eight areas, the mean level of protracted joblessness rose from 26 percent in 1969 to 39 percent in 1979. In the worst fifth of all census tracts, the rate rose from about 40 percent to 58 percent. In the best fifth it rose from about 12 percent to 19 percent.[33] The absolute increase was thus much larger in the worst tracts. Since this was true in all eight cities that Hughes studied, one can feel confident that the social consequences of rising joblessness were more severe in bad neighborhoods.[34]

32. Hughes (1988). This paper appeared in the *Journal of Policy Analysis and Management* 8 (1989), pp. 274–82, but without the tables I discuss here.

33. The percentages in the text are unweighted means for all eight metropolitan areas. My estimates for the best and worst fifths of all census tracts assume that the distribution of tract means is normal and hence that the best and worst fifths of all tracts average 1.4 standard deviations above and below the mean for their metropolitan area. Because the estimates of joblessness include both students and the elderly, the absolute level of protracted joblessness is much higher than it would be for 25- to 54-year-olds. Including the elderly may also make the proportional difference between the best and worst tracts smaller.

34. Hughes believes that his findings contradict Wilson's argument that the underclass grew, because he construes Wilson as arguing that joblessness rose proportionally more in bad neighborhoods than in good ones. But Wilson's argument is only that there were more lower-class families living in predominantly lower-class neighborhoods in 1980 than in 1970. A change of this kind can occur either because neighborhoods become more residentially segregated or because the lower class gets bigger.

The proportional increase in joblessness was slightly larger in the best tracts, implying that residential segregation along economic lines diminished slightly.[35] But the decline in economic segregation was very small, and it did not occur in all eight cities. Since neither Reynolds Farley nor Douglas Massey and Mitchell Eggers found much change in residential segregation by income using larger samples of cities, I infer that economic segregation did not in fact change much during the 1970s.[36]

There are no trend data on the geographic distribution of poor jobless men, but the existing data allow some educated guesses. Table 3 showed that the proportion of prime-age men who were *both* long-term jobless and poor grew from 5.3 to 6.6 percent among blacks and from 1.3 to 1.5 percent among whites during the 1970s. The proportion who were currently jobless and poor did not change at all. Since there was not much change in the degree of economic segregation during the 1970s, a poor jobless man's chances of having a poor jobless neighbor cannot have risen much. Those who see the jobless underclass as including only jobless men with jobless neighbors cannot, therefore, argue that it grew much during the 1970s, though it may have grown a little among blacks.

The same logic also allows us to make educated guesses about the 1980s. Both poverty and joblessness increased slightly between 1979 and 1988, and the economic statistics currently available for 1989 look a lot like those for 1988. When 1990 census data become available, therefore, we are likely to find that more prime-age men were both poor and chronically jobless in 1989 than in 1979, but the increase is unlikely to be large. No one yet knows whether cities became more segregated along economic lines during the 1980s, but since there was not much change during the 1970s, I doubt that there was much during the 1980s. If poor jobless men became slightly more numerous and economic segregation did not change, the number of poor jobless men with poor jobless neighbors probably rose a little but not a lot.

---

35. Conclusions about trends in residential segregation are highly sensitive to the measure used. While the coefficient of variation for protracted joblessness hardly changed during the 1970s, tract-to-tract differences accounted for 8 percent of the individual-level variance in protracted joblessness in 1979, compared with only 5 percent in 1969. This contradiction reflects the fact that a 1 percent increase in the mean level of joblessness raises the individual-level standard deviation by less than 1 percent.

36. Reynolds Farley in this volume; and Massey and Eggers (1990).

The Effects of Education

Most versions of the underclass story agree that job opportunities declined after 1970 for men without high school diplomas. There are at least two theories about why this happened.

The "weak aggregate demand" hypothesis claims that overall demand for labor has lagged behind the supply since 1970. Poorly educated workers are always the last hired and the first fired, so any protracted labor surplus makes a lot of them redundant.

The "skills mismatch" hypothesis claims that the problem was not (or not just) weak aggregate demand but a shift in the composition of demand. Firms wanted more skilled workers and fewer unskilled workers. Although the men and women who entered the labor force during the 1970s and 1980s were considerably better educated than those who retired, the rate of improvement was, according to this hypothesis, less than the shift in demand. As a result, unskilled and semiskilled workers had more trouble finding steady jobs, and those who found jobs had to accept lower real wages than they had received in the 1960s.

Table 4 shows the proportion of men at different educational levels who worked 50 or more weeks, primarily at full-time jobs, in 1967, 1973, 1979, and 1987, all relatively good years. Steady employment decreased dramatically among men without higher education. Between 1967 and 1987 the proportion of high school graduates with steady jobs fell from 85 to 74 percent, while the proportion of high school dropouts with steady jobs fell from 77 to 59 percent.

The deteriorating position of less educated workers is consistent with both weak aggregate demand and a skill mismatch. But if aggregate demand for labor had remained strong, one would expect the decline in steady employment among the least educated to be matched by an increase among the most educated. Table 4 shows no such increase. The chances of finding a steady job did not diminish as much among college graduates as among less educated workers, but they did diminish, especially among those over the age of 35. This change argues against the view that firms faced a serious shortage of skilled workers. Had such a shortage existed, employers would have snapped up all the college-educated workers they could find.

Table 5 shows the relationship between education and long-term joblessness. The absolute increase was much greater among the least educated than among the most educated. At any given educational level, moreover, the absolute increase was larger among blacks than among

TABLE 4. Percentage of Men Employed Full-Time, Year-Round, by Age and Years of School, Selected Years, 1967–87

Age and schooling	1967	1973	1979	1987
Age 25–34				
0–8	68.6	58.4	50.7	53.3
9–11	74.8	72.3	59.2	53.0
12	83.6	79.4	72.0	71.4
13–15	83.2	74.1	72.1	74.7
16 or more	80.8	78.4	79.5	79.3
All	79.8	75.7	71.9	71.3
Age 35–44				
0–8	70.0	65.4	60.3	52.4
9–11	78.0	74.4	68.1	56.0
12	86.9	85.4	81.2	75.0
13–15	89.8	87.7	85.2	78.2
16 or more	92.3	90.9	87.9	87.0
All	83.1	82.1	80.0	76.5
Age 45–54				
0–8	69.7	64.7	57.0	53.5
9–11	78.7	75.7	72.8	67.7
12	84.5	82.6	78.5	77.1
13–15	85.4	84.5	79.8	80.9
16 or more	90.9	91.4	88.8	86.4
All	80.2	79.3	76.1	76.6

SOURCES: *Current Population Reports*, series P-60, no. 162, table 35; series P-60, no. 129, table 52; series P-60, no. 97, table 58; and series P-60, no. 60, table 4. All estimates exclude inmates of institutions and members of the armed forces but include other men without income.

whites. This pattern is broadly consistent with the underclass story, but with two important caveats.

—The increase in long-term joblessness, like the decrease in steady employment, was not confined to the least educated. It affected even the college educated.

—The increase in long-term joblessness is not confined to the 1970s. It is also apparent during the 1960s, when the economy was booming. (Black college graduates are the only exception.)

Table 5 also shows the proportion of men at different educational levels who were both jobless and poor. Again, several trends deserve comment:

—Jobless poverty increased substantially among both blacks and whites without high school diplomas.

—Jobless poverty also increased among black high school graduates.

—Jobless poverty shows some sign of having increased among black

TABLE 5. Percentage of Men Age 25 to 54 Who Were Jobless or Jobless and Poor, by Race and Years of School, Selected Years, 1959–79

Race and schooling	Did not work			Did not work and were poor			Did not work in census week and were poor		
	1959	1969	1979	1959	1969	1979	1959	1969	1979
Whites									
0–8	6.6	9.2	16.3	3.1	3.7	5.5	5.3	5.5	6.5
9–11	2.7	3.9	9.0	1.2	1.1	2.8	2.0	1.9	3.5
12	1.7	2.3	4.2	0.6	0.7	1.0	1.2	0.9	1.4
13–15	1.8	2.1	2.9	0.6	0.6	0.7	0.9	0.9	0.8
16 or more	1.0	1.5	2.2	0.4	0.5	0.6	0.5	0.4	0.5
All	3.2	3.7	5.3	1.4	1.3	1.5	2.4	1.8	1.8
Blacks									
0–8	8.9	14.1	28.8	5.3	8.0	12.4	9.8	11.8	14.4
9–11	10.2	12.8	20.1	4.4	5.1	7.6	7.5	7.0	7.2
12	5.8	7.4	14.7	2.3	3.1	6.3	4.6	3.5	6.3
13–15	2.1	6.6	7.3	0.7	3.3	2.2	2.8	2.8	2.6
16 or more	4.0	2.0	6.2	0	0.7	2.1	0	0	2.9
All	8.2	10.9	16.4	4.3	5.3	6.6	8.0	7.1	7.0

SOURCE: 1/1000 public use samples of census records. Poverty estimate is based on family income in the year prior to the census. Sample includes members of the armed forces and inmates but excludes students. For whites, sample sizes are all 2,900 or more. For blacks, sample sizes for 1959, 1969, and 1979 are 1,748, 1,115, and 648 in the "elementary or less" category; 638, 884, and 920 in the "some high school" category; 432, 863, and 1,387 in the "high school graduate" category; 141, 212, and 587 in the "some college" category; and 101, 146, and 374 in the "college graduate" category.

college graduates, but it remained rare, and the samples of such men are too small to be certain that the apparent trend was real.

—Joblessness also increased among whites with a high school diploma or more, but it did not lead to more poverty.

Joblessness among Younger Men

Many descriptions of the underclass emphasize joblessness among teenagers and young adults rather than among older men. In part, this is because the official teenage unemployment rate is much higher than the adult rate. In 1989, for example, the official rate among 16- to 19-year-old blacks averaged 32 percent for men and 33 percent for women, more than three times the rates for blacks over the age of 20. Among white teenagers, unemployment averaged 14 percent for men and 12 percent for women.[37] Official unemployment statistics for young people can be

37. *Economic Report of the President* (1990), p. 339.

FIGURE 4. Men Age 18 to 19 and 20 to 24 Not Employed, Enrolled in School, or in the Military, by Race, 1964–85

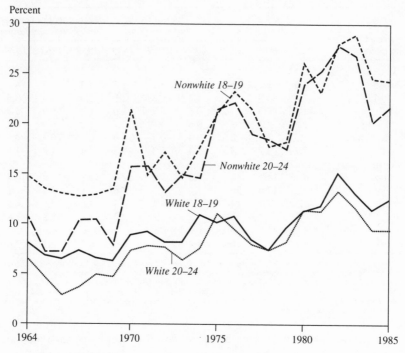

SOURCE: Mare and Winship (1984).

misleading, however, because they include students looking for part-time jobs and exclude men in the armed forces.

How many young men are truly doing nothing the larger society regards as useful? At present, the best approximation of this number is probably the percentage who are not in school, not in the armed forces, and not working in a civilian job. Robert Mare and Christopher Winship have estimated the proportions of young men who were idle in this sense during a typical week between 1964 and 1985.[38] Figure 4 shows their estimates for 18- to 19-year-olds and 20- to 24-year-olds.

Figure 4 is not strictly comparable to figure 3 because figure 3 ignores members of the armed forces and counts men who are enrolled in school

38. For a description of the way they constructed this series, see Mare and Winship (1984).

as jobless if they have no job during the survey week. But most 25- to 54-year-old students work at least part-time; and ignoring members of the armed forces does not appreciably affect the percentage who are jobless. Comparing figure 4 with figure 3 should, therefore, give a rough notion of whether idleness diminishes with age. It does not. For nonwhite men in 1985, for example, idleness averaged 25 percent among 18- to 19-year-olds, 22 percent among 20- to 24-year-olds, and 22 percent among 25- to 54-year-olds. Age differences among whites were also small.

Figure 4 also shows that race affects idleness among 18- to 24-year-olds in much the same way that it affects joblessness among older men. The nonwhite rate is about double the white rate. Both rates are sensitive to the business cycle, but the rates at the peak (or trough) of a business cycle have risen fairly steadily since the late 1960s.

Figure 4 shows the proportions of young men who were idle in the week they were surveyed. It does not show how long such men remained idle. The proportion of young men who reported that they did not work at any time during a calendar year has not risen. Only 10 percent of all 20- to 24-year-old men reported that they did not work during 1987, compared with 8 percent in 1979, 10 percent in 1969, and 8 percent in 1959.[39]

So far as I know, nobody has tried to explain why both short-term and long-term joblessness rose between 1959 and 1987 among mature men, while only short-term joblessness rose among younger men. My tentative hypothesis has five parts:

—"Good" jobs (that is, steady jobs that paid enough to support a family) became scarcer after 1970.

—Firms increasingly reserved these jobs for the college educated and for men with good work histories.

—Young men without higher education therefore found it harder to get good jobs. They responded by postponing marriage and by taking poorly paid, short-term jobs.

—The substitution of short-term jobs for steady jobs drove up the percentage of young men who were idle in a typical week but had little effect on the percentage who were idle for long periods.

—As young men get older, they become increasingly reluctant to take poorly paid short-term jobs. Some find steady jobs. Others drop out of the labor market entirely.

39. Bureau of Labor Statistics, *Handbook of Labor Statistics* (1989), table 48.

A rigorous test of this argument is obviously beyond the scope of this paper.

The Jobless Female Underclass

While almost all Americans think working-age men should have regular jobs, there is no such consensus regarding women. Many women of all social classes still marry and depend entirely on their husbands for support. Some Americans now regard such dependency as old-fashioned, but few regard it as evidence of shiftlessness. If a woman cannot persuade a man to support her, however, most Americans now think she should work, even if she has children.

The consensus that single mothers (those who are widowed, divorced, separated, or never married) ought to work is relatively recent. Until the 1960s, legislators thought single mothers should stay home and care for their children, even if that meant the government had to pay their bills. As the baby boom ended, however, the proportion of married mothers who worked outside their home began to rise (table 6). Feminist ideology, growing recognition that many marriages break up, and stagnant male earnings pushed still more married mothers into the labor market in the 1970s and 1980s. As more and more married mothers took jobs, legislators saw less and less reason to pay single mothers for staying home.

Congress made its first major effort to encourage work among single mothers in 1967, when it allowed welfare recipients to retain part of their earnings. Since then both federal and state legislators have devised dozens of different schemes for moving single mothers "off the welfare rolls and onto payrolls." Yet the proportion of single mothers with paid jobs only rose from 52 percent in 1960 to 57 percent in 1988 (table 6).[40] Since the proportion of married mothers with jobs rose from 26 percent to 62 per-

---

40. Table 6 covers all women who head families with children under age 18. Bureau of the Census, "Household and Family Characteristics," *Current Population Reports,* series P-20, table 1 (Department of Commerce, issued annually), shows that roughly an eighth of all female-headed families with children are headed by a woman other than the children's mother. Bureau of the Census, "Marital Status and Living Arrangements," *Current Population Reports,* series P-20, table 4 (issued annually), shows that more than half of these women are the children's grandmothers. Thus while I use the term single mothers to describe all female heads of families with children under age 18, it is not entirely accurate. Most female-headed families with children do, however, include the child's mother, even when she is not the head of the family.

TABLE 6. Income Sources of Female-Headed Families with Children, Selected Years, 1960–88

Characteristics	1960	1964	1968	1972	1976	1980	1984	1988
Families with children headed by women (percent)	9.4	10.0	11.0	13.3	16.3	18.6	20.2	21.2
Families with children headed by women on welfare (percent)	2.5	2.9	4.1	8.4	9.9	10.2	9.9	9.5
Working women with children (percent)								
Spouse present	26	30	35	38	42	51	55	62
No spouse present	52	n.a.	52	49	49	56	53	57
Percent of women heading families with children who:								
Collect AFDC	27	29	37	63	61	55	49	45
Collect AFDC and work	n.a.	n.a.	6	10	10	8	2	3
Mean monthly value of AFDC and food stamps (1988 dollars)	560	554	609	774	782	715	670	660

SOURCES: Row 1. *Current Population Reports*, series P-60, no. 166, table 20. Data are designated as applying to the previous year in the source but are based on the March CPS for the year shown here.

Row 2. See sources for row 1 and row 5. Estimate does not include families with male heads who received AFDC, either because they were unemployed or because they were disabled.

Row 3. Bureau of Labor Statistics, *Handbook of Labor Statistics* (Department of Commerce, 1989), p. 242.

Row 4. Robert Moffitt, "Work and the U.S. Welfare System," special report 46, Institute for Research on Poverty, University of Wisconsin, 1988, table 4. I estimated the values for 1972, 1976, and 1980 by interpolation from Moffitt's data on the immediately preceding and immediately following years. The value for 1988 is taken from *Current Population Reports*, series P-60, no. 166, table 22. The value for 1960 is from a 1/1,000 public use sample of 1960 census records.

Row 5. The rate shown here is the number of AFDC families headed by single women divided by the total number of families with children under 18 headed by single women. For number of female-headed families with children, see source, row 1. The total number of families receiving AFDC comes from *Social Security Bulletin: Annual Statistical Supplement, 1988*, table 9.G1. I estimated the proportion of AFDC families headed by women by interpolation and extrapolation from data on the number of AFDC families that included a disabled or unemployed husband, taken from *Background Material and Data on Programs within the Jurisdiction of the Committee on Ways and Means*, Committee Print, House Committee on Ways and Means (1989), table 22. I assumed that Puerto Rico, Guam, and the Virgin Islands accounted for 1.5 percent of the caseload in all years. I estimated the AFDC count for 1988 from data supplied by Emmett Dye of the Social Security Administration for fiscal years 1986–88 by assuming that the count for calendar 1988 = 0.75(fiscal 1988) + 0.25(fiscal 1989).

Row 6. Estimated from row 5 and data on the employment status of AFDC recipients in *Background Material*, Committee Print, 1989, p. 563; and Moffitt, "Work and the U.S. Welfare System."

Row 7. *Background Material and Data on Programs within the Jurisdiction of the Committee on Ways and Means*, Committee Print, House Committee on Ways and Means (1987), table 28. I readjusted the published estimates for inflation using the fixed-weight price index for personal consumption expenditures from the National Income and Product Accounts, taken from *Economic Report of the President, Fiscal Year 1988*, table B-4. All estimates are for a family of four. Estimates for 1960 through 1968 assume that a family did not receive food stamps; estimates for 1972 through 1988 assume that a family did receive food stamps. In reality, food stamps expanded gradually. In May 1969, 53 percent of all AFDC households got either food stamps or surplus food. This figure had reached 68 percent by 1973 and 83 percent by 1983. It was still 83 percent in 1987. See *Background Material*, Committee Print (1989), table 22. The estimate for 1988 assumes that AFDC benefits for a family of four rose at the same rate between 1986 and 1988 as the average monthly benefit per family, that food stamps constituted 30.5 percent of total benefits (see *Background Material*, Committee Print [1986], p. 662), and that the value of food stamps rose at the same rate as the consumer price index between 1986 and 1988.

n.a. Not available.

cent during this period, it seems reasonable to infer that the rewards of work increased far less for single mothers than for married mothers.

Confronted with statistics of this kind, most people have an easy explanation: single mothers do not work because they can get welfare instead. Some see their decisions as a simple matter of economics: those who can get a good job do so, but those who can get only low-wage work choose welfare because it pays better. Others deny that single mothers are income maximizers, arguing that many are now enmeshed in a "welfare culture" that makes them unlikely to work even if work pays significantly better than welfare. Advocates of this view conjure up images of women who grew up on welfare, had a baby out of wedlock while they were still teenagers, went on welfare themselves, and have never lived with anyone who held a regular job.

Surprisingly little research has been done on the relationship between welfare and work. Popular concern has focused largely on the number of single mothers collecting welfare rather than the number who work, so scholars have done the same. Most people assume that when more single mothers collect welfare, fewer work, and that when fewer collect welfare, more work. But the truth is that few Americans care whether single mothers work, so long as they do not collect welfare. The federal government did not calculate the number of single mothers who worked until 1981, and even today such statistics get almost no attention.

Table 6 shows that the proportion of single mothers collecting welfare has fluctuated dramatically since 1960, rising from 29 percent in 1964 to 63 percent in 1972, and then gradually declining to about 45 percent in 1988. These fluctuations had almost no effect on the proportion of single mothers who worked, which remained roughly constant.

One reason more single mothers began collecting welfare in the late 1960s was that Congress allowed them to supplement their meager welfare checks with low-wage work. Under the "$30 and a third" rule, welfare recipients who worked could keep the first $30 of their monthly earnings, plus a third of all additional earnings. In practice, the way in which welfare agencies calculated work-related expenses often allowed them to keep more. These rules remained in effect from 1967 to 1981, and during these years roughly a sixth of all welfare recipients told the welfare department that they worked. In 1981 the Reagan administration persuaded Congress to abandon this policy, once again reducing a welfare mother's check by the full amount of her earnings (except for work-related expenses). As a result, far fewer recipients told the welfare department that they worked. Some left the welfare rolls entirely. Others continued to work, but took off-the-books employment or worked under false social security numbers.[41]

Unfortunately, the weak relationship between trends in employment and trends in welfare receipt also raises questions about the quality of the data in table 6. From 1960 through 1968, about one-fifth of all single mothers appeared to be getting by without either working or collecting welfare. By 1972 such mothers had disappeared. The magnitude and speed of this change seem implausibly large, suggesting that the basic data may contain errors.[42] Thus it may be premature to conclude that changes in welfare benefits do not affect the proportion of single mothers who work.

Who Collects Welfare?

If the underclass were growing, and if welfare had played a significant role in its growth, as many believe, one would expect a rising fraction of recipients to be black, concentrated in poor inner-city neighborhoods, and raised in underclass families.

41. For rough estimates of the extent of off-the-books employment among welfare recipients in the late 1980s, see Jencks and Edin (1990). There is no way of knowing how many mothers combined work and welfare without reporting this fact before 1981. Nor is there any way of knowing how many of those who combined work and welfare told the CPS that they worked, how many said they collected welfare, how many said they did both, or how many refused to be interviewed or refused to answer the relevant questions.

42. Table 6 uses CPS data to estimate the employment rate among women who head households with children under age 18. It does not use CPS data to estimate the proportion who collect welfare or who combine work and welfare, because welfare receipt is seriously underreported in the CPS. We do not know whether this is because welfare recipients have high refusal rates (perhaps because they are cheating and fear detection) or because they simply refuse to report that they are on welfare. Table 6 therefore estimates the rate of welfare receipt by comparing the number of women heading families with children under age 18 with administrative estimates of the number collecting welfare in a given month.

We do not know how many women combined work and welfare in an average month during 1960, but the figure was presumably low, since working had no economic benefits for welfare recipients who reported their earnings to the welfare department. If 52 percent of single women who headed households with children under age 18 worked and 27 percent collected welfare in an average month, 21 percent must have survived without either working or collecting welfare. In 1968 the figure was $100 - 52 - (37 - 6) = 17$ percent. By 1972 such women had vanished, since 53 percent collected welfare without working and 49 percent worked. (Totals can exceed 100 percent because of sampling error, because the numerator and denominator of the welfare rate do not cover precisely the same universe, or because some welfare mothers tell the CPS but not the welfare department that they worked.) After 1972 all single mothers appeared to be either working, collecting welfare, or both.

In reality, blacks constitute a declining fraction of all welfare recipients (40 percent in 1987 compared with 45 percent in 1969).[43] Roughly one-third of all single mothers were black in both years, so the effect of race on a single mother's chance of collecting welfare must also have declined slightly between 1969 and 1987.[44]

Mark Hughes has investigated neighborhood differences in the proportion of households receiving public assistance.[45] The proportion of households collecting public assistance in the eight metropolitan areas discussed earlier rose from 6 percent in 1969 to 10 percent in 1979. The absolute difference between the best and the worst census tracts grew substantially in all eight cities. Any adverse effects of having neighbors who live on welfare must therefore have increased more in bad neighborhoods. The proportional difference between the best and worst tracts decreased, however, so the fraction of public assistance recipients living in the worst census tracts fell.[46]

I have not been able to locate data on changes over time in the family background of welfare recipients.

The Educational Underclass

Americans constantly use cultural cues to estimate one another's social standing. These cues include the way people talk, what they know, their taste in consumer goods and services, and how they spend their time. Sometimes we use these cues because we do not know how much money a person has or where it comes from. But most Americans also think these cultural attributes are important in their own right.

America does not collect much data on the distribution of social and cultural skills. We do not know, for example, how many Americans can

43. *Background Material and Data* (1989), p. 564.

44. For counts of female heads of households with children under age 18 from 1971 through 1988, see Bureau of the Census, "Money Income and Poverty Status in the United States: 1988," *Current Population Reports*, series P-60, no. 166 (Department of Commerce, 1989), table 20. Blacks constituted 34 percent of all female-headed families with children in both 1971 and 1987, so I assumed the same was true in 1969. Counts of female heads with children under age 18 are not identical to counts of single mothers with children under age 18, but almost all such households include a single mother.

45. Hughes (1988). Note that public assistance includes those receiving general assistance as well as AFDC. Because of underreporting and misunderstandings about what constitutes public assistance, these data are not very accurate.

46. Although the proportion of recipients living in the worst tracts fell, 14.5 percent of the individual-level variance was between tracts in 1979 compared to 10.4 percent in 1969.

speak middle-class English or how many could do so in the past.[47] Nor do we know, to take another example, how well different sorts of workers can meet a middle-class supervisor's expectations regarding punctuality, courtesy, friendliness, meticulousness, or bringing problems to the supervisor's attention. Still less do we know how well random samples of workers would have been able to meet such expectations in the past.

This section therefore focuses on only two crude measures of cultural competence: the proportion of people who finish high school and the proportions who can read and calculate at various levels of competence. I will describe young people who do not complete high school or do not learn the basic cognitive skills that schools try to teach as the "educational underclass."

High School Graduation Rates

High school graduation can mean two different things in America: graduating from a regular high school or earning a certificate of General Educational Development (GED) by passing a test. The Census Bureau treats high school diplomas and GED certificates as equivalent.

Broadly speaking, three-quarters of all American teenagers graduate from high school, and another 10 percent earn GED certificates. Table 7 shows that neither figure has changed much since the mid-1960s. The proportion of teenagers earning high school diplomas peaked around 1970, declined slightly over the next ten years, and recovered a bit in the 1980s.[48] But while the regular graduation rate declined slightly in the

47. Although America has a reputation for not placing much emphasis on the "right" accent (at least as compared with Britain), Americans can estimate an individual's social class quite accurately on the basis of the way he or she talks. Dean Ellis (1967) reported a series of studies in which panels of undergraduates listened to tape recordings of different people retelling Aesop's fables. A panel's estimate of the speaker's social class correlated 0.8 with the speaker's score on the Hollingshead index (which is based on education and occupation). Even when all the speakers were college freshmen who had graduated in the upper third of their high school class, their *fathers'* Hollingshead scores correlated 0.8 with the panel's estimate of their social class. When Ellis told speakers to make themselves sound as "upper class" as possible, the correlation between the panel's estimates and the Hollingshead index fell from 0.8 to about 0.65. When he told speakers to count from one to twenty instead of reading a story aloud, the correlation also fell to 0.65. White panels judged the social class of blacks about as accurately as they judged the class of whites. Unfortunately, Ellis did not report the inter-rater reliability of individual judgments.

48. Because high school graduates are often 18 or 19 years old, comparing the number of graduates in a given year with the number of persons who were 17 years old in that year can somewhat understate or overstate the graduation rate in years when the number of 17-

1970s, more young adults earned GED certificates. As a result, the proportion of 25- to 29-year-olds with either a high school diploma or a GED certificate remained roughly constant (about 85 percent). The data in table 7 imply that this figure is unlikely to change much over the next decade.[49]

Racial and Ethnic Differences in Dropping Out

Because high schools do not report the race of those who earn diplomas, one must rely on census surveys to see how graduation rates vary by race. The Census Bureau publishes two statistical series that throw light on dropout rates: the proportion of 25- to 29-year-olds who had neither a high school diploma nor a GED in a given year, and the proportion of 16- to 24-year-olds who were no longer in school and had neither a diploma nor a GED.

Most people who will eventually earn a GED have done so by the time they are in their late twenties, so the proportion of 25- to 29-year-olds with neither a high school diploma nor a GED is a good proxy for the proportion of the birth cohort that will never earn either credential. The main drawback of this measure is that it cannot tell us much about recent trends in dropping out. The percentage of 25- to 29-year-olds without a high school diploma in 1985, for example, reflects the holding power of high schools in the mid-1970s.

The proportion of 16- to 24-year-olds who are not in school and have neither a diploma nor a GED provides a better picture of recent trends. Some of the 16-, 17-, and 18-year-olds currently enrolled in school will drop out before earning a diploma, and some older dropouts will eventually earn a GED. Experience suggests, however, that these two sources

---

year-olds differs substantially from the number of 18- and 19-year-olds. Table 7 uses five-year averages to minimize this problem. The ratio of high school graduates to 17-year-olds exceeded 76 percent between 1966 and 1970. It was less than 72 percent in 1980 and 1981.

49. The estimates in row 3 come from different sources and cover different populations from the estimates in rows 1 and 2, so rows 1 and 2 need not add to row 3. The numerators of rows 1 and 2 come from administrative data, which are likely to be incomplete. Row 3 comes from the Current Population Survey, which misses a disproportionate number of young male dropouts but may elicit exaggerated estimates of educational attainment from those whom it interviews. Row 3 includes people who attended school in other countries and subsequently immigrated to the United States, so if all else were equal it would be slightly lower than the sum of rows 1 and 2. But row 3 also excludes those who are in the armed forces or in institutions, which on balance probably has the opposite effect.

TABLE 7. High School Graduation Rates, by Year of Expected Graduation, 1948–89

Item	1948–52	1958–62	1963–67	1968–72	1973–77	1978–82	1983–87	1988–89
High school graduates as percentage of 17-year-olds	56.3	67.5	74.5	76.3	74.1	72.2	73.2	73.9
GED certificates 5 years after graduation year as percentage of 17-year-olds	n.a.	n.a.	n.a.	8.5	10.8	10.3	n.a.	n.a.
Percentage of 25- to 29-year-olds reporting high school diploma or GED	60.7	75.4	83.1	85.4	86.1	n.a.	n.a.	n.a.

SOURCES: Row 1. National Center for Education Statistics, *Digest of Education Statistics: 1989* (1989), table 89. The estimates shown are averages for the five-year interval, based on states' reports of the number of high school graduates and Current Population Survey estimates of the number of 17-year-olds.
Row 2. National Center for Education Statistics, *Digest of Education Statistics: 1989*, table 89. The proportion of the cohort receiving a GED certificate is estimated from the mean number of GED certificates awarded in the five-year interval when the cohort was 22 years old. This approximation is based on age distributions given in the source.
Row 3. National Center for Education Statistics, *Youth Indicators 1988: Trends in the Well-Being of American Youth* (1988), p. 52. The estimates cover 25- to 29-year-olds surveyed ten years after the midpoint of the graduation interval shown at the top of the table.
n.a. Not available.

of bias roughly offset one another. As a result, the proportion of 16- to 24-year-old dropouts is about the same as the proportion of 25- to 29-year-old dropouts seven years later. Thus while table 8 presents both measures, I will concentrate on the results for 16- to 24-year-olds.

The proportion of 16- to 24-year-old whites who had left school and had neither a regular diploma nor a GED hardly changed between 1970 and 1988. This apparent stability is somewhat misleading, however, because a rapidly growing fraction of all whites are Hispanic, and they have a much higher dropout rate than either blacks or non-Hispanic whites.[50] The obvious solution to this problem would be to look at trends among non-Hispanic whites, but the Census Bureau does not report data for this group. Table 8 therefore uses a second-best approximation, namely the dropout rate for all non-Hispanic whites, Asians, and native Americans. After excluding Hispanics, the dropout rate for whites, Asians, and native Americans was 2 points lower in 1988 than it had been in 1975 (9.5 versus 11.5 percent).

For blacks the story is far more encouraging. Their dropout rate fell from 28 percent in 1970 to 15 percent in 1988. Most of this decline occurred in the 1970s, but the rate continued to fall in the 1980s. As a result, the disparity between blacks and non-Hispanic whites, Asians, and native Americans declined from 11 points in 1975 to 5 points in 1988.

If not finishing high school is a good measure of coming from an underclass family, as many believe, table 8 shows that the underclass is not only getting smaller but also getting whiter. Likewise, if not finishing high school indicates that a person will grow up to be part of the underclass, the underclass will be smaller and whiter tomorrow than it is today.

Parental Education of Dropouts

Advocates of the underclass hypothesis often argue that while the overall black dropout rate may have declined, that is because the black middle class has grown. Poor blacks, they say, are even worse off than they used to be.

Table 9 tests this theory using data collected by the General Social Survey (GSS) between 1972 and 1989. The top half of the table shows dropout rates for blacks and whites whose parents had different amounts of schooling.

—The dropout rate declined more among children whose parents had

50. Unlike the 1980 census, the CPS classifies almost all Hispanics as white.

TABLE 8. High School Dropout Rates and College Graduation Rates, by Race, Selected Years, 1960–88

Percent

Category	1960	1970	1975	1980	1985	1988
25- to 29-year-olds without high school diploma or GED						
White	36.3	22.2	15.6	13.1	13.2	n.a.
Nonwhite	61.4	41.6	26.2	23.0	17.6	n.a.
Black	n.a.	43.8	29.0	23.1	19.4	n.a.
Hispanic	n.a.	n.a.	48.3	42.1	39.0	n.a.
Non-Hispanic whites, Asians, and native Americans	n.a.	n.a.	13.4	11.2	10.4	n.a.
16- to 24-year-olds not in school and not high school graduates						
Total	n.a.	15.0	13.9	14.1	12.6	12.9
White	n.a.	13.2	12.6	13.3	12.2	12.7
Black	n.a.	27.9	22.8	19.3	15.7	14.9
Hispanic	n.a.	n.a.	29.2	35.2	27.6	35.8
Non-Hispanic whites, Asians, and native Americans	n.a.	n.a.	11.5	11.4	10.4	9.5
16- to 24-year-old dropouts						
Black	n.a.	22.6	20.6	17.9	16.8	16.5
Hispanic	n.a.	n.a.	11.9	17.4	18.4	27.6
25- to 29-year-olds with 4 or more years of college						
White	11.8	17.3	22.8	23.7	23.2	n.a.
Nonwhite	5.4	10.0	15.4	15.2	16.7	n.a.
Black	n.a.	7.3	10.7	11.7	11.5	n.a.

SOURCES: Rows 1–5 and 13–15. National Center for Education Statistics, *Youth Indicators 1988*, p. 52. Rows 6–12. Mary J. Frase, *Dropout Rates in the United States: 1988*, NCES 89-609 (Washington: National Center for Education Statistics, 1989), tables A4 and A5. I made the estimates for non-Hispanic whites, Asians, and Native Americans by subtracting blacks and Hispanics from the total population. In 1980, 2.7 percent of all Hispanics classified themselves as black; Bureau of the Census, *1980 Census of Population: General Social and Economic Characteristics, United States Summary*, PC80-1-C1 (Department of Commerce, 1983), table 75. My estimates exclude these individuals twice.
n.a. Not available.

not completed high school than among children with better-educated parents.

—The dropout rate declined more among blacks than among whites whose parents had the same amount of schooling.

—The dropout rate among blacks whose parents had not completed high school declined less after 1970 than in earlier decades. Indeed, their apparent gains after 1970 could be due to sampling error ($p = .06$). But there is no evidence that disadvantaged black children did *worse* after 1970 than in earlier decades. Nor did the gap between disadvantaged and advantaged black children widen after 1970.

TABLE 9. Students Not Completing High School, by Parents' Race and Educational Attainment, 1940–82[a]

Father's or mother's race and schooling	Percent not completing high school			
	1940–49	1950–59	1960–69	1970–82
White				
No high school	38.0	29.8	23.3	26.5
Some high school	23.2	17.1	13.9	17.4
High school graduate	14.7	12.7	5.6	6.6
Attended college	6.7	4.5	2.4	2.6
Total	29.1	20.6	11.9	10.6
Sample size	2,655	2,836	4,029	2,493
Black				
No high school	64.5	49.2	28.5	25.0
Some high school	41.0	26.5	29.5	18.9
High school graduate	46.5	26.0	11.2	11.3
Attended college	22.7	17.2	7.2	6.3
Total	56.7	39.1	22.6	16.7
Sample size	335	414	567	503
Regression coefficients of child's schooling on father's (or mother's) schooling				
Whites				
Regression coefficient	.326	.315	.324	.315
Standard error	(.014)	(.013)	(.010)	(.012)
Constant	9.445	9.788	10.016	9.778
R^2	.166	.179	.209	.220
Blacks				
Regression coefficient	.331	.260	.214	.199
Standard error	(.044)	(.033)	(.026)	(.024)
Constant	7.861	9.631	10.831	10.893
R^2	.142	.125	.104	.121

SOURCE: General Social Survey, cumulative file, 1972–89. The dependent variable in the regressions is the number of years of school completed by respondents older than age 25 who were surveyed between 1972 and 1989. The independent variable is the education of the man who headed family when respondent was age 15, or, when that is not available, the education of the woman who headed the respondent's family. Neither item is available for 12.7 percent of the sample. The white sample sizes for the cells in the top half of table all exceed 275. The black sample sizes are as follows (by educational level): 1940–49, 231/39/43/22; 1950–59, 244/68/73/29; 1960–69, 260/122/116/69; 1970–82, 168/106/150/79. Among students who reached the age of 17 between 1970 and 1982, in other words, there were 168 black respondents whose father (or mother) had not attended high school and 79 whose father (or mother) had attended college.

a. Years in which graduation was expected.

—The dropout rate for white children whose parents had not completed high school may have risen slightly after 1970, although this too could be sampling error ($p = .06$).

Trends in high school graduation rates could be misleading if family background were exerting more influence on graduates' chances of attending college. Thus the bottom half of table 9 uses parental education to predict the total number of years of school or college that GSS respondents completed. Among whites, an extra year of parental schooling yielded an extra 0.33 years of schooling for their children. This relationship hardly changed between 1940 and 1982.[51] In the 1940s an extra year of parental education had about the same impact on black and white children. After 1950, however, disadvantaged black children made bigger gains than either advantaged black children or white children. As a result, the effect of parental education on black children's attainment declined steadily. Among teenagers who finished high school during the 1970s or early 1980s, an extra year of parental education had only two-thirds as much effect on blacks as on whites.[52]

The declining effect of family background on black educational attainment is precisely the opposite of what the underclass hypothesis predicts. Why class background counts for less among today's blacks than among today's whites or yesterday's blacks remains a puzzle.

The Geographic Distribution of Dropouts

Mark Hughes examined the geographic distribution of dropouts in the eight metropolitan areas discussed earlier. He found that the proportion of 16- to 19-year-olds who had left high school without graduating fell from 22 percent in 1970 to 16 percent in 1980. The absolute decline was greatest in tracts with high initial rates. Thus if we are concerned with the social consequences of dropping out, there was more improvement in underclass areas. The proportional decline was greatest in tracts with low dropout rates, however, so a larger fraction of young dropouts lived in bad neighborhoods in 1980 than in 1970.[53]

Cognitive Skills

Just as everyone knows that dropout rates have risen in inner-city schools, so too everyone knows that academic standards have fallen.

51. Results not shown here indicate that the coefficient was significantly higher for whites who reached the age of 17 before 1930.

52. Results not shown here indicate that before 1940 the effect of parental education on children's education was even larger among blacks than among whites. Among blacks who would have finished high school in the 1920s and 1930s, an extra year of parental education boosted children's expected attainment by 0.43 years.

53. The standard deviation of tract means fell in all eight metropolitan areas, from an average of .167 to an average of .145. Since the grand mean for all eight metropolitan areas fell from .217 to .155, the coefficient of variation rose in all eight areas. Nonetheless, the total variance declined more than the between-tract variance (Hughes, 1988).

TABLE 10. Percentage of High School Students Age 17 with Reading and Mathematics Skills above Selected Thresholds, by Race, Selected Years, 1971–88

Skill level and race	1971	1975	1980	1984	1988
Reading					
Basic					
White	97.7	98.6	99.1	99.1	99.5
Black	82.0	81.1	84.9	95.8	97.1
Intermediate					
White	83.5	86.1	87.3	87.9	89.3
Black	39.7	42.4	43.9	66.0	76.0
Adept					
White	43.3	44.0	44.1	46.3	46.3
Black	7.5	7.9	6.7	16.3	25.8
Advanced					
White	7.5	7.0	6.3	6.5	5.7
Black	0.3	0.3	0.2	0.9	1.9

			1978	1982	1986
Mathematics					
Basic operations and beginning problem solving					
White		...	...	95.8	96.3	98.3
Black		...	...	70.0	75.3	86.0
Moderately complex procedures and reasoning					
White		...	...	57.3	54.5	58.0
Black		...	...	18.0	17.3	21.7
Multistep problem solving and algebra					
White		...	...	8.6	6.3	7.6
Black		...	...	0.4	0.6	0.3

SOURCES: Ina V. S. Mullis and Lynn B. Jenkins, *The Reading Report Card, 1971–88: Trends from the Nation's Report Card,* no. 19-R-01 (Princeton: Educational Testing Service, 1990), pp. 63–64; and John A. Dossey, Ina V. S. Mullis, Mary M. Lindquist, and Donald L. Chambers, *The Mathematics Report Card: Are We Measuring Up?* no. 17-M-01 (Princeton: Educational Testing Service, 1988), p. 141.

News stories about illiterate inner-city valedictorians reinforce this conviction, and so does the widely reported decline in SAT scores. SAT scores are not very useful for estimating the size of the educational underclass, however, because students do not take the SAT unless they plan to attend college. If we want to know whether high schools are losing the battle with illiteracy, we need data on *all* high school students, not just the college bound. The National Assessment of Educational Progress (NAEP), begun in 1970, is the best source of such data.

The top half of table 10 shows the percentage of 17-year-old high school students reading at various levels. More than half of all 9-year-olds can read at what NAEP calls the "basic level." [54] A teenager who

54. The labels that NAEP gives the four reading levels shown in table 10 have no intrinsic meaning. To construct these cutoff points, NAEP sets the mean for the combined sample

cannot read at this level comes close to being illiterate in the traditional sense of the term. Yet 18 percent of the black 17-year-olds who were still in school and 2 to 3 percent of the whites could not read at this level in 1971. By 1988 the proportion of 17-year-olds who were still in school had risen, yet all but 2.9 percent of the blacks and 0.5 percent of the whites could read at the basic level. The proportion unable to read at what NAEP calls the intermediate level had also fallen (from 60 to 24 percent among blacks and from 16 to 11 percent among whites).[55]

NAEP did not test 17-year-olds who had left school until the late 1970s, and it still excludes dropouts from trend statistics. As a result, table 10 overstates the percentage of all 17-year-olds who can read at any given level. The proportion of black 17-year-olds who were not in school fell between 1970–71 and 1987–88.[56] It follows that 17-year-old blacks' reading scores probably improved even more than table 10 implies.[57]

The first NAEP mathematics tests were administered in 1972–73, but the results are not available in the form shown in table 10. Question-by-question comparisons show little change between 1973 and 1978, however, so trends from 1978 to 1986 are probably good indicators of trends from 1973 to 1986. Table 10 does not show much improvement in whites' math skills during this period, but the proportion of blacks who could do basic mathematical operations rose sharply.

---

of 9-, 13-, and 17-year-olds at 250 and sets the standard deviation at 50. The labels in table 10 then represent scores above 200, 250, 300, and 350.

55. The gains in table 10 look steadier than they should because the Educational Testing Service and the Department of Education have suppressed the results of a 1985–86 reading assessment that showed a large, inexplicable, one-time drop in reading skills. The reasons for this drop remain murky, but the fact that the 1987–88 results are in line with the long-term upward trend convinces me that 1985–86 was indeed an aberration.

56. The proportion of 16- to 17-year-old whites enrolled in school was 90.6 percent in October 1970 and 91.8 percent in October 1987. For blacks, the proportions were 85.7 percent in 1970 and 91.5 percent in 1987; see Bureau of the Census, "School Enrollment—Social and Economic Characteristics of Students: October 1988 and 1987," *Current Population Reports*, series P-20, no. 443 (Department of Commerce, 1989), table A-3. There are no trend data for 17-year-olds alone, but in October 1987 the enrollment rate for 17-year-olds was 88.0 percent among whites and 88.2 percent among blacks (*Current Population Reports,* series P-20, no. 443, table 22). It is not clear how these figures change between fall and spring, when NAEP does most of its testing. NAEP also misses 17-year-olds who are already enrolled in college, but while 5 percent of all 17-year-olds are enrolled in college in October of a typical year, most of them have probably turned 18 by the time NAEP does its testing.

57. One way to check this conclusion is to look at 13-year-olds, almost all of whom are in school. The proportion of black 13-year-olds reading above both the basic and intermediate levels rose dramatically between 1971 and 1988, but there was no comparable increase among white 13-year-olds.

Social Origins of Poor Readers

NAEP also reports trend data for students whose parents had different amounts of education. Among those whose parents had not completed high school, the proportion reading at the basic or intermediate level rose, while the proportion reading at the adept or advanced level fell. This same pattern of homogenization recurs among 17-year-olds with college educated parents, although the changes are smaller. These findings lead me to two conclusions:

—The performance of the worst readers improved between 1971 and 1988, regardless of family background. The biggest gains were made by children whose parents had very little education, presumably because they were the worst off to begin with.

—The performance of the best readers, which looked roughly stable in table 10, deteriorated when parental education was held constant. This could mean that parents with college (or high school) diplomas were a less elite group in 1988 than in 1971. Or it could mean that schools did less to challenge good readers in the 1980s than they had done earlier.

Since both children of high school dropouts and children of blacks improved their performance during this period, it would be astonishing if the children of black dropouts had not improved. The inference that black children whose parents had very little education were making significant gains during these years is also consistent with table 9, which showed that the children of black dropouts stayed in school somewhat longer after 1970 than before.

Geographic Distribution of Reading Gains

Lyle Jones has used NAEP data to analyze trends in reading scores among blacks in poor inner-city schools. He found that the reading scores of black 17-year-olds in these schools rose substantially between 1971 and 1984.[58] These findings are obviously at odds with the widespread view that inner-city schools have deteriorated over the past generation. The conflict between Jones's findings and the conventional wisdom may, however, be more apparent than real. Despite sizable gains, blacks still do far worse than whites on reading and math tests. This means that when a predominantly white school becomes predominantly

58. Jones (1987a, 1987b) reported that NAEP samples only about 250 blacks a year in poor inner-city schools. The sampling errors of his trend estimates are therefore likely to be large.

black, as many inner-city schools have, its reading scores are likely to fall. The concern here, however, is not with the fate of specific schools but with the fate of demographic groups. This means we need to compare schools that were already all black or Hispanic in 1970 to similar schools today. Jones's data suggest that if we make this kind of comparison, test scores went up, not down. The widespread conviction that inner-city schools got worse may also reflect a revolution of rising expectations about what schools serving poor nonwhites should be able to accomplish.

Inequality and the Educational Underclass

The skills a person needs to get a steady job, understand a tax form, or put together a "partially assembled" item from a mail-order catalogue are not fixed for all time. Nor do they depend on some impersonal technological imperative. They depend on the skills that other members of the society have. When most people are illiterate, society organizes itself on that assumption. Work is arranged so that very few workers have to read instructions, taxes are levied on the assumption that ordinary citizens cannot be expected to fill out forms, and Sears does not sell items that only a Swiss watchmaker can put together. When most people can read relatively complicated material, society reorganizes itself to take advantage of this fact, and those who cannot read such material are left behind.

It follows that if most citizens significantly improve their reading and mathematics skills, while the least adept improve only a little, the least adept may become more of an underclass, even if they are more skillful than their counterparts were a generation earlier. Likewise, if college graduation replaces high school graduation as the normal level of educational attainment, the fact that more youngsters are finishing high school may not be enough to prevent the growth of an underclass. Reducing the size of the educational underclass may, in short, depend not just on raising the competence of those at the bottom but on making competence more equal.

The available evidence suggests that even by this demanding standard America made progress between 1970 and 1988. Table 8, for example, shows college graduation rates among 25- to 29-year-olds in various years. Both black and white college graduation rates leveled off around 1970. Since black high school dropout rates declined substantially after

1970, and white dropout rates declined a little, inequality in years of schooling decreased.

The same pattern holds for the reading skills of 17-year-olds. Table 10 shows that the number of advanced white readers declined slightly between 1971 and 1988, which is what one would expect given the decline in SAT verbal scores. The number of advanced black readers rose, but even among blacks the proportion of good readers grew far less rapidly than the proportion of poor readers fell. As a result, the distribution of reading skills among 17-year-olds was more equal in 1988 than in 1971.[59]

The Violent Underclass

Journalists, politicians, cab drivers, and graduate students are all convinced that violent crime has increased over the past generation, especially in poor black areas. Indeed, one reason the underclass hypothesis appeals to many Americans is that it seems to explain the breakdown of law and order in these areas.

The federal government collects three kinds of statistics on the level of violence in the United States. The National Center for Health Statistics (NCHS) uses statistics provided by state and local health departments to estimate the proportion of people murdered each year. The Bureau of Justice Statistics uses the Census Bureau's ongoing victimization survey to estimate the number who were raped, robbed, or assaulted in a given year. And the Federal Bureau of Investigation uses data provided by state and local police departments to estimate the number of violent crimes "known to the police." I will take up these three sources of evidence in turn.

Homicide

Homicide rates have several advantages as indicators of the overall level of violence.[60] Unlike other forms of violence, homicide is relatively

59. The standard deviation of 17-year-olds' reading scores fell from 42 to 36 points among whites and from 44 to 36 points among blacks. The black-white differential fell from 1.15 standard deviations in 1971 to 0.55 standard deviations in 1988 (Mullis and Jenkins, 1990, p. 65).

60. Here and throughout, I use the term homicide to include both murder and nonnegligent manslaughter. For a more detailed discussion of the advantages and disadvantages of using homicide rates as evidence of changes in the level of violence, see Archer and Gartner (1984).

TABLE 11. Murders per 100,000 Persons, by Race and Sex of Victims, Selected Years, 1950–87[a]

Race and sex	1950	1960	1965	1970	1975	1980	1985	1987
Total population	5.2	4.7	5.5	8.3	10.0	10.7	8.3	8.7
Whites								
Male	3.8	3.6	4.4	6.7	9.1	10.9	8.2	7.9
Female	1.4	1.4	1.6	2.1	2.9	3.2	2.9	3.0
Blacks								
Male	47.3	36.6	n.a.	67.6	62.6	66.6	48.4	53.3
Female	11.5	10.4	n.a.	13.3	13.8	13.5	11.0	12.6
Black males								
Age 15–24	58.9	46.4	n.a.	102.5	n.a.	84.3	66.1	85.6
Age 25–34	110.5	92.0	n.a.	158.5	n.a.	145.1	94.3	98.9
Age 35–44	83.7	77.5	n.a.	126.2	n.a.	110.3	76.3	78.4
Age 45–54	54.6	54.8	n.a.	100.5	n.a.	83.8	51.1	46.0
Age 55–64	35.7	31.8	n.a.	59.8	n.a.	55.6	37.8	32.8

SOURCES: National Center for Health Statistics, *Health United States: 1989* (Department of Health and Human Services, 1990), table 33; and Bureau of the Census, *Statistical Abstract of the United States: 1979*, 100th ed. (1979), table 298.
n.a. Not available.
a. Rates include deaths from executions as well as murder, but the effect of this is trivial.

easy to define and hard to conceal. When a husband assaults his wife, neither she nor anyone else is likely to report the incident, either to the police or to a victimization survey. If he kills her, her death will almost always be discovered, and the fact that she was murdered will usually be obvious, even if the identity of the killer remains uncertain. The same logic often applies to violence between strangers. If two teenage gangs get in a fight, they usually try to conceal it. If one of the teenagers is killed, the others may want to conceal the fact, but they are unlikely to succeed. Furthermore, the incentives to conceal homicides have been fairly stable over time. Thus there is no obvious reason for supposing that the authorities' chances of detecting a homicide have changed.

Table 11 shows NCHS estimates of the homicide rate from 1950 to 1987. The rates declined slightly during the 1950s, rose dramatically during the 1960s, rose more moderately during the 1970s, and fell during the early 1980s. The 1987 rate was only 5 percent higher than the 1970 rate. FBI estimates suggest that the overall murder rate rose about 2 percent in 1988 and another 4 percent in 1989.[61] Nonetheless, the 1989 rate was below the 1980 rate and only slightly above the 1970 rate.

61. The Federal Bureau of Investigation, *Crime in the United States: 1988* (Department of Justice, 1989), p. 9, reported a 1 percent increase between 1987 and 1988, but its count seems to imply a 2 percent increase. A subsequent FBI press release on April 8, 1990, re-

The crack epidemic became national news in 1986. Both the police and the news media believe that crack unleashed an unprecedented wave of violence in poor neighborhoods. Table 11 suggests that this increase in lethal violence was confined to black men between the ages of 15 and 24, whose risk of dying violently rose 30 percent between 1985 and 1987. Homicide rates did not increase systematically among older black men, and they declined among white men. Since selling crack is predominantly an adolescent occupation, the fact that homicides increased only among 15- to 24-year-olds is not surprising.

The rough stability of the overall homicide rate since 1970 could, of course, conceal an increase among nonwhites offset by a decline among whites. But table 11 shows precisely the opposite pattern. The white homicide rate rose during the 1970s, while the black rate remained constant. After 1980, both the black and white rates declined sharply. (NCHS does not report separate rates for Hispanics.)

Table 11 shows the race of homicide victims, not that of murderers. If the violent black underclass mostly murdered whites, its growth might not have had much impact on blacks' chances of dying violently. In reality, however, about 90 percent of those arrested for murder are of the same race as their alleged victim. Furthermore, while the proportion of interracial murders appears to have increased slightly since 1976, when the FBI first reported such data, the change has not been large.[62] Changes in the race of homicide victims therefore provide a fairly reliable index of changes in the race of murderers.

Robbery and Aggravated Assault

The Census Bureau began its National Crime Survey in 1973. Every month the NCS asks roughly 8,000 teenagers and adults whether they have been victims of various crimes during the previous six months. The Bureau of Justice Statistics uses these data to estimate the number of persons over the age of 12 who were raped, robbed, or assaulted each year. There are too few rapes for the NCS to yield reliable data about their frequency. But if murder data are a reliable indicator of long-term trends

---

ported a 3 percent increase between 1987 and 1988 and a 4 percent increase between 1988 and 1989.

62. Roughly 70 percent of all homicides result in an arrest, so arrest data are a fairly good guide to the characteristics of suspected murderers. For data on the race of those arrested by race of victim, see Federal Bureau of Investigation, *Crime in the United States* (1976, 1986).

TABLE 12. Aggravated Assaults and Robberies per 100,000 Persons, by Race of Assailant, Selected Periods, 1973–88

Crime	1973–75	1976–78	1979–81	1982–84	1985–86	1987–88
Aggravated assaults	792	792	782	712	656	681
White assailant	515	531	532	470	427	n.a.
Black assailant	226	198	188	185	168	n.a.
Other, mixed, or unknown	63	65	66	57	61	n.a.
Robberies	544	498	549	511	415	428
White assailant	180	204	198	179	158	n.a.
Black assailant	305	239	285	276	208	n.a.
Other, mixed, or unknown	60	55	66	56	49	n.a.
FBI estimate of murders	9.6	8.9	9.9	8.3	8.3	8.3

SOURCES: Population estimates and estimates of the number of aggravated assaults and robberies for 1973 through 1986 are taken from Timothy J. Flanagan and Katherine M. Jamieson, eds., *Sourcebook of Criminal Justice Statistics: 1988* (Albany, N.Y.: Hindelang Criminal Justice Research Center), pp. 283, 427. The 1987 and 1988 figures are from Bureau of Justice Statistics, "Bulletin: Criminal Victimization 1988." The proportions of offenses committed by whites, blacks, and others in the relevant year were estimated from Bureau of Justice Statistics, *Criminal Victimization in the United States* (issued annually). The estimated racial mix of assailants combines data on offenses involving a single assailant and offenses involving multiple assailants. The category "other, mixed, or unknown" includes offenses in which the victim reported that the assailant was neither white nor black, that the assailant's race was impossible to determine, or that there were several assailants of different races. Offenses committed by white, black, and other assailants may not add to the total number of offenses because of rounding.
n.a. Not available.

in violence, as I have argued, the NCS should find much the same trend for robbery and aggravated assault between 1973 and 1988 that NCHS finds for homicide.[63]

Table 12 shows how the aggravated assault and robbery rates changed from 1973 to 1988, pooling adjacent years to minimize the effects of sampling error. For comparison, it also shows the FBI estimate of the murder rate in these years.[64] There was no clear trend in murder, aggravated assault, or robbery from 1973–75 through 1979–81. After 1981 all three forms of violence decreased significantly. By 1987–88 both the murder and aggravated assault rates were 14 percent lower than they had been in 1973–75, and the robbery rate was 21 percent lower.[65]

Table 12 also estimates the likelihood of being assaulted or robbed by offenders of different races. The risk of being assaulted or robbed by a

63. An aggravated assault is one involving a weapon or resulting in serious injury. A robbery is a theft from a person that is carried out by force or the threat of force.

64. The FBI estimate of the homicide rate is always slightly lower than the NCHS estimate. I have used the FBI estimate here because NCHS data are not yet available for 1988. The FBI and NCHS murder series show essentially the same trend.

65. The NCS also shows a decrease in rape after 1981.

black person decreased fairly steadily from 1973 to 1986. Thus there is no evidence that the overall decline in aggravated assault and robbery masked an increase in black assaults or robberies. Quite the contrary.

The Census Bureau's victimization surveys thus tell the same story as the NCHS and FBI estimates of homicide. Taken together, these data suggest five conclusions:

—Violence increased dramatically among both blacks and whites between about 1964 and 1974.

—Violence decreased significantly among both blacks and whites after 1980.

—Violence increased again among 15- to 24-year-old blacks from 1985 to 1987, but it did not increase much for other groups.

—Blacks are still far more likely than whites to engage in murder, aggravated assault, and robbery.

—Nonetheless, both the absolute and the proportional differences between black and white levels of violence declined between 1970 and 1987.

Police Estimates of Violent Crime

Every year most local police departments try to count the number of crimes committed within their jurisdiction. These estimates get a lot of attention from the local news media. Most police departments also forward their estimates to the FBI, which uses them to estimate the national crime rate. The FBI's estimates get far more attention than those based on victimization surveys.

Local police statistics suggest that violent crime rose by a factor of four between 1960 and 1988. They also suggest that while the increase slowed after 1980, it did not stop. Since these estimates have helped shape both popular and scholarly beliefs about crime, it is important to understand how they are generated and why they are misleading.

The FBI index of violent crime (which is also widely used by local police departments) is the unweighted sum of the number of murders, forcible rapes, robberies, and aggravated assaults occurring in a given year. Since murder and rape are relatively rare, trends in this index depend largely on trends in robbery and aggravated assault. To be included in the FBI count, a robbery or aggravated assault must come to the attention of the police, either because someone reports it or because the police see it occurring. The police must then investigate, conclude that a crime really occurred, and record the allegation as founded rather than unfounded.

FBI estimates of robbery and aggravated assault differ from estimates based on victimization surveys for two main reasons. First, citizens do not report every robbery or aggravated assault to the police. Second, the police do not record all the crimes that citizens report. The NCS asks robbery and assault victims whether they reported the crime to the police. Victims were slightly more likely to report robberies and assaults in the late 1980s than in the early 1970s, but the change was not large.[66] NCS and FBI estimates of change appear to differ mainly because local police departments have changed the way they handle victims' complaints.

NCS data imply, for example, that citizens reported 565,000 robberies to the police in 1973. The police reported about two-thirds that number of robberies to the FBI. By 1987, NCS data indicate that a larger population reported about 578,000 robberies to the police. The police, however, reported 90 percent of these robberies to the FBI. Much the same story recurs for aggravated assault. In 1973 citizens reported twice as many aggravated assaults to the police as the police reported to the FBI. But by 1987 citizens reported only 8 percent more aggravated assaults to the police than the police reported to the FBI.[67]

The reason for these changes in police reporting practice is not obscure. The Justice Department initiated the NCS in response to a widespread belief that local police departments were recording far fewer crimes than really occurred. The first NCS confirmed this suspicion. Partly as a result, the Justice Department spent a lot of money helping local departments improve their record keeping. Records were computerized, completing each record became a higher priority, and police officers spent more time on paperwork. As a result, most local police departments recorded big increases in most crimes. The exception was homicide, which was already well recorded.

The contrast between FBI and NCS estimates of trends in violent crime also raises serious doubts about FBI estimates of violent crime before

66. Among those telling the NCS that they were victims of an aggravated assault, for example, 57 percent claimed they had reported it to the police in 1987–88, compared with 53 percent in 1973–75. For robbery, the reporting rate was 56 percent in 1987–88, compared with 53 percent in 1973–75. See Bureau of Justice Statistics, "Bulletin: Criminal Victimization 1988" (Department of Justice, 1989), p. 5.

67. Compare Bureau of Justice Statistics, *Sourcebook of Criminal Justice Statistics, 1988* (Department of Justice, 1989), pp. 283, 427; and Bureau of Justice Statistics, "Bulletin," p. 5.

1973. The question is not whether FBI estimates were too low—everyone agrees that was the case—but whether the FBI overestimated the *increase* in crime between 1960 and 1973. The FBI's index of violent crime rose 159 percent between 1960 and 1973, while its estimate of the murder rate rose only 84 percent. I therefore suspect, though I cannot prove, that some police departments improved their record-keeping arrangements for nonlethal crime between 1960 and 1973 as well as after 1973.

The moral of this story seems clear. If we want to understand trends in violence, we should ignore local police estimates of nonlethal crime and rely instead on murder statistics and victimization surveys. These two measures offer no support for the hypothesis that violence in general or black violence in particular has become appreciably more common since the early 1970s. On the contrary, they suggest that violence has declined somewhat.

Who Commits Violent Crimes?

While violence was almost certainly less common in America in the late 1980s than it had been in 1980 or even 1970, this might not mean that the underclass has become less violent. Violence could have increased among members of the underclass while declining among more advantaged groups. Unfortunately, there are no reliable data on changes in the economic background of violent criminals.

Violence could also have increased in poor inner-city neighborhoods while decreasing elsewhere. It should be possible to test this hypothesis using data from victimization surveys, but the Bureau of Justice Statistics does not report victimization rates for census tracts with different characteristics.[68] Most big-city police departments report homicides by geographic area, but so far as I know, nobody has used these data to see whether homicide rose faster in poor neighborhoods than in rich ones after 1970.

Drug-related violence did increase dramatically in some poor non-white neighborhoods during the late 1980s. It is therefore important to

68. Early in the 1980s BJS did release data tapes that included some information on the characteristics of the neighborhoods in which NCS respondents lived. The neighborhoods were not census tracts, however, and some of the data appear to have been erroneous. Using these data, Samuel Myers and William Sabol (n.d.) concluded that the fraction of all black victims living in neighborhoods with poverty rates above 25 percent in 1970 had fallen from 27 percent in 1973 to 20 percent in 1981. This decline is hard to interpret, since the neighborhoods in question were losing population during the 1970s. What is needed are changes in victimization *rates* for rich and poor neighborhoods.

ask whether this change implies that the underclass was growing in such neighborhoods. I think not. When drug sales are illegal, drug sellers almost always use violence to eliminate competitors and collect their debts. When new, popular drugs are introduced, as happened in the late 1980s, the hierarchy that controls the trade is likely to be disrupted, and violence is likely to increase. In due course, a new hierarchy is likely to emerge, and drug-related violence is likely to decline. We should not mistake upheavals in the drug trade for changes in the underlying class structure of American society.

Age and Crime

Men between the ages of 15 and 24 are about three times as likely as men over 25 to be arrested for violent crimes. Thus when the proportion of men between the ages of 15 and 24 increases, as it did during the 1960s, violent crime is likely to increase. When the proportion of 15- to 24-year-olds declines, as it did in the 1980s, violent crime is likely to decline. But while demographic change certainly contributed to increased violence between 1964 and 1974 and reduced violence after 1980, age-specific crime rates also changed in both periods.

Among all men older than 15, the fraction who were under the age of 24 rose from 19.7 percent in 1960 to 25.3 percent in 1975 and then fell back to 20.1 percent in 1987.[69] If age-specific rates of violence had remained constant, and if they were three times as high for 15- to 24-year-olds as for older men and women, violent crime would have risen about 8 percent between 1960 and 1975 and would then have fallen about 7 percent between 1975 and 1987.[70]

Judging by the homicide rate, violence actually increased by more than 100 percent between 1960 and 1975. Changes in age-specific rates of violence therefore appear to have accounted for something like 92 percent of this change. Homicide and aggravated assault fell 14 percent between 1973–75 and 1987–88, while robbery fell 21 percent. Declines in the proportion of men between the ages of 15 and 24 could account for between one-third and one-half of this change. The rest must have been due to declines in age-specific rates of violence.

69. Bureau of the Census, *Statistical Abstract of the United States: 1989*, p. 13. In a crude effort to adjust for the undercount of young males, the estimates in the text are based on data for both sexes combined.

70. If the violent crime rate for men age 25 and over is R and the rate for men age 15 to 24 is $3R$, the overall rate in 1960 would be $(.197)(3R) + (.803)(R) = 1.394R$. The analogous rates would be $1.506R$ in 1975 and $1.402R$ in 1987.

Demographic changes may also affect age-specific rates of violence. When the baby boomers reached adolescence, their sheer numbers may have shifted the balance of power between those who supported authority and those who resisted it. This shift may have made angry young men readier to express their feelings in violent ways. The graying of the baby boomers after 1980 may, in turn, have made violence less socially acceptable.

Incarceration and Crime

The likelihood that violence will lead to imprisonment has also changed. Changes in the murder rate suggest that violent crime rates doubled between 1950 and 1975. Yet the fraction of the nation's population in federal and state prisons hardly changed during these years, averaging 0.11 percent.[71] Assuming that violent felons accounted for about the same fraction of the prison population in both years, time served per offense must have fallen by about half.

The prison population began to rise after 1975, largely because sentences became longer. By 1980, 0.14 percent of the population was in state or federal prisons, and by 1987 the proportion had reached 0.23 percent. Since violent crime did not increase during these years, violent offenders must have been spending twice as much time in prison for each offense in 1987 as in 1975, although the great majority of violent offenders still served no time at all.

Changes in the prison population can affect the incidence of violent crime in three ways. First, incarceration obviously prevents inmates from murdering, raping, robbing, or assaulting noninmates. A panel convened by the National Research Council estimated that because of this "incapacitation effect," doubling the prison population might reduce the crime rate by about 10 percent.[72] Second, serving time in prison puts a violent offender in touch with many other violent offenders, while also making it harder to find a legitimate job after release. As a result, imprisonment may increase the number of crimes that felons commit after they are released. Third, increasing the time violent criminals can expect to spend behind bars is likely to have some effect on the number of offenses they commit. The magnitude of this deterrent effect is uncertain and controversial.

Whatever the cause, violence was somewhat less common in the late

71 Bureau of the Census, *Statistical Abstract of the United States: 1989*, table 318.
72. Blumstein and others (1986), p. 123.

1980s than it had been in 1980 or 1970. This was especially true in the black community. The black homicide rate was lower in 1987 than it was in 1980 or 1970 and not much higher than it was in 1950. Robberies and aggravated assaults involving black assailants were also less common in 1987–88 than they had been in 1973 when the NCS began. These facts do not quite suffice to prove that the violent underclass was getting smaller or that the underclass was getting less violent, but they certainly point in that direction.

The Reproductive Underclass

Middle-class Americans have always believed that adults should refrain from having children unless they could care for them properly. Until the 1960s this general principle led most Americans to espouse three norms regarding childbearing.

—Couples should not have children unless they were prepared to get married: conceiving a child out of wedlock was irresponsible, and not marrying before the child was born was even more irresponsible.

—Couples should not have children unless the prospective father could support them. Since teenage boys could seldom earn enough to support a family, teenage fatherhood was irresponsible. Teenage motherhood was acceptable so long as the father was old enough to support a family.

—Couples with modest incomes should limit their fertility. This norm was largely confined to the middle class. Children had been an economic asset on farms. Small families became advantageous once America became an urban nation, but this fact did not become widely understood for several generations.

After 1960 these three norms changed in important ways. American women cut their fertility in half, so we stopped worrying about married couples having too many children. College enrollments soared, so we began to think of adolescence as continuing until people were in their early twenties and became increasingly dubious about teenage girls' readiness for parenthood. Concern about teenage motherhood ("children having children") was exacerbated by the fact that fewer teenage mothers had sexual partners old enough to marry and support them. And while Americans continued to believe that children were better off when they lived with both their natural parents, we became considerably more tolerant of unwed mothers than we had been earlier in the century.

As a result of these changes, America entered the 1980s with only two widely accepted norms about parenthood:

TABLE 13. Expected Fertility, by Age, Race, and Sex, Selected Years, 1960–86

Fertility	1960	1965	1970	1975	1980	1986
Expected births before age 20 per 100 women						
White women	40	30	29	24	23	21
Black women	80	74	73	58	52	51
White men	9	8	11	9	8	7
Black men	22[a]	23[a]	29	23	20	21
Percent of lifetime births occurring before age 20						
White women	11.3	10.8	12.1	14.2	13.1	12.1
Black women	17.6	19.3	23.5	25.9	22.9	22.9
White men	2.6	2.8	3.9	4.3	3.6	3.4
Black men	4.0[a]	4.8[a]	6.8	6.9	6.0	7.0

SOURCES: National Center for Health Statistics, *Vital Statistics of the Untied States: 1986*, vol. 1: *Natality*, (Department of Health and Human Services, 1988), tables 1–6 and 1–7.

a. Estimated from data on all nonwhites, on the assumption that the fertility of black 15- to 19-year-old men increased at the same rate between 1960 and 1970 as the fertility of nonwhite 15- to 19-year-old men.

—Potential parents should not have children until they are in their twenties.

—Potential parents should not have children out of wedlock unless they can support them, and probably not even then.

What I will call the "reproductive underclass" is composed of couples who violate these behavioral norms. Almost everyone assumes that such violations have become more common. In reality, however, teenage motherhood has become less common, teenage fatherhood remains rare, and out-of-wedlock births have increased only a little. The big change is that married couples are having far fewer children.

Teenage Parenthood

There was a lot of talk during the 1980s about an epidemic of teenage childbearing in urban ghettos. In reality, however, teenage girls were having fewer babies than at any time since 1940. Black teenagers were having more babies than white teenagers, but the gap was narrowing rather than widening. Table 13 shows that in 1960 a representative sample of 100 black girls would have had 80 babies by the time they reached the age of 20. In the mid-1980s they would have had only 51 babies. Among whites, the numbers fell from 40 to 21.[73]

73. The estimates in table 13 are not in fact based on the experience of women who turned 20 in a given year. Instead, the estimates are projections of what would happen if the age-specific birth rates in a given year were to continue indefinitely.

Most teenage mothers become pregnant by older men. As a result, teenage fatherhood has never been as common as teenage motherhood. In 1986, for example, only 1.8 percent of 15- to 19-year-old boys became parents, compared with 5.1 percent of girls.[74] The age difference between teenage mothers and their sexual partners appears to be diminishing, however. In 1960 there were four times as many teenage mothers as teenage fathers. By 1986 there were less than three times as many.

Teenage boys have never been able to earn enough to support a family, so they have seldom married.[75] When teenage girls started dating younger men, therefore, two changes occurred: fewer teenage girls had babies, but when they did, they were less likely to marry before the baby's birth (see table 13).

The first big drop in teenage girls' fertility came between 1960 and 1965, when oral contraceptives were introduced and other forms of contraception became more readily available. The second big drop came between 1970 and 1975, when abortion became legal. The proportion of teenage pregnancies ended by abortion continued to rise after 1975, however, so the number of live births to teenagers continued to fall in the late 1970s.[76]

Births to teenagers are seldom intentional, whereas births to adults often are. If all else were equal, therefore, improvements in contraception and easier access to abortion should have lowered teenage fertility more than adult fertility. Between 1960 and 1975, however, adult fertility fell not just because contraception and abortion became more available but also because adults wanted fewer children. Since teenagers seldom wanted children even in 1960, the gap between teenage and adult preferences narrowed, and teenagers accounted for a rising fraction of all births.

After 1975 adult fertility leveled off, while teenage fertility continued to fall. As a result, the proportion of all babies born to teenagers began

74. *Vital Statistics of the United States: 1986*, vol. 1: *Natality* (1989), tables 1–6, 1–7. The estimates in the text assume that no teenage father or mother had more than one child a year.

75. For statistics on marriage rates by age, see the paper by Mare and Winship in this volume.

76. The number of illegal abortions before 1973 is unknown. The "abortion ratio" among 15- to 19-year-olds (that is, the ratio of legal abortions to the sum of legal abortions and live births) was 0.283 in 1973, 0.364 in 1975, 0.450 in 1980, and 0.465 in 1985. Bureau of the Census, *Statistical Abstract of the United States: 1982–83*, pp. 61, 68; and *1990*, tables 82, 101. If there were no spontaneous miscarriages, these ratios would imply 8.1 pregnancies per 100 girls age 15 to 19 in 1973, 8.7 in 1975, 9.7 in 1980, and 9.5 in 1985. These estimates probably overstate the increase in the pregnancy rate, however, since some pregnancies ended by abortion would otherwise end in a miscarriage.

TABLE 14. Expected Fertility, by Marital Status, Race, and Sex,
Selected Years, 1960–87

Fertility	1960	1965	1970	1975	1980	1987
Expected lifetime births while unmarried						
White	0.08	0.11	0.14	0.12	0.18	0.29
Black	1.05	1.08	1.16	1.09	1.25	1.43
Expected lifetime births while married						
White	3.45	2.67	2.25	1.56	1.57	1.47
Black	3.49	2.75	1.93	1.15	1.01	0.87
Total						
White	3.53	2.78	2.39	1.69	1.75	1.77
Black	4.54	3.83	3.10	2.24	2.27	2.29
Births while unmarried as percent of lifetime births						
White	2.3	4.0	5.7	7.3	10.2	16.7
Black	23.2	28.2	37.6	48.8	55.5	62.2

SOURCE: National Center for Health Statistics, *Vital Statistics of the United States: 1987*, vol. 1: *Natality*, tables 1–6, 1–7, and 1–31. Expected births while married and unmarried assume that age-specific birth rates in the relevant year continue and that the percentage of births to unmarried women in that year continues. Expected births while married and unmarried may not add to total births because of rounding.

to fall. This decline was apparent among boys as well as girls, and among blacks as well as whites.

I have not been able to find trend data on births to poor teenagers or on births to teenagers in poor neighborhoods. But it is hard to see how births to black teenagers could have fallen by 36 percent between 1960 and 1986 if the decline were confined to affluent blacks.

Out-of-Wedlock Births

Unlike teenagers, unmarried adults are having more babies. The best (though not the most common) way of estimating trends in out-of-wedlock births is to ask how many children a woman could expect to have while unmarried if the age-specific birth rates observed in a given year persisted throughout her childbearing years. Table 14 shows that in 1960 the typical black woman could expect to have 1.05 out-of-wedlock births over her lifetime.[77] By 1987 the figure had risen to 1.43. The typical white woman could have expected 0.08 out-of-wedlock births over her lifetime in 1960 and 0.29 in 1987.

These increases in out-of-wedlock childbearing would not have at-

77. I estimated marital and nonmarital fertility by dividing expected lifetime fertility between marital and nonmarital births in the same way that actual births were divided in the relevant year.

tracted much attention if married women had continued to have as many children as they had in 1960. In 1960, for example, black women could expect to have 3.49 children while married. Had they continued to have that many children while married, the proportion of black babies born out of wedlock would have risen only from 23 percent in 1960 to 29 percent by 1987. A change of this kind would have passed almost unnoticed. In reality, however, births to married women plummeted, and the proportion of all black children born out of wedlock (which I will call the "illegitimacy ratio") rose from 23 percent to 62 percent. Among whites, it rose from 2 percent to 16 percent.[78]

These changes have probably had an adverse effect on children's life chances, but the effect has almost certainly been far smaller than most commentators assume. All else equal, growing up in a single-parent family is a handicap.[79] But having a lot of brothers and sisters is also a handicap, for many of the same economic and psychological reasons. Since unwed mothers have fewer children than mothers who marry, the adverse effect of unwed mothers on children is likely to be quite small.[80]

Class Differences in the Spread of Unwed Motherhood

The illegitimacy ratio has risen in all strata of American society. We must therefore ask whether the increase was especially marked in the economic or educational underclass. I have not been able to find trend data on the economic background of unwed mothers, but table 15 shows how the illegitimacy ratio has changed for women with different amounts of schooling.

78. Although the term "illegitimacy ratio" implies a moral judgment that now seems outmoded, alternative phrases, such as "the ratio of babies born out of wedlock to all babies," are so cumbersome that no reader should be expected to put up with them.

79. For a summary of recent evidence regarding the impact on children of growing up in a mother-only family, see McLanahan (1988).

80. David L. Featherman and Robert M. Hauser (1978), tables 5.9, 6.9, and 6.19, present regression equations predicting years of school completed, occupational status, and earnings for national samples of men in 1962 and 1973. The independent variables are the education and occupational status of the head of the respondent's family when the respondent was 16 years old, number of siblings, and dummies for race, farm origin, and "living with both your parents most of the time up to age 16." The coefficient of growing up in a broken family is typically 2 to 4 times the coefficient of the number of siblings. If this pattern also holds for sons born out of wedlock, the positive effects of declining family size would outweigh the negative effects of the increase in out-of-wedlock births between 1960 and 1986.

TABLE 15. Percentage of Children Born Out of Wedlock and of
Women Not Living with a Husband Who Have Children under Age 18,
by Race and Years of School, Selected Years, 1969–87

Mother's race and years of school	Children Born out of wedlock		Women with children under 18 not living with a husband			Women with children under 18 not living with a husband	
	1969 NCHS	1986 NCHS	1960 census	1970 census	1980 census	1980 CPS	1987 CPS
White							
0–8	7.9	34.8	10.1	15.7	20.6	22.2	24.3
9–11	8.8	38.2	5.7	10.5	16.8	20.3	27.7
12	4.1	13.9	4.1	6.7	12.7	12.3	15.3
13–15	4.1	7.2	4.6	7.8	12.9	14.0	16.6
16 or more	1.2	2.2	4.9	5.5	8.9	9.0	11.0
Total	5.1	14.5	5.8	8.7	13.5	13.9	16.5
Black							
0–8	41.9	79.4	28.6	40.1	50.3	55.9	55.7
9–11	43.3	82.9	17.9	33.4	51.7	57.3	66.7
12	28.0	61.9	12.9	27.7	41.1	46.2	51.9
13–15	21.5	45.5	10.5	21.4	43.6	44.9	42.7
16 or more	6.6	20.8	14.3	18.4	20.7	29.8	28.3
Total	35.1	62.6	21.7	32.3	44.3	48.1	50.3

SOURCES: Columns 1 and 2 are from National Center for Health Statistics, *Vital Statistics of the United States: 1969*, vol. 1: *Natality*, table 1–69, and *1986*, table 1–78. The 1969 data cover 31 states; 1986 data cover 47 states and the District of Columbia. Totals include mothers whose education was unknown. Such mothers' illegitimacy ratios typically fall between those of high school dropouts and high school graduates.
Columns 3 through 5 are from census 1/1,000 public use samples; columns 6 and 7 are from March CPS samples. Women are classified as having children under 18 if they are the female head of a family in which there is a child under 18. They are classified as not living with a husband if they are the female head of such a family and are separated, divorced, or never married. This procedure leads to classification errors when the woman in question is the grandmother, aunt, or sister of the relevant children rather than the mother. In the census data, all white percentages are based on cell sizes of more than 1,000; black percentages are based on samples of more than 500 except for women with 12 or more years of schooling in 1960, 13 or more in 1970, and 16 or more in 1980. The only census cell with less than 100 cases is black college graduates in 1960. CPS estimates for blacks are based on less than 500 cases except for high school graduates in 1987. CPS estimates for black college graduates in 1980 and 1987 and for blacks with fewer than 9 years of schooling in 1987 are based on 60 to 75 cases.

The illegitimacy ratio is much higher among blacks than among whites
with the same amount of schooling. Among college graduates, for example, the illegitimacy ratio in 1986 was 2 percent for whites but 21
percent for blacks.

Education also has a big effect on the illegitimacy ratio, regardless of
race. Among black women, for example, the ratio in 1986 was 21 percent
among college graduates and 83 percent among high school dropouts.
The corresponding figures for white women were 2 percent and 38
percent.

The absolute increase in the illegitimacy ratio has been greater among blacks than among whites and greatest of all among blacks without high school diplomas. This is consistent with the underclass hypothesis.

The proportional increase has been greatest among whites without high school diplomas. Their illegitimacy ratio increased by a factor of 4.3 between 1969 and 1986.

College-educated whites are the only group that remains strongly committed to marrying before they have children. In 1986, 98 percent of the white college graduates who had babies were married.

Why Has Unwed Motherhood Become More Acceptable?

William Julius Wilson and Kathryn Neckerman have argued that the two-parent family lost its appeal to blacks partly because fewer black men earned enough to support a family.[81] Subsequent research supports their contention that steady employment has a major impact on a man's chance of marrying.[82] Declines in the proportions of black men with jobs must, therefore, have contributed *something* to the decline in marriage rates among blacks. This decline has been far too large for male joblessness alone to explain it, however. The simplest way of illustrating this point is to look at changes among mature black men with steady jobs. Since this group is in increasingly short supply, its marriage rate should have risen between 1960 and 1980. In reality its marriage rate fell from 80 percent in 1960 to 66 percent in 1980, a 14 point drop. For all black men in this age range, including those who did not work regularly, the proportion who were married fell from 75 percent to 58 percent, a 17 point drop.[83] This comparison suggests that four-fifths of the decline in marriage rates among mature black men would have occurred even if their employment status had not changed at all. Robert Mare and Chris-

81. Wilson and Neckerman (1986).

82. See the paper by Mare and Winship in this volume; and Ellwood and Rodda (1989). For estimates of how employment affects marriage among expectant fathers, see Testa and others (1989).

83. These estimates are based on 1/1,000 public use samples of 1960 and 1980 census records. "Married" refers here to those who were actually living with a spouse. I have done these same calculations using detailed breakdowns by age, weeks worked, and earnings with essentially the same results. The change in employment status accounts for less than a fifth of the change in marriage rates no matter how the computation is done, and in some cases it accounts for almost none of the shift.

topher Winship in this volume reach much the same conclusion using different methods.[84]

Whereas Wilson and Neckerman blame the decline in two-parent families on fewer job opportunities for men, some conservatives blame improved job opportunities for women. Mare and Winship find, however, that a woman's employment status does not have much net effect on her chances of marrying.[85] Furthermore, as table 6 showed, employment rates for single mothers have hardly changed since 1960. Improvements in women's job opportunities are not, therefore, a plausible explanation for rising illegitimacy ratios.

Most conservatives believe that the generosity of the welfare system has contributed to the increase in unwed motherhood. The purchasing power of AFDC plus food stamps did rise between 1964 and 1976, but table 14 shows that while births to married women declined in this period, out-of-wedlock births hardly increased at all. The number of out-of-wedlock births did rise after 1975, but by then real AFDC benefits were falling. This history hardly suggests that raising benefits encourages out-of-wedlock births. Nor do unmarried women in high-benefit states have appreciably more babies than those in low-benefit states.[86] Welfare benefit levels do not, therefore, provide a very convincing explanation for the spread of unwed motherhood.

Changes in men and women's economic situations may, however, have encouraged out-of-wedlock births indirectly by altering broader cultural assumptions about relations between the sexes. The moral norm that a man should marry a woman if he has gotten her pregnant lost much of its force between 1960 and 1990. That norm rested on the assumption that since women could not support themselves or their children without male help, men had to assume economic responsibility for their children. As women's earning power rose, more of them were able to get along without male help. To support a family comfortably without any male help, a woman usually had to be highly skilled and have a small family, but such women's existence still helped undermine the idea that marriage was the only way to keep children from going hungry. Wishful thinking did the rest.

Women's growing ability to control their own fertility may also have

84. See also Ellwood and Rodda (1989).

85. Ellwood and Rodda (1989).

86. The best analysis of welfare benefit levels and out-of-wedlock births is still Ellwood and Bane (1985). See also the review in Garfinkel and McLanahan (1986), pp. 55–63. For contrary evidence, see Plotnick (forthcoming).

weakened men's feeling that they were morally obligated to marry a woman who was about to have their baby. When the pill replaced the condom as the contraceptive of choice, contraception was redefined as a woman's responsibility. When the Supreme Court legalized abortion and defined it as a procedure that only a woman could initiate, an even larger share of the responsibility for having a baby ended up in women's hands. If a woman can get a legal abortion but chooses not to, her boyfriend is unlikely to feel that her pregnancy is his responsibility and that he has an obligation to marry her (except, perhaps, when he is strongly opposed to abortion himself).

Improved contraception and abortion also lowered the economic cost of not marrying. In 1960 a sexually active woman could expect to have four or five children. Then as now, a woman with four or five children had almost no chance of earning enough to keep herself and her children out of poverty. By 1975 most married women had only two children, and many unwed mothers had only one. A woman's chances of earning enough to avoid poverty were thus considerably better, and her need for a husband was reduced. Knowing this, we may have become more tolerant of men who decided not to marry a woman they had gotten pregnant.

Single Parenthood

Up to this point I have taken the traditional view that unwed parenthood is bad for children, and that society's ability to prevent out-of-wedlock births is a measure of its ability to protect the interests of the next generation. Some feminists reject this assumption on the grounds that women should not have to marry men to have babies. If our concern is with children rather than parents, however, this position is hard to defend. Raising a child is difficult under any circumstances, and it is even more difficult when you try to do it alone than when you share the responsibility. Single mothers have less money than two-parent families, and they also have less time for their children than a couple does. There are exceptions, of course. Some single mothers earn high salaries and some get as much help from their own mothers as married mothers get from their husbands. On the average, however, children raised by single mothers do somewhat worse on most measures of success than children raised by married couples.

If our concern about unwed parenthood derives from its effect on children, however, we must worry not only about whether couples marry before they have children but also about whether they stay married after having children. It is not obvious that anyone benefits when teenagers who conceive a child out of wedlock marry for a year or two and then divorce—especially if, as often happens, they conceive a second child before divorcing. Divorced fathers tend to have somewhat stronger emotional and economic ties to their children than never-married fathers do. But neither group contributes much economic support, and neither is in a strong position to give their children the supervision and attention they need.

While out-of-wedlock births are far more likely in lower-class than in middle-class families, divorce is more evenly distributed across social classes. This means that children's class backgrounds have far more impact on their chances of being born into a single-parent family than on their chances of living in such a family when they are teenagers. It also means that if we want to look at the class distribution of family breakdown, we need to consider not only out-of-wedlock births but the proportion of all children living with single mothers. Table 15 does this. Several points deserve comment.

—A woman's chance of having a child out of wedlock is less than her chance of later being a single mother. For example, only 6 percent of the white women who had babies in 1970 were unmarried. Ten years later, 14 percent of white mothers with children under age 18 were unmarried. Among black women who had babies in 1970, 28 percent were unmarried. Ten years later, 48 percent of black mothers with children under age 18 were unmarried.

—While the proportion of mothers who are unmarried increases as their children get older, the absolute size of this increase is not strongly related to the mother's education or race. It follows that the proportionate increase is much larger for groups with low illegitimacy ratios. (To verify this claim, the reader should compare the illegitimacy ratios for 1969 to the proportions of mothers with children under 18 who were unmarried in 1980.)

Table 15 does not distinguish mothers who are still married to their child's father from those who have divorced and remarried. It therefore underestimates the degree to which children are exposed to marital disruption. But even if trend data on the proportion of children living with their natural fathers existed, there would surely be large class differences, and the absolute size of these differences would probably have grown since the 1960s. Thus, we would probably still conclude that the glue holding families together had weakened more in the underclass than in the middle class.

But while class differences in family structure seem to have widened over the past generation, this trend may not continue, at least among blacks. Among black high school dropouts, to take an extreme case, 83 percent of all babies were born out of wedlock in 1986, and the proportion is probably even higher today. The illegitimacy ratio for black high school dropouts cannot go much higher. Among black college dropouts, in contrast, the illegitimacy ratio was only 46 percent in 1986. That ratio can rise a lot, and past experience suggests that it will. If the trends that prevailed from 1969 to 1986 continue, something like 70 percent of black college dropouts who have babies in the year 2003 will be unmarried. If that happens, the gap between college dropouts and high school dropouts will be somewhat smaller than it is today.

This point dramatizes the difficulties that arise when we think of family breakdown as a hallmark of membership in the underclass. The two-parent family is becoming less common in almost all strata of American society. Until now, the rate of change has been fastest in the underclass, but no group has been immune. The cost of the change has also been greatest for the underclass, because its members have fewer resources for coping with every form of adversity. In the long run, however, single parenthood will prove to be an American problem, not just an underclass problem.

Is the Underclass a Useful Idea?

Americans started talking about the underclass during the 1980s because they sensed that their society was becoming more unequal. The rich were getting richer, but the poor were as numerous as ever. Skilled professionals and business executives commanded ever higher salaries, but a growing fraction of working-age men had no job at all. At the same time, the fabric of lower-class society seemed to be unraveling. Poor couples were having more of their babies without marrying, and millions of single mothers were trying to live on welfare checks that paid less than the rich spent every month amusing themselves. Crime was rampant in many poor neighborhoods. Inner-city schools seemed unable to teach most of their students even basic skills. As a result, poor children no longer seemed to have much chance of escaping from poverty, as earlier generations had.

If all these problems had arisen more or less simultaneously, the idea that shrinking economic opportunities were creating a new underclass would be hard to resist. In reality, however, while economic conditions began to deteriorate for less skilled workers in the 1970s, most of the other problems that led Americans to start talking about an underclass followed different trajectories. Some had been getting worse for a long time. Some got worse between 1965 and 1975 but then leveled off. Some never got worse. Some have actually gotten better. Thus, when we try to link changes in family structure, welfare use, school enrollment, academic achievement, or criminal violence to changes in economic opportunity, the connections prove elusive. To see why, it is helpful to compare the timing of changes in different areas.

Which Problems Have Gotten Steadily Worse?

Male joblessness. Long-term joblessness is somewhat sensitive to the business cycle, but the underlying rate among 25- to 54-year-old men rose in both the 1970s and 1980s. Among whites the new jobless were not poor. Among blacks, however, the kinds of poor men who had worked episodically in 1960 often withdrew from the labor force, increasing the proportion of all blacks who were both long-term jobless and poor.

Unwed parenthood. The number of babies born to unmarried women did not rise much from 1960 to 1975, but the number of babies born to married women fell a lot, so the proportion of babies born out of wedlock rose. After 1975 the number of babies born to unmarried women also began to rise. Since divorce has also become more common, the fraction of women raising children without male help has also increased.

Which Problems Have Stopped Getting Worse?

Welfare. While single motherhood increased steadily after 1960, the proportion of single mothers collecting welfare rose only from 1964 to 1974. After that, it began to decline again. As a result, the proportion of all mothers collecting welfare rose dramatically between 1964 and 1974 but then leveled off.

Violence. Violent crime doubled between 1964 and 1974, remained roughly constant during the late 1970s, declined significantly in the early 1980s, and edged up in the late 1980s. As a result, violence was somewhat less common in the late 1980s than in 1980 or 1970. This was especially true among blacks.

Which Problems Have Gotten Steadily Better?

Dropouts. Both non-Hispanic whites and blacks were more likely to earn a high school diploma or GED certificate in the late 1980s than at any time in the past. The disparity between blacks and whites was also smaller. Improvements on these indices were, however, somewhat slower in the 1980s than in the 1960s or 1970s.

Reading and mathematics skills. The proportion of 17-year-olds with basic reading skills rose steadily during the 1970s and 1980s, especially among blacks. The increase among whites was much smaller. Disparities between the best and worst readers, while still huge, diminished significantly. The proportion of 17-year-old blacks with basic math skills also rose during the 1980s.

Which Problems Have Stopped Getting Better?

Teenage parenthood. Teenage motherhood declined during the 1960s and 1970s. There was no clear trend during the 1980s. Teenage fatherhood rose during the 1960s, declined during the 1970s, and was roughly constant during the 1980s.

Poverty. The proportion of individuals with family incomes below the poverty line, which had fallen steadily from 1940 to 1970, has not changed much since 1970. Only the character of poverty has changed. It has become less common among the elderly and more common among children. Poverty has also become more concentrated among families in which the head does not work regularly.

Which Problems Have I Ignored?

Drugs. Drug use is a persistent problem, especially among the underclass. I have not discussed it because I have not been able to find any convincing quantitative evidence about the prevalence or severity of the problem. Surveys of high school students show dramatic declines in almost all forms of drug use during the 1980s. Yet people who spend time in poor communities are convinced that drugs became a more serious problem during the 1980s. Both claims may be correct.

Intergenerational inheritance. Among blacks, educational attainment became less dependent on family background between 1940 and 1980.

As a result, black children from disadvantaged backgrounds had better educational prospects in the 1980s than in 1970. Among whites, there was little change after 1970. Unfortunately, I found no evidence on whether disadvantaged children's chances of growing up to be poor, jobless, or dependent on welfare have changed over time.

The Underclass and Social Change

The trends I have described do not fit together in any simple or obvious way. Those who think that everything has gotten worse for people at the bottom of the social pyramid since 1970 are clearly wrong. Economic conditions have deteriorated for workers without higher education, and two-parent families have become scarcer, but welfare dependency has not increased since the early 1970s, and illiteracy, teenage motherhood, and violence have declined somewhat.

So far as I can see, the claim that America has a growing underclass does not help us to understand complex changes of the kind I have described. On the contrary, arguments that use class as their central explanatory idea obscure what is going on. The reasons for this deserve brief discussion.

We use terms such as "middle class" and "underclass" because we know that occupation, income, educational credentials, cognitive skills, a criminal record, out-of-wedlock childbearing, and other personal characteristics are somewhat correlated with one another. Class labels provide a shorthand device for describing people who differ along many of these dimensions simultaneously. The term "middle class," for example, evokes someone who has attended college, holds a steady job, earns an adequate income, got married before having children, and has never murdered, raped, robbed, or assaulted anyone. The term "underclass," in contrast, conjures up a chronically jobless high school dropout who has had two or three children out of wedlock, has very little money to support them, and probably has either a criminal record or a history of welfare dependence.

Relatively few people fit either of these stereotypes perfectly. Many people are "middle class" in some respects, "working class" in others, and "underclass" in still others. Those who use class labels always assume, however, that everyone is a member of some class or other. In order to assign everyone to a class, they allow their classes to be internally heterogeneous. If they assign people to classes on the basis of how they make their living, for example, they allow the members of these classes to differ with regard to income, educational credentials, cognitive skills, family structure, and arrest record. Everyone who stops to think recognizes that the world is untidy in this sense. We use class labels precisely because we want to make the world seem tidier than it is. The purpose of these labels is to draw attention to the differences between classes. But by emphasizing differences between classes, such labels inevitably encourage us to forget about the much larger differences that exist *within* classes.

The illusion of class homogeneity does no harm in some contexts, but it encourages two kinds of logical error when we try to describe social change. First, whenever we observe an increase in behavior that has traditionally been correlated with membership in a particular class, we tend to assume that the class in question must be getting bigger. If more working-age men are jobless, for example, we assume that the underclass must be getting bigger, without stopping to ask whether the men who have become jobless are in fact poor or have other attributes that might make them part of the underclass. The second error is a mirror image of the first. Once we decide that a class is growing, we tend to assume that every form of behavior associated with membership in that class is becoming more common. Having concluded that the underclass is getting bigger, for example, we assume that dropout rates, crime, and teenage parenthood must also be rising. The underlying logic here is that if one correlate of membership in the underclass is rising, all must be rising.

To understand what is happening to those at the bottom of American society, we need to examine their problems one at a time, asking how each has changed and what has caused the change. Instead of assuming that the problems are closely linked to one another, we need to treat their interrelationships as a matter for empirical investigation. When we do that, the relationships are seldom as strong as our class stereotypes would have led us to expect. As a result, some problems can become more common while others become less so.

Exaggerating the correlations among social problems can have political costs as well. Portraying poverty, joblessness, illiteracy, violence, unwed motherhood, and drug abuse as symptoms of a larger metaproblem, such as the underclass, encourages people to look for metasolutions. We are frequently told, for example, that "piecemeal" reform is pointless and that we need a "comprehensive" approach to the problem of the underclass. Some even believe we need "revolutionary" change, although that view is so out of favor at the moment that few express it publicly.

Our most pressing need, it seems to me, is for schools, employers, police forces, churches, health maintenance organizations, and welfare offices that can deal with poor people's problems in more realistic ways—ways that build on people's strengths without ignoring their weaknesses. Changes of this kind require an immense amount of trial and error. Unfortunately, America has never been very good at learning from its mistakes. Instead of looking for ways to improve our institutions, we tend to blame some politician for every failure and look for a replacement. Politicians therefore become specialists in avoiding blame, not solving problems. This may be unavoidable in a large, diverse society. But if we cannot manage piecemeal reforms, looking for metasolutions is almost certain to be time wasted so far as the American underclass is concerned. If we want to reduce their poverty, joblessness, illiteracy, violence, or despair, we will surely need to change our institutions and attitudes in hundreds of small ways, not one big way.

References

Adams, Terry K., Greg J. Duncan, and Willard L. Rodgers. 1988. "The Persistence of Poverty." In *Quiet Riots: Race and Poverty in the United States,* edited by Fred R. Harris and Roger Wilkins. Pantheon.

Aponte, Robert. 1988. "Conceptualizing the Underclass: An Alternative Perspective." Department of Sociology, University of Chicago.

Archer, Dane, and Rosemary Gartner. 1984. *Violence and Crime in Cross-National Perspective.* Yale University Press.

Auletta, Ken. 1982. *The Underclass.* Random House.

Background Material and Data on Programs within the Jurisdiction of the Committee on Ways and Means. 1989. Committee Print. House Committee on Ways and Means.

Blumstein, Alfred, Jacqueline Cohen, Jeffrey A. Roth, and Christy A. Visher, editors. 1986. *Criminal Careers and "Career Criminals,"* vol. 1. Washington: National Academy Press.

Bound, John. 1989. "The Health and Earnings of Rejected Disability Insurance Applicants." *American Economic Review* 79 (June), pp. 482–503.

Clark, Kim B. and Lawrence H. Summers. 1979. "Labor Market Dynamics and Unemployment: A Reconsideration." *Brookings Papers on Economic Activity* 1, pp. 13–60.

Danziger, Sheldon. 1988. "Economic Growth, Poverty, and Inequality in an Advanced Economy." Discussion paper 862–88. Institute for Research on Poverty, University of Wisconsin.

Duncan, Greg, and Willard Rodgers. 1989. "Has Poverty Become More Persistent?" Institute for Social Research, University of Michigan.

Ellis, Dean S. 1967. "Speech and Social Status in America." *Social Forces* 45 (March), pp. 431–37.

Ellwood, David T. 1988. *Poor Support: Poverty in the American Family*. Basic Books.

Ellwood, David T., and Mary Jo Bane. 1985. "The Impact of AFDC on Family Structure and Living Arrangements." In *Research in Labor Economics 7*, edited by Ronald G. Ehrenberg. Greenwich, Conn.: JAI Press.

Ellwood, David T., and David Rodda. 1989. "The Hazards of Work and Marriage: The Influence of Male Employment on Marriage Rates." John F. Kennedy School of Government, Harvard University.

Featherman, David L., and Robert M. Hauser. 1978. *Opportunity and Changes*. Academic Press.

Garfinkel, Irwin, and Sara S. McLanahan. 1986. *Single Mothers and Their Children: A New American Dilemma*. Washington: Urban Institute Press.

Hannerz, Ulf. 1969. *Soulside: Inquiries into Ghetto Culture and Community*. Columbia University Press.

Haveman, Robert H., and Barbara L. Wolfe. 1984. "The Decline of Male Labor Force Participation: Comment." *Journal of Political Economy* 92 (June), pp. 532–41.

Hughes, Mark Alan. 1988. "Concentrated Deviance or Isolated Deprivation? The 'Underclass' Idea Reconsidered." Woodrow Wilson School, Princeton University.

Jencks, Christopher, and Kathryn Edin. 1990. "The Real Welfare Problem." *American Prospect* (Winter), pp. 31–50.

Jencks, Christopher, and Susan E. Mayer. Forthcoming. *Poverty and Hardship in America*.

Jones, Lyle. 1987a. "Achievement Trends for Black School Children." Department of Psychology, University of North Carolina.

———. 1987b. "Trends in School Achievement of Black Children." Department of Psychology, University of North Carolina.

Juhn, Chin-hui, Kevin Murphy, and Brooks Pierce. 1989. "Wage Inequality and the Rise in Returns to Skill." University of Chicago Graduate School of Business.

Levy, Frank. 1977. "How Big Is the American Underclass?" Washington: Urban Institute.

Liebow, Elliott. 1967. *Tally's Corner: A Study of Negro Streetcorner Men*. Boston: Little, Brown.

McLanahan, Sara S. 1988. "The Consequences of Single Parenthood for Subsequent Generations," *Focus* 11 (Fall), pp. 16–21.

Mare, Robert D., and Christopher Winship. 1984. "The Paradox of Lessening Racial Inequality and Joblessness among Black Youth: Enrollment, Enlistment, and Employment, 1964–1981." *American Sociological Review* 49 (February), pp. 39–55.

Massey, Douglas S., and Mitchell L. Eggers. 1990. "The Ecology of Inequality: Minorities and the Concentration of Poverty, 1970–1980." *American Journal of Sociology* 95 (March), pp. 1153–88.

Mayer, Susan E., and Christopher Jencks. 1989. "Poverty and the Distribution of Material Hardship." *Journal of Human Resources* 24 (Winter), pp. 88–113.

Mincey, Ronald. 1988. "Is There a White Underclass?" Washington: Urban Institute.

Mullis, Ina V. S., and Lynn B. Jenkins. 1990. *The Reading Report Card, 1971–88: Trends from the Nation's Report Card.* Princeton, N.J.: National Assessment of Educational Progress.

Myers, Samuel, and William Sabol. n.d. "Crime and the Black Community: Issues in the Understanding of Race and Crime in America." Department of Economics, University of Maryland.

Orshansky, Mollie. 1965. "Counting the Poor: Another Look at the Poverty Profile." *Social Security Bulletin* 28 (January), pp. 3–29.

Parsons, Donald O. 1980. "The Decline in Male Labor Force Participation." *Journal of Political Economy* 88 (February), pp. 117–34.

———. 1984. "Disability Insurance and Male Labor Force Participation: A Response to Haveman and Wolfe." *Journal of Political Economy* 92 (June), pp. 542–49.

Plotnick, Robert. Forthcoming. "Determinants of Out-of-Wedlock Childbearing: Evidence from the National Longitudinal Survey of Youth." *Journal of Marriage and the Family.*

Ruggles, Patricia, and William P. Marton. 1986. "Measuring the Size and Characteristics of the Underclass: How Much Do We Know?" Washington: Urban Institute.

Sider, Hal. 1985. "Unemployment Duration and Incidence, 1968–82." *American Economic Review* 75 (June), pp. 461–72.

Testa, Mark, Nan Marie Astone, Marilyn Krogh, and Kathryn M. Neckerman. 1989. "Employment and Marriage among Inner-City Fathers." *Annals of the American Academy of Political and Social Science* 501 (January), pp. 79–91.

Van Haitsma, Martha. 1989. "A Contextual Definition of the Underclass." *Focus* 12 (Summer), pp. 27–31.

Wilson, William Julius. 1987. *The Truly Disadvantaged: The Inner City, the Underclass, and Public Policy.* University of Chicago Press.

Wilson, William Julius, and Kathryn M. Neckerman. 1986. "Poverty and Family Structure: The Widening Gap between Evidence and Public Policy Issues." In *Fighting Poverty: What Works and What Doesn't,* edited by Sheldon M. Danziger and Daniel H. Weinberg. Harvard University Press.

Part Two ─────────────────────────────
The Economic Condition of the Underclass

Employment and Earnings of Disadvantaged Young Men in a Labor Shortage Economy

RICHARD B. FREEMAN

How do disadvantaged young men fare when there is a relative shortage of labor? To what extent do low unemployment rates change their employment and earnings prospects? Does a labor shortage bring disadvantaged young black men, many of whom are viewed as part of the "underclass," into the mainstream of the economy or does it pass them by?

This paper examines these questions for out-of-school young men in the 1980s with twelve or fewer years of schooling. Focusing on youths who have left school eliminates consideration of the decision to drop out of school and of the work behavior of students. Focusing on young men eliminates consideration of how family formation, fertility, the welfare system, and so forth affect the labor market activity of women. I treat high school graduates as well as dropouts as disadvantaged because the economic opportunities for young male graduates deteriorated greatly in the 1970s and 1980s.[1]

My research strategy was to contrast the economic position of young men across local labor markets that differ in their rates of unemployment. To reduce the danger of making incorrect inferences because of the sampling and other vagaries of a single data set, I relied on data from two surveys: the annual merged files of the Current Population Survey (CPS) and the National Longitudinal Survey of Youth (NLSY).[2]

Bill Rodgers and Alida Castillo provided invaluable research assistance for this paper.

1. Blackburn, Bloom, and Freeman (1990).
2. The Current Population Survey is the regular monthly survey of about 59,500 households from which the national unemployment rate is derived. The CPS gathers data on average weekly earnings and average hours worked from a subsample of households in each month, as well as diverse other data.

The National Longitudinal Survey of Youth is a detailed survey of more than 12,000 young people from 1979 through 1987. The original 1979 sample contained 12,686 youths age 14 to 21, of whom 6,111 represented the entire population of youths and 5,295 represented an oversampling of civilian Hispanic, black, and economically disadvantaged non-Hispanic, nonblack youth. An additional 1,280 were in the military. The survey had a re-

Local Labor Market Shortages

The rate of unemployment was relatively high in the United States in the 1980s, continuing the decade-by-decade increase that marked the post–World War II period.[3] But recovery from the 1982–83 recession created major economic booms and labor shortages in several areas of the country, largely though not exclusively in the Northeast. The "Massachusetts miracle" that achieved considerable national publicity because of the presidential candidacy of Michael Dukakis was typical. From 1983 to 1987 unemployment in the state was 3 percentage points lower than the national average; personal per capita income and average hourly earnings in manufacturing rose from below the national average to above it. In 1987, when the rate of unemployment was 6.2 percent in the country as a whole, the rate in Boston was just 2.7 percent. From 1983 to 1987 the help-wanted index for the city rose more rapidly than for the United States as a whole. Help-wanted signs on store windows, want ads on radio and television, job applications strategically placed at checkout counters of local stores, extended waits for the services of skilled craftsworkers, and wages more than 50 percent above the minimum at fast food stores confirmed the pervasiveness of the labor shortage. Many other states and metropolitan areas also had levels of unemployment that reflected labor shortages. In 1987 thirty-six metropolitan areas had unemployment rates lower than 4 percent, and several—including Anaheim–Santa Ana, California; Stamford, Connecticut; and Nashua, New Hampshire—had rates lower than 3 percent. The popular view of young blacks as residing in high-unemployment localities notwithstanding, some 22 percent of out-of-school young black men with twelve or fewer years of schooling were in metropolitan areas with unemployment rates lower than 4 percent.[4]

---

markably low attrition rate—4.9 percent through 1984—and thus represents the largest and best available longitudinal data set on youths in the period under study.

3. The unemployment rate averaged 4.5 percent in the 1950s, 4.8 percent in the 1960s, 6.2 percent in the 1970s, and 7.3 percent in the 1980s. Although demographic factors explain some of the upward trend, there is no doubt that the economic recession of 1982–83 created the highest rates of joblessness since the Great Depression. Data are from Council of Economic Advisers (1990), table C-32.

4. This figure is from my tabulations of the annual demographic files of the Current Population Survey that provide most of the data in this paper.

Tight Labor Markets and Youth Employment

One expects that in a tight labor market the proportion of young people who are employed will increase and their unemployment will decrease, absolutely and relative to adult employment or unemployment. As new entrants to a labor market, youths constitute a margin of adjustment for employers that makes hiring them especially sensitive to the state of demand. Past studies have, in fact, found that a 1 percentage point drop in adult unemployment improves the job prospects of youths by more than 1 percentage point, particularly among men.[5] Whether the employment of the young with the fewest skills was as sensitive to labor market conditions in the 1980s, when the national labor market turned against such workers, is, however, open to question.

By contrast, neither theory nor previous empirical studies show whether the pay of young workers will be higher or lower in labor markets with low unemployment. On one side, the economic theory of job search suggests that local labor markets with high rates of unemployment should have high wages. The argument is that wages in an area are largely determined by union policies, the mix of industries in the area, or government policies such as a generous unemployment insurance system or, in the case of young workers, the minimum wage. Unemployment adjusts to the given wage level. An area with high wages attracts migrants from other areas, induces additional people to participate in the labor force, and creates long durations of unemployment as the jobless search for the high-wage opportunities. In equilibrium, these labor supply adjustments equate the present value of working across areas, which requires that rates of unemployment be higher in areas with high wages. Reinforcing this tendency is the fact that the youngest and least skilled gain jobs when unemployment falls so that a disproportionately large number of workers in areas with low unemployment will be young and relatively unskilled, reducing the average wage in those areas.

On the other side, competitive pressures should lead employers to increase wages in tight labor markets. If these pressures are strong and persistent, they can cause wages to be higher in areas with low unemployment.[6] The active-labor-market hypothesis that current market developments have a greater effect on entering workers than they do on older workers who are relatively insulated by implicit contracts, specific train-

5. Clark and Summers (1981); and Freeman (1982)
6. This gives the "wage curve" that Blanchflower and Oswald (1989) have found for several European countries.

ing, and seniority rules in internal labor markets suggests further that the wages of young people will be more responsive to economic changes than will other wages, rising sharply in tight labor markets and declining sharply in loose markets. In the 1970s the wages of the young showed just such flexibility, falling in real and relative terms as the baby boom generation entered the labor market.[7] The tendency for wages in low-paying industries and occupations to increase when unemployment falls also suggests that the wages of disadvantaged youths will be higher in markets with low unemployment, because these people invariably begin their working lives in low-wage industries and occupations.

Surprising as it may seem to some, research on the relation between wages and unemployment in the 1970s found that unemployment of adult workers was higher in high-wage cities, such as Detroit, in the industrial North Central region than in low-wage cities, such as Houston, in the South or Southwest.[8] This pattern did not, however, hold for youths, whose unemployment rate was similar in high-wage and low-wage metropolitan areas and whose ratio of employed workers to the population was lower in low-wage areas, possibly because the federal minimum wage reduced youth employment most in these areas.[9] As the minimum wage, unionism, and other nonmarket wage-setting forces became less important in the 1980s, one might have expected demand-side market pressures to dominate the relationship between wages and unemployment in a way that they did not in the 1970s.

Employment Patterns in 1987

To determine how the employment and earnings of disadvantaged young men varied with local labor market conditions in the 1980s, I contrasted the economic position of youths across metropolitan statistical areas (MSAs), primary metropolitan statistical areas, and consolidated metropolitan statistical areas with different rates of unemployment.[10]

7. Freeman (1979)

8. Hall (1972); Reza (1978); Marston (1980); and Browne (1978).

9. Freeman (1982).

10. An MSA is defined by the Census Bureau as "an urban area that meets specified size criteria—either it has a city of at least 50,000 inhabitants . . . or it contains an urbanized area of at least 50,000 inhabitants and has a total population of at least 100,000." Primary and consolidated MSAs are larger urban metropolitan areas. For their precise definition see appendix C in Bureau of Labor Statistics (1988). For ease of discussion I use MSA to refer to metropolitan statistical areas, primary metropolitan statistical areas, and consolidated metropolitan statistical areas.

These three types of MSAs are the most disaggregate measures of geographic locale in the Current Population Survey and thus of the local labor market in which a person resides. In 1987 the CPS identified 202 such areas. Rates of unemployment for these areas, based on the full year's surveys, are published by the Bureau of Labor Statistics in each year's May *Employment and Earnings* and in the various editions of *Geographic Profile of Employment and Unemployment.*

In analyzing the CPS data I categorized MSAs into areas with labor shortages—those with unemployment rates of 4 percent or less—and into four additional groups—areas with unemployment rates of 4 to 5 percent, 5 to 6 percent, 6 to 7 percent, and 7 percent or higher. I compared the labor market outcomes for youths in these areas in 1987 and compared 1987 outcomes with 1983 outcomes in the same areas. I did this to control for the possibility that differences in employment or earnings across areas in 1987 reflected the effect on outcomes of relatively permanent area factors that had been omitted from the analysis rather than the effect of 1987 local labor market conditions. Under plausible assumptions the difference between the 1987 and 1983 outcomes in areas classified by 1987 unemployment removes persistent omitted factors and thus helps identify the structural impact of a labor shortage on outcomes.[11] Unfortunately, extending the analysis back to 1983 limited the sample to the 45 standard metropolitan statistical areas (SMSAs) identified in the 1983 merged annual file.[12] Because more than half the U.S. work force is in this SMSA sample and because results for the sample of 45 in 1987 are similar to those for the full 202-MSA sample, I believe that the findings are not distorted.

Table 1 shows the 1987 and 1983 percentage of unemployed and

11. To see the logic of this procedure, assume that there are two groups of cities: those with high unemployment and those with low unemployment. Outcomes depend on whether the youth lives in a high- or low-unemployment area and on unobserved city characteristics that happen to be correlated with the 1987 group in which a city is found. If there is no correlation between the 1987 category and the 1983 category in which a city falls, then the only reason for differences in 1983 youth outcomes between cities that differ in their 1987 unemployment category is the effect of the unobserved city factor on outcomes. Hence, taking the 1983–87 change in outcomes for cities in the same 1987 category eliminates the effect of the omitted factor. If, more realistically, there is a positive correlation between a city's 1983 and 1987 category, the difference estimator is likely to understate the true effect of 1987 market conditions on outcomes.

12. Standard metropolitan statistical areas were used to identify areas in the 1983 CPS and are the geographic equivalent of the MSAs. They were based on 1970 census of population definitions, whereas the MSAs are based on 1980 census of population definitions. I matched the relevant areas for comparability.

TABLE I. Unemployment Rates and Employment-Population Ratios for Out-of-School Young Men with Twelve or Fewer Years of Schooling, 1983, 1987

Percent

Area unemployment rate (1987)	Rate of unemployment				Employment-population ratio			
	202 MSAs (1987)	45 MSAs (1987)	45 MSAs (1983)	Change (1983– 87)	202 MSAs (1987)	45 MSAs (1987)	45 MSAs (1983)	Change (1983– 87)
All youths								
Less than 4	5.1	5.8	15.4	−9.6	81	79	72	7
4–5	5.2	5.7	14.5	−8.8	80	78	71	7
5–6	8.6	9.9	17.6	−7.7	73	72	65	7
6–7	10.1	11.1	12.8	−1.7	71	69	68	1
More than 7	10.1	9.7	13.8	−4.1	69	68	64	4
Black youths								
Less than 4	9.1	7.2	40.5	−33.3	71	73	43	30
4–5	12.2	12.1	37.1	−25.0	65	65	46	19
5–6	19.6	21.6	33.3	−11.7	56	54	47	7
6–7	23.4	24.3	37.0	−12.7	52	49	39	10
More than 7	20.2	24.6	33.3	−8.7	48	44	41	3

SOURCE: Calculated from the Current Population Survey annual merged files, 1983 and 1987. The statistics are based on the ESR variable on the public CPS annual merged file. Everyone whose major activity is in school was dropped. Youths include blacks and whites only. The unemployment rate is the ratio of the number of people looking for work to the sum of the number looking for work, the number working, and the number with a job but not working. Employment is the number working and the number with a job but not working.

employment-population rates and the 1983–87 changes in those rates for all youths and for black youths in metropolitan areas classified by their 1987 levels of unemployment. The unemployment rates for all youths were markedly lower in areas with low unemployment in 1987. Unemployment rates showed relatively small differences in 1983 youth unemployment by 1987 area unemployment rates. This suggests that the 1987 differences are due more to 1987 labor market conditions than to area characteristics that have been omitted. Consistent with this, the 1983–87 change in rates shows greater decreases in areas with low 1987 unemployment rates. The employment-population ratios tell a similar story: youths had higher chances of employment in low-unemployment areas, though here the pattern is more uneven. In each group the increase in the employment-population ratio is comparable to the decrease in the unemployment rate. This implies that most of the growth of employment came from the pool of the unemployed rather than from those outside the labor force.

The figures for black youths tell a more dramatic story, particularly for

TABLE 2. Unemployment Rates and Employment-Population Ratios
for Men Age 25–64 with Twelve or Fewer Years of Schooling, 1983–87

Area unemployment rate (percent)	Change in employment-population ratio (percentage points)	Change in unemployment rate (percentage points)
Less than 4	5	−2.0
4–5	3	−2.3
5–6	5	−2.8
6–7	4	−1.8
More than 7	2	−2.0

SOURCE: Calculated from the Current Population Survey annual merged files, 1983 and 1987.

areas having unemployment rates of 4 to 5 percent and less than 4 percent. The differences in unemployment rates and employment-population
ratios between tight and loose labor markets in 1987 are 15 to 20 percentage points as opposed to the 5 to 10 points for all youths. The 1983–
87 changes in unemployment and employment-population ratios show,
in addition, an extraordinary improvement in the employment prospects
for young blacks in the areas with labor shortages in 1987. Although the
small numbers of black youths in the various categories (roughly 150 in
each) and the vagaries of the CPS, which often produces sharp changes
from year to year, suggest that the magnitudes should be considered cau-
tiously, the pattern is clear and impressive: young blacks are major beneficiaries of tight labor markets. Still, even in areas with the least unemployment, the unemployment rates of black youth remain markedly
higher and the employment-population ratios markedly lower than comparable rates for whites. In 1987 the black youth employment-
population ratio in areas with less than 4 percent unemployment is only
marginally better than that for whites in areas with unemployment rates
of 6 to 7 percent.

To see whether youth employment is more sensitive than adult male
employment to labor market conditions, I also calculated the 1983 and
1987 unemployment and employment-population rates for adult males
with twelve or fewer years of education (table 2). These figures show
much smaller changes for adult men, implying that youth employment is
more sensitive than adult male employment to cyclical swings.

As a concise way to summarize the effect of area unemployment on
youth unemployment, I estimated a linear probability model in which the
dependent variable was a 0–1 dummy variable for whether a youth was
employed in 1987 and the independent variables were the 1987 MSA

unemployment rate and measures of demographic characteristics: age, years of schooling, and race. The resultant regression coefficients and standard errors (in parentheses) on area unemployment were −0.019 (0.002) for all youths and −0.043 (0.007) for black youths. Because the area unemployment rate is measured in percentage points, the implication is that a 1-point decrease in area unemployment raises youth employment by 1.9 points and black youth employment by 4.3 points. This supports the inference from the means in table 1 that tight markets improve employment prospects more for black youths than for white youths.

Hourly Earnings

To see how tight labor markets affect earnings, I regressed the log (natural log) usual hourly earnings (the usual weekly earnings divided by the usual hours worked per week) of young, less educated, out-of-school men in 1987 on two separate indicators of local area unemployment: categorical variables for 1987 area unemployment, or the unemployment rates themselves, and demographic controls for the characteristics of the individual—age, age squared, years of schooling, and race. In addition, to assess the possibility that the results are due to area factors that were omitted from the regressions, I performed two additional analyses of the sample of forty-five MSAs. In one set of calculations I regressed both 1983 earnings and 1987 earnings on dummy variables for the category in which the area's unemployment rate fell in 1987. Under plausible assumptions the differences in the coefficients on 1987 area unemployment between the 1987 and the 1983 regressions reflect the "true" effect of 1987 unemployment on 1987 earnings.[13] In the other set, I regressed log earnings in 1987 and in 1983 on the rate of area unemployment in 1983

13. Let the true relation between area unemployment (U) and the outcome variable (Y) be $Y = B U + B_a A + e$, where A is the omitted area variable. The expected value of the regression coefficient of Y on U is then $B + B_a b_{au}$, where b_{au} is the regression coefficient of the omitted area variable on area unemployment.

Now consider the regression of Y' on U, where Y' is the outcome in a different period of time t'. In this regression I have omitted A and U', the unemployment rate in t' period. Assuming that U has no true effect on Y', the regression coefficient of Y' on U is $0 + B_a b_{au} + B b_{uu}'$ where B reflects the influence of the omitted variable U' on Y'.

Then, if $bu'_u = 0$, the difference between the regression coefficient of Y on U and of Y on U' is just B. If bu_u is not zero but rather positive (unemployment across areas is correlated over time), the difference in coefficients underestimates B by $1 - b_{u'u}$.

and 1987. This also provided a control for area variables potentially omitted in the analysis.[14]

One further statistical point about the calculations. Because area unemployment rates relate to groups with common group components in their residuals, the standard errors in the regressions are likely to be biased downward. Intuitively, this is because the area differences reflect 202 or 45 independent treatments rather than the thousands of observations the regression program used to calculate the standard error. The degree of bias depends on the correlation of disturbances within areas and the average number of persons in each area.[15] I have investigated the extent of this bias using a random effects regression design, in which the error term is modeled as $U_{ij} = a_i + v_{ij}$ for area effect a_i and where v_{ij} is a residual with the usual properties.[16] I fit this model in a two-stage procedure, first estimating the magnitude of the MSA group correlations and then using generalized least squares to estimate the earnings equation.[17]

14. In this analysis one can obtain an estimate of the effects of area unemployment on outcomes by subtracting the coefficient on the 1987 unemployment in a 1983 outcome equation from the coefficient in a 1983 outcome equation. One can also obtain an estimate of the effect of area unemployment on outcomes by subtracting the coefficients on 1987 and 1983 unemployment in the two separate outcome equations.

In the first case, consider the regression coefficients of the outcome variables Y or Y' on U and U' in regressions in which there is an omitted area variable A. The coefficients in the regression of Y on U and U' are

$b_{yu.u'} = b_{yu.u'a} + b_{ya.uu'} \, b_{au.u'}$ and
$b_{yu'.u} = b_{yu'.ua} + b_{ya.uu'} b_{au'.u}$.

Similarly, the coefficients in the regression of Y' on U and U' are

$b_{y'u.u'} = b_{y'u.u'a}b + b_{y'a.uu'}b_{au.u'}$, and
$b_{y'u'.u} = b_{y'u'.ua} + b_{y'a.uu'} \, b_{au'.u}$.

The true equation in each period is $Y = BU + B_a A + e$. The expected value of the coefficient of U in the regression of Y on U and U' is $B + b_{ya.uu'} \, b_{au.u'}$. The expected value of the coefficient of U in the regression of Y' on U and U' is $b_{y'a.uu'} \, b_{au.u'}$ because U does not enter the equation for Y' except as a proxy for the omitted area variable. Hence the difference between the coefficient on U in the regression of Y on U and U' and the coefficient on U in the regression of Y' on U and U' should be B.

Alternatively, since the expected value of the coefficient of U' in the regression of Y' on U and U' is $b_{ya.uu'} \, b_{au'.u}$ if $b_{au'.u} = b_{au.u'}$, the difference between the coefficients of U and U' in this regression should also be B. I have not exploited this estimate in the paper. I have also not combined all of the information in the four estimated coefficients to obtain a single B and a single "omitted variable" effect.

15. Moulton (1988).

16. To do this I used a program written by Alan Kreuger that handles the unbalanced design of the data, with differing numbers of people in different MSA cells.

17. Johnston (1983), pp. 410–15.

I obtained results similar to those in the least squares calculations in table 1.[18]

Table 3 presents the coefficients and standard errors for the impact of local labor market conditions on the log earnings of all youths and of black youths in the CPS samples. The upper portion of the table records the coefficients on dummy variables for four of the five unemployment groups differentiated in table 1; the omitted group comprises areas with the highest rates of unemployment. The bottom portion of the table records the coefficients from a regression in which I replaced the dummy categories with the area unemployment rate in the 202-MSA sample and with 1987 and 1983 area unemployment in the 45-MSA sample. The results for all youths show a significant inverse relation between unemployment and log earnings in 1987 that runs counter to the positive relation between area unemployment and earnings found for all workers in the 1970s. Earnings are markedly higher in areas with less than 4 percent unemployment: the 0.18 coefficient on log earnings suggests a 20 percent differential in youth earnings in 1987 between, say, Boston (with low unemployment) and Detroit (in the group with the highest unemployment). The results are much the same for the smaller MSA sample. By contrast, the regression of 1983 earnings on the same variables shows only modest differences among youths in the same areas. This implies that the area pattern in hourly earnings, like that in unemployment rates, arose during the economic recovery. Indeed, the difference between the coefficients on 1987 area unemployment from the 1987 and 1983 earnings regressions shows that, corrected for the potential effect of omitted area characteristics, youths in areas with especially low 1987 unemployment had markedly higher 1987 earnings. Looking at the underlying data, the geometric mean earnings for young men in areas with less than 4 percent unemployment rose by 21 percent between 1983 and 1987, compared with an increase of 10 percent for those in areas with unemployment of 7 percent or more in 1987. With a rate of inflation of 14 percent for the period, this implies a sizable real wage gain for youths in areas with labor shortages compared with real pay losses in areas with high joblessness. In the late 1980s McDonald's and other fast-food employers paid $5.00 to $6.00 an hour in markets with labor shortages but paid minimum or near-minimum wages in areas with high rates of unemployment.

18. In addition I estimated the effects of area unemployment on outcomes using a two-stage procedure in which I added area dummies to the individual outcome regressions and then regressed the coefficients on the dummies on the area unemployment rates. These results are similar to those reported in the paper.

TABLE 3. Effect of Area Unemployment Rates on Log Hourly Earnings of Young Men, by Race, 1983, 1987[a]

Item	All youths				Black youths			
	202 MSAs (1987)	45 MSAs (1987)	45 MSAs (1983)	Change (1987–83)	202 MSAs (1987)	45 MSAs (1987)	45 MSAs (1983)	Change (1987–83)
Area unemployment rate, 1987 (percent)								
Less than 4	.18 (.02)	.18 (.02)	.03 (.02)	.15	.22 (.05)	.19 (.06)	−.03 (.09)	.22
4–5	.11 (.02)	.09 (.02)	−.01 (.02)	.10	.18 (.05)	.17 (.06)	−.09 (.08)	.26
5–6	.08 (.02)	.06 (.02)	0 (.02)	.06	.17 (.05)	.12 (.06)	−.09 (.08)	.21
6–7	.02 (.02)	.02 (.03)	.03 (.02)	−.01	.05 (.05)	.03 (.06)	−.02 (.09)	.05
More than 7	...	...	...	...	...	...	...	...
Black	−.14 (.02)	−.15 (.02)	−.13 (.02)	−.02	...	...	...	...
R²	.22	.21	.22	...	.16	.17	.09	...
Unemployment variable								
1987 unemployment	−.029 (.002)	−.025 (.004)	.012 (.004)	−.037	−.043 (.008)	−.019 (.010)	.039 (.014)	−.058
1983 unemployment	...	−.011 (.004)	−.013 (.003)	.002	...	−.017 (.009)	−.027 (.012)	.010
Black	−.15 (.02)	−.15 (.02)	−.13 (.02)	−.02	...	...	...	...
R²	.22	.21	.22	...	.16	.16	.10	...
Sample size	5,912	3,342	3,571	...	687	497	414	...

SOURCE: Calculated from the Current Population Survey annual merged files, 1983 and 1987.
a. All regressions include variables for age, age squared, years of schooling, sex, and race. Standard errors are in parentheses.

The bottom portion of the table records the results of regressing the log earnings of young men on the rate of area unemployment in the 202-MSA sample and on the 1987 rate of unemployment and the 1983 rate of unemployment in the 45-MSA sample. The estimated coefficient on 1987 unemployment in the 202-MSA sample indicates that a 1-percentage-point increase in unemployment rates is associated with a substantial 2.9-point decrease in hourly earnings. In the 45-MSA sample the estimated coefficient on 1987 unemployment is −0.025 on 1987 log earnings but 0.012 on 1983 log earnings, implying a −0.037 effect of unemployment on log earnings corrected for the assumed omitted area factor. At the same time, however, the coefficient on 1983 unemployment is nearly identical in the two regressions, implying that differences in unemployment rates across areas had relatively little effect on area earnings, possibly because aggregate unemployment was so high in that year.

The estimated coefficients show that tight labor markets had an even greater effect on the earnings of young blacks. In the upper part of table 3, however, the hourly earnings of blacks appear to rise sharply even in areas with more than 6 percent unemployment. Because the sample size for blacks is relatively small and the standard errors for the coefficients on the area dummies in the 1983 regressions are sizable, however, the more useful estimates for black youths are from the bottom part of the table. Here, the coefficient on 1987 unemployment in the 1987 regression is roughly the same as for all young men, but the coefficient on 1987 unemployment in the 1983 regression is a substantial 0.039. Taking the difference between these coefficents as the best estimate of the effect of 1987 unemployment on the earnings of black youth, I obtained −0.058, which is markedly greater than the effect of 1987 unemployment on the earnings of all youths. For black as well as for all young men, however, 1983 unemployment is estimated to have had a relatively modest effect on hourly earnings.

The higher coefficients on local area unemployment for black youths than for all youths imply that racial differentials in earnings are smaller in tight labor markets than in loose ones. For example, the estimated coefficients on area unemployment of −0.029 for all youths and of −0.043 for black youths in the 202-MSA sample imply that when the area unemployment rate is 3 percentage points lower, the black-white earnings differential is 4.2 percentage points lower: 3 × (0.043 − 0.029). Because the national unemployment rate fell by roughly 3 points from 1983 to 1987, one would expect a 4-point improvement in the earnings of blacks relative to those of whites. In fact, the mean differential between the earnings of black youths and all youths was virtually constant from 1983 to 1987. The modest increase in the coefficient on the 0–1 black dummy variable between the 1983 and 1987 earnings regressions (with area unemployment held fixed) counterbalanced the effect of economic recovery.

All told, tables 1 and 3 show that tight local labor markets substantially benefited less educated young men, particularly blacks.

Longitudinal Progress

Do tight labor markets increase the growth of young men's wages or do they simply improve prospects for being hired and raise initial wage levels? Economic theory provides little guidance on what to expect. Companies may find it profitable to offer additional promotion and training opportunities to attract labor in a tight market, or they may postpone training, producing slower increases in earnings as workers age, because the market demands immediate production. To verify the CPS finding that decreases in area unemployment increase youth employment and earnings, and to see what happens to the growth of individual earnings in a tight labor market, I examined data from the National Longitudinal Survey of Youth on the employment and hourly earnings of out-of-school young men with twelve or fewer years of education. The age group covered by the NLSY differs slightly from that in the CPS: the young men are 17 to 25 years old in 1983 and 21 to 29 in 1987. The geographic areas covered also differ somewhat: because the NLSY file contains unemployment rates for both inside and outside metropolitan areas, I treated both areas in this analysis. To control for any differences in the economic position of youths caused by their place of residence, I included a dummy variable for urban status in all regressions. Finally, to obtain the largest possible sample of disadvantaged youths, I included young men from both the national representative sample and from the special targeted subsample of blacks, Hispanics, and economically disadvantaged whites. Because the targeted subsample is not randomly drawn from the population, coefficients on dummy variables for race may not reflect population differences in outcomes by race. There is, however, no reason to expect any bias in the estimated effects of area unemployment on the employment and earnings of the disadvantaged.

Table 4 records the estimated effect of 1983 and 1987 area unemployment rates on youth employment, unemployment, and log hourly earnings in 1983 and 1987. The results on employment and unemployment

TABLE 4 Effect of Area Unemployment Rates on Youth Employment and Unemployment, and Log Hourly Earnings of Young Men, by Race, 1983, 1987[a]

Independent variable	Employment			Unemployment			Log hourly earnings		
	1987	1983	Difference	1987	1983	Difference	1987	1983	Difference
All youths[b]									
1987 area unemployment	-.020	-.006	-.014	.018	.002	.016	-.023	.012	-.035
	(.003)	(.004)	...	(.005)	(.004)	...	(.008)	(.008)	...
1983 area unemployment	-.002	-.018	.016	.003	.020	-.017	.005	-.012	.017
	(.003)	(.004)	...	(.002)	(.003)	...	(.006)	(.006)	...
Black	-.15	-.18	.03	.089	.139	-.05	-.35	-.28	-.07
	(.02)	(.02)	...	(.016)	(.022)	...	(.04)	(.04)	...
Black youths[c]									
1987 area unemployment	-.018	-.002	-.016	.022	-.007	.029	-.072	.002	-.074
	(.008)	(.004)	...	(.007)	(.008)	...	(.017)	(.017)	...
1983 area unemployment	.002	-.018	.020	.001	.040	-.039	-.001	-.002	.001
	(.003)	(.004)	...	(.006)	(.009)	...	(.014)	(.015)	...

SOURCE: Calculated from the National Longitudinal Survey of Youth.

a. Employment and unemployment regressions include age, years of schooling, and an urban dummy. The ln earnings regressions also include an age-squared term. Standard errors are in parentheses.

b. Sample sizes for all youths were 1,818 in employment regressions, 1,648 in the 1983 unemployment regression, 1,672 in the 1987 unemployment regression, 1,649 in the 1983 unemployment regression, 1,542 in the 1987 earnings equation, and 1,519 in the 1983 earnings equation.

c. Sample sizes for black youths were 601 in employment regressions, 515 in the 1983 unemployment regression, 522 in the 1987 unemployment regression, 464 in the 1987 earnings equation, and 468 in the 1983 earnings equation.

for all youths yield a pattern much like that in table 1: a positive cross-section relation between 1987 area unemployment rates and 1987 youth unemployment. The results also show no relation between 1987 area unemployment and 1983 youth unemployment, supporting the interpretation of the 1987 cross-sectional pattern as reflecting the effect of 1987 local labor markets on outcomes. More important, the coefficient on 1987 area unemployment in the 1983 regression is a bare −0.006, implying the absence of any significant omitted area effect. In this case the estimate of the effect of local market conditions based on the difference between the 1987 and 1983 coefficients on 1987 unemployment is −0.014. By contrast, the estimated effect of 1983 area unemployment on the youth employment–population ratio based on differences in coefficients between the 1987 and 1983 equations is of a similar magnitude, 0.016. This implies that 1983 area unemployment has virtually the same effect on 1983 employment-population rates, controlling for 1987 employment-population rates, as 1987 area unemployment had on 1987 employment-population rates, controlling for 1983 rates: the reversal of sign reflects the fact that the table reports both statistics in terms of the difference between 1987 and 1983. Similarly, when the outcome variable is youth unemployment, the estimates in columns 4 and 5 show that youth unemployment in a given year depends almost entirely on that year's area unemployment rate. Here, the difference in coefficients estimated for 1987 area unemployment is 0.016, while the comparable estimate for 1983 area unemployment on 1983 youth unemployment is −0.017 (the sign reversal again occurs because I report the statistic in terms of the difference between 1987 and 1983). As in the CPS calculations, the similarity in coefficients between the employment and unemployment regressions implies that the bulk of the response to a tight labor market comes in the form of jobs for those looking for work rather than from an influx of youth into the labor force. Finally, the regressions of 1983 and 1987 log earnings on 1983 and 1987 area unemployment rates also confirm the CPS finding that tight markets substantially raise the earnings of disadvantaged youths. In fact, the estimated coefficients are surprisingly similar to those in the CPS calculations of table 3: the −0.023 effect of 1987 area unemployment on 1987 log hourly earnings in the NLSY is roughly the same as the −0.029 and −0.025 coefficients in the lower half of table 3.

Table 4 shows that tight labor markets also raised blacks' employment and reduced their unemployment. But it does not show the markedly greater effect of local labor market conditions on outcomes that is found

TABLE 5. Effect of Area Unemployment Rates on Longitudinal
Earnings Growth of Young Men, by Race, 1983–87[a]

Variable	All youths	Black youths
1987 area unemployment	−.038	−.067
	(.009)	(.022
1983 area unemployment	.013	.011
	(.007)	(.020)
Black	.03	...
	(.05)	...
Sample size	1,360	396

SOURCE: Calculated from the National Longitudinal Survey of Youth.
a. All regressions include age, years of schooling, and an urban dummy. Standard errors are in parentheses.

in the CPS data. Where the NLSY data show greater sensitivity of the black economic position to market conditions is in earnings: the coefficients on area unemployment in the log earnings regressions for blacks are much larger than those for the sample as a whole. As in the CPS-based regressions, however, the coefficient on the 0–1 black dummy variable in the earnings equations is larger in absolute value in 1987 than in 1983. In part this may be the result of the general pattern of growing earnings differentials between races as workers age. It may also reflect the change in the earnings pattern that was unfavorable for lower-paid workers in general in the 1980s (that is, one would expect smaller 1983–87 changes in earnings for blacks simply because they were at lower wages in 1983), and the gradual erosion of the earnings of young blacks relative to young whites that characterized the late 1970s and the 1980s.[19]

Finally, I exploited the longitudinal aspect of the NLSY by regressing changes in the log earnings of youths on 1987 and 1983 unemployment rates, using the same control variables as in table 4. This regression reduced the sample size moderately—some youths had earnings in 1983 and not in 1987 and conversely—but had the virtue of allowing the examination of the same individuals in both years. The estimated coefficients, given in table 5, confirm the implication of the cross-sectional analyses that youths in areas with low 1987 unemployment rates received noticeably larger increases in pay in the 1983–87 recovery than youths in areas with higher 1987 unemployment rates. In addition, the difference in coefficients between blacks and all youths indicates that, as in the CPS, black youths enjoyed especially rapid increases in earnings in tight labor markets. However, although these results show that improved market

19. Juhn, Murphy, and Pearce (1989); and Bound and Freeman (1989).

conditions affected longitudinal earnings profiles, they do not indicate how youth earnings grew in a persistent labor shortage.

Conclusion

Local labor market shortages greatly improve the employment opportunities of disadvantaged young men, substantially raising the percentage employed and reducing their unemployment rate. Employment of black youths is particularly sensitive to the state of the local labor market.

Labor market shortages also significantly increase the hourly earnings of disadvantaged youths, particularly blacks. In the 1980s the increase for young men in tight labor markets was large enough to offset the deterioration in the real and relative earnings of the less skilled that marked these years.[20]

Youths in areas with labor shortages had greater increases in earnings as they aged than those in other areas, implying that improved labor market conditions raise the longitudinal earnings profiles as well as the starting prospects of youths. Again, the greatest gains were achieved by young blacks.

These findings show that despite the social pathologies that plague disadvantaged young men, particularly less educated black youths, and despite the 1980s twist in the American labor market that worked against those with fewer skills, tight labor markets substantially improved their economic position. Although a strong job market may not be a panacea for all the problems of the disadvantaged, it does improve their employment and earnings. In addition, the strong link between area unemployment and the economic position of black youths lends support to William Julius Wilson's claim in *The Truly Disadvantaged* that many of the problems of the inner city are the direct result of the loss of jobs in local labor markets. *If* demographic changes produce the labor market shortages that many expect in the next decade, the employment and earnings of young, less educated male entrants into the labor market will improve markedly, and disadvantaged blacks will be special beneficiaries of these market conditions. For the country as a whole to attain the levels of unemployment in those areas that have shortages, however, would require the national unemployment rate to drop from the 5.5 percent of the late 1980s to the 3 to 4 percent that made Boston and Anaheim areas of opportunity for disadvantaged youths in those years. Whether this is pos-

20. Murphy and Welch (1988); Katz and Revanga (1989); and Blackburn, Bloom, and Freeman (1990).

sible without setting off a round of massive inflation, as most macroeconomists fear, is another story.

References

Blackburn, McKinley L., David E. Bloom, and Richard B. Freeman. 1990. "The Declining Economic Position of Less Skilled American Men." In *A Future of Lousy Jobs? The Changing Structure of U.S. Wages,* edited by Gary Burtless. Brookings.

Blanchflower, David G., and Andrew J. Oswald. 1989. "The Wage Curve." National Bureau of Economic Research working paper 3181 (November).

Bound, John, and Richard B. Freeman. 1989. "Black Economic Progress: Erosion of the Post-1965 Gains in the 1980s?" In *The Question of Discrimination: Racial Inequality in the U.S. Labor Market,* edited by Steven Shulman and William Darity, Jr. Wesleyan University Press.

Browne, Lynne. 1978. "Regional Unemployment Rates—Why Are They So Different?" *New England Economic Review* (July-August), pp. 5–26.

Bureau of Labor Statistics. 1988. *Geographic Profile of Employment and Unemployment, 1987,* bulletin 2305. Department of Labor.

Clark, Kim B., and Lawrence H. Summers. 1981. "Demographic Differences in Cyclical Employment Variation." *Journal of Human Resources* 16 (Winter), pp. 61–79.

Council of Economic Advisers. 1990. *Economic Report of the President.*

Freeman, Richard B. 1979. "The Effect of Demographic Factors on Age-Earnings Profiles." *Journal of Human Resources* 14 (Summer), pp. 289–318.

———. 1982. "Economic Determinants of Geographic and Individual Variation in the Labor Market Position of Young Persons." In *The Youth Labor Market Problem: Its Nature, Causes and Consequences,* edited by Richard B. Freeman and David A. Wise. University of Chicago Press.

Freeman, Richard B., and Harry J. Holzer, eds. 1986. *The Black Youth Employment Crisis.* University of Chicago Press.

Hall, Robert E. 1972. "Turnover in the Labor Force." *Brookings Papers on Economic Activity* 3, pp. 709–64.

Johnston, Jack. 1983. *Econometric Methods.* McGraw-Hill.

Juhn, Chin-lui, Kevin Murphy, and Brooks Pearce. 1989. "Accounting for the Slowdown in Black-White Wage Convergence." University of Chicago.

Katz, Larry, and Ana Revanga. 1989. "Changes in the Structure of Wages: U.S. vs. Japan," National Bureau of Economic Research working paper 3021 (July).

Marston, Stephen T. 1980. "Anatomy of Persistent Local Unemployment." Paper prepared for the National Commission for Employment Policy Conference (October).

Moulton, Brent. 1988. "An Illustration of a Pitfall in Estimating the Effects of Aggregate Variables on Micro Units." Bureau of Labor Statistics working paper 181 (April).

Murphy, Kevin, and Finis Welch. 1988. "Wage Differentials in the 1980s: the

Role of International Trade." Paper prepared for the Mont Pelerin Society Meeting.

Rees, Albert. 1986. "An Essay on Youth Joblessness." *Journal of Economic Literature* 24 (June), pp. 613–28.

Reza, Ali M. 1978. "Geographical Differences in Earnings and Unemployment Rates." *Review of Economics and Statistics* 60 (May), pp. 201–08.

Wilson, William Julius. 1987. *The Truly Disadvantaged: The Inner City, the Underclass, and Public Policy.* University of Chicago Press.

Gains from Growth?
The Impact of Full Employment
on Poverty in Boston

PAUL OSTERMAN

A COMMON THEME in all discussions of how to reduce poverty has been the salutary effects of full employment. The 1960s and 1970s stand as the example. During the economic boom between 1959 and 1969 the official poverty rate fell from 22.4 percent to 12.1 percent.[1] Then progress halted, and as the economy suffered through the crises of the 1970s, the poverty rate drifted within a narrow range.

The 1980s call the universal aptness of this simple story into question. Despite sustained expansion and falling unemployment, the poverty rate increased slightly. Part of the problem was doubtless that the nature of the population in poverty changed. The elderly constituted a smaller fraction of the poor, and groups with seemingly more intractable problems, such as single parents, counted for a larger share. The problem may also have involved the uneven nature of recent economic growth, which was accompanied by growing income inequality and perhaps also by a rise in the proportion of jobs which were, as the Europeans put it, precarious.

Is it true therefore that full employment has lost its power? The recent national time-series data cannot provide a clear answer because they mask substantial variation across geographic areas and because contemporaneous structural economic shifts make the data difficult to interpret. The ideal test would be to identify and study an area in which economic structure was relatively constant and in which the economy was strong for a sustained period of time. Boston provides such a test case, and this paper brings original survey data on Boston to bear on the problem.

Understanding whether economic opportunity, in the form of full employment, reduces poverty is also important for resolving recent schol-

The survey on which this paper is based was supported by the Rockefeller Foundation and the Boston Foundation. Preparation of this paper was supported by the Social Science Research Council. I also thank Edward Gramlich for comments on an earlier version.

1. Sawhill (1988), p. 1084.

arly and political debates about poverty. The debates have been conducted in an intellectual climate very different from that which prevailed when the War on Poverty was declared. The early 1960s was a period of optimism about what government could accomplish. However, fueled by the perceived failure of the War on Poverty and the Great Society, a strong intellectual counterattack was mounted by conservative critics. Their general point has been that persistent poverty is caused, or at least worsened, by government efforts to cure it. Opportunity in the form of a strong economy is not enough; the poor must have an incentive to work, and the only way to provide that incentive is to cut back on liberal public programs.

Only recently has a strong response been marshaled against these arguments. This response takes the conservative viewpoint seriously but seeks to rebut it by linking behavior to opportunity. One element of the response is to deny that the poor, even during this period of job growth, have had real opportunities. Jobs, so the argument goes, have left the inner city and moved to the suburbs, and those jobs that do remain downtown are high-level white-collar work that is simply out of the reach of ghetto residents.

In addition, some researchers now argue that there is an element of self-perpetuating or self-destructive behavior among the poor, an assertion with which many liberals in the past have disagreed. Specifically, the idea of an underclass has been advanced as a powerful explanation of the persistence of poverty. This view emphasizes the environment in which poor people live: the adverse effects of social isolation from the middle class and the harm done by inappropriate role models. And in communities in which few adults work, the percentage of single-parent families is high, welfare dependency is common, and crime is widespread, it is difficult for a person to succeed in the mainstream world.

The underclass argument is similar in some respects to the arguments in the older literature on the culture of poverty. It differs, however, in its more optimistic assessment of the effects of opportunity. If good jobs, good role models, and richer networks of contacts were available, the conditions in which the underclass live could be changed.

In this debate between the two camps, a crucial piece of information has been missing. What would happen to urban poverty in a city that experienced sustained full employment? Would poverty rates fall as people responded to opportunity? Would poverty stagnate at discouragingly high rates because the welfare state dulled the urge to get ahead? To date both sides have had either to speculate on the answer to these questions or to rely on the distant experience of the 1960s, an era that is not representative of the past decade demographically, in terms of economic structure, or with respect to the possible long-term deleterious effects of welfare and other public policies.

Boston offers a natural experiment with which to confront these questions. The so-called Massachusetts Miracle of the 1980s created a full-employment economy. Furthermore, no one can claim of Boston, as is done with respect to the national expansion, that job growth did not extend to the inner city. Learning whether the incidence of poverty decreased in response to full employment puts competing explanations to the test.

Boston's experience is also appropriate because Massachusetts is among the most generous states in the country in its welfare and other social policies. In 1989 the average AFDC grant for a nonworking mother heading a family of three averaged $579, the fourth highest in the nation.[2] Although the state innovated in welfare and work programs, its Employment and Training program, unlike those in many other states, was entirely voluntary. Massachusetts is generous in other respects: for example, 49.6 percent of those in Boston with incomes below 125 percent of the federal poverty line either live in public housing or receive subsidized rent, a rate considerably higher than in most other cities. Finally, Massachusetts is well known nationally for its wide array of employment and training programs, business-government partnerships, and so on. In short, in an era of conservative national policies, Massachusetts remained a very activist state.[3]

If the neoconservatives are right, generosity should have inhibited the response of poor people to the economic opportunities afforded by long-term growth. If the liberals are right, the combination of full employment and active social policy should have paid off in a reduction of poverty rates.

This paper therefore addresses two interrelated matters. The first is the long-standing issue of the extent to which full employment reduces pov-

2. This was the monthly payment as of January 1989 and is based upon Family Support Administration data published in the *New York Times* national edition, March 15, 1989, p. A16. Data from 1986 published in the *Social Security Bulletin: Annual Statistical Supplement* (1988), p. 335, show a similar pattern: in 1986 the monthly average payment per recipient in Massachusetts was exceeded by only three other states.

3. This may be changing in response to the current state budget crisis, but the description is accurate for the decade preceding and including the survey.

erty. The second concerns the benefits and costs of active government programs for reducing poverty.

To answer these questions, a survey was conducted that was unique in its representative coverage of the city in a noncensus year.[4] Because the survey was conducted in the winter of 1988 and spring of 1989, before the recent downturn in the Massachusetts economy, it provides a description of the economy at its peak after a sustained period of full employment. The survey was a combination random-digit-dial and door-to-door interview sample of Boston with some oversampling to generate adequate numbers of Hispanics. Interviews were conducted in English and Spanish and were representative of the city except that the homeless, households with no one under the age of sixty, households headed by college students, and people in institutions were excluded. The appendix provides a fuller description.

Poverty Rates

One obvious starting point is to compare past and current poverty rates in Boston, and this is accomplished by presenting 1980 and 1988 data for the city. However, because it is desirable to have a standard against which the Boston changes can be judged, I also present data for 1980 and 1987 for all U.S. central cities. In all cases the same sample limitations as in the original survey are imposed.

Table 1 shows data using a poverty cutoff of 125 percent of the federal poverty line and the federal line itself.[5] The patterns are the same, although Hispanics in Boston show relatively greater improvement using the official federal cutoff. I will focus on the 125 percent cutoff to simplify the discussion and because the analysis in the remainder of the paper uses this broader group.

In 1980 poverty in Boston was slightly worse than in U.S central cities as a whole, but the levels and patterns were very similar. Blacks in Boston tracked the U.S. pattern almost exactly; white and Hispanic families were somewhat worse off than elsewhere. There is nothing in the 1980 data to

4. The survey was designed and supervised by Paul Osterman, executed by the University of Massachusetts Center for Survey Research, and funded by the Rockefeller Foundation and the Boston Foundation. It is not possible to use Current Population Survey data for as small an area as Boston.

5. The federal poverty line takes no account of local differences in cost of living. Furthermore, eligibility for many poverty programs is based upon a family income closer to the 125 percent rate. For a family of three in 1980 the federal line was $7,641.

TABLE I. Poverty Rates for Boston and Average for All Central Cities, by Race and Ethnicity, 1980, 1987, 1988
Percent

Location and family status	White	Black	Hispanic	All
125 percent of federal standard				
Boston 1980				
Families	14.5	36.8	52.7	23.5
Unrelated individuals	19.3	32.3	37.9	22.5
Boston 1988				
Families	8.4	22.3	45.4	19.0
Unrelated individuals	3.2	9.0	23.0	5.9
All central cities 1980				
Families	9.5	33.0	37.6	19.7
Unrelated individuals	17.8	37.0	38.9	24.5
All central cities 1987				
Families	10.5	38.2	38.8	22.2
Unrelated individuals	20.9	37.2	34.0	25.8
Federal standard				
Boston 1980				
Families	10.6	29.1	42.9	18.0
Unrelated individuals	14.3	26.5	28.0	17.2
Boston 1988				
Families	5.6	13.4	24.8	11.5
Unrelated individuals	2.0	5.3	12.8	3.5
All central cities 1980				
Families	6.8	25.9	28.6	15.0
Unrelated individuals	14.0	30.8	32.7	19.9
All central cities 1987				
Families	7.4	32.3	30.7	17.7
Unrelated individuals	15.0	31.2	24.3	19.0

SOURCES: Data for 1980 are from Bureau of the Census Current Population Survey public use tapes. U.S. data for 1987 are from Bureau of the Census (1988). Boston data for 1988 are from Boston Foundation (1989). U.S. data are limited to central cities, and all the data refer to households headed by an adult between the ages of 18 and 60 who does not (and whose spouse, if any, does not) attend college full time. Family data include all family units with two or more people related by blood or marriage. Single-parent families are a subset of all families. In these data and throughout the paper, the categories "white," "black," and "Hispanic" are exclusive and do not overlap.

suggest that Boston structurally was better off than the rest of the nation. Yet by 1988, after years of economic growth, Boston's relative position had changed dramatically. Three points stand out.

For all ethnic groups the situation of single people improved sharply as a strong labor market succeeded in lifting incomes significantly. In 1980 unrelated persons accounted for 45.1 percent of all household units in poverty in Boston (using the 125 percent standard); in 1988 they accounted for only 15.1 percent.

Both white and black families experienced considerable improvement in their financial situation. The poverty rates of both groups declined at the same pace, and thus in that sense both groups shared equally in the improving economy. But the strong economy did not succeed in helping income levels of blacks catch up with those of whites; in this sense there was no gain for blacks.

Finally, Hispanic families shared only modestly in the rewards of growth. This is the one conclusion, however, that would be modified by looking at the federal standard, a fact that implies considerable bunching of Hispanic families between the federal cutoff and the 125 percent standard. But regardless of the standard, the incomes of Hispanics did not improve at the same rate as those of whites and blacks.

Full employment is thus a powerful weapon against poverty. Poverty rates fell substantially in Boston, including the rates for single-parent black and white families. But full employment is hardly a panacea. Poverty rates remained stubbornly high for Hispanics. Furthermore, most people would not consider even the reduced rates for blacks to be acceptable. A dramatic way of seeing this is to ask about the poverty rates of children younger than six years of age. In 1988 this rate (using the 125 percent standard) was 35.7 percent in Boston. It was 17.5 percent for whites, 33.1 percent for blacks, and 73.2 percent for Hispanics. Even after half a decade of sustained growth, there was a long way to go.[6]

Characteristics of the Poor

Basic demographic characteristics of Boston's poor are shown in table 2 and compared with those of Bostonians who are not poor. There are few surprises. The poor are badly educated and mostly female; about half are single parents. The poor are not new migrants who came to Boston in response to the boom. Three-quarters of them had lived in Boston for more than five years. Even among poor Hispanics, 68 percent reported having lived continuously in Boston for more than five years.

This profile of Boston's population closely matches what is known from national data. Of particular interest is that nearly half of Boston's poor are female single parents. This compares with the average of 41.8

6. Because the survey is limited to Boston, migration out of the city may have influenced the findings. If large numbers of the poor left the city in search of cheaper housing in surrounding areas (for example, Chelsea or Lawrence), the falling poverty rates may be overstated. If, however, as people are lifted out of poverty they move elsewhere for better schools, the improvement is understated. I have no way of knowing which way, if either, the bias goes.

TABLE 2. Survey Characteristics of Boston Poor and Nonpoor,
1988–89
Percent

Characteristics	Poor	Nonpoor
Less than twelve years of school	46.7	7.3
Twelve years of school exactly	35.4	25.1
More than twelve years of school	17.9	67.6
Female single parent	46.1	8.7
Single	15.1	48.4
Living in Boston more than five years	75.4	n.a.
Living in Boston three to five years	9.6	n.a.
Living in Boston less than two years	14.9	n.a.

SOURCE: Boston survey.
n.a. Not available.

percent for all central-city poor. A natural question, which parallels the
discussion of poverty rates, is what impact has full employment had on
the incidence of single-parent families in Boston? In 1980 the rate of
single-parent families for all demographic groups was higher in Boston
than in the nation as a whole and dramatically higher for Hispanics
(table 3). Between 1980 and 1987 the rate of single-parent families in the
national data increased for each subgroup, but it declined in Boston for
blacks and Hispanics. The rate for whites in Boston increased in rough
step with the national pattern.

One implication is that the strong economy did have some impact on
family formation, with Boston bucking the national trend of increased
single-parent families for blacks and Hispanics. What is more striking,
however, is that the incidence of single-parent families in Boston did not
fall very much, not nearly as much as the unemployment rate or poverty
rate. By the end of the period Boston still looked much like the rest of the

TABLE 3. Families with Children Headed by a Female Single Parent,
Boston and Average for All Central Cities, 1980, 1987, 1988
Percent

Location	White	Black	Hispanic	All
Boston 1980	25.3	56.8	50.0	38.2
Central cities 1980	19.1	49.7	31.9	30.9
Boston 1988	28.5	54.9	45.4	39.4
Central cities 1987	21.4	55.8	33.7	33.5

SOURCE: Boston survey.

TABLE 4. Work History of Boston Poor, 1986-89
Percent

When last worked	All poor	Female single parents	Other poor
At time of interview	43.6	29.2	57.7
1988	20.4	21.5	19.3
1987	5.5	6.2	4.8
1986	5.9	9.3	2.6
Before 1986	14.7	21.7	7.7
Never	9.9	12.0	7.8

SOURCE: Boston survey. The sample is limited to those who did not report having total permanent disabilities; 13 percent of the sample of all poor people reported such disabilities. Family status is as of the interview; people may not have been in that family status in earlier years.

nation, with over a third of all families and far more than that of minority families headed by single mothers. This implies that what is driving family formation patterns is by and large not the economy. What the economy has done is to alter the consequence of being a single parent.[7]

To complete the picture of Boston's poor, I now turn to the labor market. As table 4 shows, more than 60 percent of Boston's poor were working at the time of the interview or had worked sometime during the year of the interview. Even among the group that faced the most difficulties, female single parents, 50 percent worked sometime during the interview year. But a significant number of the poor are long-term jobless: if one places into this category people who have not worked at all since 1986, then 30.5 percent are long-term jobless. For female single parents the rate rises to 43 percent.

Again, the national data suggest that the poor in Boston are not very different from their counterparts elsewhere: 50.7 percent of female single parents in Boston worked sometime during the year; the comparable nationwide figure is 48.9 percent.

These patterns suggest that there are two groups among the poor and that somewhat different issues need to be thought through for each. Most of the poor work at least part of the time, yet they nonetheless remain poor. Even a casual look at the data shows the importance of some of the obvious reasons: 48.8 percent of the jobs held by the poor in the Boston sample paid $5.00 an hour or less, and 39 percent of the people in poverty worked less than full time. A deeper question, and one that space

7. For whites in Boston the 125 percent poverty rate among single parents fell from 56.7 percent in 1980 to 25.7 percent in 1988. For blacks it fell from 59.9 percent to 35.2 percent. For Hispanics it rose from 74.1 percent to 78.2 percent.

precludes addressing here, is the nature of the barriers that prevented this group from finding better jobs or moving up the ladder in the jobs they did hold. At the same time, a substantial minority of the poor seem to have virtually no attachment to the labor market. It is important to understand how this group differs from those who do manage to work at least some of the time.[8]

Conclusion

This paper represents a first effort to grapple with a large and complex data set, but some useful conclusions do emerge. Full employment does in fact deliver many of the benefits its advocates have promised. Poverty rates fell substantially in Boston, and it is very clear that the poor did respond to economic opportunity when it was offered. The sharp drop in the incidence of poverty and the high percentage of the poor who are working undercuts the idea that an active government social policy is debilitating. That these gains took place in a heavily white-collar city also raises questions about the 1980s explanation that poverty resulted from a mismatch of skills and available jobs.[9]

Although the benefits of full employment are clear, it is also apparent that problems remain. The poverty rates of children are especially troubling. There is ample reason to believe that policies to supplement the benefits of a strong economy are necessary.

In some respects Boston's poor are different from those elsewhere. Poverty among single people was nearly eliminated between 1980 and 1988, and Hispanics did worse relative to blacks than in other cities. However, with respect to education, family structure, and, most important, what appears to be a real if intermittent commitment to the labor market, the poor in Boston are much like their counterparts in other cities. There is also, consistent with the argument for the existence of an underclass, a significant minority that seems to have no attachment to the labor mar-

---

8. Preliminary analysis suggests that two family factors are very important. Not surprisingly, single parents with young children have a much harder time working than do others. But even among single parents there is variation; an important factor appears to be the presence or absence of an extended family-support network. However, these observations are only the beginning, and questions about the hiring practices of firms, job search patterns, and other topics remain to be asked.

9. Manufacturing and construction accounted for only 14.4 percent of total employment among all Boston residents in the sample.

ket.[10] If one takes relationship to the labor market as an axis, then why the first group is unable to use the labor market to make sustainable gains and why the second group is so isolated seem to be questions crucial for further work.

Although a strong economy did reduce poverty, it did not alter patterns of family formation very much. There was some decline in the rate of single-parent families, but the changes were not enough to alter the family profile of Boston. Thus although arguments that poverty results from lack of opportunity are valid, it is less clear that similar arguments about family structure are correct.

Racial patterns in the data are also revealing. Many models of the underclass focus on blacks and suggest that, given the reduction of overt racism, what perpetuates the underclass are dysfunctional cultural norms. My data raise some complications for this view. Blacks have benefited a good deal from full employment in Boston; thus, given opportunity, they evidently responded in "acceptable" ways. Also significant is that the black poor are the most connected among the three racial groups in the city.[11] The people in most difficulty, Hispanics, have a history very different from that of blacks, and any explanation of their problems seemingly should turn on a different set of considerations.

To understand the underclass one needs a more general theory of poverty against which to judge the circumstances of any subgroup. Obviously, many researchers have devoted a great deal of effort to this challenge, and we certainly understand more than in the past. Yet the patterns presented here seem to pose puzzles that require further work.

Appendix: The Boston Poverty Survey

The Boston survey, sponsored by the Rockefeller Foundation and the Boston Foundation, was a combination telephone and door-to-door survey of both poor and nonpoor in Boston.

Three separate sampling frames were created. The first was based on a citywide random-digit-dial (RDD) approach. A total of 14,135 house-

---

10. If one follows a more strict definition and asks what percentage of the permanently disabled had not worked since 1987 and did not have children under the age of five (a "legitimate" excuse), then the percentage of long-term jobless among the poor falls to 10.2 percent.

11. The survey asked a number of questions about knowledge of community groups, church attendance, and knowledge of the labor market. The responses of the black poor consistently indicated more attachment to institutions and to the labor market than was true for other groups.

holds were called and received a five-minute screening interview. If the family income fell below 125 percent of the federal poverty line (and met other conditions described below), a thirty-minute questionnaire was administered. A total of 862 RDD poverty interviews was conducted. In addition, a random sample of 903 nonpoor families was administered a ten-minute questionnaire. The response rate to the screening questionnaire was 85.7 percent, to the poverty questionnaire 67.1 percent, and to the nonpoverty questionnaire 79.4 percent.

The second sampling frame was designed to determine the bias introduced by the telephone survey method. An area probability sample was created based on a listing of city blocks and residences on those blocks. A sample of residences was drawn and an attempt was made to contact each residence by phone. If that was not possible, a field worker went out to conduct the interview. A total of 1,440 households was contacted using this method, and from this group 103 poverty interviews were conducted. The response rate to the screening questionnaire was 84.5 percent and to the poverty questionnaire (among those eligible) 66.5 percent.[12]

The final sampling frame was similar in structure to the second in that it was geographic and person-to-person, but it was aimed at generating a Hispanic oversample. Hence it was limited to Jamaica Plain, Roxbury, Dorchester, and the South End. A total of 1,341 households were contacted and 100 poverty interviews with Hispanics conducted. The response rate to the screening interview was 93.5 percent and to the poverty interview 87.7 percent.

A total of 16,916 households in Boston was contacted for screening interviews and 1,065 poverty interviews and 903 nonpoverty interviews conducted. In addition, interviews with two samples, Asians who do not speak English and nonpoor Hispanics, are now being completed.

The data reported in this paper are drawn from several combinations of the samples described above.

Poverty rates were calculated from the combined file of the first two

12. Actually, an attempt to reach them by telephone was made first, and if that failed, interviews were conducted in person. The purpose of this sample was to assess the bias introduced by the phone sampling. Of the 103 households in this sample 12 percent lacked working telephones. This implies that the 13.0 percent family poverty rate should be 14.4 percent. The households without telephones were slightly worse off than other poor households. For example, 50.0 percent of the households with phones were headed by a high school dropout compared with 66.6 percent of the households without phones; 57.3 percent of the households with phones fell below the federal poverty line, but 66.6 percent of those without phones did so. This implies that the data presented on the percentage of the poor population that is underclass are slightly understated.

samples, the RDD, and citywide screening interviews. Appropriate weights were used to create a merged file. With this file one can identify households, single people, and families that fall below and above the 125 percent poverty rates. The federal poverty rates were calculated by combining the information just described on the 125 percent poverty rates with data from the poverty interviews on the proportion (by race) of the 125 percent poverty population that falls above and below the federal poverty level.

For the poverty population as a whole and for poor whites and blacks broken out separately, a combined file (with appropriate weights) of the RDD and area samples was used. The sample size of this file was 962 total poor, 297 white poor, and 372 black poor.

When poor Hispanics were analyzed separately, a combined file of the citywide RDD poverty sample, the citywide area sample, and the area Hispanic oversample was used (with appropriate weights). The sample size of this file was 373.

When the nonpoor were analyzed as a group, the nonpoor RDD sample was employed. The sample size was 903.

There were several additional limitations in the sampling. First, interviews were conducted in English and in Spanish; hence, non-English, non-Spanish speakers were not included. Second, residents of institutions, such as college dormitories, prisons, and army facilities, were excluded, as were the homeless and others with no fixed address.

These limitations aside, the screening interviews are a representative sample of the Boston population. However, for the longer poverty and nonpoverty interviews additional limitations were imposed. Households in which no adult was younger than sixty-one years old were excluded (unless that household had responsibility for a child). Households headed by full-time college students were also excluded. Finally, households in which the head was younger than eighteen years old were excluded.

The survey included both single people and families. Families were defined by the standard census definitions as a group of people related by blood or adoption (although for some purposes data were also collected on foster children and live-in boy friends or girl friends). If there was more than one family in a household, all were interviewed. Within a family the respondent was selected randomly from among all adults older than eighteen who had some connection to the labor market (that is, worked or looked for work) in the past year. If no such adult existed, the respondent was selected randomly from among the adults.

A final matter concerns a possible undercount of men, particularly minority men. This is a problem that has concerned many researchers. To judge the extent, if any, of this problem, I calculated sex ratios for the Boston survey and for central city populations in the 1988 Current Population Survey (with the same restrictions as the other sample). These calculations are for the entire population because focusing on the poverty sample would be inappropriate in that one effect of a strong economy may be to improve the lot of men relative to that of women. If true, this would distort a comparison between Boston and the rest of the nation.

The data are displayed below.

	Ratio of adult women to men	
	Boston Survey	Current Population Survey
All	1.17	1.14
White	1.06	1.05
Black	1.66	1.48
Hispanic	0.99	1.10

It is apparent that the Boston survey does find, particularly for blacks, considerably fewer men than women in poverty. At the same time, it tracks the pattern in the Current Population Survey quite closely. To some extent the sex disparity represents reality and to some extent it reflects an undercount. I cannot judge the relative importance of these two effects, but at least the results are essentially as good as those drawn from far more complex and expensive Current Population Surveys.

References

Boston Foundation. 1989. *In the Midst of Plenty: A Profile of Boston and Its Poor: An In-Depth Study on the Working Age Population of Boston.*

Bureau of the Census. 1988. *Current Population Survey, March 1988: Technical Documentation.* Department of Commerce.

Sawhill, Isabel V. 1988. "Poverty in the U.S.: Why Is It So Persistent?" *Journal of Economic Literature* 26 (September), pp. 1073–1119.

Social Security Administration. 1988. *Social Security Bulletin: Annual Statistical Supplement, 1988.* Department of Health and Human Services.

Joblessness and Shiftlessness: Labor Force Activity in Chicago's Inner City

MARTA TIENDA *and* **HAYA STIER**

AMERICANS expect able-bodied adults to work for a living, but there are troubling signs that people are increasingly falling short of this expectation. Most adult men hold steady jobs, and more than anytime in the past, mothers with young children work outside the home. Yet labor force participation varies appreciably by age, gender, race and ethnicity, and place of residence. Minorities living in decaying inner cities were increasingly likely to be out of work or out of the labor force entirely during the 1970s and 1980s, and this development has rekindled debates about the relative importance of individual and structural factors in shaping the lives of the poor. At one extreme, observers blame welfare, which offers an alternative to work in dead-end jobs, for the decreasing percentage of minority men who work.[1] Others attribute rising joblessness to fewer unskilled and semiskilled jobs in and around urban ghettos.[2]

In this paper we document the pervasiveness of idleness among parents living in Chicago's inner-city neighborhoods and explore the reasons for it. Chicago is important because it experienced an increased concentration of poverty and high levels of minority unemployment during the 1970s and 1980s. Although the boundary between shiftlessness and chronic joblessness is blurry, we propose a way to distinguish various states of joblessness and to estimate the pervasiveness of shiftlessness. Our goal is to ascertain whether and how jobless parents differ from those who are employed and to explore reasons for racial and ethnic differences.

This research was supported by grants from the Rockefeller Foundation to the University of Chicago, and from the Office of the Assistant Secretary for Planning and Evaluation of the Department of Health and Human Services to the Institute for Research on Poverty of the University of Wisconsin. William Julius Wilson provided permission to analyze the Urban Poverty and Family Life Survey, for which we are grateful. We acknowledge technical assistance from Adelle Hinojosa and Kelly Mikelson.

    1. Murray (1984).
    2. Wilson (1987).

Theoretical and Definitional Considerations

The underclass can be characterized by behavior associated with extreme poverty or by spatial and social arrangements that place people outside the social mainstream.[3] So-called weak labor force attachment, however, is the common denominator undergirding most current definitions.[4] Not joblessness per se, but chronic idleness buttressed by impoverished social environments, distinguishes the underclass from the poor in general. Most people believe the work ethic of the underclass differs from that of the working poor: the working poor prefer a low-wage job to public assistance; members of the underclass prefer welfare or illegitimate sources of support, or both.

If the concern about the underclass is the chronic joblessness among the able-bodied and their unwillingness to work, then weak labor market attachment is a polite way of saying that those at the bottom of the income ladder are essentially shiftless.[5] But to advance understanding of how joblessness differentiates the underclass from the poor in general, one must indicate clearly what kinds of nonparticipation constitute deviant behavior and what kinds are socially acceptable. This task is complicated because the linkage between work and material conditions is imperfect.[6]

Demarcating the boundary between joblessness and shiftlessness is theoretically important because people have many different reasons for not working or not being willing to work. All these reasons bear on *who* is jobless, for how long, and whether their joblessness is socially acceptable. To represent these distinctions, we use the following categories:

—the *unemployed,* which includes people who are actively seeking work;

—the *discouraged,* consisting of those who want a job but have ceased searching because they believe no work is available, at least to them;

—the *constrained,* consisting of the disabled, mothers with young chil-

3. Auletta (1982); and Wilson (1987).

4. McLanahan and Garfinkel (1989).

5. The *Random House Dictionary of the English Language* defines shiftlessness as: 1. lacking in resourcefulness; inefficient. 2. lacking in incentive, ambition, or aspiration; lazy.

6. The extremes of labor supply and income distributions illustrate this point. There are some very poor people who do not work and rely exclusively on public aid for maintenance. There are also rich people who rely on their wealth for support. Although both may be deemed shiftless, most likely only the poor will be so classified. The absence of a work ethic among the affluent is tolerated because they pose no apparent burden to society (Davidson, 1979).

dren who are unable (or unwilling) to secure child care, and to some extent students; and

—the *shiftless,* which includes those who are idle and do not want to work, either because they are independently wealthy and see no need to do so or because they are lazy and prefer other forms of support, even if the support is grossly inadequate to maintain a decent life-style.

The labor market attachment of the unemployed is generally not questioned because they are actively seeking jobs, although some observers wonder whether they are too choosy about the jobs they will accept. The duration of joblessness differs for residents of inner-city and suburban neighborhoods, and for minority and nonminority groups, but it is unclear whether these differences result from unequal job opportunities, discrimination, or unrealistic expectations about wages and working conditions. The probability that prolonged joblessness will result in discouragement increases with the duration of each episode of unemployment.[7] However, the labor market commitment of discouraged workers is not apparent unless one inquires about *willingness* to work and about expected wages and working conditions.

The work commitment of those who are jobless because personal constraints prevent them from seeking employment is more difficult to classify. For them, clues about labor market attachment must be derived from their previous experiences: whether they have worked at all and whether their reasons for not working are socially legitimate. Legitimate reasons include permanent disability and, under some circumstances, family commitments and school attendance. Unacceptable reasons include preference for public aid, unrealistic wage expectations, and preferences for illegal sources of income. Even students who receive financial aid are expected to work part time (for example, in work-study programs), and successive reforms in welfare have made explicit the expectation that poor mothers with young children also should work. This means that women with children are excused from work obligations only if their husbands support them or if they are independently wealthy.

The proposition that members of inner-city neighborhoods are less interested in working and have a higher incidence of shiftlessness than the population in general has not been examined except through ethnographic accounts that speak neither to the prevalence nor to the duration of joblessness. Also undocumented is the extent to which joblessness is voluntary or involuntary, except implicitly (and occasionally) through

7. Clark and Summers (1979).

distinctions between the states of unemployment and discouragement. Nonparticipation generally is assumed to be voluntary, even though the reasons for its occurrence range from socially acceptable, such as most forms of disability, to reluctantly tolerated (female headship) to unacceptable (laziness).[8]

In documenting the distribution and prevalence of joblessness and shiftlessness in Chicago's inner city, we draw comparisons among black, white, Mexican, and Puerto Rican parents. The comparisons are important to determine whether shiftlessness is confined to the black population or is more general in poor ethnic neighborhoods. Comparisons with a national sample of parents of similar age help establish whether those living in poor Chicago neighborhoods are unique.

The primary data sources for our analyses are the 1987 Urban Poverty and Family Life Survey of Chicago (UPFLS) and the 1987 National Survey of Families and Households (NSFH).[9] The UPFLS is a sample of parents age 18 to 44 who lived in poverty areas in Chicago in 1986.[10] These areas were defined as census tracts where 20 percent or more of families had incomes below the 1980 federal poverty line. Completed interviews were obtained from 2,490 respondents: 1,184 black, 365 white, 488 Mexican, and 453 Puerto Rican.[11] The 1987 National Survey of Families and Households includes 13,017 respondents interviewed between March 1987 and May 1988.[12] Both surveys are based on cross-sectional designs and both contain several retrospective sequences on earlier experiences that are similar or virtually identical. To maximize comparability with the Urban Poverty and Family Life Survey of Chicago, we used an extract of parents age 19 to 44 from the National Survey of Families and Households.

8. Substance dependence leads to disability, but it is not a socially acceptable form of disability.

9. William Julius Wilson directed the Urban Poverty and Family Life Survey. Larry Bumpass and James Sweet directed the National Survey of Families and Households.

10. Although the original study was conceived as a survey of parents, a few blacks who were not parents were also interviewed. Other racial and ethnic groups are not represented among the nonparent subsample.

11. These are the unweighted sample counts. Statistical analyses require that the sample be weighted to generate representative population parameters.

12. It included a main sample of 9,643 respondents representing the noninstitutional U.S. population age 19 or older. In addition, several population groups were oversampled by a factor of two, including blacks, Puerto Ricans, and Chicanos; single parents; persons with stepchildren; persons cohabiting; and persons recently married.

Joblessness, Shiftlessness, or Normative Work Activity?

The labor force includes people who are employed and those who are looking for work. But a snapshot based on their current status is insufficient to document degrees of labor market attachment because it does not reveal which people worked in the past or whether the jobless are willing to work, and under what conditions. Figure 1 provides a mapping of these alternatives for the UPFLS and, in parentheses, the parent subsample from the NSFH.

Because mothers account for more than 60 percent of the respondents in the UPFLS, and because of popular beliefs that single mothers residing in poor inner-city neighborhoods are detached from the labor market, we expected extremely low rates of labor force participation. Surprisingly, two-thirds of the men and women were economically active at the time of the survey: 87 percent of the economically active had a job and 13 percent were actively searching for one. The participation rate was 14 percentage points lower than that of parents in the national sample and their unemployment rate two and one-half times higher. These differences suggest that job opportunities may be more limited in the inner city of Chicago than in the nation as a whole, that inner-city Chicago parents might expect higher wages, that shiftlessness is more pervasive in poor Chicago neighborhoods, or some combination of these explanations.

Most employed parents worked full time, a feature common both to the Chicago and national samples. Furthermore, among those unemployed, 21 and 16 percent were new entrants to the labor force in the inner-city and national samples, respectively. Because the majority of unemployed parents had previous job experience and because all but four job seekers reported intensive job searches, one would be hard pressed to conclude that unemployed parents in poor Chicago neighborhoods do not want to work.[13] High unemployment rates coupled with extensive job search activities suggest that opportunities to work may be more limited in the inner city than in the nation as a whole.

The samples of parents not in the labor force at the time of the surveys presented greater contrasts. About 35 percent of Chicago inner-city parents were not in the labor force, as opposed to 21 percent nationally, and

13. Job search activities identified in the UPFLS include checking with state or private employment agencies, checking directly with employers, friends, or relatives, and other ways, including placing or answering newspaper ads and using a school employment service. Most respondents engaged in several activities simultaneously.

FIGURE 1. Work Status of Parents Age 18 to 44, Chicago Inner City and United States, 1987

Percent unless otherwise specified

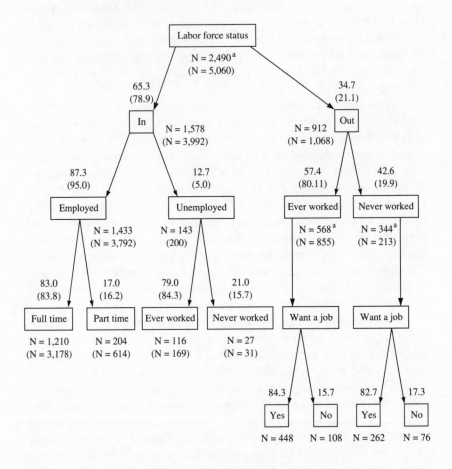

SOURCE: 1987 Urban Poverty and Family Life Survey of Chicago and, in parentheses, 1987 National Survey of Families and Households. Chicago sample includes 183 nonparents.

a. Raw frequencies may not total because of missing data. Percentages are weighted; sample numbers are unweighted.

the share of those who had never worked was more than double the national rate. Still, 57 percent of nonparticipating inner-city parents reported some work experience, and most of these said they wanted a job. Furthermore, four out of five jobless respondents with no experience said they wanted to work. Thus for the jobless who want employment, the challenge is to ascertain what circumstances constrain their ability to seek and find stable jobs and whether their employment expectations are realistic, given their skill levels and work experience.[14] Similarly, for the handful who did not want a job, it is appropriate to ask who they are and why they do not want to work.[15]

Supplementary tabulations (available from the authors) revealed that those who had ever worked and did not want a job at the time of the survey had on average, ten years of formal schooling, were approximately 35 years of age, and had about 3 children. Furthermore, 87 percent were women, 46 percent were unmarried (but 70 percent had been married), and more than half were receiving AFDC or another form of public assistance. Those who had never worked and did not want a job had, on average, 9.5 years of formal schooling, were 31 years of age, and had 2.6 children. Approximately 80 percent were women—all but eight were mothers—and 60 percent received AFDC or another form of public assistance. Mexicans and Puerto Ricans were disproportionately represented (relative to their sample shares) among those who had never worked; whites were overrepresented among those with work experience.

Before concluding that parents who did not want a job are shiftless, one needs to consider their reasons. Some 91 percent of those surveyed reported poor health or family responsibilities, and an additional 5 percent said they did not want to work because they attended school. Thus only 4 percent of those with work experience approached our definition of shiftlessness. However, among respondents with no work experience, 12 percent reported reasons other than family, health, or school for not wanting a job. These responses included "supported by parents or kids," "supported by public aid," "don't want to work," "pay is too low," "cannot work," and "illegal status."

14. Those who were not actively seeking jobs but reported wanting one may have been discouraged workers. Unfortunately, we cannot confirm this speculation with the UPFLS data.

15. The 144 people who said they did not want a job represented 5.8 percent of the entire survey and 16 percent of the jobless.

Although poor health is generally considered a socially acceptable reason for not wanting to work, and under very special circumstances so are family responsibilities and school attendance, these other reasons are not. At a minimum, one-half of 1 percent of inner-city parents qualified as shiftless. For the others who were not in the labor force and did not want a job—151 respondents, or 6 percent of the UPFLS sample—the evidence of weak labor market attachment might be excused as stemming from socially legitimate constraints. However, as social tolerance for welfare dependence wanes, the public will increasingly believe that single mothers on public assistance are shiftless.

It is also fair to question what respondents meant when they said they wanted a job, and in particular whether they would have taken one paying the minimum wage if it had been offered. Three-quarters of the men and two-thirds of the women who reported they had worked before and currently wanted a job relied on public aid for their primary support.[16] But whether these people would have been willing to take a low-paying job as an alternative to welfare is another matter, particularly because such jobs seldom offer benefits, while public assistance often includes medical care, subsidized housing, food stamps, and other in-kind benefits.

None of the men who had worked before but did not want a job and only 36 percent of the women received public aid. For all the men and two-thirds of the women with work experience who did not want to work, derived market benefits—social security, unemployment compensation, or spousal earnings—provided the main source of support, thereby legitimating their unwillingness. Informal activities—odd jobs, babysitting, and illegal activities—provided the main support for only 5 percent of the men and 2 percent of the women who wanted steady work and had some experience. Relatives provided the primary support for approximately 2 percent of these respondents.

A different picture emerged for respondents with no work experience. Of those who did not want a job, public assistance provided the primary support for fewer than half the women and about one-third of the men; derived market benefits, including spousal employment, were the primary support for about half the women and one-third of the men. Those who

16. This tabulation was based on 474 respondents who had ever worked, including 62 men and 339 women who wanted a job and 12 men and 61 women who did not. The total number who had never worked was 360, which included 83 men and 213 women who wanted a job and 23 men and 41 women who did not.

apparently preferred welfare to work would qualify as shiftless, but they represented only 1 percent of the sample and, in any event, have been included in our original estimate of shiftlessness. Nearly 17 percent of the men who did not want a regular job and had never worked supported themselves through informal activities, including those recognized as illegal. Only 2 percent of women with similar histories relied on informal market activities. Public assistance was the primary support for 80 percent of the women and 40 percent of the men with no work experience who said they did want a job. For this group, the response of wanting a job is believable if they perceived income from work to be higher than income from public assistance and if their expectations of wages, days, and hours were reasonable.

Our supplementary tabulations also showed that the average wage rate expected by those who had worked and wanted a job was $5.50 an hour for black men, $6.20 for Mexican and Puerto Rican men, and $10.20 for white men. Black men appeared most willing and white men least willing to accept low-paying jobs. Desired wages for women varied less by race and ethnicity: those who said they wanted a job and had experience expected to receive between $5.10 (Puerto Ricans) and $5.60 (whites) an hour; for those who had never worked, the wages expected ranged from $4.70 an hour for Puerto Ricans to $7.50 for whites.[17] Although the sample of men who did not want to work was too small to generate reliable analyses of the wages they expected, the tabulations for women who did not want a job indicated that higher wages might induce them into the labor force. Wage rates needed averaged $8.40 an hour for white women who had experience and $5.90 for black women.

On balance, this overview provided little evidence that shiftlessness was pervasive in Chicago's inner city, even though rates of joblessness were much higher than the national average for parents of similar age. Yet a handful of cases fit the stereotype of persons sufficiently detached from the world of work that they qualified as truly shiftless. About 6 percent of Chicago's inner-city residents qualified as potentially shiftless, but this share varied by gender, ethnicity, and neighborhood. However, the estimate may be conservative because the truly shiftless may have been underrepresented in the survey. We have no way of assessing this underrepresentation, but a disaggregation of the incidence of joblessness

17. There were too few men who wanted a job but had never worked to generate reliable reservation wage rates by race and ethnicity.

by race, ethnicity, gender, and degree of neighborhood poverty will help decipher the meaning of the pervasive joblessness in Chicago's inner city.

Racial and Ethnic Variation in Employment Status

For the United States as a whole, black women have reported higher rates of labor force participation than Latinas, but less than 45 percent of black mothers living in Chicago's inner city were employed when interviewed in 1987, and only an additional 6 percent were looking for work. Their participation rate of about 50 percent was almost 24 points below the national rate for comparably aged black mothers (table 1). They also differed from the national population in that the proportion of nonparticipants with no work experience was more than double.

That black fathers residing in Chicago's inner city were almost 17 percentage points less likely to be employed than black fathers nationally and their unemployment rate was 50 percent higher attests to either the difficulties they confronted in securing jobs or their unwillingness to take the jobs available. The former does not imply a weaker labor market attachment or a less robust work ethic; the latter may. Of the 18 percent of black fathers who were not in the labor force in 1987, just under half had never worked. Although work experience may indicate some degree of labor market attachment, there was no correlation between previous and current willingness to work. In the national sample less than 6 percent of black fathers age 18 to 44 were out of the labor force, and less than 1 percent reported no work experience. Thus, while most black parents reported either current or former involvement in the labor market, there is evidence of weak attachment, and this is more true for inner-city black parents than for the national population of black parents.

Black women who were not parents had significantly higher employment rates than black men, whose unemployment rate exceeded 20 percent. Labor force participation among black childless men was slightly lower than among childless women, and about one-fifth of the childless men who were out of the labor force at the time of the survey had never worked, compared with about one-tenth of the childless women. This segment of the black nonparent sample appears to fit our operational definition of shiftlessness. In many cases, however, their lack of job experience reflected their youth and the well-documented difficulties young blacks experience getting jobs.

Among white parents, 91 percent of fathers and 56 percent of mothers from Chicago's inner city worked or were looking for work in 1987. Al-

TABLE I. Employment Status of Parents Age 18 to 44 in Chicago's
Inner City and United States, by Race or National Origin and Sex, 1987

Percent unless otherwise specified

Race, area, and gender	In labor force		Not in labor force		
	Employed	Unemployed	Ever worked	Never worked	Number[a]
Black					
Chicago					
Parents					
Men	69.6	12.6	9.4	8.3	300
Women	43.9	6.4	30.5	19.2	715
Nonparents					
Men	53.6	20.8	5.9	19.9	112
Women	75.5	2.1	11.1	11.1	51
United States					
Men	86.1	8.2	5.2	0.5	411
Women	63.6	10.3	17.4	8.7	716
White					
Chicago					
Men	87.0	4.3	8.7	n.a.	127
Women	52.6	3.3	35.7	8.4	237
United States					
Men	94.3	2.2	3.2	0.2	1,591
Women	62.7	2.9	28.8	5.6	2,026
Mexican					
Chicago					
Men	93.1	1.7	4.4	0.9	228
Women	50.9	1.9	30.4	16.9	261
United States					
Men	93.0	4.2	2.8	0	147
Women	50.3	9.8	23.3	16.6	198
Puerto Rican					
Chicago					
Men	76.7	7.6	13.1	2.7	147
Women	34.0	1.3	36.4	28.3	306
United States					
Men	78.1	12.5	9.4	0	32
Women	30.6	4.8	30.6	33.9	62

SOURCES: U.S. data from 1987 National Survey of Families and Households; Chicago data from 1987 Urban Poverty and Family Life Survey.

a. Numbers are unweighted; percentages are weighted to approximate universe.

n.a. Not available.

though these rates were lower than those of their national counterparts, the differences were small in comparison with differences observed among blacks. Furthermore, four out of five white mothers who were not in the labor force reported having worked in the past, compared with three out of five black mothers. On balance, Chicago's inner-city white mothers differed less from their national counterparts than did black mothers.

Unemployment rates of white parents, moreover, were far lower than those experienced by black parents. This finding is crucial because it brings into focus the relative importance of race and residence in producing persistent poverty, chronic welfare dependence, and alienation from the labor market. Three interpretations are plausible: living in a poor neighborhood has fewer effects on the work activity of whites than of blacks, Chicago's poor white neighborhoods are not nearly as poor as its black neighborhoods, or some combination of the two.

Table 2 lends support to the third interpretation. It shows that black fathers were four times more likely than white fathers and black mothers nearly seven times more likely than white mothers to live in neighborhoods where 40 percent of all families were poor. The participation rates of blacks were much lower than those of whites who lived in similarly poor neighborhoods. Black men participated less in the labor force than their white counterparts in all poor neighborhoods, but the differential was greatest in neighborhoods where 30 to 39 percent of all families were poor. This is the modal residence category for poor blacks, but not for poor whites. Among women, black participation rates exceeded those of whites in neighborhoods where less than 40 percent of all families were poor—probably because of greater economic need and the unavailability of support from spouses—but whites had the market advantage in the poorest neighborhoods. These differences indicate a moderate neighborhood effect, a strong race effect, and a strong gender effect that depends on neighborhood context.

To return to table 1, the highest and lowest levels of participation occurred among Chicago's Latino parents, with Puerto Rican mothers having the lowest rates among women and Mexican fathers the highest among men. Participation rates of Mexican fathers from Chicago were similar to those of Mexican fathers nationally, but unemployment was higher in the national sample. Participation rates of Puerto Rican fathers in Chicago's inner city, however, were 6 percentage points lower than those reported nationally. The national population had higher unemployment rates but lower nonparticipation rates than Chicago's inner-city

TABLE 2. Labor Force Participation of Parents in Chicago's Inner City, by Neighborhood Poverty Rate, Race or National Origin, and Sex, 1987

Percent unless otherwise specified

Neighborhood poverty rate	Black		White		Mexican		Puerto Rican	
	In labor force	Living in neighborhood	In labor force	Living in neighborhood	In labor force	Living in neighborhood	In labor force	Living in neighborhood
Men								
Less than 30 percent poor	60.9	52.1	81.6	79.6	93.7	75.7	76.7	67.2
30–39 percent poor	50.6	28.1	79.8	15.8	82.2	19.1	65.9	20.8
More than 40 percent poor	53.5	19.8	70.8	4.6	91.6	5.2	67.3	12.0
Average poverty rate	56.5	…	80.8	…	91.4	…	73.3	…
Number[a]	415		127		228		148	
Women								
Less than 30 percent poor	51.5	47.1	47.1	79.9	45.2	79.1	29.4	63.0
30–39 percent poor	46.0	27.2	34.3	16.3	52.8	18.0	35.7	28.5
More than 40 percent poor	27.4	25.7	49.8	3.8	36.9	2.9	5.4	8.5
Average poverty rate	43.8	…	45.1	…	46.3	…	29.2	…
Number[a]	768		237		261		306	

SOURCE: Urban Poverty and Family Life Survey.
a. Numbers are unweighted; percentages are weighted to approximate universe.

population.[18] Unemployment among Mexican fathers and mothers and Puerto Rican mothers in Chicago was generally low, but Puerto Rican men experienced high unemployment. Labor force nonparticipation rates of black and Puerto Rican fathers were similar but far higher than those of Mexican fathers. Among nonparticipant fathers, blacks were three times as likely as Puerto Ricans to have never worked.

As occurs in the general population, Puerto Rican mothers residing in Chicago's inner city showed the lowest participation rates.[19] Labor force activity among Mexican mothers from Chicago was lower than that of Mexican women nationally, a circumstance that may be related to the immigrant composition of the Chicago sample. Yet only 17 percent of both the national and local samples reported no work experience, whereas 28 percent of local Puerto Rican mothers reported no work experience.

It is unlikely that differences in work activity between Mexicans and Puerto Ricans resulted solely from unequal job opportunities. Such an interpretation may be tenable for the national sample because Puerto Ricans have been disproportionately concentrated in the Northeast, where blue-collar employment opportunities declined steeply during the 1970s and 1980s.[20] But it is difficult to argue that geography was a major factor in the differences in labor force activity of Mexicans and Puerto Ricans living in poor Chicago neighborhoods. Instead, unequal participation may have reflected differences in willingness to accept available jobs, given that Puerto Ricans are eligible for public aid but Mexicans in Chicago, 80 percent of whom were foreign born, may not be.

Participation differences classified by neighborhood poverty levels in table 2 show that Puerto Ricans were more likely than Mexicans to reside in highly concentrated poverty areas. That Mexican participation rates exceeded those of Puerto Ricans in both high- and relatively low-poverty neighborhoods raises questions about the importance of ethnicity and residence in determining labor market success. Although the lower labor force activity among Puerto Ricans may have reflected more limited job opportunities close to their neighborhoods, institutionalized discrimination and lower commitment to work remain viable explanations.

This overview of racial and ethnic variations in labor force activity

18. The rates based on the National Sample of Families and Households must be interpreted with some caution because of the small sample sizes. Nonetheless, they accord with independent estimates based on census and survey data (see Bean and Tienda, 1987).

19. For general population, see Bean and Tienda (1987).

20. Tienda (1989).

warrants three generalizations. First, Chicago's inner-city blacks are worse off than blacks nationally with respect to employment, but this is not so for whites or Mexicans. Second, Puerto Ricans are worse off than Mexicans even when they reside in the same city or in equally poor neighborhoods. Third, blacks and Puerto Ricans may be worse off than whites and Mexicans because they tend to live in poorer neighborhoods, but this result may also be caused by less attachment to the labor market and a tendency for the jobless to live in the same areas. How much the poor labor market standing of blacks and Puerto Ricans can be traced to institutionalized racism, how much to more limited employment opportunities commensurate with fewer job skills, and how much to values that denigrate work and render welfare an acceptable means of support cannot be ascertained with the available data.

The Duration of Joblessness

Table 3 summarizes the job history of the experienced labor force, that is, persons who ever worked, by focusing on periods of joblessness. The job history is based on the criterion of steady full-time or part-time work that lasted at least six months, exclusive of after-school jobs.[21] For those who had worked, we computed time spent between jobs in months, which we called wait times. "Percent censored" is the share of jobless episodes in progress at the time of the survey; the category combines permanent and transitory episodes of nonwork.

The average duration of wait times was 4.5 years for Puerto Rican women and 4 years for black mothers, but for Mexican and white mothers durations were 3.8 and 3.3 years, respectively. On average, men had shorter jobless spells than women, but differences by race and ethnicity were evident. Black and Mexican men experienced the longest average waits, 2.9 and 2.7 years, respectively; the average wait for Puerto Rican and white men was 2.3 and 1.9 years.

The shorter periods of unemployment for men largely reflected the fact that fathers' work behavior is less constrained than mothers' by family responsibilities. However, this does not explain the racial and ethnic variations in waiting times, nor why jobless episodes are longer for Mexican than for Puerto Rican men. To appreciate these differences, one must understand that episodes rather than individuals are the unit of analysis

21. Because the UPFLS did not include questions about activities pursued during spells of joblessness, we could not examine unemployment behavior retrospectively or determine with accuracy which persons had withdrawn permanently from the labor market.

TABLE 3. Unemployment of the Experienced Labor Force Residing in Chicago's Inner City, by Race or National Origin, Sex, and Age[a]
Months unless otherwise specified

Joblessness	Black		White		Mexican		Puerto Rican	
	Men	Women	Men	Women	Men	Women	Men	Women
Average wait	34.6	47.4	22.6	39.9	32.2	45.9	27.5	54.1
Percent censored[b]	14.1	9.2	12.6	7.9	16.9	11.0	12.9	8.8
Average wait, by age								
18–24	10.1	22.5	19.4	25.3	8.9	27.8	19.2	27.7
25–34	27.6	41.2	25.5	32.8	27.8	43.8	24.3	43.6
35 or older	48.4	57.3	21.2	47.9	37.9	55.0	30.8	72.1
Number[c]	747	1,155	390	521	408	292	301	364

SOURCE: 1987 Urban Poverty and Family Life Survey.
a. Excludes persons who never worked.
b. Permanent and transitory jobless episodes in progress at time of survey.
c. Unit of analysis is spells of joblessness.

for computing average waiting times between jobs, and that the incidence of periods of joblessness is much lower among Mexicans and whites than among blacks and Puerto Ricans. However, when joblessness occurs, the wait is longer for whites and Mexicans.

Mothers age 18 to 24 showed relatively little variation in the duration of unemployment, but minority women age 25 to 34 experienced wait times 8.4 to 11 months longer than their white counterparts. Average waits of women age 35 and older were equally heterogeneous, ranging from 4 years for white women to 6 for Puerto Rican women. Although other studies have pointed out the low levels of work activity among Puerto Ricans, the reasons for its occurrence are not well understood.[22]

Wait times experienced by men generally varied less widely than those of women, yet racial and ethnic differences remained well defined. Among young men, Puerto Ricans and whites weathered periods of unemployment that were twice as long as those experienced by black men. These averages pertain only to those workers who actually experienced periods of joblessness, which is higher for Puerto Rican and black men than for white and Mexican men. In the absence of information about whether jobless respondents intended to return to the labor market, inferences about withdrawal based on the data in table 3 must be regarded as tentative. Nonetheless, the patterns are consistent with those derived from cross-sectional data in showing that withdrawal is more pervasive among women than among men, and in particular, Puerto Ricans and blacks. The racial and ethnic differences in the duration of joblessness square with an image of the urban underclass as consisting largely of minorities, but blacks and Puerto Ricans in particular.

Conclusion

Our results do not support the claim of widespread shiftlessness among inner-city parents. We broadened the definition of labor market attachment to include work experience and aspirations for work to better distinguish between involuntary and voluntary idleness. People who were not working, had never worked, and did not want to work for reasons other than those deemed socially tolerable were the truly shiftless, but they were a small subset of those most other people consider shiftless. Most of the evidence showed that willingness to work was the norm in Chicago's inner city. We gathered only indirect evidence on the incidence of discouragement, but the large share of unemployed parents who re-

22. See Bean and Tienda (1987); and Tienda (1989).

ported wanting a job suggests that discouragement may be pervasive in Chicago's inner-city neighborhoods.

Compared with parents age 19 to 44 nationally, those residing in poor Chicago neighborhoods participated less in the labor force and experienced higher levels of unemployment. Other things being equal, mothers worked outside the home less than fathers because of family constraints and fewer skills. This finding, however, constitutes evidence neither of weaker labor force attachment nor of greater shiftlessness in the inner city than in the nation as a whole. That most inner-city parents had held jobs showed some commitment to work, but the connection between previous labor market position and position at the time of the survey was tenuous and probably weaker among the poor and discouraged. Few of those who were unemployed did not want a job, and most of these gave family responsibilities, poor health, or school attendance as reasons. In an ideal world, such reasons may be legitimate, but not in a world where public assistance is the main alternative to work. Black men who were not parents were a possible exception to this generalization: little more than half were employed, and more than one-quarter were not looking for work. Of that one-quarter, most had never worked and hence provided the closest fit to our definition of shiftlessness. At most, 6 percent of adults in Chicago's inner-city neighborhoods would meet our criteria for being shiftless.

On balance, we conclude that shiftlessness is not pervasive among parents living in Chicago's inner-city neighborhoods. However, the absence of widespread shiftlessness is not incompatible with high levels of joblessness. Unemployment is pervasive in the inner city, and its occurrence, as well as the reasons for its occurrence, varies appreciably by ethnicity and gender. Inner-city residents expected jobs that paid more than the minimum wage, but whether this expectation reflected a desire to compensate for the medical and food benefits provided welfare recipients was not obvious. Until this is clarified, the responses indicating that people wanted work must be treated with caution.

Although few would question the legitimacy of a disabling physical condition as a valid reason for not working, exactly what constitutes family responsibilities as an acceptable reason has become increasingly blurry. Tolerance for mothers who do not work outside the home has waned since the original conception of aid to dependent children, and the idea of getting mothers off welfare rolls and onto payrolls has been the main theme of welfare reform since 1967. The major obstacle has been the cost of providing mothers of young children with job training and adequate child care to ensure long-term self-sufficiency. It remains to be seen whether, in fact, family responsibilities will remain a reason excusing women from the work requirements originally intended to apply only to men.

The diversity of labor force experiences among ethnic and gender groups requires further analysis to determine what life events—marriage, divorce, births, training, and so forth—and what social circumstances— plant closings, work slowdown, relocation—precipitate changes in work status. For married women, unemployment is generally not a social problem because their spouses usually provide economic support. Unmarried mothers are a different case, however, particularly when their former partners do not provide child support.[23] Unmarried fathers who do not work present special problems because they do not generate income to support their dependents and, unless identified by the mothers, may not be held accountable for the support of their children. If fathers do not provide child support and mothers do not work, taxpayers become surrogate parents.

Our evidence raises several policy matters that deserve close attention. If society really expects single mothers with limited skills to work, social policy must specify the income guarantees, child care assistance, and other supports that will be provided so that the work will not aggravate the economic deprivation of their children with social deprivation. Another matter that must be addressed is unemployment among minority men in poor neighborhoods. Our survey has shown not the absence of a work ethic, but limited opportunities to secure employment. This is revealed by the higher levels of unemployment that men in Chicago's inner city experience compared with minority men nationally, the longer wait times between jobs, and tentative evidence of higher rates of dropping out of the labor market, possibly because of discouragement. It is not simply limited skills that produce the different employment experiences of white and minority parents.

Black fathers have an educational advantage over Mexican and Puerto Rican fathers when measured by years of school completed, but not necessarily when other measures of job readiness are used. That parents from Chicago's inner-city neighborhoods did not differ from a national sample of parents with respect to educational attainment drives home the point that formal schooling is a necessary but insufficient condition to guarantee employment. Employers care about skills, and they continue to

23. McLanahan and Garfinkel (1989).

prefer white and Mexican workers. Whether such preferences are justified on grounds of expected differences in productivity or simply reflect prejudice will remain a matter of debate, but discrimination based on race and national origin remains a plausible explanation for the pronounced racial and ethnic differences we have documented.

References

Auletta, Ken. 1982. *The Underclass*. Random House.

Bean, Frank D., and Marta Tienda. 1987. *The Hispanic Population of the United States*. Russell Sage Foundation.

Clark, Kim B., and Lawrence H. Summers. 1979. "Labor Market Dynamics and Unemployment: A Reconsideration." *Brookings Papers on Economic Activity* 1, pp. 13–72.

Davidson, Chandler. 1979. "On the Culture of Shiftlessness." In *Twenty-Five Years of Dissent: An American Tradition*, edited by Irving Howe. Methuen Press.

McLanahan, Sara, and Irwin Garfinkel. 1989. "Single Mothers, the Underclass, and Social Policy." *Annals of the American Academy of Political and Social Science* 501 (January), pp. 92–104.

Murray, Charles. 1984. *Losing Ground: American Social Policy, 1950–1980*. Basic Books.

Tienda, Marta. 1989. "Puerto Ricans and the Underclass Debate." *Annals of the American Academy of Political and Social Science* 501 (January), pp. 105–19.

Wilson, William Julius. 1987. *The Truly Disadvantaged: The Inner City, the Underclass, and Public Policy*. University of Chicago Press.

Teenage Underclass Behavior and Subsequent Poverty: Have the Rules Changed?

GREG J. DUNCAN *and* SAUL D. HOFFMAN

LIMITED EDUCATION, living in a single-parent family, and giving birth out of wedlock are among the most familiar correlates of poverty. These empirically tested associations have often been converted into rules of behavior needed to avoid poverty. Charles Murray, for example, has concluded,

> If you follow a set of modest requirements, you are almost surely going to avoid poverty. . . . For women, one option is to get an education, acquire skills, and get a job. . . . Another option is to marry a man who will be a good and conscientious provider. . . . Whatever else she does: A poor woman who wishes to get out of poverty ought not to have a baby out of wedlock. This is not a moral statement but an empirical one. . . . The main policy question is: *"How can policies affecting poor people encourage them to do the very ordinary things that need to be done to avoid poverty?"*[1]

The correlates of poverty also figure prominently in thinking about the underclass. The problems of the underclass are, as William Julius Wilson has emphasized, very much a result of geographic and social isolation.[2] But they are also the product of individual behavior. Limited education and unwed motherhood are widely regarded as prime credentials for membership in the underclass.

In this regard, the popular consensus regarding the behavior of teenagers is that young people, especially minority and inner-city youth, are increasingly choosing "bad" behavior—failing to complete high school

This research was supported by grant 1RO1 HD 19339-02 from the National Institute for Child Health and Human Development and grant 890-0047 from the Ford Foundation. We have benefited from the expert research assistance of Deborah Laren and suggestions from Sheldon Danziger, Dorothy Duncan, David Ellwood, and Jeff Lehman.

1. Murray (1986), p. 90.
2. Wilson (1987).

or giving birth out of wedlock—over "good." By doing so, they find themselves in the ranks of the underclass, thus perpetuating the economic disadvantages of their own childhoods.

It is argued by many that an important cause of these disturbing trends is a deterioration during the past thirty years in the relative attractiveness of the economic reward for good behavior. Conservatives such as Murray have blamed this on the expansion of Great Society welfare programs, which have, they suggest, provided benefits that are often very attractive compared with those of steady work and marriage.[3] In other words, the economic cost associated with bad behavior has diminished.

Wilson and Neckerman, among others, have blamed instead the economic conditions of the past two decades that have eliminated many well-paid but unskilled manufacturing jobs and substituted, at best, low-paying service jobs. The decrease in the number of young men, especially minority men, with these manufacturing jobs has meant dismal marriage prospects for minority women, thus reducing the rewards associated with their good behavior.[4]

We seek in this paper to evaluate various assumptions about the relationships between behavior during the teenage years and the incidence of poverty in later life. We focus on two kinds of behavior, high school graduation and childbearing out of wedlock. In most of the analysis we concentrate on two groups of women: those who graduated from high school and did not bear a child out of wedlock during their teenage years, and those who did not graduate from high school, or bore a child out of wedlock as a teenager, or both.

We first describe trends in fertility and schooling since the late 1960s.[5] We then investigate the extent to which fertility and schooling choices made during the teenage years affect economic well-being nearly a decade later. And in the final part, we test a crucial assumption in the debate

3. Murray (1984).

4. Wilson and Neckerman (1986).

5. Our empirical work uses national data throughout, although some trends differ sharply between the urban North and other areas (Wilson, 1987; Massey and Eggers, 1989). Our choice of national data was dictated by several considerations, including the lack of appropriate data for individual cities and a desire to maintain a national perspective. As shown by David Ellwood (1988) and others, poor families living in areas of concentrated poverty in big cities account for a small fraction of the nation's poor or welfare-dependent population. And it is potentially misleading to presume that trends and behavior displayed in certain geographic areas hold true for other areas as well. In addition, much of the debate over trends in fertility, marriage, and poverty and their causes (see, for example, Wilson, 1987, chaps. 3, 4) has been argued from a national perspective.

about teenage behavior: that choices made in the teenage years in fact respond to the likely economic consequences of these choices.

Trends in Schooling, Fertility, Earnings, Welfare Benefits, and Marriage

Evidence from Current Population Survey data on national trends in the schooling and fertility of young women shows that larger proportions of both white and black women completed high school or college in the 1980s than did so in the late 1960s (table 1). High school completion rates for black and white women living in inner cities were only marginally lower than the national estimates. Over the same period, out-of-wedlock birth rates for teenagers declined slightly for blacks and rose modestly from a much lower base for whites. Taken together, these data show no alarming national trends in the schooling or fertility behavior of either black or white teenagers.

Although out-of-wedlock birth rates among young women have changed little since the late 1960s, the percentage of all births accounted for by unmarried mothers has risen dramatically for both whites and blacks, but especially for blacks, in large part because of the falling rates of marriage. In 1970 four of five white women and three of five black women 25 to 29 years old were married and living with a spouse; by 1987 only three of five white women and one of three black women were married. Indeed, by the late 1980s, black women 25 to 29 years old who had never married far outnumbered married black women. These falling marriage rates figure prominently in William Wilson's work and also in our attempt to explain the links between teenage behavior and subsequent economic status.

Declining marriage rates, especially for black women, are often linked to worsening marriage prospects or improved welfare benefits or both. The decline in marriage prospects, accompanied by the sharp downturn in young men's average earnings, has indeed been accurately depicted in popular discussions. As table 1 shows, the average real earnings of young white men fell by nearly 20 percent between 1969 and 1984 and by 25 percent for black men. A much smaller percentage of black men held jobs in 1984 than in 1969, and the average real earnings of those who did were lower. Wilson and other observers have shown how much more dramatic these changes have been in northern central cities than elsewhere.

Not as widely known is the deterioration in the real value of welfare benefits. Although the combined value of benefits from the AFDC and

TABLE 1. Schooling, Rates of Marriage and Birth, Earnings, and Welfare Benefit Levels, by Race and Age Group, Selected Periods, 1967–88

Characteristic	1967–72	1973–79	1980–85	1986–88
Schooling, women age 25–29 (percent)[a]				
Four years of high school or more				
White	76	85	87	87
Black	58	75	80	82
Four years of college or more				
White	13	21	22	23
Black	8	14	13	11
Births per thousand unmarried women age 15–19[b]				
White	11	12	19	22
Black	97	90	86	90
Married, spouse present, women age 25–29 (percent)[c]				
White	83	76	65	61
Black	60	45	37	35
Annual earnings, men age 25–34 (thousands of 1984 dollars)[d]				
White	23.7	21.9	19.3	n.a.
Black	15.2	13.4	11.4	n.a.
AFDC and food stamp benefit levels, family of four with no income (thousands of 1986 dollars)[e]	7.5	9.1	7.3	7.5

SOURCES: See notes a–e.

n.a. Not available.

a. Bureau of the Census, "Educational Attainment in the United States: March 1987 and 1986," *Current Population Reports*, series P-20, no. 428 (Department of Commerce, 1988), table 12. Figures are for 1970, 1976, 1983, and 1987.

b. National Research Council, *Risking the Future*, vol. 2 (Washington: National Academy Press, 1987), table 6.4; and *Monthly Vital Statistics*, vol. 37, no. 3 (1988). Figures are for 1970, 1976, 1983, and 1986.

c. Bureau of the Census, "Marital Status and Family Status: March 1970," *Current Population Reports*, series P-20, no. 212 (Department of Commerce, 1971), table 1; "Marital Status and Living Arrangements: March 1976," *Current Population Reports*, series P-20, no. 306 (1977), table 1; "Marital Status and Living Arrangements: March 1983," *Current Population Reports*, series P-20, no. 389 (1984), table 1; and "Marital Status and Living Arrangements: March 1987," *Current Population Reports*, series P-20, no. 423 (1988), table 1. Figures are for 1970, 1976, 1983, and 1987.

d. Unpublished tabulations by Reynolds Farley. Figures are for 1969 and 1979 from the 1970 and the 1980 decennial census and for 1984 from the 1985 Current Population Survey.

e. *Background Material and Data on Programs Within the Jurisdiction of the Committee on Ways and Means, 1987 Edition* (1987), table 28. Figures are for 1968, 1976, 1984, and 1986, and are population-weighted state averages.

food stamp programs rose through the mid-1970s, they have since fallen precipitately as inflation has eroded their value.

Much has been made by some observers of the way changing economic incentives have depressed marriage rates and increased out-of-wedlock births. But the data shown in table 1 reveal no consistent direction of net change in those incentives. Looking only at falling welfare benefits, for example, one might predict a decrease in out-of-wedlock births and an increase in marriage rates. But the relative attractions of welfare and marriage are crucial to an incentives model, and diminished levels of male earnings, which reduce the attractions of marriage, confound simple predictions based on welfare benefit levels alone.

Teenagers' Behavior and Economic Well-Being

We first examine trends and economic consequences of teenagers' fertility and schooling behavior, using longitudinal information available in the Panel Study of Income Dynamics. The PSID, a study of nationally representative families, has been collecting information on economic well-being, schooling, and family formation annually since 1968. Our sample includes all women in the PSID who reached age 25 between 1967 and 1985. We divided these women into two groups according to schooling and childbearing during their teenage years—those who completed high school and did not have an out-of-wedlock birth, and those who did not complete high school or had an out-of-wedlock birth or both. With some trepidation, we will describe the first group as displaying "good" teenage behavior or "following the rules" and the second as displaying "bad" behavior or "breaking the rules."

Table 2 shows trends in the relative sizes of these two groups, by race (black and nonblack, referred to as "white" hereafter), and according to the time period in which the women reached age 25: 1967–72, the period of economic growth and low unemployment before the first oil crisis; 1973–79, a turbulent period of low productivity and relatively high rates of inflation; and 1980–85, in which a sharp recession was followed by sustained economic growth. Women in these three periods completed their teenage years in the early 1960s, late 1960s and early 1970s, and late 1970s, respectively.[6]

A first striking result is the absence of trends in behavior: contrary to

6. Sample sizes for white women with good and bad behavior range from 236 to 387 and from 59 to 84, respectively. Comparable ranges for black women are 47 to 197 and 88 to 212.

TABLE 2. High School Graduation and Teenage Out-of-Wedlock
Births for Women, by Race, Selected Periods, 1967–85
Percent

Teenage behavior and time period[a]	White	Black
High school graduate, no out-of-wedlock birth		
1967–72	82	49
1973–79	84	57
1980–85	86	51
Not high school graduate and/or had out-of-wedlock birth		
1967–72	18	51
1973–79	16	43
1980–85	14	48
Not high school graduate and had out-of-wedlock birth		
1967–72	1	19
1973–79	2	16
1980–85	3	15

SOURCE: Panel Study of Income Dynamics.
a. Time period is the calendar year in which a woman was age 25.

conventional wisdom, but consistent with Census Bureau evidence, there
has been no decrease in the percentages of either black or white women
showing good behavior. The proportion of white women who completed
their teenage years with a high school degree and no out-of-wedlock birth
actually increased slightly. Although the comparable figures for black
women are much lower and more erratic, the proportion with good behavior in the latest time period is still slightly higher than for the first
period.[7] And as the bottom portion of the table shows, the percentage of
women breaking both rules—those not completing high school *and* having children out of wedlock—fell several percentage points for black
women and rose by about the same amount for white women. Despite
the modest racial convergence, the proportion of black women who did
not graduate and who had a child out of wedlock was five times that of
whites in the 1980s.

Table 3 shows the economic consequences of these behaviors, mea-

7. The distribution of schooling and out-of-wedlock births within the group of women
exhibiting bad behavior does, however, show some change. Consistent with Census Bureau
evidence in table 1, dropping out of high school became much less common relative to births
out of wedlock. The economic consequences within each time period for those who dropped
out but did not have births out of wedlock were similar to those of teenagers with babies
who completed high school.

TABLE 3. Poverty and Family Income of Women as of Age 25, by Teenage Behavior and Race, Selected Periods, 1967–85[a]

Economic status	White			Black		
	High school graduate, no out-of-wedlock teenage birth	Not high school graduate and/or had out-of-wedlock teenage birth	Difference	High school graduate, no out-of-wedlock teenage birth	Not high school graduate and/or had out-of-wedlock teenage birth	Difference
Poor (percent)						
1967–72	3	6	–3	15	25	–10
1973–79	2	10	–8	12	24	–12
1980–85	3	22	–19	13	48	–35
Median family income (thousands of 1985 dollars)						
1967–72	30.6	21.7	8.9	26.1	14.3	11.8
1973–79	29.9	21.8	8.1	22.1	15.6	6.5
1980–85	28.6	17.6	11.0	17.7	8.3	9.4

SOURCE: Panel Study of Income Dynamics.
a. Time period is the calendar year in which a woman was age 25.

sured in the year in which each woman reached age 25, an age at which we believe the medium-term consequences of teenage behavior first begin to appear. A simple calculation of poverty rates at age 25 for women who had followed the rules during their teenage years is consistent with Charles Murray's observations: both white and black women who completed their teenage years with a high school diploma and no out-of-wedlock birth consistently have had very high (about 97 percent for white women and 87 percent for black women) chances of avoiding poverty.

But although poverty rates have not changed for women exhibiting good behavior during their teenage years, their median family incomes have declined—rather sharply for black women. The typical black woman who finished her teenage years in the 1960s having followed the rules enjoyed at age 25 a family income of $26,100 in 1985 dollars, while her counterpart in the 1980s could expect an income of only $17,700. Family incomes for white women also fell, but not by as much.

An economic model of teenage behavior should focus on the relative payoff for good behavior—that is, the difference in likely poverty or median income between teenagers who did and did not follow the rules. Here the poverty trends are striking: the difference in poverty rates between the two groups of women has increased substantially because both black and white teenagers who dropped out of school or had babies out of wedlock were much worse off when they reached their mid-twenties in the early 1980s than were such women twenty years earlier. Poverty rates of white women who either dropped out of high school or had a child out-of-wedlock more than tripled and nearly doubled for black women. Median family incomes at age 25 for these groups dropped sharply as well. In the 1980s the median income at age 25 for black women who dropped out of school or had a child out of wedlock was only $8,300.

These findings of rising poverty for bad behavior stand in sharp contrast to the conservative view that the absolute reward for such behavior has increased. Teenage women who broke the rules were much worse off at age 25 in the early 1980s, not only relative to a comparable group of women twenty years earlier, but also compared with women who completed high school and did not have a child out of wedlock.

Accounting for the Changes

What causes the trends in poverty and income associated with good and bad teenage behavior? Table 4 provides data on some of the behaviors that may be responsible.

We first looked at schooling and fertility behavior after the teenage years, thinking that a decrease in the proportion of women who returned to school or limited the number of births after the first might account for the deepening poverty of women with bad teen behavior. Instead we found just the opposite: recent cohorts of both white and black women who either dropped out of high school or had children out of wedlock as teenagers were much more likely to have completed school and limited family size by age 25 than were previous cohorts. Thus in terms of schooling and fertility behavior, those who followed and those who broke the rules have become more alike by age 25, which makes the growing gap in poverty rates all the more puzzling.

Wilson has emphasized marriage as the key to understanding the patterns of poverty among blacks. Consistent with the Census Bureau evidence shown in table 1, the rates of marriage at age 25 fell steadily for both white and black women. But by far the biggest decrease occurred for women who had either dropped out of high school or had a child out of wedlock during their teenage years. Before 1980, marriage rates were typically lower for the women who had graduated from high school and had not had a child out of wedlock. But by the 1980s this historical pattern was reversed: the teenagers who had broken the rules were the ones now much less likely to be married at age 25. This was especially true for black women.

Table 4 also shows that the difference in the average income of the husbands of women following and breaking the rules as teenagers was surprisingly small. For white women, the average difference was about $4,800; for black women, about half that, except in the 1980s when the difference almost disappeared. Also surprising is that the median earnings of husbands of black women in the 1980s were as high as or higher than in the late 1960s, suggesting that the dramatic decline in the earnings of black men shown in table 1 has been more than offset by the increased selectivity of black women in choosing partners.

Marriage patterns during the past two decades appear consistent with the presumption that women consider marriage only if a prospective husband earns more than some minimum threshold. The combination of an unchanging threshold and worsening labor market prospects of potential mates has meant far fewer marriages.

If the increased poverty in the 1980s associated with bad teenage behavior is largely a consequence of schooling, fertility, and marriage, then controlling for these variables, measured at age 25, ought to account for the trends in poverty. A regression analysis confirmed that the rising pov-

TABLE 4. Demographic and Labor Market Characteristics of Women as of Age 25, by Teenage Behavior and Race, Selected Periods, 1967–85[a]

Percent unless otherwise specified

Characteristic	White			Black		
	High school graduate, no out-of-wedlock teenage birth	Not high school graduate and/or had out-of-wedlock teenage birth	Difference	High school graduate, no out-of-wedlock teenage birth	Not high school graduate and/or had out-of-wedlock teenage birth	Difference
Acquired additional schooling[b]						
1967–72	25	2	23	18	3	15
1973–79	31	13	18	22	8	14
1980–85	25	13	12	17	14	3
Three or more births						
1967–72	15	45	−30	24	50	−26
1973–79	6	36	−30	11	43	−32
1980–85	5	20	−15	7	29	−22
Married[c]						
1967–72	85	91	−6	53	50	3
1973–79	73	69	−4	39	44	−5
1980–85	67	58	9	41	23	18

Median spousal earnings[d]					
1967–72	25.2	19.4	5.8	17.6	15.4	2.2
1973–79	24.7	22.1	2.6	17.0	14.2	2.8
1980–85	21.8	15.7	6.1	17.6	17.1	0.5
Receiving AFDC					
1967–72	1	10	−9	1	22	−21
1973–79	1	23	−22	26	30	−4
1980–85	3	22	−19	12	48	−36
Working at least 1,000 hours					
1967–72	42	30	12	75	44	31
1973–79	55	24	31	72	52	20
1980–85	64	45	19	77	35	42
Median earnings[e]					
1967–72	13.8	5.0	8.8	9.3	7.7	1.6
1973–79	13.5	6.9	6.6	12.4	8.4	4.0
1980–85	12.8	5.2	7.6	11.1	4.9	6.2

SOURCE: Panel Study of Income Dynamics.
a. Time period is the calendar year in which a woman was age 25.
b. For teenage high school graduates, percent who had completed college by age 25. For dropouts, percent who had graduated from high school by age 25.
c. Includes living with long-term partner.
d. Thousands of 1985 dollars.
e. For women who worked at least 250 hours. Thousands of 1985 dollars.

erty rate for whites was largely the result of these demographic trends. Those trends do not, however, adequately explain the very high poverty rate in the 1980s for black women with bad behavior as teenagers. Even after taking into account schooling, fertility, and marriage, the poverty rates for this group remain well above those of previous cohorts.

Our final attempt to understand the deepening poverty of black women who did not follow the rules as teenagers consisted of compiling more complete information about the composition of family income at age 25 for these and other women in the sample. Table 4 clearly shows that a far smaller percentage of black women who had either dropped out of high school or had a child out of wedlock by the 1980s were working regularly, and their reliance on AFDC had more than doubled. Despite their smaller families, barely one-third worked at least half-time, a rate well below that of any other group.[8] The rate of receiving AFDC benefits grew much more rapidly for them as well, and they were the only group for whom receiving benefits was much more likely than working steadily.

It is tempting to attribute this shift from work to welfare to the fact, noted by both liberals such as David Ellwood and conservatives such as Charles Murray and Lawrence Mead, that work provides very few rewards that welfare does not.[9] However, such an explanation alone cannot reconcile the fact that at the same time market work was diminishing and AFDC usage was increasing for black women with bad teenage behavior, among white women who had shown similar behavior, the percentage engaged in market work was increasing rapidly and AFDC usage had leveled off. And falling real levels of welfare benefits and smaller family sizes should have increased the attractions of work relative to welfare. Thus although the shift from work to welfare among black women exhibiting bad teenage behavior accounts for much of their increased poverty, it does not conform to any simple explanation based on trends in incentives.

Economic Incentives and Teenage Underclass Behavior

Liberals such as Wilson and conservatives such as Murray agree that economic incentives exert an important influence on individual behavior.

8. The falling labor income of the black women with bad behavior shown in table 4 results primarily from fewer work hours. Median real hourly wage rates for these women for the three periods were $4.66, $4.89, and $4.46.

9. Ellwood (1989); Murray (1984); and Mead (1988).

But they disagree strongly over which incentives matter. Wilson stresses the influence of the labor market and Murray that of the welfare system. In fact relatively little empirical work has tested whether incentives do influence an individual's fertility and schooling decisions, and no research at all has examined carefully the effects of welfare and nonwelfare income simultaneously.

In this section we test the incentive theories by estimating a model relating teenage behavior to welfare, employment, and marital opportunities. For example, some women live in states where welfare benefits are relatively high and work and marriage opportunities relatively poor. Other women may experience just the opposite situations. Are the former more likely than the latter not to complete high school or to have a child out of wedlock? Do both welfare opportunities and work opportunities make a difference?

The teenage behavior we focus on here differs slightly from that emphasized thus far. "Good" teenage behavior is defined exactly as before: graduating from high school and having no children out of wedlock. For "bad" behavior, however, schooling is ignored, and the focus is instead on teenage out-of-wedlock births that are accompanied by the receipt of AFDC income.[10]

Our sample included all women from the Panel Study of Income Dynamics who were teenagers between 1968 and 1978, were 25 years old between 1980 and 1985, and were part of the PSID throughout their entire teenage years. Because teenage out-of-wedlock births are rather rare for whites, a study the size of the PSID simply does not yield a large enough sample to have estimated our model on white teenagers. Thus we confined our analysis to black women. The resulting sample included 232 women, about 30 percent of whom had an AFDC-related out-of-wedlock teenage birth.[11]

In developing a model relating AFDC teenage births to welfare, labor market, and marital opportunities, we assumed that the decision-makers—the teenage women—were reasonably well informed about the

10. This produced a sample with a sharper division of teenage behavior and made some of our assumptions, noted below, more reasonable. Excluded from the sample were teenagers who did not complete high school but had no children out of wedlock and those who had a child out of wedlock but did not receive AFDC.

11. If an unwed teenage mother or the family in which she resided reported AFDC income in either of the first two years following an out-of-wedlock birth, the birth was treated as AFDC-related. If no AFDC was reported, but other welfare was, we examined the interviews individually to assess whether the income was likely to be misreported AFDC income.

economic consequences of their actions: specifically, that they looked forward about a decade and, on average, understood correctly the likely consequences of their actions for their economic well-being when they reached their mid-twenties.[12]

We measured the economic opportunities that would be available to a woman were she to have a child out of wedlock and receive AFDC by the amount of AFDC benefits that she would be eligible to receive. Because AFDC benefit levels vary significantly from state to state and among regions, we could compare the behavior of women who lived in high-benefit states with that of otherwise similar women living in low-benefit states.[13] As a measure of the likely consequences of good behavior, we used a woman's earned (nontransfer) family income when she was 25 years old. This measure included both her own earned income and that of her husband if she was married and thus incorporated information about both her labor market and her marriage opportunities.

Our analysis was complicated by the fact that we did not observe "counterfactual" conditions—the consequences of bad behavior for teenagers who followed the rules and the consequences of good behavior for women who broke them. For women not having AFDC-related teenage births, we can presume that state AFDC benefits measured the economic value of this unchosen path. For the women who did have such births, we had to construct some estimate of what would have happened had they made the other choice. This was crucial because, for Wilson, the poor marriage opportunities that are not accepted and thus not directly observed are the important part of the story.

To construct such an estimate, we looked at the family income at age 25 of women who did complete high school and did not have a child out of wedlock, but who were in other respects, such as family background, similar to women who did have a child out of wedlock. In doing this, we were aided by the information the PSID provides on the economic attainments of a woman's siblings; the sibling information captures some of the within-family variation in opportunities and enabled us to make far more accurate predictions of income at age 25.[14]

12. This does not mean that they were necessarily correct, only that they were not systematically too optimistic or pessimistic in their assessment of consequences.

13. Welfare benefits are typically much lower in the South than elsewhere. For example, in January 1987, maximum benefits for a two-person family ranged from $88 in Alabama to more than $500 in Alaska and some counties in New York state (Committee on Ways and Means, 1987, table 9).

14. Our estimates of nonwelfare opportunities were obtained by regressing family income at age 25 (for women who completed high school and did not have a child out of

Our key underclass behavior equation used welfare and nonwelfare income measures and additional characteristics of a woman and her parental family to estimate the probability that she would have a child out of wedlock as a teenager and receive AFDC benefits.[15] Thus our empirical model of behavior captured the incentives emphasized by Wilson and Murray and allowed for effects via differences in preferences. Our estimation used a logit regression model suitable for analyses of this kind.

Table 5 presents estimates of our model of teenage out-of-wedlock births and receipt of AFDC benefits. Two sets of results are shown. The first column shows coefficients from a specification that includes only the two measures of economic opportunities, along with a constant. It corresponds to a situation in which only economic incentives matter, and all other family background factors are assumed to be irrelevant. There is clear evidence that incentives do, indeed, matter. Women with higher predicted family incomes at age 25 are less likely to have had children out of wedlock as teenagers. Women living in states with higher AFDC benefits are more likely to have had such births. The estimated effect of income at age 25 is highly significant in a statistical sense, while the coefficient on AFDC benefits falls just short of the 10 percent significance level. Interestingly, the effect of family income at age 25 is nearly twice as large (in absolute value) as that of AFDC benefits, which suggests that a dollar of

---

wedlock as a teenager) on a large set of family background characteristics and the economic attainments (earned income and AFDC receipt) of her siblings. In estimating this relationship, we accounted for the possibility of sample selection bias, which might exist if there were important unmeasured differences in opportunities that affected the observed choices. An examination of predicted incomes for various sample subgroups was reassuring. For example, the predicted earned family income at age 25 for women who had graduated from high school and did not have a child out of wedlock was 25 percent higher than for those who had a child and received AFDC. Even larger predicted income differences existed between women from families that received AFDC income and those that did not. The lowest predicted income figures were for women whose sisters had received AFDC, and the largest difference was between that group and those whose sisters never received AFDC. See appendix table A-1 for further information.

15. The two income measures were converted to natural logs and inflated to 1985 price levels using the Consumer Price Index. AFDC benefits were measured by the AFDC guaranteed level for a family of two for a teenager's state of residence between ages 15 and 19. Additional characteristics included in the behavior equation were dummy variables for parental family income ($10,000–$20,000 and more than $20,000), whether the parental family received AFDC or other welfare, and residence in the South or urban North. We used the geographic measures to help control for unmeasured geographic differences that might influence AFDC usage and the parental income and AFDC receipt measures because they were consistently significant across various specifications and provided interesting evidence on the intergenerational transmission of economic status.

TABLE 5. Effects of Economic Incentives and Personal Characteristics on Likelihood of AFDC-Related Out-of-Wedlock Teenage Birth[a]

Variable	Model 1	Model 2
Ln earned income at age 25	−.639[b]	−.524[c]
	(.216)	(.235)
Ln AFDC benefits	.358	.132
	(.227)	(.311)
Parental income $10,000 to $20,000	...	−.197
		(.392)
Parental income greater than $20,000	...	−.734
		(.445)
Parental income from AFDC	...	.596
		(.330)
Urban North	...	.355
		(.493)
South	...	−.189
		(.513)
Constant	2.395	3.264
	(2.622)	(3.407)
χ^2	11.48[b]	24.46[b]
Sample size (unweighted)	232	232

SOURCE: Authors' calculations.

a. Black women reaching age 25 between 1980 and 1985. Entries in table are logistic regression coefficients. Standard errors are in parentheses. Parental income and residence variables are measured in the year a woman is age 14.

b. Statistically significant at the 1 percent level.

c. Statistically significant at the 5 percent level.

AFDC income is valued far less than a dollar of a woman's own earnings or the earnings of her spouse. By standard statistical criteria, however, the equation is not a particularly powerful predictor of behavior.

The second column of table 5 presents results from a model that includes family characteristics. If only economic incentives mattered, these variables should be unimportant and coefficients in the second column should be essentially identical to those in the first. Instead, this augmented model is statistically superior to the simpler one. In this specification the effect of earned family income at age 25 persists, but the coefficient on AFDC benefits falls sharply, and is now less than half its standard error.[16] Higher parental family income decreases the probability of having an AFDC-related teenage birth, while receipt of AFDC by the parental family increases it, even after controlling for effects on economic opportunities. In our sample, which covered teenage behavior in the early

16. This appears to be due to the inclusion of a variable measuring residence in the urban North or in the South.

to mid-1970s, there was no difference in underclass behavior in northern urban areas. Although the estimated effect of urban northern residence relative to residence elsewhere is positive, it is well below standard levels of statistical confidence.

One way to assess the importance of economic incentives on teenage behavior is to predict the changes in behavior that would result if family income or AFDC benefits were substantially different. The quantitative effects are modest. Using the coefficients from the model in table 5, column 2, we estimated that a 25 percent increase in family income at age 25 would decrease the proportion of black women having a child out of wedlock as a teenager by about 2 percentage points. A comparable increase in AFDC benefits would increase the proportion by only 1 percentage point. Put differently, although economic incentives do matter, they appear to have had a relatively small effect on the choices made by black women who were teenagers in the 1970s.

Receipt of AFDC benefits by both parents and siblings has a substantial impact. When the direct effect of parental receipt of AFDC benefits and the indirect effects of parental and sibling AFDC receipt in predicting income at age 25 are eliminated, the predicted proportion of teenagers having children out of wedlock decreases by 8 percentage points.

Conclusion

Our survey of changes in the consequences of schooling and childbearing by teens was conducted with an eye toward the work of both Wilson and Murray. In particular, we have focused on differences since the late 1960s in the subsequent economic well-being and demographic status of women who completed high school and did not have a child out of wedlock as a teenager and those who failed to complete high school or had a child or both.

Not surprisingly, we found that teenagers who "followed the rules" had much lower chances of subsequent poverty. More surprising is that the gap between the two groups grew substantially by the 1980s as a result of a very sharp jump in the poverty rate for women who did not graduate from high school or had a child out of wedlock as a teenager or both. Differences in median family income were also large and persistent, although they did not grow as much. By the 1980s, women who exhibited underclass behavior as teenagers were doing very poorly as young adults on all measures. The apparent economic incentives for avoiding bad behavior had become very large indeed.

A closer look at women exhibiting underclass behavior as teenagers showed a reversal in the marriage rates at age 25 of the two groups of teenage women. In the 1960s marriage had been more common among women who had not completed high school or had had a child out of wedlock than among other women; by the 1980s exactly the opposite was true. We also found evidence of a sharp drop in the labor market involvement of black women who had either dropped out of high school or had a child out of wedlock, a drop that was in sharp contrast to the trend among all other groups.

Whether teenage behavior regarding schooling and childbearing responds to changes in economic consequences is obviously a crucial issue for research on the underclass and for public policy. A very specific underclass behavior—bearing a child as a teenager and receiving AFDC—responded positively but weakly to AFDC benefit levels and negatively and much more strongly to nonwelfare economic opportunities. Women with the least to lose were indeed most likely to have a child as a teenager. But although significant in a statistical sense, our estimates imply rather modest changes in behavior in response to modest changes in opportunities.

Our descriptive work on the consequences of teenage behavior shows that one rule does not appear to have changed: national data still support the claim that schooling and delayed childbearing are sufficient conditions for most women, black and white, to avoid poverty as adults. Our evidence does not tell us whether this rule continues to hold (or indeed ever held) for women living in the concentrated poverty areas of our nation's cities. Wilson and others have shown how profoundly marital and economic opportunities have changed for these women. If our estimates of linkages between underclass behavior and economic opportunities hold as true in highly concentrated urban areas as for the entire nation, then the deteriorating opportunities may be crucial in explaining the extraordinarily high rates of births to teenagers and welfare dependence in some of our nation's cities.

At a more general level, social policy can have a major impact on the consequences of teenagers' actions through the rewards for good behavior and penalties for bad behavior built into the system of tax and transfer programs. One particularly noteworthy "reward" policy is the earned income tax credit, which supplements the income of low-wage workers and could be expanded into a much more effective program.

Those who promote the social "goal" of penalizing teenage rule breakers can take satisfaction in the remarkable progress made in the past two decades. Teenagers who break the rules are punished economically as never before. Common decency and elementary psychology, however, call for more attention to the rewards offered for good behavior. Here the picture is very disheartening. As we urge teenagers to follow the rules, the rewards for doing so are becoming smaller and smaller.

References

Bane, Mary Jo, and David T. Ellwood. 1983. *The Dynamics of Dependence: The Routes to Self-Sufficiency.* Department of Health and Human Services.

Bureau of the Census. 1971. "Educational Attainment: March 1970." *Current Population Reports,* series P-20, no. 207. Department of Commerce.

———. 1986. "Educational Attainment in the United States: March 1982 to 1985." *Current Population Reports,* series P-20, no. 415. Department of Commerce.

Committee on Ways and Means, House of Representatives. 1987. *Background Material and Data on Programs Within the Jurisdiction of the Committee on Ways and Means.*

Ellwood, David T. 1988. *Poor Support: Poverty in the American Family.* Basic Books.

———. 1989. "The Origins of 'Dependency': Choices, Confidence, or Culture?" *Focus* 12 (Spring–Summer), pp. 6–13.

Massey, Douglas S., and Mitchell L. Eggers. 1989. "The Ecology of Inequality: Minorities and the Concentration of Poverty 1970–1980." Population Research Center, University of Chicago (January).

Mead, Lawrence M. 1988. "The Hidden Jobs Debate." *Public Interest* 91 (Spring), pp. 40–58.

Murray, Charles C. 1984. *Losing Ground: American Social Policy, 1950–1980.* Basic Books.

———. 1986. "According to Age: Longitudinal Profiles of AFDC Recipients and the Poor by Age Group." Paper prepared for the Working Seminar on the Family and American Welfare Policy.

Wilson, William Julius. 1987. *The Truly Disadvantaged: The Inner City, the Underclass, and Public Policy.* University of Chicago Press.

Wilson, William Julius, and Kathryn M. Neckerman. 1986. "Poverty and Family Structure: The Widening Gap Between Evidence and Public Policy Issues." In *Fighting Poverty: What Works and What Doesn't,* edited by Sheldon M. Danziger and Daniel H. Weinberg. Harvard University Press.

Appendix Table

TABLE A-1. Predicted Earned Family Income for Black Women at Age 25 and Proportion with Teenage AFDC-Related Out-of-Wedlock Birth, by Selected Characteristics[a]

Characteristic	Predicted earned family income (dollars)	Teenage out-of-wedlock birth with AFDC receipt (percent)	Unweighted number of observations
All	9,452	29.8	232
High school graduate, no out-of-wedlock birth, no AFDC receipt	10,097	0	150
Out-of-wedlock birth with AFDC receipt	8,062	100.0	82
Characteristics at age 14			
Family received AFDC	7,605	43.5	86
Family did not receive AFDC	10,826	21.3	146
Urban North	10,570	36.4	51
South	9,132	30.5	150
Other	9,413	25.3	31
Sibling characteristics			
Brothers' average earned income (ages 26–30)			
Less than $10,000	8,091	63.8	41[b]
More than $10,000	9,716	18.1	84[b]
Sisters ever received AFDC	6,180	47.8	93[b]
Sisters never received AFDC	15,260	16.8	81[b]

SOURCES: Panel Study on Income Dynamics and authors' calculations.
a. Includes PSID black women who reached age 25 between 1980 and 1985.
b. Numbers do not sum to total sample size because of missing data.

Socioeconomic Change and the Decline of Marriage for Blacks and Whites

ROBERT D. MARE *and* **CHRISTOPHER WINSHIP**

THE PROPORTION of people who are married and living with their spouses has decreased greatly since the 1960s; the decline has been especially dramatic among blacks. For example, 60 percent of black women 25 to 29 years old were married in 1960, but only 32 percent in the mid-1980s. For white women of the same age, the percentage married dropped from 83 to 62 percent. Marriage became less common partly because women were marrying at a later age and partly because more women, again especially blacks, were remaining single throughout their lives.[1] Higher rates of divorce and separation also contributed to the decrease, but in lesser measure.[2]

That fewer black women are marrying has substantially undermined their socioeconomic well-being. The number of women having babies out of wedlock has grown considerably. This in turn has been the main cause of the tripling in the number of black families headed by women since 1940 and is a major source of the persistently large gap between family incomes of blacks and whites.[3] Half of all households headed by women are poor. Children from these families have lower cognitive abilities and fewer years of schooling. They have less desirable jobs and lower incomes and are more likely to be poor as adults. Daughters from such households are more likely to form female-headed households themselves.[4] Thus fall-

Our research was supported in part by grants from the National Institute of Child Health and Human Development, the National Science Foundation, and the Institute for Research on Poverty of the University of Wisconsin. Computations were performed using the facilities of the Center for Demography and Ecology at the University of Wisconsin, Madison, which are supported by the Center for Population Research of the National Institute of Child Health and Human Development (HD-5876). The authors are grateful to Judith Seltzer for helpful comments on an earlier draft of the paper and to Julia Gray, Cheryl Knobeloch, Linzhu Tian, and Meei-Shenn Tzeng for research assistance.

1. Espenshade (1985)
2. Garfinkel and McLanahan (1986); and Sweet and Bumpass (1987).
3. Espenshade (1985); Garfinkel and McLanahan (1986); and Farley (1984).
4. See Garfinkel and McLanahan (1986) for a review of the literature.

ing marriage rates have been an important contributor to high rates of poverty among blacks.

In *The Truly Disadvantaged,* William Julius Wilson argued that blacks have been marrying less because labor market conditions for young black men steadily grew worse in the 1970s and 1980s. As rates of employment for young black men and their rates of labor force participation dropped, he argued, the number of attractive potential marriage partners for black women also decreased. His evidence is the decrease in the ratio of marriageable (employed) black men to black women of the same age since the 1950s. This decline is particularly large for blacks in their teens and early twenties.[5]

An alternative view is that the changes in marriage rates have been caused by improvements in the economic position of black women.[6] Since the 1950s their average earnings have increased substantially relative to those of black men. Such changes may have led black women to depend less on marriage for financial security, and marriage has to that extent become less attractive and has led to greater female "independence."

Both arguments focus on changes in blacks' labor market position, ignoring other important changes in the socioeconomic situation of young blacks, especially their rates of school enrollment, which have risen significantly since 1940. Students have lower marriage rates than nonstudents, in part because they are less likely to be employed and, when employed, have lower earnings. Birthrates are also high among black students. Increases in school enrollment may therefore have also contributed to the increase in births to unmarried women.

The total effect of increases in school enrollment on marriage is complex and difficult to predict, however, because higher enrollments eventually lead to higher average levels of educational attainment. Additional schooling improves a person's marriageability, partly because it is an important indicator of future economic success. But whether increases in the overall level of education raise the overall marriage rate is unclear. Among women, higher educational attainment may contribute to greater economic independence and a lower likelihood of marrying.

This paper investigates the effects of labor market and educational trends on marriage rates since 1940. We find some support for Wilson's hypothesis. Changes in the employment of young black men explain about 20 percent of the decline in their marriage rates since 1960, but the

---

5. Wilson (1987), pp. 84–89.
6. Espenshade (1985); Farley and Bianchi (1987); and Farley (1988).

changes are simply not large enough to account for much more.[7] In addition, the earnings of young black men have increased substantially, which should have increased their rates of marriage and offset much of the effect of decreased employment.

Employment rates for black women have remained relatively stable since World War II, and their earnings have increased both absolutely and relative to those of black men. The increase however, seems to have had little effect on marriage rates. Higher earnings may enhance a woman's attractiveness in the marriage market but also decrease her incentive to marry. Our results suggest that these effects offset each other.

Changes in school enrollment have had varying effects on the marriage rates of young adults. For young men, the changes have had little effect except among black teenagers, for whom increased school enrollment explains about 12 percent of the decline in their marriage rates since 1960. For women under the age of 24, increases in enrollment account for 13 to 29 percent of the decline in marriage rates. The effects of educational attainment on marriage are also mixed. For black women older than age 20, higher levels of educational attainment lead to higher rates of marriage. In fact, their increased years of schooling since 1940 would, in the absence of offsetting changes, have raised marriage rates.

Three Hypotheses about Marriage

We consider three broad hypotheses about decreases in marriage rates: William Julius Wilson's "male marriageable pool" hypothesis; Thomas Espenshade's, Reynolds Farley's, and Suzanne Bianchi's "female independence" hypothesis; and the schooling hypothesis.

The Supply of Marriageable Men

The current and prospective economic statuses of men have always influenced their position in the marriage market.[8] When economic prospects are poor, marriages occur later and less frequently.[9] Economic deprivation may also increase rates of separation and divorce. Since World War II the socioeconomic position of blacks has improved both absolutely and relative to that of whites in terms of educational attainment,

7. Our results are similar to those of Ellwood and Rodda (1990), who use different data and methods.
8. England and Farkas (1986).
9. Hajnal (1965).

economic returns of schooling, and earnings for most age groups but worsened since 1970 in terms of withdrawal from the labor force, relative family income, and earnings for teenagers.[10]

Wilson argued that marriage rates respond mainly to the employment position of young men. This argument is tentatively supported by the parallel trends in employment among young black men and rates of marriage for blacks, both of which declined gradually in the 1960s and rapidly in the 1970s. He showed that the ratio of employed black men to women of the same age, his "male marriageable pool" index, has fallen since the 1960s.[11] The decline of the index among the young is, however, partly the result of rising school enrollment. Increases in enrollment explain almost half of the drop in employment between 1964 and 1981 for black men between the ages of 16 and 19. The increases also explain 20 to 25 percent of the decline among black men between the ages of 20 and 24.[12] Rising enrollments have had little impact on the index for men older than 25; it has declined far less than their rate of marriage.

In its simplest form, Wilson's argument also implies that marriage rates for employed black men should *increase* as they age because of their more favorable position in the marriage market. But this has not occurred. Rates of marriage have declined for employed black men as well as those without jobs.[13]

Women's Incentives to Marry

Some social scientists also consider the improved economic independence of women incompatible with universal and stable marriage. Thomas Espenshade and Lenore Weitzman have argued that marriage contracts are gradually shifting away from permanent commitment and toward short-term involvement.[14] Valerie Oppenheimer has added that women's economic independence increases uncertainty in the marriage market.[15] Uncertainty about their own career prospects compounds the uncertainty about the economic prospects of prospective spouses that women in the marriage market have traditionally faced, leading to delays in marriage, somewhat higher rates of cohabitation, and, in the short run,

10. Farley (1984); Mare and Winship (1984); and Smith and Welch (1986).
11. Wilson (1987); and Bennett, Bloom, and Craig (1989).
12. Mare and Winship (1984).
13. Jencks (1988).
14. Espenshade (1985); and Weitzman (1981).
15. Oppenheimer (1988).

higher rates of divorce, although the uncertainty is consistent with wide-spread and stable marriage.

Some of these observers have also stated that increases in the economic independence of black women have lowered rates of marriage. At first glance the argument is puzzling; the percentage of black unmarried women who work has remained relatively stable since 1940, except for declines among the youngest women. For those who do work, however, wages have increased relative to those of black men.[16] The higher a woman's earnings and the greater her permanent commitment to the work force relative to her husband's, the less likely she is to remain married.[17] This finding suggests that women whose earnings are high relative to those of their potential husbands may also be less likely to marry at all. But although rising wages may have reduced black women's economic need to marry, the higher wages may also have made them more attractive to prospective husbands.[18] Whether this has indeed happened depends on whether men, like women, are attracted to partners who have good labor market prospects.

School Enrollment and Later Marriages

Students are less likely to marry than nonstudents. Those who have recently left school may also be less likely to marry than those who have been out of school for several years, because they may need some time to find stable employment or a suitable spouse.[19] Increases in enrollment are therefore likely to reduce marriage rates more among teenagers and young adults. Because women marry younger and closer to the time they leave school, the effect of increased enrollment may be greater for them than for men. In due course, however, rising enrollment leads to increased educational attainment, which may make both men and women more likely to marry because they probably are able to get better jobs.

Data

To investigate trends in marrying we used the 1 percent Public Use Microdata Samples (PUMS) of the 1940–80 censuses and the March and June Current Population Surveys (CPS) for 1985–87. The data provide

16. Farley (1984, 1988).
17. Espenshade (1985).
18. Preston and Richards (1975).
19. Oppenheimer (1988).

large numbers of observations and comparable measurement. Our multivariate analyses of entry into marriage were based on persons age 16 to 39 who had never been married or who entered their first marriage during the year before the census. With this focus we analyzed the association between people's characteristics and the rates at which they marry rather than simply whether or not they were married, which reflects both marital disruption and entry into marriage at an unspecified time before the census.[20] Because the 1940 census records only age in years (and not months) of first marriage, for 1940 we included persons who entered their first marriage when their age was the same as or one year less than their age at the census date.[21] Our descriptions of trends in marriage are also based on the 1940–80 censuses and the 1985–87 March and June CPS. To obtain stable estimates, we pooled the CPS estimates for these three years.[22]

20. We focused on first marriages because the census provides no information on the timing (age) of later marriages, and the determinants of entry into first marriage may be distinct from those for remarriage.

21. By this procedure our sample included all marriages occuring during the twelve months prior to the 1940 census, plus about one-half of marriages occurring thirteen to twenty-four months before the 1940 census. In our analysis of marriage rates, however, we adjusted the number of marriages to estimate an annual marriage rate comparable to our estimates for 1950–80. If the marriage rate was uniform between April 1938 and March 1940, we observed about 50 percent more marriages than occurred between April 1939 and March 1940. Thus, we deflated observed marriages by one-third, both for the calculation of rates (table 1) and multivariate models (table 2).

Although each PUMS file is a 1 percent sample, the 1940 persons included in our analysis were less than 1 percent of those marrying just before the 1940 census. We included only recently married persons for whom we could ascertain age at first marriage. Age at first marriage was obtained only for couples in which the wife was part of the 5 percent person sample within the 1940 census (Bureau of Census, 1973). In the 1940 PUMS, all households contained at least one person who was part of the 5 percent sample, but not all sample households contained an ever-married woman who was a sample person (Bureau of the Census, 1983). Only persons from the latter households were included in our sample. The sampling rate for these persons was about 0.4 percent.

Similarly, the 1950 census obtained information on duration of marriage only for persons who were part of the 3.33 percent person sample (Bureau of the Census, 1973). Only persons who were part of the 1950 PUMS and the 3.33 percent person sample were included in our analysis. The sampling rate for this procedure was about 0.3 percent (Bureau of the Census, 1984).

22. We used the March surveys to estimate marital status and the June surveys to estimate rates of entry into marriage. The CPS provides insufficient information to permit us to extend the multivariate analysis to the 1985–87 period. The March surveys contain comparable measures on earnings and weeks worked but no information on age at marriage and school enrollment. The June surveys contain information on age at marriage and enrollment but not earnings and weeks worked.

Trends in Marital Status and Marriage Rates

Trends in marital status and entry into marriage from 1940 to the mid-1980s are summarized in table 1. The percentage of married black men has declined since 1940 within every age group. Among those 20 to 23 years old, for example, it fell from over 30 percent to just under 10 percent, a result of changes both in marriage rates and rates of marital disruption by separation, divorce, and death. For black men, divorce and separation break up far more marriages than do the deaths of their wives, but for those under age 30, rates of divorce and separation have not increased since 1940. Indeed, since 1960 those rates have declined. For black men age 30 to 39, however, the prevalence of divorce and separation has nearly doubled.

Among black men 20 to 23 years old the share of those who are single has increased from about 60 percent in 1940 to nearly 90 percent in the mid-1980s. Since 1950, the percentages of men who have never married has more than doubled among those age 24 to 29 and 30 to 39, and marriage has virtually disappeared among teenagers. The major source of the decreasing percentages of young black men who are married has been the drop in rates of entry into marriages. Except for men in their thirties, marital disruption has not reduced the percentage of those married; the prevalence of divorce and separation has declined because the percentage of men who are married has declined.

Trends in marital status for black women closely mirror those for black men except that declines in the percentage married and increases in percentages never married have occurred more dramatically among those age 16 to 19 and 20 to 23. Nearly 20 percent of those 16 to 19 were married in 1940; less than 2 percent were in 1985–87. These sex differences mainly reflect the historically lower ages at which women marry.

Trends in marital status among whites have followed the same pattern as trends among blacks since 1960 but have been less dramatic. Between 1940 and 1960 the average age at marriage fell and the percentages of persons who were married rose steadily. In most age and sex groups, percentages of people currently married and ever married peaked in 1960, returning in the mid-1980s to levels similar to those observed in 1940. This development was in marked contrast to blacks, for whom percentages of those never married in 1985–87 far exceeded the percentages in 1940. In 1940, for every age and sex group, whites exceeded blacks in percentages never married; by the 1980s, just the opposite was true.

Trends in marital status reflect the cumulative impact of changes in

TABLE I. Marital Status and Marriage Rates, by Race, Sex, and Age, Selected Years, 1940–80

Percent

Age and year	Black marital status[a]					White marital status[a]				
	Married	Widowed	Divorced/ separated	Never married	Marriage rate[b]	Married	Widowed	Divorced/ separated	Never married	Marriage rate[b]
Men										
Age 16–19										
1940	3.1	0.1	1.2	95.7	2.1	1.5	0.1	0.6	97.9	1.1
1950	3.1	0.1	1.7	95.1	2.1	2.3	0.1	1.1	96.6	1.7
1960	3.1	0.0	1.6	95.2	3.3	3.7	0.0	1.1	95.1	3.2
1970	3.3	0.1	1.6	95.0	2.6	3.9	0.1	1.0	95.1	3.1
1980	0.9	0.0	1.3	97.8	1.4	2.5	0.0	0.9	96.6	2.3
1985–87	0.5	0.0	0.3	99.1	0.1	1.5	0.0	0.3	98.2	0.6
Age 20–23										
1940	31.5	0.5	5.4	62.6	12.1	20.5	0.2	2.0	77.3	8.8
1950	31.3	0.4	7.4	60.9	7.6	28.7	0.1	3.4	67.7	10.4
1960	31.2	0.2	9.2	59.5	15.6	38.0	0.1	4.6	57.4	18.0
1970	28.6	0.2	9.3	61.9	15.7	35.3	0.2	5.0	59.6	18.0
1980	13.0	0.1	5.1	81.7	6.5	24.3	0.0	4.6	71.0	11.0
1985–87	9.7	0.1	1.6	88.5	2.1	19.1	0.1	2.6	78.2	6.1
Age 24–29										
1940	59.1	1.2	9.2	30.6	10.7	56.2	0.3	3.6	39.9	13.1
1950	61.2	0.7	11.9	26.3	10.8	68.3	0.2	4.3	26.8	14.2
1960	58.5	0.5	13.8	27.3	16.8	72.3	0.2	5.2	22.3	20.5
1970	58.3	0.7	13.2	27.8	18.6	72.3	0.2	6.4	21.1	23.1
1980	38.9	0.2	15.3	45.6	11.3	56.3	0.1	9.9	33.7	15.1
1985–87	35.4	0.1	8.5	56.1	4.7	51.9	0.1	8.0	40.1	12.1

Women

Age 30–39

1940	69.4	2.5	10.9	17.3	5.3	76.5	0.9	4.6	18.1	7.2
1950	77.0	1.3	11.8	10.0	4.8	86.1	0.4	3.8	9.7	8.3
1960	68.8	1.2	16.0	14.0	11.7	84.4	0.3	5.3	10.1	10.3
1970	68.8	1.2	15.5	14.5	11.1	84.4	0.4	6.3	8.9	10.9
1980	56.9	0.7	22.6	19.8	8.8	76.7	0.2	11.8	11.3	10.4
1985–87	57.3	0.4	18.0	24.4	6.6	74.4	0.2	11.4	14.0	12.0

Age 16–19

1940	19.4	0.5	3.8	76.2	12.6	12.1	0.2	1.3	86.5	8.3
1950	16.2	0.4	6.5	76.9	7.4	14.0	0.2	2.7	83.1	7.6
1960	14.7	0.2	5.0	80.0	9.6	16.9	0.1	3.1	80.0	10.4
1970	9.7	0.3	4.5	85.5	7.1	11.9	0.2	2.8	85.1	8.3
1980	3.8	0.1	2.0	94.1	3.1	9.3	0.1	2.0	88.6	6.1
1985–87	1.8	0.0	0.4	97.0	0.5	6.4	0.0	1.3	92.3	2.5

Age 20–23

1940	51.0	2.0	10.2	36.9	13.6	44.5	0.4	3.4	51.8	14.2
1950	45.7	1.1	16.2	37.0	14.3	55.2	0.4	5.9	38.6	15.7
1960	45.6	0.6	16.0	37.8	20.1	62.3	0.2	6.6	30.9	26.0
1970	37.1	1.1	15.5	46.4	16.8	53.2	0.6	7.7	38.6	24.8
1980	20.4	0.3	9.2	70.1	8.1	39.8	0.2	7.5	52.5	15.4
1985–87	13.8	0.1	5.5	80.7	2.6	33.8	0.1	5.8	60.3	11.0

TABLE 1. (continued)

Women

Age and year	Black marital status[a]					White marital status[a]				
	Married	Widowed	Divorced/ separated	Never married	Marriage rate[b]	Married	Widowed	Divorced/ separated	Never married	Marriage rate[b]
Age 24–29										
1940	61.8	4.0	14.3	20.0	6.8	69.8	1.0	4.6	24.7	12.0
1950	63.5	2.1	18.8	15.7	7.7	80.0	0.7	5.7	13.6	13.1
1960	60.3	1.5	21.3	16.9	16.8	82.9	0.5	6.0	10.4	19.9
1970	53.9	1.9	21.7	22.5	12.1	78.5	0.9	8.2	12.4	20.0
1980	37.8	0.9	21.6	39.6	8.5	65.7	0.4	12.5	21.4	15.6
1985–87	31.8	0.6	14.3	53.2	4.6	61.5	0.4	11.8	26.3	14.6
Age 30–39										
1940	63.5	11.2	15.2	10.1	4.5	78.4	2.7	5.8	13.1	4.3
1950	70.5	5.6	17.1	6.9	7.9	86.6	1.6	5.1	6.8	6.9
1960	63.5	4.2	23.7	8.7	9.1	86.3	1.4	6.3	6.1	7.7
1970	57.9	4.3	26.2	11.6	7.3	83.6	1.5	8.9	6.1	8.2
1980	47.2	3.2	30.6	19.0	5.8	76.8	1.0	14.5	7.7	8.3
1985–87	43.1	2.3	29.2	25.4	1.2	73.6	0.9	16.0	9.5	8.0

SOURCE: See text.

a. Married denotes married spouse present; divorced/separated includes divorced, separated, and married, spouse absent. Percentages may not sum to 100 because of rounding.

b. Rate is annual number of first marriages per 100 never-married persons in age, sex, and race group.

TABLE 2. Labor Market and Education Indicators, by Race, Sex, and Age, Selected Years, 1940–80

Percent unless otherwise specified

	Black					White				
Indicator	1940	1950	1960	1970	1980	1940	1950	1960	1970	1980
Men										
Age 16–19										
Earnings ($/week)[a]	30.4	45.7	52.5	80.0	65.2	32.7	65.3	86.4	108.4	105.6
Employment probability[b]	.498	.521	.357	.292	.272	.373	.455	.454	.443	.470
12 grades	4.7	6.7	10.6	16.0	19.0	18.3	19.2	19.5	23.2	25.2
More than 12 grades	0.9	1.3	1.4	3.5	3.4	4.6	4.8	5.0	7.3	5.5
Enrolled	33.3	45.7	59.1	61.8	70.9	50.4	57.8	67.1	73.2	71.2
Age 20–23										
Earnings ($/week)[a]	48.1	80.6	106.6	150.8	151.4	82.7	121.7	165.6	195.3	209.2
Employment probability[b]	.662	.693	.660	.630	.560	.731	.715	.747	.700	.708
12 grades	7.0	16.1	29.6	38.6	42.0	32.8	32.6	36.0	34.2	41.2
More than 12 grades	4.5	8.5	10.3	21.8	27.7	16.9	25.6	33.3	51.2	43.8
Enrolled	4.3	14.0	14.9	17.7	23.5	11.0	26.0	27.8	35.4	32.8

TABLE 2. (*continued*)

Indicator	Black					White				
	1940	1950	1960	1970	1980	1940	1950	1960	1970	1980
					Men					
Age 24–29										
Earnings ($/week)[a]	59.6	103.6	137.0	187.1	188.5	110.8	142.7	206.2	261.8	261.1
Employment probability[b]	.682	.685	.695	.701	.630	.808	.767	.808	.808	.809
12 grades	6.8	13.6	21.9	35.0	38.9	25.8	29.4	30.3	32.0	30.6
More than 12 grades	4.2	10.3	13.3	18.0	33.6	21.4	29.0	37.8	47.9	57.6
Enrolled	1.4	12.7	8.9	7.4	13.1	4.1	18.3	16.1	14.8	17.2
Age 30–39										
Earnings ($/week)[a]	67.3	106.3	140.3	177.5	196.6	115.7	148.1	216.1	272.7	281.3
Employment probability[b]	.640	.624	.643	.680	.605	.757	.804	.795	.786	.801
12 grades	3.8	13.0	17.8	24.6	33.5	16.0	25.7	26.4	29.1	25.0
More than 12 grades	5.0	8.7	9.5	12.8	27.6	16.4	17.8	27.5	35.5	58.5
Enrolled	.8	0	2.5	3.6	7.8	1.5	0	4.0	4.9	8.7
					Women					
Age 16–19										
Earnings ($/week)[a]	16.7	29.3	36.7	57.8	50.1	20.5	49.4	66.4	76.4	79.9
Employment probability[b]	.258	.221	.188	.195	.218	.217	.316	.318	.329	.433
12 grades	9.8	11.5	15.1	21.1	23.5	25.9	25.6	23.7	26.9	28.0
More than 12 grades	2.4	2.8	2.7	4.9	6.1	5.5	5.8	5.6	7.9	7.3
Enrolled	36.8	58.1	60.8	62.9	72.4	49.2	60.3	67.7	71.8	73.6

Age 20–23										
Earnings ($/week)[a]	32.3	59.6	77.5	129.0	111.4	58.8	105.5	137.9	165.4	155.6
Employment probability[b]	.489	.469	.479	.532	.474	.573	.685	.655	.651	.698
12 grades	15.3	22.2	34.7	41.8	39.3	45.7	45.0	43.1	37.2	36.9
More than 12 grades	9.0	17.3	18.7	29.5	39.2	19.5	29.9	37.5	53.0	54.6
Enrolled	6.7	18.7	17.2	20.2	29.8	10.5	19.2	23.5	30.2	35.7
Age 24–29										
Earnings ($/week)[a]	44.9	72.1	93.2	151.3	159.0	83.7	132.4	170.7	222.8	216.0
Employment probability[b]	.614	.603	.554	.597	.604	.672	.765	.746	.775	.814
12 grades	10.8	21.4	27.0	37.1	38.7	36.4	43.2	38.4	34.3	28.8
More than 12 grades	11.4	13.2	16.0	19.4	38.7	25.4	26.0	34.4	48.5	62.4
Enrolled	1.6	5.6	6.3	5.6	13.0	3.4	6.9	9.5	9.4	16.8
Age 30–39										
Earnings ($/week)[a]	42.6	79.4	93.9	133.6	174.3	100.7	125.3	172.7	219.7	244.7
Employment probability[b]	.621	.627	.630	.602	.628	.721	.739	.760	.747	.794
12 grades	7.6	13.0	22.5	29.5	38.1	26.1	33.6	38.0	36.4	28.9
More than 12 grades	9.6	11.3	12.9	14.0	29.9	29.4	26.3	27.6	34.2	56.1
Enrolled	1.4	0	2.9	4.0	8.8	2.5	0	3.1	5.6	10.7

SOURCE: See text.
a. Constant 1979 dollars.
b. Estimated expected probability of employment, which is similar to observed proportions employed at the date of each census.

rates of marriage and marital dissolution. For persons under age 24, a drop in rates of entry into marriage has been the main source of decline since 1940 in percentages of persons who are married. The marriage rate columns of table 1 show the percentages of men and women who married twelve months before each census and Current Population Survey. Except for teenage women, marriage rates for black men and women of all ages increased between 1940 and 1960 and then fell precipitously. Among black women age 20 to 23, for example, the annual rate dropped from 20.1 percent in 1960 to 2.6 percent in 1985–87. In the four broad age groups in table 1, the modal age of marriage was 24 to 29 in 1960 and 30 to 39 in 1985–87 for black women.

Trends in marriage rates for whites resemble those for blacks, but the declines are less pronounced, so that the race difference in rates has widened. Among white women age 20 to 23 the rate exceeded that for black women by about 30 percent in 1960, but by the mid-1980s it was more than four times greater.

If the extremely low rates of marriage in 1985–87 persist, and if rates for marital dissolution remain constant, the relative numbers of people who are married will continue to decline, the number never married will continue to grow, and the number divorced or separated will continue to decline.

Labor Market and Schooling Status of Young Adults

Earnings and employment changed substantially between 1959 and 1979. Table 2 shows that average weekly earnings (in constant 1979 dollars) rose by factors of two to three. Most of the growth occurred before 1970. Real weekly earnings were stable from 1970 to 1980, except among black teenagers, for whom they declined. For blacks age 20 or older, earnings growth was somewhat more rapid than for whites, resulting in some convergence.

Among black men in each age group the employment rate has also declined, but especially for those age 16 to 23 and between 1960 and 1980. The decline was greatest for teenagers, although this was largely the result of their increasing rates of school enrollment.[23] In addition, the labor market position of young black men eroded. For black women, employment rates were essentially stable between 1940 and 1980 because increases in unemployment offset increases in labor force participation.

23. Mare and Winship (1984).

Employment rates for white men were generally stable with the exception of teenagers, for whom the rates have increased since 1940, particularly among students. Employment rates for white women increased substantially between 1970 and 1980.

Table 2 also shows that enrollment rates grew rapidly since 1940, especially among blacks and women. For teenagers, black and white rates converged to near parity by 1980, despite the somewhat lower levels of educational attainment still experienced by blacks. For older groups, black enrollment rates were less than half those of whites in 1940 and grew to approximately 75 percent of the white rates by 1980. Rising school enrollment unambiguously reduces rates of marriage because students delay marrying until schooling is completed. The dramatic increase in enrollment from 1940 to 1980, therefore, may be a source of decline in marriage rates for younger groups.

Because enrollment rates have risen, educational attainment has also risen. Within each period, table 2 shows that the percentages of young persons with twelve or more years of schooling were lower for blacks than for whites. Educational growth, however, was more rapid for blacks, leading to narrower racial differentials in schooling in 1980 than there were in 1940. Among women age 24 to 29, for example, only 22 percent of blacks but more than 60 percent of whites had at least a high school degree in 1940. By 1980 almost 80 percent of black women and 90 percent of white women in this age group had a high school degree.

Labor Market and Schooling Effects on Entry into Marriage

Determinants of Entry into Marriage

We estimated school enrollment, educational attainment, weekly earnings, and employment status expected after marriage on the probability of entry into marriage from 1940 to 1980. The equation reported in appendix table A-1 is based on a logistic regression that also includes dummy variables for census year and two-year age groups. Although we experimented with numerous model specifications, we report a single additive model for these effects within each age group, race, and sex.[24]

One variable, expected employment status, requires explanation. Marriage decisions are affected by the employment status people expect

24. We considered models that included separate effects for labor markets and schooling for each year. We found no large or systematic change in these effects over time.

after marriage. Their actual employment status after marriage is observed, but this is a consequence as well as a cause of entry into marriage.
To avoid this problem, we used an estimate of employment potential
based on educational attainment and work experience during the previous year, characteristics that are not affected by marriage. We constructed
this measure by regressing the employment status for all respondents at
the time of the census on their weeks of work during the previous year
and their educational attainment.[25]

For men, both expected employment and earnings positively affected
the marriage rate at all ages, although the effects were somewhat larger
for men less than 24 years old. For example, a 0.1 increase in the expected
probability of employment in the census year raised the odds of marriage
in the twelve months leading up to the census by about 25 percent for
black men age 20 to 23 and by about 15 percent for those age 30 to 39.[26]

25. An equivalent view of this method is that "weeks worked last year" and "educational attainment" are instrumental variables for current employment status. This enabled
us to estimate the effects of employment on marriage, while taking into account their potential simultaneous relationship.

The measure was constructed as follows. Using a logit model estimated over the five
censuses, we predicted the probability of employment at the date of the census from age,
educational attainment, weeks worked during the preceding year, and census year. Given
the estimated logit coefficients, we predicted the probability of employment for each person.

We estimated the logit model for current employment separately for each race-sex group
and, within these groups, separately for four age categories (16 to 19, 20 to 23, 24 to 29,
and 30 to 39). The independent variables included three categories of weeks worked (fewer
than 20, 20 to 39, and more than 39), three categories of educational attainment (fewer
than 12, 12, and more than 12 years), categorical variables for whatever two-year age
groups were included in the four broad age groups, and five categories for year. Within each
age-race-sex group, the model included main effects for education, weeks worked, age, and
year, plus interactions between census year and each of the other three variables in the
model.

The predicted probability entered the models for marriage as a continuous variable. The
schooling and employment measures differ in the degree to which they can be precisely
timed relative to marriage. The educational attainment of most persons does not change
between their date of marriage and the census date. The census measures the number of
weeks worked, and earnings summarize work experience between 4 and 16 months before
the census (for example, January 1969 to December 1969), whereas our sample marriages
occurred between 0 and 12 months before the census (for example, April 1969 to April
1970). For some persons, therefore, the temporal order of these measures and marriage is
unknown. Finally, school enrollment status was measured at the census date and thus followed recent changes in marital status. This may result in some overstatement of the effect
of school enrollment status on the entry into marriage.

26. This percentage is calculated as 100 times the difference in the exponent of
the amount due to the increase, that is, $\exp(\beta \times 0.1) = \exp(2.179 \times 0.1) = 1.243$,
minus the base amount, $\exp(\beta \times 0) = 1$. Stated as a single expression this is
$100[\exp(2.179 \times 0.1) - 1] = 24.3$.

A $100 increase in weekly earnings raised the odds of marriage by about 30 percent for black men age 20 to 23 and by about 20 percent for those age 30 to 39. The employment and earnings effects for white men were remarkably similar to those for black men in every age group. For both races, these effects were large.

The effects of expected employment and earnings were much weaker for women than for men and differ by race and age. For black women less than 50 years old, expected employment prospects had almost no effect on the chances of marrying. For those age 30 to 39, a 0.1 point increase in the probability of employment reduced the odds of marriage by about 4 percent. High weekly earnings during the previous year increased black women's chances of marrying, but the effect was small both absolutely and relative to the corresponding effect for men. These results suggest that for black women good labor market prospects have two offsetting effects, increasing their attractiveness to potential husbands but making them feel less pressure to marry.

For white women, good employment prospects reduced the chances of marriage, and the effect increased with age. A 0.1 increase in the expected probability of employment reduced the odds of marriage by 3 percent for women age 16 to 19. This effect increased to 13 percent for those age 30 to 39. Among those age 30 to 39 the negative effect of employment on marriage was as large as the corresponding positive effect for white men. It is not clear why employment should be negative for white women but neutral or positive for black women. The effect of earnings on the odds of marriage was as weak for white women as for blacks.

The labor market's effects on marriage were much larger for men than women. Both employment and high earnings raised men's readiness to marry and their ability to attract a wife. This is consistent with Wilson's claim that employment is a critical aspect of a man's marriageability. But for a woman, labor market success may increase marriage prospects while it reduces the economic need for marriage.

School Enrollment and Educational Attainment. For most groups, students were less likely to marry than those who were out of school, even when employment and earnings were controlled for, although this difference waned with age and was stronger for women than for men. Among 20- to 23-year-old black men, the odds of marriage for students were less than one-half those for nonstudents. For black women of the same age, the odds were less than one-third those for nonstudents. The effects of school enrollment were negligible for 24- to 39-year-old men, but substantial for all age groups of women. These results suggest that although young adults typically finish school before marriage, men are more likely than women to combine schooling with marriage, at least after labor market factors are taken into account.[27]

White high school graduates were less likely than high school dropouts to marry, although teenagers with some college were somewhat more likely to marry than those with just a high school degree. Among black teenagers the pattern was similar but the effects were weaker. The effects of educational attainment weakened with age for men, although for white men 30 to 39 years old with some college, odds of marrying remained about 15 percent lower than for high school dropouts. For women age 20 to 39, greater educational attainment increased the marriage rate.

These patterns suggest that long-term increases in educational attainment may have contributed to declines in the marriage rate among white teenagers since 1960. Among blacks, however, the within-year effect of educational attainment was weak for men at all ages and for teenage women. For women 20 to 39 years old, moreover, education improved marriage prospects, suggesting that educational trends have tended to raise teenage marriage rates.

Residual Trends in Marriage Rates. Table A-1 also shows the additive effects of census year on the odds of marriage after labor market and schooling factors are considered. The net effects of year on marriage resemble the trends in marriage rates documented in table 1. For all groups except teenage black women, the net odds of marriage peaked or reached a plateau between 1960 and 1970 and then declined. The net changes for 1960–80 were substantial for most age groups and were greater for blacks than for whites. For 20- to 23-year-old black men, for example, the odds of marriage in 1980 were only 40 percent of the odds in 1960. Despite the strong within-year effects of several of the labor market and schooling factors included in the logit models, the net year effects suggest that trends in these factors did not account for trends in marriage.

27. The large effects for women may reflect their tendency to leave school when they marry rather than solely the inhibiting effect of school attendance on marriage. The census measures current enrollment status whereas entry into marriage occurs during the year before the census. The estimated effects of enrollment status, therefore, may be somewhat overstated.

Contributions to Change in the Odds of Entry into Marriage

Appendix table A-2 shows the relative contributions of various influences to the changes in the odds of marriage from 1960 to 1980, the period when most of the decline in marriage rates occurred. The breakdown is based on the coefficients in table A-1 and the means in table 2. We omitted those groups in which change in the marriage rate was less than one marriage for each one hundred people who had never married.

Employment and Earnings. The downward trend in the expected probability of employment was an important component of the decrease in marriage rates for black men of every age group. For those age 20 to 23, who experienced the largest change in marriage rates, about 20 percent of the decrease in the odds of marriage was attributable to trends in employment. However, a significant part of the change engendered by declining employment rates was offset by growth in real earnings between 1960 and 1980. Indeed, for men age 30 to 39, earnings growth did more to increase marriage rates than reduced employment did to reduce them. The overall effect of labor market trends on the marriage rates of black men was modest.

The contribution of labor market changes to the marriage rates of white men was even smaller. For 20- to 23-year-olds, employment accounted for about 14 percent of the decline in the odds of marriage but was entirely offset by growth in average earnings. For 24- to 29-year-olds, employment changes had no effect; the growth in earnings, however, implied significant increases in the odds of marriage.[28]

Trends in employment and earnings among women had little effect on their marriage rates. Labor market factors had negligible net effects on rates for black women within census years, implying that changes in average levels of employment and earnings between censuses did not strongly affect changes in marriage rates. For 24- to 29-year-old white women the trend in expected employment probabilities accounted for about 23 percent of the decline in marriage rates. For older and younger white women, labor market effects were very small.

28. A hypothesis we have not tested is that relative earnings within the black community, not absolute earnings, affect marriage rates. In such a case long-term increases in average earnings would have no effect on marriage rates. This hypothesis would not change our conclusions about the importance of trends in employment.

Overall, employment trends had relatively small effects on changes in rates of marriage. About 20 percent of the changes in marriage rates for black men from 1960 to 1980 are attributable to decreasing employment rates, but much of this change was offset by increased earnings. For black women and whites, employment effects were negligible.

School Enrollment and Educational Attainment. Table A-2 shows that increases in school enrollment and educational attainment accounted for little of the trend in marriage for men. For black teenage men, about 12 percent of the small decline in marriage rates was due to rising enrollment, but enrollment and attainment did not affect marriage trends in other groups. For women, however, school enrollment trends were important to the decrease in rates of marriage. For black women younger than age 24 and white women younger than 30, between 13 and 29 percent of the decline in marriage rates was due to increased school enrollment. For women older than 24, however, growth in educational attainment seems to have led to large increases in rates of marriage. Among black women age 24 to 29, for example, increases in educational attainment completely offset other changes in schooling and the labor market that might have accounted for the decline in marriage rates.

Women's marriage trends are more responsive to changes in enrollment and educational attainment than the corresponding trends for men because women typically marry earlier and marriage and schooling are more likely to be competing activities. Long-term growth in their enrollment rates and educational attainment, therefore, is more likely to alter the marriage behavior of women than of men.

Taken together, the labor market and schooling factors considered here accounted for only modest portions of the decline in marriage rates between 1960 and 1980. The significant residual changes for all ages of both black and white men and women indicate that changes in marriage rates were largely the result of factors not measured in the census.[29]

29. For example, we have relied on a simple specification of labor market effects on marriage. But work experience, wage history, occupational position, local labor market conditions, and other elements that we have not included may also have had effects. In addition, a person's propensity to marry is affected not only by his or her own traits but also those of potential partners. The absolute and relative frequencies of potential partners with varying labor market prospects may affect rates of marriage. But given the modest and sometimes offsetting effects of those aspects of employment and earnings that we have measured, additional labor market factors are unlikely to affect marital trends significantly.

Conclusion

Our results suggest that socioeconomic factors cannot account for the drastic decreases in marriage rates during the past thirty years. It is necessary therefore to seek alternative explanations. Compared with their counterparts a generation ago, young people of both races now come of age much more uncertain about their future family life. Successive cohorts of young adults are increasingly likely to have been raised in unstable or disrupted marriages, and they themselves face higher probabilities of divorce. They are more likely to cohabit without marrying, to want few children or perhaps none, and to consider the separation of childbearing from marriage as feasible and socially acceptable. Therefore young adults may be more likely to view marriage with apprehension and skepticism. Each of these trends is interdependent with downward trends in rates of marriage and in itself requires explanation. But taken together they create a climate of expectations that may contribute to further decreases in marriage rates. Labor market conditions are catalysts for changes in marriage and family life, but a fuller understanding of marriage trends requires attention to the way that family trends, once set in motion, may continue by their own momentum.

References

Bennett, Neil G., David E. Bloom, and Patricia H. Craig. 1989. "The Divergence of Black and White Marriage Patterns." *American Journal of Sociology* 95 (November), pp. 692–722.

Bureau of the Census. 1973. "Population and Housing Inquiries in U.S. Decennial Censuses, 1790–1970." Working paper 39. Department of Commerce.

———. 1983. *Census of Population, 1940: Public Use Microdata Sample Technical Documentation.* Department of Commerce.

———. 1984. *Census of Population, 1950: Public Use Microdata Sample Technical Documentation.* Department of Commerce.

England, Paula, and George Farkas. 1986. *Households, Employment, and Gender: A Social, Economic, and Demographic View.* Aldine Press.

Ellwood, David T., and David Rodda. 1990. "The Hazards of Work and Marriage: The Influence of Male Employment on Marriage." Unpublished paper, Harvard University.

Espenshade, Thomas J. 1985. "Marriage Trends in America: Estimates, Implications, and Underlying Causes." *Population and Development Review* 11 (June), pp. 193–245.

Farley, Reynolds. 1984. *Blacks and Whites: Narrowing the Gap?* Harvard University Press.

————. 1988. "After the Starting Line: Blacks and Women in an Uphill Race." *Demography* 25 (November), pp. 477–95.

Farley, Reynolds, and Suzanne M. Bianchi. 1987. "The Growing Racial Difference in Marriage and Family Patterns." Research report 87–107. Population Studies Center, University of Michigan.

Garfinkel, Irwin, and Sara S. McLanahan. 1986. *Single Mothers and Their Children*. Washington: Urban Institute Press.

Hajnal, John. 1965. "European Marriage Patterns in Perspective." In *Population in History,* edited by D. V. Glass and D. E. C. Eversley. Aldine Press.

Hogan, Dennis P. 1981. *Transitions and Social Change*. Academic Press.

Jencks, Christopher. 1988. "Deadly Neighborhoods." *New Republic*, June 13, 1988, pp. 23–32.

Lerman, Robert I. 1988. "Employment Opportunities of Young Men and Family Formation." Paper prepared for a joint session of the American Economic Association and the National Economic Association.

Mare, Robert D., and Christopher Winship. 1984. "The Paradox of Lessening Racial Inequality and Joblessness Among Black Youth: Enrollment, Enlistment, and Employment, 1964–1981." *American Sociological Review* 49 (February), pp. 39–56.

Marini, Margaret M. 1978. "The Transition to Adulthood: Sex Differences in Educational Attainment and Age at Marriage." *American Sociological Review* 43 (August), pp. 483–507.

Oppenheimer, Valerie K. 1988. "A Theory of Marriage Timing." *American Journal of Sociology* 94 (November), pp. 563–91.

Preston, Samuel H., and Alan Thomas Richards. 1975. "The Influence of Women's Work Opportunities on Marriage Rates." *Demography* 12 (May), pp. 209–22.

Smith, James P., and Finis R. Welch. 1986. *Closing the Gap: Forty Years of Economic Progress for Blacks*. Santa Monica: Rand.

Sweet, James A., and Larry L. Bumpass. 1987. *American Families and Households*. Russell Sage Foundation.

Weitzman, Lenore. 1981. *The Marriage Contract*. Free Press.

Wilson, William Julius. 1987. *The Truly Disadvantaged: The Inner City, The Underclass, and Public Policy*. University of Chicago Press.

TABLE A-1. Logit Parameter Estimates for Models of Entry into Marriage

Parameter	Black men		White men		Black women		White women	
	β	SEª	β	SEª	β	SEª	β	SEª
Age 16–19								
Intercept	-5.416	.249	-5.941	.111	-1.596	.109	-1.760	.042
Age 16–17 (vs. 18–19)	.686	.116	.778	.046	.404	.065	.590	.026
12 grades (vs. <12)	-.185	.101	-.584	.033	-.146	.067	-.448	.024
>12 grades (vs. <12)	-.120	.240	-.180	.063	-.039	.135	-.395	.043
Enrolled (vs. not)	-1.030	.106	-1.727	.039	-2.153	.071	-2.953	.026
Weekly earnings (/100)	.290	.052	.340	.018	.147	.045	-.092	.012
Weekly earnings**2	-.014	.005	-.017	.002	-.020	.006	.002	.001
Expected employment	1.929	.156	2.154	.061	-.083	.125	-.267	.041
1950 (vs. 1940)	.023	.282	.455	.124	-.388	.151	.163	.056
1960 (vs. 1940)	.952	.228	1.308	.104	-.019	.111	.844	.043
1970 (vs. 1940)	.787	.231	1.411	.103	-.334	.110	.690	.043
1980 (vs. 1940)	.285	.237	.932	.104	-1.075	.116	.383	.044
scaled deviance/d.f.	672	930	2107	1827	863	829	5556	1570
# obs./ # marriages	28,401	636	201,307	5,459	27,547	1,696	185,948	15,053

TABLE A-I. (*continued*)

Parameter	Black men		White men		Black women		White women	
	β	SE[a]	β	SE[a]	β	SE[a]	β	SE[a]
Age 20–23								
Intercept	-3.478	.141	-4.028	.054	-1.780	.130	-1.367	.041
Age 20–21 (vs. 22–23)	-.202	.049	-.296	.016	.004	.050	-.107	.017
12 grades (vs. <12)	-.155	.059	-.345	.021	.129	.061	.228	.026
>12 grades (vs. <12)	-.072	.080	-.258	.024	.235	.073	.195	.028
Enrolled (vs. not)	-.726	.095	-.529	.024	-1.179	.085	-1.736	.028
Weekly earnings (/100)	.265	.027	.296	.009	.066	.026	.004	.010
Weekly earnings**2	-.010	.002	-.012	.001	-.002	.002	-.002	.001
Expected employment	2.179	.115	2.310	.044	.011	.091	-.542	.034
1950 (vs. 1940)	-.670	.166	.128	.051	.031	.170	.172	.051
1960 (vs. 1940)	.217	.117	.711	.040	.405	.131	.857	.039
1970 (vs. 1940)	.198	.118	.818	.040	.146	.129	.866	.038
1980 (vs. 1940)	-.682	.121	.137	.040	-.619	.130	.327	.038
scaled deviance/d.f.	1389	1353	4006	2459	1335	1124	7211	1907
# obs./# marriages	18,508	2,022	142,688	20,595	16,514	2,100	104,275	21,100

Age 24-29

Intercept	-3.479	.150	-3.523	.057	2.925	.201	-1.810	.055
Age 24-25 (vs. 28-29)	.138	.067	.250	.024	.344	.082	.398	.032
Age 26-27 (vs. 28-29)	.028	.072	.126	.025	.114	.089	.237	.034
12 grades (vs. <12)	.111	.066	-.096	.026	.327	.084	.391	.039
>12 grades (vs. <12)	.076	.076	-.185	.026	.507	.096	.549	.041
Enrolled (vs. not)	-.02	.094	-.041	.028	-.539	.128	-.918	.046
Weekly earnings (/100)	.174	.025	.199	.009	.085	.034	.054	.014
Weekly earnings**2	-.004	.002	-.008	.001	-.004	.003	-.005	.001
Expected employment	1.674	.116	1.707	.053	.034	.116	-1.036	.050
1950 (vs. 1940)	-.115	.173	.017	.050	.041	.265	.116	.066
1960 (vs. 1940)	.297	.129	.323	.038	.878	.194	.577	.051
1970 (vs. 1940)	.292	.129	.403	.038	.401	.195	.526	.049
1980 (vs. 1940)	-.221	.128	-.113	.038	-.072	.192	.268	.047
scaled deviance/d.f.	1648	1647	4320	3313	1204	1307	4403	2441
# obs./# marriages	12,790	1,782	88,396	15,989	11,213	1,171	52,649	9,068

TABLE A-I. (continued)

Parameter	Black men β	Black men SE[a]	White men β	White men SE[a]	Black women β	Black women SE[a]	White women β	White women SE[a]
Age 30–39								
Intercept	-4.201	.227	-4.387	.094	-3.312	.291	-2.969	.101
Age 30–31 (vs. 38–39)	.518	.138	.878	.058	.706	.176	.883	.075
Age 32–33 (vs. 38–39)	.413	.145	.688	.061	.446	.188	.525	.079
Age 34–35 (vs. 38–39)	.185	.153	.381	.065	.295	.196	.385	.083
Age 36–37 (vs. 38–39)	.208	.158	.291	.068	.431	.201	.023	.091
12 grades (vs. <12)	-.072	.099	-.079	.043	.267	.119	.423	.060
>12 grades (vs. <12)	-.097	.115	-.154	.042	.284	.147	.498	.066
Enrolled (vs. not)	-.105	.193	-.207	.073	-.662	.262	-.647	.107
Weekly earnings (/100)	.175	.041	.183	.014	.079	.051	.088	.025
Weekly earnings**2	-.004	.004	-.005	.001	-.003	.004	-.008	.003
Expected employment	1.324	.161	1.446	.082	-.418	.161	-1.349	.080
1950 (vs. 1940)	.250	.266	-.007	.076	.553	.322	.502	.103
1960 (vs. 1940)	.724	.182	.144	.057	.666	.258	.624	.084
1970 (vs. 1940)	.536	.186	.127	.060	.373	.259	.630	.085
1980 (vs. 1940)	.322	.187	.023	.058	.033	.256	.579	.081
scaled deviance/d.f.	1435	1681	3447	3767	1009	1446	3118	2972
# obs./# marriages	7,744	770	48,162	5,000	7,228	494	32,293	2,551

SOURCE: Authors' calculations.
a. Standard error.

TABLE A-2. Components of Change in Marriage Rates, by Race, Sex, and Age, 1960–80[a]

Component	Black Men		White Men		Black Women		White Women	
	Change	%	Change	%	Change	%	Change	%
Age 16–19								
Age	.036	-4.1	n.a.	n.a.	.027	-2.1	.042	-6.4
Education	-.018	2.0	n.a.	n.a.	-.013	1.1	-.026	3.9
Enrollment	-.111	12.4	n.a.	n.a.	-.249	19.4	-.174	26.3
Earnings	.028	-3.2	n.a.	n.a.	.009	-0.7	-.013	1.8
Employment	-.164	18.3	n.a.	n.a.	-.003	0.2	-.030	4.6
Residual	-.667	74.5	n.a.	n.a.	-1.056	82.2	-.461	69.8
Total (logit)	-.894	100.0	n.a.	n.a.	-1.285	100.0	-.660	100.0
Change in rate	-1.9		-0.9		-6.5		-4.3	
Age 20–23								
Age	.005	-0.5	.007	-1.2	-.000	0	.006	-0.9
Education	-.032	2.8	-.044	7.0	.054	-4.9	.019	-2.6
Enrollment	-.062	5.6	-.026	4.1	-.149	13.6	-.212	28.6
Earnings	.090	-8.1	.090	-14.2	.019	-1.7	-.001	0.2
Employment	-.216	19.4	-.091	14.2	-.000	0	-.023	3.2
Residual	-.899	80.7	-.574	89.9	-1.023	93.0	-.529	71.5
Total (logit)	-1.114	100.0	-.639	100.0	-1.100	100.0	-.740	100.0
Change in rate	-9.1		-9.0		-12.0		-10.6	

TABLE A-2. (continued)

Component	Black Men		White Men		Black Women		White Women	
	Change	%	Change	%	Change	%	Change	%
Age 24–29								
Age	.003	-0.6	.005	-1.2	.002	-0.2	.018	-5.9
Education	.033	-6.4	-.037	9.4	.154	-19.4	.117	-38.8
Enrollment	-.001	0.2	-.000	0.1	-.036	4.6	-.067	22.3
Earnings	.075	-14.5	.077	-19.7	.041	-5.2	.011	-3.6
Employment	-.110	21.3	.001	-0.3	.002	-0.2	-.070	23.3
Residual	-.518	100.1	-.436	111.6	-.951	120.5	-.309	102.7
Total (logit)	-.517	100.0	-.390	100.0	-.789	100.0	-.301	100.0
Change in rate	-5.5		-5.4		-8.3		-4.3	
Age 30–39								
Age	.037	-10.1	n.a.	n.a.	.040	-8.1	n.a.	n.a.
Education	-.029	7.8	n.a.	n.a.	.090	-18.2	n.a.	n.a.
Enrollment	-.006	1.5	n.a.	n.a.	-.039	7.8	n.a.	n.a.
Earnings	.080	-21.6	n.a.	n.a.	.048	-9.8	n.a.	n.a.
Employment	-.050	13.5	n.a.	n.a.	.001	-0.2	n.a.	n.a.
Residual	-.402	108.9	n.a.	n.a.	-.632	128.5	n.a.	n.a.
Total (logit)	-.369	100.0	n.a.	n.a.	-.492	100.0	n.a.	n.a.
Change in rate	-2.9		0.1		-3.3		0.6	

SOURCES: Authors' calculations based on table 2 and table A-1.

n.a. Not available.

a. The components shown are differences in means between 1960 and 1980 of the independent variables weighted by their respective logit coefficients. For variables such as education with two or more coefficients, the weighted differences are summed. "Total" is the difference in the predicted log odds of marriage between 1960 and 1980. "Change in rate" is the difference in observed marriage rates between 1960 and 1980 as reported in columns 5 and 10 of table 1. Percentages of change may not sum to 100 because of rounding.

"We'd Love to Hire Them, But . . .": The Meaning of Race for Employers

JOLEEN KIRSCHENMAN and KATHRYN M. NECKERMAN

DESPITE BLACKS' disproportionate representation in the urban underclass, however defined, analyses of inner-city joblessness seldom consider racism or discrimination as a significant cause. In *The Truly Disadvantaged*, for instance, William Julius Wilson explains increased rates of inner-city unemployment as a consequence of other social or economic developments.[1] Job opportunities for unskilled workers are fewer, he argues, because employers have moved elsewhere or upgraded the skills they require. Because of increased social isolation in the inner city, poor blacks have fewer ways of finding out about the unskilled jobs that do remain. Social isolation has also contributed, he maintains, to a decline in the quality of this labor pool. Lacking the mainstream role models they once had, inner-city blacks no longer learn and value the habits associated with steady work. Wilson and other analysts acknowledge the importance of historical discrimination in education and employment, racial segregation in residence, and ghetto-specific culture; but in their analyses of blacks' current problems of employment, race itself is of little importance.

In this paper we explore the meaning of race and ethnicity to employers, the ways race and ethnicity are qualified by—and at times reinforce—other characteristics in the eyes of employers, and the conditions

The survey on which this research is based was conducted as part of the Urban Poverty and Family Structure project directed by William Julius Wilson at the University of Chicago. This project received funding from the Ford Foundation, the Carnegie Foundation, the Department of Health and Human Services, the Lloyd A. Fry Foundation, the Rockefeller Foundation, the Institute for Research on Poverty, the Spencer Foundation, the William T. Grant Foundation, the Joyce Foundation, and the Woods Charitable Fund. We gratefully acknowledge their support. We also thank Daniel Breslau, Judy Mintz, Lori Sparzo, and Loic Wacquant, who helped conduct the interviews. Finally, we thank Rebecca Blank, Kermit Daniel, Mark Alan Hughes, David Laitin, George Steinmetz, and William Julius Wilson for helpful comments on earlier versions of this paper.

1. Wilson (1987).

under which race seems to matter most. Our interviews at Chicago-area businesses show that employers view inner-city workers, especially black men, as unstable, uncooperative, dishonest, and uneducated. Race is an important factor in hiring decisions. But it is not race alone: rather it is race in a complex interaction with employers' perceptions of class and space, or inner-city residence. Our findings suggest that racial discrimination deserves an important place in analyses of the underclass.

Race and Employment

In research on the disadvantages blacks experience in the labor market, social scientists tend to rely on indirect measures of racial discrimination. They interpret as evidence of this discrimination the differences in wages or employment among races and ethnic groups that remain after education and experience are controlled. With a few exceptions they have neglected the processes at the level of the firm that underlie these observed differences.[2] This neglect is more striking in contrast with research on gender and employment, in which the importance of firm-level characteristics and processes has received much attention.[3] So, despite intense interest in the relation of race to employment, very few scholars have studied the matter at the level of the firm, much less queried employers directly about their views of black workers or how race might enter into their recruitment and hiring decisions.

The theoretical literature conventionally distinguishes two types of discrimination, "pure" and "statistical." In pure discrimination, employers, employees, or consumers have a "taste" for discrimination, that is, they will pay a premium to avoid members of another group.[4] Statistical discrimination is a more recent conception that builds on the discussions of "signaling."[5] In statistical discrimination, employers use group membership as a proxy for aspects of productivity that are relatively expensive or impossible to measure. Those who use the concept disagree about whether employers' perceptions of group differences in productivity must reflect reality.[6] In this discussion, we are concerned with statistical dis-

2. One of the exceptions is Braddock and McPartland (1987).
3. Bielby and Baron (1986); England (1982); and Reskin and Roos (1990).
4. Becker (1957).
5. Phelps (1972); Arrow (1973); and Spence (1973).
6. See, for example, Thurow (1975); Aigner and Cain (1977); and Bielby and Baron (1986).

crimination as a cognitive process, regardless of whether the employer is correct or mistaken in his or her views of the labor force.[7]

Economists note that pure discrimination and "mistaken" statistical discrimination are both costly. With a market in equilibrium, and given certain assumptions, employers who indulge their prejudices or make incorrect inferences about the correlation between race and productivity will be driven out of business by their competitors.[8] This well-known implication of neoclassical models may, in fact, account for the limited research attention given to racial discrimination. Because discrimination itself has seemed theoretically implausible, many social scientists interpret differences in earnings between races as a reflection of unmeasured productivity differences. But neoclassical economists do not predict that firms will never discriminate; they simply argue that, all other things being equal, and under certain assumptions, competitive pressures will tend to drive discriminating firms out of business. If employees or consumers have a taste for discrimination, or if the industry is not competitive, the economic prediction need not hold.[9] In short, neoclassical economics does not imply that discrimination will never occur unless it is based on differences in group productivity, nor does it imply that evidence of discrimination must be taken as prima facie evidence of such differences.

Characteristics of the firm and workplace may also militate against antidiscriminatory competitive pressures, at least in the short term. Incentives for individuals within the firm may differ from incentives for the firm as a whole. A personnel officer might, for instance, prefer simple—and from his or her perspective, cost-efficient—discriminatory practices regardless of their implications for the productivity of the work force and the rational conduct of the firm.

The distinction between pure and statistical discrimination is a useful one. However, it is also useful to recognize the relationship between the

7. Although the question of whether group differences in productivity exist is a critical one for public policy, it is not one we can settle with our data. It is, moreover, a very complex empirical question. Overall group differences in productivity may in fact be irrelevant to employers, who are more likely to be concerned with the correlation of productivity with race among the particular applicants they attract. The composition of the applicant pool depends on factors such as the firm's location, the wage rate and type of work, and the firm's recruitment practices, which in turn are influenced by employers' perceptions of black and white workers.

8. See Becker (1957), especially pp. 44–45, for conditions under which discrimination is completely eliminated.

9. Becker (1957).

two. There are several ways in which a taste for discrimination in employment practices may lead to perceived and actual productivity differences between groups, making statistical discrimination more likely. Social psychological evidence suggests that expectations about group differences in productivity may bias evaluation of job performance.[10] These expectations may also influence job placement. In particular, workers of lower expected productivity may be given less on-the-job training. Finally, and most important for our study, productivity is not an individual characteristic; rather, it is shaped by the social relations of the workplace. If these relations are strained because of tastes for discrimination on the part of the employer, supervisor, coworkers, or consumers, lower productivity may result.[11] Thus what begins as irrational practice based on prejudice or mistaken beliefs may end up being rational, profit-maximizing behavior.

Data

This research is based on face-to-face interviews with employers in Chicago and surrounding Cook County between July 1988 and March 1989. Inner-city firms were oversampled; all results here are weighted to adjust for this oversampling. Our overall response rate was 46 percent, and the completed sample of 185 employers is representative of the distribution of Cook County's employment by industry and firm size.[12]

Interviews included both closed- and open-ended questions about employers' hiring and recruitment practices and about their perceptions of Chicago's labor force and business climate. Our initial contacts, and most of the interviews themselves, were conducted with the highest ranking official at the establishment. Because of the many open-ended questions, we taped the interviews.

Most of the structured portion of the interview focused on a sample job, defined by the interview schedule as "the most typical entry-level position" in the firm's modal occupational category—sales, clerical, skilled, semiskilled, unskilled, or service, but excluding managerial, professional, and technical. The distribution of our sample jobs approximates the occupational distribution in the 1980 census for Cook County, again excluding professional, managerial, and technical categories. In ef-

10. See Bielby and Baron (1986) for a discussion.
11. Anderson (1980).
12. The sample and survey methods are described in more detail in the "Employer Survey Final Report," available from the authors.

fect, what we have is a sample of the opportunities facing the Chicago job-seeker with minimal skills.

The answers to the open-ended questions were coded, categorized, and, when it was meaningful to do so, counted. Given the nature of qualitative data, there are times when it does not make sense to tabulate. For instance, even though all employers were asked the same questions, the interviews varied in the amount of information they yielded. Some respondents were expressive, some were relaxed and gave longer interviews, while others were more pressed for time or more guarded and refused to commit themselves on controversial issues. Frequency of comment does not, therefore, equal significance.

Although we do not present our findings as necessarily representative of the attitudes of all Chicago employers, as the rules of positivist social science would require, they are representative of those Chicago employers who spoke to a particular issue. A standard rule of discourse is that some things are acceptable to say and others are better left unsaid. Silence has the capacity to speak volumes. Thus we were overwhelmed by the degree to which Chicago employers felt comfortable talking with us—in a situation where the temptation would be to conceal rather than reveal—in a negative manner about blacks. In this paper we make an effort to understand the discursive evidence by relating it to the practice of discrimination, using quantitative data to reinforce the qualitative findings.

We'd Love to Hire Them, But . . .

At least since 1915, when Emile Durkheim wrote *Elementary Forms of Religious Life,* sociologists have recognized the importance of categorization as a cognitive instrument for people in general as well as for social scientists.[13] Explanations for the high rates of unemployment and poverty among blacks have relied heavily on the categories of class and space.[14] We found that employers also relied on those categories, but they used them to refine the category of race, which for them is primary. Indeed, it was through the interaction of race with class and space that these categories were imbued with new meaning. It was race that made class and space important to employers.

Although some employers regarded Chicago's workers as highly

13. Durkheim (1965).

14. Wilson (1980, 1987); and Kasarda (1985). We use the term "space" in the tradition of urban geography. We do this to draw attention to the way people categorize and attach meaning to geographic locations.

skilled and having a good work ethic, far more thought that the labor force had deteriorated. When asked why they thought business had been leaving Chicago, 35 percent referred to the inferior quality of the work force. As one said, "Some of it has to do, I think, with the quality of the worker—the work force that they have to recruit from. We have talked about that several times ourselves, but we've made a commitment to the churches to stay in those communities. So we will be there, but it makes it very difficult to recruit staff." Employers needing machinists or nurses or other skilled workers worried about the short supply and high cost of these employees. City employers believed most skilled workers had fled to the suburbs and had no desire to commute back to Chicago: "They got out of here, why would they want to come back?" Several firms in our sample were relocating or seriously considering a move to the South in a search for cheap skilled labor. Employers of less skilled labor can find an ample supply of applicants, but many complained that it was becoming more difficult to find workers with basic skills and a good work ethic.

These employers coped with what they considered a less qualified work force through various strategies. Some restructured production to require either fewer workers or fewer skills. These strategies included increasing automation and deemphasizing literacy requirements—using color-coded filing systems, for example. But far more widespread were the use of recruiting and screening techniques to help select "good" workers. For instance, employers relied more heavily on referrals from employees, which tend to reproduce the traits and characteristics of the current work force: the Chicago Association of Commerce and Industry has reported a dramatic increase in the use of referral bonuses in the past few years. Or employers targeted newspaper ads to particular neighborhoods or ethnic groups. The rationale underlying these strategies was, in part, related to the productivity employers accorded different categories of workers.

For instance, whether or not the urban underclass is an objective social category, its subjective importance in the discourse of Chicago employers cannot be denied. Their characterizations of inner-city workers mirrored many descriptions of the underclass by social scientists. Common among the traits listed were that workers were unskilled, uneducated, illiterate, dishonest, lacking initiative, unmotivated, involved with drugs and gangs, did not understand work, had no personal charm, were unstable, lacked a work ethic, and had no family life or role models.

Social scientists discover pathologies; employers try to avoid them.

After explaining that he hired "the best applicant," the owner of a transportation firm added, "Probably what I'm trying to say is we're not social minded. We're not worried about solving the problems of sociology. We can't afford to." But despite not being worried about the "problems of sociology," employers have become lay social theorists, creating numerous distinctions among the labor force that then serve as bases for statistical discrimination. From their own experiences and biases, those of other employers, and accounts in the mass media, employers have attributed meaning to the categories of race and ethnicity, class, and space. These have then become markers of more or less desirable workers.

These categories were often confounded with each other, as when one respondent contrasted the white youth (with opportunities) from the North Shore with the black one (without opportunities) from the South Side. Although the primary distinction that more than 70 percent of our informants made was based on race and ethnicity, it was frequently confounded with class: black and Hispanic equaled lower class; white equaled middle class. And these distinctions also overlapped with space: "inner-city" and at times "Chicago" equaled minority, especially black; "suburb" equaled white. In fact, race was important in part because it signaled class and inner-city residence, which are less easy to observe directly. But employers also needed class and space to draw distinctions within racial and ethnic groups; race was the distinguishing characteristic most often referred to, followed respectively by class and space. Consider the use of race and ethnicity, class, and space in the following response from the owner of a Chicago construction firm who thought that for minorities in general "the quality of . . . education is not as great as white folk from the suburbs. . . . And it shows in the intellectual capability of the labor force." Furthermore, "The minority worker is not as punctual and not as concerned about punctuality as the middle-class white. So they're not as wired to the clock in keeping time and being on time as someone else who was raised in a family where the father went to work every day and the mother was up at the same time every day to make breakfast or go to work herself. It's just a cultural difference."

Race and Ethnicity

When they talked about the work ethic, tensions in the workplace, or attitudes toward work, employers emphasized the color of a person's skin. Many believed that white workers were superior to minorities in their work ethic. A woman who hires for a suburban service firm said, "The Polish immigrants that I know and know of are more highly motivated than the Hispanics. The Hispanics share in some of the problems that the blacks do." These problems included "exposure to poverty and drugs" as well as "a lack of motivation" related to "their environment and background." A man from a Chicago construction company, expressing a view shared by many of our informants, said, "For all groups, the pride [in their work] of days gone by is not there, but what is left, I think probably the whites take more pride than some of the other minorities." (Interviewer: "And between blacks and Hispanics?") "Probably the same."

In the discourse of "work ethic," which looms large among the concerns of employers, whites usually came out on top. But although white workers generally looked good to employers, East European whites were repeatedly praised for really knowing how to work and caring about their work. Several informants cited positive experiences with their Polish domestic help. In the skilled occupations, East European men were sought. One company advertised for its skilled workers in Polish- and German-language newspapers, but hired all its unskilled workers, 97 percent of whom were Hispanic, through an employee network.

When asked directly whether they thought there were any differences in the work ethics of whites, blacks, and Hispanics, 37.7 percent of the employers ranked blacks last, 1.4 percent ranked Hispanics last, and no one ranked whites there. Another 7.6 percent placed blacks and Hispanics together on the lowest level; 51.4 percent either saw no difference or refused to categorize in a straightforward way. Many of the latter group qualified their response by saying they saw no differences once one controlled for education, background, or environment, and that any differences were more the result of class or space.

Although blacks were consistently evaluated less favorably than whites, employers' perceptions of Hispanics were more mixed. Some ranked them with blacks; others positioned them between whites and blacks: "[According to] the energy that they put into their job and trying to be as productive as possible, I would have to put the white native-born at the high end and the Hispanic in the middle and the blacks at the bottom." Some employers recognized ethnicity within Hispanicity: "Well, if you exclude Mexicans from the Hispanic group . . . you have Puerto Ricans, Cubans—their work ethic basically in our experience has been poor, as a group. We have exceptions. And I would say the work ethic that we see from blacks is superior to that of Puerto Rican people." (Interviewer: "And what? Do you think white folks have the best work ethic of all?") "Not in every case, but, as a group, I guess, yes." Finally, some employers believed that Hispanics, as immigrants, had superior work habits.

They also believed that a homogeneous work force serves to maintain good relations among workers. As a respondent from a large Chicago insurance company put it,

> I wanted a person who was going to fit into this area. And sometimes just to satisfy affirmative action, I don't know if that's the hidden agenda here at all.
>
> (Interviewer: No, there isn't a hidden agenda.)
>
> You have to pick somebody who is black or Hispanic or whatever, not that that's a big thing, but you want that person to feel comfortable with the rest of your work force, you want that person to be, if they have phone skills to be articulate, you want them to be neat in their dress, and probably all those little fuzzy feelings that say I know what my current staff is, I want to bring somebody in who I know can deal with Mr. A and Ms. B and all that sort of thing.
>
> (Interviewer: So to some degree it's personality?)
>
> Exactly. You're looking for skills, but you are looking for someone who will fit in, and who will stick with the [company].

A personnel manager from a large, once all-white Chicago manufacturing concern lamented the tensions that race and ethnic diversity had created among workers: "I wish we could all be the same, but, unfortunately, we're not." An employer of an all-white work force said that "if I had one [black worker] back there it might be okay, but if I have two or more I would have trouble." But although some employers found a diverse work force more difficult to manage, few actually maintained a homogeneous labor force, at least in terms of race and ethnicity.

Employers worried about tensions not only between white and minority workers but also between Mexicans and blacks, Mexicans and Puerto Ricans, and even African and American blacks. A restaurateur with an all-white staff of waiters and a Hispanic kitchen said, "The Mexican kids that work in the kitchen, they're not, they're not kids anymore, but they don't like to work with black guys. But they don't like to work with

Puerto Rican guys either." Another manufacturer distinguished among Hispanics and noted workplace tensions when she said,

> I would even break down the Hispanics. Well, it's only my observation, I'm not out in the plant working, but initially when I started with [this company] we employed mostly Mexicans, and it just seemed that things operated better and, of course, then there are immigration laws and we abided by the immigration laws, and also coming into this neighborhood, we've hired more Puerto Ricans.
>
> (Interviewer: And you find them to be less reliable workers?)
>
> Not so much, but there's more, there's actually friction in the groups to some degree.

A service employer in the suburbs mentioned that some black American workers had filed discrimination suits against their Nigerian supervisors. These respondents called attention to potential tensions that may arise from a heterogeneous workplace.

Blacks are by and large thought to possess very few of the characteristics of a "good" worker. Over and over employers said, "They don't want to work." "They don't want to stay." "They've got an attitude problem." One compared blacks with Mexicans: "Most of them are not as educated as you might think. I've never seen any of these guys read anything outside of a comic book. These Mexicans are sitting here reading novels constantly, even though they are in Spanish. These guys will sit and watch cartoons while the other guys are busy reading. To me that shows basic laziness. No desire to upgrade yourself." When asked about discrimination against black workers, a Chicago manufacturer related a common view: "Oh, I would in all honesty probably say there is some among most employers. I think one of the reasons, in all honesty, is because we've had bad experience in that sector, and believe me, I've tried. And as I say, if I find—whether he's black or white, if he's good and, you know, we'll hire him. We are not shutting out any black specifically. But I will say that our experience factor has been bad. We've had more bad black employees over the years than we had good." This negative opinion of blacks sometimes cuts across class lines. For instance, a personnel officer of a professional service company in the suburbs commented that "with the professional staff, black males that we've had, some of the skill levels—they're not as orientated to details. They lack some of the leadership skills."

One must also consider the "relevant nots": what were employers not talking about? They were not talking about how clever black workers were, they were not talking about the cultural richness of the black community, nor were they talking about rising divorce rates among whites. Furthermore, although each employer reserved the right to deny making distinctions along racial lines, fewer than 10 percent consistently refused to distinguish or generalize according to race.

These ways of talking about black workers—they have a bad work ethic, they create tensions in the workplace, they are lazy and unreliable, they have a bad attitude—reveal the meaning race has for many employers. If race were a proxy for expected productivity and the sole basis for statistical discrimination, black applicants would indeed find few job opportunities.

Class

Although some respondents spoke only in terms of race and ethnicity, or conflated class with race, others were sensitive to class distinctions. Class constituted a second, less easily detected signal for employers. Depending somewhat on the demands of the jobs, they used class markers to select among black applicants. The contrasts between their discourse about blacks and Hispanics were striking. Employers sometimes placed Hispanics with blacks in the lower class: an inner-city retailer confounded race, ethnicity, and class when he said, "I think there's a self-defeating prophecy that's maybe inherent in a lot of lower-income ethnic groups or races. Blacks, Hispanics." But although they rarely drew class distinctions among Hispanics, such distinctions were widely made for black workers. As one manufacturer said, "The black work ethic. There's no work ethic. At least at the unskilled. I'm sure with the skilled, as you go up, it's a lot different." Employers generally considered it likely that lower-class blacks would have more negative traits than blacks of other classes.

In many ways black business owners and black personnel managers were the most expressive about class divisions among blacks. A few believed poor blacks were more likely to be dishonest because of the economic pressures they face. A black jeweler said the most important quality he looked for in his help was "a person who doesn't need a job."

(Interviewer: That's what you're looking for?)
That's what we usually try to hire. People that don't need the job.
(Interviewer: Why?)
Because they will tend to be a little more honest. Most of the people

that live in the neighborhoods and areas where my stores are at need the job. They are low-income, and so, consequently, they're under more pressure and there's more of a tendency to be dishonest, because of the pressure.

He elaborated later:

I have a great deal of reluctance to hire a divorcee that lives by herself that doesn't have a source of income. I mean, you know, and she doesn't have to live in the projects, she could live right around the corner, she could live in a good neighborhood. Because the type of job that I have to offer her does not offer enough wage to justify a continuation of that type of lifestyle. I mean, I don't pay enough, $4 doesn't pay enough to support an apartment and a car and kids in school, it doesn't pay that much. So if I'm going to give you a job, and I know that it's not going to pay enough to maintain that lifestyle, what's going to happen? I mean, you've got to have an alternate source, you've got to have a boyfriend, you've got to have a rich parent, or it's going to be my jewelry.

Other employers mentioned problems that occur in the workplace when there are class divisions among the workers. These are reminiscent of the tensions created by the racial and ethnic diversity described earlier. One black businesswoman told of a program wherein disadvantaged youths were sent to private schools by wealthy sponsors. She herself was a sponsor and held the program in high regard, but she hired some of these youths and they did not get along with her other young employees: "Those kids were too smart 'cause they were from a middle-class background." (Interviewer: "So these were primarily middle-class kids?") "No, they're not middle class, but they have middle-class values because they're exposed to them all the time." They made excellent employees, she said, "if you kept your store filled with just them. They're more outgoing and less afraid of the customers. But they're very intimidating to the supervisors because they know everything by the time they get to be a sophomore in high school." A Chicago retailer talked about his "good" black women employees and his "bad" ones: the "good" employees ridiculed their "bad" coworkers and called them "ghetto chicks."

Thus, although many employers assumed that black meant "inner-city poor," others—both black and white—were quick to see divisions within the black population. Of course, class itself is not directly observable, but markers that convey middle- or working-class status will help a black job applicant get through race-based exclusionary barriers. Class is primarily signaled to employers through speech, dress, education levels, skill levels, and place of residence. Although many respondents drew class distinctions among blacks, very few made those same distinctions among Hispanics or whites; in refining these categories, respondents referred to ethnicity and age rather than class.

Space

Although some employers spoke implicitly or explicitly in terms of class, for others "inner-city" was the more important category. For most the term immediately connoted black, poor, uneducated, unskilled, lacking in values, crime, gangs, drugs, and unstable families. "Suburb" connoted white, middle-class, educated, skilled, and stable families. Conversely, race was salient in part because it signaled space; black connoted inner city and white the suburbs. A communications employer associated Chicago with a minority work force: "Chicago has a people base maybe not all businesses would like. Spanish and black are very good for the things that we want, perhaps other companies don't think that." When asked what it would take for their firm to relocate to the inner city, respondents generally thought it an implausible notion. They were sure their skilled workers would not consider working in those neighborhoods because they feared for their safety, and the employers saw no alternative labor supply there.

The skepticism that greets the inner-city worker often arises when employers associate their race and residence with enrollment in Chicago's troubled public education system. Being educated in Chicago public schools has become a way of signaling "I'm black, I'm poor, and I'm from the inner city" to employers. Some mentioned that they passed over applicants from Chicago public schools for those with parochial or suburban educations. If employers were looking at an applicant's credentials when screening, blacks in the inner city did not do well. As one employer said, "The educational skills they come to the job with are minimal because of the schools in the areas where they generally live."

A vice president of a television station complained of the inner-city work force:

They are frequently unable to write. They go through the Chicago public schools or they dropped out when they were in the eighth grade.

They can't read. They can't write. They can hardly talk. I have another opinion which is strictly my own and that is that people who insist on beating themselves to the point where they are out of the mainstream of the world suffer the consequences. And I'm talking about the languages that are spoken in the ghetto. They are not English.

Employers were clearly disappointed, not just in the academic content and level of training students receive, but in the failure of the school system to prepare them for the work force. Because the inner city is heavily associated with a lack of family values, employers wished the schools would compensate and provide students the self-discipline needed for worker socialization. Additionally, they complained that black workers had no "ability to understand work." As the Hispanic vice president of personnel for a large Chicago manufacturing concern said of black men,

> If you're handicapped by not having some of the basic, basic skills you need, if you're hired and you can't make it on the job because you don't even have the basic skills, that's part of the problem. Part of the problem may be role models in the families. The business of the discipline of having to be at work every day. If it's not in the school, and they didn't experience it in schools, when you put them in this work environment and all of a sudden try to change habits when there are no role models anywhere, it's not going to work.

It is not only educational content per se that employers were looking for; some were concerned with the educational "experience." One talked about how it just showed "they could finish something." Thus inner city is equated with public school attendance, which in turn signifies insufficient work skills and work ethic.

Address is another signal of an applicant's inner-city residence. Most employers we talked to about "address discrimination" said they did not care where an employee lived, or would not know in what kind of neighborhood a given address was located. However, ghetto residents interviewed earlier for the Urban Poverty and Family Structure project told us they thought their address had hurt them in their job search. A few even said they lied about where they lived. One employer who was from a large company in which one vice president came from the Robert Taylor Homes, a black public housing project, did not think it mattered where an employee lived, but "if I were at a small company, small plant that's located close to either one of those homes, and that the only candidates I saw were from there . . . my feelings, my attitudes might be different." A large Chicago manufacturer offered this reasoning: "The address does have an indication or suggests that, okay, here is an applicant that'll probably fall into a pattern that others have. The result would be low job offers."

"Inner city" also connoted a "culture" that could be signaled by attributes other than address. For instance, employers talked about West Side blacks and South Side blacks. A few expressed a preference for those from the West Side because their roots were closer to the rural South; hence, they had more "understanding of work." The migration pattern was such that the South Side of Chicago was settled first and only then did the West Side become a black ghetto, so they were seeking out the more recent migrants. This was consistent with employers' generally higher regard, mentioned earlier, for immigrant labor. Another employer used space to refine the category of race: "We have some black women here but they're not inner city. They're from suburbs and . . . I think they're a little bit more willing to give it a shot, you know, I mean they're a little bit more willing [than black men] to give a day's work for a day's pay."

Employers readily distinguished among blacks on the basis of space. They talked about Cabrini Green or the Robert Taylor Homes or referred to the South Side and West Side as a shorthand for black. But they were not likely to make these distinctions among whites and Hispanics. They made no reference to Pilsen (a largely immigrant Mexican neighborhood), Humboldt Park (largely Puerto Rican), or Uptown (a community of poor whites and new immigrants).

For black applicants, having the wrong combination of class and space markers suggested low productivity and undesirability to an employer. The important finding of this research, then, is not only that employers make hiring decisions based on the color of a person's skin, but the extent to which that act has become nuanced. Race, class, and space interact with each other. Moreover, the precise nature of that interaction is largely determined by the demands of the job.

They Don't Have What It Takes

This section provides evidence about what race and ethnicity signal for different types of employers, and how they seem to respond. We compare three categories of occupations with distinctive sets of hiring criteria: sales and customer service jobs, clerical jobs, and semiskilled, unskilled,

TABLE 1. Employee Prerequisites and Employer Hiring Criteria for
Sample Job, by Occupational Category
Percent

Criteria	Sales and customer service	Clerical	Low-skilled
Most important			
Communications skills	52.3	20.7	14.0
Appearance	46.6	20.7	14.9
Ability to deal with public	36.4	23.0	14.9
Dependable	14.8	20.7	32.4
Wants to work	12.5	6.3	22.1
Works well in a team	0	14.0	20.3
Job history	0	19.8	17.6
Specific job experience	8.0	18.9	7.2
Attitude	18.2	6.3	11.7
Work ethic	3.4	6.8	18.0
Skills	4.5	17.1	7.2
Technical skills	0	9.9	0.9
Prerequisites			
None	68.2	10.9	63.5
High school diploma	16.5	22.4	18.2
Skills test	11.8	16.7	15.1
High school diploma and skills test	3.5	50.0	3.1
Unweighted number	27	66	67

SOURCE: Authors' survey.

and other service jobs. Race enters into hiring decisions in different ways,
depending on the observability of key job requirements and particular
occupational demands.

Sales and Customer Service Jobs

For sales and customer service jobs, employers' key criteria are appearance, communications skills, and personality. When asked about the
most important qualities for the sample job, one said, "Probably the ability to communicate, you know. Can they communicate with you. That's
very important. And their appearance is very important also. As far as
qualities, that's really about everything." Honesty and simple mathematics skills were occasionally mentioned, as were intelligence, flexibility,
and aggressiveness. But as table 1 shows, job skills and specific work experience were relatively unimportant. How workers look, talk, and inter-

act with customers or clients were clearly more important. As one respondent said, "A cheerful person can get by with fewer skills."

To most respondents in sales and service, appearance simply meant "someone who dresses neat and clean. They don't have on anything expensive but [they care] about their hygiene." These employers were not as concerned as the employers of clerical staff about professional or corporate appearance, although a few were dubious about unconventional styles such as "dangly earrings" and long hair or earrings on men.

Communication was considered crucial; employees who speak English and who have good voices are sought. When employers talked about the ability to communicate, some also seemed to mean the ability to think on one's feet or converse with customers. A few respondents looked for a certain style. A restaurateur with an all-white staff of waiters described his initial telephone screening: "I talk to them to see if they speak English, if they sound slightly sophisticated, that they've eaten in nice restaurants." But this was unusual: another said simply of the waitress he hired, "She's got to be able to use her mouth."

The ability to deal with the public was an important requirement for sales and service positions. Some respondents talked about it in terms of personality. One restaurateur said, "Personality is very important, an outgoing personality, a pleasing personality." A hotel manager looked for a houseman who "has a personality in that does he seem to like people and get along with them?" Asked what aspects of personality were important, another employer said, "Be nice and courteous when you treat the customers, courtesy towards the customer, give the customer some help." A respondent hiring commissioned sales staff wanted "what I call sales personality—has to be charismatic but at the same time has to be very aggressive." Others spoke in terms of attitude: the manager of a luggage store looked for "personality, attitude. We're looking for a smile, positive attitude, good communication skills. Our philosophy is we can train anybody as long as they're friendly and open and can talk to another individual." An important aspect of job performance, then, was how well the employee established rapport with the customer and, depending on the setting, flattered, reassured, or persuaded.

Sales and service employers' hiring criteria and processes were relatively simple, with minimal screening for skills or education. Asked how he identified good employees, one respondent said,

If an applicant comes in and they're dressed neatly and they can spell correctly and fill out an application form with common sense, they're usually a pretty good job prospect. If people come in looking, I don't mean they have to wear a suit, but if people come in looking like the clothes haven't been washed for two weeks, and they can't spell and read, they're usually a pretty poor source for a job. Believe it or not, I know that sounds pretty basic, but that's really kind of what the job market is like out there.

The important attributes for someone who deals with the public can readily be observed, and in fact some employers made explicit analogies between the job interview and interaction with customers. A restaurant manager hiring waitresses paid close attention to how a job applicant talked to him, "because if she's not going to communicate to me, she's certainly not going to be able to talk to a customer who's dissatisfied at that moment."

Given the significance of interaction with the public for sales and service employers, one might expect to have found some discussion of "black" styles of interaction and speech, as we found among clerical employers. But sales and service employers' discussions of race made little reference to customers. The two respondents who made specific references to "black English" or black culture spoke in terms of interaction with supervisors or coworkers rather than with the public. One retailer said that if the employer is a middle-aged white man "and this kid comes in with his hair in braids, and he doesn't speak the same language, [the employer] says 'oh uh, what've I got?' Whereas if this kid is white, give him a slap on the back of the head and say 'get to work.' He wouldn't be afraid of him but he's afraid of the other one." A florist, describing a black male employee who did not get along with coworkers, said, "He did not speak really white English American. He spoke black American English. And there's a big discrepancy there. A lot of black people are very bright and speak both black and white, but some don't speak white, and that makes it very hard."

Evidence of consumer discrimination appeared in a more direct form. One city restaurateur acknowledged that he discriminated by race because his customers did: "I have all white waitresses for a very basic reason. My clientele is 95 percent white. I simply wouldn't last very long if I had some black waitresses out there." A suburban restaurateur who hired blacks from Chicago because he could not get suburban teenagers to work for him reported that some of his white customers chided him, saying, "Why do you have all *those* people out here?" These two examples illustrated the dilemma employers found themselves in when adjudicating between competitive pressures and consumer tastes. Although no one else reported consumer discrimination, it seems likely that other retailers in white neighborhoods or suburbs face similar pressures.

And when retail employers told us that appearance, communications skills, and personality were important, they may have been giving us code words for white skin or white styles of interaction. Sales employers who said they valued communications skills or ability to deal with the public hired fewer blacks and Hispanics than those who did not. These patterns are difficult to interpret, given the respondents' silence on the matter of race and styles of interaction, but they suggest that consumer discrimination has some influence on the hiring of sales employees.

Although most important qualities for sales and customer service workers are observable in the hiring interview, race, class, and space might also function as signals for at least one unobservable characteristic: honesty. A suburban drug store manager said,

> It's unfortunate, but, in my business I think overall [black men] tend to be known to be dishonest. I think that's too bad but that's the image they have.
> (Interviewer: So you think it's an image problem?)
> Yeah, a dishonest, an image problem of being dishonest men and lazy. They're known to be lazy. They are [laughs]. I hate to tell you, but. It's all an image though. Whether they are or not, I don't know, but, it's an image that is perceived.
> (Interviewer: I see. How do you think that image was developed?)
> Go look in the jails [laughs].

The two black retailers cited earlier both noted the economic pressures on low-income black workers.

Clerical Jobs

Clerical jobs are the most highly skilled of the jobs we consider here. When asked what qualities were most important to them, employers of clerical workers emphasized job experience and skills, communications skills, and specific skills such as mathematics or typing (see table 1) but also mentioned personal qualities such as appearance.

Language ability and other clerical skills can readily be tested, and in fact two-thirds of clerical employers administered some kind of basic (language and mathematics) skills test. A few tested for writing, asking applicants to write brief essays or letters. Informal "tests" were also common; one insurance company solicited letters from job applicants to get a sense of their writing skills. A law firm employer scanned the format of the resume. Requiring a high school degree was common, although the poor reputation of the Chicago public schools was reflected in significant differences between city and suburb: 90.9 percent of suburban employers required a high school diploma, compared with only 61.2 percent of city employers.

But clerical employers looked for other qualities as well. As table 1 suggests, employers are often concerned with interpersonal skills such as the ability to deal with the public or cooperate with coworkers. Employers in law firms, public relations agencies, and similar businesses emphasized the need for secretaries to get along with the hard-driving and demanding professionals they worked for. When hiring receptionists and others who dealt with clients or the public, employers looked for applicants who could represent the company with a polished, professional, and friendly manner—they had to know whom to serve coffee to, how to talk to clients, or in case of a hospital admitting clerk, how to "have a good effect on customers." Asked what she meant by attitude, an employer responded, "Mannerisms, speaking, well-bred, 'thank you, may I help you, I'm here to serve you, you're not here to serve me' kind of thing because there is a lot of contact [with clients] even though it's on the telephone."

Interpersonal skills were considered important even for clerical workers who would have little contact with senior employees or with the public. Respondents often spoke of wanting someone who would fit in, who would know how to behave and get along with other employees. "We have, like I said, more of a family-type relationship here. . . . It's one of our main things that we do look for, to get along with other people. We like to keep it so that, you know, we don't have people in the department fighting." An employer in a small downtown law firm was more succinct: "If you don't have that interpersonal skill of being able to get along with everybody, you're history."

Appearance signaled whether an applicant had a personal style compatible with the staff and image of the firm. One respondent, the placement director for a secretarial school, expressed her frustration with the students' styles of dress: "They don't realize what they're doing to the employers. They're turning them off before they have the interview. . . . I tell them the image is very, very important to the employer. It has nothing to do with the skills. They have to have a professional image going into the company or the employers will not hire. And the employers agree. They must have an image." [15] Employers were also sensitive to speech patterns. Readily observable in interviews, appearance and voice are themselves productive criteria because of what they signal to others about the firm, but they may also signal other characteristics about an applicant to the employer.

Some white-collar employers told us that they felt blacks' styles of presentation and speech were inappropriate. The placement director quoted earlier complained that "a lot of the blacks still will wear their hair in tons and millions of braids all over their head. They're sort of hostile. They will [say] 'I never wear make-up.' " A black personnel officer said, "Unfortunately, there is a perception that most of [Chicago public high school] kids are black and they don't have the proper skills. They don't know how to write. They don't know how to speak. They don't act in a business fashion or dress in a business manner, in a way that the business community would like." Black speech patterns were an immediate marker of an undesirable job candidate; a former counseler said that one of the first things job seekers were taught was "you don't 'ax' nobody for a job, you'll *ask* them." Another respondent, who screens out most job applicants on the telephone on the basis of their "grammar and English," defended his methods: "I have every right to say that that's a requirement for this job. I don't care if you're pink, black, green, yellow, or orange, I demand someone who speaks well. You want to tell me that I'm a bigot, fine, call me a bigot. I know blacks, you don't even know they're black. So do you." Another believed that the styles of interaction characteristic of many blacks were out of place in the business world:

> I think for most middle-class white people there's a big cultural gap between them and the culture . . . I would call typical of many Chicago black men, and it's not something that a lot of white people are comfortable with. There's a certain type of repartee that goes on between black guys; even in this building you see it. We have a security guard and a couple of his friends that come in, I'm real uncomfortable with that. You know, I do my best to realize it's a cultural thing, but I don't

15. The potential significance of image is evident in a suit filed in 1989 against four New York City employment agencies that were charged with discriminating against minority job applicants. According to newspaper reports, most of the discrimination cases involved highly visible jobs, such as receptionist or secretary, that employers "wanted a certain look for." Employers indicated their preference for white job candidates by using code words such as "all-American," "front-office appearance," and "corporate image" (Craig Wolff, "New York Sues Job Agencies in Bias Case," *New York Times,* September 29, 1989, p. B1).

like it, I don't think it's being professional, and I don't think it's the right atmosphere for a building.

Clerical employers were notable for their sensitivity to class distinctions among blacks, and their responses were often framed in terms of speech patterns:

> I think it's primarily what I mentioned—the cultural thing. We have a couple of black workers—a friend of mine, one of the black secretaries who's been here several years, said, "Well, they're black but their soul is white" and, because culturally, they're white. They do not have black accents. They do not—I think the accent is a big part of it. If someone—it doesn't matter—if someone is black but they speak with the same accent as a Midwestern white person, it completely changes the perception of them. And then dress is part of it. So, you're dealing with what is almost more socioeconomic prejudice than purely racial prejudice.

Another said, "In many businesses the ability to meet the public is paramount, and you do not talk street talk to the buying public. Almost all your black welfare people talk street talk." Occasionally, a respondent referred to other characteristics perceived to be correlated with class: "I find that the less skilled, the less educational background of—and now I'll say black—the more belligerent they are."

Less common was reference to inner-city residence. One respondent described her interview with an applicant from the projects:

> The person came in, made a very, very poor impression physically. . . . I mean she was already for the interview in a state of pretty bad disarray. And I just did not feel she would mix in with the people that I already had, and I didn't want to start explaining that she'd have to show up for work in the morning and you go home at this time, and I think this company gives our clerical employees a fair amount of latitude. . . . I didn't really want to explain these small nuances of behavior to somebody like that.

To her, "inner city" connoted the inability to fit in with other employees or to apprehend and accept subtle rules of the workplace. Another respondent described how a job applicant can signal that these stereotypes did not apply: "You take somebody from the inner city, they may be right out of the ghetto, they may be right out of the projects, if we feel confident they're not going to steal, I mean, they're sincere. They may be going to school nights or something. They have a little background. They interview well. They're neat and clean. They fill out an 'ap.' We don't have any problems." However, it is likely that most inner-city applicants are screened out by the education and skill requirements of clerical jobs. So while the category "inner city" may be familiar from newspaper accounts, it is not one that is prominent in their hiring and recruitment decisions, other than through its correlation with lower class. Rather, the primary criteria that distinguish appropriate black clerical applicants are those based on class.

Low-Skilled Blue-Collar and Service Jobs

Like sales and customer service employers, most employers of low-skilled blue-collar and service workers do not require job skills (see table 1). In fact, several employers said explicitly that they valued trainability over experience. One looked for a "bright" job applicant, one with an attitude that "I don't have any of the basic skills but I can learn them in a hurry." A few said they wanted candidates who were familiar with factory work, "someone who has worked in or has an interest in working in this type of environment, running a machine, 'cause it's not a real clean job and the working conditions, it's hot in the summer, it's dirty, some of the work is heavy."

What is crucial in these jobs is dependability: "Every day coming to work on time." Common complaints about low-skilled workers focused on those who were hired and never showed up, or quit without warning. Respondents tended to use terms such as "stability," "dependability," "good work history," and "attendance record" interchangeably, and many said explicitly that they saw an applicant's work record as an index of stability: "As far as dependability, and that's why I said earlier that past work record, that's important, so I almost automatically disqualify someone who has moved from position to position, numerous positions within a very short period of time." Rapid turnover was a more important warning sign than a long spell of unemployment. Some respondents immediately ruled out "job hoppers" but were willing to consider applicants with long periods of unemployment if they had a good reason for being out of work.

Closely related to dependability in employers' discussions were work ethic, "willingness to work," or "desire to have a job." This phrasing almost never occurred in interviews with other types of employers, but these respondents took its meaning for granted when discussing the most important qualities of a worker with few skills: "Desire to have a job and do a good job, willingness to come to work." "Just the characteristic stuff. You know, if they're willing to work, if they're willing to take the job." As this last quotation suggests, "willingness to work" is a conventional phrase; the context suggests that employers want workers who have a good work ethic, who "do a day's work for a day's pay."

Work history is not the only marker of reliability and motivation. A few employers said they looked at whether an employee was a family man, assuming that married men were more stable because they needed the job: "Well, I think that you know you can tell during an interview process how eager they are to work. What the family situation is. Usually if they have, if they're married, I would say that would have an influence because we found here that people who are in these entry-level positions, if they are married they generally have more, feel more, a bigger sense of responsibility and would be less likely to either screw around or leave." Most semiskilled and unskilled workers are not in the public eye, so appearance is not part of job performance. However, it is a common indicator of desire to work: "Well, I think probably the first major factor is an enthusiasm to want to work. And that enthusiasm gets symbolized by a lot of different factors, like showing up on time, your appearance, just all the little subtle things that convey how badly, or how sincerely, you want to do your work." Finally, as these statements suggest, employers relied on their gut feeling from the interview: "You can tell a certain amount just by talking to them."

Willingness to cooperate with others and take instructions were other crucial characteristics for low-skilled workers. Employers were concerned not with brief interactions with the public but with day-to-day working relations over the long term. Some respondents said they would use the interview to "get a fix on" how well someone worked with others. But one employer stressed the difficulty of assessing this quality:

You know they have to be able to get along with the other employees that we have up there. We've had in the past years people who just cannot get along, they're always arguing with each other and so forth and so on and we try to avoid that type of thing where possible. But, of course, you never know until after they are hired. When you are interviewing them, everybody is on good behavior.

(Interviewer: I know one thing I've learned from the study is that all

of you folks that do the hiring have to be sort of lay psychologists, I
think.)
Yeah.
(Interviewer: Figure out how to read people.)
We try, we try. But sometimes you get fooled.

Only a few respondents made an explicit connection between racial heterogeneity and workplace tensions. But those employers of low-skilled
workers who valued teamwork were twice as likely to have racially and
ethnically homogeneous work forces in the sample job—37.8 percent
versus 16.4 percent.[16]

Unlike employers of clerical and sales workers, employers of low-
skilled labor had no direct measures of the most important qualities for
the sample job. Work history was the only more or less objective measure
of dependability and stability. Employers gauged work ethic or willingness to work largely from their impressions in the interview. Even the
qualities of personality that make someone a cooperative employee and
good team member may be difficult to assess in an interview: job interviews are similar to the short-term encounters with the public that employers of clerical and sales and service workers were concerned about,
but they are relatively unlike the longer-term working relationships that
low-skilled employees may need to establish.

Because the most desired traits in low-skilled workers are unobservable, employers of such labor seemed more likely to engage in statistical
discrimination. According to some of our respondents, the widespread
perception that black workers were unreliable or had a poor work ethic
hurt them in the labor market:

> In talking about reasons black men don't get jobs, you know, I think a
> lot of people see that group as being quote lazy unquote, which is a
> stereotypical image that you would have, and a lot of employers have
> had experience with hiring people like that and if they get enough of
> them who tend to make that a reality—that yes, they are. They're not
> reliable. They're not dependable. They don't show up. When they do
> show up they don't do a good job. They're just going to say, "Well, I'm
> not going to hire anybody like that anymore." And that's human
> nature.

16. Homogeneous work forces were defined as those in which 90 percent or more of
sample job workers were either white, black, or Hispanic.

An inner-city manufacturer reported that "when we hear other employers talk, they'll go after primarily the Hispanic and Oriental first, those two, and, I'll qualify that even further, the Mexican Hispanic, and any Oriental, and after that, that's pretty much it, that's pretty much where they like to draw the line, right there."

Like those cited above, some employers talked only in terms of race and ethnicity. But in most cases race did not disqualify a job applicant: many employers praised their "good" black employees, often speaking in terms of their long tenure at the firm. Rather, employers perceived the black labor force as relatively heterogeneous. The significance of race for them was that black job applicants were scrutinized more carefully. As one manufacturer said, "I meet people who look at the black males with a little more finely tuned eye than they would someone else."

In contrast to employers of clerical workers, who were concerned with class and paid little attention to space, employers of low-skilled workers were most concerned with characteristics associated with the distinction between inner-city blacks and other blacks. Some drew this distinction explicitly, as one responded to the question about "address discrimination": "If you take a perceived bigoted position that black males are lazy, which I probably unfortunately did earlier, then how do you sort through that and find those who are not? Well, you sure as hell don't go to the projects to look for someone who is not. Now a lot of great people come out of the projects, but you know, that's not where I'd go looking for the exception." Another commented, "I think the stereotyping of if you live in a housing project or if you're black or if you're Hispanic or if you're, you know, you have big gaps in your work record, you put all those things together and you've got an undesirable animal. And many times that's probably, maybe, true. You may have a person who you're not going to get anywhere with. And you're going to spend a lot of money training these people and you're going to have a high turnover." But they also did this implicitly, relying on markers associated with inner city as a cultural pattern rather than a physical location. These markers may include family status, dress, or style of speech. Finally, personal references may also be more important for black job applicants than for others: "All of a sudden, they take a look at a guy, and unless he's got an in, the reason why I hired this black kid the last time is 'cause my neighbor said to me, yeah, I used him for a few, he's good, and I said, you know what, I'm going to take a chance. But it was a recommendation. But other than that, I've got a walk-in, and, who knows? And I think that for the most part, a guy sees a black man, he's a bit hesitant, because I don't know." Other respondents who hired low-skilled black men also relied on informal networks or formal referral systems such as school-work cooperative programs to screen for good black workers.

One would expect racial stereotypes to influence hiring decisions most when there are few other indicators of an applicant's quality. Although the employer survey was not designed to examine statistical discrimination, we can test this briefly using a distinction between jobs that require basic skills and those that do not. Many employers wanted low-skilled workers who could speak English, read and write, or do basic mathematics, either because the job itself required it or because employers wanted to be able to communicate with workers in writing. If racial stereotypes influence hiring decisions most when reliable information about productivity is lacking, and if Hispanics are regarded as more reliable workers than blacks, then one would expect employers to favor Hispanics for less skilled jobs requiring no language or math skills.

We compared the race and ethnic composition of these jobs by occupation and city or suburban location (table 2). City employers who did not seek basic skills placed more Hispanics than blacks in the sample job. By contrast, those who wanted language or mathematics skills had, on average, larger proportions of blacks. The relationship was reversed among suburban firms. Jobs requiring no language or math skills had higher proportions of blacks than Hispanics, while jobs requiring some skills had more Hispanics.[17]

Without information about the labor supply for these jobs, table 2 can only be suggestive.[18] But one interpretation is that when employers of low-skilled labor have some other criteria on which to screen, racial stereotypes become less important. Whether basic skills requirements for less skilled workers are important for the job or simply help the employer screen out applicants with undesirable personal qualities is irrelevant; what matters is that these criteria give the employer objective information about the applicant that supplements the fact of skin color. Another interpretation is simply that employers prefer Hispanic workers as long as they have the requisite skills. It seems likely that the Hispanic workers in the suburbs are more proficient at English and thus are more equipped to

17. City-suburban differences remained when we controlled for percent black and Hispanic residents in the neighborhood or suburb.

18. The question of statistical discrimination is examined in more detail in Neckerman and Kirschenman (1990).

TABLE 2. Black and Hispanic Employees in Blue-Collar and Non–Customer Service Jobs, by Location of Firm and Basic Skills Requirement

Percent

Firm location and basic skills requirement	Black	Hispanic	Unweighted number
City			
Semiskilled			
Not required	19.7	64.6	3
Required	26.0	17.9	7
Unskilled			
Not required	24.4	37.6	8
Required	40.9	20.3	15
Service			
Not required	20.6	39.5	5
Required	47.9	19.3	6
Average			
Not required	22.3	42.8	16
Required	39.0	19.5	28
Suburbs			
Semiskilled			
Not required	51.7	13.3	3
Required	6.0	45.3	3
Unskilled			
Not required	35.4	1.6	2
Required	24.6	41.3	2
Service			
Not required	...	...	0
Required	50.0	25.0	2
Total			
Not required	45.2	8.6	5
Required	19.5	40.6	7

SOURCE: Authors' survey.

compete for jobs requiring language skills, while the reverse is true in the city. In either case, employers appear to be acting on their beliefs that Hispanics are better workers than blacks.

Conclusion

Chicago's employers did not hesitate to generalize about race or ethnic differences in the quality of the labor force. Most associated negative images with inner-city workers, and particularly with black men. "Black" and "inner-city" were inextricably linked, and both were linked with "lower-class."

Regardless of the generalizations employers made, they did consider the black population particularly heterogeneous, which made it more important that they be able to distinguish "good" from "bad" workers. Whether through skills tests, credentials, personal references, folk theories, or their intuition, they used some means of screening out the inner-city applicant. The ubiquitous anecdote about the good black worker, the exception to the rule, testified to their own perceived success at doing this. So did frequent references to "our" black workers as opposed to "those guys on the street corner."

And black job applicants, unlike their white counterparts, must indicate to employers that the stereotypes do not apply to them. Inner-city and lower-class workers were seen as undesirable, and black applicants had to try to signal to employers that they did not fall into those categories, either by demonstrating their skills or by adopting a middle-class style of dress, manner, and speech or perhaps (as we were told some did) by lying about their address or work history.

By stressing employers' preconceptions about inner-city workers, we do not mean to imply that there are no problems of labor quality in the inner city: the low reading and mathematics test scores of Chicago public school students testify to these problems. But if the quality of the inner-city labor force has indeed deteriorated, then it is incumbent on employers to avoid hiring inner-city workers. This is precisely the result one would expect from William Julius Wilson's account of increased social dislocations in the inner city since the early 1970s. Because race and inner-city residence are so highly correlated, it would not be surprising if race were to become a key marker of worker productivity.

However, productivity is not an individual characteristic. Rather it is embedded in social relations. The qualities most likely to be proxied by race are not job skills but behavioral and attitudinal attributes—dependability, strong work ethic, and cooperativeness—that are closely tied to interactions among workers and between workers and employers. Our evidence suggests that more attention should be paid to social relations in the workplace. Antagonisms among workers and between workers and their employers are likely to diminish productivity. Thus employers' expectations may become self-fulfilling prophecies.

References

Aigner, Dennis J., and Glen G. Cain. 1977. "Statistical Theories of Discrimination in Labor Markets." *Industrial and Labor Relations Review* 30 (January), pp. 175–87.

Anderson, Elijah. 1980. "Some Observations on Black Youth Employment." In *Youth Employment and Public Policy,* edited by Bernard E. Anderson and Isabel V. Sawhill. Prentice-Hall.

Arrow, Kenneth. 1973. "The Theory of Discrimination." In *Discrimination in Labor Markets,* edited by Orley Aschenfelter and Albert Rees. Princeton University Press.

Becker, Gary S. 1957. *The Economics of Discrimination.* University of Chicago Press.

Bielby, William T., and James N. Baron. 1986. "Men and Women at Work: Sex Segregation and Statistical Discrimination." *American Journal of Sociology* 91 (January), pp. 759–99.

Braddock, Jomills Henry II, and James M. McPartland. 1987. "How Minorities Continue to Be Excluded from Equal Employment Opportunities: Research on Labor Market and Institutional Barriers." *Journal of Social Issues* 43, pp. 5–39.

Durkheim, Emile. 1965 (1915). *The Elementary Forms of Religious Life,* translated by Joseph Ward Swain. Free Press.

England, Paula. 1982. "The Failure of Human Capital Theory to Explain Occupational Sex Segregation." *Journal of Human Resources* 17 (Summer), pp. 358–70.

Kasarda, John D. 1985. "Urban Change and Minority Opportunities." In *The New Urban Reality,* edited by Paul E. Peterson. Brookings.

Neckerman, Kathryn M., and Joleen Kirschenman. 1990. "Hiring Strategies, Racial Bias, and Inner-City Workers: An Investigation of Employers' Hiring Decisions." Paper prepared for American Sociological Association Meeting.

Phelps, Edmund S. 1972. "The Statistical Theory of Racism and Sexism." *American Economic Review* 62 (September), pp. 659–61.

Reskin, Barbara F., and Patricia A. Roos. 1990. *Job Queues, Gender Queues: Explaining Women's Inroads into Male Occupations.* Temple University Press.

Spence, Michael. 1973. "Job Market Signalling." *Quarterly Journal of Economics* 87 (August), pp. 355–74.

Thurow, Lester C. 1975. *Generating Inequality: Mechanisms of Distribution in the U.S. Economy.* Basic Books.

Wilson, William Julius. 1980. *The Declining Significance of Race: Blacks and Changing American Institutions.* 2d ed. University of Chicago Press.

———. 1987. *The Truly Disadvantaged: The Inner City, the Underclass, and Public Policy.* University of Chicago Press.

Part Three ——————————————————
Causes and Consequences of Concentrated Poverty

Ghetto Poverty in the United States, 1970–1980

PAUL A. JARGOWSKY *and* **MARY JO BANE**

AFTER YEARS of neglect, a series of developments in the 1980s rekindled public interest in the problems of urban poverty. Homeless people became more and more visible in urban areas. The media began to pay attention to an "underclass"—people, mostly black and living in urban areas, who were said to be outside the American class system.[1] And academic interest in social problems among urban blacks was rekindled by University of Chicago sociologist William Julius Wilson, whose book, *The Truly Disadvantaged*, represented a return to the study of the urban ghetto that had been choked off in the 1960s by the furor over the Moynihan report on the problems of the black family.[2]

Despite the intense interest, however, no consensus has emerged on how to define and measure ghettos, whether ghetto poverty has become worse, whether ghettos harm their residents, and what if anything public policy can do about the problem. One of the primary reasons for the confusion is that various concepts of poverty are contending simultaneously for attention:

—*Persistent poverty:* individuals and families that remain poor for long periods of time, and perhaps pass poverty on to their descendants.

—*Neighborhood poverty:* geographically defined areas of high pov-

Support for this project was provided by the Ford Foundation and the Russell Sage Foundation. David Ellwood, Naomi Goldstein, and Julie Wilson provided helpful comments on the paper. We also thank the Philadelphia regional office of the Census Bureau, Tennessee State Representative Karen Williams, and the officials of the Memphis Free the Children project for their aid. An earlier version of this article appeared as "Ghetto Poverty: Basic Questions," in *Inner-City Poverty in the United States*, edited by Laurence E. Lynn, Jr., and Michael G. H. McGeary (Washington: National Academy Press, 1990).

1. For prominent examples of this coverage see Auletta (1982); Moyers (1986); and Lehmann (1986).

2. Wilson (1987); and Moynihan (1965).

erty, usually characterized by dilapidated housing stock or public housing and high levels of unemployment.

—*Underclass poverty:* defined in terms of attitudes and behavior, especially behavior indicating deviance from social norms—weak attachment to the labor force, bearing children out of wedlock, dependence on public assistance, and drug use and habitual criminal behavior.

The first concept is defined in terms of time, the second in terms of space, and the third in terms of behavior.[3] Sometimes the concepts are combined—for example, in journalistic depictions of third-generation welfare families living in bad neighborhoods and using drugs. Nevertheless, it is important to keep the separate dimensions of the problem clear.

We have focused on the spatial dimension, the poverty of neighborhoods. We set up a criterion for defining some neighborhoods as ghettos based on their level of poverty and attempted to identify ghetto neighborhoods in metropolitan areas. We then developed a summary measure for SMSAs describing the proportion of all poor people who live in ghetto neighborhoods. Finally, we reviewed data from various SMSAs and regions and the trends between 1970 and 1980.

We have not attempted to define or measure an "underclass." The term is used by too many people in too many ways. Formally, it refers to a "heterogeneous grouping of families and individuals who are outside the mainstream of the American occupational system . . . a reality not captured in the more standard designation *lower class*." [4] Thus the claim that the underclass is growing implies that the lowest income or social class is now more isolated from the mainstream in terms of opportunity for upward mobility. The census data we worked with cannot answer questions about economic mobility, at least not directly, because they are not longitudinal.

In a less formal use of the term, saying that an underclass has developed amounts to little more than a shorthand way of saying that on various measures the poor are worse off now than they once were. There is plenty of evidence for this: the rate of labor force participation among the poor has declined, the proportion of children in single-parent families has increased, and so forth. On some measures, however, the poor are

3. The concept of persistent poverty is used by Adams, Duncan, and Rogers (1988), among others. The underclass concept, defined on the basis of behavior measured at the neighborhood level, is developed by Ricketts and Sawhill (1988). A neighborhood concept is also used by Hughes (1989) in identifying what he calls impacted ghettos.

4. Wilson (1987), p. 8.

better off than in the past: high school graduation rates have increased, for example.[5] We are troubled by the vagueness of the term when it is used this way.

To reiterate, we have not defined or measured the underclass. Instead, we have defined ghettos and counted the ghetto poor in all metropolitan areas in the United States.[6] Then we have asked basic questions about ghetto poverty:

—How can we apply the concept of ghetto poverty so that we can measure it over time and across cities?

—How extensive is the problem nationally?

—What are the characteristics of ghetto areas?

—How serious is the problem of ghetto poverty within specific urban areas?

—How does it vary by region and race?

—Has the problem been growing?

—What are the typical patterns associated with the growth of ghetto poverty?

We have not attempted to explain why ghetto poverty has been increasing in some areas and decreasing in others. We do, however, present a framework for thinking about these matters.

Defining and Measuring Ghetto Poverty

A ghetto is defined in the *Random House Dictionary* as "a section of a city, especially a thickly populated slum area, inhabited predominantly by members of a minority group, often as the result of social or economic restrictions." Historically, the term has referred to segregated Jewish areas of European cities. In the United States it has often been used to refer to any racial or ethnic enclave, without emphasis on its economic status. Current usage, however, almost always implies impoverished residents and rundown housing: completely black but middle-class neighborhoods, increasingly common in the United States, are not called ghettos.

People have an idea of what and where ghetto neighborhoods are;

5. Jencks (1989).

6. Because most definitions of the underclass assume implicitly or explicitly that they live in ghetto neighborhoods, our work could be seen as a starting point from which a national study on the underclass could be done. Van Haitsma (1989), for example, argues that the underclass is defined by poor attachment to the labor force and a social context that supports and encourages poor attachment to the labor force.

most officials in urban areas could show on a map the neighborhoods they consider ghettos. But not everyone would agree on the boundaries. One person's ghetto might be another's up-and-coming neighborhood ripe for gentrification. If ghetto neighborhoods are to be studied on a national scale, the concept must be defined in a manner that can be consistently applied to available national data.

There are two basic ways to measure ghetto poverty. One calculates a summary measure for a metropolitan area.[7] Douglas Massey and Mitchell Eggers, for example, define poverty concentration as the probability that a black poor person has poor neighbors. This measure allows for the characterization of SMSAs according to their overall level of ghetto poverty. It does not, however, identify specific neighborhoods that are ghettos and others that are not. The second strategy classifies specific neighborhoods as ghettos based on set criteria. Using Chicago's well-known community areas, William Julius Wilson defines an underclass neighborhood as one with a poverty rate greater than 30 percent. Erol Ricketts and Isabel Sawhill define underclass areas as neighborhoods that are one standard deviation worse than the national norm on four separate measures: high school graduation, labor force participation of men, welfare receipt, and single-parent families.[8]

For the reasons already described, we have not used the term underclass and we have not attempted to define or measure underclass neighborhoods. However, we have taken an approach similar to Wilson's, using census tracts as our proxy for neighborhoods.[9] We then created a summary measure for an SMSA based on the population in ghetto tracts.[10]

7. Massey and Denton (1988a) define five summary measures in the context of racial segregation: evenness, exposure, concentration, centralization, and clustering. These measures and techniques can also be applied in the context of residential segregation of the poor from the nonpoor. Race and poverty are both involved in creating ghetto neighborhoods. See Massey and Eggers (1989) and Massey, Eggers, and Denton (1989) for examples of applying aggregate measures of ghetto poverty.

8. Wilson (1987); and Ricketts and Sawhill (1988).

9. Census tracts are areas defined by the Census Bureau, typically containing 2,000 to 8,000 people. In a densely settled neighborhood, a census tract may be the size of four or five city blocks.

10. Massey and Eggers argue against "ad hoc and arbitrary definitions" of poverty neighborhoods. Further, they argue that standard measures of segregation "use complete information on the spatial distribution of income" (1989, p. 4). This is not entirely true, however. Such standard measures of segregation as the dissimilarity index and the exposure measure treat each census tract as if it were an isolated entity. An area's segregation score would not change if all the tracts were scrambled like the pieces of a jigsaw puzzle. Our

We have defined a ghetto as an area in which the overall poverty rate in a census tract is greater than 40 percent. The ghetto poor are then those poor, of any race or ethnic group, who live in such high-poverty census tracts. We have defined the level of ghetto poverty in an SMSA as the percentage of the SMSA's poor living in ghetto census tracts. However, we usually report levels of ghetto poverty separately for blacks and Hispanics, that is, the percentage of black poor living in ghetto census tracts and the percentage of Hispanic poor living in them.

In earlier work we were limited to the poverty rate cutoffs—either 20, 30, or 40 percent—used in data published by the Census Bureau.[11] Visits to various cities confirmed that the 40 percent criterion came very close to identifying areas that looked like ghettos in terms of their housing conditions.[12] Moreover, the areas selected by the 40 percent criterion corresponded closely with the neighborhoods that city officials and local Census Bureau officials considered ghettos. Even though we now have the flexibility to choose any poverty rate as the ghetto criterion, we have continued to use 40 percent as the dividing line between ghettos and mixed-income neighborhoods. With somewhat less justification, we have used 20 percent poverty as the dividing line between mixed-income and non-poor neighborhoods.

Any fixed cutoff is inherently arbitrary. A census tract with a 39.9 percent poverty rate is not very different from one with a 40.1 percent rate. Moreover, the poverty rate in a given tract is an estimate based on a sample. This potential for inaccuracy will not affect aggregate numbers, because errors will cancel one another out; but individual census tracts, especially near the boundaries of ghettos, may be misclassified.[13] Nonetheless, we are convinced that the 40 percent criterion appropriately identifies most ghetto neighborhoods. To illustrate this, we have mapped cen-

---

strategy has enabled us to identify and map census tracts, which becomes important to understanding the pattern of population movements that led to the observed changes between 1970 and 1980. It is reassuring, however, that Massey's and Eggers's main measure of poverty concentration (the exposure of the black poor to poor persons) is highly correlated with the level of ghetto poverty for blacks as we have defined it. Both measures appear to reflect the same underlying reality.

11. See Bane and Jargowsky (1988); and Bureau of the Census (1973b, 1985).

12. We visited Baltimore, Boston, Detroit, Little Rock, Memphis, Omaha, Philadelphia, San Antonio, and a number of smaller cities. The correspondence of tract poverty rates with the conditions we observed was especially striking because we were using 1980 census tract data as our guide to cities in 1987, 1988, and 1989.

13. Coulton, Chow, and Pandey (1990).

FIGURE I. Philadelphia SMSA, by Neighborhood Poverty Rate, 1980

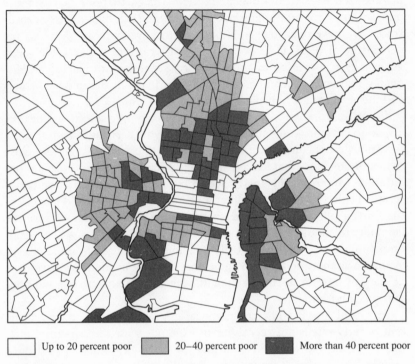

☐ Up to 20 percent poor   ▨ 20–40 percent poor   ■ More than 40 percent poor

SOURCE: See text.

sus tracts in Philadelphia and Memphis, showing nonpoor tracts (0 to 20 percent poverty), mixed-income tracts (20 to 40 percent poverty), and ghetto tracts (greater than 40 percent poverty).

In figure 1 the large North Philadelphia ghetto (the island in the middle is Temple University) consists of densely packed three- to five-story row houses, many boarded up and vacant.[14] In addition, several high-rise and low-rise housing projects dot the region. The signs of urban decay are overwhelming: broken glass, litter, stripped and abandoned automobiles, and many young men hanging out on street corners. The other major ghetto areas are West Philadelphia and Camden, New Jersey, on the other side of the Delaware River. A smaller area occurs in South Philadelphia. The areas of 20 to 40 percent poverty are basically working-class and

14. Because most tracts were not poor in 1970 and did not become ghettos by 1980, the maps seem to focus on the downtown areas, where most ghetto and mixed-income tracts are located.

FIGURE 2. Philadelphia SMSA, Neighborhoods by Race and Poverty
Status, 1980

☐ White, nonpoor	▦ White, ghetto	▨ Mixed, nonpoor	

☐ Mixed, ghetto	▥ Minority, nonpoor	■ Minority, ghetto

SOURCE: See text.

lower-middle-income neighborhoods. In our visit to Philadelphia the 40
percent census tracts, especially in North Philadelphia, looked and felt
very different from the other areas.

It is important to distinguish our definition of ghetto tracts based on a
poverty criterion from a definition based on racial composition. Not all
majority black tracts are ghettos under our definition nor are all ghettos
black. In general, ghetto tracts are a subset of a city's majority black or
Hispanic tracts. Figure 2 shows this relationship for Philadelphia. Census
tracts are divided into three groups by race: less than one-third minority
(white), one-third to two-thirds minority (mixed), and more than two-
thirds minority (minority).[15] Each group is divided into ghetto and non-

15. "Minority" includes blacks and "other races" and Hispanics.

FIGURE 3. Memphis SMSA, by Neighborhood Poverty Rate, 1980

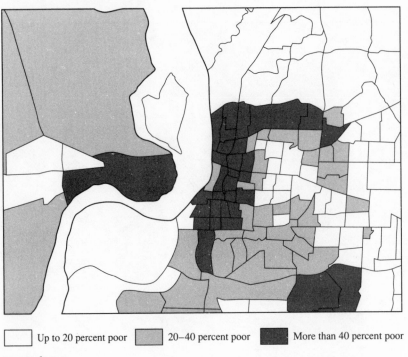

☐ Up to 20 percent poor   ▨ 20–40 percent poor   ■ More than 40 percent poor

SOURCE: See text.

ghetto tracts on the basis of their poverty rates. Given that minorities make up 20 percent of the city's population, the existence of so many census tracts that are more than two-thirds minority indicates a high degree of racial segregation. There are few mixed-race tracts. Most of the ghetto tracts are more than two-thirds minority: only a few are mixed race and even fewer non-Hispanic white. There are, however, many segregated minority areas in Philadelphia that are not ghettos by our criterion, as there are in all the cities we visited that had substantial black populations.

Figure 3 shows the census tracts of Memphis. The ghetto area of North Memphis is predominantly single-family houses, many in dilapidated condition, although there are a few low-rise housing projects such as Hurt Village. North of Chelsea Avenue, one of the main corridors in this area, the housing stock is mostly run-down shacks. The high-poverty area continues south to the east of downtown along the Mississippi River.

The South Memphis ghetto is mostly two- and three-story housing projects. The one large ghetto tract on the Arkansas side of the river is largely
swampland. The other Arkansas ghetto tracts are in West Memphis City;
here the housing stock is a mixture of single-family homes and rusting
trailers.

In both cities, mixed tracts (20 to 40 percent poor) had a look and feel
very different from ghetto tracts: the housing stock was in better condition and corner markets and other businesses more numerous. These
mixed tracts appeared to be working-class or lower-middle-class neighborhoods. Although outside appearances can be deceiving, city and Census Bureau officials and other knowledgeable people generally confirmed
our assessments.

Having set up a criterion to identify ghetto neighborhoods, we needed
a way to assess how serious a problem ghetto poverty was in a given
metropolitan area. Although one measure could be the percentage of census tracts that are ghettos, the tracts vary in population, and this criterion
would be misleading. Other possibilities included the proportion of the
population in ghetto areas, the proportion of the poor in ghetto areas,
and the proportion of the black and Hispanic poor in ghetto areas. All
three measures are interesting. The percentage of the population in ghetto
areas is, however, affected by both the overall poverty rate in the SMSA
and the proportion of the poor in ghetto areas. Using it as the summary
measure for SMSA-level ghetto poverty would make the two phenomena
hard to distinguish. Another possibility is the percentage of the poor who
live in such census tracts, but this measure is also potentially misleading:
white poor almost never live in ghettos, Hispanic poor sometimes do, and
black poor frequently do. As a result, the percentage of all poor living in
ghettos can vary dramatically with the racial composition of the SMSA
and is partly a proxy for percentage of minorities.[16]

To solve this problem, we defined levels of ghetto poverty separately
by race and ethnicity. In most of our analyses, we looked at the percentage of black poor and Hispanic poor living in ghettos. The percentage of
white poor living in ghettos was extremely low and varied little among
regions and cities; consequently we generally omit whites from our discussions of levels of ghetto poverty.[17] A potential pitfall of this measure is

16. Data reported in Bane and Jargowsky (1988) used this definition of the level of
ghetto poverty.

17. The only places where the level of ghetto poverty among whites was greater than 20
percent were college towns such as Madison, Wisconsin, and Texas towns where many of
the whites were probably Hispanic.

that it fails to take geographic proximity into account. It seems reasonable to assume that a city with twenty-five contiguous high-poverty tracts has a worse ghetto problem than one with twenty-five tracts scattered throughout the metropolitan area.[18] However, because most of the ghetto tracts in metropolitan areas occur in one or two clusters, the lack of a geographic dimension in our measure of ghetto poverty is not a significant problem. Moreover, because our measure identifies specific tracts, we were able to map ghetto tracts and visually inspect their geographic relationships. The value of this approach will be evident later.

Having settled on a measure, we compiled data for all metropolitan census tracts (approximately 40,000) in 1970 and 1980.[19] The data improve on those in our earlier work because they cover entire metropolitan areas, not merely central cities, and because all metropolitan areas are included, not just the hundred largest.[20] Although it is dangerous to judge a trend from only two data points (1970 and 1980), the most recent of which is a decade old, there is simply no source other than the decennial census that has a sample large enough to allow analysis at the neighborhood level.[21] We relied therefore on 1970 and 1980 census data.

Characteristics of Ghetto Neighborhoods

What are the ghetto neighborhoods defined by our 40 percent poverty criterion like? What do we know about the quality of life for people who

18. Those in the scattered tracts will have partial access to the amenities of their better-off nearby neighbors, more role models, and so forth. If this seems unconvincing, consider whether you would rather live in one of the scattered tracts or in the center of the twenty-five contiguous tracts.

19. The data for 1980 are from Bureau of the Census (1983d). Outside metropolitan areas, county data were included from Bureau of the Census (1983e), so that the 1980 data set is national in scope. The 1970 data are from Bureau of the Census (1973b) and include all metropolitan tracts. Jargowsky and Bane (1990, appendix B) discuss issues related to processing the tapes and compiling the data set, such as complementary suppression in 1980 and changes in SMSA boundaries between 1970 and 1980.

20. Bane and Jargowsky (1988). Ghettos such as East St. Louis, Illinois, and Camden, New Jersey, were excluded from our earlier data simply because they were outside the political boundaries of the central cities of their metropolitan areas.

21. The Census Bureau's Current Population Survey (CPS) does report "poverty area data" annually, but these data are not as useful. First, the criterion used is a 20 percent rate of poverty, which does not identify ghetto poverty very well. Second, the CPS uses tract poverty rates from a previous decennial census until the next one becomes available, so the rates are derived from data that may be ten or more years out of date. With the rapid changes and movements common in ghetto areas, this procedure is simply too flawed to make the data it generates useful.

TABLE 1. Distribution of Memphis and Philadelphia Residents, by Race and Ethnicity and Neighborhood Poverty Level, 1980
Percent

SMSA and race	SMSA total	Neighborhood poverty level		
		Up to 20 percent poor	20–40 percent poor	More than 40 percent poor
Memphis				
Black	39.8	15.8	75.6	88.9
Hispanic	0.8	0.7	1.0	0.9
Non-Hispanic white and other races[a]	59.4	83.6	23.5	10.2
Philadelphia				
Black	18.6	7.9	62.3	69.1
Hispanic	2.3	1.0	4.8	14.5
Non-Hispanic white and other races[a]	79.2	91.0	32.9	16.4

SOURCES: Bureau of the Census (1983d); and authors' calculations. Percentages may not total 100 because of rounding.
a. See text note 23.

live in ghettos, especially poor people? A separate question is whether living in a ghetto makes poverty worse. Does living in a ghetto have an independent effect on poor persons? One could attempt to answer this question by comparing characteristics of poor people who live in ghettos with those of poor people who do not. Unfortunately, this strategy ignores the possibility of unobserved differences between the two groups that are directly related to their residential status. For example, it could be that employed adults move out of ghettos, leaving the unemployed behind. The resulting difference in employment rates would reflect selection, not effects of the neighborhoods themselves. Controlled experiments or longitudinal data or both are needed to sort this out.[22] For the balance of this section, however, we are not dealing with neighborhood effects but are simply describing differences in neighborhood characteristics.

Race and Ethnicity

The distribution of Memphis and Philadelphia residents by race and Hispanic origin and the level of poverty in their neighborhoods is shown in table 1. The poorer the neighborhood, the greater the proportion of

22. Christopher Jencks and Susan Mayer (1990) have reviewed the data on what is known about neighborhood effects.

TABLE 2. Distribution of Memphis and Philadelphia Families, by Type and Race, SMSA Averages and Ghetto Neighborhoods, 1980
Percent

Family type	Memphis		Philadelphia	
	SMSA	Ghetto	SMSA	Ghetto
All families				
Married couples				
With children	39.1	21.1	38.7	20.1
Without children	36.4	24.7	39.9	20.4
Single parent	14.7	35.0	11.0	39.6
All other families	9.8	19.1	10.5	20.0
Black families				
Married couples				
With children	31.8	19.5	27.2	15.9
Without children	23.1	22.1	24.2	17.7
Single parent	29.2	38.1	30.1	44.3
All other families	15.9	20.3	18.6	22.1

SOURCES: Bureau of the Census (1983d); and authors' calculations. Percentages may not total 100 because of rounding.

residents who are members of a minority group. In Memphis, where there are very few Hispanics, ghettos are nearly 90 percent black; in Philadelphia, blacks and Hispanics account for nearly 85 percent of ghetto residents. Nonpoor neighborhoods, those with poverty rates less than 20 percent, have just the opposite race-ethnicity composition. Non-Hispanic whites make up the vast majority of persons in nonpoor neighborhoods and only a small proportion of those in ghettos.[23]

Family Structure and Demographics

Family structure in ghetto neighborhoods is also different from that in other neighborhoods (table 2). Three in four families in the Memphis and Philadelphia SMSAs are married couples. Only 11 to 15 percent are single-parent families. In ghetto neighborhoods, however, fewer than half of all families are headed by a married couple, and fewer than a quarter

23. Our estimate of the number of non-Hispanic whites is not completely accurate because tract level data are not categorized simultaneously by race, Hispanic origin, and poverty status. While it is true that Hispanics can be either white or black, most identified themselves on the 1980 census as either white or "other race." Only 2.6 percent identified themselves as black (Bureau of the Census, 1983a). Therefore a good approximation can be achieved with aggregate data by subtracting black and Hispanic data from the total, yielding non-Hispanic whites and other races.

are married couples with children. Single-parent families account for 65 percent of all families with children. Considering only blacks reduces the differences in family type but by no means eliminates them. On average, children of single parents are poorer in income and other resources. In addition, one parent often cannot provide the same level of guidance and discipline as two. Children in single-parent families do significantly worse on average than other children in educational attainment, earnings, and rates of family formation, and are somewhat more likely to be arrested.[24]

Economic Characteristics

Given that the stratifying variable is the neighborhood poverty rate, one would expect differences on economic measures. Nevertheless, it is interesting to note how large the differences are (table 3). Although nearly 90 percent of the prime-age men in the SMSAs are employed, in ghettos only two-thirds in Memphis and just over half in Philadelphia are employed. And a far greater proportion of ghetto men are not in the labor force at all. Those who are in the labor force are two to three times more likely to unemployed than those in the rest of the metropolitan area. Once again, this is partly an effect of the racial composition of the neighborhoods, but after controlling for race, substantial differences remain.

Table 3 also shows the median earnings of men who worked full-time year-round—in effect, the wage rate for full-time male workers multiplied by 2,000 (40 hours times 50 weeks). The average wage rate in Memphis for such workers was about $8.00 an hour in 1979 dollars. For blacks the rates were $5.60 for the SMSA as a whole and $4.62 for ghetto residents. (In Philadelphia the wage rates were generally higher, though the pattern of differences was the same.) Although considerably higher than the minimum wage in 1979 ($2.90), these rates suggest that the kinds of jobs ghetto residents have, even when they work full-time all year, are low paid and probably require only minimum skills. Wage rates for part-year or part-time work are undoubtedly lower.

The numbers have implications for the sources of support for families. The average earnings of all prime-age men in the Memphis and Philadel-

24. Garfinkel and McLanahan (1986); Dornbusch and others (1985); and Dembo (1988). We have focused on families in this section mainly because we did not find important differences between ghetto areas and the rest of the SMSA in the proportion of non-family households. Only about 10 percent of residents live in non-family households or group quarters.

TABLE 3. Memphis and Philadelphia Economic Characteristics, SMSA Averages and Ghetto Neighborhoods, by Race, 1980

Percent unless otherwise specified

	Memphis		Philadelphia	
Characteristic and race	SMSA	Ghetto	SMSA	Ghetto
All races				
Men age 25–44				
Employed	86.7	63.6	86.3	51.8
Unemployed	5.2	11.9	5.8	14.4
Not in labor force	8.1	24.5	7.9	33.8
Total unemployment rate	5.7	15.8	6.3	21.8
Median earnings, full-year, full-time adult male workers (dollars)	16,067	9,701	18,933	12,019
Proportion of households with income from:				
Earnings	82.1	60.3	79.3	52.6
Public assistance	11.1	33.1	10.0	42.8
Black				
Men age 25–44				
Employed	75.5	62.1	69.2	49.7
Unemployed	10.1	13.9	12.0	17.0
Not in labor force	14.3	24.1	18.8	33.3
Total unemployment rate	11.8	18.3	14.8	25.5
Median earnings, full-year, full-time adult male workers (dollars)	11,195	9,241	13,916	11,653
Proportion of households with income from:				
Earnings	74.4	59.0	71.0	50.5
Public assistance	24.4	36.5	28.4	47.5

SOURCES: Bureau of the Census (1983d); and authors' calculations. Percentages may not total 100 because of rounding.

phia ghettos were about $5,700 a year, well below the $7,421 that was needed in 1979 to support a family of four at a poverty level.[25] It is perhaps not surprising, therefore, that so many ghetto families are headed by women and that so many rely on income from public assistance.

25. The $5,700 estimate was obtained by multiplying the earnings of full-year, full-time workers by the percentage who are employed. Because it assumes that all the employed are working full-year, full-time, it is an overestimate of average earnings.

TABLE 4. Memphis and Philadelphia Social Indicators for Blacks of Selected Age Groups, SMSA Averages and Ghetto Neighborhoods, 1980

	Memphis		Philadelphia	
Indicator	SMSA	Ghetto	SMSA	Ghetto
Median years of school completed, age 25 and older	10.8	9.5	11.7	10.8
Hang-out rate, age 16–21 (percent)[a]	25.7	31.1	29.5	40.3
Ratio of employed men to women, age 25–44	60.3	44.5	53.2	32.7

SOURCES: Bureau of the Census (1983d); and authors' calculations.
a. See text for explanation.

Social Characteristics

One common thread of both academic and popular studies is that the harshness of living in a ghetto is only partly economic. For example, ghetto residents are more likely to be victims of crime, and more often perpetrators of crime, than others. They are more likely to have problems with substance abuse and to have been victims of racial discrimination, police brutality, and environmental health hazards.[26]

The census does not provide such details. There are, however, a few useful measures available at the level of the census tract. Differences between ghetto residents and others in attachment to the labor force and in the incidence of welfare recipiency were noted earlier. Several other differences are shown in table 4. All figures are for blacks only, so none of the differences between neighborhoods are the result of racial composition. The table shows a large difference between ghetto residents and residents of the SMSA in years of schooling completed. This difference may reflect the socioeconomic level of ghetto residents, lower educational aspirations in these neighborhoods, or the quality of education in ghetto schools. Whatever the reason, ghetto residents have low levels of education. The median adult in a Memphis ghetto, for example, has not finished his or her sophomore year in high school.[27]

The other two indicators in the table require some explanation. The hang-out rate, an attempt to measure idleness or exclusion from the

26. Anderson (1989); Wilson (1987); Coulton, Chow, and Pandey, (1990); and O'Regan and Wiseman (1989).
27. The median level for all adults in the SMSA is 12.1 years, indicating some postsecondary education.

mainstream economy among young people, is the proportion of civilians 16 to 21 years old who are not in school and not working (either unemployed or not in the labor force).[28] This figure should almost certainly be interpreted differently for men and women, but unfortunately they are grouped together in the census tract data.[29] Among young men, those hanging out may be thought of as the pool available for criminal enterprises, though by no means do all of them turn to crime. Among young women, a significant proportion is likely to be poorly educated, unemployed young mothers, many (at least in the ghetto) unmarried. In the Philadelphia ghetto, 40 percent of the young black adults are hanging out; in the SMSA as a whole the rate is just under 30 percent, so the difference is not as great as one might have guessed.

The third measure in table 4 is the ratio of employed men ages 25 to 44 to women of the same age. William Julius Wilson and Katheryn Neckerman have argued that women are not inclined to marry men who are not in a position to support them and that the low levels of this "male marriageable pool index" in ghetto communities help explain the high levels of female-headed families.[30] In Philadelphia ghettos, there is one employed man for every three women in the 25–44 age group; in Memphis, about one for every two. In part, the ratios reflect the census undercount of urban black males, but no one alleges an undercount large enough to account for a ratio of one man to two or three women. A second factor contributing to such low ratios in the ghettos is the number of men who have died, joined the army, or gone to prison. A third factor is the low employment level of the remaining men.

Public Policy and Ghettos

Ghettos, then, contain a concentration of economic and social problems that census data barely suggest. Those who live and work in these communities could doubtless paint a much more vivid picture. Although we have not attempted to argue that ghettos have effects on their residents, in some ways it does not matter. There are enough people with economic hardships, educational deficits, and social problems clustered in these neighborhoods that a compassionate society should worry about

28. See Mare and Winship (1984) for a discussion of the importance of considering the employment of black youth in the context of their school enrollment and military enlistment.

29. The data are from Bureau of the Census (1983d), table PB49.

30. Wilson and Neckerman (1986).

TABLE 5. Distribution of Poor Persons, SMSA Averages and Ghetto Neighborhoods, by Race and Ethnicity, 1980

Race	United States (thousands)	Metropolitan areas		Ghetto areas	
		Thousands	Percent	Thousands	Percent of total poor
All	27,388	18,820	68.7	2,449	8.9
Black	7,548	5,734	76.0	1,590	21.1
Hispanic	3,348	2,869	85.7	534	15.9
Non-Hispanic white[a]	16,492	10,217	62.0	325	2.0

SOURCES: Bureau of the Census (1983d); and authors' calculations.
a. See text note 23.

their quality of life. If further research shows that living in a ghetto makes it even harder for the poor to escape poverty, that will provide one more incentive to tackle the problem.

Ghetto Poverty, 1970–80: The National Picture

In 1980 there were 27 million poor people in the United States—12.4 percent of the population.[31] Of these, 18.8 million (nearly 70 percent) lived in the 318 SMSAs defined at the time of the census.[32] It would be a mistake, however, to assume that all people who were poor and lived in metropolitan areas lived in ghettos. The total number of poor who lived in a metropolitan census tract where the poverty rate was greater than 40 percent was 2.4 million. The number of metropolitan poor, ghetto poor, and poor living outside metropolitan areas is shown in table 5. Fewer

31. Although the census uses income figures from the previous year, in this case 1979, it reports residence in the census year. The census somewhat overstates poverty. The Current Population Survey poverty rate in 1979 was somewhat lower—11.7 percent. In general, the CPS seems to do a better job of measuring income than the census, resulting in a lower measured poverty rate. Underreporting of public assistance and other unearned income may be particularly serious in the census. The general direction of bias should be toward some overstatement of poverty rates and perhaps poverty concentrations as well.

32. Several more SMSAs were defined after the census, and major changes were made in metropolitan area boundaries in 1983. In addition, the terminology was changed. The term SMSA was eliminated, replaced by Consolidated Metropolitan Statistical Areas (CMSAs), Primary Metropolitan Statistical Areas (PMSAs), and Metropolitan Statistical Areas (MSAs). CMSAs contain more than one PMSA. PMSAs and MSAs, taken together, are roughly comparable to the pre-1983 SMSAs (Bureau of the Census, 1989, appendix II, p. 890). We continue to use the term SMSA to indicate that our data are based on the pre-1983 concepts and boundaries.

than 9 percent of all poor lived in ghettos in 1979.[33] Even within metropolitan areas, only 13 percent did; the rest lived in mixed-income and
nonpoor neighborhoods. Thus ghetto poverty is a relatively small part of
overall poverty in the United States. This is not to say that poverty in
ghettos is not important—it may be far more degrading and harmful to
be poor in an urban ghetto than elsewhere—but poverty in the United
States is certainly not confined to urban ghettos.

Table 5 also shows that the proportion of the poor in ghettos varies
dramatically by race. Only 2 percent of the non-Hispanic white poor
lived in ghettos, compared with 21 percent of black poor and 16 percent
of Hispanic poor. Within metropolitan areas, almost three in ten poor
blacks lived in a ghetto. As a result, the 2.4 million ghetto poor were 65
percent black, 22 percent Hispanic, and 13 percent non-Hispanic white
and other races. Thus ghettos are predominantly populated by blacks and
Hispanics, and black and Hispanic poor are much more likely than white
poor to live in a ghetto.

The Growth of Ghetto Poverty

Much of the concern about urban poverty stems from a sense that
ghettos, and the social problems they represent, have been getting worse.
To evaluate these claims, we present data on the changes in ghetto poverty between 1970 and 1980.[34]

Between 1970 and 1980 the number of poor living in ghettos in metropolitan areas increased by 29.5 percent, from 1,890,925 to 2,449,324.
This is much less than the 66 percent growth reported by Richard Nathan
and John Lego in 1986 and by us in 1988. Those estimates were based on
published data for the fifty largest central cities. The difference is mainly
due to the inclusion in this analysis of smaller SMSAs, many of them
southern and many showing substantial decreases in ghetto poverty. Thus
the focus on large central cities left out an important part of the story.
The number of black ghetto poor grew by 27 percent from 1970 to 1980

33. Bane and Jargowsky (1988) reported that 6.7 percent of the poor lived in ghettos in
the 100 largest central cities. The increase here to 8.9 percent reflects the addition of smaller
SMSAs and suburbs, that is, portions of SMSAs that are not central cities.

34. Not all metropolitan areas that existed in 1980 were defined in 1970, and there
were numerous boundary changes. We tried to adjust for significant boundary changes by
recoding the 1970 data to be consistent with 1980 boundaries. For more information, see
Jargowsky and Bane (1990), appendix B.

TABLE 6. Number of Black and Hispanic Ghetto Poor, All SMSAs, 1970, 1980

Race and origin	Number of SMSAs (1980)	Ghetto poor (thousands)			Percent change
		1970	1980	Change	
All races	318	1,891	2,449	558	29.5
Increases	107	785	1,712	927	118.1
No change	44	0	0	0	0
Decreases	88	1,106	668	−438	−39.6
New in 1980	79	. . .	67	67	. . .
Black	318	1,247	1,590	343	27.5
Increases	96	558	1,121	563	100.9
No change	62	0	0	0	0
Decreases	81	689	426	−263	−38.2
New in 1980	79	. . .	42	42	. . .
Hispanic	318	385	534	149	38.7
Increases	116	96	361	265	276.0
No change	86	0	0	0	0
Decreases	37	289	170	−119	−41.2
New in 1980	79	. . .	3	3	. . .

SOURCES: Bureau of the Census (1973b, 1983d); and authors' calculations.

and the number of Hispanic poor by 39 percent.[35] These figures, however, are misleading: the aggregate increase of more than one-half million ghetto poor obscures the fact that some metropolitan areas had large increases and some large decreases.

Table 6 shows the number of SMSAs with increases and decreases in the number of all ghetto poor, black ghetto poor, and Hispanic ghetto poor. More SMSAs experienced decreases or no change than experienced increases. The number of ghetto poor in those SMSAs with increases more than doubled; for Hispanics the number tripled. Metropolitan areas with decreases had more than one-third fewer ghetto poor in 1980. It is also important to note that the addition of new SMSAs between 1970 and 1980 does not account for much of the growth in ghetto poverty— only for about 12 percent of it.[36]

To further understand the variations in the level of ghetto poverty and changes over time, one must look at specific SMSAs. As we will see, the

35. However, the aggregate level of concentration—the percent of the metropolitan poor living in ghettos—increased only modestly among blacks (from 26.4 to 27.7 percent) and decreased among Hispanics (from 23.7 to 18.6 percent).

36. In the 239 SMSAs that were defined in both years, there was a net increase of just under one-half million, and a growth rate of 25.9 percent.

TABLE 7. SMSAs with Most Ghetto Poor, 1970, 1980

SMSA	Number of ghetto poor	Cumulative percent
1970		
New York	134,139	7.1
McAllen-Pharr-Edinburg, Texas	80,477	11.3
Memphis	77,589	15.5
Chicago	74,370	19.4
New Orleans	71,932	23.2
San Antonio	54,749	26.1
Brownsville–Harlingen–San Benito, Texas	53,632	28.9
Philadelphia	49,657	31.5
Baltimore	45,732	34.0
Los Angeles–Long Beach	41,885	36.2
Remaining 229 metropolitan areas	1,206,763	100.0
1980		
New York	477,621	19.5
Chicago	194,338	27.4
Philadelphia	127,134	32.6
Baltimore	60,983	35.1
McAllen-Pharr-Edinburg, Texas	58,222	37.5
Memphis	56,915	39.8
New Orleans	56,504	42.1
Newark	54,720	44.4
Detroit	54,572	46.6
Los Angeles–Long Beach	51,306	48.7
Remaining 308 metropolitan areas	1,257,009	100.0

SOURCES: Bureau of the Census (1983d); and authors' calculations.

often-cited aggregate figures mask considerable regional variation and, to a lesser degree, city-to-city variation within regions.

Where Are the Ghetto Poor?

The most visible ghetto poor are those who live in the largest urban areas, and these areas in fact contain a large proportion of the ghetto poor. In 1980, slightly more than one-fourth of all ghetto poor lived in New York and Chicago. The ten metropolitan areas with the largest concentrations accounted for almost half of all ghetto poor (table 7). Every region of the United States was represented: the South contributed four areas, the Northeast three, the North Central two, and the West one. Large black populations accounted for most of the ghetto poor. The exception was the McAllen-Pharr-Edinburg SMSA, which had a large His-

FIGURE 4. Largest Increases in Number of Ghetto Poor, by SMSA and Race, 1970–80

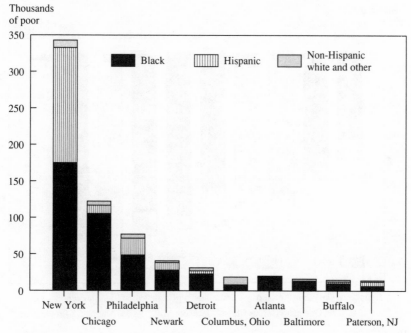

SOURCE: See text.

panic population. The top ten in 1970 were somewhat different. They accounted for only one-third of the ghetto poor instead of one-half. And southern cities were more prominently represented (six of ten), both in the Southeast where the ghetto poor were predominantly black and in Texas where they were predominantly Hispanic.

The ten cities with the largest increases in the number of ghetto poor from 1970 to 1980 accounted for three-fourths of the total increase (figure 4). New York alone accounted for more than one-third, and New York and Chicago together for half. Adding Philadelphia, Newark, and Detroit brings the total to two-thirds. Atlanta and Baltimore, unlike many other cities in the South, also had large increases. The eight northern cities doubled or tripled their ghetto populations. The increases were largely among blacks, though there was a significant Hispanic increase in New York. The SMSAs with large decreases were of two types: Texas cities with large decreases in the number of Hispanics living in ghettos,

FIGURE 5. Largest Decreases in Number of Ghetto Poor, by SMSA and Race, 1970–80

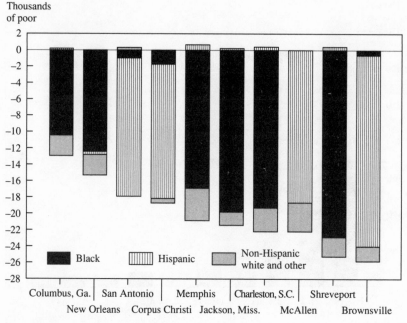

SOURCE: See text.

and other southern cities with large decreases among blacks (figure 5). The decreases were not limited to a few cities, as were the increases. The ten cities with the largest decreases accounted for less than half the total decrease.

These facts begin to explain the widespread impression of rapidly increasing ghetto poverty. In some cities the area of the ghetto and the number of people affected have both increased rapidly. These cities include some of the nation's largest population centers, where many large foundations, universities, and news organizations are located. But because many of the largest decreases have occurred in small- to medium-size metropolitan areas in the South, they have received less attention. These regional patterns are shown in table 8. Relative to all metropolitan poor, the ghetto poor in 1980 were more likely to live in the northeast and north central regions and in the largest cities. A substantial majority lived in central cities.[37] Moreover, most of those in suburbs were probably in

37. A few tracts were split by central city boundaries; we have included these in suburbs. A comparable variable is not available on the 1970 census tapes.

TABLE 8. Distribution of Metropolitan Poor, by Region,
Neighborhood Type, and SMSA Size, 1970, 1980
Percent unless otherwise specified

Item	Metropolitan areas		Ghetto areas	
	1970	1980	1970	1980
Poor (thousands)	15,240	18,820	1,891	2,449
Region				
Northeast	25.0	24.2	13.0	32.7
North Central	22.1	21.3	14.2	21.8
South	34.4	34.5	65.0	39.4
West	18.5	19.9	7.7	6.1
Neighborhood type				
Central city	n.a.	51.2	n.a.	86.6
Suburb	n.a.	48.4	n.a.	13.4
SMSA population				
Less than 500,000	26.7	30.2	38.5	24.0
500,000–1,000,000	16.6	16.0	16.2	13.1
More than 1,000,000	56.6	53.8	45.4	62.9

SOURCES: Bureau of the Census (1973b, 1983d); and authors' calculations.
n.a. Not available.

places such as East St. Louis, Illinois, and Camden, New Jersey, which
are suburbs only in a technical sense. In 1970, in contrast, almost two-
thirds of the ghetto poor lived in the South, and more than half in cities
of less than a million people.

The Level of Ghetto Poverty

Because the distribution of the total numbers of metropolitan poor by
region and SMSA size changed very little between 1970 and 1980,
changes in the distribution of the ghetto poor must have been caused by
increases or decreases in the percentage of the poor living in ghettos,
which we call the level of ghetto poverty.[38] The level of ghetto poverty
increased 1.2 percentage points among blacks and decreased 5.1 points
among Hispanics (table 9). As with the changes in the numbers of ghetto
poor, however, the aggregate levels conceal considerable variation. Some
cities experienced large increases in the percentage of the poor living in
ghettos, others large decreases. Among Hispanics, ghetto poverty

38. Both the number of poor living in ghettos and the total number of poor in an area
can change. Thus the change in the number of ghetto poor, described earlier, and the change
in the level of ghetto poverty described here, can be quite different.

TABLE 9. Level of Black and Hispanic Ghetto Poverty, 1970, 1980

Percent unless otherwise specified

Race	Number of SMSAs	Level of ghetto poverty		
		1970	1980	Change
Black	176	26.5	27.7	1.2
Increases	89	19.1	31.8	12.7
Decreases	87	37.7	23.9	−13.8
Hispanic	151	23.7	18.6	−5.1
Increases	99	14.2	28.1	13.9
Decreases	52	32.4	14.4	−18.0

SOURCES: Bureau of the Census (1973b, 1983d); and authors' calculations.

doubled in the 99 cities in which it increased, and fell by more than half in the 52 in which it decreased.[39]

The possibility of strong regional shifts mentioned earlier is borne out in changes in the level of ghetto poverty in the metropolitan areas aggregated by region. The Northeast, dominated by New York, had an increase of nearly 20 percentage points in the level of ghetto poverty among blacks (table 10). The north central region also had a substantial increase. The South and West showed decreases.

Table 10 also shows the levels of ghetto poverty by size of the metropolitan area. In 1970 the highest level of concentration of blacks was in the smallest metropolitan areas; by 1980 the opposite was true. Disaggregating by region shows that the general decline in the level of black ghetto poverty in the South is most evident in smaller SMSAs. In the northeast and north central regions, even smaller SMSAs showed increases, though not as large as bigger SMSAs. The West also had larger decreases in the smaller SMSAs. Hispanic poverty concentrations followed similar patterns.

In the North, all large cities except Boston had increases in levels of ghetto poverty among blacks, although the size of the increase varied considerably.[40] In the South, the picture was more mixed. Most cities had decreases among blacks, some of them large. But Baltimore, Atlanta, and Miami saw modest increases and Fort Lauderdale a large increase. There were also increases in a few smaller cities.

39. The aggregate level of ghetto poverty as reported in table 9 is the weighted average of SMSAs in the group; some SMSAs were not included because they did not exist in 1970 or they existed but had no blacks or no Hispanics in 1970 or 1980 and, therefore, did not have a level of ghetto poverty (division by zero).

40. Jargowsky and Bane (1990), appendix A, shows data for individual cities, organized by region and size of metropolitan area.

TABLE 10. Percentage of Black and Hispanic Poor in Ghettos, by SMSA Population and Region, 1970, 1980

Race and region	SMSA population 1970				SMSA population 1980			
	Less than 0.5 million	0.5– 1.0 million	1.0 million or more	All SMSAs	Less than 0.5 million	0.5– 1.0 million	1.0 million or more	All SMSAs
Black								
Metropolitan average	37	29	22	27	22	25	31	28
Northeast	4	7	17	15	17	17	38	34
North Central	7	8	23	20	20	21	33	30
South	45	35	29	36	24	28	28	26
West	21	47	14	16	6	23	11	11
Hispanic								
Metropolitan average	48	12	14	24	22	10	19	19
Northeast	4	7	21	19	22	18	42	37
North Central	4	0	4	3	5	4	10	9
South	64	17	23	45	32	11	11	21
West	11	13	6	8	2	3	5	4

SOURCES: Bureau of the Census (1973b, 1983d); and authors' calculations.
a. Table contains data for 239 SMSAs in 1970 and 318 SMSAs in 1980. See Jargowsky and Bane (1990), appendix B.

Ghetto Poverty and the SMSA Poverty Rate

What accounts for these strong regional variations? Many factors are potentially involved, including differences in racial and economic segregation, changes in the economic structure of metropolitan areas, and interregional migration.[41] However, the SMSA poverty rates among blacks and Hispanics are clearly important. Figure 6 shows the change in the level of ghetto poverty among blacks plotted against the change in the black poverty rate between 1970 and 1980. Each point represents an SMSA, and the symbol indicates the region and size of the metropolitan area.[42]

41. To cite just a few examples of research concerning the importance of these different factors: Wilson (1987) argues that changes in economic segregation among blacks play a key role; Massey and Eggers (1989) argue that interactions between black poverty and racial segregation are more important than economic segregation among blacks; others (Hughes, 1989; Kasarda, 1988) examine the role of changes in the location of jobs within the metropolitan area. Jargowsky and Ellwood (1990) are examining the relationship between the household distribution of income and the neighborhood distribution of income.

42. The graph only includes SMSAs which were defined in both decades and which had at least 10,000 blacks in 1970. Of 318 SMSAs, 148 satisfy both conditions. We exclude the

FIGURE 6. Changes in Black Ghetto Poverty and Poverty Rates, by Region and SMSA Size, 1970–80

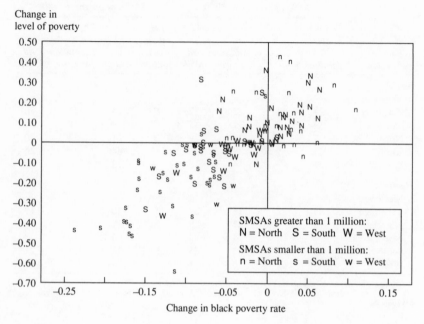

SOURCE: See text.

There was a strong relationship between the change in the black poverty rate and the change in the level of ghetto poverty.[43] Moreover, most SMSAs with decreases in poverty were smaller cities in the South. Large northern cities more often experienced increases in black poverty and in ghetto poverty among blacks.

The strength and consistency of the relationship might lead one to conclude, erroneously as it turns out, that the increases and decreases in levels of ghetto poverty arose mechanically from changes in the poverty rate. In other words, as the poverty rate rose more tracts fell into the 40 percent or higher poverty category, and thus more of the poor lived in

---

smaller SMSAs because the level of ghetto poverty in such cities depends on the poverty rate of just one or two tracts and is therefore highly subject to random noise.

43. The relationship is similar among Hispanics. Plotting the levels of poverty against the level of ghetto poverty, rather than changes, also shows a relationship, but a less strong one.

ghettos. This is part of what happened, but the full picture was much more complex.

The Geography of Ghetto Poverty

In the preceding section we described changes in the number of persons living in ghettos and also in the level of ghetto poverty, but said little about the physical extent of the ghettos, their locations, or the patterns of economic changes and population movements typical of them. This set of topics, which we refer to as the geography of ghetto poverty, is the subject of this section. It examines four cities, two with large increases in the level of black ghetto poverty, one with a modest increase, and one with a large decrease, and describes what actually happened to the geography of the ghetto (none of the cities had a significant Hispanic population). We also describe the population changes that took place in different areas of the city, as a way of beginning to understand the complicated process by which groups of census tracts remain, become, or stop being ghettos. Finally, we examine the relationship between the black poverty rate and ghetto poverty across SMSAs.

Understanding Increases in Ghetto Poverty

The percentage of the black poor living in ghetto areas could have risen between 1970 and 1980 for several reasons:

—More of the black poor could have moved from other areas of the city into the ghetto.

—The poverty rate could have risen, causing some additional census tracts to exceed the 40 percent cutoff and be classified as ghettos.

—Nonpoor persons could have moved out of mixed-income tracts. This would cause the group left behind to be poorer, and some additional tracts would exceed the 40 percent cutoff.

—Several of the above could have happened simultaneously, with differences in fertility and mortality and changes in family structure also playing a role.

Each explanation can be checked against the data for specific census tracts. If poor people had moved into the ghetto and had caused the increase in ghetto poverty, there would be no new ghetto tracts, and the number of people in the existing ghetto tracts would have increased. If new ghetto tracts had been added by changes in the poverty rate, we would expect the number of ghetto tracts to have increased. We would

FIGURE 7. Cleveland (Top) and Memphis (Bottom) SMSA Changes in Census Tract Poverty, 1970–80

New, split, or no data	Not poor in 1970; not ghetto in 1980	Not poor in 1970; ghetto in 1980
Mixed in 1970; not ghetto in 1980	Mixed in 1970; ghetto in 1980	Ghetto in 1970; not ghetto in 1980
Ghetto in 1970 and 1980		

SOURCE: See text.

FIGURE 8. Milwaukee (Top) and Philadelphia (Bottom) SMSA
Changes in Census Tract Poverty, 1970–80

New, split,
or no data

Not poor in 1970;
not ghetto in 1980

Not poor in 1970;
ghetto in 1980

Mixed in 1970;
not ghetto in 1980

Mixed in 1970;
ghetto in 1980

Ghetto in 1970;
not ghetto in 1980

Ghetto in 1970 and 1980

SOURCE: See text.

also expect the total number of people in both the 1970 ghetto tracts and the new tracts not to have changed much. The number of poor would have gone up, but by about the same as the decrease in the number of nonpoor: people would simply be reclassified from nonpoor to poor. If the increase in ghetto poverty had been caused by movement of the non-poor out of mixed-income tracts, we would again expect the number of ghetto tracts to have increased, but now we would expect the new ghetto tracts to have had fewer people in 1980 than in 1970.

To investigate these mechanics, we examined the location of the 1970 and 1980 ghetto census tracts and the movements of people into and out of different areas in Cleveland, Memphis, Milwaukee, and Philadelphia. But identifying who was moving where does not tell us anything about why they moved. The causes of the increases in ghetto poverty lie beyond these mere descriptions. Understanding the dynamics, however, is an important first step and can help frame the right questions to ask about the deeper causes.

The four cities showed different patterns of change. Cleveland was a large north central city with a high level of poverty concentration in 1970 (32.8 percent) and a modest growth in concentration (3.8 percentage points) from 1970 to 1980. Memphis, a large southern city with a large black population, had an extremely high level of poverty concentration in 1970 (56.2 percent) and a large decrease in concentration (16.9 percentage points) between 1970 and 1980. Milwaukee had a low level of poverty concentration in 1970 (8.6 percent), but one that experienced very rapid growth (15.5 percentage points). Philadelphia had a moderate level of poverty concentration in 1970 (21.3 percent) that also experienced rapid growth (15.6 percentage points.

Figures 7 and 8 are maps of these cities showing seven categories of census tracts:

—Tracts that were ghettos in 1970 and either remained ghettos in 1980 or improved.

—Tracts that were mixed income (20 to 40 percent poor) in 1970 and either became ghettos by 1980 or did not.

—Tracts that were not poor (less than 20 percent poor) in 1970, again divided into those that became ghettos by 1980 and those that did not.

—Tracts that were added to the SMSA between 1970 and 1980, and existing tracts that were split, virtually none of which were poor in 1980.

Table 11 shows the total number of tracts that fell into the various categories. The table and the maps illustrate some important aspects of how changes in poverty concentration actually took place.

TABLE 11. Numbers of Ghettos in Four SMSAs, 1980, by Neighborhood Type in 1970

Neighborhood type	Cleveland	Memphis	Milwaukee	Philadelphia
Ghetto tracts, 1970	19	37	11	26
Stayed ghetto in 1980	18	30	7	19
Improved by 1980	1	7	4	7
Mixed-income tracts, 1970	51	31	43	99
Became ghetto by 1980	21	4	11	43
Did not become ghetto	30	27	32	56
Tracts not poor, 1970	340	57	303	1,047
Became ghetto by 1980	3	1	1	4
Did not become ghetto	337	56	302	1,043
Total ghetto tracts, 1980	42	35	19	59

SOURCES: Bureau of the Census (1983d); and authors' calculations.

Geographic Spread of the Ghetto

The geographic extent of the ghetto areas in Philadelphia, Milwaukee, and Cleveland expanded dramatically. Even in Memphis, where the proportion of the poor living in high-poverty areas declined substantially, the net number of ghetto tracts decreased by only two. In general, the areas that became ghettos by 1980 had been mixed-income tracts in 1970 that were contiguous to ghetto areas. But the maps show that the process was not completely orderly. Some 1970 ghetto tracts were no longer ghettos in 1980, even in the cities where ghetto poverty increased. Some 1980 ghetto tracts were not contiguous to 1970 ghettos, and a few were not poor in 1970. Nonetheless, the basic pattern was one of expansion of the ghetto into adjacent mixed-income tracts.

The expansion rules out the hypothesis that the increase in ghetto poverty in the three cities with increases was caused by poor people moving into the ghetto. To distinguish between the other two hypotheses—that tracts became ghettos simply because of changes in the poverty rate or because the nonpoor moved out—one needs to look at population movements.

Movements from Ghetto and Mixed-Income Tracts

Between 1970 and 1980 both ghettos and mixed-income areas experienced population decreases (table 12). This pattern suggests that the nonpoor were moving out of mixed-income areas, causing them to "tip" and

TABLE 12. Population Loss in Ghettos and Mixed-Income Tracts in Four SMSAs, 1970–80

Type of tract	Cleveland	Memphis	Milwaukee	Philadelphia
Ghetto areas, 1970				
Population, 1970	62,233	143,951	17,319	111,622
Percent change in population, 1970–80	−36.2	−21.6	−31.5	−24.2
Percent change in black poor, 1970–80	−26.3	−23.5	−30.4	−14.2
Percent of black poor, 1970	32.8	54.2	15.5	21.3
Percent of black poor, 1980	21.9	38.2	7.1	14.8
Mixed-income areas, 1970				
Population, 1970	151,638	134,609	119,090	491,169
Percent change in population, 1970–80	−36.8	−7.0	−20.9	−23.8
Percent change in black poor, 1970–80	−12.8	−6.1	18.5	−1.6
Percent of black poor, 1970	38.0	27.4	66.4	46.4
Percent of black poor, 1980	30.0	23.7	52.0	37.0

SOURCES: Bureau of the Census (1983d); and authors' calculations.

become ghettos. The patterns are complicated, however, and it is useful to lay them out in some detail.

Table 12 shows what may appear to be a paradox: the 1970 ghetto areas contained a smaller proportion of the black poor in 1980 than in 1970, even in cities where the level of ghetto poverty increased substantially. The percentage of the poor who were living in ghettos, therefore, would have declined in these cities had not additional tracts been classified as ghettos. Mixed-income areas in all four cities—what we can think of as potential ghettos—also experienced substantial population losses, even in Memphis, were the metropolitan population as a whole was growing rapidly. In all four cities, the proportion of the black poor living in mixed-income areas declined substantially between 1970 and 1980.

This pattern is most consistent with the hypothesis that the increase in ghetto poverty was caused by movements of nonpoor people out of the 1970 mixed-income areas. The poor were moving out as well, but the nonpoor left in greater numbers, leaving behind a group of people in 1980 that was poorer than in 1970. As a result, some of the 1970 mixed-income tracts became ghettos by 1980. In three of the cities the addition of the black poor in these new ghetto tracts to the shrinking proportion of the poor in the old ghetto tracts was enough to result in an increase in the proportion of the poor living in ghettos. In other words, the level of ghetto poverty went up only because new areas were classified as ghettos.[44]

Perhaps it is not surprising that ghettos lost population during the decade. The data are consistent with the emptying out of downtown areas that has been observed in many cities. Given the harsh conditions of life in these neighborhoods, anyone who could leave probably did. However, the fact that mixed-income areas also lost many residents is somewhat surprising. One might have predicted increases in the number of black poor in these areas, at least in the cities where ghetto poverty increased, because these are the areas from which new ghetto tracts formed. And one might have expected the people leaving the ghetto to settle there. Some may have, but on balance the population—poor and nonpoor—declined substantially. The population, poor and nonpoor, black and white, was spreading out from poor and mixed-income tracts into other areas. The next ring, areas that were not poor and mostly white, became mixed-income and often mixed-race, becoming home to a larger proportion of the black and poor population. The white nonpoor left these areas, which also lost population overall. Population growth took place mostly in tracts at the outskirts of the SMSAs, some of which were added to the metropolitan areas after 1970.

Tracts That Become Ghettos

In the three cities in which ghetto poverty increased, a part of what had been the mixed-income area became a ghetto. The number of mixed-income tracts that tipped into ghetto status varied by city, but was substantial in all three. Comparing the mixed-income tracts that became ghettos with those that did not reveals some interesting commonalities and contrasts.

Table 13 shows population changes by race and poverty status in the 1970 mixed-income tracts that had and had not become ghettos by 1980. The 1970 mixed-income tracts that became ghettos lost population in all three cities. The number of black poor in these tracts generally increased, but the number of blacks who were not poor decreased by a much greater number. Because each of the three cities had an increase in the black poverty rate, the increase in the number of black poor came from a change of

44. This is a general pattern. In Jargowsky and Bane (1990), appendix A shows the number of ghetto census tracts in 1970 and 1980. In almost all the areas where the level of ghetto poverty increased, and even in many areas where it decreased, the ghetto area was spreading.

TABLE 13. Population Changes in Mixed-Income Tracts in Three SMSAs, by Race, 1970–80

Type of Change	Cleveland	Milwaukee	Philadelphia
Mixed-income tracts in 1970 that became ghettos in 1980			
Population, 1970	53,382	27,113	246,623
Change in black poor, 1970–80	1,085	1,231	4,164
Change in black not poor, 1970–80	−10,556	−3,149	−39,604
Change in whites, 1970–80	−11,124	−3,886	−26,034
Mixed-income tracts in 1970 that did not become ghettos in 1980			
Population, 1970	98,256	91,977	244,546
Change in black poor, 1970–80	−5,075	2,269	−5,686
Change in black not poor, 1970–80	−16,323	−4,220	−26,619
Change in whites, 1970–80	−12,751	−18,228	−20,883

SOURCES: Bureau of the Census (1983d); and authors' calculations.

poverty status among some blacks. Declines in the white population occurred among both poor and nonpoor.

In all three cities the mixed-income areas that did not become ghettos showed patterns of population change basically similar to what occurred in the mixed-income tracts that became ghettos—though with somewhat different proportions of black and white, poor and nonpoor, among the movers and stayers. The mixed-income areas that did not become ghettos also lost population, both black and white. The difference between tracts that became ghettos and tracts that did not seems to be more a matter of degree than of kind.

These data suggest that at least in these four cities the process by which geographic areas stayed, became, or stopped being ghettos was complicated. In none was the process a simple matter of the poor moving into ghetto areas or the nonpoor moving out. Nor can the situation in any city be described as one in which people basically stayed put but that changes in the poverty rate caused more areas to be pushed over the 40 percent line. Instead there was a general pattern of dispersion—probably part of a longer historical trend—interacting with changes in the poverty rate and continuing high levels of racial segregation.

Conclusions

We have attempted to determine the size and extent of the ghetto problem in the United States and to learn whether the problem was getting worse. We began with a belief in the conventional wisdom that urban ghettos were large and growing and deserved focused policy attention. Our answers to questions about urban poverty reveal a much more diverse picture than we had anticipated.

—There were 2.4 million ghetto poor in the United States in 1980, about 9 percent of all poor persons, living predominantly in the central cities of large metropolitan areas.

—About half the ghetto poor lived in the northeast or north central regions, and another 40 percent in the South.

—The level of ghetto poverty varied tremendously from city to city.

The impression that ghetto poverty is growing rapidly turns out to be only partly true. The data on the growth of ghetto poverty from 1970 to 1980 indicates that:

—Between 1970 and 1980 the number of ghetto poor increased by 29.5 percent, but the level of ghetto poverty (the percent of the poor living in ghettos) increased only modestly among blacks and decreased among Hispanics.

—The aggregate numbers concealed substantial regional variation. Ghetto poverty increased dramatically in large northern cities, and decreased equally dramatically in many southern cities, especially small and medium-sized southern cities.

—Changes in the regional distribution of the ghetto poor were driven by changes in levels of ghetto poverty, which were very different among regions, and to some extent varied from city to city within regions.

—Within the four cities that we studied in detail, there was a pattern of emptying out of downtown neighborhoods. Ghettos and mixed-income neighborhoods generally had substantial decreases in population.

—In cities where ghetto poverty increased, many census tracts that were not ghettos in 1970 became ghettos by 1980. The process was driven by a combination of increases in the poverty rate and differential outmigration of the poor and nonpoor.

There are large and growing ghetto poverty populations in perhaps a dozen large northern SMSAs. But the phenomenon characterizes only a minority of SMSAs. Previous work on this subject, including but not limited to our own, usually focused on the 50 or 100 largest metropolitan areas or central cities. The focus missed an important part of the picture. The data for all SMSAs indicate that many had small increases in ghetto poverty, and in the South most SMSAs had substantial decreases.

The implications of these findings for public policy are not entirely clear. For one thing, SMSAs differ dramatically in the scope and nature of their urban poverty problems. Much more needs to be learned, both in the aggregate and at the level of individual SMSAs, before we can draw firm conclusions about the growth of poverty areas and their effects on their residents. However, the data would lead us to support the following guidelines for public policies concerning ghetto poverty:

—It probably makes sense to have policies that focus specifically on those SMSAs with large and growing problems rather than a national policy based on an assumption that all cities are alike.

—The policies and programs for those SMSAs with large and growing problems should recognize the strong relationship between the general economic vitality of SMSAs and regions and the problems of particular neighborhoods and population groups.

—Policies that affect the geographic mobility of the poor and nonpoor may play an important role in ghetto formation. Thus housing and development policies may have an important role to play in many cities.

We offer these as preliminary suggestions; more detailed recommendations would need to be based on a better understanding of the causes of the changes and variations documented here. We are continuing to investigate these causes, and we hope that the basic data presented here encourage others to do the same.

References

Adams, Terry, Greg Duncan, and Willard Rodgers. 1988. "The Persistence of Poverty." In *Quiet Riots: Race and Poverty in the United States,* edited by Fred R. Harris and Roger W. Wilkins. Pantheon Books.

Anderson, Elijah. 1989. "Sex Codes and Family Life among Inner-City Youth." In *Annals of the American Academy of Political and Social Science* 501 (January), pp. 59–78.

Auletta, Ken. 1982. *The Underclass.* Random House.

Bane, Mary Jo, and Paul A. Jargowsky. 1988. "Urban Poverty Areas: Basic Questions Concerning Prevalence, Growth and Dynamics." Center for Health and Human Resources policy discussion paper series, Harvard University.

Bean, Frank D., and Marta Tienda. 1987. *The Hispanic Population of the United States.* Russell Sage Foundation.

Bureau of the Census. 1970. *1970 Census User's Guide*. Department of Commerce.

———. 1973a. *1970 Census of Population, Detailed Characteristics, United States Summary*, PC1-D1.

———. 1973b. *1970 Census of Population, Subject Reports, Low-Income Areas in Large Cities*, PC2-9B.

———. 1982a. *Census of Population and Housing, 1980: Summary Tape File 3C* [machine-readable data file, processed by the Inter-university Consortium for Political and Social Research, SMSA totals only].

———. 1982b. *Census of Population and Housing, 1980: Summary Tape File 3, Technical Documentation*.

———. 1982c. *User's Guide*, PHC80-R1.

———. 1983a. *Census of Population, 1980*. Vol. 1: *Chapter C: General Social and Economic Characteristics*. Part 1: *U.S. Summary*, PC80-1-C1.

———. 1983b. *Census of Population and Housing, 1980: Geographic Identification Code Scheme*, PHC80-R5.

———. 1983c. *Census of Population and Housing, 1980: Census Tracts*, PHC80-2 [various volumes and census tract maps, including Boston SMSA, Cleveland SMSA, Memphis SMSA, Milwaukee SMSA, and Philadelphia SMSA].

———. 1983d. *Census of Population and Housing, 1980: Summary Tape File 4A* [machine-readable data file, processed by National Planning Data Corp., census tract totals only, all states].

———. 1983e. *Census of Population and Housing, 1980: Summary Tape File 4, Technical Documentation*.

———. 1985. *Census of Population and Housing, 1980*. Vol. 2: *Subject Reports. Poverty Areas in Large Cities*, PC80-2-8D.

———. 1989. *Statistical Abstract of the United States*, 109th edition.

Coulton, Claudia J., Julian Chow, and Shanta Pandey. 1990. *An Analysis of Poverty and Related Conditions in Cleveland Area Neighborhoods: Technical Report*. Center for Urban Poverty and Social Change, Case Western Reserve University.

Dembo, Richard. 1988. "Delinquency among Black Male Youth." In *Young, Black, and Male in America: An Endangered Species*, edited by Jewelle Taylor Gibbs. Dover, Mass.: Auburn House.

Dornbusch, Sanford M., and others. 1985. "Single Parents, Extended Households, and the Control of Adolescents." *Child Development* 56 (April), pp. 326–41.

Ellwood, David T. 1986. "The Spatial Mismatch Hypothesis: Are There Teenage Jobs Missing in the Ghetto?" In *The Black Youth Employment Crisis*, edited by Richard B. Freeman and Harry J. Holzer. University of Chicago Press.

Farley, Reynolds. 1984. *Blacks and Whites: Narrowing the Gap?* Harvard University Press.

Garfinkel, Irwin, and Sara S. McLanahan. 1986. *Single Mothers and Their Children: A New American Dilemma*. Washington: Urban Institute Press.

Hughes, Mark Alan. 1989. "Misspeaking Truth to Power: A Geographical Perspective on the 'Underclass' Fallacy." *Economic Geography* 65, pp. 187–207.

Jargowsky, Paul A., and Mary Jo Bane. 1990. "Ghetto Poverty: Basic Questions." In *Inner-City Poverty in the United States,* edited by Laurence E. Lynn, Jr. and Michael G. H. McGeary. Washington: National Academy Press.

Jargowsky, Paul A., and David T. Ellwood. 1990. "Ghetto Poverty: A Theoretical and Empirical Framework." Malcolm Wiener Center for Social Policy, working paper H–90–7 (October).

Jencks, Christopher. 1989. "What is the Underclass—and is it Growing?" *Focus* 12 (Spring and Summer), pp. 14–26.

Jencks, Christopher, and Susan E. Mayer. 1990. "The Social Consequences of Growing Up in a Bad Neighborhood." In *Inner-City Poverty in the United States,* edited by Laurence E. Lynn Jr. and Michael G. H. McGeary. Washington: National Academy Press.

Kasarda, John D. 1988. "Jobs, Migration, and Emerging Urban Mismatches." In *Urban Change and Poverty,* edited by Michael G. H. McGeary and Laurence E. Lynn, Jr. Washington: National Academy Press.

Lehmann, Nicholas. 1986. "The Origins of the Underclass." *Atlantic Monthly,* June, pp. 31–55 (part 1), and July, pp. 54–68 (part 2).

Mare, Robert D., and Christopher Winship. 1984. "The Paradox of Lessening Racial Inequality and Joblessness among Black Youth: Enrollment, Enlistment, and Employment, 1964–1981." *American Sociological Review* 49 (February), pp. 39–55.

Massey, Douglas S., and Nancy A. Denton. 1987. "Trends in the Residential Segregation of Blacks, Hispanics, and Asians: 1970–1980." *American Sociological Review* 52 (December), pp. 802–25.

———. 1988a. "The Dimensions of Residential Segregation." *Social Forces* 67 (December), pp. 281–315.

———. 1988b. "Suburbanization and Segregation in U.S. Metropolitan Areas." *American Journal of Sociology* 94 (November), pp. 592–626.

———. 1989. "Hypersegregation in U.S. Metropolitan Areas: Black and Hispanic Segregation along Five Dimensions." *Demography* 26 (August), pp. 373–91.

Massey, Douglas S., and Mitchell L. Eggers. 1989. "The Ecology of Inequality: Minorities and the Concentration of Poverty, 1970–1980." Population Research Center discussion paper series, University of Chicago.

Massey, Douglas S., Mitchell L. Eggers, and Nancy A. Denton. 1989. "Disentangling the Causes of Concentrated Poverty." Population Research Center, University of Chicago.

Moyers, Bill. 1986. "The Vanishing Family: Crisis in Black America" (television documentary). CBS broadcast, January 25.

Moynihan, Daniel Patrick. 1965. *The Negro Family: The Case for National Action.* Office of Policy Planning and Research, Department of Labor.

Nathan, Richard. 1986. "The Underclass—Will It Always Be with Us?" Paper presented at the New School for Social Research, New York.

Nathan, Richard, and John Lego. 1986. "The Changing Size and Concentration of the Poverty Population of Large Cities, 1970–1980." Memorandum, Princeton University.

O'Regan, Katherine, and Michael Wiseman. 1989. "Birth Weights and the Geography of Poverty." *Focus* 12 (Fall and Winter), pp. 16–22.

Ricketts, Erol R., and Ronald Mincy. Forthcoming. "The Growth of the Underclass, 1970–1980." *Journal of Human Resources.*

Ricketts, Erol R., and Isabel V. Sawhill. 1988. "Defining and Measuring the Underclass." *Journal of Policy Analysis and Management* 7 (Winter), pp. 316–25.

Van Haitsma, Martha. 1989. "A Contextual Definition of the Underclass." *Focus* 12 (Spring and Summer), pp. 27–31.

Wilson, William Julius. 1987. *The Truly Disadvantaged: The Inner City, The Underclass, and Public Policy.* University of Chicago Press.

———. 1988. "The American Underclass: Inner City Ghettos and the Norms of Citizenship." Godkin lecture, John F. Kennedy School of Government, Harvard University, April 26.

Wilson, William Julius, and Katheryn M. Neckerman. 1986. "Poverty and Family Structure: The Widening Gap Between Evidence and Public Policy Issues." In *Fighting Poverty: What Works and What Doesn't,* edited by Sheldon H. Danziger and Daniel H. Weinberg. Harvard University Press.

Residential Segregation of Social and Economic Groups among Blacks, 1970–80

REYNOLDS FARLEY

In *The Truly Disadvantaged* William Julius Wilson argues that residences of blacks in the underclass are increasingly segregated from those of middle-class blacks. This situation has deleterious consequences because poor blacks, especially young people, no longer have middle-class neighbors to provide them with the information and opportunities they need to be socially mobile.

> I believe that the exodus of middle- and working-class families from many ghetto neighborhoods removes an important "social buffer" that could deflect the full impact of the kind of prolonged and increasing joblessness that plagued inner-city neighborhoods in the 1970s and early 1980s, joblessness created by uneven economic growth and periodic recessions. This argument is based on the assumption that even if the truly disadvantaged segments of an inner-city area experience a significant increase in long-term spells of joblessness, the basic institutions in that area (churches, schools, stores, recreational facilities, etc.) would remain viable if much of the base of their support comes from the more economically stable and secure families. Moreover, the very presence of these families during such periods provides mainstream role models that help keep alive the perception that education is meaningful, that steady employment is a viable alternative to welfare, and that family stability is the norm, not the exception.[1]

My analysis used 1970 and 1980 data for census tracts in large metropolitan areas to investigate whether the residential segregation of social class or economic groups within the black community indeed increased. There seems to have been little, if any, increase in the residential segrega-

1. Wilson (1987), p. 56.

tion of social classes among either blacks or whites. At least in the major metropolises, there is no evidence of increasing geographic segregation of economic groups. But it is reasonable to conclude that the average proportion of the impoverished population in the census tract of the typical poor black increased between 1970 and 1980. This came about because of increases in the overall proportion impoverished in northeastern and midwestern metropolises rather than because of increases in the residential segregation of poor blacks from prosperous blacks.

Trends in Black-White Residential Segregation

The change Wilson describes, if it has occurred, needs to be put in the context of the long-run geographic isolation of blacks from whites in cities. Racial residential segregation emerged early in this century primarily because whites desired to exclude blacks from their neighborhoods.[2] Urban historians who describe southern cities distinguish an antebellum period when there was little residential segregation from a postbellum era of growing racial isolation.[3] Those who have analyzed northern cities in the interval between the Civil War and the First World War have observed that blacks were one of many immigrant groups concentrated in low-income areas, but that those who wished to do so and had the means could live throughout the city. Allan Spear, for instance, has argued that a black ghetto did not exist in Chicago before World War I, and Olivier Zunz has pointed out that as late as 1915 blacks lived throughout Detroit.[4]

As blacks moved to cities in large numbers, this situation changed. By 1940 a thorough system of racial residential segregation had developed in large cities in both South and North. This segregation was abetted in the South by the Jim Crow system, which legislated racial segregation in all areas of public life. In the North segregation developed because of real estate practices—sometimes enforced by restrictive covenants—and because of the violence directed toward blacks who entered formerly white neighborhoods.[5] Black-white competition for urban space was violent in many cities, especially during World War I and again after World War II

2. DuBois (1899), p. 349.
3. Blassingame (1973); and Rabinowitz (1978).
4. Spear (1967), p. 7; and Zunz (1982), p. 374.
5. Conot (1974), pp. 300–03; Kusmer (1976), p. 167; and Zunz (1982), p. 374.

when patterns of black-white segregation were rigidly enforced.[6] In the North, segregation remained at high levels between 1940 and 1960, although some slight declines may have occurred between 1960 and 1970. In the South, black-white residential segregation increased in the 1950s and then held steady at high levels in the 1960s.[7]

The 1970s were different because black-white segregation decreased much more than in previous periods. Indeed, this was the first decade in which there was an unambiguous pattern of lessening black-white segregation throughout the country. Figure 1 shows black-white residential segregation indexes for metropolises with 200,000 or more black residents in 1980. These results are taken from a study that involved 203 metropolises in which at least 4 percent of the population was black in 1980.[8]

Throughout this analysis, residential segregation will be measured by the index of dissimilarity, which assesses how evenly blacks and whites are distributed across the urban landscape. The numerical value of this index indicates the percentage of either group who would have to move from one census tract to another to eliminate segregation, that is, to produce an index of zero, while keeping the population size of each tract fixed. An index of 50, for example, means that 50 percent of either blacks or whites would need to move to end residential segregation. Were a system of apartheid so thorough that all blacks lived in exclusively black neighborhoods and all whites in all-white neighborhoods, the index

6. Chicago Commission on Race Relations (1922); and Hirsch (1983).

7. Many investigators studied trends before 1980 data were released. The analyses differed in whether they focused on central cities or entire metropolises and whether they used blocks or census tracts and in the measures of segregation. Some investigators detected small changes, sometimes rises, sometimes declines. See Taeuber and Taeuber (1965); Farley and Taeuber (1968); Sørenson, Taeuber, and Hollingsworth (1970); Van Valey, Roof, and Wilcox (1977); Schnare (1978); and Massey and Denton (1987).

8. Wilger and Farley (1989). Metropolises with small black populations were excluded because it is not meaningful to analyze segregation where blacks are rare. The locations in this study included 97 percent of the total black metropolitan population in 1980 and 79 percent of the white; see Bureau of the Census (1983a), table 69.

Data for 1980 were obtained from the Master Area Reference File Two for census tracts, geographic areas containing about 5,000 persons. This investigation compares the residential distributions of those who identified themselves as either black or white on the race question that was asked of all individuals. Fifty-six percent of those who claimed they were Hispanic on the Spanish-origin question also said that their race was white, but 42 percent defined themselves as "other" by race and so are excluded from this analysis; see Bureau of the Census (1983a), table 49. For studies of segregation of Hispanics or Asians, see Langberg and Farley (1985); Massey and Denton (1987); and Woolbright and Hartman (1987).

FIGURE 1. Indexes of Black-White Residential Segregation,
by Metropolitan Area, 1960–80[a]

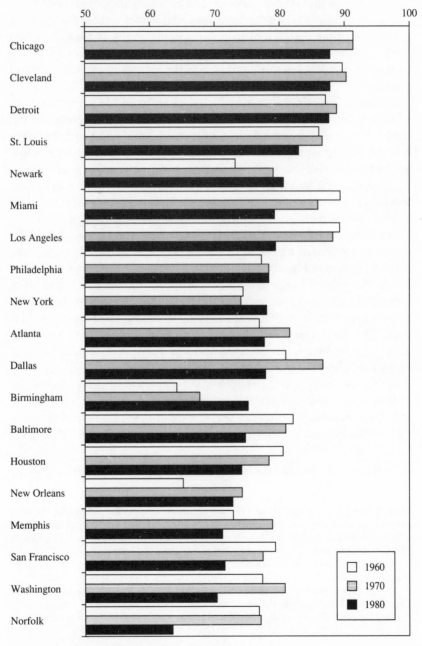

SOURCES: Van Valey, Roof, and Wilcox (1977), table 1; and Wilger and Farley (1989).
a. Metropolitan areas with 200,000 or more blacks in 1980.

would be 100. If people were randomly assigned to census tracts, the index would be zero.[9] The numerical value of this index is statistically independent of the relative sizes of the black and white populations.[10]

Figure 1 shows that during the 1960s, residential segregation declined in only six of the nineteen metropolises; in the 1970s, declines occurred in fifteen. The average change in the 1960s was an increase of about 1.5 points in the index, but during the 1970s the average decrease was nearly 5 points.

For the 203 metropolises for which data are available, segregation fell in 85 percent during the 1970s. In contrast, residential segregation declined in only 43 percent having data for both 1960 and 1970. By 1980, one out of nine of the cities had a black-white segregation score below 50, compared with just 3 percent in 1970 and 1 percent in 1960.

What is meant by a high or low level of segregation? Table 1 shows the metropolises with the highest and lowest black-white segregation levels in each census year. In 1980 Gary was most thoroughly segregated, followed closely by Ft. Myers, Cleveland, Chicago, and Detroit. Six of the ten most segregated places were old midwestern industrial centers; the other four were in Florida. Even though indexes remained high, the average for the ten most segregated places dropped from 91 in 1960 to 90 in 1970 and to 86 in 1980. Seven of the top ten in 1960 were also on the 1970 list, and six from that year's ranking were also listed for 1980. Chicago, Cleveland, Gary, and Milwaukee were on all lists, but four of the areas with highest levels of segregation in 1980 were rapidly growing Florida retirement areas.

The least segregated metropolises also experienced decreasing segregation; their average index decreased from 57 in 1960 to 39 in 1980. Lawrence, Kansas, had the least segregation in 1980, but several others— all with small populations—had indexes below 40. Four of the most in-

9. Duncan and Duncan (1955a); Farley and Johnson (1985); White (1986); and Massey and Denton (1988).

10. Zoloth (1976); and James and Taeuber (1985). To analyze changes over time, measures of residential segregation for 1980 are compared with similar indexes for the same metropolises for 1970 and 1960 computed by Van Valey, Roof, and Wilcox (1977) using census tract data in every year. The indexes for 1960 compare the residential distributions of nonwhites and whites; those for 1970 and 1980, blacks and whites.

Between 1970 and 1980 the nonwhite population that was not black grew more rapidly than the black population, and the Census Bureau changed its procedure concerning who is white, but there were no similar changes in the 1960s. Thus the 1960 and 1970 comparison basically describes changes in the segregation of blacks. For additional information about the use of black-white or nonwhite-white segregation scores, see White (1987), table 6.2.

TABLE 1. Metropolitan Areas with Greatest and Least Black-White Residential Segregation, 1960–80

1960		1970		1980	
City	Index	City	Index	City	Index
Metropolises with greatest segregation					
Las Vegas	98	Ft. Lauderdale	95	Gary	89
Lubbock	93	Chicago	91	Ft. Myers	88
Chicago	91	Oklahoma City	91	Cleveland	88
Oklahoma City	91	Cleveland	90	Chicago	88
Dayton	91	Milwaukee	90	Detroit	88
Milwaukee	90	Detroit	89	Flint	86
Cleveland	90	Los Angeles	89	Bradenton	85
Miami	90	Gary	88	Milwaukee	84
Los Angeles	89	Kansas City	87	Ft. Lauderdale	84
Gary	89	Dayton	87	Sarasota	84
Average	91	Average	90	Average	86
Metropolises with least segregation					
Greenville, S.C.	38	Texarkana	39	Lawrence, Kans.	29
Macon	56	Greenville, S.C.	43	Danville, Va.	33
Topeka	56	Fayetteville, N.C.	45	Jacksonville, N.C.	34
Raleigh	57	Lynchburg, Va.	48	Anchorage	39
Norwalk	59	Ann Arbor	52	Fayetteville, N.C.	59
Trenton	59	Champaign	52	Lawton, Okla.	40
Stamford	61	Lawton, Okla.	53	Clarksville, Tenn.	42
Springfield, Ohio	61	Tuscaloosa	53	Vineland, N.J.	43
Gadsden, Ala.	62	Bloomington, Ill.	54	Victoria, Tex.	43
Waco	62	Vineland, N.J.	54	Texarkana	44
Average	57	Average	49	Average	39

SOURCE: Wilger and Farley (1989).

tegrated places, Clarksville, Tennessee, Fayetteville and Jacksonville, North Carolina, and Lawton, Oklahoma, were dominated by the military.

Concomitants of Black-White Residential Segregation

Residential segregation in 1980 varied greatly from one location to another, but there was a pattern of differences. To understand the causes of segregation, metropolises were classified by their characteristics (figure 2).[11]

Previous studies have reported that larger places are the most segre-

11. For additional information, see Wilger (1988).

FIGURE 2. Indexes of Black-White Residential Segregation in 203 Metropolitan Areas, by Size and Selected Characteristics, 1960–80[a]

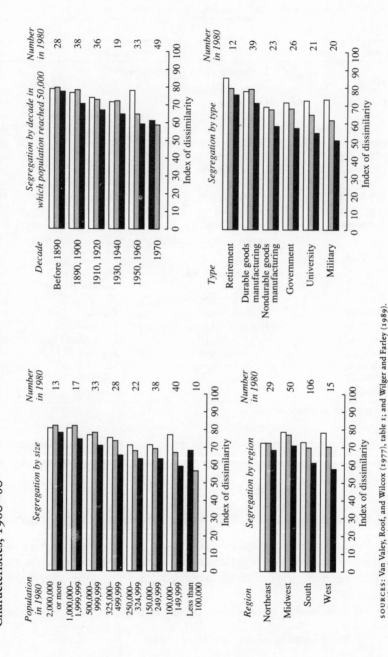

SOURCES: Van Valey, Roof, and Wilcox (1977), table 1; and Wilger and Farley (1989).
a. See figure 1 for legend.

gated, a pattern that continued in 1980.[12] Metropolises with populations exceeding 2 million had the highest average segregation score while those with fewer than 100,000 were least segregated. Between 1970 and 1980 all population size groups experienced declines in segregation, the largest and smallest categories having the least relative declines. The upper right panel of figure 2 shows areas by the decade in which their central city first reached 50,000. Blacks and whites were much more segregated in older locations than they were in those places that reached metropolitan size more recently. There was also a clear pattern of change in the 1970s because the largest percentage declines occurred in the youngest areas, and once again declines far exceeded those of the 1960s for every category.

At least since 1960, residential segregation has been more thorough in the Midwest than in the nation's three other regions. In 1980 the South had average segregation levels 9 points lower than the Midwest and only 3 points higher than the West, the region in which metropolises were least segregated. Regional changes in the 1970s differed greatly from those of the 1960s when black-white segregation declined only in the West. In the 1970s the West had the largest average decline, 15 percent, while the Northeast had the smallest, 4 percent.

Black-white residential segregation may be influenced by the economic and social structure of a community. A metropolis whose economic base is a military post will have a different stock of housing and will attract a different demographic mix than another that specializes in heavy industry or a third that is a retirement center.[13] Retirement communities had exceptionally high levels of black-white segregation. Probably relatively few blacks have the requisite savings to move into these areas, so they attract almost exclusively white populations, although marketing policies may also exclude minorities.[14] Durable goods manufacturing centers had un-

12. Van Valey, Roof, and Wilcox (1977), table 2.

13. Each metropolis was classified according to the following variables, using data from the census of 1980: percentage of total population age 65 and older (retirement communities); percentage of employed work force in durable goods manufacturing industries (durable goods manufacturing communities); percentage of employed work force in nondurable goods manufacturing industries (nondurable goods manufacturing communities); percentage of employed work force in public administration (government communities); percentage of population age 18 to 24 enrolled in college (university communities); and percentage of total labor force in the armed forces (military communities). If a community was one standard deviation or more above the national metropolitan average on any of these measures, it was classified in one of the functional specializations. Diversified places were those that were less than one standard deviation above the mean on none of the six measures.

14. FitzGerald (1986), chap. 4.

usually high levels of segregation. Brian Berry hypothesized that people in such places show a strong attachment to their communities and that the purchase of a home is their only major financial commitment, so they may try to preserve its value by excluding racial minorities.[15] Places emphasizing nondurable goods manufacturing were considerably less segregated, but eighteen of the twenty-three were in the South where blacks were generally less segregated from whites. Both durable and nondurable goods manufacturing centers had much larger declines in segregation during the 1970s than in the 1960s. Government, university, and military communities attract populations that differ in important ways, especially in educational attainment, from metropolises that have a manufacturing base. In addition, the military, and perhaps some universities, exerts pressures to make certain that equal housing opportunities are provided in their environs. Several southern university locations, including Athens, Georgia, Charlottesville, Virginia, and Gainesville, Florida, had unusually low segregation scores and, in the Midwest, the least segregated communities included Columbia, Missouri; Champaign; and Ann Arbor. Four of the five least segregated metropolitan areas in the South were military communities, and two military centers, Colorado Springs and Anchorage, were the least segregated western metropolises.

Michael White thoroughly investigated black-white residential segregation from 1940 to 1980 and observed that there was no change between 1940 and 1970, but in the 1970s the index of dissimilarity declined in almost every city he examined. Wondering if the change were real or a statistical artifact, he analyzed different measures of segregation and the consequences of the Census Bureau's change in the definition of whites after 1970. He concluded that "the decline in racial segregation in the 1970s is not an artifact; it is real, appreciable, and quite widespread."[16]

Even though segregation was reduced in the 1970s, blacks remain uniquely apart. The census of 1980 asked all respondents their race and whether their origin was Spanish. A 19.3 percent sample answered an additional open-ended question about ancestry. To assess the unique segregation of blacks, I considered the larger racial and ethnic groups and compared their geographic distributions with those of people who claimed English ancestry. The English, of course, were the group most influential in the development of the nation and were, in 1980, the most

15. Berry and others (1976).
16. White (1987), p. 189.

numerous group, with more than 49 million identifying this as their ancestry.[17]

Figure 3 shows the segregation of major racial and ethnic groups from the English in Chicago. There were moderate levels of ethnic residential segregation in 1980. Descendants of those groups coming to the United States in large numbers before the Civil War—Germans, Scots, and Irish—were least segregated from the English. Descendants of Italians, Poles, Hungarians, Ukrainians, and others who arrived later in the nineteenth century were more segregated from the English. The Europeans most highly segregated were the Russians, whose residential choices were once limited because many were Jewish.[18] Clearly, European ethnicities were much less residentially segregated than blacks.

The uniqueness of black-white segregation may be seen by analyzing patterns for other racial and ethnic groups that have come to the United States recently: Hispanics and Asians. They differ from blacks in that their populations have grown more rapidly and they have entered Chicago and other cities in large numbers since 1960.[19] Many might be expected to settle in immigrant enclaves and thus be highly segregated from the English-origin population, perhaps at a level exceeding that of blacks. That is not the case. Although they are more highly segregated from the English than are any of the European groups, with the possible exception of Russians, Hispanics and Asians are considerably less segregated than blacks.

Assessing the Residential Segregation of Social Classes

The analysis of residential segregation by social class dates from the 1950s, when Dudley and Beverly Duncan published findings from Chicago.[20] They defined class in terms of broad occupational categories and then used 1950 data for census tracts and the index of dissimilarity to demonstrate that residential patterns mirrored patterns of occupational status or prestige. When geographic distributions of occupational groups that were similar in earnings or education, such as professionals and managers, were compared, the indexes of residential segregation were

17. Bureau of the Census (1983b), table 2. For analyses of ethnic residential segregation in the 1980s, see White (1987), pp. 93–98; and Farley and Allen (1987), table 5.9.
18. Rosenthal (1975).
19. Bureau of the Census (1984), table 253.
20. Duncan and Duncan (1957).

FIGURE 3. Index of Residential Segregation of Ethnic and Racial
Minorities from Respondents of English Ancestry, Chicago
Metropolitan Area, 1980[a]

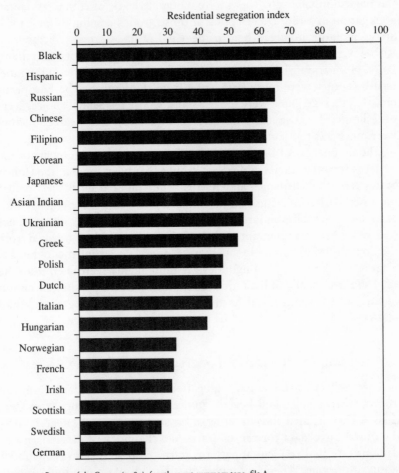

SOURCE: Bureau of the Census (1984), fourth count summary tape, file A.
a. Racial groups are defined on the basis of the race question from the 1980 census, Hispanics on the basis of the question on Spanish origin. Ethnic groups were defined on the basis of the first or only reported ancestry. Indexes of dissimilarity compare each ethnic or racial group to the distribution of those who said English was their ancestry.

low. When groups such as professionals and laborers were compared, the indexes were larger.

More important for this research was the evidence regarding the segregation of one social class from all others. When those at the top of the occupational rank, professionals, or those at the bottom, laborers, were compared with all other employed men, residential segregation scores were relatively high, about 35. When those in the middle-ranking occupational categories, sales and clerical workers, were compared with all others, their residential segregation scores were low, about 15. Those with prestigious jobs had the money to live in costly areas; men with the lowest ranking jobs could only rent or buy in the bottom of the housing market.

Among the first to analyze residential segregation of social classes within racial groups was Nathan Kantrowitz. He assumed that racial residential segregation overpowered the normal operation of the housing market and argued, "One might expect, given prejudice against blacks and Puerto Ricans by whites, that only minimal separation would exist between the wealthy and the poor within these groups." [21] His findings surprised him. The residential segregation of family income groups was actually greater within the nonwhite community than among whites.

Brigitte Erbe focused on residential segregation of social classes among blacks in Chicago in 1970. [22] She believed that even if a black had an extensive education, a prestigious job, or a high income, he or she would likely live in a neighborhood with many impoverished blacks, thereby losing one of the benefits of status that accrues to prosperous whites. Her interest was the opposite of Wilson's; she was concerned about the problems prosperous blacks presumably faced because they could not segregate themselves from poor blacks. Her findings paralleled those of Kantrowitz. The extent of residential segregation based on occupation and education was about the same for Chicago-area blacks and whites. Controlling for family income, segregation was greater among blacks than among whites.

In an important advance, Erbe calculated measures of the composition of neighborhoods, known as intergroup contact indexes, and found a large racial difference. Because the black and white distributions of education, occupation, and income differ greatly, blacks are exposed to neighborhood mixes different from those of whites, even when the levels

21. Kantrowitz (1973), p. 37.
22. Erbe (1975).

of social class segregation are identical. For example, black families that had incomes exceeding $25,000 (1969 dollars) in Chicago in 1970 on average lived in census tracts in which 23 percent of their black neighbors had incomes higher than $15,000 and 24 percent had incomes less than $6,000. Thus prosperous blacks lived in neighborhoods where poverty was not rare. But white families in Chicago with incomes of $25,000 or more lived in neighborhoods in which 50 percent of their white neighbors had incomes higher than $15,000 and only 8 percent less than $6,000.[23] Despite similar levels of segregation as measured by the index of dissimilarity, middle-class blacks had proportionally fewer middle-class peers than did middle-class whites. Similarly, low-income blacks lived in areas with proportionally more poor residents than did low-income whites. This came about because of black-white differences in income, not because of racial differences in residential segregation by social class.

Although these results may appear confusing at first, an example may help to elucidate Erbe's findings. Suppose a military base *randomly* assigns personnel to barracks. At this base, one-half of the personnel are white and one-half black. At another base, personnel are also randomly assigned to living quarters, but the staff is 95 percent white and 5 percent black. If indexes of residential dissimilarity are calculated for both bases, they both approach zero, implying no residential segregation. However, both blacks and whites at the first base will be living in barracks that are 50 percent black; at the second base everyone will be in quarters that are only 5 percent black. In Chicago, residential segregation by class was much the same among blacks and whites, but blacks had much lower incomes than whites, producing a situation in which poor blacks lived with proportionally more poor neighbors than did poor whites.

Trends in Residential Segregation of Social Classes

To test William Wilson's hypothesis that residential segregation by class is increasing, I used educational attainment and family income to estimate class and then measured the residential segregation of a specific category from all others. If the values for these indexes of segregation were generally higher in 1980 than in 1970, this would be evidence of increasing segregation by class. In particular, there would be strong support for Wilson's hypothesis if blacks at the bottom of the educational or

23. Erbe (1975), table 7.

family income distributions were more residentially segregated from other blacks in 1980 than in 1970.[24]

Figure 4 compares residential segregation of blacks and whites on the basis of income. When the geographic distributions of black and white families in the lowest income category in 1970, families with incomes less than $1,700 in 1987 dollars, were compared, their segregation score was 91 (top line). For black and white families in the highest income category, more than $78,000 in 1987 dollars, the index of dissimilarity was 93 (top line). Income made virtually no difference in the extent of residential segregation because prosperous blacks and whites were as residentially segregated from each other as impoverished blacks were segregated from poor whites. In 1980 increasing income among blacks may have led to higher standards of living and better housing, but in Chicago and other large metropolises, it did not lead to residential integration. However, 1980 segregation levels, controlled for family income, were about 10 points lower than 1970 levels, reflecting the general decline in black-white segregation during the 1970s (second line).

The lines in the lower half of figure 4 refer to blacks only, and report the residential segregation score that results when one family income category is compared with all other income categories. Those at the extremes of the income distribution were more residentially segregated than those in the middle-income range. In 1980 black families reporting incomes less than $7,800 in 1987 dollars had a segregation score of 29 compared with black families with higher incomes. Those in the top-ranked income category, $78,000 or more, had a segregation score of 36. When social class residential segregation measures for 1970 and 1980 are

24. The findings that follow are based on three studies conducted at the University of Michigan's Population Studies Center. The first analyzed social class and racial residential segregation using 1970 census tracts for twenty-nine urbanized areas (Farley, 1977). The second studied the residential segregation of blacks, Asians, and Hispanics in 1980 in metropolitan areas (Langberg and Farley, 1985), and the third studied black-white residential segregation in 1980 (Wilger, 1988; Wilger and Farley, 1989).

Researchers are restricted to census tract data as released on public use files from the two most recent enumerations. These do not provide data for individuals but rather grouped data for residents of census tracts classified by race. Studies are thus limited to an analysis of groups defined on the basis of educational attainment for persons age 25 and older, occupation for employed men and women, or family income. In most metropolises, census tract boundaries were redrawn, although the effect on this analysis was presumably small. In addition, the number of educational categories for which data were tabulated declined from ten to five between 1970 and 1980, and the number of family income categories from fourteen to nine. Because the procedures used to classify occupations changed after 1970 (Rytina and Bianchi, 1984), no analysis of the residential segregation of occupational groups appears in this research.

FIGURE 4. Black-White Residential Segregation, by Family Income, Chicago Metropolitan Area, 1970, 1980

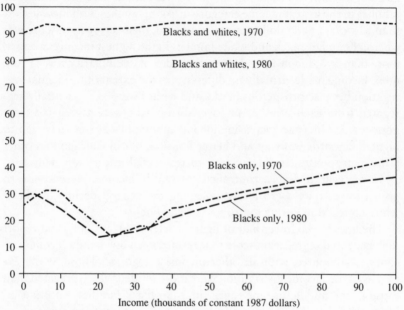

Residential segregation scores

SOURCE: Bureau of the Census (1973), fourth count summary tape file 3A.

compared, there is little change. This suggests that, controlling for race, residential segregation of social classes neither increased nor decreased very much.

In both years racial residential segregation was more thorough than class segregation. That is, the index of dissimilarity comparing blacks in the $78,000 and greater category with whites in the same category in 1980 was 82. The score comparing blacks in the $78,000 and greater category with blacks in the $7,800 or less category was 51 (data not shown). Prosperous blacks were much less segregated from poor blacks than they were from equally prosperous whites.

There was no increase in residential segregation by income level among blacks in Chicago between 1970 and 1980, and a parallel analysis (not shown) found that there was no increase when educational attainment was used as the index of class. Are the findings for Chicago's black population typical? To answer this question, I considered data for twenty-one large metropolitan areas. Figures 5 and 6 show data for the three largest, New York, Chicago, and Los Angeles, and for the other eighteen cities grouped by region.[25] To provide trend lines comparable for 1970 and 1980, a curve was fitted to the observed values, such as those shown in figure 4.[26]

Figure 5 tests the hypothesis of increasing segregation by using education as the index of class. The segregation scores for 1980 were similar to those for 1970. For educational attainment levels of eleven years or more, the segregation of the group from all other attainment groups was less in 1980 than in 1970, suggesting a decline in social class segregation among those at or above the middle of the educational distribution. If there had been a substantial rise in the residential segregation of those at the very bottom of the class ladder, one would expect to find that their segregation scores increased after 1970. There is limited evidence that this occurred. In four of the six panels in figure 5 the segregation score for those with eight years of attainment was greater in 1980 than in 1970, but only in southern metropolises was the segregation score for those with nine years of education greater in 1980 than it was a decade earlier.

Figure 6 shows estimated residential segregation scores for blacks classified by family income. There is no evidence to support the hypothesis that those at the bottom of the income distribution were more residentially segregated from other blacks in 1980 than in 1970. Blacks with incomes of approximately $10,000 in 1987 dollars were less segregated from all other black families in four of the six locations in 1980 than they were in 1970.

For whites in these locations, residential segregation by social class, as defined by either education or family income, generally diminished between 1970 and 1980 (data not shown). In almost all comparisons, residential segregation by class was somewhat less common among whites than among blacks.[27]

25. Metropolises were grouped as follows: South: Atlanta, Dallas, Houston, Miami, New Orleans, and Washington; Northeast and Midwest: Boston, Cleveland, Detroit, Minneapolis, Philadelphia, and St. Louis; West: Denver, Portland, San Diego, San Francisco, and Seattle.

26. The census categories of income and years of schooling were not identical in 1970 and 1980. Because the indexes of dissimilarity measuring the segregation of one social class from all others approximate a U-shaped pattern, a second-degree polynomial was fit to observable values. This permitted the estimation of scores for any social class, allowing a comparison of 1970 and 1980, holding social class constant.

27. This finding is consistent with those of Massey and Eggers (1989), table 2; and Erbe (1975).

FIGURE 5. Estimated Residential Segregation of One Educational
Attainment Group of Blacks from All Other Blacks, by Metropolis
and Region, 1970, 1980

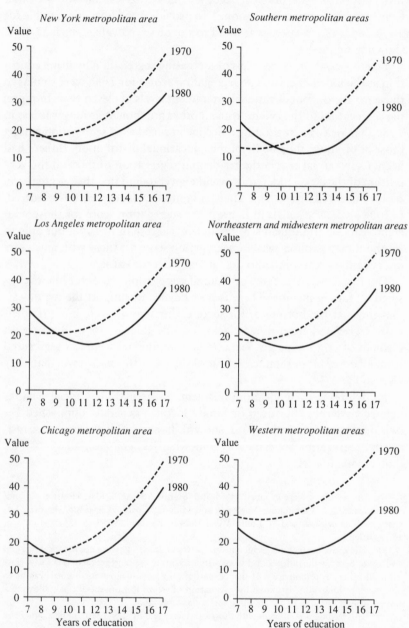

SOURCE: See figure 4.

FIGURE 6. Estimated Residential Segregation of Black Families in
One Income Category from All Other Black Families, by Metropolis
and Region, 1970, 1980

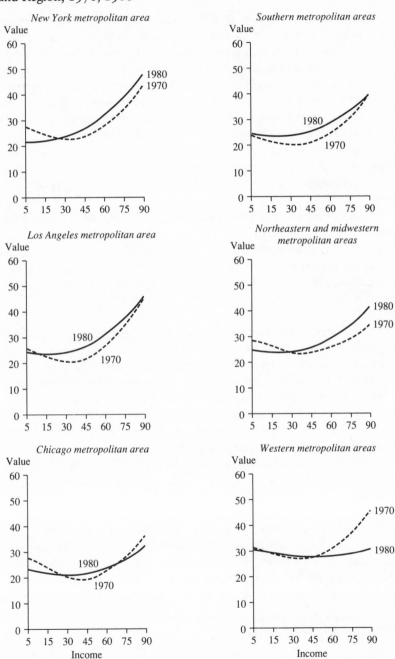

Income
(thousands of constant 1987 dollars)

SOURCE: See figure 4.

Conclusion

William Wilson's account of urban change involves two assumptions and one conclusion. First, at some point in the past, he suggests, there was much greater economic heterogeneity in black urban neighborhoods, presumably because the residential choices of well-to-do blacks were rigidly constrained by patterns of residential segregation. Second, during the 1960s and 1970s barriers to residential segregation were challenged, and some, perhaps many, middle-income blacks had new options. As a result, they moved away from traditional black neighborhoods, thus increasing the concentration of poverty and diminishing prospects for upward mobility for those who remained behind because they no longer had middle-class neighbors who could assist them in locating jobs or better opportunities.

Evidence presented in this paper and the findings of other scholars challenge the first two assumptions and lead to qualifications—but not rejections—of the conclusion. First, residential segregation of social classes has apparently not increased since World War II. Concerning such segregation, Dudley and Beverly Duncan, writing a third of a century ago, concluded,

> The Negro is segregated residentially from the white population in Chicago; but within both the Negro and the white community, high-status groups tend to share residential areas and to be residentially segregated from low-status groups. Apparently, the selective forces which produce differentiation of residential areas in the urban community operate in somewhat the same way upon the Negro and white population. This is also in line with the findings that patterns of inter-area differentiation with respect to physical characteristics of the area and social and economic characteristics of the residents tend to be maintained under the impact of succession from white to Negro occupancy.[28]

The findings of Douglas Massey and Mitchell Eggers and those presented in this paper demonstrate that there was almost no change in the extent of residential segregation by social class between 1970 and 1980.[29] Although the census classifications are not exactly comparable, an inspection of my data for Chicago in 1980 and the data compiled by the

28. Duncan and Duncan (1957), p. 298.
29. Massey and Eggers (1989).

Duncans for the 1950s implies that there has been little change in the extent to which blacks in the top social class are residentially segregated from those in the bottom.

There undoubtedly was migration of prosperous blacks from the inner cities in the 1970s, but that was not a new process nor did it lead to any more than modest decreases in black-white segregation. As several scholars have observed, the process of black migration from inner cities has been occurring for decades.[30] Studies consistently show that the higher-status members of the community have led the migration.

The 1970s also witnessed the increasing suburbanization of blacks, a process that perhaps accelerated in the 1980s.[31] This suburbanization has involved selectivity; high-income blacks are choosing suburban rather than city residences.[32] At first glance, this appears to be a new pattern that will, as Wilson hypothesized, segregate a black elite in the suburbs from a black underclass in the cities. However, the innovation of the 1970s was not the process of selective black migration to better residential areas. Rather, blacks in all economic groups crossed city boundaries and moved into the suburban ring in large numbers. As the investigation in this paper shows, this change did not alter the levels of social class residential segregation among blacks.

One cannot so readily reject Wilson's conclusions that poor blacks in Chicago lived in proportionally more impoverished neighborhoods in 1980 than in 1970. This is an accurate conclusion, but the situation has occurred because of overall increases in black poverty rather than because of higher levels of residential segregation by social class or a new outmigration of prosperous blacks.

Table 2 presents indexes measuring the residential segregation of the poor from the nonpoor in 1980. In Chicago the score comparing the geographic distribution of poor and nonpoor whites was 34; among blacks it was 31, leading to the conclusion that residential segregation of social classes was moderate and existed at the same level for both races. However, the asymmetric segregation measures, frequently identified as P* measures, show that the typical impoverished Chicago-area white lived in a tract where 12 percent of the whites were poor. Poor blacks lived in tracts where 35 percent of the blacks were poor.

Because the residential segregation of social classes has hardly changed

30. Edwards (1970); Taeuber and Taeuber (1965), chaps. 4, 5; and Duncan and Duncan (1957), chaps. 5, 6.

31. Bureau of the Census (1989).

32. Frey and Speare (1988), chap. 9.

TABLE 2. Residential Segregation of Poor and Nonpoor, by Race and Metropolitan Area, 1980

Metropolitan area	Index of dissimilarity[a]		Average percent poor in census tract of poor	
	White	Black	White	Black
Atlanta	25	29	10	32
Baltimore	29	31	11	34
Boston	29	24	12	31
Chicago	34	31	12	35
Cleveland	32	31	12	34
Dallas	29	32	11	33
Denver	32	39	12	35
Detroit	30	27	11	31
Houston	29	29	10	29
Los Angeles	31	28	16	29
Miami	26	26	16	34
Minneapolis	28	36	10	39
Philadelphia	28	29	12	37
New Orleans	25	26	11	38
New York	36	30	20	36
Portland	23	29	11	35
St. Louis	28	26	10	32
San Diego	24	30	12	27
San Francisco	29	28	12	29
Seattle	25	28	10	28
Average	29	29	12	33

SOURCE: Bureau of the Census (1983), summary tape file 3A.

a. Indexes of dissimilarity are based on census tract data and compare the distribution of the population below the poverty line with that of the population above the povery line.

in recent decades, shifts up or down in the poverty rate alter the percentage of poor in the tract of the typical poor person. Table 3 shows poverty rates for blacks and whites in fourteen metropolises for 1969, 1979, and 1986–87. The mid-decade estimates were obtained from March Current Population Surveys. Because there were few blacks in the mid-1980 samples for seven metropolitan areas, places such as Denver, Seattle, and Portland have been omitted.

Three metropolises—Chicago, Cleveland, and Detroit—stand out for their abrupt increases in black poverty. There poor blacks are now living in neighborhoods where poverty levels are, presumably, much higher than they were for poor blacks in 1970, even though the residential segregation of the poor from the prosperous has apparently not increased.

TABLE 3. Black and White Populations below Poverty Line,
by Metropolitan Area, 1970, 1980, 1987–88[a]

Percent

	Black			White		
Metropolitan area	1970 census	1980 census	Current Population Survey 1987–88	1970 census	1980 census	Current Population Survey 1987–88
Atlanta	29	28	20	7	7	4
Baltimore	26	32	29	7	10	6
Chicago	24	29	36	6	6	9
Cleveland	25	27	40	6	6	8
Dallas	31	25	11	8	7	7
Detroit	22	26	34	8	6	7
Houston	31	22	33	8	6	11
Los Angeles	24	23	21	9	9	12
Miami	32	30	33	11	9	12
Philadelphia	25	29	23	7	7	7
New Orleans	43	35	43	10	9	7
New York	24	28	28	7	8	11
San Francisco	23	22	11	8	7	7
Washington	18	17	10	5	5	3
U.S. total	35	30	32	11	9	11

SOURCES: Bureau of the Census (1973), tables 90, 95; (1984), Table 245; and public use micro data files from March 1987 and March 1988 Current Population Surveys.

a. Data were obtained from the 1970 census, the 1980 census, and from the Current Population Surveys conducted in March 1987 and March 1988. Poverty rates from the census of 1970 refer to blacks and nonblacks; those from the census of 1980 and the Current Population Survey refer to persons identified as black or white by race.

Atlanta, Dallas, the San Francisco Bay area, and Washington are distinguished by decreases in black poverty. Poor blacks there are very likely living in census tracts where the proportion of poor blacks has declined for twenty or more years.

If poverty rates increase substantially—and table 3 shows that the rate for Chicago-area blacks went up from 24 percent in 1970 to 36 percent in the mid-1980s—and the residential segregation of social classes remains about the same, the population in poverty will increase and proportionally more of their neighbors will be poor. The demographic evidence for Chicago is unambiguous about these matters. The change that Wilson describes in The Truly Disadvantaged is the rise in poverty among blacks, not an increase in residential segregation among social classes. A similarly thorough analysis of blacks from 1970 to the present in San Francisco or Washington would likely report that poverty decreased and that poor blacks now have somewhat fewer poor neighbors than they did in the past.

References

Berry, Brian J. L., and others. 1976. "Attitudes Toward Integration: The Role of Status in Community Response to Racial Change." In *The Changing Face of the Suburbs,* edited by Barry Schwartz. University of Chicago Press.

Blassingame, John W. 1973. *Black New Orleans: 1860–1880.* University of Chicago Press.

Bureau of the Census. 1973. *Census of Population, 1970: Detailed Characteristics: United States Summary,* PC(1)-D1. Department of Commerce.

———. 1983a. *Census of Population, 1980.* PC80-1-B1. Department of Commerce.

———. 1983b. *Census of Population, 1980.* PC80-S1-10. Department of Commerce.

———. 1983c. *Census of Population, 1980: General Social and Economic Statistics: Illinois,* PC80-1-C15. Department of Commerce.

———. 1984. *Census of Population, 1980: Detailed Population Characteristics: United States Summary,* PC80-1-D1-A. Department of Commerce.

———. 1989. "Population Estimates by Race and Hispanic Origin for States, Metropolitan Areas, and Selected Counties: 1980 to 1985." *Current Population Reports,* series P-25, no. 1040-RD-1. Department of Commerce.

Chicago Commission on Race Relations. 1922. *The Negro in Chicago: A Study of Race Relations and a Race Riot.* University of Chicago Press.

Conot, Robert E. 1974. *American Odyssey.* Bantam Books.

DuBois, W. E. B. 1899. *The Philadelphia Negro.* University of Pennsylvania Press.

Duncan, Otis Dudley, and Beverly Duncan. 1955a. "A Methodological Analysis of Segregation Indexes." *American Sociological Review* 20 (April), pp. 210–17.

———. 1955b. "Residential Distribution and Occupational Stratification." *American Journal of Sociology* 60 (March), pp. 493–503.

———. 1957. *The Negro Population of Chicago: A Study of Residential Succession.* University of Chicago Press.

Edwards, Ozzie L. 1970. "Patterns of Residential Segregation within a Metropolitan Ghetto." *Demography* 7 (May), pp. 185–93.

Erbe, Brigitte Mach. 1975. "Race and Socioeconomic Segregation." *American Sociological Review* 40 (December), pp. 801–12.

Farley, Reynolds. 1977. "Residential Segregation in Urbanized Areas of the United States in 1970: An Analysis of Social Class and Racial Differences." *Demography* 14 (November), pp. 497–518.

Farley, Reynolds, and Walter R. Allen. 1987. *The Color Line and the Quality of Life in America.* Russell Sage Foundation.

Farley, Reynolds, and Robert Johnson. 1985. "On the Statistical Significance of the Index of Dissimilarity." *American Statistical Association: Proceedings of the Social Statistics Section*. Washington: ASA.

Farley, Reynolds, and Karl Taeuber. 1968. "Population Trends and Residential Segregation since 1960." *Science* 159 (March), pp. 953–56.

FitzGerald, Frances. 1986. *Cities on a Hill: A Journey through Contemporary American Cultures*. Simon and Schuster.

Frey, William H., and Alden Speare, Jr. 1988. *Regional and Metropolitan Growth and Decline in the United States*. Russell Sage Foundation.

Hirsch, Arnold R. 1983. *Making the Second Ghetto: Race and Housing in Chicago, 1940–1960*. Cambridge University Press.

James, David E., and Karl E. Taeuber. 1985. "Measures of Segregation." In *Sociological Methodology 1985*, edited by Nancy Brandon Tuma. San Francisco: Jossey-Bass.

Kantrowitz, Nathan. 1973. *Ethnic and Racial Segregation in the New York Metropolis: Residential Patterns among White Ethnic Groups, Blacks and Puerto Ricans*. Praeger.

Kusmer, Kenneth L. 1976. *A Ghetto Takes Shape: Black Cleveland, 1870–1930*. University of Illinois Press.

Langberg, Mark, and Reynolds Farley. 1985. "Residential Segregation of Asian Americans in 1980." *Sociology and Social Research* 70 (October), pp. 71–73.

Massey, Douglas S., and Nancy A. Denton. 1987. "Trends in the Residential Segregation of Blacks, Hispanics, and Asians: 1970–1980." *American Sociological Review* 52 (December), pp. 802–25.

———. 1988. "The Dimensions of Residential Segregation." *Social Forces* 67 (December), pp. 281–315.

Massey, Douglas S., and Mitchell L. Eggers. 1989. "The Ecology of Inequality: Minorities and the Concentration of Poverty 1970–1980." Population Research Center, University of Chicago (January).

Rabinowitz, Howard N. 1978. *Race Relations in the Urban South, 1865–1890*. Oxford University Press.

Rosenthal, Erich. 1975. "The Equivalence of United States Census Data for Persons of Russian Stock or Descent with American Jews: An Evaluation." *Demography* 12 (May), pp. 275–90.

Rytina, Nancy F., and Suzanne M. Bianchi. 1984. "Occupational Reclassification and Changes in Distribution by Gender." *Monthly Labor Review* 107 (March), pp. 11–17.

Schnare, Ann Burnet. 1978. *The Persistence of Racial Segregation in Housing*. Washington: Urban Institute.

Sørenson, Annemette, Karl E. Taeuber, and Leslie J. Hollingsworth, Jr. 1970. "Indexes of Racial Residential Segregation for 109 Cities in the United States, 1940 to 1970." *Sociological Focus* 8 (April), pp. 125–42.

Spear, Allan H. 1967. *Black Chicago: The Making of a Negro Ghetto, 1890–1920*. University of Chicago Press.

Taeuber, Karl E., and Alma F. Taeuber. 1965. *Negroes in Cities: Residential Segregation and Neighborhood Change*. Chicago: Aldine Press.

Van Valey, Thomas L., Wade Clark Roof, and Jerome E. Wilcox. 1977. "Trends in Residential Segregation: 1960–1970." *American Journal of Sociology* 82 (January), pp. 826–44.

White, Michael J. 1986. "Segregation and Diversity Measures in Population Distribution." *Population Index* 52 (Summer), pp. 198–221.

———. 1987. *American Neighborhoods and Residential Differentiation*. Russell Sage Foundation.

Wilger, Robert. 1988. *Black-White Residential Segregation in 1980*. Ph.D. dissertation, University of Michigan.

Wilger, Robert, and Reynolds Farley. 1989. "Black-White Residential Segregation: Recent Trends." University of Michigan, Population Studies Center.

Wilson, William Julius. 1987. *The Truly Disadvantaged: The Inner City, the Underclass, and Public Policy*. University of Chicago Press.

Woolbright, Louis Albert, and David J. Hartman. 1987. "The New Segregation: Asians and Hispanics." In *Divided Neighborhoods: Changing Patterns of Racial Segregation*, edited by Gary A. Tobin. Newbury Park, Calif.: Sage Publications.

Zoloth, Barbara S. 1976. "Alternative Measures of School Segregation." *Land Economics* 52 (August), pp. 278–98.

Zunz, Olivier. 1982. *The Changing Face of Inequality: Urbanization, Industrial Development, and Immigrants in Detroit, 1880–1920*. University of Chicago Press.

Effects of Neighborhoods on Dropping Out of School and Teenage Childbearing

JONATHAN CRANE

DO THE NEIGHBORHOODS they live in affect the lives of teenagers in important ways? The conventional wisdom is that they do. The media, lawyers in the courtroom, and people in everyday conversation often presume that the tribulations of living in a bad neighborhood lead young people astray, as if this were an incontrovertible fact. But it is not. Christopher Jencks and Susan Mayer have found that strong conclusions about the existence and extent of neighborhood effects could not be drawn from the empirical work done so far. There are a number of reasons for their conclusion, but the main one is that just a handful of studies have been done on the effects of neighborhoods.[1]

There have been just two previous studies of the effects of neighborhoods on educational attainment. Linda Datcher used the Panel Study of Income Dynamics (PSID) to do a longitudinal study of urban young men age 13 to 22 living with their parents in 1968.[2] She estimated the effects that the average family income in certain zip code areas in 1968 had on the number of years of school completed by 1978. She controlled for the parents' age, educational attainment, and income, and family size, region, community size, and the aspirations of the head of the family for his or her children's education. She found that an increase in average income of $1,000, or 10 percent, raised the young men's educational attainment by a tenth of a school year for both blacks and whites.

I wish to thank Mary Jo Bane, David T. Ellwood, Naomi Goldstein, Glenn Loury, and Lee Rainwater for their advice and helpful comments on earlier drafts.

The data in this paper were made available in part by the Inter-university Consortium for Political and Social Research. The data for the Public Use Samples of Basic Records from the 1970 census and for the *Census of Population and Housing, 1980: Summary Tape File 3* were originally collected by the Bureau of the Census. Neither the collector of the original data nor the consortium bear any responsibility for the analyses or interpretations presented here.

1. Jencks and Mayer (1990). There is a relatively large literature on the effects of the social composition of schools, but it has not generated clear findings either.

2. Datcher (1982).

Mary Corcoran and colleagues expanded Datcher's analysis by look-ing at all people age 10 to 17 in the PSID in 1968.[3] They examined the effects of four characteristics of the 1968 zip code area—median income, the proportion of homes headed by women, the male unemployment rate, and the proportion of people receiving some form of public assistance—on the young people's educational attainment in 1983. They controlled for race, region, city size, religion, family structure, family income in 1968, welfare receipt, and the educational attainment and work hours of the family head and spouse. For male students, living in an area in which the proportion of female-headed families was two standard deviations (8 percentage points) higher than the mean meant that educational attain-ment was reduced by a quarter of a year. An increase of two standard deviations (10 percentage points) in the rate of welfare receipt reduced schooling by half a year. Neither median income nor the male unemploy-ment rate had an effect. For female students, living in areas in which the male unemployment rate was two standard deviations higher than the mean meant that educational achievement was reduced by half a year. An increase of 8 points in the proportion of female-headed families reduced schooling by a quarter of a year, and an increase of 8 points in the rate of welfare receipt reduced it by a little less than half a year. Median income had no effect.

There have been no previous studies of neighborhood effects on teen-age childbearing per se, but there is one each on pregnancy and contra-ception. Dennis Hogan and Evelyn Kitagawa studied a 1979 sample of unmarried black girls between the ages of 13 and 19 in Chicago census tracts.[4] They constructed a composite measure of neighborhood quality using the tracts' poverty rates, median family incomes, male-female ra-tios, number of children per ever-married woman, and several indexes of juvenile delinquency among teenage boys. They divided the tracts into three groups: the top quarter of the composite index, the middle half, and the bottom quarter. The other neighborhood variable was a dummy in-dicating whether the girl lived in Chicago's west side ghetto. They con-trolled for social class, parents' marital status, and number of siblings. They found no significant difference in rates of teenage pregnancy be-tween the high-status neighborhoods and the middle-status ones. But a teenager's chances of becoming pregnant were a third higher in the low-status neighborhoods. Living on the west side increased pregnancy risk by almost two-fifths. Because two measures at very different geographic

3. Corcoran and others (1987).
4. Hogan and Kitagawa (1985).

levels were used, the overall influence of the neighborhood could not be determined precisely. It was probably larger than the effect of either one, but less than the sum.

Using the same data, Dennis Hogan, Nan Marie Astone, and Evelyn Kitagawa examined the practice of contraception among black girls in Chicago.[5] They found that those in low-status neighborhoods were about half as likely as those in better neighborhoods to use contraception when they first had sex.

In short, what little evidence there is suggests that the effects of the neighborhoods on educational attainment are minimal, but effects on pregnancy are large. It is possible, however, that the two studies of educational attainment underestimated the importance of neighborhoods because zip code areas are poor proxies for true neighborhoods. These areas are usually larger than most neighborhoods, and they are not designed to be socioeconomically or ethnically homogeneous. As a result, the estimates might be unduly conservative because the error in measurement introduces randomness.[6] The results were also highly sensitive to random measurement error because the samples were small. This is a particularly serious problem if residence in a given neighborhood affects only some types of people or if only some types of neighborhoods have large effects.

Most of the public concern about neighborhoods focuses on very bad ones, particularly urban ghettos. It may be that the effects of living in a certain type of neighborhood are relatively small in most communities, but that inner-city environments have a very large impact on residents' lives. In this study, I analyze the effects of various levels of neighborhood quality to determine whether the strength of the effects varies with the type of community. This analysis required a very large data set that would provide information on both people and their neighborhoods. Luckily, one does exist.

Methodology

Just once, in 1970, the Census Bureau defined the geographic unit called a neighborhood and made data on individuals' neighborhoods publicly available. This enormous data set includes information on more than two million people and thus enables researchers to examine the ef-

5. Hogan, Astone, and Kitagawa (1985).
6. Of course it is also true that the effects of neighborhoods in all three studies may have been over- or underestimated for a number of other reasons. Most of the potential sources of bias in my analysis, which I discuss later, apply to these studies as well.

fects of living in a certain type of neighborhood, such as an urban ghetto. The data set was the 1/100, 15 percent neighborhood characteristics file of the 1970 Public Use Microdata Sample. Neighborhoods were specially defined for this version of the PUMS.[7] They were about the same size as census tracts, averaging 4,000 to 5,000 people. They were formed by computer, using geographic keys associated with each household record, and were normally contiguous and relatively compact. However, because socioeconomic and demographic data were not used to define them, these geographic units were not necessarily neighborhoods in any meaningful social sense.

For my study of teenage childbearing and school dropout rates, I included only teenagers living with their parents, because social problems almost certainly affected both the probability that teenagers would move out of their parents' homes and the quality of the neighborhoods into which they moved. In a model that assumed one-way causality and made no adjustment for this simultaneity effect, the effects of neighborhoods on teenage behaviors would probably be overestimated.[8] Some teenagers were also excluded on the basis of two data-cleaning criteria. Those with inconsistencies in their records were left out, as were those with certain values allocated by the Census Bureau for the outcome variables.[9]

The 1970 PUMS included 113,997 people 16 to 19 years old; 56,219 were female. After the exclusions, the study samples consisted of 92,512 for the analysis of dropping out and 44,466 for the analysis of childbearing. I will discuss the ramifications of the exclusions later.

I used a piecewise linear logit model to analyze the pattern of effects across the neighborhood distribution.[10] For blacks and Hispanics, the neighborhood quality distribution was divided into seven intervals. Percentiles of individuals were used to establish boundaries for the intervals.[11] For example, the bottom group included the 5 percent of the black population living in the worst neighborhoods. The intervals are percentiles 0–5, 6–10, 11–25, 26–50, 51–75, 76–90, and 91–100. I used the

---

7. Bureau of the Census (1973).

8. No instrument could be found to distinguish the effects in each direction, so it was not possible to specify a simultaneous equation model. The problem does not apply to children, but there was no information on their social problems in the data set.

9. If a question is left unanswered or the response is ambiguous, the Census Bureau may allocate a response in the PUMS. One method of allocation was to substitute the response of the previous person of the same type. Those with dropout and childbearing responses allocated in this way were excluded.

10. For a description of the model, see Amemiya (1981).

11. Approximations were necessary because the raw data were provided in discrete form.

same intervals for whites. I added an eighth interval for the purpose of comparison, in the same range of the bottom interval for blacks. It comprised percentiles 0–0.10. In other words, just 0.1 percent of white teenagers lived in neighborhoods as bad as those in which 5 percent of black teenagers lived.

The index of neighborhood quality in the models was the percentage of workers in the neighborhood who held professional or managerial jobs. I chose the index because it had a larger effect on both dropping out and childbearing than any of fifteen others as well as several composites.[12] It also dominated the other indexes when they were run together in various combinations. And it alone explained almost as large a proportion of the variation in each outcome variable as all sixteen of the indexes together.

Just why the percentage of workers who held high-status jobs had the strongest effects is not entirely clear. It could be that if young people see a lot of role models for traditional success in their neighborhoods, they have more incentive to stay in school and avoid having children. Or it may be that high-status people use their affluence and influence in society to bring resources into their neighborhoods, which makes the local institutions and services better. Although these hypotheses may be valid to some extent, my guess is that for the most part the relationship reflects a selection process. Affluent people can live wherever they want. They choose to live in good neighborhoods. If few such people live in a neighborhood, it is probably because the neighborhood is unattractive. This hypothesis is predicated on the assumption that people can gain better information about neighborhood quality in their everyday lives than social scientists can with statistical instruments.

I chose the control variables in the models of dropping out on the basis of previous empirical work. There is a large literature on determinants of educational attainment. Parents' educational attainment, family income, and father's occupational status are important factors.[13] Cognitive ability,

12. The fifteen other measures were poverty rate, family poverty rate, median income, unemployment rate, male labor force participation rate, female labor force participation rate, proportion of families headed by women, percentage of the population that was black, percentage Hispanic, percentage of the population between the ages of 16 and 21, median level of educational attainment, percentage of adults who had completed fewer than eight years of school, percentage of families who had moved within the previous five years, percentage of households with more than one person per room, and a Gini coefficient of income distribution. A correlation matrix showing the relationship between ten of these indexes can be found in Crane (1991).

13. Corcoran and others (1987); Sewell, Hauser, and Wolf (1980); and Jencks and others (1972).

academic achievement, attitudes, and aspirations also have effects.[14] Christopher Jencks and his colleagues found that race had no effect on educational attainment, after they controlled for background variables, but Mary Corcoran and coworkers found a significant black advantage in years of schooling. William Sewell, Robert Hauser, and Wendy Wolf found that gender affected the pattern of attainment and that family size, number of parents in the home, rural origin, and maternal employment had indirect effects.

Eight of these variables were available in the PUMS data: family income, parents' educational status, family head's occupational status, household structure, family size, rural origin, gender, and race. I included the first six as controls in the models of dropping out. Gender and race (and also Hispanic ethnicity) were accounted for by estimating separate equations for various subgroups. Measures of ability, achievement, attitudes, and aspirations were not available. I included the population of the place, the region, and residential mobility because it seemed plausible that they might have effects. Finally, I included variables for whether the head of the family was in the military and whether he or she lacked a census-designated occupation, because in both cases the occupational status score was zero.

Demographic analyses of the determinants of teenage childbearing have tended to yield equivocal results. But Hogan and Kitagawa did find significant effects of a composite variable of social class, parents' marital status, the presence of a sister who was a teenage mother herself, and parental control of dating on the childbearing age of black teenagers in Chicago.[15] And Melvin Zelnick, John Kantner, and Kathleen Ford found that the number of parents in the home had a significant effect.[16] For the sake of comparison and because it seemed plausible that they might have an effect, I also included in the childbearing models the same measures of socioeconomic status and family structure and all the other controls that were in the models of dropping out. The one exception was household size, which I excluded because it is endogenous.

Results

Figure 1 shows the effect of changes in the percentage of high-status workers in the neighborhood on the probabilities that black, Hispanic,

14. Sewell, Hauser, and Wolf (1980); and Jencks and others (1972).
15. Hogan and Kitagawa (1985).
16. Zelnick, Kantner, and Ford (1981).

FIGURE 1. Probability of Dropping Out of School as a Function
of Percentage of High-Status Workers in the Neighborhood,
by Race or Ethnicity

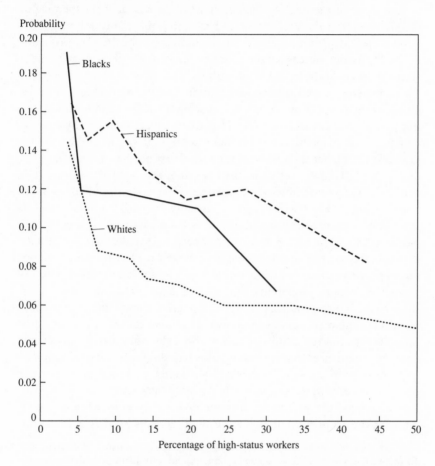

and white teenagers will drop out of high school.[17] This figure and the
ones that follow are structured to highlight the effects of decreases in the
percentage of high-status workers. The figure reads from right to left,
from higher percentages to lower ones, that is, from better neighborhoods to worse ones.[18]

17. The "white" category contained all individuals who were neither blacks nor Hispanics, including Asians, native Americans, and other minorities. Because whites comprised
such a high percentage of this group, the term is used as shorthand.

18. The equations that generated these estimates, as well as those in each of the other
figures in this chapter, can be found in Crane (1991).

The estimates of dropout probabilities were calculated for teenagers with average background characteristics for their racial or ethnic group. In other words, the control variables are fixed at their mean levels.

The slope of the line between each set of points indicates the magnitude of the effect the neighborhood has in that portion of the neighborhood quality distribution. For example, in figure 1 the dropout probability for Hispanics increases from 0.083 to 0.121 as the percentage of high-status workers living in the neighborhood falls from 43.3 to 27 percent. The slope is −0.0023, which means that for each percentage point decrease in the proportion of high-status workers in the neighborhood, the dropout probability of an average Hispanic teenager increases by 0.0023. As figure 1 clearly shows, the dropout rates of both blacks and whites are dramatically higher if they live in the very worst neighborhoods. And the discontinuity is severe—that is, the rates alter very greatly and very suddenly. For Hispanics, however, the pattern of neighborhood effects is essentially linear. For blacks, there is virtually no neighborhood effect in the middle range of the distribution: as the proportion of high-status workers falls from 20.7 percent to 5.6 percent, the dropout probability increases from 0.111 to 0.120, that is, from about 11 in 100 to 12 in 100. But as the proportion of high-status workers falls just 2 percentage points more, the dropout probability shoots up to 0.192. The ratio of the steep slope to the flat slope is 52.3, a very sharp discontinuity indeed: the effect of living in the very worst neighborhoods is more than fifty times greater than the effect in the middle. There is also a discontinuity for black students at the other extreme, although it is less sharp. As the proportion of high-status workers living in the neighborhood increases from 20 percent or so to 30 percent, the dropout rate decreases quickly.[19]

For whites, the estimated dropout probability rises from 0.049 to 0.090 as the proportion of high-status workers falls from 49.4 percent to

19. Is it likely that the discontinuities resulted from random variation in the estimates? To address this question, I tested a null hypothesis of linearity, that is, that the slope in the middle of the distribution was the true slope for the entire distribution. To do this, I extrapolated from the line fitted to the middle five points by extending it in each direction, down to 3.5 percent high-status workers and up to 31 percent. I then checked to see if the dropout probabilities at these points were significantly different from the extrapolated values. The dropout probability in the worst neighborhoods was significantly higher than the corresponding extrapolated value. (The boundaries of the confidence intervals of the estimates for the worst neighborhoods in each figure are shown in table A-1.) But the dropout probability in the best neighborhoods was not significantly lower than the corresponding extrapolated value. The criterion for significance is the 0.5 level of a one-tailed test. The value at 31 percent was significant at the level of 0.10 but not at 0.05. The value at 3.5 percent was significant at 0.01.

7.7 percent. As the proportion of high-status workers falls to 3.6 percent, the dropout probability jumps to 0.146, which means the neighborhood effect is almost fifteen times greater than it was at 7.7 percent. Although only 0.1 percent of white teenagers lived in those very worst neighborhoods, the ones who did were not immune to epidemics of dropping out.

For Hispanics, neighborhood effects are fairly large and increase steadily as the percentage of high-status workers decreases. There is no evidence of an epidemic of dropping out. But the validity of the results is questionable because of problems with the definition of Hispanic ethnicity in the 1970 census—different criteria were used in different regions of the country. If the estimates are actually composites in which the dropout probabilities of very different populations are averaged together, discontinuities within each separate population could be masked. Of course, there is no evidence that this is in fact the case.

To determine whether these sharp jumps in the rates were concentrated in or confined to inner cities, I estimated separate equations for blacks living in the largest cities and those living in other places.[20] Figure 2 shows the patterns of neighborhood effects for the two groups. In the cities, all neighborhoods had significant effects on dropout probabilities, which rise from 0.063 to 0.145 as the proportion of high-status workers falls from 28 percent to 5 percent. But as the proportion falls just 1.6 percentage points further (to 3.4 percent), the probability leaps to 0.226. Outside the largest cities the discontinuity is even sharper, but this is because there is virtually no neighborhood effect at all in the center of the distribution. The dropout probability is almost constant until the proportion of high-status workers falls below 6.7 percent. There also appears to be a discontinuity at the top of the distribution. But the level, the absolute increase, and the rate of increase in dropout probabilities are all greater within the largest cities than outside of them.

To ensure that these probabilities are not just the result of the arbitrary grouping, I also estimated several models in which progressively smaller cities were included in the big-city category. As expected, the slope below the discontinuity diminished as more cities were added, but the discontinuity itself remained quite sharp. Equations were also estimated for whites inside and outside the largest cities. The results were similar to those for blacks.

Although all inner-city teenagers suffer from social problems, people

---

20. The cities were central cities in urbanized areas that had populations of more than 1 million.

FIGURE 2. Probability of Black Teenagers Dropping Out of School as a Function of Percentage of High-Status Workers in the Neighborhood, by Location of Neighborhood

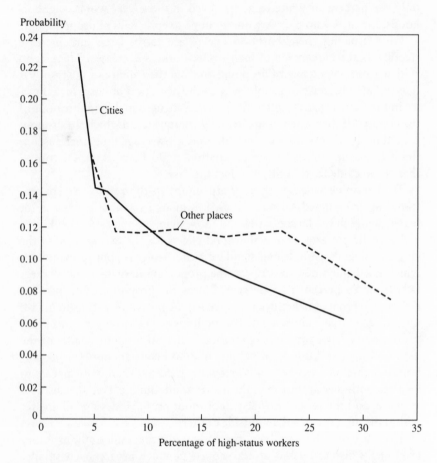

have become particularly concerned about the dropout rates for young black men. Thus I estimated separate models for young black men and women in the largest cities, to see if teenage males were particularly prone to large so-called ghetto effects. As figure 3 shows, black male teenagers from inner-city neighborhoods were at considerably higher risk of dropping out than were black female teenagers. As the proportion of high-status workers falls from 5.6 percent to 3.4 percent, the male dropout probability explodes from 0.146 to 0.345. Neighborhood effects be-

FIGURE 3. Probability of Black Teenagers Dropping Out of School as a Function of Percentage of High-Status Workers in Big-City Neighborhoods, by Sex

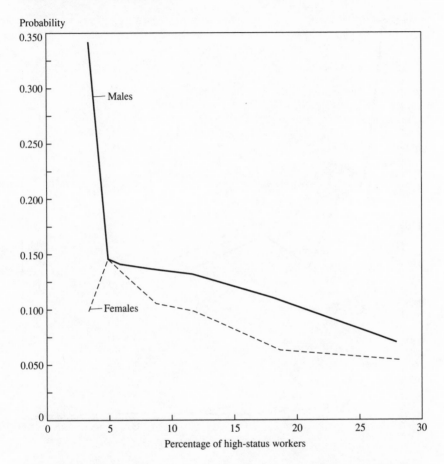

Probability

come thirty-eight times greater. Black female teenagers experience no such crisis.

The special concern for young black men may thus be more well placed than anyone ever imagined, but it is hard to believe that there could really have been a difference of this magnitude. When I estimated models for black male and female teenagers outside the largest cities and for white teenagers within them, discontinuities appeared for all and were about the same size for both sexes. This suggests that one or both of

FIGURE 4. Probability of Teenage Childbearing as a Function of Percentage of High-Status Workers in the Neighborhood, by Race and Location of Neighborhood

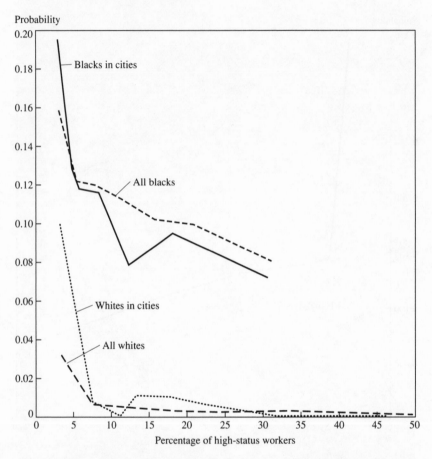

Probability

0.20
0.18   — Blacks in cities
0.16
0.14
0.12   — All blacks
0.10
0.08
0.06   — Whites in cities
0.04   — All whites
0.02
0

0   5   10   15   20   25   30   35   40   45   50

Percentage of high-status workers

the observations for inner-city blacks in the worst neighborhoods may have been bad estimates. Random error could be responsible. The upper bound of the 95 percent confidence interval of the observation for females is 0.182, which would create a discontinuity. The lower bound for males is 0.229, still quite high. Another possibility is that the observation may be too conservative for females, a possibility that I will discuss later.

Neighborhood effects on teenage childbearing also showed some sharp discontinuities. Figure 4 presents the results for four groups: black females in the largest cities, all black females, white females in the largest cities, and all white females. Neighborhood effects were not significant in the equation estimated for Hispanic females, probably because there were very few with children in the study sample.[21]

For black females as a whole, the probability of having a child rises from 0.082 to 0.124 as the proportion of high-status workers in the neighborhood falls from 31.2 percent to 5.6 percent. As the proportion falls to 3.5 percent, the probability jumps to 0.161. The slope after the discontinuity is thirteen times greater than the slope before it, but the increase in childbearing probability is not significant. I also estimated models for young black women in smaller cities, suburbs, towns, and rural areas, but none of the increases was significant.

For black teenagers in the largest cities, the probability of having a child rises from 0.074 to 0.120 as the proportion of high-status workers falls from 31.2 percent to 6 percent. As it falls to 3.5 percent, the probability jumps to 0.198. The discontinuity occurs at the third-to-last point rather than the second-to-last, as in all the other cases. Because these two observations are so close together, this aberration could be generated by a small random error in either one. But the basic story is the same either way. Childbearing probability is highest by far in the very worst neighborhoods. Taking the third-to-last observation as the point of discontinuity, the ratio of the slopes is sixteen. The increase in childbearing probability is significant for the last observation, though not for the second-to-last.

The results are similar for white teenagers. There is a discontinuity at the bottom for white females as a whole, but the increase in childbearing probability is not significant for this group or for any subgroup outside the largest cities. Within these cities, however, the effects of the poorest neighborhoods are huge. Childbearing probability increases from 0.001 to 0.01 as the proportion of high-status workers falls from 46.3 percent to 7.5 percent. As it falls to 3.5 percent, the probability explodes to 0.102. The slope after the discontinuity is almost one hundred times greater than the slope before it. Those few white teenagers who lived in the worst neighborhoods of the largest cities were more like black teenagers than other whites in terms of childbearing.

The pattern of results found here could be sensitive to the scale of measurement. The choice of scales was not completely arbitrary. The nonlinear pattern of effects in this linear scale suggests that there was a "social effect." If the pattern of effects had been linear, it could be argued that

21. Crane (1989).

neighborhood effects were generated directly and entirely by the high-status workers and thus were directly proportional to the percentage of such workers in the community. The nonlinear results suggest that neighborhood effects were the product of social interaction, that the whole was greater than the sum of its parts, at least in the worst neighborhoods.

Nevertheless, I also estimated equations scaled in percentiles. The results were essentially the same in each case, except that effects tend to be a little larger for the best neighborhoods, and there are small discontinuities for several subgroups in these neighborhoods.

Bias

Sampling bias, measurement error, and endogeneity bias are the most important potential sources of bias in estimating neighborhood effects. Wherever possible, I structured the analysis so that estimates of both the overall neighborhood effect and the relative size of the effect for the worst neighborhoods would be biased downward to make the estimates as conservative as possible.

The most important potential source of bias was the exclusion of some teenagers from the study sample. Those that were not living with their parents had to be excluded because the direction of causality could not be identified for them; that is, it cannot be known whether they live in the neighborhood because they have social problems or they have social problems because they live in the neighborhood. I also left out those who showed inconsistencies or other problems in their records. Unfortunately, dropouts and teenagers who had borne a child were disproportionately excluded, and thus the total bias may be very large. Almost half the dropouts and about two-thirds of the childbearers were excluded. Fortunately, the net bias was probably toward underestimating the effects of living in a given neighborhood, especially in the worst neighborhoods. So the estimates of neighborhood effects are probably conservative.

The estimates may also be biased if the correlation between the dropout or childbearing probabilities and neighborhood is different for the excluded group than for the group included in the study sample. If the partial correlation is more negative among the excluded teenagers than in the sample, the estimates are biased downward. If the correlation is less negative or positive, the estimates are biased upward.

For the group excluded in the data-cleaning process, I had information on dropout rates, childbearing rates, and the percentage of high-status workers in the neighborhood, but I do not know how reliable it is. For the teenagers excluded because they lived away from home, dropout and

TABLE 1. Dropout and Childbearing Rates of Groups Included in and Excluded from the Study Sample

Group	Dropping out		Childbearing	
	Number	Rate	Number	Rate
Total PUMS	113,997	11.4	56,219	7.5
Study sample	92,512	7.7	44,466	3.0
Total excluded	21,485	27.4	11,753	24.6
Blacks in sample	10,459	12.7	5,280	12.4
Blacks excluded	3,952	32.8	1,942	35.7
Whites in sample	77,508	6.8	37,007	1.7
Whites excluded	16,236	25.0	9,092	21.0
Excluded by data cleaning	2,698	20.9	1,235	20.6
Not living with parent	18,787	28.3	10,518	25.1
Students in dormitories	4,318	0	2,221	0.4
Living on own or in institution	9,368	43.5	5,569	38.6
Living with relatives	5,101	24.4	2,728	17.5

childbearing rates were known, but I did not have any information about the neighborhoods they lived in when they dropped out or became pregnant. Their neighborhoods at the time of the census may have been a good proxy for those who lived with relatives but not for those living independently. Many teenagers living on their own probably moved out after (and often because) they left school or became pregnant. And the neighborhoods they moved to were almost surely poorer on average than the ones they moved from. So any conclusions drawn for this group about the correlation between neighborhood quality and social problems, and thus about bias, have to be conditioned on assumptions about where they lived before dropping out or bearing a child.

Table 1 compares the dropout and childbearing rates of the various groups that were included or excluded. Teenagers that I left out of the sample were much more likely to have left school or have had a child than those whom I included. The dropout rates of the excluded are three and one-half times greater than those included. Females excluded were more than eight times as likely as those included to have given birth. This is not only because blacks and Hispanics were disproportionately excluded. The excluded minorities were also much more likely to have given birth than the included minorities.

Teenagers excluded because of inconsistencies in their records lived in very low-quality neighborhoods. The mean neighborhood for those in the sample had 23 percent high-status workers. The mean for those with inconsistencies had 7.4 percent. The dropout rate of this excluded group was more than 4 percentage points higher than that of those from comparable neighborhoods in the sample. The childbearing rate was 12 percentage points higher.[22] So if the data for this group are accurate, then the data cleaning may have biased estimates of neighborhood effects downward, especially in the models of childbearing.

To analyze bias for the teenagers living away from home, I divided them into three mutually exclusive subgroups: students in college dormitories, teenagers living on their own or in institutions, and teenagers living with relatives other than their parents. A little less than a quarter of those away from home were students living in college dorms. By definition, their dropout rate was zero. The childbearing rate was 0.4 percent.[23] The students almost certainly came from above-average neighborhoods. The incidence of childbearing or dropping out among teenagers from comparable neighborhoods in the sample was probably low, but not that low. So excluding college students who lived in dorms probably underestimated the effects of neighborhoods.

Half of those who lived away from home were on their own or in institutions. As table 1 shows, their dropout and childbearing rates were extremely high. Nothing certain was known about the neighborhoods they lived in when they dropped out or became pregnant, but these teenagers probably lived originally in low-quality neighborhoods with high rates of social problems that caused them to strike out on their own or become institutionalized. If so, excluding them probably biased estimates of neighborhood effects downward. However, it is conceivable that affluent teenagers from rich neighborhoods were also more likely to live independently because they could get enough financial help from their parents. If that was the case, excluding this group could have biased estimates upward.

A little more than a quarter of those living away from home lived with relatives. The mean value of neighborhood status for this group was 18.6 percent. The dropout and childbearing rates for these teenagers were considerably higher than for those in the sample from comparable neighborhoods.[24] If all these teenagers actually grew up with their relatives, leaving them out almost certainly underestimated the influence of neighborhoods. But these high rates of dropping out or bearing a child prob-

22. For this comparison, I used teenagers in the sample who lived in neighborhoods in which the proportion of high-status workers was 7 or 8 percent.

23. Because the average age of 16- to 18-year-olds living in dormitories was 17.96, the relevant comparison group in the sample was 18-year-olds. Their childbearing rate was 5.8 percent.

24. For this comparison, I used teenagers in the sample who lived in neighborhoods in which the proportion of high-status workers was 18 or 19 percent.

ably reflected the fact that dropouts and teenage mothers were more likely to move in with relatives (which is precisely why they were excluded from the study sample). In that case, the size and direction of the bias depends on the difference in quality between the neighborhoods of the parents and the relatives. If the parents lived in neighborhoods of quality similar to or better than those of the relatives, then excluding the teenagers probably biased estimates downward. If the parents lived in neighborhoods that were moderately worse than those of the relatives, then there is probably very little bias. The estimates could only be biased upward if the parents lived in neighborhoods much worse than those of the relatives.

For the sake of comparison, I estimated models that included some or all of these groups. Because the models suffered from simultaneity bias, one would expect them to generate higher estimates of neighborhood effects. They did. The estimates were consistently larger, by up to about three-fourths. There were discontinuities at the very bottom of the distributions, although in most cases they were not as sharp, because neighborhood effects before the discontinuities were larger.

Analysis of biases on the overall neighborhood effects does not necessarily say much about whether the huge effects found for teenagers from inner cities were biased in any way. The dropout rate for excluded teenagers from these neighborhoods was 49.4 percent, compared with 19.9 percent for those in the sample; the childbearing rate was 40.7 percent, compared with 16.5 percent for girls in the sample. Of course, these differences probably resulted at least partly from endogeneity, that is, the tendency for teenagers with these problems to leave home and move to bad neighborhoods. But these differences are so large they suggest that even the estimates of large neighborhood effects in the worst neighborhoods may be underestimated because of the exclusions.

There is a discontinuity for those living in the worst neighborhoods in all cases except for black females in the largest cities. One possible reason for this exception is that black females living in inner cities were the ones most likely to be living away from home and were thus excluded from the sample. If so, the dropout probability for these girls may be underestimated more than any other. It is conceivable that a discontinuity could be masked by such bias, though it would have to be very large.

Among black females in the worst neighborhoods of the largest cities, the dropout rate for those in the sample is just 10.3 percent.[25] But among

25. This includes all neighborhoods in which the proportion of high-status workers was less than or equal to 4 percent.

the black females in these neighborhoods who were excluded from the sample, the rate is 50 percent. In marked contrast, the difference for young black men in inner cities is only about 10 percent. This suggests that a lot more black female than male teenagers who originated from these neighborhoods were excluded, probably because females with children were most likely to leave home. Thus the estimate for black females in ghettos may very well be biased downward by a large amount. Whether the bias is in fact great enough to mask a sharp discontinuity is impossible to say.

The census undercount of minorities is a second possible source of sampling bias. Supplemental surveys designed to identify people left out of the census suggest that those who were missed tend to lack family attachments.[26] So the census probably did not leave out many teenagers who lived at home or with relatives. But it may have missed a considerable number of those living on their own. It seems likely that those missed were disproportionately concentrated in bad neighborhoods and perhaps also in cities. Their dropout rate was almost certainly extremely high. Thus neighborhood effects on dropping out for blacks and Hispanics may be underestimated to some extent by the census undercount. The relative childbearing rate among those missed is less certain because having a child may make a woman less mobile and easier to find. But in general, the teenagers left out of the census were probably the ones who were most likely to develop social problems. Unfortunately, this is the catch-22 for statistical analyses of problems of the inner cities. It is hard to find the people who matter most.

Measurement error is another possible source of bias. The most fundamental problem in measuring neighborhood effects is defining the neighborhoods themselves. The concept of neighborhood is a little like the concept of obscenity: it is hard to define, but most people know it when they see it. Essentially, a neighborhood is a geographic area with unbroken borders in which the density of social ties among residents is significantly greater than the density of ties between residents and nearby nonresidents. In practice, neighborhoods are defined by using socioeconomic criteria, subjective conceptions, or geographic features to determine the boundaries. But no one knows how well these methods work. Measurement error could very well be quite large even when all three methods are used together. This is probably the most fundamental problem in attempting to measure neighborhood effects. The census used only

26. Bound (1986).

geographic criteria to define the neighborhoods in the sample I used; this aggravated the problem.

There is one saving grace, however. The bias that measurement error generates is unambiguously downward, thus making estimates of neighborhood effects conservative because overlaps between true boundaries and operational boundaries make the operationally defined neighborhoods weighted averages of separate actual neighborhoods. This averaging adds an element of randomness to the measured association between neighborhood characteristics and the dependent variable.

Another possible source of bias is the endogeneity of the control variables. The model used here assumed that the control variables were unaffected by neighborhoods. But family income, occupational status, family structure, and residential tenure could very well have been affected by neighborhood quality. If so, estimates of neighborhood effects were once again biased downward. The total neighborhood effect would be the measured effect, which is direct, plus the sum of indirect effects through these other variables.[27]

In sum, most of the potential biases would contribute toward conservative estimates of the influence of neighborhoods. There is no way to be absolutely sure that the estimates are as conservative as they could be because the magnitudes of the actual biases cannot be calculated, but unless the net bias is tilted toward overestimating effects and is especially large for inner cities, the basic finding that neighborhood effects are much more serious in the poorest areas than they are anywhere else is valid.

Conclusion

Neighborhood effects on dropping out and teenage childbearing among both blacks and whites in 1970 were extremely large in very bad neighborhoods, particularly in urban ghettos. Elsewhere, the effects were much smaller, though not trivial. The surge in probabilities of dropping out was significant for blacks as a group, young black men, whites as a group, young white men, and young white women in the largest cities. The surge in childbearing probabilities was significant for both black and white teenagers in the largest cities. Outside these cities, there were some nonlinear increases in dropout probabilities for both blacks and whites and in childbearing probabilities for blacks, but they were not significant.

27. There are several other possible sources of bias, but they are less important and more technical. They are discussed in Crane (1991).

Neighborhood effects on childbearing were essentially linear for white teenagers living outside the largest cities. In each case of a nonlinear increase, the point of discontinuity fell at approximately the same point in the distribution, in neighborhoods where only 4 percent or so of the workers held high-status jobs.

The influence of inner-city residence on dropping out was very great for black male teenagers but not for black females. However, there is evidence that the probabilities that young women would drop out may have been underestimated, possibly by a very large amount. Dropout probabilities for Hispanics were approximately linear. However, the validity of this finding is open to question because the Census Bureau used different definitions of Hispanic ethnicity in different regions of the country. There were too few Hispanic teenagers with children in the study sample to distinguish any effects of neighborhoods on childbearing.

In terms of policy, these findings suggest that small improvements in inner-city environments, and perhaps also in the worst neighborhoods outside large cities, might be able to reduce the rates of dropping out and teenage childbearing a great deal. The rates were much lower in neighborhoods that were even slightly better than the very worst.

Unfortunately, the findings do not indicate how to go about improving neighborhoods. If the presence of high-status workers improves neighborhoods because of their personal contact with young people and the role models they present, perhaps a limited amount of gentrification should be encouraged in poor neighborhoods. But this index may have only reflected the judgment of high-status workers to avoid certain neighborhoods because they were bad. If so, other strategies will have to be pursued. High-status workers may also improve neighborhoods by using their affluence and influence to bring social and economic resources into the community. If so, these resources could be supplied directly. However, given political impediments to redistributing resources to poor communities, encouraging gentrification might be the better strategy after all.

If the presence of high-status workers is a proxy for the general socioeconomic composition of the neighborhood, desegregation by class (and race to the extent that it is correlated with class) should be actively encouraged. The nonlinear pattern of the model's results implies that desegregation would have large net benefits. It would greatly reduce dropping out and childbearing among teenagers from the worst neighborhoods yet would increase these problems among those from other communities very little.

It is also possible that neighborhood effects work in a more complicated way. The sharp discontinuities found here may reflect a process of social contagion that generates epidemics of social problems, and America's inner cities may be neighborhoods that experience such epidemics.[28] Clearly, more research is needed on the mechanics of neighborhood effects.

28. Crane (1991).

References

Amemiya, Takeshi. 1981. "Qualitative Response Models: A Survey." *Journal of Economic Literature* 19 (December), pp. 1483–1536.

Bound, John. 1986. "Appendix: NBER-Mathematica Survey of Inner-City Black Youth: An Analysis of the Undercount of Older Youths." In *The Black Youth Employment Crisis,* edited by Richard B. Freeman and Henry J. Holzer. University of Chicago Press.

Bureau of the Census. 1972. *Public Use Samples of Basic Records from the 1970 Census: Description and Technical Documentation.* Department of Commerce.

———. 1973. *Supplement No. 1 to Public Use Samples of Basic Records from the 1970 Census: Description and Technical Documentation.* Department of Commerce.

Corcoran, Mary, and others. 1987. "Intergenerational Transmission of Education, Income and Earnings." Unpublished paper.

Crane, Jonathan. 1989. "The Epidemic Theory of Ghettos," Center for Health and Human Resources Policy discussion paper series. John F. Kennedy School of Government, Harvard University.

———. 1991. "The Epidemic Theory of Ghettos and Neighborhood Effects on Dropping Out and Teenage Childbearing." *American Journal of Sociology* 96 (March).

Datcher, Linda. 1982. "Effects of Community and Family Background on Achievement." *Review of Economics and Statistics* 64 (February), pp. 132–41.

Hogan, Dennis P., Nan Marie Astone, and Evelyn M. Kitagawa. 1985. "Social and Environmental Factors Influencing Contraceptive Use Among Black Adolescents." *Family Planning Perspectives* 17 (July-August), pp. 165–69.

Hogan, Dennis P., and Evelyn M. Kitagawa. 1985. "The Impact of Social Status, Family Structure, and Neighborhood on the Fertility of Black Adolescents." *American Journal of Sociology* 90 (January), pp. 825–55.

Jencks, Christopher, and Susan E. Mayer. 1990. "The Social Consequences of Growing Up in a Poor Neighborhood." In *Inner-City Poverty in the United States,* edited by Laurence E. Lynn, Jr., and Michael G. H. McGeary. Washington: National Academy Press.

Jencks, Christopher, and others. 1972. *Inequality.* Basic Books.

Sewell, William H., Robert M. Hauser, and Wendy C. Wolf. 1980. "Sex, Schooling, and Occupational Status." *American Journal of Sociology* 86 (November), pp. 551–83.

Zelnik, Melvin, John F. Kantner, and Kathleen Ford. 1981. *Sex and Pregnancy in Adolescence*. Beverly Hills: Sage Publications.

Appendix Table

TABLE A-1. Confidence Intervals (95 Percent) for Estimates of Dropout and Childbearing Probabilities in the Worst Neighborhoods

Group	Percent high-status workers	Estimate	Lower bound	Upper bound
Dropping out				
Figure 1				
Blacks	3.5	.192	.140	.259
Whites	3.6	.146	.098	.213
Hispanics	4.2	.166	.110	.243
Figure 2				
Blacks in cities	3.4	.226	.156	.314
Blacks in other places	4.5	.166	.122	.221
Figure 3				
Black males in ghettos	3.4	.344	.229	.481
Black females in ghettos	3.4	.103	.022	.132
Childbearing				
Figure 4				
All black females	3.5	.161	.108	.223
Black females in cities	3.4	.198	.121	.308
All white females	3.6	.034	.012	.093
White females in cities	3.5	.102	.018	.412

How Much Does a High School's Racial and Socioeconomic Mix Affect Graduation and Teenage Fertility Rates?

SUSAN E. MAYER

MANY SOCIAL CRITICS, of whom William Wilson is probably the best known, have argued that when poor families have overwhelmingly poor neighbors, their children find it harder to escape from poverty. If this belief is true, reducing economic segregation in both schools and residential neighborhoods should significantly improve poor children's chances of escaping poverty.

The idea that economic segregation makes it harder for children to escape poverty is closely related to the idea that racial segregation makes it harder for black and Hispanic children to advance in a society dominated by whites. Indeed, the two concepts are often empirically indistinguishable, since the poorest urban neighborhoods are almost all black or Hispanic.

If a neighborhood's socioeconomic and racial or ethnic mix (which I abbreviate as simply "social mix") affects teenagers' life chances, high schools' social mix should have at least as much effect, since school is an important focus of most teenagers' social lives. In this paper I use data from the High School and Beyond survey to examine the potential impact of racial and socioeconomic desegregation of schools on students' chances of dropping out of high schools and on teenage girls' chances of having a child.

Racial and socioeconomic desegregation of schools is more likely to command the support of the majority if it improves the life chances of disadvantaged students far more than it hurts the life chances of advantaged students. For this to be the case, disadvantaged students must be more sensitive than advantaged students to changes in schools' social

The Russell Sage Foundation and the Ford Foundation provided partial funding for this project. I am indebted to Tony Bryk for comments on an earlier version of this paper, to Tony Maier for computer assistance and technical suggestions, and to Karen Rolf for computer assistance. The data used in this paper were provided by the Inter-university Consortium for Political and Social Research.

composition. To test the hypothesis, I have examined whether a school's social mix has different effects on students from different backgrounds.

Past Research

Social scientists have been interested in the effects of schools' socioeconomic and racial mix since the late 1950s. This topic was especially popular during the decade following publication of the so-called Coleman report in 1966.[1] Most of this research focused on assessing schools' effects on cognitive skills and college entrance rates, but a few recent studies have looked at the effect of schools' social mix on dropping out and teenage fertility.

Dropouts

Only one study has estimated the effect of a high school's mean socioeconomic status (SES) on students' chances of graduating. Anthony Bryk and Mary Driscoll used data from 357 High School and Beyond (HSB) schools that participated in the Administrator and Teacher survey to investigate the effects of school characteristics on tenth graders' chances of dropping out.[2] They found that dropping out was subject to two contradictory influences. As a school's mean SES fell, as its student body became more economically diverse, and as its minority enrollment increased, tenth graders of any given race, SES, and academic background were more likely to drop out. But with both the school's racial and socioeconomic mix and students' own race and SES held constant, students whose classmates had high tenth grade test scores tended to have above-average dropout rates. These findings suggest that academic competition increases attrition, while high-SES peers reduce it.[3] Since these two school characteristics are highly correlated, the net effect of having advantaged classmates is probably small, but this effect cannot be estimated from the work of Bryk and Driscoll.[4]

Bryk and Driscoll did not estimate the overall impact of a school's social mix. Instead, they estimated its effect with other endogenous school

1. Coleman and others (1966).
2. Bryk and Driscoll (1988).
3. The same contradictory influences affect the chances that high school graduates will go to college. See Jencks and Mayer (1990).
4. Using High School and Beyond data, the correlation between schools' mean reading score and mean SES is 0.73. The correlation between schools' mean math scores and mean SES is 0.75.

characteristics, such as school climate and students' mean test scores, controlled. They did not investigate whether students from different racial or economic backgrounds react differently to a change in racial or socioeconomic composition, and they did not consider the possibility that extreme concentrations of poverty or extreme levels of racial segregation have effects different from those within the "normal" range.[5]

Although the work of Bryk and Driscoll suggests that the net effect of a school's social mix on dropping out may be small, Jonathan Crane's paper in this volume finds that the mean SES of a neighborhood has substantial effects, and the effects are greater for blacks than for whites. Crane did not consider the effect of neighborhood racial composition on dropping out.

Teenage Childbearing

Using High School and Beyond date, Allan Abrahamse, Peter Morrison, and Linda Waite found that white, tenth grade girls were more likely to have a child out of wedlock if they attended high schools in which a large proportion of tenth graders reported that they would consider having a child out of wedlock.[6] This relationship held even after controlling for the girls' own professed willingness to have an out-of-wedlock child and other background measures. This relationship did not hold for black females.

Unfortunately, the authors did not investigate why the proportion of tenth graders who reported that they might have a child out of wedlock varied from school to school. The proportion of students willing to have an out-of-wedlock child is probably associated with a school's social mix, but the study did not report the strength of this relationship. In addition, a school's social mix may affect out-of-wedlock teenage childbearing independent of its effect on tenth graders' reports about their willingness to have an out-of-wedlock child.

Several other studies bear indirectly on the likely relationship between schools' social composition and teenage childbearing. Crane's paper in this volume finds substantial effects of neighborhood SES on teenage childbearing, which are greater for blacks than for whites.

Frank Furstenberg and his colleagues investigated the effect of class-

5. Jencks and Mayer (1990) discuss the general methodological limitations of the literature on the effects of neighborhoods' and schools' social mix.
6. Abrahamse, Morrison, and Waite (1988).

rooms' racial mix on teenage sexual behavior.[7] They found that 67 percent of black 15- and 16-year-olds in classrooms that were more than
four-fifths black reported having had sexual intercourse, compared with
only 40 percent of blacks of the same age in classrooms less than four-
fifths black. Controlling for mother's education had little effect on these
results. This finding suggests that racial segregation increases the rate of
sexual activity among black teenagers, but the 95 percent confidence interval for the difference between blacks in all-black classrooms and those
in mixed classrooms ranges from 7 percentage points to 47, so the true
magnitude of the effect is uncertain. There were not enough whites in
predominantly black classrooms to assess the effect of such classrooms
on white girls' sexual experience.[8]

Effective contraception can prevent pregnancy among those who are
sexually active. But Dennis Hogan, Nan Marie Astone, and Evelyn Kitagawa found that black teenage girls in low-SES neighborhoods in Chicago were only half as likely as those from high-SES neighborhoods to
use contraception at the time of first sexual intercourse.[9] Taken together,
the work of Furstenberg and his colleagues and Hogan, Astone, and Kitagawa suggests that black teenagers' social environment may affect both
sexual activity and likelihood of using contraception. Consequently, one
would also expect social environment to affect pregnancy.

Hogan and Kitagawa found that, with family background controlled,
living in a low-SES Chicago neighborhood increased the pregnancy rate
among unmarried black teenage girls by a third.[10] There was little difference in pregnancy rates between those living in middle-SES and high-SES
neighborhoods. This finding highlights the importance of nonlinearities.
Because whites in Chicago almost never live in neighborhoods as bad as
the worst third of black neighborhoods, a linear model estimated for all
teenagers in the Chicago metropolitan area would probably show that a
neighborhood's mean SES had almost no effect on teenage pregnancy.

None of these studies tried to assess the possibility that the effect of

7. Furstenberg and others (1987).
8. Furstenberg and his colleagues (1987) did not control for students' ability. One
would expect low-scoring blacks in racially mixed high schools to end up in disproportionately black classrooms. The racial mix of black students' classrooms may, therefore, be a
proxy for their own academic ability. Low test scores are correlated with an increase in the
probability that teenage girls will become pregnant. See Sum, Harrington, and Goedieke
(1986); and Eisen and others (1983). Low scores are probably associated with early sexual
activity as well.
9. Hogan, Astone, and Kitagawa (1985).
10. Hogan and Kitagawa (1985).

neighborhood or school SES is greater for low-SES girls than for higher-SES girls. Except for the study by Furstenberg and his colleagues, none tried to assess the effect of neighborhood or school racial composition on teenage childbearing.

Data and Methods

I used data from the 1980 High School and Beyond survey, a nationally representative panel study of students from 968 public and private high schools. I used data on 26,425 white, black, and Hispanic students who were in tenth grade in 1980 and were followed up in 1982.[11] HSB targeted 36 tenth graders for interviewing in each school. The actual number interviewed ranged from 38 to 3.

I defined a high school dropout as any student who was in school in 1980 but was neither in school nor a graduate in 1982. The overall dropout rate was 13.6 percent. It was 12.1 percent for whites, 16.9 percent for blacks, and 18.5 percent for Hispanics.[12]

The analysis of teenage childbearing covers only female students, 4.9 percent of whom had had a child by 1982. The childbearing rate was 3.5 percent for whites, 11.1 percent for blacks, and 7.8 percent for Hispanics.[13]

I used father's and mother's education, whether the father had a white-collar job, whether the family owned its home, whether it had two or more cars, and whether it had a dishwasher to estimate a student's SES.[14]

11. The HSB survey oversampled certain kinds of schools (especially private schools) but selected students within schools randomly. HSB provided weights intended to compensate for the oversampling of certain kinds of schools, for students' probability of selection within schools, and for nonresponse. These weights were intended to yield a nationally representative sample of students. I used the weights for all analyses reported in this paper.

12. See the appendix for a description of the variables, their means, and standard deviations.

13. Students were not explicitly asked if they had had a child. Girls were counted as having had a child if they reported that they lived with their own child or if they responded to a question about when they expected to have their first child by saying that they had already done so. This measure includes mothers who are step- or foster mothers and may include some mothers who do not live with their child.

14. I used 1980 data on students' family background. When students were missing data on one of the family background variables for 1980, I substituted the 1982 value. When students were missing data for both years, I substituted the mean for that variable. I estimated the school mean for a variable using the responses of all tenth graders in a school who had valid data on that variable. I did not use imputed values when estimating school means.

The variation in the number of students surveyed in each school suggests a potentially

The last three measures were intended as proxies for income. I did not include family income because many students did not answer this question.[15] I weighted these measures according to their relative effect on the particular dependent variable of interest to construct two composite measures of SES, one for predicting dropouts and one for predicting teenage births. (See the appendix for an explanation of the construction of this variable.)

I estimated the cumulative impact of schools' social mix on dropping out and teenage fertility. To do this, I treated the social mix of the school a student attended in the tenth grade as a proxy for the mix of the schools the student attended in grades 1 through 9 as well as in grades 11 and 12. I then controlled for only those characteristics of individual students that were clearly unaffected by school characteristics, namely race and parental SES.[16] I did not control for characteristics such as tenth grade test scores or educational plans that depended partly on the student's school experience before tenth grade.

My estimate of schools' cumulative effects is too high if, as seems likely, unmeasured parental characteristics influence both the parents' choice of a school district and the child's behavior as a teenager. My esti-

---

important selection problem. If low-SES students are less likely to participate in the survey, one would expect fewer participants in low-SES schools, and those who do participate would likely be from unrepresentatively high-SES families. In this case one would overestimate mean SES and the coefficients for the effect of mean SES would be biased downward. But the number of respondents in a school correlates only -0.12 with principals' reports of the number of dropouts, -0.06 with reports of the percent of 1978–79 students in college, and -0.04 with whether the school participates in the chapter I program. If the number of respondents was strongly correlated with these measures, one would suspect that the number of respondents was correlated with school SES. Because the correlations are so weak, it is unlikely that this source of selection bias will have much effect on the reported results.

15. I experimented with other SES measures that included a broader range of occupational categories for both mothers and fathers. In most cases the occupational categories were not statistically significant at the 0.05 level, had trivial coefficients, and added little to the explained variance. These more cumbersome SES measures all correlated greater than 0.90 with the measure used in this paper. About a third of students did not report their families' income in 1980. Using 1982 income to impute 1980 income proved difficult because the way income was coded changed between 1980 and 1982. In addition dropouts were not asked to report their family income in 1982. Once parents' education, whether the father had a white-collar job, and whether the family owned their home, a dishwasher, or two or more cars were included in an equation predicting whether students drop out, income was not statistically significant at the 0.05 level and its inclusion increased R^2 by only 0.001.

16. Jencks and Mayer (1990) discuss the rationale for considering parental SES as exogenous.

mates are too low if, as also seems likely, a student's race and SES are more highly correlated with the social mix of his or her elementary school than with the social mix of his or her high school. If individual race and SES are proxies for elementary school social mix, some part of what seems to be an effect of individual SES or race may really be an effect of elementary schools' social mix. These two sources of bias are not likely to be large, and they should offset one another.

When estimating the effects of a change in a schools' social mix, I did not control for the school's curriculum, teachers' expectations, the school's expenditures, or any other school characteristic correlated with social mix. The rationale for this approach was that in the long run all school characteristics that are currently correlated with social mix are causally dependent on it. I assumed, for instance, that teacher expectations depend on students' race and SES, not the other way around. If this assumption is correct, the best way to estimate the long-run effects of desegregating schools is to look at the effect of attending those schools that are currently desegregated. This assumption may somewhat overestimate the effect of changing schools' social mix.

Results

Table 1 shows the effect of schools' socioeconomic and racial or ethnic composition on the log odds of a student's dropping out or having a child before graduation. These estimates control only for students' SES and race or ethnicity. The first equation for each outcome shows the effect of school SES when schools' racial composition is not considered. As expected, it shows that students who attend high-SES schools are less likely to drop out and less likely to have a child than students of the same race and socioeconomic background who attend lower-SES schools.[17]

17. The parameter estimates for the school means may be less accurate than those for student characteristics because they are based on only 968 schools. In principle these standard errors can be adjusted for degrees of freedom lost in using school means by adjusting the number of cases to equal the number of schools. This would increase the standard errors of the parameter estimates. However, one would also need to account for the fact that the variance of school means is less than the variance of individual characteristics. This adjustment would reduce the variance of the dependent variable and lower the standard errors of the parameter estimates. I have not made these corrections.

Because school means are assigned to each student, this procedure implicitly accounts for the fact that estimates of the school mean are more reliable in some schools than others by giving less weight to schools with fewer respondents. In estimating school effect models such as this one, hierarchical linear models and similar estimation procedures weight school

TABLE 1. Effect of School Social Mix on Log Odds of Dropping Out and Teenage Childbearing[a]

Independent variable	Dropping out			Teenage childbearing		
	(1)	(2)	(3)	(1)	(2)	(3)
School mean socioeconomic status	−2.834	...	−1.984	−8.966	...	−7.461
	(.348)		(.426)	(2.063)		(2.452)
Student socioeconomic status	−4.539	−4.934	−4.595	−12.206	−13.759	−12.343
	(.175)	(.161)	(.180)	(1.079)	(.982)	(1.085)
Black	−.157	−.198	−.186	.280	.207	.220
	(.029)	(.035)	(.036)	(.054)	(.068)	(.068)
Hispanic	.028	−.047	−.038	.177	.148	.163
	(.026)	(.030)	(.030)	(.058)	(.066)	(.066)
Proportion black	...	.230	.090	...	.344	.172
		(.055)	(.063)		(.105)	(.119)
Proportion Hispanic	...	.464	.341	...	.199	.024
		(.063)	(.069)		(.137)	(.150)
Intercept	4.773	4.453	4.650	4.281	3.889	4.203
	(.034)	(.020)	(.046)	(.085)	(.051)	(.115)
Chi-square	24,736	23,974	24,632	11,718	11,559	11,702
Degrees of freedom	23,859	22,997	23,857	12,408	11,916	12,406

SOURCE: Author's calculations based on data from the High School and Beyond survey; see appendix. Standard errors are in parentheses.

a. Equations were estimated using SPSS-X (1986), which uses the algorithm: $[Ln\,(p/1-p)/2] + 5 = bX + a$, where a is the intercept and B is the parameter estimate.

The second equation for each outcome shows the effect of schools' racial or ethnic composition when the schools' socioeconomic mix is not considered. It shows that students in predominantly black or predominantly Hispanic schools are more likely to drop out and more likely to have a child than students of the same race and socioeconomic background who attend predominantly white high schools.

The third equation for each outcome shows the combined effects of schools' racial or ethnic and socioeconomic mix. For both outcomes, some of the apparent effect of schools' socioeconomic mix is accounted for by racial composition. However, once I controlled for schools' socioeconomic mix, the proportion of students who are black had only a small and statistically insignificant effect on dropping out or on teenage child-

means proportional to their precision and consequently could produce more accurate estimates of standard errors for school characteristics.

TABLE 2. Effect of School Social Mix on Log Odds of Dropping Out and Teenage Childbearing, by Student Race and Ethnicity[a]

Independent variable	Dropping out			Teenage childbearing		
	White	Black	Hispanic	White	Black	Hispanic
School mean socio-economic status	−2.636	−2.208	−1.908	−11.318	−1.119	−6.975
	(.560)	(.951)	(.960)	(3.523)	(4.543)	(5.611)
Student socio-economic status	−5.637	−2.341	−2.908	−13.311	−10.307	−13.005
	(.225)	(.420)	(.442)	(1.462)	(2.054)	(2.550)
Proportion black	.146	−.036	.173	.506	.109	−.106
	(.100)	(.109)	(.125)	(.205)	(.177)	(.264)
Proportion Hispanic	.823	.060	.171	.760	.042	−.427
	(.113)	(.212)	(.101)	(.259)	(.356)	(.234)
Intercept	4.696	4.491	4.545	4.293	4.207	4.562
	(.062)	(.112)	(.109)	(.164)	(.232)	(.272)
Chi-square	17,779	3,163	3,276	8,205	1,703	1,464
Degrees of freedom	15,466	3,352	4,330	8,088	1,819	2,145

SOURCE: Author's calculations. See appendix. Standard errors are in parentheses.
a. See table 1, note a.

bearing, and the proportion of students who are Hispanic had a statistically reliable effect only on dropping out.

Reducing socioeconomic segregation would increase the school SES of disadvantaged students and reduce the school SES of advantaged students. Table 1, therefore, suggests that socioeconomic desegregation would help disadvantaged students but hurt advantaged students. To see if disadvantaged students gain more from desegregation than advantaged students lose, table 2 estimates the effects of schools' racial and socioeconomic mix separately for whites, blacks, and Hispanics, while table 3 investigates these effects for students from different socioeconomic backgrounds.[18]

These tables estimate the effect of a unit change in school SES on the odds that students with different characteristics will drop out or have a baby before graduation. A coefficient of 5.68 would imply that a decrease of two standard deviations in school SES doubled a student's odds of dropping out. Because SES has a different metric in the equation predicting childbearing, it would take a coefficient of 14.43 for a decrease of two standard deviations in school SES to double a girl's odds of having a child.

Tables 2 and 3 provide little evidence that disadvantaged students gain

18. The appendix explains the system for classifying students according to their socioeconomic background.

TABLE 3. Effect of School Social Mix on Log Odds of Dropping Out and Teenage Childbearing, by Student Socioeconomic Status[a]

Independent variable	Dropping out[a]			Teenage childbearing		
	Low SES	Medium SES	High SES	Low SES	Medium SES	High SES
School mean socio-economic status	−2.614	−1.779	−1.564	−11.173	−7.090	−.108
	(.715)	(.557)	(1.492)	(3.912)	(3.269)	(11.983)
Student socio-economic status	−3.308	−5.362	−2.367	−11.363	−11.298	−13.972
	(.509)	(.393)	(2.242)	(3.112)	(2.410)	(16.202)
Black	−.192	−.166	.019	.254	.200	.957
	(.053)	(.048)	(.189)	(.099)	(.095)	(.372)
Hispanic	−.077	.005	−.247	.273	.105	.143
	(.050)	(.036)	(.181)	(.101)	(.089)	(.536)
Proportion black	−.190	.233	.639	−.069	.270	.635
	(.100)	(.079)	(.294)	(.176)	(.165)	(.709)
Proportion Hispanic	−.132	.519	1.301	−.617	.387	.963
	(.116)	(.084)	(.270)	(.241)	(.190)	(.940)
Intercept	4.832	4.674	3.899	4.449	4.109	3.389
	(.180)	(.070)	(.436)	(.180)	(.174)	(1.366)
Chi-square	4,680	16,228	4,179	2,338	7,817	1,464
Degrees of freedom	4,719	15,183	4,031	2,438	7,995	2,145

SOURCE: Author's calculations. See appendix. Standard errors are in parentheses.
a. See table 1, note a.

proportionately more from increases in schools' mean SES than advantaged students lose from decreases in mean SES. However, because blacks and Hispanics are more likely to drop out of high school and have children as teenagers, the same proportionate change in either behavior implies a greater absolute change for blacks and Hispanics than for whites. The same is true for low-SES students compared with higher-SES students. Direct comparisons of coefficients for black and Hispanic students or for high- and low-SES students are therefore likely to be misleading. Table 4 shows predicted dropout and childbearing rates for students with various characteristics in low-SES schools, average-SES schools, and high-SES schools.

Racial Differences

Moving an average-SES white student from an average-SES school to a low-SES school increases his or her chances of dropping out from 14.2 percent to 17.1 percent. Moving an average-SES black student to a low-

TABLE 4. Estimated Probability of Dropping Out and Having a Child between the Tenth and Twelfth Grades, by Student Race and Socioeconomic Status and School Socioeconomic Status[a]

Student socioeconomic status and race	Probability of dropping out			Probability of having a child		
	Low-SES school	Average-SES school	High-SES school	Low-SES school	Average-SES school	High-SES school
Low						
White	.285	.243	.184	.109	.074	.050
Black	.184	.165	.138	.130	.123	.116
Hispanic	.238	.206	.162	.110	.104	.100
Average						
White	.171	.142	.117	.064	.042	.028
Black	.145	.129	.115	.086	.079	.076
Hispanic	.181	.155	.132	.063	.058	.056
High						
White	.096	.079	.064	.037	.024	.016
Black	.113	.100	.089	.055	.052	.049
Hispanic	.135	.114	.097	.036	.034	.032

SOURCE: Author's calculations. See appendix.

a. To get these dropout rates and teenage childbearing rates I estimated separate equations for whites, blacks, and Hispanics that included only student SES and school SES so these estimates do not control for schools' racial or ethnic mix. Low-SES schools are one standard deviation below the sample mean for school SES. High-SES schools are one standard deviation above the sample mean, and average schools are the remainder. Similarly, low-SES students are one standard deviation below the sample mean for student SES. High-SES students are one standard deviation above the sample mean, and average-SES students are at the sample mean for student SES.

SES school increases his or her chances of dropping out from 12.9 percent to 14.5 percent. The situation is similar for teenage childbearing. Moving an average-SES white girl from an average-SES school to a low-SES school raises her chances of having a baby from 4.2 percent to 6.4 percent. Transferring an average-SES black girl from an average-SES school to a low-SES school raises her chances of having a baby from 7.9 percent to 8.6 percent.

In general blacks and Hispanics are less sensitive than whites to changes in their school's mean SES. This finding suggests that socioeconomic desegregation may hurt whites more than it helps blacks and Hispanics. However, these estimates do not control for schools' racial or ethnic mix.

High- and Low-SES Students

Table 4 also suggests that a change in school SES has a greater absolute effect on the chances that low-SES students will drop out or have a child

TABLE 5. Probability of Dropping Out and Having a Child between the Tenth and Twelfth Grades for Students with Selected Characteristics Transferring to Schools with Average Racial and Socioeconomic Composition[a]

	Dropping out		Teenage childbearing	
Characteristic	Actual probability	Predicted probability	Actual probability	Predicted probability
With race interaction				
White	.121	.132	.035	.040
Black	.169	.156	.111	.108
Hispanic	.185	.169	.078	.085
All	.136	.139	.049	.054
With student SES interaction				
Low socioeconomic status	.258	.243	.113	.110
Medium socioeconomic status	.127	.128	.042	.043
High socioeconomic status	.042	.054	.008	.010
All	.136	.136	.049	.050

SOURCE: Author's calculations. See appendix.
a. To estimate probabilities I used the results from the equations reported in tables 2 and 3. I substituted the sample means for school mean socioeconomic status, proportion black, and proportion Hispanic to estimate the predicted probabilities of dropping out and teenage childbearing.

than on the chances that high-SES students will do so. Moving a high-SES white student from a high-SES school to an average-SES school only increases his or her chances of dropping out from 6.4 percent to 7.9 percent. Moving a low-SES white student from a low-SES school to an average-SES school reduces his or her chances of dropping out from 28.5 percent to 24.3 percent. The same is true for black and Hispanic students. Similarly, the same change in school SES has a greater absolute effect on teenage childbearing for low-SES girls than for high-SES girls, regardless of their race. The proportionate effect is often greater for low-SES students, so the coefficient of mean SES in table 3 is somewhat higher for low-SES students. Again, these estimates do not control for schools' racial or ethnic mix.

From table 4 one cannot tell what the overall change in the incidence of dropping out and teenage childbearing would be if there were both racial and socioeconomic desegregation of schools. The overall change depends both on the current distribution of students across schools and the absolute effect of a change in school social mix on students from different family backgrounds. Table 5 uses the equations in tables 2 and 3 to estimate the overall changes in the dropout rate and teenage fertility rate that one would expect if students were randomly assigned to schools. The conclusions are the same whether one estimates the changes from the equations within race groups or within SES groups.

Racial and socioeconomic desegregation would improve schools' social mix for black and Hispanic students but worsen the mix for white students. Therefore, the black and Hispanic dropout rates would decrease, and the white rate would increase if students were randomly assigned to schools. The overall dropout rate between tenth and twelfth grades would remain about the same, but dropping out would be slightly redistributed from black and Hispanic to white students and from low-to high-SES students.

My best estimate is that if students were randomly distributed among schools, the overall rate at which teenage girls have children between tenth and twelfth grades would not decrease. There might be a slight redistribution from black to white and Hispanic students and from low- to higher-SES students. However, because of the large standard errors in the equations for black and Hispanic girls, these estimates should be considered very tentative.

Nonlinear Effects of Schools' Social Mix

If the effect of raising the social mix of a low-SES school is the same as the effect of a comparable reduction in the mix of a high-SES school, socioeconomic desegregation will not change the overall graduation rate or teenage fertility rate. It will simply distribute these behaviors more evenly across schools. Similarly, if the effect of decreasing minority enrollment is the same in schools with high minority enrollment as it is in those with low minority enrollment, racial desegregation will not change the overall dropout or teenage fertility rates. Racial and economic desegregation will change the overall rate if the effect of changing a school's social mix is greater in schools with low socioeconomic status or schools with high minority enrollments.

To test this possibility I estimated logistic regressions that included dummy variables for schools with high, medium, and low SES and for various concentrations of blacks and Hispanics. (The appendix explains the construction of these dummy variables.) These results are not shown because they are very weak. I found no statistically significant or substantively large nonlinear effects of either school mean SES, proportion black, or proportion Hispanic on dropping out or teenage childbearing once I accounted for interactions with race and student SES. This result may simply indicate that there is not enough statistical power in these data to test simultaneously for interactions and nonlinearities.

That there are no statistically reliable nonlinear effects of school SES suggests that low-SES schools have the same proportionate effect on students' chances of dropping out or having a child as high-SES schools. Because students in low-SES schools are more likely to drop out or have a child, low-SES schools have a greater absolute effect on students' chances of dropping out or having a child than higher-SES schools.

Conclusion

These results suggest that students who attend high-SES schools are less likely to drop out of high school between the tenth and twelfth grades and that girls who attend high-SES schools are less likely to have a child between the tenth and twelfth grades than students with the same family background who attend lower-SES schools. White students who attend predominantly black or predominantly Hispanic schools are more likely to drop out and more likely to have a child than white students with the same family background who attend predominantly white high schools. Among black and Hispanic students, however, the effect of attending predominantly black schools on both dropping out and teenage fertility is largely accounted for by the low mean socioeconomic status of these schools.

A change in school SES has a greater absolute effect on dropping out and teenage fertility for low-SES students than for high-SES students. But it also has a greater absolute effect for white students than for black or Hispanic students.

These results are at odds with Jonathan Crane's finding that the same absolute change in a neighborhood's SES had a greater effect on both dropping out and teenage childbearing for black teenagers than for white teenagers. This difference could mean that neighborhoods and schools do not have the same effects or that things have changed since 1970. The disparities could also be caused by differences in the way the results were estimated.

My results are also at odds with the findings of Hogan and Kitagawa that black teenagers living in the worst Chicago census tracts have higher pregnancy rates than black teenagers with the same family background who live in higher-SES black census tracts. This difference may occur because there are few high schools in the United States whose mean SES is as low as the mean SES of the worst census tracts in Chicago or because neighborhoods may affect pregnancy rates differently from the way schools do.

References

Abrahamse, Allan F., Peter A. Morrison, and Linda J. Waite. 1988. *Beyond Stereotypes: Who Becomes a Single Teenage Mother?* Santa Monica: Rand.

Altonji, Joseph. 1988. "The Effects of Family Background, School Characteristics and High School Curriculum on Wages and the Return to Education." Paper presented at the NBER Summer Institute.

Bryk, Anthony S., and Mary Evina Driscoll. 1988. "The High School as Community: Contextual Influences, and Consequences for Students and Teachers." Madison, Wis.: National Center on Effective Secondary Schools.

Bryk, Anthony, and Stephan Raudenbush. 1988. "Toward a More Appropriate Conceptualization of Research on School Effects: A Three-Level Hierarchical Linear Model." *American Journal of Education* (November), pp. 65–108.

Coleman, James, and others. 1966. *Equality of Educational Opportunity.* Department of Health, Education, and Welfare.

Eisen, Marvin, and others. 1983. "Factors Discriminating Pregnancy Resolution Decisions of Unmarried Adolescents." *Genetic Psychology Monographs* 108 (August), pp. 69–95.

Furstenberg, Frank F., Jr., and others. 1987. "Race Differences in the Timing of Adolescent Intercourse." *American Sociological Review* 52 (August), pp. 511–18.

Hogan, Dennis, Nan Marie Astone, and Evelyn Kitagawa. 1985. "Social and Environmental Factors Influencing Contraceptive Use among Black Adolescents." *Family Planning Perspectives* 17 (July-August), pp. 165–69.

Hogan, Dennis P., and Evelyn M. Kitigawa. 1985. "The Impact of Social Status, Family Structure, and Neighborhood on the Fertility of Black Adolescents." *American Journal of Sociology* 90 (January), pp. 825–55.

Jencks, Christopher, and Marsha Brown. 1975. "Effects of High Schools on Their Students." *Harvard Educational Review* 45 (August), pp. 273–324.

Jencks, Christopher, and Susan E. Mayer. (1990). "The Social Consequences of Growing Up in a Poor Neighborhood." In *Inner-City Poverty in the United States,* edited by Laurence E. Lynn, Jr., and Michael G. H. McGeary. Washington: National Academy Press.

National Center for Educational Statistics. 1984. *High School and Beyond: A National Longitudinal Study for the 1980s.* Department of Education.

SPSS-X User's Guide. 1986. McGraw-Hill.

Sum, Andre, Paul Harrington, and William Goedicke. 1986. "Basic Skills of America's Teens and Young Adults: Findings from the 1980 National ASVAB Testing and Their Implications for Education." Report submitted to the Ford Foundation.

Wilson, William Julius. 1987. *The Truly Disadvantaged: The Inner City, the Underclass, and Public Policy.* University of Chicago Press.

Appendix

Means and standard deviations for the following variables are shown for all black, white, and Hispanic students in table A-1 and for girls only in table A-2.

Dropout: a binary variable coded 1 if the student had not graduated and was not enrolled in school in 1982.

Teenage mother: a binary variable coded 1 for girls who in 1982 reported that they lived with their own child or responded that they already had a child when asked when they expected to have their first child.

Black: a binary variable equal to 1 if the student reported his or her race as black.

Hispanic: a binary variable equal to 1 if the student answered "Hispanic or Spanish" to the question, "What is your origin or descent?"

Proportion black: proportion of respondents in a school who are black.

Proportion hispanic: proportion of respondents in a school who are Hispanic.

TABLE A-1. Means and Standard Deviations for Variables for All Students, by Race and Student Socioeconomic Background[a]

Variable	White	Black	Hispanic	Low SES	Medium SES	High SES	Total
Dropout	.121	.169	.185	.258	.127	.042	.136
	(.326)	(.374)	(.388)	(.438)	(.333)	(.201)	(.343)
Student socio-economic status	.114	.060	.078	.010	.105	.109	.102
	(.055)	(.063)	(.058)	(.032)	(.030)	(.017)	(.060)
School socio-economic status	.109	.075	.089	.077	.102	.127	.102
	(.027)	(.034)	(.033)	(.033)	(.026)	(.029)	(.031)
Proportion black	.062	.456	.141	.225	.107	.065	.121
	(.112)	(.268)	(.209)	(.265)	(.186)	(.124)	(.201)
Proportion Hispanic	.096	.150	.290	.178	.125	.091	.129
	(.092)	(.118)	(.252)	(.183)	(.137)	(.106)	(.144)
Black	...	...	...	.277	.100	.035	.124
				(.448)	(.300)	(.184)	...
Hispanic	...	...	...	.213	.125	.051	.132
				(.410)	(.331)	(.221)	...
Number	19,654	3,281	3,490	4,757	17,308	4,360	26,425

a. Standard errors are in parentheses.

TABLE A-2. Means and Standard Deviations for Variables for Girls, by Race and Student Socioeconomic Background[a]

Variable	White	Black	Hispanic	Low SES	Medium SES	High SES	Total
Teenage	.035	.111	.078	.113	.042	.008	.049
mother	(.183)	(.314)	(.268)	(.316)	(.201)	(.089)	(.216)
Student SES	.050	.030	.035	.011	.046	.082	.045
	(.022)	(.024)	(.023)	(.010)	(.012)	(.008)	(.023)
School SES	.048	.036	.041	.036	.046	.056	.046
	(.011)	(.012)	(.012)	(.011)	(.010)	(.012)	(.012)
Proportion	.064	.471	.145	.233	.110	.069	.126
black	(.114)	(.270)	(.209)	(.271)	(.190)	(.135)	(.207)
Proportion	.097	.150	.307	.177	.125	.093	.129
Hispanic	(.091)	(.118)	(.260)	(.182)	(.138)	(.103)	(.144)
Black	...	...	...	.288	.103	.044	.129
				(.453)	(.303)	(.206)	(.333)
Hispanic	...	...	...	.204	.108	.047	.118
				(.403)	(.311)	(.213)	(.320)
Number	9,978	1,714	1,567	2,378	8,756	2,125	13,259

a. Standard errors are in parentheses.

SES: a composite index consisting of the following variables:
Education—Both father's and mother's education is coded as follows:

    0 = less than high school
    1 = high school graduate
    2 = two or fewer years of vocational training
    3 = more than two years of vocational training
    4 = two or fewer years of college
    5 = two to four years of college
    6 = college graduate
    7 = master's degree or equivalent
    8 = advanced professional degree

Father, white collar: a binary variable equal to 1 if the father's occupation is professional or teacher, manager, proprietor, or owner.

Owns home: a binary variable equal to 1 if the student reports that his or her family owns the home in which they live.

Owns cars: a binary variable equal to 1 if the student reports that his or her family owns two or more cars.

Dishwasher: a binary variable equal to 1 if the student reports that his or her family owns a dishwasher.

School mean SES: mean SES of respondents in a school.

Procedures for Calculating SES Measures

To devise a measure for estimating the effect of school mean SES on dropping out, I estimated the within-school effect on dropping out of the components of SES. Students in the same school are presumably influenced by characteristics of the school and its surrounding neighborhood. Consequently, it is necessary to estimate the within-school effect of the components of SES to avoid correlation of the independent variables and the error term.[19] To devise the measure for estimating the effect of SES on dropping out, I did the following:

—Subtracted each student's score on each component of SES from the school mean for that component to get a deviation score for each SES component.

—Subtracted each student's dropout score (1 if the student dropped out, 0 otherwise) from the school dropout rate to get a dropout deviation score.

—Used ordinary least squares to regress the dropout deviation score on the deviation scores for the SES components. This procedure is equivalent to estimating regression equations within each school and averaging the results.[20]

—Used the unstandardized regression coefficient of each component of SES as a weight to estimate each student's parental SES score.

—Used these parental SES scores to estimate each school's mean SES.

I followed an analogous procedure for computing a second composite measure of SES for use in equations predicting teenage childbearing. The correlation between the two measures was 0.76.

The dependent variable was dichotomous and highly skewed, suggesting that a logit model might provide a better estimate of the effect of SES components and consequently a better estimate of students' SES. Fortunately, an SES index computed using logistic regression weights and transformed from log odds to probabilities correlated 0.98 with the index computed using the OLS weights. Thus the two models provide essentially the same within-school SES scale for dropping out and teenage childbearing.

19. See Altonji (1988) for a discussion of this problem.
20. See Jencks and Brown (1975) for an explanation of this technique.

TABLE A-3. Estimates of Within-School Effects of Student
Characteristics on Dropping Out and Teenage Childbearing[a]

Characteristic	Dropping out	Teenage childbearing
Father's education	−.009	−.004
	(.001)	(.000)
Mother's education	−.008	−.004
	(.001)	(.001)
Father white-collar	−.010	−.001
	(.005)	(.004)
Owns two or more cars	−.003	−.012
	(.006)	(.005)
Owns dishwasher	−.015	−.009
	(.005)	(.004)
Owns home	−.069	−.020
	(.006)	(.005)
Father's education, MD[b]	.023	.021
	(.007)	(.006)
Mother's education, MD[b]	.061	−.024
	(.009)	(.009)
Father white-collar, MD[b]	.061	−.021
	(.011)	(.006)
Owns car, MD[b]	.027	−.013
	(.016)	(.015)
Owns dishwasher, MD[b]	.009	.027
	(.014)	(.013)
Owns home, MD[b]	.011	−.004
	(.011)	(.011)
Constant	−.014	−.002
	(.002)	(.002)
R^2	.031	.010
Number	27,117	13,552

a. All variables are differences from the mean. Standard errors are in parentheses.
b. MD denotes a dummy variable for missing data on that variable. The coefficient represents the difference between students at the mean on the variable and students with missing data.

Table A-3 shows the within-school contribution of the components of family SES on dropping out and teenage childbearing. These equations also include a dummy variable for each SES component that is equal to 1 if the student did not answer the relevant question and was assigned the mean. These coefficients can be interpreted as the amount that a particular characteristic changes a student's probability of dropping out from the average school's mean dropout or childbearing rate. For instance, this equation suggests that students who live in a home owned by their parents have a probability of dropping out that is 0.069 less than students in the same school who live in rental housing.

To be precise it is necessary to correct the standard errors of the parameter estimates in this within-school equation for the degrees of freedom lost in the computation of the school means. I have not done this correction because the standard errors were irrelevant for constructing an SES scale.

Variables Used in Testing for Interactions and Nonlinearities

Low-, medium-, and high-SES students. Students were classified as low SES if they were at least one standard deviation below the mean student SES score, high SES if they were at least one standard deviation above the mean student SES score, and medium SES otherwise. For both the total sample and the sample of girls, about 18 percent of the sample was low SES and 16 percent high SES.

This classification assumed that students' SES rank relative to everyone else's was relevant. It ignored the possibility that students' rank relative to that of some other group, for instance, their own racial group, was relevant. Abrahamse, Morrison, and Waite found some evidence that a race-specific measure of relative socioeconomic standing had a greater effect on teenage childbearing than a measure of overall SES rank.[21] I have not tested this possibility.

Low-, medium-, and high-SES schools. Low-SES schools were those whose mean SES was at least one standard deviation below the average school mean SES. High-SES schools were those whose mean SES was at least one standard deviation above the average school mean SES. The remaining schools were classified as medium-SES schools.

Schools' racial composition. Classifying schools according to their racial composition was more difficult because groupings that make sense for one racial group often meant that there were no cases in some categories for other racial groups. I classified schools as having a high concentration of black students if the proportion black was at least one standard deviation above the average proportion black for black students. I classified schools as having a medium concentration of black students if between 32 percent and 72 percent of their students were black, a low concentration if between 10 percent and 32 percent of their students were black, and very low if fewer than 10 percent of their students were black.

I classified schools as having a high concentration of Hispanic students

21. Abrahamse, Morrison, and Waite (1988).

if the proportion Hispanic was at least one standard deviation above the average proportion. I classified schools as having a medium concentration if between 27 percent and 55 percent of their students were Hispanic, a low concentration if between 5 percent and 27 percent of their students were Hispanic, and very low if fewer than 5 percent of their students were Hispanic.

Employment and Earnings of Low-Income Blacks Who Move to Middle-Class Suburbs

JAMES E. ROSENBAUM *and* SUSAN J. POPKIN

How would moving low-income blacks to middle-class suburbs affect their participation in the labor market? If, as William Julius Wilson contends, the migration of low-skill jobs to the suburbs is a major cause of growth of the urban underclass, then low-income blacks who move to the suburbs should experience employment gains.[1] If, as other scholars argue, work disincentives in welfare programs and recipients' own lack of motivation are to blame, then suburban moves should have little effect on their employment.[2]

This paper tests this question with a study of a highly unusual experiment in racial and economic integration, the Gautreaux program, which helps low-income black families move from public housing into private-market housing in Chicago and throughout the six-county metropolitan area. Gautreaux locates available apartments and arranges for participants to receive Section 8 federal housing subsidies.[3] Begun in 1976, the program has placed more than 3,900 families in private-sector apartments, more than half in the suburbs. Some families have lived in these communities for more than ten years.[4] The program permits us to compare the employment experiences of low-income blacks who moved to the suburbs with the experiences of those who moved within the city.

Because the Gautreaux program arose from a consent decree in a housing discrimination case, it is designed only to improve housing op-

---

1. Wilson (1987).

2. Murray (1984); and Mead (1986).

3. Section 8 is a federal program that subsidizes low-income people's rents in private-sector apartments, either by giving them a certificate that allows them to rent apartments on the open market or by moving them into a new or rehabilitated building whose owner has taken a federal loan that requires some units be set aside for low-income tenants. Both types of subsidies last for thirty years, or until the participant's income exceeds the eligibility cutoff.

4. For a complete description of the program and the Gautreaux decision, see Rosenbaum and Popkin (1990).

portunity, not to promote labor market participation. The program provides no counseling, training, or encouragement about employment. Participants are expected to be good tenants, but there are no expectations about employment, either explicit or implicit. Consequently, the program provides a good test of the conflict between the structural and motivational theories of the causes of long-term poverty. Participants who move to the suburbs are similar to those who move within a city in their level of motivation, and they are subject to the same work disincentives from the welfare system. However, the suburban movers relocated to middle-class suburbs, which offered much better job opportunities—if they wanted to take advantage of them. Did the people who moved to the suburbs respond to those new opportunities or did they simply accept this program as a housing improvement and nothing more? This question is the subject of this paper.

Theories of Poverty

Some scholars contend that the primary problem of the urban underclass is lack of motivation and social obligation among inner-city residents. In the 1960s Oscar Lewis's theory of the culture of poverty was hotly debated. Lewis argued that low-income children are socialized into a value system that reduces their motivation to succeed in the labor market. "By the time slum children are age six or seven, they have usually absorbed the basic values and attitudes of their subculture and are not psychologically geared to take full advantage of changing conditions or increased opportunities which may occur in their lifetime."[5] Although Lewis later modified his position, the idea that deeply ingrained habits prevent low-income people from taking advantage of improved circumstances has gained a large following.[6]

In recent years, some scholars have revived the culture of poverty theory in their critiques of the welfare system.[7] They argue that the system has contributed to the growth of an urban underclass by permitting low-income people to expect that they need never work. This situation has created a class of people who remain poor because they feel no obligation to contribute to the larger society and who exhibit high rates of out-of-wedlock births, teen pregnancy, long-term unemployment, crime, and drug use.

5. Lewis (1968), p. 188.
6. Steinberg (1981).
7. Mead (1986).

The structural explanation is the other major explanation of long-term poverty. Scholars have proposed that poverty is caused by the structure of the welfare system, the economic structure of low-skill jobs, and the location of these jobs.[8] This study examines the last contention.

In recent decades large numbers of low-skill jobs have left the cities and relocated in suburbs.[9] The Chicago area has undergone a radical change in the past twenty years. Between 1975 and 1978, for example, 2,380 firms in Illinois moved from the city to the suburban ring.[10] However, low-income blacks have not followed the jobs because of housing discrimination, housing costs, and personal preferences. As a result, "low-skilled jobs have been leaving the city faster than low-skilled workers."[11]

The spatial mismatch hypothesis posits that geographical distance between home and work has limited employment for low-income blacks, who are largely constrained to inner cities.[12] If distance is indeed a serious barrier to employment, then the Gautreaux program provides a way for them to overcome this barrier, and one would expect those who move to the suburbs to experience increased employment.

However, the hypothesis has received mixed research support. Some studies find that suburbs increase black employment and earnings; others do not.[13] The review by Christopher Jencks and Susan Mayer suggests that although suburbs had little effect on employment in the 1960s, by 1980 black men worked more weeks and earned more in the suburbs than in the city. One possible interpretation is that "the spatial mismatch between black job opportunities and black housing options, that Kain described in 1968, while exaggerated at that time, has become quite important since then."[14] However, they note that it is also possible that "black migration between central cities and suburbs became far more selective than it had previously been." In other words, the problem with previous research is that the causal direction of the correlation may be the opposite of the hypothesis: that jobs cause residential choice rather than that residential choice determines employment.

The Gautreaux participants are particularly interesting because they

8. Wilson (1987).
9. Kasarda (1989).
10. Wilson (1987), p. 135.
11. Ellwood (1986), p. 148.
12. Kain (1968).
13. Studies finding increases, see Kain (1968); and Price and Mills (1985). For studies not finding such a change, see Harrison (1972, 1974); Bell (1974); and Kasarda (1989).
14. Jencks and Mayer (1989b), p. 33.

circumvent the financial barriers to living in the suburbs, not by their jobs or personal finances but by getting into the program. The program gives them subsidies that permit them to live in suburban apartments with moderately high rents for the same cost they had paid to live in public housing projects. Moreover, unlike the usual case of black suburbanization—working-class blacks living in working-class suburbs—Gautreaux permits low-income blacks to live in a wide variety of suburbs with different income levels.[15]

William Julius Wilson's argument incorporates elements of both the cultural and structural perspectives. He contends that the primary cause of the growth of the urban underclass is economic—the loss of access to low-skilled jobs as industry has left the inner cities. However, the departure of the middle class from the cities has also left low-income blacks increasingly isolated from mainstream culture and "made it more difficult to sustain the basic institutions in . . . [ghetto] neighborhoods (including churches, stores, schools, recreational facilities, etc.)."[16] The decline of these institutions undermines norms and sanctions against aberrant behavior and reduces the opportunities to gain a positive sense of community. Members of the underclass are so socially and economically isolated that they have given up trying to improve their economic status. Without either appropriate role models or access to economic opportunity, they have little incentive to alter their behavior. But although Wilson's theory shows how the influences of values and economic structure are related, whether ghetto residents could and would get jobs if suburban employment were suddenly made accessible to them has remained unclear.

The Gautreaux program provides a chance to test these theories. The participants are all former public housing residents, and they have lived much of their lives as part of the inner-city underclass. All have been poor their entire lives and many are second-generation welfare recipients. If the theory of the culture of poverty is correct and their early socialization has made them unwilling to participate in mainstream society, then moving to middle-class suburbs should make little difference in their lives, aside from providing better housing. If the structural theory is correct and they have been held back by lack of opportunity, then the suburban move, which puts them in a growing labor market with a strong demand for low-skill workers, should increase their labor force participation. If Wilson is correct, those who move to the suburbs may also benefit from

15. Jencks and Mayer (1989b).
16. Wilson (1987), p. 138.

positive role models (neighbors with full-time jobs), good public schools, and stable community institutions. Those who stay in the city will experience little or no change in labor market opportunity and community characteristics, so their employment behavior should be little affected.

Methods and Sample

In the fall of 1988 we surveyed a random sample of 342 female heads of household. After excluding 10 respondents age sixty-five or older, we had a sample of 224 in the suburbs and 108 in the city. Because participants usually took the first apartment the program offered, and unit availability often permitted no choice of location, there should have been few differences between city and suburban movers. In fact, our analyses found no initial differences in demographic characteristics or employment. Therefore, any differences in employment outcomes were not likely to be the result of a dissimilarity other than location.

Respondents were randomly selected from a list of participants for whom the program had valid addresses. Because so few Gautreaux households are two-parent, we surveyed only female heads of household. Respondents were mailed a questionnaire about their experiences in their new communities and were sent a reminder after two weeks if they did not return it. The response rate for the survey was 67.0 percent. To understand respondents' experiences better, interviews were conducted with 95 participants in their homes (52 suburban movers and 43 city movers).[17]

Because program participants had little latitude for choosing where they would move, we expected city and suburban movers to be highly comparable. The results confirmed that expectation. There were few differences between the demographic characteristics of the two groups.[18]

17. Our refusal rate on the interviews was less than 7 percent. There are no systematic differences between the interview and survey respondents, but the interview sample is used only for qualitative analysis. Responses to the questionnaire were consistent with those from the interviews.

18. Counselors offer participants units as they become available, regardless of the clients' preference for location. Although participants are allowed to refuse two housing offers, most accept the first offer they receive. As a result, their preferences for city or suburbs have little to do with where they end up moving: fewer than half moved to their preferred location.

City movers average about a year older than suburban movers, as do their children. However, the two groups are very similar in other ways. The average length of time since moving into the program is about five years for both groups. The mean number of children is about 2.5. Half of both samples reported receiving AFDC. About 8 percent of city movers and 6 percent of suburban movers were married at the time of the survey and 44 percent of

Generalizing from this basis to all low-income blacks was more diffi-cult. The program had three kinds of selection criteria. First, because there are few large apartments in the suburbs, it tends to select families with four or fewer children. This is not a serious restriction, however, because 95 percent of AFDC families have four or fewer children and 90 percent have three or fewer.[19] Second, as in the Section 8 program, Gau-treaux applicants are screened to make sure that they regularly pay their rent and that they have some source of income (usually AFDC). The Leadership Council estimates that about 12 percent are rejected by the credit check or rental record. Third, counselors visit applicants' homes to determine which people are such bad housekeepers that they would be undesirable tenants. About 13 percent of families are rejected on this cri-terion.[20] Therefore, Gautreaux participants are somewhat different from public housing residents in general: they have smaller families, they have good rent-paying records, and they meet housekeeping standards (on the day of the counselor's appointment).

However, the requirements of the program are not so stringent as to make participants totally atypical. Experience indicates that the three cri-teria sequentially eliminated 5 percent, 13 percent, and 12 percent, so together they reduced the eligible pool by less than 30 percent. Self-selection may further reduce generalizability, but if these factors are cor-related with the three criteria, their additional impact may be very small. From the experience of our previous work, we would guess that Gau-treaux families represent more than half of public housing residents, but that is a very rough guess. With some 100,000 families in Chicago hous-ing projects, the program participants are likely to represent a large num-ber of people.

Study Design and Results

The study had two main designs: a comparison of experimental and control groups and a retrospective comparison. The city movers were used in these analyses as a no-change control group that could be com-pared with the suburban movers to determine the effects of residential integration. Using this group allowed us to control for the selection ef-

---

both groups had never been married. Both groups have similar education: about 20 percent lack a high school diploma and 35 percent have some college education.

19. Office of Family Assistance (1987).
20. Office of Policy Development and Research (1979).

TABLE I. City and Suburban Respondents Employed after Moves, by Employment Status before Moves

Status	City	Suburbs
Employed premove and postmove		
(percent)	64.6	73.6
Number	65	144
Unemployed premove but employed postmove		
(percent)	30.2	46.2
Number	43	80
Total employed postmove (percent)	50.9	63.8
Number	108	224

fects of Gautreaux participation and of improved housing. The retrospective comparison asked respondents in both groups to compare their experiences after the move with their previous situations.[21]

Table I compares the two groups' employment status before and after the move. The work experiences before moving were virtually identical. Just under two-thirds of both city and suburban movers had jobs before they moved. The average hourly wage was about $4.90 and the average hours worked each week was thirty-two. Thus suburban movers had no advantages over city movers that would suggest that they would do better in the labor market.

Although both groups started from the same baseline, after moving, suburban residents were 13 percent more likely to have had jobs than city movers (table 1). The retrospective analysis provides further evidence that suburban residents participated more in the labor market after they moved than those who remained in the city. Among respondents who were employed before moving, suburban movers were about 9 percent more likely than city movers to have a job after moving. Of those who were never employed before their move, 46 percent found work after moving to the suburbs; for the city the figure was only 30 percent.

Table 2 shows that despite these differences in employment, there were few differences between city and suburban movers in average hourly wages or number of hours worked each week. Among those who had a job before and after moving, both city and suburban movers reported gains in hourly wages and little change in hours worked. Although this

21. To measure job experiences before the move, we asked respondents whether they had had any jobs before they got into the Gautreaux program. If they had, we asked questions about the last job they had before moving: the type of job, hourly wage, number of hours worked each week, and how long they stayed. We then asked the same questions about jobs after the move.

TABLE 2. City and Suburban Respondents' Average Wages and Hours Worked

Wages and hours	Premove	Postmove	t-statistic	p
City postmove (N = 55)				
Hourly wages (dollars)	5.04	6.20	6.52	0.00
Hours per week	33.27	31.92	-0.60	0.55
Suburban postmove (N = 143)				
Hourly wages (dollars)	4.96	6.00	6.50	0.00
Hours per week	33.62	33.39	-0.60	0.55

increase in earnings is partly a result of inflation, many city workers may have experienced gains because of job tenure: 18 percent had the same job before and after moving; the comparable figure for the suburbs was 3 percent.

Multivariate Analysis

To understand more about the differences in employment experiences of city and suburban movers, we used multiple regression analyses to explain possible determinants of having a job and of hourly wages after the move. We controlled for respondents' previous work history, education, training, age, and long-term AFDC recipiency (five years or more), family circumstances (having a child under six years of age), motivation (internal sense of control), family background (whether the respondent's mother received AFDC), and postmove education. Finally, we controlled for the number of years since the respondent first moved on the Gautreaux program.[22]

Table 3 shows the results of the model explaining who had a job after moving.[23] Suburban movers were significantly more likely to have a job

22. Job training after the move could not be added to the model because of multicollinearity. Internal sense of control was measured by respondents' answers to four items on a four-point scale from strongly agree to strongly disagree: good luck is more important than hard work for success; every time I try to get ahead, something stops me; when I make plans, I can usually carry them out; and planning only makes a person unhappy because plans hardly ever work out anyway. These four items were combined to make an index of fate control.

23. This model was run using both OLS and probit models. Probit models are appropriate for dichotomous dependent variables (Hanushek and Jackson, 1977). Since there were no differences between the results of the two procedures, only the OLS results were reported because the coefficients have a more direct interpretation. The probit results are available from the authors.

TABLE 3. Effects of Respondent Characteristics on Having a Job after Moves

Variable	Coefficient
Suburb[a]	0.14[b]
Years since move	0.02[b]
Age	−0.01[c]
Child under age 6[d]	−0.24[c]
Internal control	0.09[b]
Long-term AFDC recipient[e]	−0.09
Second-generation AFDC recipient[f]	−0.01
Premove education	0.02
GED postmove	0.04
Attended college postmove	0.03
Job training premove[g]	0.09
Premove job	0.21[c]
Number 332	
R^2 23.2	
R^2 adjusted 20.1	

a. Dummy variable with 1 indicating a suburban mover and 0 indicating a city mover.
b. $p < .01$.
c. $p < .001$.
d. Dummy variable with 1 indicating that the respondent has a child who is younger than six years old.
e. AFDC recipient for five years or more.
f. Dummy variable within 1 indicating that the respondent's mother received AFDC.
g. Dummy variable indicating respondent reported getting job training before move.

than city movers. Indeed, after controls, the suburban advantage increased slightly over the raw figures to 14 percent. Postmove employment was also more likely for respondents who had previous work experience, were younger, had no children under six years old, and had been in the area more years. Two "culture of poverty" variables (low internal sense of control and long-term AFDC recipiency) reduced the likelihood of employment, but being a second-generation AFDC recipient had no effect. Education had little net effect, and additional education had no effect. In sum, even after we controlled for these factors, the results supported the spatial mismatch hypothesis: suburban movers are more likely to find jobs than city movers.

To explain postmove hourly wages, we used a similar model and controlled for the effect of job tenure (months of employment). Suburban movers earned the same wages as city movers after we controlled for premove wages, job tenure, years since move, and personal characteristics (table 4). Job tenure and premove pay had significant effects on postmove wages. Again the variables for internal sense of control and long-term AFDC recipiency had significant effects. Other variables had no net effects.

TABLE 4. Effects of Respondent Characteristics on Hourly Wages of Workers after Moves[a]

Variable	Coefficient
Suburb[b]	−0.04
Years since move	0.02
Age	−0.02
Child under age 6[c]	−0.09
Internal control	0.28[d]
Long-term AFDC recipient[e]	−0.33
Second-generation AFDC recipient[f]	0.10
Premove education	0.06
GED postmove	0.06
Attended college postmove	0.20
Job training premove[g]	−0.12
Months on job	0.02[h]
Premove pay per hour	0.12[h]
Number 197	
R^2 26.5	
R^2 adjusted 21.3	

a. Respondents who had no job premove were assigned a premove wage of 0. Mean replacement was used for all missing cases, with suburban respondents given the suburban mean and city respondents given the city mean.
b. Dummy variable with 1 indicating a suburban mover and 0 indicating a city mover.
c. Dummy variable with 1 indicating that the respondent has a child who is less than six years old.
d. $p < .05$.
e. AFDC recipient for five years or more.
f. Dummy variable with 1 indicating that the respondent's mother received AFDC.
g. Dummy variable indicating respondent reported getting job training premove.
h. $p < .001$.

In sum, we found some support for the culture of poverty hypothesis. Long-term AFDC and fatalistic attitudes reduced earnings and likelihood of employment, although being a second-generation AFDC recipient had no effect. These results also supported the spatial mismatch hypothesis: suburban movers are more likely than city movers to have jobs postmove. Most strikingly, of those who had never been employed, suburban movers were 16 percent more likely than city movers to find work after a move.

However, spatial mismatch is not the only barrier to employment. Other factors still prevent more than one-third of suburban movers from working. Moreover, spatial mismatch does not explain the lack of difference in the earnings of suburban movers and those who remain in the city.

Respondents' Perceptions of Opportunities and Barriers

To supplement this quantitative analysis, we examined what respondents said about their experiences—the type of jobs they got, what made it easier to get jobs in the suburbs, and what difficulties remained that prevent many from getting jobs.

According to respondents, the greater number of jobs in the suburbs was the major factor that made it easier for them to find employment there. Nearly all mentioned job availability.

The second most important factor was greater safety for respondents and their children in the suburbs. One respondent had worked in a plastics factory in the suburbs. The only job she had before she moved was in the navy. After noting that there were more jobs and better pay in the suburbs, she also stressed that improved neighborhood safety made a big difference: "I can advance now. When I was discharged from the service, life stopped. You can't walk up and down the streets in the city." Another suburban mover quit her last premove job because "I'd have to use the subway late at night. I was just scared." And another noted, "I've moved up. You don't get robbed here, so I can better myself."

Many mothers also said they were reluctant to take a job when they lived in the projects because they needed to be home to watch their children. If they did not watch, their children would get hurt or get in trouble with the gangs. As one respondent said, "When I got out here [to the suburbs] I saw how comfortable everything was and I knew I could feel comfortable going to school and leaving her here at school without worrying."

Finally, many said that living in the suburbs gave them stronger motivation to improve themselves and get jobs. One respondent went from being a nurse's aide before her move to being a phlebotomist at a suburban blood bank. She believed her new job was much better than her old one because it paid more, was more secure, and offered her opportunity for advancement. She believed it was easier to find jobs in the suburbs because there were more jobs available. But she also believed she had been changed by moving to a better environment: "[The housing project] deteriorates you. You don't want to do anything. . . . [Living in the suburbs] made me feel that I'm worth something. I can do anything I want to do if I get up and try it."

Another respondent who was a clerical worker in both the city and suburbs believed that moving had motivated her to pursue new opportunities: "Once I had moved, it was a different type of environment. Most of the people around me were more advanced than I was. I had a job in which I wanted a promotion. So more education was the answer." She learned how to present herself more positively: "You present yourself the way you want to be respected. Don't leave any blank spaces on applications."

Still, barriers remained that made it difficult to get a good job in the suburbs. The major obstacles were lack of transportation, lack of day care, discrimination, and the higher level of skill that suburban employers expected.

Although she enjoyed her suburban job as a clerical worker, one respondent considered lack of transportation a barrier to getting ahead. She believed that it was easier to find a job in the suburbs because there were more jobs and no safety concerns, but, as she said, "I need a car and I could get [the kind of job I want] right now if I had a car." Another reported, "It is easier to find a job here, but getting to it is the problem."

Child care is always difficult for one-parent families, but it is particularly a problem for suburban movers. Having lived in the city all their lives, participants often had relatives and friends who could help with child care. The move to the suburbs deprived them of inexpensive baby-sitting. Many suburban movers reported that they had not looked for work because they could not locate affordable day care.

Many respondents identified employer discrimination and their own lack of skills as preventing them from getting an adequately paid job. One worked as a clerk and a manager at a discount store before moving. She transferred to a suburban store but quit because "they didn't want to pay me what I'd been making and wouldn't keep me as manager. . . . If you have a skill, then you can find a job, but if you don't, you have to take a job at McDonald's."

The respondents clearly believed that the suburbs offered more jobs and more encouragement to get jobs, and living in the suburbs freed them from the safety worries that prevented some of them from working in the city. However, lack of public transportation and child care, discrimination, and their own lack of skills were barriers that made it difficult for them to take jobs. While the move to the suburbs improved employment by reducing spatial mismatch, some mismatch still remained because of poor public transportation.

Conclusion

These findings have important implications for the debate on the nature of the underclass. First, the increased employment among suburban movers supports the spatial mismatch hypothesis.[24] The Gautreaux par-

24. Although those moving to the suburbs are participating in the labor force at a greater rate, they are not able to be self-supporting on $200 a week (the average earnings; see table 2). To pay suburban rents, which average more than $550 a month for a two-bedroom apartment, they still need the housing subsidy and other financial assistance. As

ticipants responded to the improved employment opportunities in middle-class suburbs even though they came from low-income communities and had presumably been exposed to both negative attitudes about work and the work disincentives of the welfare system.[25] However, our results also provide some support for the culture of poverty hypothesis. People who had received AFDC a long time and those who had fatalistic attitudes were less often employed and had lower wages. Yet in all analyses, second-generation AFDC recipients were no less successful than others at finding jobs, so our results provide no support for fears about the harmful effects of multigenerational welfare dependence. Most noteworthy, even after we controlled for training, education, and previous jobs, moving to the suburbs led to greater employment than moving within the city. That is, even respondents who were relatively disadvantaged did better in the suburbs than they did in the city.

Some participants in both the city and suburbs did show the kinds of fatalistic attitudes reminiscent of Lewis's culture of poverty. Our analyses found that these people were less likely to have a job and received lower wages (but did not work any fewer hours a week), which suggests that fatalistic attitudes may indeed impede employment (although causality may run in the opposite direction). In any case, even if a fatalistic attitude does affect chances for employment, it is only one of many influences, and its influence is relatively small compared with that of education or work experience or the suburban environment.

The fact that long-term AFDC recipients fare worse in the labor market suggests that the ill effects of lengthy spells of economic hardship are not easily overcome. We do not know whether their inability to get jobs is a reflection of their relative lack of work experience or of reduced motivation, but the effect of this factor is relatively small. However, because

---

Ellwood (1988) stated, it is unrealistic to expect that a female head of household can support herself and her family at the same level as a two-parent family. First, women tend to work in low-paying service-sector jobs. In 1987 black women working full time earned an average of $16,211 as compared with $19,385 for black men (Bureau of the Census, 1987). Second, because female heads of household have sole responsibility for their children's care, it is extremely difficult for them to work full time, which means they earn even less. Because of these difficulties, probably few Gautreaux movers work their way off Section 8 assistance. In fact, the eligibility cutoff for Section 8 for a family of two (a mother and one child) is approximately equal to the average wage for black female full-time workers. Given this situation, a more realistic criterion for success is that suburban movers contribute a larger share of their own support.

25. Virtually all Gautreaux participants had received public assistance and about 63 percent received AFDC for five years or more.

being a second-generation AFDC recipient has no effect on employment outcomes, this dependency is probably not insurmountable.

Finally, our qualitative results support Wilson's contentions about the importance of role models and social norms. These respondents see the suburbs as offering good role models and social norms that encourage work—both absent in their city neighborhoods—and they believe that these factors have encouraged them to enter the labor force.

These findings have clear implications for policymakers. They provide new evidence about neighborhood effects on underclass behavior and how recipients of public assistance can be helped in moving from welfare to work. They should provide policymakers and scholars with hope because they indicate that it is possible to help long-term public housing residents move into the labor force and become at least partially self-supporting. It is difficult to know exactly what it is about the move to the suburbs that causes these changes, and the subject certainly merits further research. However, the people moving to the suburbs clearly experienced improved employment, even though the program provided no job assistance or encouragement. A program that provided such support might produce even more encouraging results.

References

Bane, Mary Jo, and David T. Ellwood. 1989. "One Fifth of the Nation's Children: Why Are They Poor?" *Science* 245 (September), pp. 1047–53.

Bell, Duran, Jr. 1974. "Residential Location, Economic Performance, and Public Employment." In *Patterns of Racial Discrimination*, vol. 1: *Housing*, edited by George M. von Furstenberg, Bennet Harrison, and Ann R. Horowitz. Lexington, Mass.: Lexington Books.

Bureau of the Census. 1987. "Money Income of Households, Families, and Persons in the United States: 1987." *Current Population Reports*, series P-60, no. 162. Department of Commerce.

Ellwood, David T. 1986. "The Spatial Mismatch Hypothesis: Are There Teenage Jobs Missing in the Ghetto?" In *The Black Youth Unemployment Crisis*, edited by Richard B. Freeman and Harry J. Holzer. University of Chicago Press.

———. 1988. *Poor Support: Poverty in the American Family*. Basic Books.

Hanushek, Eric Alan, and John E. Jackson. 1977. *Statistical Methods for Social Scientists*. Academic Press.

Harrison, Bennett. 1972. "The Intrametropolitan Distribution of Minority Economic Welfare." *Journal of Regional Science* 12 (April), pp. 23–43.

———. 1974. "Discrimination in Space: Suburbanization and Black Unemployment in Cities." In *Patterns of Racial Discrimination*, vol. 1: *Housing*, edited by George M. von Furstenberg, Bennett Harrison, and Ann R. Horowitz. Lexington, Mass.: Lexington Books.

Jencks, Christopher, and Susan E. Mayer. 1989a. "The Social Consequences of Growing Up in a Poor Neighborhood: A Review." Center for Urban Affairs and Policy Research working paper, Northwestern University.

————. 1989b. "Residential Segregation, Job Proximity, and Black Job Opportunities." Center for Urban Affairs and Policy Research working paper, Northwestern University.

Kain, John F. 1968. "Housing Segregation, Negro Employment, and Metropolitan Decentralization." *Quarterly Journal of Economics* 82 (May), pp. 175–97.

Kasarda, John D. 1989. "Urban Industrial Transition and the Underclass." *Annals of the American Academy of Political and Social Science* 501 (January), pp. 26–47.

Lewis, Oscar. 1968. "The Culture of Poverty." In *On Understanding Poverty: Perspectives from the Social Sciences,* edited by Daniel P. Moynihan. Basic Books.

Mead, Lawrence M. 1986. *Beyond Entitlement: The Social Obligations of Citizenship.* Free Press.

Murray, Charles. 1984. *Losing Ground: American Social Policy, 1950–1980.* Basic Books.

Office of Family Assistance. 1987. *Characteristics and Financial Circumstances of AFDC Recipients: Aid to Families With Dependent Children, 1986.* Department of Health and Human Services.

Office of Policy Development and Research. 1979. *Gautreaux Housing Demonstration: An Evaluation of Its Impact on Participating Households.* Department of Housing and Urban Development.

Price, Richard, and Edwin Mills. 1985. "Race and Residence in Earnings Determination." *Journal of Urban Economics* 17 (January), pp. 1–18.

Rosenbaum, James E., and Susan J. Popkin. 1990. *Economic and Social Impacts of Housing Integration.* Report of the Center for Urban Affairs and Policy Research, Northwestern University.

Steinberg, Stephen. 1981. *The Ethnic Myth: Race, Ethnicity, and Class in America.* Atheneum.

Wilson, William Julius. 1987. *The Truly Disadvantaged: The Inner City, the Underclass, and Public Policy.* University of Chicago Press.

The Political Behavior of Poor People

JEFFREY M. BERRY, KENT E. PORTNEY, *and* **KEN THOMSON**

AMONG THE MANY ills that afflict the poor is their low level of political involvement. Survey research demonstrates clearly that voting and other forms of political activity are highly correlated with social class. The people who most need help from government make the least demands of it.

Although we can paint the broad contours of political participation by the poor, we do not know much else about their political behavior. Fortunately, this failure to study such political activity is not symptomatic of social scientists' current attitude toward the subject of poverty in America. Scholars have recently paid a great deal of attention to welfare policy, income inequality, and social deviance among the poor. A vigorous debate has emerged over the idea of an underclass of Americans who have little opportunity to escape the big city ghettos they live in.

As defined by William Julius Wilson, the underclass includes those "who lack training and skills and either experience long-term unemployment or are not members of the labor force, individuals who are engaged in street crime and other forms of aberrant behavior, and families that experience long-term spells of poverty and/or welfare dependency." Even if these people were to find full-time employment, it would be in menial jobs with little opportunity for advancement. Members of the underclass are particularly disadvantaged because they live in areas of core poverty isolated from middle-class role models and institutional support. As Ken Auletta puts it, these Americans "do not assimilate." [1]

Understanding the relationship of this underclass to the political system presents a particularly difficult challenge for those who study political behavior. Sociologists, economists, and others who do research on the

This research has been supported by Ford Foundation grants #850-0780 and #850-0870A. The authors thank Linda Williams for her careful reading of an earlier draft of this paper.

1. Wilson (1987), p. 8; and Auletta (1982), p. xvi.

underclass are able to draw on census data to analyze neighborhoods on the basis of income, unemployment, racial composition, and family makeup. But rich as it is, the Census Bureau's data base is not sufficient for the study of political participation. Political scientists have to depend on other surveys. Yet the sample surveys most suitable for analysis of political behavior usually have a national focus and contain only limited information on place of residence. For all practical purposes, scholars wishing to study neighborhood politics must conduct specialized surveys themselves. Our own neighborhood-based survey work has allowed us to make some initial inquiries relevant to the effects of core poverty on political behavior.

First we asked, does neighborhood make a difference? Wilson argues that underclass neighborhoods are unique not simply because they are the lowest in income but also because of their social isolation, which makes worse whatever inherent problems the poor have. As a consequence of the isolation, residents of underclass neighborhoods are not sufficiently exposed to the norms of mainstream society. The "underclass condition," Richard Nathan has written, is "attitudinal and behavioral. It involves alienation, and . . . a feeling of 'learned helplessness.' "[2] If this logic holds, such attitudes should have political manifestations. If neighborhood has an independent effect on how residents view themselves in relation to the broader community, one would expect to find that poor residents of poor neighborhoods trust government less, feel less politically effective, and are less likely to participate in politics than poor people who do not live in such areas.

Second, we asked, does race make a difference? Are poor blacks politically distinct from poor whites? By controlling for income, one can examine the behavior of these two groups to see whether race drives the development of political attitudes or the level of political involvement. Furthermore, poor blacks living in impoverished areas can be identified and compared with other blacks. This comparison helps determine whether the combination of race, income, and concentration of poverty produces neighborhoods that have been depoliticized by cynicism and isolation from mainstream America.

The data we have used come from a study of participation and democracy in five large American cities—Birmingham, Dayton, Portland (Oregon), St. Paul, and San Antonio. These cities were chosen because they were judged to have exemplary programs for involving residents in the

2. Nathan (1987), p. 58.

political process at the neighborhood level.[3] In four of them local government sponsors a citizen participation program through a citywide network of neighborhood associations. Government funds pay for a small staff of community organizers and for a central office at city hall. In St. Paul, for example, the city is divided into seventeen neighborhoods, each with its own autonomous district council. These councils control zoning and have other impressive powers that give residents reason to take them seriously. In the fifth city, San Antonio, a grassroots advocacy group, Communities Organized for Public Service (COPS), has organized the most heavily Hispanic sections of town. There is no city sponsorship of COPS, which is a potent force in San Antonio politics.

Sample surveys of 1,100 residents in each city taken in 1986 and 1987 constitute our primary source of data. The surveys were stratified by neighborhood to facilitate comparisons. In the four cities with government-sponsored citizen participation programs, an elaborate process was used by city planners to determine neighborhood boundaries. Lines were drawn in consultation with the people of each community to ensure that the resulting boundaries would encompass a coherent neighborhood with which residents already identified. Because we can pinpoint the location of every respondent by neighborhood and because each city participates in the Census Bureau's neighborhood statistics program, we can use this data set to investigate the propositions discussed earlier.

Neighborhood Comparisons

In the first stage of the analysis we classified all neighborhoods and all respondents as poor or nonpoor. Thus we could isolate poor people living

3. The cities were chosen through an elaborate screening process. We began by conducting a survey of citizen participation programs around the country. We also sent a questionnaire to many practitioners and experts in the field of citizen participation who had been identified over the years through various projects, conferences, and publications sponsored by the Lincoln Filene Center for Citizenship and Public Affairs. We winnowed the list of all nominated programs to those that seemed the most promising. Research was then done on these programs, and after this additional information was collected, we judged that these five cities had the most impressive public involvement programs. In making our decisions, we looked in particular at the breadth and depth of the citizen participation program. By breadth, we mean the degree to which an opportunity is offered to every community resident to participate at all stages of the policymaking process. By depth, we mean the extent to which citizens who choose to participate have the opportunity to determine the final policy outcomes. One additional criterion was that we looked only at cities with populations over 100,000. We wanted to ensure that the cities selected faced the range of serious urban problems the country is most concerned about.

in poor neighborhoods, poor people living in nonpoor neighborhoods, nonpoor people living in poor neighborhoods, and nonpoor people living in nonpoor neighborhoods.

Poor people were respondents who told our interviewers their family income was less than $5,000 a year. This standard is much stricter than the official government poverty index. Poor neighborhoods are those in which, according to the Census Bureau, 20 percent or more of the people have incomes below the official poverty line.[4] There is, of course, no general agreement on what characteristics define a poor neighborhood, and the debate over what constitutes underclass areas has been particularly contentious.[5] Wilson uses a straightforward set of definitions, with 20 percent of the population in poverty as the threshold for a neighborhood to be defined as a poverty area. Neighborhoods in "extreme poverty" are those in which at least 40 percent of the people are poor.[6] Because there are virtually no neighborhoods in the five cities surveyed where the poverty level exceeds 40 percent, the analysis was restricted to neighborhoods that cross the 20 percent threshold. (The data below do not include the interviews from San Antonio because the government there has not defined all the city's neighborhoods in the precise manner necessary for this particular analysis.)[7]

The hypothesis growing out of Wilson's work is that when the poor are isolated they believe that government institutions are uncaring, distant, and difficult to deal with. The drug abuse, poor schools, inadequate housing, and teenage pregnancy so prevalent in poor neighborhoods may cause residents to perceive government as uncommitted to solving the ills

4. When these interviews were conducted the official poverty line for a two-person family was slightly more than $5,000 and, of course, was higher for larger families. In our coding, the next highest family income category was $5,000 to $10,000, which would include some families below the poverty line but some above it as well. Thus all respondents who indicated that they had a family income of $5,000 or more were excluded. In the four cities examined, there were some sixty-nine neighborhoods which met our definition of being poor. Of these, thirty-nine were in Birmingham, twelve in Dayton, fifteen in Portland, and three in St. Paul.

5. Various studies have estimated the size of the underclass as between 0.4 and 5.3 percent of the population. As a percentage of the poverty population, estimates of the underclass run from 2.9 percent to 50.0 percent (Ricketts and Sawhill, 1988; Hughes, 1989; Sawhill, 1989).

6. Wilson (1987).

7. There is significant variation in the percentage of minorities living in these cities. St. Paul (4.9 percent black and 7.9 percent Hispanic and other minority) and Portland (7.6 percent black and 8.1 percent Hispanic and other minority) do not have heavy concentrations of minorities. Dayton, however, is 36.9 percent black, and Birmingham (54.7 percent black) has a black voting majority in city politics.

of their communities. We assumed that holding highly cynical attitudes about politics and government and failing to participate in local politics are behaviors damaging to poor neighborhoods and compound whatever social isolation they experience. However, holding negative attitudes about government or failing to participate politically are not behaviors that one can expect to find only in poor or racially isolated neighborhoods. On the contrary, such behavior can be found among all social classes and in all areas of a city. Our intention was to find out if neighborhood isolation leads to greater tendencies of these common forms of behavior than would otherwise be true.

To test our hypotheses we used five survey questions on trust in government, two questions on feelings of personal political efficacy, one question on sense of community, and five questions on political activity. Except for the two about personal political efficacy, our questions concerned attitudes and activities relevant to local government. A number of the questions were based on those used in the National Election Studies or the General Social Survey.

We identified 122 respondents in the four cities whom we considered to be poor people living in poor neighborhoods. Of these, 48.4 percent were from Birmingham, 26.2 percent from Dayton, 15.6 percent from Portland, and 9.8 percent from St. Paul. Not all of them gave answers to all the questions used as dependent or control variables. When the attitudes on trust in government held by the poor living in poor neighborhoods were compared with those of the poor living in nonpoor neighborhoods, no significant differences were evident.[8] When the same type of

8. Space limitations do not permit us to display the data on trust and personal political efficacy. The complete data are contained in Berry, Portney, and Thomson (1989). The questions on trust and on personal political efficacy are worded as follows. *Trust in government:* 1. "How much of the time do you think you can trust the government in (*respondent's city*) to do what is right—just about always, most of the time, or only some of the time?" 2. "Would you say that the government in (*respondent's city*) is pretty much run by a *few big interests* looking out for themselves, or that it is run for the *benefit of all* of the people?" 3. "Over the years, how much attention do you feel the government in (*respondent's city*) pays to what people think when it decides what to do—a good deal, some, or not much?" 4. "Overall, how would you rate the way (*respondent's city*) is run? Would you say the way it is run is *excellent, very good, good enough, not so good, or not good at all?*" 5. "How do you think the people who run your city or town would react if you let them know about a major neighborhood problem you are having? If you explained your point of view to the officials, what effect do you think it would have? Would they give your point of view serious consideration, would they pay only a little attention, or would they ignore what you had to say?" *Personal political efficacy:* 1. (agree or disagree) "People like me don't have any say about what government does." 2. (agree or disagree) "Sometimes politics and government seem so complicated that a person like me can't really understand what's going on."

comparison was made on personal political effectiveness, the two sub-samples again failed to show consistent differences. Neighborhood did not seem to affect the political attitudes of poor people, but it did seem to matter for the nonpoor. The nonpoor who lived in poor neighborhoods were somewhat less trusting of government and felt less politically effective than their nonpoor counterparts who lived in nonpoor neighborhoods.

We also asked people about their sense of community. This question was especially relevant because it offered the most direct assessment of people's attitudes about their own neighborhood. In his study of neighborhood politics in Baltimore, Matthew Crenson found that the poor have less sense of identity with their neighborhoods than others do.[9] "Identity" may get at something slightly different from "sense of community," but it seems safe to assume that these two concepts are generally related to the sense of feeling that one is a part of one's neighborhood. For the two groups of respondents who were poor, those who lived in nonpoor neighborhoods manifested a slightly greater inclination (36.8 percent to 30.8 percent) to say they felt a "strong sense of community with others" in their neighborhood than did those in poor neighborhoods (table 1). What is striking, however, is that there was no significant difference between the poor and the nonpoor. What people feel about their neighbors and the degree to which they feel a part of their community is not related to social class.

Overall, the results of the attitudinal questions did not support the idea that poor people in poor neighborhoods become so isolated from mainstream society that they develop unusually cynical or fatalistic attitudes toward the political system. Their views are not usually different from those of poor people who live in middle-class neighborhoods. In one important respect—sense of community—they are not even different from the attitudes of middle-class people living in middle-class neighborhoods.

It would be a mistake, however, to rely solely on attitudinal measures. One also needs to look at people's actual political behavior. The concern here is with the active involvement of individuals in the local political system. We focused very little on voting because it requires relatively little time and occurs so infrequently. It is also difficult to interpret rates of voting. Some people may vote because they feel angry; other people's electoral participation reflects a strong and positive attitude toward the

9. Crenson (1983).

TABLE I. Activity in Local Politics, by Respondent Neighborhood and Financial Status

Percent

Response	Poor in poor neighborhood	Poor in nonpoor neighborhood	Nonpoor in poor neighborhood	Nonpoor in nonpoor neighborhood
Have you ever personally gone to see, or spoken to, or written to some member of the local community about some need or problem?				
Yes	29.7	17.8	37.6	40.3
No	70.3	82.2	62.4	59.7
Number	91	197	665	2,673
$X^2 = 42.6^a$				
Have you ever worked with others in this community to try to solve some community problem?				
Yes	31.4	26.3	41.6	42.3
No	68.6	73.7	58.4	57.7
Number	86	190	647	2,627
$X^2 = 22.0^a$				
Have you ever actually been active in any community or citizen groups or neighborhood organizations?				
Yes	26.1	31.1	38.4	44.3
No	73.9	68.9	61.6	55.5
Number	88	193	661	2,665
$X^2 = 28.8^a$				
Have you ever taken part in forming a new group or a new organization to try to solve some community problem?				
Yes	13.1	9.6	12.5	12.2
No	86.9	90.4	87.5	87.8
Number	84	188	646	2,605
$X^2 = 1.33$				
Have you personally taken part in the activities of your neighborhood association [district council; priority board] in the last two years?				
Yes	13.2	8.3	19.4	20.5
No	86.8	91.7	80.6	79.5
Number	88	72	550	1,360
$X^2 = 7.5^b$				
Some people say they feel like they have a sense of community with the people in their neighborhood. Others don't feel that way. How about you? Would you say that you feel a strong sense of community with others in your neighborhood, very little sense of community, or something in-between?				
Strong sense	30.8	36.8	32.0	34.2
In-between	43.6	40.1	43.2	43.5
Little sense	25.6	23.1	24.8	22.3
Number	78	182	622	2,570
$X^2 = 3.48$				

a. Significant at 0.01 level or beyond.
b. Significant at 0.05 level.

political system. For the cities we selected, with their institutions for bringing people into the political process at the neighborhood level, we wanted to find out how often citizens interacted with city officials, with their neighborhood associations, and with other citizen groups. In a straightforward way, questions about political activity measured involvement directly connected to the immediate community.

The results of the questions on political involvement were generally consistent: on four of the five questions the poor in poor neighborhoods were more active than the poor in nonpoor neighborhoods (table 1), perhaps because people in poor neighborhoods are faced with more problems and recognize that they cannot wait for government to solve them.[10] It may also be that poor people living in middle-class neighborhoods do not feel as comfortable in local political organizations or feel that their problems are not ones that concern their middle-class neighbors. The research of Jeffrey Henig and Dennis Gale, which compares blacks living in white suburbs with whites living in inner-city neighborhoods that are undergoing gentrification, offers some support for these ideas.[11] Although both groups are middle class and well educated, black suburbanites were much less active than inner-city whites.

The differences between poor and nonpoor shown in table 1 are to be expected because income and education are reliable predictors of political participation. However, a strong sense of community has an effect on political participation independent of social class. The sense of community is a powerful predictor of participation in neighborhood politics even after controlling for social class.[12] We attribute this at least in part to the impact of the neighborhood associations that work to involve rank-and-file citizens in their activities.

Race and Participation

The debate about the underclass is a debate about poor urban blacks. Only a small proportion of poor whites live in neighborhoods of extreme poverty. Controversy has surrounded attempts to sort out the respective weights of the effects of race and class in perpetuating the black underclass. Wilson's conclusion that "class has become more important than race in determining black life-chances in the modern industrial period" has attracted a host of critics who contend that race is as important as

10. Crenson (1983).
11. Henig and Gale (1987).
12. Thomson, Berry, and Portney (1988).

ever or even growing in importance.[13] The data set did not allow us to measure whether the significance of race has declined, but race can be brought into the analysis to see how it affects the relationship between class, neighborhood, and political involvement.

In the cauldron of big city politics, race can be the only thing that matters at election time. Yet Birmingham and Dayton, the two cities in this study with large minority populations, are not plagued by the dominance of race in local politics as are cities such as Chicago and New York.[14] By no means is race absent; whites in Birmingham are concerned about the growing power of Mayor Richard Arrington's machine, and Dayton whites' concern about an increasingly black student body has helped make the future of the city's schools an important issue. Still, the evidence indicates that racial matters are not the dominant concern in these two cities.

To investigate the impact of race we broke the sample into three sets of comparisons. Relying on the same questions used earlier, we compared all black respondents with all white respondents. Controlling for income, we then compared the responses of poor blacks with those of poor whites. An annual family income of less than $5,000 was again used to divide the poor from the nonpoor. We made another set of comparisons between nonpoor blacks and nonpoor whites. Comparisons within and between these sets helped determine the effect race has on attitudes about personal political efficacy and trust in government and whether race influences the level of political participation independent of class effects.

The questions about trust in government produced consistent responses across all categories. The differences between blacks and whites were small and statistically insignificant. When poor blacks and poor whites were compared, there were no statistically significant differences in their attitudes; nor did important differences occur between nonpoor blacks and nonpoor whites. The comparison between blacks and whites on their feelings of personal political efficacy, however, revealed a sizable difference in opinion: blacks were more likely to perceive that they do not have much say in government and that government is too complicated.

13. Wilson (1980), p. 150; Willie (1978); Thomas and Hughes (1986); and Lowi (1988).

14. We interviewed a total of 664 black respondents in the four cities. Of this number, 42.3 percent were in Birmingham, 43.8 percent in Dayton, 8.3 percent in Portland, and 5.6 percent in St. Paul. In each city except Birmingham the proportion of the total sample that was black was well within the range of sampling error of the actual size of the black population.

These differences remained when the control for income was applied. The answers on sense of community also showed differences between blacks and whites, with poor and nonpoor blacks being more likely than their white counterparts to say they felt a strong sense of community (table 2).

Although race does influence people's sense of their effectiveness, the less positive attitudes of blacks do not seem to carry over into apathetic behavior. When all blacks were compared with all whites, blacks proved more active. On four of the measures of participation, they scored higher than whites, though differences are insignificant in two cases. When income was taken into account, differences between poor blacks and poor whites were insignificant. Consequently, the overall differences between blacks and whites were due to the fact that nonpoor blacks were the more active group. It may be that the very positive environment for blacks in Birmingham, with a black mayor and a black majority on the city council, provided unusual encouragement for participation. The small number of minority people in Portland and St. Paul prevented us, however, from comparing the behavior of blacks across the four cities.

Because the underclass thesis concerns poor blacks living in areas with high concentrations of poverty, we again isolated those families with incomes less than $5,000 who lived in neighborhoods in which at least 20 percent of the population had incomes below the poverty line (table 3). Three sets of comparisons were made. The first was between all poor people in poor neighborhoods with all others. This comparison served as a baseline for further analysis that controlled for race. In the second set of comparisons, all blacks interviewed were divided into those who were poor and lived in poor neighborhoods and all others. The same breakdown was then applied to whites.

When we compared the political activity of poor blacks in poor neighborhoods with that of all other blacks, we found little difference. The questions about trust in government show a similar pattern: poor blacks who live in poor neighborhoods are about as trusting as those who live outside poor neighborhoods. Poor blacks in poor neighborhoods do, however, feel less personally effective than all other blacks.

On the question about the sense of community, socially isolated whites had a much weaker feeling of identity with their neighborhood than did other whites. For blacks though, there was no statistically significant difference between the two sets of respondents. Small subsample sizes made comparisons between socially isolated whites and blacks difficult, but 51.9 percent of the black poor people in poor areas had a strong sense of identity with their neighborhoods and only 16.3 percent of the white PPN

TABLE 2. Activity in Local Politics, by Respondent Financial Status and Race

Percent

Response[a]	All respondents		Poor respondents		Nonpoor respondents	
	Black	White	Black	White	Black	White
Contacted anyone?						
Yes	32.6	40.0	17.9	22.3	35.1	41.1
No	67.4	60.0	82.1	77.7	64.9	58.9
Number	571	2,670	84	166	487	2,504
	$X^2 = 10.83^b$		$X^2 = 0.66$		$X^2 = 6.15^b$	
Worked with others?						
Yes	44.0	40.7	30.4	26.9	46.3	41.6
No	56.0	59.3	69.6	73.1	53.7	58.4
Number	554	2,614	79	160	475	2,454
	$X^2 = 2.15$		$X^2 = 0.32$		$X^2 = 3.6^b$	
Active in citizen group?						
Yes	43.6	42.1	23.1	31.5	47.0	42.8
No	56.4	57.9	76.9	68.5	53.0	57.2
Number	559	2,667	78	165	481	2,502
	$X^2 = 0.47$		$X^2 = 1.83$		$X^2 = 2.92$	
Formed a new group?						
Yes	15.5	11.5	13.5	8.8	15.9	11.7
No	84.5	88.5	86.5	91.3	84.1	88.3
Number	547	2,605	74	160	473	2,445
	$X^2 = 6.82^b$		$X^2 = 1.25$		$X^2 = 6.32^b$	
Took part in neighborhood association?						
Yes	24.4	18.5	10.3	9.1	26.3	18.9
No	75.6	81.5	89.7	90.9	73.7	81.1
Number	328	1,325	39	55	289	1,270
	$X^2 = 5.79^c$		$X^2 = .03$		$X^2 = 7.98^b$	
Sense of community?						
Strong	42.9	32.4	42.9	29.0	42.9	32.6
In-between	40.2	44.1	40.3	43.9	40.2	44.1
Very little	16.8	23.5	16.9	27.1	16.8	23.3
Number	594	2,705	77	155	517	2,550
	$X^2 = 26.9^b$		$X^2 = 5.3^c$		$X^2 = 22.8^b$	

a. See table 1 for full wording of questions.
b. Significant at 0.01 level or beyond.
c. Significant at 0.05 level.

TABLE 3. Activity in Local Politics, by Respondent Neighborhood Status and Race

Percent

Response[a]	Blacks and Whites		Blacks		Whites	
	Poor in poor neighborhoods	All others	Poor in poor neighborhoods	All others	Poor in poor neighborhoods	All others
Contacted anyone?						
Yes	29.7	38.5	25.0	33.1	29.8	40.1
No	70.3	61.5	75.0	66.9	70.2	59.9
Number	91	3,535	36	535	47	2,623
	$X^2 = 2.95$		$X^2 = 1.00$		$X^2 = 2.06$	
Worked with others?						
Yes	31.4	41.3	32.4	44.8	27.3	40.9
No	68.6	58.7	67.6	55.2	72.7	59.1
Number	(86)	3,464	34	(520)	44	2,570
	$X^2 = 3.37^b$		$X^2 = 2.00$		$X^2 = 3.33^b$	
Active in citizen group?						
Yes	26.1	42.6	18.2	45.2	27.7	42.3
No	73.9	57.4	81.8	54.8	72.3	57.7
Number	88	3,520	33	526	47	2,620
	$X^2 = 9.59^c$		$X^2 = 9.24^c$		$X^2 = 4.08^b$	
Formed a new group?						
Yes	13.1	12.1	18.8	15.3	6.8	11.6
No	86.9	87.9	81.3	84.7	93.2	88.4
Number	84	3,439	32	515	44	2,561
	$X^2 = 0.07$		$X^2 = 0.27$		$X^2 = 0.97$	
Took part in neighborhood association?						
Yes	13.2	19.8	20.0	24.6	5.0	18.7
No	86.8	80.2	80.0	75.4	95.0	81.3
Number	38	1,782	15	313	20	1,305
	$X^2 = 1.04$		$X^2 = 0.16$		$X^2 = 2.45$	
Sense of community?						
Strong sense	30.8	33.9	51.9	42.0	16.3	32.6
In-between	43.6	43.3	40.7	40.4	46.5	43.9
Little sense	25.6	22.8	7.4	17.6	37.2	23.5
Number	3,374	78	495	27	2,562	43
	$X^2 = 0.49$		$X^2 = 2.14$		$X^2 = 6.94^b$	

a. See table 1 for full wording of questions.
b. Significant at 0.05 level.
c. Significant at 0.01 level or beyond.

group felt that way. For blacks, living in a poor community does not lead to a weak bonding with that neighborhood. If sense of community is a foundation from which civic-minded activity emerges, then poor, black neighborhoods have large quantities of an important and precious resource.

Overall, poor blacks living in poor neighborhoods were not politically distinct from blacks living elsewhere. Large numbers of poor blacks concentrated in the same neighborhood does not work against their inclination to become politically involved. They are not any less trusting of government than those blacks outside areas of high poverty. They have the same strong sense of community that other blacks have. Although poor blacks may feel less effective politically, these attitudes do not translate into political inactivity. Conceivably, the lack of difference between blacks in poor neighborhoods and other blacks could come about because nonpoor blacks are disproportionately inactive in politics. But this is not the case. When the "white all others" category is compared with the "black all others" category, blacks show a modest tendency to be more active.

In sum, there are strong community bonds in the poor, black areas of the cities in our survey, and many residents appear to believe that political activism can make things better for themselves and for their neighborhoods. Despite the problems that afflict neighborhoods with high incidences of poverty, poor blacks still believe that the system can be made to work.

Finally, we sought to verify the basic patterns of relationship we found by using multiple regression and logit analysis.[15] We examined the independent influences exerted by race, controlling for personal and neighborhood poverty status, and poverty status, controlling for race, on the five types of political behavior and on sense of community. The results confirmed the initial findings. Race was consistently more strongly related to political activity and sense of community than was personal or neighborhood poverty. Poverty tended to suppress political activities and sense of community, while being black tended to increase them.

Politically Viable Neighborhoods

In a period of pessimism about the endless problems of hard-core poverty areas, there is a glimmer of hope. In the poor, heavily black areas of

15. Berry, Portney, and Thomson (1989).

Birmingham, Dayton, Portland, and St. Paul, there are politically active citizens who see the political process as a means of helping themselves and helping their neighborhoods. These communities have not become depoliticized by the many economic and social ills that afflict them. Whatever general isolation they are subject to, the neighborhoods remain integrally involved in citywide politics.

The results from the surveys show that poor people living in poor neighborhoods differ little in their attitudes from poor people living in middle-class areas. Poor people from poor neighborhoods are actually more politically active than poor people living elsewhere. When race is added to the analysis, poor blacks have the same levels of trust in government as do poor whites. Poor blacks are less positive than poor whites in their perceptions of personal political effectiveness, but poor blacks and poor whites are similar in their propensity to become involved in politics. Finally, when poor blacks living in poor neighborhoods are compared with all other blacks, they are similar in levels of trust but more cynical about personal political efficacy. There are no significant differences in the political activity of blacks living in poor neighborhoods and that of other blacks.

We found no evidence that concentrations of poor blacks led to distinctive patterns of political behavior. Although poor blacks may be more cynical about their chances of influencing government than those in the appropriate comparison groups, these attitudes seem of little importance when it comes to deciding whether to become involved in politics. Possibly the attitudes reflect their frustration with the political system, but such frustration is not sufficient to keep them from becoming active. In short, poor blacks in poor neighborhoods are not a politically disenfranchised subpopulation beset by apathy and alienation. By itself, though, race is a stronger factor than class in its effect on political attitudes and levels of involvement.

The concentrations of poor blacks are not as great in the four cities in the study as in some of the nation's largest urban areas. It may be that at some greater level of concentration of poverty in black neighborhoods, political attitudes and behavior do become distinct from what would be found for other poor people and other blacks. Consequently, our data cannot categorically refute Wilson's thesis. However, the poverty line used in our surveys is lower than the official government poverty line, and the neighborhoods examined are very poor communities deeply troubled by high rates of unemployment and welfare.

Clearly, in the cities we studied, neighborhoods with high concentrations of poor blacks are politically viable communities. Poor blacks have a strong sense of community, and this characteristic seems to help propel them into the political arena.

The four cities we studied all have excellent programs for involving people in local politics. The neighborhood associations provide a meaningful channel of communication with city government and create an environment conducive to citizen participation. Each neighborhood association serves a small area and encompasses a coherent community with a long-standing identity.[16] The associations have a good deal of power over their communities, and city politicians and civil servants have strong incentives to cooperate with them and seek their support. They are run by volunteers from their neighborhood, and their leadership changes frequently. They use city funds for outreach and to communicate with residents through handbills and newsletters.

The common strategy for empowering neighborhoods used by each of these local governments was to establish neighborhood associations with roughly equal resources in all areas of the city. This plan emulates Wilson's strategy for developing politically acceptable solutions for the underclass. He argues that the most feasible option for policymakers interested in helping the underclass is to create programs "to which the more advantaged groups of all class and racial backgrounds can positively relate." [17]

Efforts by government designed to stimulate political activity of the poor may seem of little consequence if they are not connected to efforts aimed directly at eradicating the underlying causes of poverty. Political activism, however, must be seen as part of the solution to the problems of the poor; passivity can only compound their misery. Poor communities are not inherently apolitical, and our data show a strong reservoir of activism in low-income areas. Governmental structures designed to facilitate political participation are important tools for those who wish to improve the quality of life in their neighborhoods.

16. Dayton is a partial exception to the pattern of creating citizen participation units along existing community boundaries. The city is divided up into pie-shaped wedges that, along with a district for the downtown area, form the city's priority boards. The purpose for drawing the boundary lines for the priority boards in this fashion was to include a variety of communities within each one. However, each board is wholly divided into officially recognized neighborhoods, and each one of these has a neighborhood association.

17. Wilson (1987), p. 163.

References

Auletta, Ken. 1982. *The Underclass*. Random House.

Berry, Jeffrey M., Kent E. Portney, and Ken Thomson, 1989. "The Political Behavior of Poor People." Paper presented at the Conference on the Truly Disadvantaged.

Crenson, Matthew A. 1983. *Neighborhood Politics*. Harvard University Press.

Henig, Jeffrey R., and Dennis E. Gale. 1987. "The Political Incorporation of Newcomers to Racially Changing Neighborhoods." *Urban Affairs Quarterly* 22 (March), pp. 399–419.

Hughes, Mark Alan. 1989. "Concentrated Deviance and the 'Underclass' Hypothesis." *Journal of Policy Analysis and Management* 8 (Spring), pp. 274–81.

Lowi, Theodore J. 1988. "The Theory of the Underclass: A Review of Wilson's *The Truly Disadvantaged*." *Policy Studies Review* 7 (Summer), pp. 852–58.

Massey, Douglas S., and Nancy A. Denton. 1987. "Trends in the Residential Segregation of Blacks, Hispanics, and Asians: 1970–1980." *American Sociological Review* 52 (December), pp. 802–25.

———. 1989. "Hypersegregation in the U.S. Metropolitan Areas." *Demography* 26 (August), pp. 373–91.

Nathan, Richard P. 1987. "Will the Underclass Always Be with Us?" *Society* 24 (March-April), pp. 57–62.

Ricketts, Erol R., and Isabel V. Sawhill. 1988. "Defining and Measuring the Underclass." *Journal of Policy Analysis and Management* 7 (Winter), pp. 316–25.

Sawhill, Isabel V. 1989. "An Overview." *Public Interest* 96 (Summer), pp. 3–15.

Thomas, Melvin E., and Michael Hughes. 1986. "The Continuing Significance of Race: A Study of Race, Class, and Quality of Life in America, 1972–1985." *American Sociological Review* 51 (December), pp. 830–41.

Thomson, Ken, Jeffrey M. Berry, and Kent E. Portney. 1988. *Directions for Democracy*. Report 1 to the Ford Foundation. Medford, Mass.: Lincoln Filene Center for Citizenship and Public Affairs.

Wacquant, Loïc J. D., and William Julius Wilson. 1989. "The Cost of Racial and Class Exclusion in the Inner City." *Annals of the American Academy of Political and Social Science* 501 (January), pp. 8–25.

Willie, Charles V. 1978. "The Inclining Significance of Race." *Society* 15 (July-August), pp. 10–15.

Wilson, William Julius. 1980. *The Declining Significance of Race: Blacks and Changing American Institutions*, 2d ed. University of Chicago Press.

———. 1987. *The Truly Disadvantaged: The Inner City, the Underclass, and Public Policy*. University of Chicago Press.

Part Four ────────────────────────

The Rationale of Inner-City Life

Neighborhood Effects on Teenage Pregnancy

ELIJAH ANDERSON

An IMPORTANT FACTOR influencing the prevalence of teenage parenthood in underclass neighborhoods is the outlook of the young people involved. It is strongly affected by their perceived options in life. These perceptions are shaped by the fortunes of immediate peers, family, and others with whom the youths identify. One of the most important factors working against pregnancy is teenagers' belief that they have something to lose by presently becoming a parent; many believe they have something to gain.[1]

In many of these neighborhoods, it is the strong, financially stable, tightly knit "decent" (as neighborhood residents say) family, often but not always nuclear, that works to instill high aspirations in children and expectations of a good future that would be undermined by youthful parenthood. With the connections and examples of such families and their representatives in a neighborhood, a youth may hope to prevail in life despite presumed obstacles—financial, cultural, or other. The presence of these models can serve as a powerful inspiration to those who may be otherwise disadvantaged, and it can work socially as a bastion against the street culture. This street culture is characterized by support for and encouragement of an alternative life style that appears highly attractive to many adolescents, regardless of family background. Its activities are centered on the "fast life," and may include early sexual activity and drug experimentation and other forms of delinquency. But while relatively advantaged youths with clear options may dabble in this culture, becoming hip enough for social approval and then moving on, those with fewer apparent options, a limited sense of the future, may more fully invest themselves in the culture, attempting to gain status according to its prin-

This paper draws from and expands on my ethnographic field work in black underclass neighborhoods in Philadelphia and Chicago in the past twenty years. See Anderson (1978, 1989, 1990).

1. Dash (1989).

375

ciples and norms. The relative prominence of this culture in the poorest inner-city neighborhoods brings about not only the prevalence of much antisocial behavior but the high incidence of teenage parenthood as well.[2]

The Neighborhood Context

Amid crumbling houses and abandoned stolen automobiles whose carcasses are constantly picked at by some impoverished residents for spare parts, children rip and run, playing double dutch (jump rope games) and stick ball. At the corner store, young children pass in and out. Mostly they buy cigarettes (for parents or other adults), candy, Slim Jims, potato chips, bread, and soda.

The summer streets are populated by these children and sometimes their mothers, grandmothers, older sisters, and female cousins. It is mostly a very poor neighborhood of women and small children, who make up extremely important kinship networks that work to sustain their members; at times others are enlisted as fictive kin for needed help.[3] These residents, if they are employed, work as dishwashers, mechanics, domestics, and in other menial jobs. Some working poor people survive by living with kin and thus sharing household duties and close family life—joys as well as troubles. A large number of the women are single and on welfare, and eligible men seem a scarce presence in their lives.[4]

When present at all, men appear most prominently in the roles of nephew, cousin, father, uncle, boyfriend, and son, but seldom as husband. A few older men are retired and sit on the stoops, laughing and talking with their friends. Some will extend themselves to women in need of support, at times driving them on errands for a negotiated fee or for sexual favors.

In a crisis, say when young women with children become strung out on crack and other drugs to the point of being unable to function as mothers, a friend or relative may help out, but in some of the most desperate situations, the oldest children may take over, procuring and preparing food and performing other household duties. At other times, a grandmother takes over a crack addict's household chores and steps in to raise her daughter's children. In the neighborhood, stories circulate about this or that crack-addicted young mother abusing her children in favor of

2. Anderson (1989).
3. Stack (1974).
4. Wilson (1987).

the pipe. Everyone knows someone or knows about someone with a drug habit, their lives having been touched in some way by drugs.

While most residents struggle with poverty, there are some solidly working-class nuclear families living here, at times with a man still employed by a local factory, but this is rare. As many of the working-class residents as are able have left, routed by crime, incivility, and persistent poverty.

Small groups of seven- and eight-year-old street kids hang out on the corners or in the local alleys; they watch the traffic go by, observing the recurring drug sales, though many pretend not to see. Streetlore is that local drug dealers employ some of them as lookouts for crack houses or to signal dealers when a new shipment of drugs has arrived at a pickup point.

On a summer day residents hang out of their windows to catch a breeze or sit on stoops to watch the traffic go by. There is much street life here: young men, young women, old people, middle-aged people. To walk the streets is to observe many pregnant young women, walking or standing around with one or two children. Their youthful faces belie their distended bellies, but they carry on.

The streets are noisy and very much alive with sociability—yells, screams, loud laughter and talk, car screeches, rap music, and honking horns. A car pulls up and honks its horn for a passenger; another honks to urge the stopped car in the middle of the street to move on. But people are basically courteous, not wanting to provoke others. There are smiles and a certain level of camaraderie. Everybody knows everybody here, and as best they can, some try to watch out for others.

But many have their hands full watching out for themselves. Like aluminum siding at an earlier time, decorative iron bars have become a status symbol in the neighborhood, and residents acquire them for downstairs windows and doors as serious protection against thieves and "zombies" (crack addicts). And they show real concern about any stranger who seems at all questionable.

Now and again, a young boy appears, dressed in an expensive athletic suit and white sneakers (usually new; some boys have four or five pairs), and carrying an expensive boom box with the bass sound turned up loud as he walks to the beat of rap music, his self-presentation serving as a kind of dare, demonstrating to others that he has enough nerve to walk up and down the neighborhood streets with such an expensive item.

On certain street corners or down certain alleys, small groups of boys pass the time in the middle of the day. They "profile" in stylized poses, almost always dressed in expensive clothes that belie their unemployed status. They leave others to the easy conclusion that they clock (work) in the drug trade. A common view on the streets among the corner men is that the families of some of these boys "know about" their involvements, because they "get some of the money" for help with household expenses. Corner men talk of parents' tacit acceptance and willing ignorance of their youngster's drug dealing, expressing their worry about the boy, the random gunshots that sometimes come from a passing automobile, the occasional drug wars that sometimes start up spontaneously, and the possibility of his arrest by the police, not just because of the prospect of incarceration but because the family in some cases has come to rely on the drug money.

In the underclass neighborhood, the drug trade is everywhere; and it becomes ever more difficult to separate the drug culture from the experience of poverty. The neighborhood is sprinkled with crack dens located in abandoned buildings or in someone's home. On corner after corner, young men peddle drugs the way a newsboy peddles papers. To those who pass their brief inspection, they say, "Psst psst, I got the news. I got the news. 'Caine, blow. Beam me up, Scotty," code words easily understood by those in the know. At times, they sell drugs to passing motorists, who stop in broad daylight and hold up traffic during the transaction. When customers drive up, sometimes small children will be sitting in the back seat, which seems to faze neither the dealers nor the customer. Some of these young men carry beepers, which they use in conjunction with the telephone to make their sales; in fact, as pressure has been placed on the local crack houses and on the open air street sales, the beeper and telephone have become more important. For some, the beeper has become a status symbol, emblematic of the possession of money, daring, coolness, and drugs.

Almost any denizen of these streets has come to accept the area as a tough place, a neighborhood where the strongest survive and where, if people are not careful and streetwise, they can become ensnared in the games of those who could hurt them. When the boys admire another's property, they may simply try to take it; this includes another person's sneakers, jacket, hat, and other personal items. In this sense the public spaces have an air of incivility about them, particularly at night, and the implication is that many of the younger people are uncivilized. But the viewpoints of the young are to be distinguished from those of the older people, who sometimes proudly claim they were *raised* under a different system with different opportunities and abilities to realize them, while offering that "kids today just grow up." The older people try to live out their values of decency and law-abidingness; and while these continue to be important values in the neighborhood, the young generally do not seem as committed to them as the older residents.

Street Culture and "Decency"

For social purposes, working poor residents distinguish those values they see as "decent" from others they associate with "the street." Generally, decency is a highly regarded personal quality, and the assignation of a street orientation to a person is usually deeply discrediting. In the underclass neighborhood the meanings of the terms sometimes overlap, compete, and even support one another; their interaction is highly complex. But in fact these distinctions operate more or less to identify social polarities; and particularly among the young, their social referents may be used to distinguish the socially "lame" from the "hip."

Essentially, residents of the underclass neighborhood divide their neighbors into those who are decent and those whom they associate with the street.[5] The culture of decency is usually represented by close and extended families, often characterized by low-income financial stability. It emphasizes the work ethic, getting ahead, or "having something" as an important goal.[6] Decency becomes an organizing principle against which others are then judged. The family unit, often with the aid of a strong religious component, instills in its members a certain degree of self-respect, civility, propriety, and often, despite prevailing impoverished living conditions, a positive view of the future. Many such decent families become highly protective of their children and motivated to leave the neighborhood. Those who cannot afford to leave try to accomplish socially what they cannot accomplish otherwise: they attempt to isolate their children from the children whom they associate with the street. For they believe that teenage pregnancy, early involvement with drugs and crime, and other difficulties begin in early childhood, in deep involvement with the play groups proliferating on the streets. Decent local role models, sometimes through direct mentoring, allow young people to observe the possibilities and opportunities available for people like themselves.

To negotiate this setting effectively, particularly its public places, one must to some degree be hip or down or streetwise, demonstrating the

5. Matza (1966); Hannerz (1969); and Anderson (1978).
6. Anderson (1978).

ability to see through troublesome street situations and to prevail.[7] Thus
to survive in the setting is to be somewhat adept at handling the streets.
But to be streetwise is to risk one's claim to decency, for decency is often
associated with being lame or square. Thus, growing up, young people of
the neighborhood must walk something of a social tightrope. When some
youths, for instance, go away to college and return, they are sometimes
challenged by their more street-oriented peers with the mocking question,
"Can you still hang?" [Can you still handle the streets?] Hence those who
would be socially mobile often feel they must be hip enough to get along
with their more street-oriented peers, but they must be square enough to
keep out of trouble or avoid those habits and situations that would hurt
their chances for social mobility or even simple survival. It is in this sense
that so many adolescents, simply by growing up in an underclass neighborhood, are at special risk.

But they are at risk in other ways as well. Youths observe the would-
be legitimate role models around them, and many find them unworthy of
emulation. Conventional hard work seems not to have paid off for the
old, and they see the relatively few hardworking people of the neighborhood struggling to survive. At the same time, through unconventional
role models, a thriving underground economy beckons to them, in which
enormous sums are promised, along with a certain thrill, power, and
prestige. Streetwise and impoverished young men can easily deal in the
drug trade, part-time or full-time. They may even draw their intimate
female counterparts along with them, "hooking them up," and smoothly
initiating them into prostitution.

Given that persistent poverty is so widespread in the neighborhood,
for many residents, particularly the young, values of decency and law-
abidingness are more easily compromised. Needing money badly, they
feel social pressure and see the chance for making sometimes huge sums
outside their front door. With all the vice and crime occurring within the
neighborhood, those who are able to tend to leave, isolating even further
the very poor and the working poor. This exodus further demoralizes the
neighborhood, contributing to its residents' vulnerability to a number of
social ills, including increasing drug use and teenage pregnancy.[8]

The manufacturing jobs that used to provide opportunities for young
people in inner-city neighborhoods and strongly, albeit indirectly, supported values of decency and conventionality have largely vanished from

7. Anderson (1990).
8. Anderson (1990).

the economy, replaced by thousands of low-paying jobs that often exist in the suburbs beyond the reach of poor neighborhoods.[9] These changes have damaged the financial health of the inner city and undermined the quality of available role models. The trust and perceptions of decency that once prevailed in the community are increasingly absent. In their place, street values, represented by the fast life, violence, and crime, become more prominent.

The consequences of these changes can be illustrated by their effect on one of the community's most important institutions, the relationship between "old heads" and young boys. The old head was once the epitome of decency in inner-city neighborhoods.[10] Strongly supported by a vibrant manufacturing economy, he had relatively stable means. His acknowledged role in the community was to teach, support, encourage, and, in effect, socialize young men to meet their responsibilities regarding work, family life, the law, and common decency. Young boys and single men in their late teens or twenties had confidence in the old head's ability to impart practical advice. Very often, he played surrogate father to those who needed his attention and moral support.

But as meaningful employment becomes increasingly scarce for young men of the neighborhood and the expansion of the drug culture offers opportunities for quick money, the old head is losing prestige and authority. Streetwise boys are concluding that the old heads' lessons about life and the work ethic are no longer relevant, and a new role model is emerging. The embodiment of the street, he is young, often a product of the street gang, and indifferent at best to the law and traditional values. If he works at the low-paying jobs available to him, he does so grudgingly. More likely he makes ends meet, either part-time or full-time, in the drug trade or some other area of the underground economy. He derides conventional family life: he has a string of women but feels little obligation toward them and the children he has fathered.

On the street corner his self-aggrandizement consumes his whole being as he attempts to impress people through expensive clothes, fancy cars, and other displays of material success. And eagerly awaiting his message are the young, unemployed black men, demoralized by a seemingly hopeless financial situation and inclined to emulate his style and values.

Traditional female role models, often paragons of decency, have also suffered decreased authority. Mature women, often grandmothers them-

9. Kasarda (1985, 1989); Wilson (1987, 1989); and Anderson (1990).
10. Anderson (1978, 1990).

selves, once effectively served the neighborhood as auxiliary parents who publicly augmented and supported the relationship between parent and child. They would discipline children and serve as role models for young women, exerting a certain degree of social control. As the neighborhoods became increasingly drug infested, ordinary young mothers and their children became some of the most obvious casualties. The traditional female old head has become stretched and overburdened; her role has become more complicated as she often steps in as a surrogate mother for her grandchildren or at times a stray neighborhood child.

These women universally lament the proliferation of drugs in the community, the "crack whores" who walk neighborhood streets, the drug dealers who recruit the youth of the neighborhood, the sporadic violence that now and then claims innocent bystanders. The demoralization and deterioration of the neighborhood are omnipresent: open-air drug sales, numerous pregnant girls, incivility, crime, the many street kids, and the relatively few upstanding (as the residents say) men. It becomes difficult for either old or young to maintain a positive outlook, to envision themselves beyond the immediate situation. As neighborhood deterioration feeds on itself, decent, law-abiding people become increasingly demoralized; many of those who are capable leave, while some succumb to the street.

The Problem of Inner-City Teenage Pregnancy

In this context the incidence of teenage pregnancy becomes complicated by peer pressure, ignorance, passion, luck, intent, conquest, religion, love, and even profound hostility between young men and women. The inner-city girl who succumbs to pregnancy at age fifteen or sixteen is often subscribing to the culture of her peer group, but she may be doing it in a way that for her mimics grown-up middle-class behavior. Pregnancy often brings with it dreams of marriage and the hope—however short-lived—of a stable future with a husband, children, and a home. The boy has promised or implied as much through his behavior. He may have been playing a game from the start, but even if he was sincere, the realization of his severely limited employment prospects and financial instability often causes him to back out, or at best to play his role of father part-time.[11]

11. Anderson (1989).

In general, the boys pursue sex for both biological and status reasons. Sexual conquests give them a certain pride and status in their peer group. The group encourages this orientation, rewarding members who are able to get over the sexual defenses of women and encouraging game behavior to succeed. For many, the object is to hit and run while maintaining personal freedom and independence from conjugal ties; when they exist, such ties should be on the young man's terms. A sense of a limited future and ignorance mixed with indifference about reproduction and sexual activity bring on pregnancies and babies. Concerned with immediate gratification, some boys want babies to demonstrate their ability to control a girl's mind and body. With job opportunities, many of the young men might attempt to play out a more conventional version of being family head, but because of their severely limited employment prospects, they often are not interested in "playing house." As a cultural manifestation of persistent poverty, a manner of adaptation that appears to have taken on a life of its own, the mating game is an end in itself and its players gain self-esteem and affirmation from their conquests.

These cultural characteristics dovetail to some extent with the girls' sexual availability. The "fast" adolescent street orientation presents early sexual experience and promiscuity as a virtue. For many such girls who have few other perceivable options, motherhood, accidental or otherwise, becomes a rite of passage to adulthood. Although an overwhelming number may not be actively trying to have babies, many are not actively trying to prevent it. One of the reasons may be the strong fundamentalist religious orientation of many underclass blacks, which emphasizes the role of fate in life. If something happens, it happens; if something was meant to be, then let it be and "God will find a way." With the dream of a mate, a girl may be indifferent to the possibility of pregnancy, even if it is not likely that pregnancy will lead to marriage. So the pregnant girl can look forward to a certain affirmation, particularly after the baby arrives, if not from the father then from her peer group, from her family, from the Lord, and ultimately from "aid" (as neighborhood residents refer to welfare) from the wider society.

Thus if or when it becomes obvious that the young father's promises are empty, the young woman has a certain amount of help in settling for the role of single parent. A large part of her identity is provided by the baby, the symbolic passage to adulthood. The baby is under her care and guidance, and for many street-oriented girls there is no quicker way to grow up. Becoming a mother can be a strong play for authority, maturity, and respect. But it is also a shortsighted and naive gamble because the girl often fails to realize that her life will be suddenly burdened and her choices in life significantly limited.

In these circumstances outlook, including a certain amount of education, wisdom, and mentoring from decent role models, becomes extremely important. The strong, so-called decent family, often with a husband and wife, sometimes with a strong-willed single mother helped by close relatives and neighbors, may instill in girls a sense of hope. Thus these families can hope to reproduce the relatively strong family form. Such units are generally regarded in the neighborhood as advantaged. Both parents, or close kin, are known as hard workers, striving to have something and strongly emphasizing the work ethic, common decency, and social and moral responsibility. Though the pay may be low, the family often can count on a regular income, giving its members the sense that decent values have paid off for them.

A girl growing up in such a family, or even living in close social and physical proximity to one, may have strong support from a mother, a father, friends, and neighbors who not only care very much whether she becomes pregnant but are also able to share knowledge about negotiating life beyond the confines of the neighborhood. The girl may then develop certain avenues of self-expression that might more realistically approach social mobility or at least delay pregnancy. In these circumstances, she has a better chance to develop a positive sense of the future and a healthy self-respect; she may come to feel she has a great deal to lose by becoming an unwed parent.

Contributing strongly to this outlook are ministers, teachers, parents, and upwardly mobile peers. At times a successful older sister sets a standard and expectations for younger siblings, who then may attempt to follow her example. The community and the decent family help place the successful one high in the sibling hierarchy by praising her achievements. At the very least such support groups come strongly to communicate their expectation that the girl will do something with her life other than have a baby out of wedlock. These points are illustrated in the following narrative by a twenty-three-year-old woman who was raised in an underclass neighborhood but who graduated from college and recently married a young lawyer.

My younger sister Shareese used to complain to my parents, "Why do we always have to hear about Kim?" 'Cause I'm the oldest, you see. "It's always what Kim did." And she's sixteen months behind me. But

I think that just the programs were there for me, and in the summer-time I wasn't outside on the steps. I was in Prime [a program geared to encouraging low-income minority youngsters to go to college], and I was on campus, and I was studying for classes and stuff. I'm not saying I love learning any more than anyone else did, but part of it was that my parents had placed me in a position where I was with other people where I was able to compete with people on a different scale. And then when I came home, I already had a full day and was ready to sit out-side. And when I got older, when I started at the university, I stayed at home the whole four years, which allowed me to see two different worlds. My neighbors used to say, "You always the same. You never change."

But sitting and talking with the girls next door and then the girl across the street [who became pregnant], I guess I had always hoped that I would not become nonsympathetic towards some of the things that were going on, because in essence really [social problems of the black community] affect all of us really.

My informant felt somewhat between worlds, which kept her from feeling strongly anchored in either, but she had a sense that if she did certain things, she would likely face impediments to achieving her goal, which was mainly to obtain an education. Her desire for success was much too important to give up in favor of becoming pregnant. Further-more, the neighborhood peer group she joined at the age of fourteen had very little subsequent hold on her. She made friends, but their influence did not control her behavior, and she was not inclined to depend upon them for social sustenance. Also important, her parents were very strict in their childrearing practices. They demanded respect from their chil-dren and others, and got it. They enforced rules of address in relations between child and adult, such as having their children answer, "Yes, sir" and "No, sir" or "Yes, ma'am" and "No, ma'am." Such so-called decent parents take pride in their own child-training practices and quickly judge others on the basis of how well behaved their children are. They also expect to know their children's whereabouts at all times, and they scruti-nize their children's friends with their own values and standards firmly in mind.

At home the father of a girl plays a particularly important role (single mothers sometimes play this role effectively as well). In effect, he watches over the home, protecting and defending it when necessary. In this role, he may quickly remind a young suitor of his place, that he cannot "come in and take over." The father's demands for respect are sometimes quite direct, to the point of warning the young man outright, and may embarrass his daughter. He often does not have to say a word: as "a man," his very presence says everything to the young man and in itself may be enough to keep him in line. As my informant continued:

> My father was over-protective. Though I didn't at the time, now I appreciate it. But a lot of [his strictness] could have had a reverse effect. My sister, for example, kinda rebelled against the strictness. And my uncle probably is more of an example. His daughter is fourteen, but she's been seen talking to people [young boys] fifteen and sixteen, which is that borderline age [when girls become pregnant]. They [boys] come in and he wants to know, "Do your parents know you're here?" It's embarrassing to her. But the boy knows. He says, "Yes sir, no sir, Mr. Turner, sir."

The girl may suffer under the strict father's behavior, but in light of her father's criticisms of her friends, she may begin to listen attentively to his arguments and see them supported when so many of her girlfriends become pregnant at an early age.

As in the case of my informant, however, the girl's reactions are affected and tempered by the distance she has from the local, street-oriented peer group. If she is close to it, her parents' messages may fall on deaf ears. If she is marginal to the group, which is often the case for "decent" young people, her chance of heeding her parents is likely to be good. With time and maturity she hears the extremely important message that her parents care about her and expect her to have a future without a youthful pregnancy, a message all the more resonant because of the relatively effective financial and social position of her parents.

Fortunate to have been raised by adults who have contributed to her self-esteem and strong belief in a positive future, the girl emerging from a stable family is inclined to "want to have something." Hence, such young women tend to put off immediate gratification. Like any teenager, they can become affected by serious love affairs gone bad, become vulnerable to the sexual games of the boys, and have their "heads turned." But in general they do not resort to seeking self-esteem and status by settling immediately on the local pool of available men or by trying to have a prize baby. Instead they become motivated to go on to college, or to obtain a good job downtown in an office building, where they can wear nice clothes and associate with those of the more conventional society.

Strikingly, these young women are sometimes viewed as naive by the boys—and thus most vulnerable to their games—but they are also among the most desirable women in the neighborhood, the top of the status hierarchy. Many young men see them as the girls to "hit on," to "pull," and to "wrap up" and sometimes "take home to mom, to show her what I found." Because of these attitudes, such young women are placed on a pedestal, but they are also placed at special risk in the neighborhood, and sometimes because of this, their parents become even more protective. In the underclass neighborhood, such protection may be difficult to establish, because the local male gangs and play groups see the girls as "our women" and seek to control them and screen their boyfriends.

In contrast, the girls who graduate to the street are products of homes in which they have relatively little parental supervision and limited family support to strive for a life much different from the one they are currently living. Hence, as indicated earlier, decent parents often forbid their own children from regular participation in such groups and label such children street kids. Something akin to the status-creating processes I observed during my field work in Chicago play themselves out in the neighborhoods among the children.[12] In the scenario most closely related to the street, the girl primarily raises herself with the help of her street-oriented peers and her mother, or as some residents say, "she just grows up." She becomes deeply involved in the apparently innocent jump-rope games of double dutch, but in such participation she becomes more fully socialized into the street-oriented peer group. Some decent parents become outraged by the sometimes obscene jump-rope rhymes.

Left largely to their own devices, these children play with their peers on the street corners in mild weather, at times until 1:00 or 2:00 in the morning on school nights. The decent children must often come in at dinner time, or they may be allowed to go no farther than their front stoops, from which they sit and observe the action. Through such constant, strictly applied sanctions by their parents, they eventually learn their place in the neighborhood, as neighborhood peer groups increasingly take on status characteristics.

By the age of eleven or twelve many of the street girls are aware of their bodies and beginning to engage in sexual relations, but they have very little biological knowledge and understand even less about the consequences of their behavior. In these circumstances the street girls become

12. Anderson (1978).

committed to their peer groups, learning to survive by their wits, as they take pride in "being cool" and pursue a certain "grown-up" sophistication. Increasingly, they "talk to people" [boys], whose sexual desires begin to mesh with the social needs of the girls. Some members of this group begin to have babies by the age of fifteen, and soon others follow. And as increasing numbers of girls become pregnant, fewer constraints are there for their peers. If "everyone else is doing it," those who are not may feel greatly outnumbered or feel they are missing out on an important aspect of life. For some, becoming pregnant may be viewed as normal and as only a matter of time.

In time, this primary group can become something of a family for many of its members who grow up lacking the emotional supports of one. When this group wins the girl's allegiance, it works to shape her dreams, social agenda, values, aspirations, and goals. At times, it competes strongly with the inner-city family, "decent" or "street."

The group is considered hip by its members and operates as an in-crowd in the neighborhood, although more conventional residents derogate it, associating it even more firmly with the street. They refer to its members as fast and believe them to have "tried everything" by an early age. The general group's decent counterparts are considered by the hip to be lame or square and may suffer social ostracism or ridicule as a result. The decent girl's reactions to such developments may well depend upon the ratio of decent to street-oriented teenagers residing in the area; the decent ones may offer each other moral and emotional support, while their parents encourage this split.

In a particular neighborhood, then, proximity to and degree of integration with certain peer groups can be significant factors in the chances of a young woman's becoming pregnant, depending on the extent to which she feels the pull of the peer group, and the extent to which the peer group is able to influence her sexual conduct.

As these social forces come together, youthful pregnancies proliferate. My informant continues, "We moved into the neighborhood when I was already fourteen. And the people there had already formed their cliques with each other. So it took me a while to get in good with anybody, since we were the new people on the block. Whereas if I had grown up with them it might have been a different thing."

This young woman felt her identity as outsider to be important in determining her sexual activity. At a certain point the adolescent female peer group places a strong cultural emphasis on babies, and so in their conversations there is constant discussion of who is sleeping with whom and who is pregnant by whom. Outsiders are not drawn in so tightly, and the norms, prescriptions, and proscriptions of group behavior do not apply so strongly. Thus where she lives and the types of influences found in the neighborhood can have a serious impact on determining a girl's inclination to become sexually active and pregnant, but social class, including outlook and family life, are important considerations. This is indicated in the following account of one of my informants in reference to a seventeen-year-old woman who was only marginally related to the neighborhood peer groups, had moved away, but had returned for a visit. My informant said, "She had come to see our neighbors [a family with teenage girls] next door. I was waiting to catch the bus and I asked her, 'Oh, you friends with Brenda?' She said, 'Yes, I used to live on this block. But now I live out in Wynnfield.' I said, 'Oh, that's nice.' She said, 'Yeah, this [becoming pregnant] is like contagious around here. Everybody gets pregnant.'" They then compared notes on common acquaintances and friends, and the visitor was surprised to find that so many of her former neighbors had become pregnant. In winding up the conversation, the visitor commented, "I'm glad I'm out of this neighborhood."

Because a girl raised in the street culture may lack the outlook that would allow her to pursue options other than pregnancy, she often lacks the ability fully to appraise its consequences. She is so downtrodden and isolated from the wider society and its values that she may feel she is doing well by becoming pregnant and receiving welfare. Girls who have become single parents before her are often her role models. She sees that their babies are almost always warmly welcomed by the family. In fact, many of the girls' mothers will take over care of the babies, both because the girls are so inexperienced and because the mothers hope that the girls will somehow recoup and not be "messed up" by the pregnancy. (Sometimes the grandmother is really "mom" or "big mama" to the child, while the real mother is called by her first name as though mother and child were siblings, and they may in fact be raised as such.) These girls often have their independence, a welfare check, and food stamps (they may gain love and attention from young men by giving them a portion of the check).

With the welfare check or income from other sources, including family and male friends, the young women can dress up their babies and show them off to their peers, in their eyes proving that they are managing just fine, living out their versions of a decent life style. Images of middle-class life come to them through television soap operas or "stories" (as the neighborhood residents say) or through the models they see around them.

But middle-class life is an abstraction to many inner-city residents. Most have little with which to compare their present quality of life, and the poorest may not fully appreciate the real extent of their deprivation.

It is in this respect that the typical impoverished girl is so profoundly different from the one who is upwardly mobile and who enjoys emotional support and social connection from her family and friends.[13] The upwardly mobile girl generally has a sense of future that is not bound by the immediate importance of the babies, informal "baby clubs," gin and coffee klatches, and men that constitute the horizon of the more street-oriented girl. But the decent families sometimes face fierce competition from the street groups. Their daughters may succumb to the lure of the street culture; sometimes it takes only one misstep. But the street peer group more often draws in those girls who are only loosely connected with other sources of social and emotional support. At special risk are members of families headed by a young woman with her hands full working, socializing, and mothering. These families stand a limited chance in the struggle for an adolescent daughter's full allegiance, and such girls become vulnerable to pregnancy.

As indicated above, by the age of fifteen or sixteen many of the young girls of the street peer group start getting pregnant. A form of social contagion spreads to other group members. Many of these young women have a dream of the good life: they want to be married to a good man ("someone who will treat me right") and settled down in a nice neighborhood. In fact, when a girl does become engaged to be married, relatives and friends express excitement and approval of her prospective life, particularly of the wedding ceremony itself. But this seldom happens. The dream of the good life usually unravels when the young men do not or cannot come through as viable providers and husbands. Thus many girls settle for babies and part-time fathers. Through the rite of pregnancy they become "grown" and work to rationalize and enhance motherhood, infusing this state with special value.

The Baby Club

When the babies arrive, the street groups become informal baby clubs.[14] The girls support one another, taking some care to praise one another and the babies. But they also use their babies to compete with

13. Waquant and Wilson (1989).
14. Anderson (1990).

each other for status. In this context the baby is viewed as an extension of the mother and reflects directly upon her. Carried on at birthday parties, weddings, church services, and spontaneous encounters, these competitions often take the form of invidious comparisons of one baby with another. First, the baby's physical features are noted: cuteness, texture of hair, skin color, and grooming and dress. To enhance her chances in such competitions, the young mother often dresses her baby in the latest and most expensive clothes, actions that provoke criticisms from more conventional and mature mothers and grandmothers. As one grandmother said:

> Oh, they can't wait until check day so they can go to the store. I listen at 'em, talking about what they gon' buy *this* time. "Next time my check come, I'm gon' buy my baby this, I'm gon' buy my baby that." And that's exactly what they will do, expensive store, too. The more expensive, the better. Some will buy a baby an expensive outfit that the baby only gon' wear for a few months. I seen a girl go . . . I think she paid $45 for an outfit. I think the baby was about six weeks old. Now, how long was that child gon' wear that outfit? For that kind of money? They do these silly, silly things.

But the apparent irresponsibility of these mothers evolves in a logical way. Lacking decent role models and peer groups, they may come under the influence of street-oriented peer groups. Along with street smartness, hipness and fashionable dress, and experimentation with alcohol and drugs, these groups emphasize sexual activity. But to be sexually active is also to risk getting pregnant. Group members are often ignorant about the facts of reproduction, but there is also a certain amount of indifference. A girl may not be actively trying to become pregnant, but the peer group generally does little to discourage her from doing so. Moreover, for many, a baby is part of the dream of marriage and bliss.

The baby club is a reaction to this experience. It deflects criticism of the young mother's "messed up" circumstances and gives her a certain status. The members then develop an ideology about their circumstances that is at odds with that of the more conventional society. In effect, they create value and status by sometimes denigrating the girls who do not become pregnant. Those girls who are only weakly oriented toward mobility and decency might become drawn into the orbit of the baby club. Some residents, as indicated in the field note quoted earlier, talk about becoming pregnant as "contagious."

Girls in the baby club participate in planned or spontaneous gatherings at the homes of various members. Mainly they come to socialize and to show off their babies, who are often dressed in expensive new outfits. They talk about their experience of giving birth and about the men in their lives, at times comparing how each other's men behaved during the pregnancy and after. They speak of the behavior of the boys' mothers and how they themselves have treated various girls in the boys' lives. They use the distinctions, or reports of how they were treated, to express their status. The amount of help given by boys and their mothers may become a measure indicating their closeness and care.

During these gatherings mother and child must "look good" to negate the generalized notion that the mother has messed up her life; when the baby and mother look good, the message is sent out publicly that she is doing all right. Mothers lobby for compliments, smiles, and nods of approval and feel good when they are forthcoming, for they signal affirmation and pride. The cutest babies are passed around.

For these reasons, babies born to unwed teenagers are highly value-laden. For the father, presumptive but not fully acknowledged fatherhood is important proof of sexual prowess. At the same time, his loose connection to the woman allows him to maintain the free life style so valued by his peer group. He may reason that he is much better off remaining single, "staying home with mama," and maintaining his freedom "to come as I want and to go as I please." Given his limited employment prospects, such a resolution may afford him a better alternative than "playing house" and being "tied down with kids, bills, and all that." Thus he has a distinct incentive for playing his role of father and "husband" part-time.

For the mother, a baby often becomes the cornerstone of status among the street-oriented peer group. The better looking the baby, the higher the mother's status. This has two implications: the girl spends a disproportionately large amount of money on dressing and grooming the baby and tends to cultivate cute boys (those with a "rap," "good hair," and "good looking" features) who she hopes will give her a "prize baby," as people of the neighborhood say. Thus in a community of severely limited resources, physical appearance works to define status, and the baby becomes the physical symbol of success of the young couple, especially of the girl.[15] The highest status accrues to the mother with the prize baby, one with "nice eyes, curly black hair, and nice complexion" and a win-

15. Rainwater (1960).

ning smile that comes easily. Conversely, the mothers and other members of the group disparage the "ugly baby." As my informant said, "There is one baby who is very dark skinned. And she has short hair, and someone said, 'Did you see Lynette's baby?! *She* even said the baby was ugly.' It was a little boy. He wasn't ugly. [But] he wasn't a really cute baby. When they saw the baby, they looked over at the baby, then they looked at me, and rolled their eyes. It really wasn't a prize. That's how they measure one another."

Mothers will go to great lengths to avoid the stigma of the ugly baby, even to the point of avoiding "ugly" men and encouraging cute ones. And what they cannot gain through physical attributes they can try to make up with clothes, which can sometimes take 75 percent of a welfare check. The clothes must be of good quality, not hand-me-downs. Among some of the newest and poorest mothers, the baby is of such paramount importance that the mother may look disheveled while the baby is decked out, though it also is important for the mother to keep up her appearance. As my informant commented,

> Once there was a sale at the church at Thirty-second and Buford. A friend of mine had some baby clothes for sale. They were some cute clothes, but they weren't new. They were sweatsuits, older things. The young girls would just pass them by. Now, the older women, the grandmothers, would come and buy them for their grandchildren. But the girls, sixteen and seventeen, had to have a decked-out baby. No hand-me-downs. Some would pay up to $40 for a pair of Nike sneakers. They go to Carl's [an expensive baby boutique downtown where many upper middle-class mothers shop]. And the babies sometimes are burning up in the clothes, but they dress them up anyway. The baby is in some ways like a doll. They sometimes do more to clothe the baby than to feed the baby.

The prize baby is not usually the prize of first choice for many of these girls. For an undetermined number, the real prize is upward mobility, the good life, having a family on the middle-class model they avidly follow in the soap operas. The wish for many is to go to college or land a job downtown. But sooner or later they make do with what they have at their disposal. In effect, they may settle for babies because there is "nothing else to do." This poverty of outlook is far different from that of their "decent" counterparts, to whom they usually defer during encounters, thus recognizing such people as their "betters" in the neighborhood's social order.

The profound absence of role models in the neighborhood is not simply the result of economic changes that have undermined financial stability for lower-class and lower-middle-class black families or the rapid departure of the black middle class.[16] It also occurs because middle-class people and others who are relatively better off than the desperately poor very often place social if not physical distance between themselves and others of the neighborhood who do not measure up to their notions of decency.

For street girls there is a profound absence of credible role models, people who are enough like them but different enough from them to motivate them to abandon the street orientation. Those who cannot go to college, who lack a positive outlook, and who fail to find a husband with whom they can become upwardly mobile adapt to the situation they see before them. If a girl does not get good grades and is not competitive in school sports, she might choose to have a baby. She may see this as the only path left for her "to do something," especially if the baby has a chance of being a prize. Thus it may not be so much whether the boy has a good job or even good job prospects that determines the sexual relationship but rather his way of contributing to the enhancement of her self-esteem. It is in this socially complicated way that having a baby fulfills a dream.

Once the girls of the peer group begin to have babies, a stronger informal segregation develops in the neighborhood. Those who have babies gravitate to social groups with others who have babies. Those without babies tend to hang out together. Differences between the street culture and decency crystallize if they have not already done so.

Many girls who get caught up in the street culture and go on to compete for status in the baby club come to realize that this is not the best to be achieved in life. Most have the presence, though in dwindling numbers, of the decent families and girls from those families to remind them of their "failings." And in the presence of girls who have avoided early pregnancy and "made something of themselves," these young mothers will be almost apologetic. The account of a girl who was successful in resisting the draw of the street culture and graduated from college sums the situation up nicely:

My neighbor next door to me . . . I think she had about seven girls, and she's like forty, almost fifty now. The oldest girls had babies

16. See Wilson (1987).

around fifteen or sixteen, and this was before I came along on the block. They had kids that you could tell they had when they were really young. The older girls were raising the young ones. If there was going to be any charming [courting], the mother was just absent from the house. And people [boys] kinda knew. The girls kinda raised themselves.

The baby girl [youngest girl in her family], who is about nineteen now, and she just had a baby. She said, "I'm gonna be like Sharon," and Sharon went on to college and never had any kids. "I'm gonna go on to the service, or I'm gonna go on to school." But as she got older, seventeen and eighteen, I started seeing her hang around with the guys more and more. Up on Adams Street. Tiger's [bar] is located there: Thirty-fourth and Adams Street. Well, I saw her last summer, and she had a baby. I guess the baby's about a couple months old, and she was pregnant then. And I don't know anything about the circumstances, you know, about the guy. I know she's not married. From what I heard, he comes and brings Pampers and stuff. But what can he really support her with? But he brings things. For her, it was really a case where she didn't think she was limited to just [single parenthood]. She thought she could go on, primarily because she had an example in her sister. She used to ask me about going to college. Hers was a different kind of case. She really had some high hopes to aspire to and she got trapped in this game or cycle. Now she has a baby girl. She graduated from high school. I don't think she plans on going to college.

The Old Baby

As the baby grows older, socially he or she becomes less an extension of the mother and more an individual—a demanding one at that. By the third year or so the mother may find herself being eased from the competition in the baby club and also losing status in her extended family network. The child may become more clearly a burden, seeming to curtail the mother's freedom. She may feel trapped and her sense of pride in being a mother may diminish.

As the novelty of having a baby begins to wear off, the young woman's tolerance for the child may suffer, particularly as feelings of abandonment by the man mount. She may begin to snap at the child and become generally intolerant of behavior that seemed so cute before. Conditions can become ripe for serious child abuse, and mothers may more frequently hit, yell, or curse at their babies in public. These points are illustrated in the following field note:

On Sunday evening at about 4:30, I visited a laundromat in the ghetto community to do my family's wash, as I do on occasion. Since few local residents can afford their own washing machines, the setting has a way of drawing some of the poorest residents of the neighborhood. And not only does it become a convenient place to do their laundry, but also sociability is often a by-product of performing the chore. Most of the clientele are women and small children, and thus it is a good place to observe family interaction among the local poor. On this day, I had been in the setting for about an hour, and was waiting for my wash to complete its cycle. Suddenly, the sounds of the television set and the socializing friends and the whirring machines were broken by the yells of a young mother, "Get yo' black ass over here and sit down!" The child, a three-year-old boy, simply cowered, as she jerked him by the arm and slammed him on the empty seat. She had become fed up with his running to and fro with a couple of other children. The small boy put his thumb in his mouth and looked down at the floor. Minutes later, he was up and tugging on his mother's dress, while she tended to her wash. But a few minutes later, he wandered off to the soap dispenser and began fingering it. When the mother discovered this, she became very impatient, and again she screamed at the child. Then she smacked him. He appeared stoic. Others watched the performance, while the mother demonstrated her control over the child, dressing the child down with a loud barrage of cursing. This is not an uncommon scene.

In these circumstances, mothers often try to show that they are in control, that they are good mothers because their children mind them in public. Some people may shake their heads in pity for the child and young mother, but most understand, for the exhibition is a culturally approved way of dealing with older children, to keep them in line and not spoil them. In publicly chastising the child, however, the mother also may be attempting to demonstrate independence and strength, trying desperately to show that she is not trapped. As the feelings of abandonment mount, a young woman's self-esteem may drop.

In these circumstances, a young mother may attempt to resolve her frustrations by becoming pregnant again, perhaps subconsciously making an effort to stay in the running for the status she once had in the baby club. Those women whose first baby lacked prize status may now seek out young men who seem to have a better chance than the last one of delivering on the promise of the prize.

Summary

Two lifestyles tug at young people of underclass neighborhoods. The stable "decent" family with its belief in upward mobility and options for the future provides one. The street culture, which revolves around violence, drugs, sex, having babies out of wedlock, and other problem behavior, provides the other. The neighborhood can be predominantly street-oriented or decent. Accordingly, its effects vary depending on the individual and on the neighborhood itself. Equally important is the class background of the young person. Virtually all teenagers are at risk and vulnerable to the alluring street culture, and most will dally with the experience; ultimately, many successfully resist. Those who are not well supervised and raised with optimism toward the future may linger in the street culture and may eventually succumb to its standards.

The street culture can proliferate. As economic conditions deteriorate, the street culture grows, and more residents adopt its standards of behavior. More of those who are better off leave. The most desperate people are left behind, increasingly isolated from the decent families and the successful role models they provide. For great numbers of young people, the culture precludes a vision of a life very different from that in which they live and observe their parents and neighbors living.

Young people who are raised with a sense of opportunity and are able realistically to picture a better life are often successful in avoiding the draw of the street culture. For girls, the belief that they can be somebody in the wider community prevails over the lure of becoming somebody by having a prize baby at age fifteen.

But such dreams are difficult to realize. Available service jobs tend to pay little or are located far from the ghetto community; the underground economy awaits, counting as participants young people who are decent as well as those who are street-oriented. And the street culture has more allure the more unyielding and unreceptive the wider society is to it. Moreover, a cute baby is proof that a girl is attractive to desirable (good-looking) men. Such recognition from her peers, along with the status of grown woman, which accrues to her upon becoming a mother, is often the most she hopes for.

Young girls growing up in such situations, strongly encouraged by their mothers and fathers, extended kin, and neighbors, are sometimes highly motivated to avoid those habits and situations that would undermine their movement toward the good life. They are in effect encouraged to adopt an outlook that places them in a world beyond their immediate circumstances. Many envision marriage, a family, and a home. In attempting to instill such an outlook, the parents tend to be relatively strict in their childrearing practices. Such parental control, along with their own developing hopes, causes the girls to watch themselves and work hard to achieve a life better than that lived by so many in the inner cities. Because they want to be somebody and to have something, they tend to avoid youthful, unwed pregnancies.

References

Anderson, Elijah. 1978. *A Place on the Corner*. University of Chicago Press.
———. 1989. "Sex Codes and Family Life among Inner-City Youths." *Annals of the American Academy of Political and Social Science* 501 (January), pp. 59–78.
———. 1990. *Streetwise: Race, Class, and Change in an Urban Community*. University of Chicago Press.
Dash, Leon. 1989. *When Children Want Children*. William Morrow.
Hannerz, Ulf. 1969. *Soulside: Inquiries into Ghetto Culture and Community*. Columbia University Press.
Kasarda, John D. 1985. "Urban Change and Minority Opportunities." In *The New Urban Reality*, edited by Paul E. Peterson. Brookings.
———. 1989. "Urban Industrial Transition and the Underclass." *Annals of the American Academy of Political and Social Science* 501 (January), pp. 26–47.
Matza, David. 1966. "The Disreputable Poor." In *Social Structure and Mobility in Economic Development*, edited by Neil J. Smelser and Seymour Martin Lipset. Chicago: Aldine Press.
Rainwater, Lee. 1960. *And the Poor Get Children: Sex, Contraception, and Family Planning in the Working Class*. Chicago: Quadrangle Books.
Stack, Carol B. 1974. *All Our Kin: Strategies for Survival in a Black Community*. Harper and Row.
Wacquant, Loïc J. D., and William Julius Wilson. 1989. "Poverty, Joblessness, and Social Transformation of the Inner City." In *Welfare Policy for the 1990s*, edited by Phoebe H. Cottingham and David T. Ellwood. Harvard University Press.
Wilson, William Julius. 1987. *The Truly Disadvantaged: The Inner City, the Underclass, and Public Policy*. University of Chicago Press.
———. 1989. "The Underclass: Issues, Perspectives, and Public Policy." *Annals of the American Academy of Political and Social Science* 501 (January), pp. 182–92.

Culture, Rationality, and the Underclass

J. DAVID GREENSTONE

DEBATES ON THE underclass typically regard underclass behavior as either a response to an economic predicament or the result of cultural commitments to dysfunctional values. Persuasive and influential as it has been, this debate is not just misleading but ultimately incoherent. On the one side, proponents of the culture of poverty thesis emphasize a culture that irrationally sanctions dysfunctional conduct. On the other side, proponents of its major antagonist, the structural thesis, claim the underclass is responding rationally to economic constraints imposed on urban minorities by a capitalistic social order.

Each side offers a carefully explicated and argued position. Yet neither is able to fully resolve the issues. Much of the difficulty follows from the complexity of the pivotal terms "culture" and "rationality." Among the many aspects of "culture" are a community's fundamental beliefs, ethical and esthetic values, revered rituals, and material preferences. But culture also includes the tools—material and linguistic, practical and theoretical—that people employ in their purposive and reflective activities.[1] Again, the instrumental side of "rationality" specifies those actions, techniques, and skills necessary to achieve specific goals, but rationality also includes the capacity to make human experience bearable by rendering it intelligible.[2] Once these more complex meanings are recognized, a sharp distinction between culture and rationality becomes untenable.

The Culture of Poverty Thesis

In attributing the dysfunctional behaviors of the underclass to deviant values, the culture of poverty thesis echoes a major conservative theme in

I wish to thank Carla Hess, David Laitin, and Paul Peterson for their helpful criticisms of earlier versions of this paper.

1. Hannerz (1969), pp. 186, 191.
2. Geertz (1973), chaps. 4, 8.

American culture: the affirmation of the values of asceticism, hard work, law-abidingness, the conventional nuclear family, and the restriction of sexual activity to relations within the marriage bond. The core ethic, then, is one of personal responsibility for one's actions. To those who advocate this ethic, obeying it entitles one to worldly success; violating it endangers the fabric of American society. A strong version of the culture of poverty thesis considers the underclass to have rather freely chosen to reject this basic morality. It is this element of free choice that justifies subjecting the underclass to moral judgment.

In explicating the grip of "black ghetto culture" on young members of the underclass, Charles Murray's *Losing Ground* offers this perspective's most sophisticated recent statement. Murray's overt concern is the role of a liberal intelligentsia in accelerating the decline of black participation in the labor force since the mid-1960s. Blaming the American economy and society for black inequality, these liberal intellectuals supported generous welfare programs and more lenient criminal justice and public education systems. The results were new outlooks, new rules, and better levels of welfare payments that encouraged choosing leisure over labor. "For the first time in American history, it became socially acceptable within poor communities to be unemployed, because working families too were receiving welfare." Social mores changed because government was now penalizing the young man who "has taken responsibility for his wife and child even though his friends with the same choice have called him a fool."[3]

So ghetto rationality is shaped by a decisive cultural fact. The rewards, monetary and otherwise, of work are valued less than those of leisure, no matter what the long-run costs. In sum, culture overrides rationality. Underclass people act on ultimately misleading incentives, and thus self-defeating values and beliefs, rather than carefully thinking through the best way to lead genuinely satisfying and productive lives.

Apart from its ideological and moral tilt, this thesis has emphasized underclass pathologies in the context of persistent urban poverty. As a result, it has proved compelling to scholars with very different political and ethical commitments. In the 1960s, Hannerz reported a "ghetto-specific complex" that included a male role emphasizing toughness, sexual activity, and liquor consumption, conflictual relations between the sexes, an extensive informal social life outside the family, and suspiciousness toward others.[4] Recently, social theorist Ralf Dahrendorf, who rec-

3. Murray (1984), pp. 185, 229.
4. Hannerz (1969), p. 177.

ognizes the impact of inequality and discrimination, has noted "a kind of underclass culture," a "life style of laid back sloppiness . . . gangs . . . hostility to normal middle class society . . . [and] often drugs and alcohol."[5]

Still, the culture of poverty thesis has clear shortcomings, quite apart from a basic philosophical error I shall consider presently. First, its overly narrow view of rationality obscures the adaptiveness of certain ghetto-specific gender roles. Constraints on employment effectively prevent many inner-city men from becoming traditional breadwinners, husbands, and fathers. The roles fashioned in response to such conditions provide genuine benefits not offered by mainstream alternatives.[6]

The thesis also views culture too simplistically. To sustain its emphasis on the importance of underclass values, its advocates must emphasize historical continuities over generations. But many scholars have found that the black family, in both North and South, largely conformed to the mainstream model, at least up to World War II.[7] A generation later, Hannerz found that most inner-city dwellers were well aware of mainstream norms that called for male breadwinners in stable, two-parent families.[8]

These theoretical deficiencies may help account for the defects in Murray's policy analysis. Because he believes that underclass people react hedonistically to strong incentives, he expects underclass women to become mothers if they receive generous welfare payments. Accordingly, lower welfare payments should change the balance of incentives and induce inner-city residents to seek employment. However, the growth of the underclass since the early 1970s has occurred at a time when the real value of welfare payments has actually been falling.[9]

The Structural Thesis

In opposition to the culture of poverty thesis, proponents of a structural interpretation argue that underclass behaviors are rational reactions to an "ungenerous social structure" that imposes constraints and limited opportunities.[10] According to William Julius Wilson's explanation for the growth of the underclass, the effects of historic patterns of racial discrim-

5. Dahrendorf (1987), pp. 4–5.
6. Hannerz (1969), pp. 50, 87–88, 94, 136. See also Wilson (1987), chap. 3.
7. Wilson (1987), p. 32.
8. Hannerz (1969), pp. 12, 15.
9. Wilson (1987), pp. 44–55; and Greenstein (1985), pp. 12–17.
10. Hannerz (1969), p. 74. See also Wilson (1987), pp. 13, 61, 104; and Wilson (1988), pp. 41–42.

ination were compounded by the disappearance of some manufacturing jobs, the movement of others away from the inner cities, and the increasing concentrations of poor people in specific neighborhoods.[11]

It is in this context that ghetto-specific practices become genuinely adaptive. Given too few decently paying jobs, men often find that they can make only unsatisfactory contributions as providers and that their ability to manage family business is small.[12] Accordingly, their quest for social recognition and self-esteem leads to frequent and informal sexual exploits, heavy drinking, and an emphasis on maintaining peer relations rather than family commitments. Because these behaviors reduce the pool of marriageable men, many underclass women have little realistic hope of becoming wives and mothers in conventional marriages. It becomes more rational to have children out of wedlock, raise them in single-parent, female-headed families, and maintain informal extramarital relations with male companions. The apparently pathological behavior of the underclass should then be analyzed "not as a cultural aberration but as a symptom of class and racial inequality."[13] Here is a determinist as well as rationalist line: the constraints on the underclass make a moral critique of its conduct largely irrelevant.

This analysis also rests on a powerful intuition: most people, most of the time, do their best to satisfy their desires or preferences. In this respect the macrostructural position belongs to the single most powerful strand of belief that permeates mainstream American culture, that whatever their social stations, Americans should choose their goals for themselves and then determine the most appropriate means for pursuing them.

In the end, however, the macrostructural argument attacks the culture of poverty thesis more persuasively than it builds an alternative explanation for the persistence of an underclass. Consider its claims about underclass rationality. If inner-city schools are ineffective and unresponsive to the community, there may indeed be a rationale for underclass parents to ignore their children's schools. But there is an obvious difficulty: a situation in which one does not attend to the education of one's children is manifestly irrational.

Nor is the ghetto-specific male role unequivocally adaptive. The young men forgo the joys, sense of accomplishment, and social status that come with responsible parenthood. On occasion, an exasperated mother may even tell her son, "I wish I'd had another girl." As for older men, to para-

11. Wilson (1987), pp. 32, 39; see also Wilson (1988), pp. 5, 18.
12. Hannerz (1969), p. 76.
13. Wilson (1987), pp. 145–46.

phrase Thomas Hobbes, life is often nasty, increasingly brutish, and relatively short: "Middle age may meet . . . [the man] well on the road downhill to alcoholism, isolation and poor health, while his ability to live up to his role, with sex, toughness, and all, becomes progressively more impaired. Several of the men [I observed] . . . were obviously near death." [14]

The macrostructural thesis also suffers from its limited, indeed epiphenomenal, view of culture. Because apparently dysfunctional behaviors are treated as responses to a lack of jobs, underclass behavior is expected to change with improving prospects. [15] This claim, however, asserts causal relationships that run from an economic condition—more employment—to a change in gender roles. Such a linkage is so long and complex that there is substantial room for intervening factors to prevent change. Nor can one simply assume that causality operates in just one direction, such that most members of the underclass will react automatically to economic change.

My intention here is not to depict people as blindly and unshakably attached to cultural values. On the contrary, the point is that underclass norms may persist even after jobs become available *precisely because the norms are rational*—that is, beneficial in the short run and in the environment in which they have been put into practice. What the world of work offers may seem uncertain. There is, in fact, a complex trade-off between the sure and immediate advantages of ghetto practices and a mere probability that taking an entry-level job will lead to a better life in the future. [16]

This same inattention to culture may help account for the apparent difficulties in Wilson's policy proposals for a tight labor market and more liberal family allowances. Policies that create tight labor markets and force employers to hire underclass workers are also likely to create politically embarrassing inflationary pressures. If the monetary authorities react by cooling down the economy, newly hired underclass workers may well be the first to be fired because they would still have the fewest relevant skills. A broad family allowance program that supports many people in different classes would be a costly way to address the underclass predicament. Because that would force unpopular tax increases, any such program could survive, even in a generous budgetary climate, only by

14. Hannerz (1969), pp. 87, 96.
15. Wilson (1987), p. 14, note 48.
16. Hannerz (1969), p. 183.

defining its recipients very restrictively. But that step would constitute the mainstream backlash that Wilson is rightly trying to avoid.

The Connection between Culture and Rationality

Thus neither the culture of poverty nor the structural thesis provides clear policy guidance. And neither is correct when it treats rationality as dichotomous. The point here is not that cultural and structural theorists consistently attribute all underclass behavior either to rational calculation or to value commitments. Ricketts and Sawhill suggest a complex interaction between the two factors, and Wilson himself rejects any "rigid either/or line." [17] But however their relative influence is assessed, rationality and culture are still treated as essentially separate: rationality refers to calculated adaptations to prevailing circumstances, and culture refers to stable values and beliefs. But any adequate concept of culture must refer, among other things, to those elements of human life that contribute to the effective exercise of human intelligence. Thus to speak of culture is necessarily to speak of human rationality.

Without the claim that the underclass's irrational culture, or subculture, is sharply distinct from that of the mainstream, the culture of poverty thesis loses its point. If such a sharp disjunction exists, then mainstream observers must overcome it if they are truly to understand and accurately report on the underclass's relevant values, concepts, and behaviors. Only then can they know that they have correctly translated the discourse with which much of underclass life is carried on. It turns out that one can count on having made such a correct translation only if one attributes to such a culture both the presence of logical canons and logical terms very much like those of the mainstream and the presence of certain skills that make instrumental activity possible.[18]

As Hannerz suggests, cultures include wide arrays of skills as well as

17. Ricketts and Sawhill (1986); and Wilson (1988), p. 46.

18. The specific question is whether the language has the equivalent of such logical operators as "not," "and," "or," and so on. Observers' options here are limited. If they answer that these operators are present, then underclass culture clearly has a rational component. Of course, they may deny that the operators are present, but if the discourse actually has them, the observers have overlooked them and mistranslated the discourse. In that case, claims about the irrationality of underclass culture also become suspect. If observers are correct and there really are no such operators, then there is, in fact, no translatable discourse at all. I mean by natural language only those sets of symbols that include the logical operators and other features necessary for all complex communication; one ordinarily does not speak of a culture when such communication is lacking.

values and preferences, rituals and artistic activities. Some skills are essential for logical analysis; some facilitate the pursuit of particular goals; others help the community produce intelligible accounts of its experiences. One could hardly say that a community had a real culture if it lacked these tools. To deny the presence of these elements of rationality is thus to deny the presence of a culture. In sum, talk about a broadly irrational culture is incoherent.

Of course, a particular culture may include some values that are self-defeating or dysfunctional from some perspective. But that possibility does not and cannot make the whole culture irrational. The issue instead must be the adequacy of particular tools or skills. Cultures primarily differ, then, not in their rationality, but in the usefulness of the tools—logical, instrumental, and interpretive—with which they address particular problems.

This basic argument, moreover, suggests that, like the culture of poverty thesis, the structural perspective overlooks the link between human rationality and human culture. If culture and rationality are tightly bound together, then the presence of rational activities and social practices indicates the presence of a culture. And if rational underclass practices are woven into a stable culture, they may not be surrendered very easily.

The Underclass Impasse

Each side of the cultural-structural debate offers a real insight into the condition of the underclass. Yet each seems seriously flawed. As the discussion so far suggests, the problem is not just social inequality and constraints but a devastating gulf between underclass and mainstream life. Accordingly, any program for change must foster communication between the mainstream and underclass cultures instead of simply replacing the latter with the former.

Just here, however, the policy recommendations of the two sides are most wanting. Given its moralistic emphasis on destructive values, the culture of poverty thesis makes the underclass largely responsible for transforming itself. There is little need for mutual interchange or any affirmative action by mainstream society and its government. Although the structural thesis calls for drastic action, in Wilson's formulation that action is mainly impersonal and technical. It would manipulate the national economy to tighten up the national labor market and develop a supplementary program of family allowances presumably to be controlled by formal rules and administered by an impersonal bureaucracy.

The picture of the underclass developed here is different from both these views. Not only is there a significant overlap between mainstream culture and underclass subculture, but the subculture exhibits both instrumental and interpretive rationality. Quite apart from its esthetic and religious achievements,[19] it has helped render underclass life intelligible, and it offers ways to secure some self-esteem, sociability, and the opportunity for relatively stable, if mainly single-parent, families. These strengths, together with the American devotion to local autonomy, argue for careful attention to the inner city's existing cultural realities.

On the other side, in some respects the underclass's skills, measured either by its own aspirations or by mainstream standards, are inadequate. Even the rational adaptations to its circumstances often hinder its members' efforts to make their way in mainstream culture and society. These difficulties lead to a profound cultural isolation. One consequence is instrumental: an unease with, and often fear of, the mainstream world that makes pursuing social and occupational success even more difficult. A second effect is intrinsic: a lack of exposure to those features of mainstream culture such as literacy that are inherently valuable. In other words, underclass people need skills clearly different from ghetto-specific orientations, skills that can only be acquired through a process sensitive to these cultural differences.

The Multicultural Perspective

These considerations culminate in an alternative policy approach that is based on the following simple claim: all cultures offer ways to solve human problems rationally, but some problems are more effectively addressed in one way than in another. Some relevant and effective skills belong to a mainstream world that members of the underclass find foreign and discriminatory. Indeed, this foreignness suggests that the process of acquiring the skills of mainstream culture must begin in early childhood with Head Start or similar programs and continue well into adolescence. Without such programs, even the best-intentioned parental and community involvement in underclass schools may be insufficient. The emphasis on Head Start is familiar to anyone acquainted with discussions of the underclass. What must be done is to make explicit the general criteria that such programs should satisfy.

19. Wilson (1987), pp. 8–9; and Hannerz (1969), pp. 144–56, 188–90.

The first criterion is a broadly pluralist outlook. The concept of rationality is sufficiently complex to accommodate very different skills. In particular, the strengths of the underclass subculture mean that, at least for the intermediate term, program efforts should add to existing skills, not replace them. It must add them in part by involving parents and other members of the community. The aim, according to Hannerz, is to create a repertoire of genuinely bicultural skills that combine the best of what both the mainstream and underclass cultures have to offer. As Hannerz notes, the people he studied in the 1960s generally followed a mainstream life-style in terms of employment and family relations. Nevertheless, they were "familiar with a large body of ghetto-specific culture," and could "identify with at least part of it as in some ways their own." [20]

Second, because of the complexity of the underclass's problem, a criterion for successful programs is that educational intervention should be as radical as Wilson's proposals are for economic intervention. In particular, these programs must go well beyond what is offered by the conventional kindergarten through twelfth grade educational system. They must address the acculturation of the child to both the underclass subculture and mainstream culture from early years through adolescence. If the place to begin is indeed an expanded Head Start program, the effort surely cannot end there.

Finally, a program of this sort must be politically feasible, that is, be supported outside the inner cities. There are three reasons for thinking that radical educational intervention would arouse both limited opposition and attract considerable support, even if the program were focused mainly on racial minorities. Poor children, who cannot readily be blamed for their plight, are relatively popular beneficiaries. A more general reason follows from the legitimating ideology of the American regime. That ideology insists on both political equality and equality of economic and social opportunity, even as it affirms human rationality as a warrant for individual freedom and links that freedom to moral accountability. The existence of a deprived and isolated underclass violates every tenet of that creed. Finally, this proposal appeals directly to a major tradition in mainstream American culture. The concern with the cultivation of human faculties sustained the antislavery crusade, other antebellum moral reform movements, and women's rights. It then supported socially conscious Progressives and the 1960s movements, including those devoted to civil rights and feminist issues. From the standpoint of this tradition, the per-

20. Hannerz (1969), pp. 38–40, 192.

408   J. DAVID GREENSTONE

sistence of the underclass is a scandal, not primarily because its members cannot get what they want, as the macrostructural thesis argues, but because they are denied the opportunity to develop their intellectual, artistic, and physical abilities according to socially shared standards of competence and excellence.[21] Given a belief in self-development, this tradition can combine a devotion to such standards with a pluralist recognition of the cultural achievements of the underclass.

The watchword here is a respect for the integrity and morality of both persons and communities, rather than a simple deference to individual preferences. Especially on so pressing and complex an issue, such a concern deserves our attention. Our object, after all, is not just to assist the underclass. We must also redeem mainstream American culture by helping it honor its own deepest commitments.

21. Greenstone (1982, 1988).

References

Dahrendorf, Ralf. 1987. "The Underclass and the Future of Great Britain." Lecture delivered at Windsor Castle, England, April 27.
Geertz, Clifford. 1973. *The Interpretation of Cultures: Selected Essays.* Basic Books.
Greenstein, Robert. 1985. "Losing Faith in 'Losing Ground.'" *New Republic,* March 25, pp. 12–17.
Greenstone, J. David. 1982. "The Transient and Permanent in American Politics: Standards, Interests, and the Concept of 'Public.'" In *Public Values and Private Power in American Politics,* edited by J. David Greenstone. University of Chicago Press.
———. 1988. "Against Simplicity: The Cultural Dimensions of the Constitution." *University of Chicago Law Review* (June).
Hannerz, Ulf. 1969. *Soulside: Inquiries into Ghetto Culture and Community.* Columbia University Press.
Murray, Charles. 1984. *Losing Ground: American Social Policy, 1950–1980.* Basic Books.
Ricketts, Erol R., and Isabel Sawhill. 1986. "Defining and Measuring the Underclass." Washington: Urban Institute discussion paper.
Wilson, William Julius. 1987. *The Truly Disadvantaged: The Inner City, the Underclass and Public Policy.* University of Chicago Press.
———. 1988. "The American Underclass: Inner-City Ghettos and the Norms of Citizenship." Paper prepared for the Godkin lecture, Harvard University.

Part Five
The Policy Response

Targeting within Universalism: Politically Viable Policies to Combat Poverty in the United States

THEDA SKOCPOL

WHAT TO DO about poverty is, once again, on the public agenda in the United States. Just a few years back, academics and research funders, whipsawed by backlashes against the War on Poverty and the Moynihan report, averted their attention from poverty and other race-related social ills. Then Charles Murray's broadsides against federal social policies in *Losing Ground* provoked outraged critics to enter the fray again; and William Julius Wilson's *The Truly Disadvantaged* revalidated discussion of "the underclass" by progressives as well as conservatives.[1] Now analysts are looking closely and talking frankly about the full range of social problems and policy solutions connected to poverty, including severe inner-city black poverty.

This new interest is good news for citizens who want to strengthen public efforts against poverty. But there are also reasons to worry, and not only because the overall tone of academic and political discourse is much less optimistic than in the 1960s. Recent debates have been imbued with presumptions of a national budget crisis, with cynicism about what government can do, and with extreme pessimism about the intractability of the problems of the inner-city poor. Thus those who want to do more to fight poverty are understandably concerned that their proposals may be stalled or perverted into purely disciplinary measures. Yet they also need to worry about how much the policy prescriptions they are debating recapitulate the flawed presumptions and tactics of the War on Poverty and the Great Society. If supporters of new social policies do find openings in the near future, they need to do better politically than did the antipoverty warriors of the 1960s and early 1970s, whose best intentions were not realized. It is not clear, however, that current debates about poverty and welfare are breaking enough new ground to make politically successful policy innovations likely.

1. Murray (1984); and Wilson (1987).

Just as the mainstream debates in the 1960s presumed that hard-core, long-term poverty was largely caused by behavioral problems or deficient skills that could be corrected by special training and community action programs, the welfare reform consensus of the mid-1980s quickly seized on the idea that the ills of the poor could be cured by mandated work and job training tacked on to existing welfare programs, perhaps supplemented with a year or so of child care and medical coverage for those making the transition from welfare.[2] During the 1960s many liberal professionals focused on rehabilitating young people; today many would accept Lisbeth Schorr's call to expand intensive and comprehensive programs targeted at impoverished families with babies and young children.[3] Similarly, after the War on Poverty got under way, many activists wanted programs to concentrate on helping poor blacks in particular; today one still hears voices such as Roger Wilkins's arguing that, because the black poor are "different," special antipoverty policies should be devised for them alone.[4] Finally, just as advocates for lower-income Americans during the Johnson and first Nixon presidencies argued for directing more benefits and services to all lower-income people, so some redistribution-minded progressives are now making similar proposals for a much larger national safety net without gaping holes.[5]

Universal versus Targeted Social Policies

Along with the small chorus of academic and political voices advocating welfare reforms or new programs and benefits targeted on low-income people (or special sectors of the poor), there are a few voices trying to sing a different tune. Proposing "universalism" rather than targeting, they argue that renewed efforts to deal with the plight of the poor, including the inner-city black poor, ought to be occasions for launching or redesigning U.S. social provision in general. The aim ought to be to ameliorate poverty through broader social programs that include whites

2. The mood of this consensus is captured in Kaus (1986).
3. Schorr (1988).
4. Wilkins (1989).
5. Sar A. Levitan and Clifford M. Johnson (1984) suggested cutting back public benefits to the middle class to fund comprehensive job training and public employment programs for the poor. Frances Fox Piven and Richard A. Cloward (1987), p. 99, argued that AFDC, unemployment insurance, and supplemental security income should be merged into a more comprehensive, financially generous, and nationally uniform system of social provision for the poor that would be without bureaucratic hassles. See also Russell (1989).

along with people of color, and middle-class citizens along with economically disadvantaged Americans.

This position has been forcefully argued by William Wilson in *The Truly Disadvantaged,* a book embodying a paradoxical message that needs to be heard with all of its nuances. The first part of the message has already been heard: that renewed attention must be given to the multiple pathologies and special problems of the inner-city black underclass, which constitutes about 10 percent of all of the poor.[6] But the second part does not follow simple-mindedly from the first. If vivid facts about severe social problems were all that mattered in shaping policy prescriptions, Wilson's focus on the truly disadvantaged would constitute a call for more finely targeted public policies. Yet he sharply criticizes both racially specific measures to aid blacks and redistributive socioeconomic programs to help lower-income people in general. Racially targeted policies primarily help socially advantaged blacks, he argues, while benefits or services restricted to the poor cannot generate sustained political support: "especially when the national economy is in a period of little growth, no growth, or decline . . . the more the public programs are perceived by members of the wider society as benefiting only certain groups, the less support those programs receive." Following this politically grounded logic, Wilson concludes that the *"hidden agenda is to improve the life chances of groups such as the ghetto underclass by emphasizing programs . . . [to] which the more advantaged groups of all races can positively relate."* [7]

Supporters of targeted antipoverty policies have arguments against such universalism. Widespread benefits, it is often said, are expensive, and Americans will not pay taxes to fund them. Furthermore, it is sometimes claimed that universal programs, whether benefits or services, give most of the available resources to those who need them least, either to those already in the middle class or, through the well-known phenomenon of "creaming," to those within the low-income population who are already best prepared to improve themselves. According to the advocates of targeted programs, the social problems now faced by America's most impoverished people, especially female-headed black families in inner cities, can be ameliorated only by highly concentrated and comprehensive benefits and social services devised especially for the poor.[8]

Rarely, however, do advocates of targeted benefits or specially tailored

6. Ellwood (1988).
7. Wilson (1987), pp. 118, 120.
8. See Russell (1989), p. 17; Schorr (1988), pp. xxiv–vi; and Wilkins (1989), p. A23.

public social services face up to the problem of finding sustained political support for them. Implicitly relying on altruistic appeals to Americans who want to help the disadvantaged, they do not explain why working-class families with incomes just above the poverty line, themselves frequently struggling economically without the aid of health insurance or child care or adequate unemployment benefits, should pay for programs that go only to people with incomes below the poverty line. Neither do these advocates explain why the American middle and working classes will not simply want to write off troubled inner-city people, or else use repressive agencies—police departments, prisons, and a "war against drugs"—to deal with their threatening behaviors. Some voters feel better about punishing the underclass than about helping it. More broadly, and especially in America, the poor serve as a negative example against which those who "make it on their own" and "earn their own way" can define themselves. Regrettable or not, this attitude is unlikely to change. Such stereotyping of the poor helps to explain why cross-national research on social expenditures has found that universal programs are more sustainable in democracies, even if they are more expensive than policies targeted solely on the poor or other "marginal" groups.[9]

Are we left, then, with a standoff in which advocates of universalism and advocates of targeting can each explain cogently why the other's prescriptions will not adequately help the truly disadvantaged? This standoff certainly exists as long as we remain at the level of logical or highly speculative arguments. Yet three conclusions can be drawn by examining the history of public policies dealing with, or including, poor people in the United States. First, when U.S. antipoverty efforts have featured policies targeted on the poor alone, they have not been politically sustainable, and they have stigmatized and demeaned the poor. Second, some kinds of relatively universal social policies have been politically very successful. Third, room has been made *within* certain universal policy frameworks for extra benefits and services that disproportionately help less privileged people without stigmatizing them. What I shall call "targeting within universalism" has delivered extra benefits and special services to certain poor people throughout the history of modern American social provision, and new versions of it could be devised today to revitalize and redirect U.S. public social provision.

9. See Korpi (1980); and Rosenberry (1982). Of course, targeted programs may succeed politically when their beneficiaries are relatively privileged—witness U.S. federal programs such as tax subsidies for private homeowners and parity payments to commercial farmers.

The Travails of Targeted Policies

Without plunging into a detailed discussion of all the government strategies devised in the United States for coping with the poor, I will consider some of the most important initiatives: poorhouses in the nineteenth century, the mothers' pensions launched in the 1910s, and the War on Poverty and associated Great Society reforms of the late 1960s and early 1970s. In each instance, reformers' high hopes of helping poor people were soon dashed against rock-hard political realities.

Poorhouses as a Failed Reform Effort

Poorhouses are the best example of a targeted antipoverty policy in the nineteenth century. Part of a general proliferation of institutions to reform people thought to be defective in a period when the disciplines of the market, wage labor, and political citizenship were being established for the majority, almshouses were intended to "cut the expense of poor relief and deter potential paupers" and at the same time "mitigate the harshness of contemporary poor relief practice by ending the auctioning of the poor to the lowest bidder and stopping the shunting of the poor from town to town regardless of their health or the weather." [10] Almshouses were also expected to improve the character and behavior of the poor: work "would be mandatory for all inmates neither too sick nor too feeble, and both idleness and alcohol would be prohibited. Able-bodied men would be pruned rigorously from the relief rolls; begging would be barred and punished; [and] children would be schooled. . . ."[11] Fueled by all these hopes, the movement for poor houses peppered them across most of the settled areas of the country (except the rural South) before the Civil War.

But by the 1850s it had become clear that poorhouses were not working as intended and a "preoccupation with order, routine, and cost replaced the founders' concern with the transformation of character and social reform." [12] Intended to cut costs (although in practice it cost more, not less, to maintain people in institutions rather than homes), few poorhouses were adequately funded. They failed to help needy inmates and quickly became prey to corrupt managers who made special deals with

10. Katz (1986), pp. 22–23.
11. Katz (1986), p. 22.
12. Katz (1986), p. 25. The following account draws on Katz, chap. 1 and the rest of part 1.

merchants and doctors. Appropriate work was often not devised for able-bodied paupers, and the very young, the old, and the insane were simply shut up and often exploited. Furthermore, poorhouses did not always discipline poor people, some of whom learned to come and go as they wished in response to the ebb and flow of outside opportunities.

Before long, poorhouses lost the support of reformers and the public. New movements were launched to abolish all public assistance for the able-bodied and to create more specialized institutions for subgroups such as orphans and the insane. Surviving poorhouses served mainly as miserable warnings to working people to avoid dependency at all costs. By the turn of the century, poorhouses were principally old-age homes for those unlucky enough to lack resources and family ties. Meanwhile, destitution and dependency proliferated along with industrialism, and the poor, including the able-bodied men who were supposed to have been cured in (or by the example of) almshouses, became more of a problem than ever.

The Marginalization of Pensions for Mothers

Laws allowing local jurisdictions to give benefits to impoverished widowed mothers (and sometimes other caretakers) in charge of dependent children were passed in forty states between 1911 and 1920 and in four more before 1931.[13] The legislation was enthusiastically urged on state legislatures by federations of local clubs whose members were elite and middle-class married women.[14] Local, state, and national associations within the National Congress of Mothers, the General Federation of Women's Clubs, and the Women's Christian Temperance Union argued that all mothers should be honored for their child-nurturing service and, like disabled veteran soldiers, should be adequately and honorably supported by government when breadwinner husbands were not available. Impoverished widowed mothers, the women's associations insisted, should not have to do low-wage labor to survive; and they should not have to give up their children to custodial institutions. Above all, they should not be stigmatized as paupers.

Despite generous intentions and broad popular support, mothers' pensions evolved into one of the most socially demeaning and poorly funded

13. Children's Bureau (1933), p. 2.
14. A full account of the role of women's associations in the campaign for mothers' pensions will appear in Skocpol (in progress), chap. 7.

parts of modern U.S. social provision.[15] The pensions were implemented only in certain (predominantly nonrural) jurisdictions, leaving many widowed mothers, including most nonwhites, unable even to apply for benefits. Where these pensions were established, the programs were starved for funds by communities reluctant to spend taxpayers' money on the poor. Consequently, benefit levels were set so low that many clients could not avoid working for wages or taking in male boarders, activities that could open clients up to charges of child neglect or immorality. Social workers, whose organizations had originally opposed mothers' pensions, moved in to become local administrators and caseworkers. Acutely sensitive to possible accusations of political corruption and lacking sufficient resources to help more than a few of the needy applicants, they applied eligibility rules and "proper home" investigations with a vengeance. Before long, these conditions turned the pensions into an often cumbersome and demeaning form of public welfare.

When mothers' pensions were federalized as aid to dependent children (ADC) under the Social Security Act of 1935, benefit levels and administrative procedures remained decentralized and the tradition of inadequate funding continued. Indeed, at first, the federal government offered only one-third matching funds to the states. The 1939 amendments to the act increased the federal proportion to one-half but removed from ADC the very "worthy widows" who had originally been the focus of reformers' efforts. Surviving dependents of contributing workers were to be covered by social security's old age and survivors' insurance, leaving poorer caretakers of children—increasingly women without morally approved family histories—to be helped by ADC (which later became aid to families with dependent children, or AFDC). Nationwide support never burgeoned for this program as it did for old age insurance. Benefits remained low and their distribution geographically uneven. And traditions of surveillance established by social workers became even more intrusive once southerners, blacks, and unmarried mothers began to represent a significant number of clients. Directly contradicting the original sponsors' intentions, mothers' pensions-ADC-AFDC evolved into the core program of what is today pejoratively known as "welfare."

Limits of the "War on Poverty"

Efforts to erase poverty again came to the fore in American politics (indeed, reached an unprecedented visibility and scale) during the admin-

15. For an overview of the historical development of mothers' pensions, aid to dependent children, and aid to families with dependent children, see Bell (1965).

istrations of John F. Kennedy, Lyndon Johnson, and Richard Nixon. The nonelderly poor were the visible targets, especially of the widely trumpeted War on Poverty. Once again reformers dreamed of reeducating the poor to take advantage of economic opportunities, especially by reforming juvenile delinquents, giving children a head start and better schools, and offering job training to adults.[16] After the winding down of the War on Poverty, a major role of the Johnson administration's Great Society was to ensure improved access to medical care for the nonelderly poor and the elderly in general. The Nixon administration witnessed large increases in transfers to the poor. Overall, "federal expenditures for cash and in-kind transfers directly targeted to the poor almost tripled from the end of FY 1969 through FY 1974, with most of the increase not in cash assistance, but in programs such as food stamps, medicaid, housing subsidies, and student aid."[17] Aid to families with dependent children was also expanded in these years as states eased eligibility rules in response to changing federal regulations and attempted to make clients eligible for more generous federally subsidized benefits linked to AFDC.[18]

An evaluation of the 1960s and 1970s initiatives against poverty must be mixed. Many people were helped. Elderly Americans, including the elderly poor, benefited enormously from medicare, increases in social security, and the nationalization of residual need-based old-age assistance through the supplemental security income program passed in 1974. Community action programs launched many local black activists into political careers. And "the expansion of cash and in-kind transfers . . . directly benefited substantial numbers of poor women and minorities and their families. The number of female-headed families receiving welfare . . . rose from 635,000 in 1961 (or 29 percent of all such families) to almost 3 million by 1979 (or 50 percent of female-headed families)."[19] Economic expansion between 1965 and 1972 lifted out of poverty perhaps only one-tenth of the 21.3 percent of Americans who were below the poverty line in 1965; government programs lifted more than half of the rest above the poverty line.[20]

But both the service strategies and the transfer strategies of the Kennedy, Johnson, and Nixon years failed to reduce poverty rates much among the nonelderly, and certainly failed to reverse such specifically

16. Katz (1986), chap. 9; and Patterson (1981), part 3.
17. Brown (1988), p. 193.
18. Patterson (1981), chap. 11; and Albritton (1979).
19. Brown (1988), p. 194.
20. Schwarz (1983), pp. 34–35.

worrisome trends as the increase in out-of-wedlock births and families sustained only by mothers. Antipoverty warriors can argue that not nearly enough was done or spent to make either services or transfers sufficient to end poverty or to reduce pathologies among the severely disadvantaged.[21] But the antipoverty services and increased expenditures for the nonelderly poor quickly generated political backlashes that ended possibilities for their continuation and improvement. To the degree that antipoverty service efforts were associated with the community action programs that tried to mobilize poor people, especially blacks, these efforts were quickly deemphasized by Johnson, who was chagrined at the anger of local Democratic political leaders, and by Nixon, who was elected through rising discontent with Johnson's domestic and foreign policies and was not about to channel services through urban politicians.[22] In unfavorable political climates, surviving social service programs were also highly vulnerable to charges of corruption.

More significantly, even the broader income transfers emphasized by the Johnson and Nixon administrations backfired politically against lower-income Americans, blacks, and the Democratic party, contributing to Jimmy Carter's retrenchments and then to the rise of Ronald Reagan and of fierce conservative intellectual and political attacks against federal social programs. During the 1970s, public opinion polls recorded that support was decreasing for government efforts to aid minorities and for public social spending, especially on service programs popularly identified with poor blacks.[23] Blacks in general remained staunchly Democratic and in favor of strengthened government social programs. Meanwhile, union members, white urban ethnics, and white southerners moved away from the Democratic party, especially in presidential elections. The perceived position of the party on racial and welfare issues contributed to these defections.[24]

This political situation was rooted in a split between the people who apparently benefited most from the changes in social policy in the 1960s and early 1970s and the people who had to pay higher taxes during the 1970s and into the 1980s. Although many working-class and middle-class families surely gained from increases in social benefits to their elderly relatives, they have not perceived gains to themselves from increased welfare transfers to the poor. Meanwhile, they faced rising finan-

21. See Schwarz (1983); and Levitan and Taggart (1976).
22. Patterson (1981), pp. 146–48.
23. Some poll results are summarized in Brown (1988), p. 198.
24. Petrocik (1981), pp. 126–32, 139–43.

cial burdens attributable to higher bites from payroll taxes, the effects of inflation and bracket creep on federal income taxes, and increases in state and local taxes. These tax increases for average workers "occurred in the context of an inflationary economy and thus a steady erosion of real income. Over the 1970s, median real family income declined by 16 percent, while regressive taxes were rising. What developed was a pincers effect on blue-collar and middle-income white-collar workers and their families: declining real income combined with a rising tax burden that appeared to yield no tangible benefits. Little wonder that [such people] began to desert the Democratic party and display hostility toward the welfare programs of the 1960s." [25]

And little wonder that many working-class and middle-class Americans found Ronald Reagan's tax cuts and his generalized attacks on government's social role appealing. Although Reagan's efforts were not as successful as is often supposed, the political and intellectual discourse of the 1980s expressed and reinforced widespread hostility toward big government and "throwing money" at poor people. Thus it seems highly unlikely that further redistributive benefits or intensive services targeted on the poor alone can succeed politically. We still live amidst the backlash against the War on Poverty and the Great Society.

Some Successes of Cross-Class Social Policies

If social policies targeted exclusively on the poor have not fared well politically, more universal policies that have spread costs and visibly delivered benefits across classes and races have recurrently flourished. Broad political coalitions have developed to protect and extend these policies, which have also been managed by federal agencies skilled in the arts of public relations and legislative maneuvering. What is more, universal policies have also sustained moral imageries within which specific programs could redistribute income and deliver special services to certain groups of disadvantaged Americans without risking public disaffection. During much of the past century, public education has helped the poor as well as more privileged children at local levels. Yet here I want to focus on federal social policies. Civil War benefits of the late nineteenth and early twentieth centuries, the Sheppard-Towner program for maternity and neonatal health education of 1921–29, and the broadly construed social security system since the 1960s are national or federal-state policies that exemplify what I call targeting within universalism.

25. Brown (1988), p. 198.

Civil War Benefits

Civil War benefits are not often considered a part of U.S. public social provision, but they should be. From the 1870s through the early 1900s, an originally delimited program of military disability and survivors' benefits evolved into a massively expensive de facto system of disability, old-age, and survivors' benefits for all American men who could demonstrate merely minimal service time in the Union armies.[26] The expansion of Civil War pensions, which sopped up from one-fifth to one-third of the federal budget between the 1880s and the 1910s, was fueled by political party competition in late-nineteenth-century patronage democracy and financed by huge "surpluses" from protective tariffs. By 1910 about 29 percent of American men 65 years of age or older (along with 8 percent of elderly women and various younger women, children, and other dependents of deceased men) were receiving old-age pensions not based on need that were remarkably generous by contemporary international standards.[27]

To be sure, Civil War pensions involved ethnic and regional biases partially correlated with differences in socioeconomic status. The benefits went to native-born northerners and to northern and central Europeans who had immigrated to the North before the 1860s, categories that by the late nineteenth century were disporportionately likely to include farmers, middle-class employees, and skilled workers. Left out of the system were southern whites and most southern blacks, disproportionately farmers and tenants, along with post–Civil War immigrants who tended to be from southern and central Europe and who mostly took unskilled industrial jobs. Nevertheless, the pensions were awarded to many blacks because more than 186,000, some of them freed slaves, had constituted 9 to 10 percent of the Union armies, and they or their survivors were fully eligible. In general, too, the pensions helped many poor whites, including people who had been relatively low-paid farmers and workers and those who had fared better during their working lives but then became impoverished when they lost income and family ties in old age.

Within the overall system of Civil War benefits, moreover, additional aid was available to the poorest veterans and their dependents, especially through the states. Some, such as Massachusetts, offered generous public

26. The story is told in Glasson (1918); McMurry (1922); and Sanders (1980).
27. The discussion in this and the following paragraph is documented in Skocpol (forthcoming), chap. 3.

assistance to needy veterans in their own homes.[28] And starting in 1888 the federal government offered subsidies for state-run veterans' homes, encouraging their establishment in twenty-eight states. By 1910 national and state institutions housed 31,830 Union veterans, about 5 percent of those still living (some served veterans' dependents as well). The men were typically former skilled workers; there were also some former unskilled workers and farmers, but very few from middle-class occupations.[29]

The generous Civil War benefits were unequivocally honorable and were defined in explicit opposition to poor relief. The argument was that they had been *earned*. The 1888 Republican platform urged that benefits "be so enlarged and extended as to provide against the possibility that any man who honorably wore the Federal uniform shall become the inmate of an almshouse, or dependent upon private charity. . . . [I]t would be a public scandal to do less for those whose valorous service preserved the government." [30] Similarly, the Massachusetts statutes concerning aid to veterans and their dependents proclaimed that their purpose was to help worthy persons "who would otherwise be receiving relief under the pauper laws." [31]

Arguments such as these convinced many northern voters and legislators. Broad political coalitions, spearheaded by the Grand Army of the Republic and supported by many native-born voters in towns and rural areas across the northern states, campaigned for ever-improved benefits.[32] Mostly these campaigns bore political fruit through the Republican party, yet they also gained the support of many northern Democratic legislators who could not afford to let Republicans outdo them in bidding for votes. That the benefits were bestowed as ostensible rewards for service also made it easy for individual recipients to take pensions (or public assistance or a place in an asylum) during what was supposedly the preeminent era of "rugged individualism" in American history. As Commissioner of Pensions Green B. Raum explained in 1891, "an old soldier can receive a pension as a recognition of honorable service with a feeling of pride, while he would turn his back with shame upon an offer of charity." [33]

28. Massachusetts Bureau of Statistics (1916), pp. 16, 34.
29. Cetina (1977), chap. 10.
30. Johnson (1978), p. 82.
31. Massachusetts Bureau of Statistics (1916), p. 30.
32. Sanders (1980).
33. Raum (1891), p. 207.

In sum, the politically viable Civil War benefits not only reached many disabled and elderly Americans, including some of the truly needy, but they did so in ways that bolstered society's esteem for the beneficiaries. So popular were these benefits that they eventually reached more than 90 percent of surviving veterans. Despite vociferous attacks against the political corruption that pension expenditures supposedly expressed, the benefits persisted until the generation of men who received them died out.

Health Education Services for Mothers and Babies

During the early twentieth century, state legislatures established mothers' pensions, child labor laws, and protective labor laws for women workers. Congress established the federal Children's Bureau in 1912, and the Federal Act for the Promotion of Welfare and Hygiene of Maternity and Infancy of 1921, better known as the Sheppard-Towner Act.[34] These "maternalist" measures were promoted by political coalitions that included educated reformers, trade unionists, and geographically widespread associations of elite and middle-class married women, and they were understood as extensions of mother love into the public sphere. Although all the policies had cross-class backing and universalistic justification, some of them, such as mothers' pensions, were finally focused on the poor alone, while others, such as the Children's Bureau and Sheppard-Towner programs, aimed at more broadly defined clienteles. The Sheppard-Towner programs expanded rapidly for some years and reached many especially needy people through efforts that never became stigmatized (as mothers' pensions unfortunately did).

The Children's Bureau was established in 1912 to "investigate and report . . . upon all matters pertaining to the welfare of children and child life among all classes of our people."[35] The bureau's chief, Julia Lathrop, mobilized women's associations and reform groups across the nation on behalf of improved birth and infant mortality statistics and public health measures for mothers and children. Working with the women's associations, Lathrop also mobilized broad public support to persuade Congress to enlarge the bureau's budget and increase its personnel.[36] After several years she began organizing similar support for the passage of what eventually became the Sheppard-Towner Act of 1921. Significantly, even

34. These summary remarks are documented in Skocpol (forthcoming), chaps. 5–8.
35. The text of the enabling act appears in Children's Bureau, *First Annual Report of the Chief* (1914), p. 2.
36. Parker and Carpenter (1981).

though her aim was to reach out to underprivileged mothers (especially in remote rural areas), Lathrop deliberately decided against a narrowly targeted program and arranged for the measures debated in Congress to carry an explanatory clause stressing that "the act is not a charity." If the services of the bill were not open to all, Lathrop believed, they would "degenerate into poor relief." [37]

The Children's Bureau was able to reach large numbers of American mothers through Sheppard-Towner, just as it had done in its previous programs. During seven years of administering the act, the bureau coordinated nationwide efforts that distributed 22 million pieces of literature, conducted 183,000 health conferences, established some 3,000 prenatal centers, and visited more than 3 million homes. [38] "Women from every geographic region, social class, and educational background wrote to the bureau as many as 125,000 letters a year," according to Molly Ladd-Taylor, and by 1929 the bureau "estimated that one-half of U.S. babies had benefited from the government's childrearing information." [39] Yet at the same time, the bureau was also effectively targeting poorly educated white and nonwhite mothers in rural areas for special help through consultations with public health nurses and clinics, and through conferences sponsored by the act. While allowing wide state-to-state variation in program design, the bureau's leadership prodded all states to improve birth statistics and channel resources toward places where infant and maternal mortality rates were highest. [40] As a result, many state programs did emphasize delivering public health information and services to rural areas and small towns.

Despite its successes in targeting within universalism, the Sheppard-Towner program cannot stand as an unequivocally successful social policy because Congress refused to make the act (briefly extended in 1927) permanent. To be sure, there was never a strong political backlash against it: it remained broadly popular with American women, and most of the elite and middle-class women's associations that had backed the law continued throughout the 1920s to lobby Congress on behalf of its extension. Many states continued Sheppard-Towner programs in new ways

37. Covotsos (1976), p. 123. Covotsos quotes from a letter by Julia Lathrop to Bleeker Marquette, December 1, 1920, Children's Bureau papers, drawer 408, National Archives, Washington.

38. Ladd-Taylor (1986), p. 28.

39. Ladd-Taylor (1986), p. 2.

40. Rothman (1978), pp. 140–41; Costin (1983), p. 136; and Children's Bureau, *Annual Reports*, 1922–29.

after the federal matching funds disappeared. And after a few years the federal program itself was revived through the Social Security Act of 1935. By the late 1920s, however, private physicians wanted to take over prenatal and postnatal health counseling themselves, and their local associations, affiliated with the American Medical Association, helped persuade President Hoover and some congressional leaders to kill the original program in legislative maneuvers.[41]

Sheppard-Towner was vulnerable to cancellation because it had not established a fixed entitlement to benefits, nor had it included a provision for the automatic renewal of yearly appropriations. Thus the broad political support that follows from a universalistic program is not the only explanation for the survival of social policies. Entitlement status or automatically renewable appropriations have also been important. Indeed, the most successful measures—Civil War pensions and social security—have been those that ensured entitlements to broad categories of beneficiaries.

Economic Security for the Elderly

The national contributory social insurance programs chartered by the Social Security Act of 1935 evolved in subsequent decades into a broad and, by international standards, reasonably generous set of income supports and medical services for retired American wage and salary workers and their dependents. Within the inclusive rubric of social security, benefits were gradually redistributed toward poorer elderly people and were larger than they would have received from a mere proportional return on their own payroll taxes collected at their preretirement wage levels. Today social security is not only the most politically unassailable part of U.S. public social provision, but also America's most effective antipoverty program.

U.S. social insurance was far from an antipoverty policy in its early years. For the first three decades, the originators and administrators of social security concentrated on building mainstream support and extending the scope of the program. They worked out effective relationships with congressional committees and maneuvered to rein in public assistance and to deflect populist demands for noncontributory need-based pensions and conservative attempts to institute universal flat-rate pensions.[42] Even though early beneficiaries reaped windfalls because they

41. Rothman (1978), pp. 142–53.
42. Cates (1983).

had not paid taxes for long, and even though tax increases for social security were repeatedly deferred while benefits were increased, the administrators deliberately portrayed the system as a set of individual "accounts" into which "contributors" paid taxes to build up "earned" benefits. They portrayed social security as very different from public assistance, much as Civil War pensions were once contrasted to charity and poor relief. Step by step, new categories of beneficiaries and taxpayers were brought into the contributory insurance system, until by the early 1970s it encompassed more than 90 percent of the labor force.[43] New types of benefits were added to the core of retirement insurance, partially filling the vacuum left by the absence of national health insurance. What was launched as old age insurance (OAI) in 1935 was modified into old age and survivors' insurance (OASI) in 1939, and further amended to become old age, survivors' and disability insurance (OASDI) in 1956. Finally, medicare was added to the system in 1965.

In a number of ways, social security has always disproportionately favored not the neediest Americans but the stably employed and the middle class: as Martha Derthick has written, "For a long time many elderly people were left out altogether because they had not been in the work force, had not been in the covered portion of it, had not been in long enough to qualify, or were not married to someone who did qualify. Among these were a large number of persons who had to fall back on public assistance."[44] Within the social security system, moreover, benefits are pegged to the wage rates at which pensioners have been paid over considerable periods during their working lives. And payroll taxes are regressive because they are set at a flat rate and not collected at all on earnings above a certain ceiling.

Nevertheless, from the start the system gave proportionately higher—although never absolutely higher—retirement benefits to formerly lower-income workers. More important, once social security was established as virtually universal for employed Americans, its administrators worked to make benefits higher for everyone, and relatively better for the less privileged, so that benefits could be closer to a sufficient retirement income.[45] Taking advantage of crucial conjunctures in favor of innovations in social policy during the 1960s and early 1970s, social security's promoters gained presidential and congressional backing for leaps forward in services and benefits for all the elderly and, at the same time, followed a

43. Achenbaum (1986), p. 59.
44. Derthick (1979), p. 215.
45. Achenbaum (1986), pp. 49–60.

strategy that Hugh Heclo has called "helping the poor by not talking about them." [46] Amidst the fuss about the War on Poverty and the Great Society, plans for medicare were brought to fruition, and social security administrators began to work for higher retirement benefits. President Nixon and the Republicans did not want to propose less than the Democrats for the elderly, and in 1972 they also saw indexing benefits to inflation as a way to time future increases automatically rather than politically. As for benefit levels, after a small increase under Johnson in 1967, Congress enacted large increases in 1969, 1971, and 1972, so that benefits, adjusted for inflation, rose by 23 percent. More significantly, the proportion of earnings subject to social security taxation and replacement rates also jumped. As Martha Derthick has pointed out, "Replacement rates in 1975 were approximately 67 percent for a married man earning average wages and 92 percent for a married man earning the federal minimum wage—up from 50 percent and 67 percent, respectively, a decade earlier, on the eve of the drive for expansion." [47]

After benefits leapt forward for everyone and at the same time increased proportionately more for the lower-wage beneficiaries, social security became by far modern America's most effective program for lifting people out of poverty. In general, social insurance does much more than means-tested transfers to raise American families from below to above the officially defined poverty line.[48] This is true even for nonelderly families, who benefit from disability, unemployment, and survivors' insurance.[49] Yet retirement benefits and medicare are chiefly responsible for the antipoverty effects of social insurance, which explains why elderly families have benefited disproportionately. Indeed, these programs have shifted the age distribution of poverty in America. According to Gary Burtless, in 1959 "the income poverty rate of the elderly was 35 percent, while the rate for the remainder of the population was only 22 percent. By 1983 the income poverty rate for the elderly had fallen to 14 percent, while for the nonelderly it was more than 15 percent." [50] For elderly Americans who might otherwise be impoverished, the Social Security Administration's practice of targeting within universalism has clearly worked well over the past quarter century.

Indeed, "helping the poor by not talking about them" has not only

46. Heclo (1986), p. 325.
47. Derthick (1979), p. 363.
48. See Weinberg (1985); and Sawhill (1988), especially pp. 1097–1101.
49. Sawhill (1988), p. 1099.
50. Burtless (1986), p. 28.

worked better, at least, for the elderly poor, but has also proved more politically durable than did the War on Poverty and the Great Society's vociferous targeted efforts to help the working-age poor and their children. The gains achieved for social security programs during the 1960s and early 1970s proved durable even in the face of Reagan administration onslaughts against social spending. Although public support for welfare declined sharply during the 1970s, some 95 percent or more of people polled continued to agree that "the government spends too little or about the right amount" on the elderly, despite substantial payroll taxes for social security.[51] Talk of a "crisis" in social security led to a few adjustments and then died away. When the first Reagan administration discussed cuts in the program, it faced immediate public resistance and soon backed down (except that it continued for a time to use administrative regulations to cut people from the disability rolls). Targeted public assistance programs for low-income people accounted for less than 18 percent of federal social spending (far less than the proportions accounted for by social security and medicare), yet these targeted programs took the brunt of the first Reagan administration's efforts to retrench domestic social expenditures.[52] Hopes of expanding the coverage of impoverished mothers and children suffered, but the elderly clients of social insurance, including those who would otherwise have been poor, preserved their improved economic standing.

There has been, in short, no political backlash against social security. Even in a generally conservative period, it has been protected by its broad constituency; and it has continued to be championed by congressional representatives of all partisan and ideological stripes.

Current Possibilities for Targeting within Universalism

U.S. history speaks loud and clear to those who would do more now to help the poor through public social policies. Rather than devising new programs narrowly focused on low-income people or the urban poor, and rather than seeking to reform or expand aid to families with dependent children and other means-tested public assistance programs, policymakers should work toward displacing welfare with new policies that could address the needs of less privileged Americans along with those of the middle class and the stable working class. New policies must speak with a consistent moral voice to all Americans who would be recipients

51. Brown (1988), p. 199.
52. Palmer and Sawhill (1982), p. 373.

and taxpayers. The policies should reinforce fundamental values such as rewards for work, opportunities for individual betterment, and family and community responsibility for the care of children and other vulnerable people. Even if new measures start small and give significant proportions of their benefits to families who seem less needy than the most desperately poor, advocates for the poor should realize that before long such measures could create new opportunities for more targeted efforts. In contrast, measures that start out small and are narrowly focused may either lose support or (even if popular, such as Head Start) fail to receive the resources they need to meet crying social needs.

To supplement social security programs for the elderly, the United States could develop what might be called a family security program available to all children and working-age citizens.[53] The new policies would include child support assurance for all single custodial parents, parental leave and child-care assistance for all working families, job training and relocation assistance for displaced workers and new entrants to the labor market, and universal health benefits.

Child support assurance would establish nationwide guidelines requiring all absent parents (most of whom are fathers) to pay proportions of their wages as child support.[54] As a substitute for the current haphazard system of judicially awarded child support, payments would be automatically fixed and collected through wage withholding, exactly as income and social security taxes now are. Checks to all custodial parents (mostly mothers) would come from the government. They would nearly equal the amounts collected from absent parents, except when the monies were not collected or fell below a minimum benefit needed to raise children, in which case the custodial parent would get the minimum payment from public funds. Such a program would express the nation's interest in helping single custodial parents with the socially crucial work of raising the approximately half of American children that are now growing up in such families. The system would address pressing social problems that cut across class and racial lines, since half of all marriages now end in divorce and only half of all divorced mothers receive child support (separated and never-married mothers fare even worse).[55] Because the program "would be sending checks to middle- and upper-income women as well as to disadvantaged ones," there would be "no stigma, no failure, and no

53. I have borrowed a number of ideas from Ellwood (1988).
54. This proposal is outlined in Garfinkel and Uhr (1984).
55. Weitzman (1985), p. xvii; and Ellwood (1988), p. 158.

isolation under this system." [56] At the same time, an adequate minimum benefit could do much to help needy mothers and, in contrast to welfare payments, would not disappear as soon as the mother went to work.

Although child support assurance could do much to ensure that all children have basic financial support, both dual-parent and single-parent families also need help with the growing challenges of balancing parenting and work outside the home. More and more married women, including mothers of young children, are working outside the home, yet current public policies do remarkably little by international standards to buffer families from the extra stresses of childbirth or adoption or to help them find and finance adequate child care while both parents work.[57] Various policies could address these problems for all families. At a minimum it surely makes sense to move toward paid parental leave for families of newborns or new adoptees, perhaps with legally mandated unpaid leave, including guaranteed reinstatement, as a first step.

Another objective should be to deliver more income through public means to all families that must combine working and parenting, but with larger benefits (proportionately and absolutely) for the neediest families. All families with children could be given larger, refundable tax credits, which would benefit families with two workers and those with full-time homemakers. Or public benefits could be tied much more directly to women's labor force participation by offering refundable tax credits to families that have to purchase child care while a single parent or both parents work.

Help for parents raising children is one part of an overall family security program. The other part must be help for all adults who are looking for jobs. This help would make it easier for families to form and for parents to support their children. And it is consonant with American values because adults are being assisted to help themselves, not put on a permanent public dole. A universally available, federally run labor market system could do several things for displaced workers (including displaced managers and skilled workers as well as unemployed low-wage workers) and for new entrants to the labor market (including young people, "welfare mothers," and divorced former homemakers). It could identify jobs and areas of the country where new workers are needed. It should provide transitional unemployment benefits and perhaps housing subsidies, if necessary, to help workers and their families relocate. And most impor-

56. Ellwood (1988), p. 169.
57. See Kamerman, Kahn, and Kingston (1983), especially pp. 16–22.

tant, this system could train or retrain people to help match their skills to available jobs.

As William Wilson and his collaborators have argued, poor job prospects for unskilled young black men are directly linked to low rates of family formation, especially in inner cities.[58] The present welfare system also unnecessarily traps many single mothers into making a stark choice between unskilled paid work at very low wages or welfare benefits that are available only to mothers who do not work.[59] The existing system rarely helps them gain new skills, nor does it urge or help them to relocate, if necessary, to take advantage of decent jobs and housing. A new public labor market system would do all these things, and it would provide help and incentives to low-income, unskilled single mothers within the same broad, nonstigmatized rubric in which aid would be offered to family heads with more education and greater skills. Everyone, moreover, could receive job training and help with job searches in the name of promoting national economic efficiency.

Some analysts believe that a new labor market system should also guarantee public jobs at the minimum wage as a last resort. But this might stigmatize the system as a make-work program, whereas emphasizing training and relocation would make the policies appealing to the working-class and middle-class public. If more jobs are needed in the end than can be generated through private and existing public labor markets, then other kinds of federal and state policies, such as measures to develop infrastructure, might be planned to create new jobs for workers in training. Furthermore, the institution of a higher earned income tax credit to subsidize low-wage workers might indirectly make more self-supporting jobs available to newly trained workers. Although this is a targeted measure, it qualifies as targeting within universalism because it arranges subsidies through the income tax system in which all workers participate.

Finally, more universally available health benefits are essential if the United States is to improve the efficiency of its labor markets and help working families raise healthy children. The present patchwork system discourages labor mobility and job redefinitions within industries and workplaces because medical insurance for many employees and their dependents is tied to certain professional and unionized jobs, and coverage is not available through other jobs (or through the part-time work that makes sense for many parents). Likewise, the present system rewards

58. Neckerman, Aponte, and Wilson (1988).
59. Ellwood (1988), pp. 137–42.

welfare recipients (and sometimes people with incomes slightly above a legally defined poverty line) with medical insurance, but leaves many working people, especially low-wage workers, without coverage. This situation discourages recipients from moving off welfare and arouses taxpayer resistance to improving the provision of public health care for impoverished families. The present uneven system of publicly provided or tax-subsidized health benefits only for the elderly, the very poor, and the unionized should be replaced either with Canadian-style universal health insurance or with some kind of residual, publicly mandated or contributory publicly funded health benefits.

Conclusion

These interrelated proposals for family support and labor market measures that would constitute a family security program for America necessarily raise questions. Could such policies be enacted in the present fiscal climate? If enacted, would they really help truly needy Americans?

The present concern about federal budget deficits is apparently inimical to new social policies that threaten to cost a lot. Some of these policies could save or generate considerable amounts of public money at the same time that they authorized new expenditures.[60] Nevertheless, a family security program of the sort outlined, especially the health insurance and child-care assistance provisions, would require major new budgetary commitments from the federal government. Although public support for addressing social problems, including those of the poor, has recently rebounded, the 1981 Reagan tax cuts did have the effect of shifting congressional debates toward cost cutting, so that many politicians now seem obsessively wary about mentioning tax increases.

Still, the history of the modern social security system demonstrates that Americans will accept taxes that they perceive as contributions toward public programs in which there is a direct stake for themselves, their families, and their friends, not just for "the poor." Perhaps the introduction of new programs on a modest scale could be accompanied by a family security payroll tax, collected up to a considerably higher wage base than social security taxes are now to avoid some of the worst regressive features. In any event, new universalistic programs and new sources of revenue, to be collected from virtually the entire population, not just

60. See Garfinkel and Uhr (1980), pp. 120–22; and Ellwood (1988), p. 169. To the extent that they put people to work, labor market policies would also generate new revenues.

small subgroups as with the unsuccessful catastrophic illness surcharge, should be discussed together. If this is done, there is reason for optimism about the willingness of Americans to accept new public policies to address family needs that are widely felt.

Of course, proposed innovations do not turn into legislation just because the public might accept them. There have to be articulate political leaders and effective social alliances behind measures if they are to wend their way through the legislative process. Here there is less room for immediate optimism but some hope for action in the next decade. Missing right now are mobilized organizations and broad, legislatively active alliances that include groups other than those advocating help for the poor. Civil rights groups tend to be preoccupied with defending affirmative action or pushing for measures targeted on the nonwhite poor. Similarly, organized feminists and antifeminists are currently engrossed with abortion issues, and their conflict undercuts the cross-class coalitions that might come together in support of new family security measures. Many old-line labor unions are so much on the defensive organizationally and economically that they are preoccupied with issues of labor law, even as emerging unions in feminine social service occupations tend to favor broad social policy agendas. All the same, on a surprisingly bipartisan basis, elected representatives and candidates are now beginning to talk regularly about new child care, parental leave, and health insurance policies, although such talk always goes on for quite some time before particular policies come into being. And business-oriented conservatives may be willing to accept new public social spending, if only to head off regulations that would burden employers with the costs for child care or expanded health coverage.

But can the American poor really be helped by the program I have outlined? Wouldn't this set of policies help principally the middle and working classes, along with the most privileged and least troubled of the poor, leaving behind many of the extremely disadvantaged, disproportionately people of color, who require intensive services to break out of cycles of social pathology and despair? Initially, this might happen. Yet an ever-deepening course of hope and improvement might soon unfold among the poor. Once genuinely new and nonstigmatizing incentives, social supports, and ways of providing job opportunities were solidly in place, the example of a few go-getters who took advantage of new policies and forged better lives for themselves might well propagate among relatives, friends, and neighbors. After the word got out that work really does lead to rewards, a certain amount of the social despair that now pervades the very poor might well begin to dissipate. In a way, this could be the greatest gift that new universalistic family security policies could give to the most disadvantaged among the American poor, for it would facilitate their moral reintegration into the mainstream of national life.

Universalistic policies would also change the attitudes of more privileged Americans, which returns us to the bedrock matter of broad and sustainable political support for antipoverty policies. Just as social security has done, new family security policies, once established, would probably nourish broad political alliances prepared to support extensions of benefits and willing to accept redistributions toward the poor at the same time. If and when new public social policies begin to help American families from all social classes and all racial and ethnic groups to meet contingencies of ill health, job loss, and the challenges of balancing paid work and parental responsibilities, then a "kinder and gentler" political nation might actually emerge. With their own values and needs recognized through a revitalized public sector, larger numbers of middle-class American citizens would be prepared to go the extra mile for especially needy minorities. Instead of policies for the disadvantaged alone, targeting within universalism is the prescription for effective and politically sustainable policies to fight poverty in the United States. This is what experience teaches us about prospects for a rebirth of political community.

References

Achenbaum, W. Andrew. 1986. *Social Security: Visions and Revisions*. Cambridge University Press.

Albritton, Robert B. 1979. "Social Amelioration through Mass Insurgency? A Reexamination of the Piven and Cloward Thesis." *American Political Science Review* 73 (December), pp. 1003–11.

Bell, Winifred. 1965. *Aid to Dependent Children*. Columbia University Press.

Brown, Michael K. 1988. "The Segmented Welfare System: Distributive Conflict and Retrenchment in the United States, 1968–1984." In *Remaking the Welfare State: Retrenchment and Social Policy in America and Europe*, edited by Michael K. Brown. Temple University Press.

Burtless, Gary. 1986. "Public Spending for the Poor: Trends, Prospects, and Economic Limits." In *Fighting Poverty: What Works and What Doesn't*, edited by Sheldon H. Danziger and Daniel H. Weinberg. Harvard University Press.

Cates, Jerry R. 1983. *Insuring Inequality: Administrative Leadership in Social Security, 1935–54*. University of Michigan Press.

Cetina, Judith Gladys. 1977. "A History of Veterans' Homes in the United States, 1811–1930." Ph.D. dissertation, Case Western Reserve University.

Children's Bureau. 1914. *First Annual Report of the Chief, Children's Bureau to the Secretary of Labor for the Year Ended June 30, 1913.* Department of Labor.
————. 1933. *Mothers' Aid, 1931,* publication 220. Department of Labor.
Costin, Lela B. 1983. *Two Sisters for Social Justice: A Biography of Grace and Edith Abbott.* University of Illinois Press.
Covotsos, Louis J. 1976. "Child Welfare and Social Progress: A History of the United States Children's Bureau, 1912–1935." Ph.D. dissertation, University of Chicago.
Derthick, Martha. 1979. *Policymaking for Social Security.* Brookings.
Ellwood, David T. 1988. *Poor Support: Poverty in the American Family.* Basic Books.
Garfinkel, Irwin, and Elizabeth Uhr. 1984. "A New Approach to Child Support." *Public Interest* 74 (Spring), pp. 111–22.
Glasson, William H. 1918. *Federal Military Pensions in the United States.* Oxford University Press.
Heclo, Hugh. 1986. "The Political Foundations of Antipoverty Policy." In *Fighting Poverty: What Works and What Doesn't,* edited by Sheldon H. Danziger and Daniel H. Weinberg. Harvard University Press.
Johnson, Donald Bruce, compiler. 1978. *National Party Platforms,* vol. 1: *1840–1956.* Rev. ed. University of Illinois Press.
Kamerman, Sheila B., Alfred J. Kahn, and Paul Kingston. 1983. *Maternity Policies and Working Women.* Columbia University Press.
Katz, Michael B. 1986. *In the Shadow of the Poorhouse: A Social History of Welfare in America.* Basic Books.
Kaus, Mickey. 1986. "The Work Ethic State." *New Republic,* July 7, pp. 22–32.
Korpi, Walter. 1980. "Social Policy and Distributional Conflict in the Capitalist Democracies: A Preliminary Comparative Framework." *West European Politics* 3 (October), pp. 296–316.
Ladd-Taylor, Molly, editor. 1986. *Raising a Baby the Government Way: Mothers' Letters to the Children's Bureau, 1915–1932.* Rutgers University Press.
Levitan, Sar A., and Clifford M. Johnson. 1984. *Beyond the Safety Net: Reviving the Promise of Opportunity in America.* Cambridge, Mass.: Ballinger.
Levitan, Sar A., and Robert Taggart. 1976. *The Promise of Greatness.* Harvard University Press.
McMurry, Donald L. 1922. "The Political Significance of the Pension Question, 1885–1897." *Mississippi Valley Historical Review* 9 (June), pp. 19–36.
Massachusetts Bureau of Statistics. 1916. *Report of a Special Inquiry Relative to Aged and Dependent Persons in Massachusetts, 1915.* Boston: Wright and Potter.
Murray, Charles. 1984. *Losing Ground: American Social Policy, 1950–1980.* Basic Books.
Neckerman, Kathryn, Robert Aponte, and William Julius Wilson. 1988. "Family Structure, Black Unemployment, and American Social Policy." In *The Politics of Social Policy in the United States,* edited by Margaret Weir, Ann Shola Orloff, and Theda Skocpol. Princeton University Press.

Palmer, John L., and Isabel V. Sawhill, editors. 1982. *The Reagan Experiment: An Examination of Economic and Social Policies under the Reagan Administration.* Washington: Urban Institute.

Parker, Jacqueline K., and Edward M. Carpenter. 1981. "Julia Lathrop and the Children's Bureau: The Emergence of an Institution." *Social Service Review* 55 (March), pp. 60–77.

Patterson, James T. 1981. *America's Struggle against Poverty, 1900–1980.* Harvard University Press.

Petrocik, John R. 1981. *Party Coalitions: Realignment and the Decline of the New Deal Party System.* University of Chicago Press.

Piven, Frances Fox, and Richard A. Cloward. 1987. "The Contemporary Relief Debate." In *The Mean Season: The Attack on the Welfare State*, edited by Fred Block and others. Pantheon Books.

Raum, Green B. 1891. "Pensions and Patriotism." *North American Review* 42 (August), pp. 205–14.

Rosenberry, Sara A. 1982. "Social Insurance, Distributive Criteria and the Welfare Backlash: A Comparative Analysis." *British Journal of Political Science* 12 (October), pp. 421–47.

Rothman, Sheila M. 1978. *Woman's Proper Place: A History of Changing Ideals and Practices, 1870 to Present.* Basic Books.

Russell, Louise. 1989. "Proposed: A Comprehensive Health Care System for the Poor." *Brookings Review* 7 (Summer), pp. 13–20.

Sanders, Heywood T. 1980. "Paying for the 'Bloody Shirt': The Politics of Civil War Pensions." In *Political Benefits: Empirical Studies of American Public Programs*, edited by Barry S. Rundquist. Lexington, Mass.: D.C. Heath.

Sawhill, Isabel V. 1988. "Poverty in the U.S.: Why Is It So Persistent?" *Journal of Economic Literature* 26 (September), pp. 1073–1119.

Schorr, Lisbeth B., with Daniel Schorr. 1988. *Within Our Reach: Breaking the Cycle of Disadvantage.* Anchor Press.

Schwarz, John E. 1983. *America's Hidden Success: A Reassessment of Twenty Years of Public Policy.* Norton.

Skocpol, Theda. Forthcoming. *Protecting Soldiers and Mothers: The Politics of Social Provision in the United States, 1870–1920.* Harvard University Press.

Weinberg, Daniel H. 1985. "Filling the 'Poverty Gap': Multiple Transfer Program Participation." *Journal of Human Resources* 20 (Winter), pp. 64–89.

Weitzman, Lenore J. 1985. *The Divorce Revolution: The Unexpected Social and Economic Consequences for Women and Children in America.* Free Press.

Wilkins, Roger. 1989. "The Black Poor Are Different." *New York Times*, August 22, p. A23.

Wilson, William Julius. 1987. *The Truly Disadvantaged: The Inner City, the Underclass, and Public Policy.* University of Chicago Press.

Universal and Targeted Approaches to Relieving Poverty: An Alternative View

ROBERT GREENSTEIN

BOTH WILLIAM JULIUS WILSON in *The Truly Disadvantaged* and Theda Skocpol in her paper in this volume call for addressing poverty through universal programs that serve all income classes.[1] Only in this fashion, they argue, are the truly disadvantaged likely to be aided very much. This viewpoint rests on the belief that programs limited to poor people inevitably have such a weak political base that they are periodically restricted, their funding is cut, or they are terminated outright. The more the society believes the programs benefit only the poor (and implicitly minorities), the argument goes, the less support the programs receive.

Skocpol is critical of those whose antipoverty agenda focuses on expanding or creating programs for low-income groups. "Rarely," she says "do advocates of targeted benefits or specially tailored public social services face up to the problem of finding sustained political support for them. . . . [T]hey do not explain why working-class families with incomes just above the poverty line, themselves frequently struggling economically without the aid of health insurance or child care or adequate unemployment benefits, should pay for programs that go only to people with incomes below the poverty line. . . . When U.S. antipoverty efforts have featured policies targeted on the poor alone, they have not been politically sustainable, and they have stigmatized and demeaned the poor." Skocpol's thinking is in line with the old adage that "programs for poor people make poor programs." The only way out of this bind is said to be universal programs, of which social security, clearly the nation's most effective antipoverty program, is the best example.

Some of Wilson's and Skocpol's statements ring true. Do universal programs have broader and therefore stronger constituencies? Yes. Do uni-

The author would like to thank Henry Aaron, Paul Leonard, Kathryn Porter, Wendell Primus, Robert Reischauer, Isabel Sawhill, and Isaac Shapiro for their helpful comments on an earlier draft of this chapter.

1. Wilson (1987).

versal programs tend to be less stigmatizing than targeted programs? Yes. Yet Skocpol's basic argument goes further, concluding that because targeted programs have a narrower base, they are doomed to yield disappointing results and that universal approaches do better, last longer, and nearly always prove preferable. This conclusion goes beyond the historical evidence, which indicates that many targeted programs are considerably stronger and more durable politically than Skocpol suggests. Medicaid, the supplemental security income program (SSI), food stamps, the earned income tax credit (EITC), and other major low-income benefit programs bounced back from the budget cuts of the early 1980s and ended the Reagan era nearly as strong or stronger than when they entered it.

The evidence also indicates that factors other than whether a program is universal or targeted have a significant bearing on the political prospects of social programs. Targeted programs, for example, are more likely to be strong politically when they serve low-income and moderate-income working families as well as the very poor. They are also more likely to succeed when they are regarded as providing an earned benefit or are otherwise linked to work, when they are entitlement programs with federally prescribed and funded benefits, when they seem effective, and when they are not provided in the form of cash welfare assistance for young, able-bodied people who do not work.

Skocpol's principal conclusion, that those seeking to develop new anti-poverty policies should rely almost exclusively on universal approaches, seems weak on another account as well: it conflicts with current fiscal constraints. Advocates of new universal programs need to acknowledge the political difficulties posed by the large costs of such programs, just as advocates of targeted programs need to acknowledge the political problems inherent in spending tax dollars on a narrow segment of the population.

Targeted Programs: What Is the Historical Record?

Skocpol provides three examples of targeted programs that are said to have failed for lack of political support. One of them, the nineteenth century movement to establish poorhouses, seems too dated; I do not examine it further here. For the second, the early twentieth century effort to provide mothers' pensions, which evolved into aid to families with dependent children (AFDC), her discussion of the program's political weakness is surely on the mark. But her analysis of the third and most relevant example, the political failure of the antipoverty programs of the 1960s and 1970s, is flawed.

Skocpol makes two distinct points about these antipoverty programs. First, she argues that the "transfer strategies of the Kennedy, Johnson, and Nixon years failed to reduce poverty levels much among the nonelderly." Second, these programs supposedly collapsed under political fire in the 1980s, as "the antipoverty services and increased expenditures on the nonelderly poor . . . generated political backlashes that ended possibilities for their continuation and improvement." She concludes, "it seems highly unlikely that further redistributive benefits or targeted intensive services for the poor alone can succeed politically. We still live amidst the backlash against the War on Poverty and the Great Society."

The assertion that the antipoverty programs of the 1960s and 1970s failed to reduce poverty rates relies on a questionable measure of their success. The principal means-tested benefit programs established in these years were food stamps, medicaid, and Section 8 housing assistance, none of which is counted in measuring the official poverty rate, and the supplemental security income program, which affects only the elderly and disabled poor. By definition, therefore, these programs could not have affected poverty rates among the nonelderly very much.

The programs could, however, have had other significant effects. Paul Starr has shown that in the decade before 1965, the infant mortality rate changed little, but from 1968 to 1980, when medicaid and other health programs were instituted and expanded, infant mortality was cut in half.[2] Similarly, a team of physicians sponsored by the Field Foundation examined the incidence of hunger and malnutrition in the late 1960s and again in the late 1970s and found dramatic improvements, which they attributed primarily to expansion of the food stamp and other food assistance programs.[3] The conclusion was underscored when a subsequent study found food purchases to have grown sharply in the nation's poorest counties as the food stamp program took hold.[4]

The disappointing failure of the poverty rate to decrease after 1973 — and its increase after 1978 — was related to such factors as general income stagnation, the erosion of wages for nonsupervisory jobs in the private sector (average hourly wages were lower in real terms in 1989 than in any year since 1970), the increase in the proportion of families headed by single women, and the large decrease in real benefit levels provided by

2. Starr (1986).
3. Kotz (1979).
4. Boehm, Nelson, and Longen (1980).

states under the AFDC program (for reasons I will discuss later, the political weakness of AFDC is much greater than that of most other targeted programs). Food stamps, medicaid, and SSI helped cushion the effects of these adverse changes, but they could not, by their nature, have much effect on the poverty rates among the nonelderly.

A more serious problem with Skocpol's discussion of the targeted programs of the 1960s and 1970s is her analysis of how the conservative political backlash in the 1980s weakened them. She is right that the Reagan budget cuts of 1981 singled out means-tested benefit programs for particularly deep reductions. Congress adopted nearly all the cuts that the administration proposed in these programs that year and legislated further reductions in 1982. Yet even by 1982 the political tide had begun to turn. The administration achieved less than one-fifth of the additional reductions in means-tested entitlement reductions it requested that year, and after 1982, the federal reductions virtually ceased. Indeed, several of these programs once again began to expand, in some cases significantly.[5]

For example, the principal 1981 cutback in medicaid was a reduction in federal matching rates for state medicaid programs, which led most states to place new restrictions on their programs. The federal reduction expired at the end of fiscal year 1984, however, and after that, the earlier matching rates were reinstated. Furthermore, in 1984, 1986, 1987, 1988, and 1989, Congress passed, and the president signed, significant expansions of medicaid coverage. Effective April 1, 1990, states were required to extend coverage to nearly all pregnant women and children under age six in families with incomes less than 133 percent of the poverty line. In some southern states, the medicaid income eligibility limit for pregnant women and young children will have risen from less than 25 percent of the poverty line in 1984. In close to half the states, many pregnant women and young children in poor two-parent families began receiving medicaid coverage for the first time. Overall, the Congressional Budget Office estimates that the expansions of the 1980s have added 1.75 million pregnant women and children to the program.[6]

Moreover, legislation enacted in the fall of 1990 contained further substantial medicaid expansions, extending coverage to large numbers of older children as well. This newest expansion is being phased in; by shortly after the turn of the century, states will have to provide medicaid

5. Unfortunately, Skocpol's principal reference here is a 1982 Urban Institute study by John L. Palmer and Gregory B. Mills that does not reflect these later developments.
6. Letter from Robert Reischauer, director, Congressional Budget Office, July 17, 1990.

coverage to nearly all children age six through eighteen whose families have incomes below 100 percent of the poverty line. Legislation was also enacted requiring state medicaid programs to pay medicare premiums and deductibles for elderly and disabled people who are not already on medicaid and who have incomes below the poverty line. By 1995 states will have to pay the medicare premiums for elderly and disabled people with incomes between 100 percent and 120 percent of the poverty line as well.[7]

Other means-tested programs also fared better than Skocpol's account would suggest. Cut substantially in 1981 and 1982, the food stamp program was expanded in 1985, 1987, and 1988, when some of the initial reductions were repealed and basic benefit levels were raised to a higher level than at any previous point in the program's history.[8] The federal supplemental security income program for the elderly and disabled poor was cut very little during the Reagan years. Instead, basic benefits were increased in 1983 as part of the social security compromise legislation.[9] In the child nutrition programs, the principal reductions came in the benefits focused on middle- and upper-income children. Federal reimbursement rates and eligibility limits for free school meals for low-income children were not affected much (in fact, federal funding rates for free school breakfasts were slightly increased).[10]

The one low-income entitlement program that has not largely recov-

7. Some states have attempted to cover a portion of the added medicaid costs by holding reimbursements to providers at unrealistically low levels or restricting services in other ways. This has affected the provision of services to beneficiaries in some areas. The overall trend for medicaid since 1984, however, has been one of significant expansion.

8. The food stamp program did experience a largely unexplained decrease in participation in the early 1980s. Sixty-eight people received food stamps in an average month in 1990 for every 100 people with incomes below the poverty line. In 1988 there were 59 food stamp recipients for every 100 people below the poverty line. An Urban Institute study in the mid-1980s found that the decline in participation could not be explained by budget reductions or economic or demographic changes. However, in 1989 and 1990, a significant increase in participation has occurred. The increase, which equalled 1.3 million people between the second calendar quarter of 1989 and the second quarter of 1990, appears to be raising the participation-to-poverty ratio part of the way back toward the 1980 levels.

9. Although federal SSI benefits were not reduced in the Reagan era, SSI supplemental benefits, which are provided in twenty-seven states, have been declining in real terms since the program started in 1974.

10. Some decreases in free school lunch participation occurred in part because a modest number of schools in middle-income school districts dropped the school lunch program following significant reductions in federal subsidies for lunches provided to children who were not from low-income families.

ered from the federal budget cuts of the early 1980s is AFDC. But even here some modest restorations of the reductions were enacted, although benefit levels, as set by the states, have continued to erode significantly in purchasing power.

Indeed, an examination of congressional budgets from 1981 through 1990 reveals that although means-tested entitlements were reduced disproportionately in 1981 and 1982, it was medicare and other universal entitlements that have borne the brunt of the entitlement cuts since 1983. In the major deficit reduction legislation enacted in 1990, for example, *none* of the entitlement cuts came from means-tested benefit programs targeted at low-income people. Nearly all the entitlement cuts (which totaled close to $100 billion over five years) came from non-means-tested programs. In addition, after the early 1980s the cost of expanding medicaid coverage for low-income people was sometimes "financed" through offsetting reductions in the universal medicare program—not at all what Skocpol's argument would lead one to expect. Using medicare cuts to "pay for" some of the medicaid increases has been explicit among several of the relevant committees on Capitol Hill.

Furthermore, although many cuts made in targeted entitlement programs were rolled back later in the 1980s, one universal entitlement, the unemployment insurance program, made up little of the ground it lost in the early Reagan budgets. In every year from 1984 through 1988 the proportion of the jobless receiving unemployment insurance benefits in an average month registered a record low. While a number of factors were at work here, including lower rates of application by eligible unemployed workers, federal and state cuts in the program played a role.

In assessing the political backlash against the targeted programs begun in the 1960s and 1970s, one should ask how they fared under the Gramm-Rudman-Hollings law, enacted in 1985 and revised in 1987 and 1990, which requires across-the-board budget cuts when the deficit ceiling for a fiscal year is breached. Only a limited number of programs are fully exempt from these cuts, but they include every major means-tested entitlement: medicaid, food stamps, SSI, child nutrition programs, and even AFDC. Although a number of universal entitlements—social security, federal retirement benefits, veterans' disability benefits—are also fully exempt, others, particularly medicare, are not.[11]

11. Under the Gramm-Rudman-Hollings law, reductions in medicare are achieved through lower payments to providers for covered health care services. These reductions cannot exceed 4 percent of the cost of the services.

Inappropriate Comparisons of Targeted and Universal Programs

The picture Skocpol presents of relatively fragile means-tested programs existing alongside politically robust universal programs is also troublesome for other reasons. She overstates the relative political strength of universal programs because she compares universal programs providing entitlements to targeted programs that are not entitlements and must have their funding levels determined in the appropriations cycle each year.[12]

Entitlement status proved especially important during the Reagan years. Except for AFDC, the low-income entitlements largely bounced back from the cuts of 1981; the picture emerging now is one of the enduring political strength of these programs. Low-income nonentitlement programs, however, fared much less well. Paul Leonard has found that after adjusting for inflation, appropriations for these programs, other than subsidized housing programs, fell 30 percent from fiscal year 1981 to fiscal year 1989.[13] Additional sharp reductions were made in subsidized housing programs, a particular problem because this retrenchment came at a time when the stock of private low-income housing was diminishing. The reductions in low-income nonentitlement programs were concentrated in employment and training, housing and community development, and programs providing social services, legal services, and assistance with high heating bills.

Even for these, however, one cannot simply assume it was the targeted

12. An entitlement is a program in which categories of individuals or families are entitled to a prescribed level of benefits if they meet specified eligibility criteria. Although some entitlement programs receive yearly appropriations, the role of Congress in setting appropriations levels for these programs is perfunctory. It must allow appropriations sufficient to provide the prescribed level of benefits to all eligible individuals or families who apply. Eligible individuals or families cannot be denied benefits because appropriations are insufficient. If the appropriation level initially provided is too low in a given fiscal year, a supplemental appropriation, termed a mandatory supplemental because Congress has no choice but to provide it to meet the terms of the entitlement, must be enacted.

13. Leonard (1989). Subsidized housing is excluded from this calculation because yearly appropriations levels are not the best measure of changes in the federal commitment to low-income housing. During the 1980s, appropriations for subsidized housing fell sharply in real terms, but outlays increased. The best measure of changes in the federal commitment to low-income housing is neither appropriations nor outlay levels but rather the number of additional units whose rent the government has made a commitment to subsidize. By this measure, subsidized housing programs were cut substantially in the 1980s. See Leonard, Dolbeare, and Lazere (1989), chap. 4.

nature of the programs that led to their poor treatment. Nonentitlement programs serving a broader population also were hit hard. Federal outlays for domestic nonentitlement programs fell 19 percent from fiscal year 1981 to fiscal year 1989, declining during this period from 5.7 percent of GNP to 3.7 percent. And the decrease would have been much larger were it not for substantial increases in spending for the National Aeronautics and Space Administration, drug interdiction efforts, prison construction and other law enforcement activities, the National Science Foundation, and some other areas of domestic nonentitlement spending that do not involve social programs.[14]

Skocpol also overstates the case for the success of universal programs by using programs for the elderly as her primary example. She compares the political success in recent years of social security, an earned entitlement for the elderly, with the problems encountered by targeted programs that are not entitlements, are not focused on the elderly, and are not considered earned benefits. Skocpol states that social security's strategy of " 'helping the [elderly] poor by not talking about them' has not only worked better . . . but has also proved more politically durable than did the War on Poverty and the Great Society's vociferous targeted efforts to help the working-age poor and their children." Such a comparison confuses the case for programs serving all income groups with the case for assisting the elderly, a politically potent group. To get a clearer sense of the relative political strength of universal and targeted programs, it would be better to compare a universal program for the elderly, such as social security, with a means-tested program for the elderly, such as supplemental security income. SSI, the basic welfare entitlement program for the elderly and disabled poor, actually fared better at the federal level in the 1980s than social security did: social security was cut modestly in 1981 and 1983; SSI was not.[15]

14. Furthermore, since 1983, most low-income nonentitlement programs have received some protection by being included in a list of "low-income/high priority" programs compiled by the House Budget Committee. Each year the budget resolution approved by the committee and passed on the House floor has included an assumption that all programs on this list would receive funding at least equal to the previous year's level plus inflation. This assumption is not binding, and several programs were reduced somewhat when the annual appropriations bills were written. Nevertheless, the protection has generally worked to the programs' benefit. In fact, some supporters of various domestic nonentitlement programs not included on the list have tried to demonstrate that their program has a major low-income component and should therefore be added.

15. SSI was cut by about 1 percent in 1982, but was expanded in 1983 and subsequent years. An Urban Institute analysis estimated that between fiscal years 1981 and 1985, outlays for SSI increased 8.6 percent over the level the outlays would have attained if no legis-

Furthermore, the component of social security that provides disability insurance benefits was tightened significantly during the 1980s. As the criteria for getting and staying on the rolls became more restrictive, the number of beneficiaries fell from nearly 4.9 million in 1978 to 4.1 million in 1989. The incidence of new disability insurance awards fell even more sharply, from an average of 5.9 new awards each year for every 1,000 insured workers in the 1970s to just 3.5 per 1,000 in the 1980s.[16] Thus being a universal program, and part of the social security system, did not insulate disability insurance from retrenchment. The fact that disability insurance payments are not popularly viewed as earned in the same way social security retirement benefits are, and charges that some beneficiaries on the rapidly growing rolls were not severely disabled and should be working, helped create an atmosphere in which the program could be trimmed.

Skocpol's comparison of the political strength of the universal social security program with the political weakness of targeted Great Society programs suffers from one other shortcoming. It does not recognize that "success" is far easier to achieve by sending beneficiaries a check than it is by attempting to lift families out of poverty through education, training, or social services. Transfer payments, both universal and means tested, generally succeed in raising income. Similarly, food stamps raise disposable income and increase food purchases, and medicaid results in more access to health care. But success is much harder to come by in the targeted programs that aim to promote self-sufficiency among the poor through the provision of services. It is likely, as Isabel Sawhill has argued, that the perceived ineffectiveness of many of the Great Society services programs added to their political weakness and made them more vulnerable.[17] For example, the public service employment and job training programs of the Comprehensive Employment and Training Administration were widely viewed in the early 1980s as yielding disappointing results. These programs were among the ones cut most sharply in the early Reagan years.

---

lative changes had been made, while social security outlays were reduced 4.6 percent below that level. Bawden and Palmer (1984), p. 185.

16. In 1989 some 3.7 disability insurance awards were granted for every 1,000 insured workers. House Committee on Ways and Means (1990), pp. 58–60.

17. Sawhill (1989). This short piece is the text of Sawhill's comments on the paper that forms the basis for Skocpol's contribution in this volume. Both the Skocpol paper and Sawhill's comments were presented at the Northwestern University conference on the underclass in October 1989.

Elements of Politically Successful Programs

What lessons emerge from these patterns? Skocpol's history of universal programs that have enjoyed political success is instructive, but I would draw somewhat different conclusions from her evidence. She cites the experiences of three universal programs: pensions provided to Civil War veterans, maternal and child health services provided in the 1920s under the Sheppard-Towner Act, and social security. For each case she concludes that the universal nature of the benefit or service was the element most important in producing political success. But her discussion paints a richer picture than she acknowledges and indicates that more factors were involved than she accounts for.

Regarding Civil War pensions, she comments, "the argument was that [generous benefits] had been *earned*" through the Union soldiers' service to the nation. She also reports that a strong underpinning of support for the pensions came from the conviction, expressed in national party platforms and state laws, that those who wore the federal uniform should not have to live off public relief or private charity and should be better off than those who did.

The approval of benefits viewed as earned is particularly significant. One reason social security enjoys such strong political support is that most Americans also regard these benefits as earned rather than as a handout. This suggests that benefits perceived as earned are likely to have political strength that benefits that are viewed as welfare, and as unrelated to some form of work or service, do not possess. As I will discuss later, this dichotomy appears to be of considerable importance in gaining public approval for a program, in addition to the dichotomy between universal and targeted approaches.

Skocpol's second example of a program that had political strength primarily because of its universality was the one that provided maternal and child health care services in the 1920s under the Sheppard-Towner Act. But was this program's universality the critical element behind its political success? The nature of the services provided may well have been as important in generating political support as the universal delivery mechanism employed.

The recent history of a targeted program providing services to pregnant and postpartum women, infants, and young children, the special supplemental food program for women, infants, and children (known as WIC), suggests that such services are popular even when they are restricted to low-income families. WIC operates through health clinics and provides nutrition benefits and services to low-income pregnant women and young children. A means-tested program that is not an entitlement, WIC was slated for deep cuts by the Reagan administration. Instead, Congress expanded it. When Reagan took office, WIC's funding level was $900 million; today it is $2.35 billion. This is one of the sharpest rates of growth for any federal program between 1981 and 1991, including programs that are not means tested. Both the nature of the services provided through WIC and impressive evidence showing it to have a powerful effect in improving pregnancy outcomes contributed to its political success.[18]

The recent history of other targeted programs also supports the idea that if the public considers benefits to be earned, or strongly approves of the services being provided, political strength can be sustained among targeted as well as universal programs. One such targeted program is the earned income tax credit. In *Family and Nation*, Daniel Patrick Moynihan recounts how in the early 1970s Congress rejected President Nixon's family assistance plan—it was considered a highly controversial form of negative income tax—only to turn around several years later and establish another form of negative income tax, the EITC. Moreover, as Moynihan notes, the EITC passed with little opposition or controversy.[19] Why did one plan fail and the other succeed? A critical factor appears to be that the family assistance plan would have raised unearned welfare benefits, whereas the EITC was presented as an earned benefit available only to low-income families that worked and was designed to reward them for their effort. Moreover, the EITC was regarded as an antidote for the supposed attractions of welfare: it would help make work more remunerative than welfare, and its benefits would be provided through the income tax system, not at the welfare office.

The EITC thus embodied some of the elements that Skocpol describes as characterizing Civil War pensions and some that mark social security as well. It was viewed as an earned benefit, one that helped make those who were entitled to its benefits, because of their work effort, better off than those who had not worked and were relying on welfare. Yet unlike Civil War pensions or social security, the EITC is a targeted program. In 1990, for example, the benefits began to decline after family income sur-

18. Even in 1981, when most administration proposals for cuts in domestic programs were being approved, the Senate Budget Committee, the administration's strongest fortress in Congress, trounced the proposed WIC cut by a 15–4 vote. The program prospered in the 1980s while many other programs with stronger constituencies were reduced.

19. Moynihan (1986), p. 157.

passed $10,730, and they were phased out entirely when income reached $20,264. (Skocpol makes an effort to claim the EITC as an example of universalism because its benefits are delivered through the tax system, but she is not convincing. The tax credit is a means-tested benefit, and only families with incomes less than $20,264, which is far below the median family income, qualify for it.)[20]

Among antipoverty programs, the EITC is the political success story of recent years. Modestly expanded in 1984, it was greatly enlarged through the tax reform legislation passed in 1986 and greatly expanded again in the deficit reduction legislation enacted in 1990. Today more than 11 million low-income working families with children receive the credit, nearly triple the number of families receiving AFDC. In addition, EITC benefit levels were more than doubled by these two pieces of legislation.[21]

Another targeted program, medicaid, has also been expanded since 1984 and is now available to categories of low-income pregnant women and children never previously covered. Most of the recent expansions reflect a principle similar to that underlying the EITC enlargements—that those who work at low wages and have children should not be worse off than those on welfare. In the case of medicaid, this has translated into the opinion that as far as pregnant women and children are concerned, it is unfair to provide coverage to those on welfare while denying it to those in low-income families that work. Accordingly, recent legislation has extended medicaid to low-income pregnant women and young children who are not on welfare. In fact, most are members of working families.

The political support for this growth has doubtless also stemmed from the services provided—health care coverage for pregnant women and children, a clientele not dissimilar to that of the WIC program. The expansions of medicaid services provide further evidence that the political

20. Median family income is expected to exceed $35,000 in 1990. It was $34,210 in 1989.

21. Under legislation enacted in 1990, EITC expansion will be phased in over four years. By tax year 1994 the maximum EITC benefit will equal $1,700 (in 1990 dollars) for a family with two or more children, and more than $2,000 if one of these children is younger than one year old. The EITC expansions enacted in 1990 will provide additional benefits of $13 billion over five years. (By comparison, the welfare reform legislation enacted in 1988 carried a price tag of $3.3 billion over five years.)

In recent years, support for EITC expansion has frequently been accompanied by statements from policymakers emphasizing that work should pay enough so that families with a full-time working parent need not be poor and so that those who work will be better off than those on public assistance.

success of the Sheppard-Towner Act in the 1920s, cited by Skocpol, may have had as much to do with its focus on health services for pregnant women and young children as with its universality.

One other feature is shared by the earned income tax credit, medicaid coverage for pregnant women and young children, and the WIC program. For each of these targeted programs, expansion has not only covered the very poor but has also included many working families with incomes modestly above the poverty line. Thus these programs (or components of programs) do not separate those modestly above the poverty line from those well below it. Instead, the programs combine these two groups.

As I have already noted, the income limit for the tax credit is about $20,000 a year. Families are eligible for WIC benefits in all but three states until their income surpasses 185 percent of the poverty line, now about $23,500 for a family of four. Recent expansions have also raised medicaid income ceilings for pregnant women and young children to 133 percent of the poverty line, now about $17,000 a year for a family of four. Moreover, states have the option of raising the medicaid ceiling for pregnant women and infants to 185 percent of the poverty line. And while the recently enacted medicaid expansions covering children age six through eighteen do not include children whose families have incomes above the poverty line, the same legislation that contained this medicaid enlargement also established a new, refundable health insurance credit for low- and moderate-income working families with children. The credit will defray a modest share of health insurance costs (including copayments charged by employers) for working families with incomes less than $20,000.

As a result, these three targeted programs have largely avoided the pitfalls described by Skocpol when she speaks of "working-class families with incomes just above the poverty line, themselves frequently struggling economically without the aid of health insurance or child care or adequate unemployment benefits" having to "pay for programs that go only to people with incomes below the poverty line." Instead, some of the very groups among whom welfare backlash has traditionally been thought to be strongest are beneficiaries of the earned income credit, the WIC program, the expansions in medicaid coverage for pregnant women and young children, and the new health insurance credit.

Including working families that earn $10,000 to $20,000 may also help these programs avoid the image of being primarily for minorities. Although AFDC is perceived in some quarters as a program primarily for black welfare mothers, the earned income tax credit and the WIC seem to have a broader focus. Thus they appear better able to meet William Julius Wilson's call for policies the public will consider race-neutral, and to do this within the framework of targeted programs.

Strategic Implications

What then creates wide political support for a social program? I would draw the following tentative conclusions.

—As a rule, universal programs are politically more successful than targeted programs. However, being targeted does not necessarily make a program unsustainable or highly vulnerable to cutbacks.

—The severe political weakness that Skocpol ascribes to targeted programs in general is more accurately ascribed to cash welfare programs for people who are not elderly, are not severely disabled, and do not work or work very little.

—Whether a benefit is linked to work and perceived as earned or whether it is seen as a welfare benefit for able-bodied adults who do not work is particularly significant. Delivering the benefit through the tax system, as is done with the earned income tax credit, rather than through the welfare office, also helps significantly.

—It also is important to ensure that the benefit is not narrowly targeted on the poorest elements in society. Covering working families that earn $10,000 to $20,000 (or roughly those with earnings between 100 percent and 200 percent of the poverty line)—and doing so without requiring that these families go on welfare—can be an important determinant of political success. This suggests that Skocpol's basic point about the importance of broadening the constituency served by a social program is correct but that the choice is not either-or between universal and targeted programs. There is a middle ground of maintaining a targeted program structure while incorporating near-poor and moderate-income working families that are struggling themselves.

—The particular groups of poor people served by a program—the elderly, pregnant women, able-bodied adults who are not working—are also relevant. Programs targeted on nonworking, nonelderly adults, as the AFDC program is and as state and local general assistance programs usually are, tend to be much weaker politically than programs that also encompass the low-income elderly or low-income working families. In this regard, the experience of the food stamp program is instructive. Although much like a welfare program and run through the welfare system, the food stamp program has fared relatively well politically during the past quarter century. Unlike AFDC benefits, food stamp benefits have kept pace with inflation, and the program has periodically been expanded. One reason it has fared better than AFDC is that it includes among its beneficiaries the low-income elderly and disabled (and to a lesser degree low-income working families as well). In fact, several cuts proposed in the program in the early 1980s failed on Capitol Hill precisely because of the impact the cuts would have had on the low-income elderly. (That the program provides its benefits in kind rather than in cash, along with its federally prescribed benefit structure, is also important.)

—Is the program seen as benefiting a national constituency or primarily a regional constituency? One of the low-income programs cut substantially in recent years is the low-income home energy assistance program, which helps households pay heating and cooling bills. That the program is viewed as primarily benefiting northern states weakens it politically. Its funding levels fell sharply as soon as former House Speaker Thomas P. O'Neill was no longer there to protect it.

—Are the benefit levels federally prescribed or are they left to the states to determine? The importance of this distinction can be seen vividly in the experience of the SSI program. By law, federal SSI benefit levels are fully indexed to inflation, and these levels rose slightly in real terms in the 1980s. By contrast, in most of the twenty-seven states that provide supplemental SSI payments, state payment levels have fallen far behind inflation in the past fifteen years. That food stamp benefits are entirely federally funded, and that food stamp eligibility and benefit levels are federally prescribed, has also been crucial to the durability of that program. Of course, whether a program has a federal funding structure of this nature is not unrelated to which groups of the poor it serves. If the food stamp program did not include the elderly and disabled and was limited to the able-bodied poor, it might never have attained its status as an entitlement program in which the benefits are 100 percent federally funded.[22]

22. Federally prescribed and funded benefits, as distinguished from benefits that are set by the states and wholly or partially state-funded, are significant for another reason. There is evidence that when state costs increase for means-tested programs such as medicaid that are partially state-funded, resources for other means-tested benefits tend to be reduced. Steven Gold (1990) has found that from 1976 to 1989, state spending for medicaid rose from 33 cents to 61 cents per $100 of personal income. During the same period, state spending for all other means-tested benefits (including AFDC, state SSI supplements, and general assistance) plunged from 68 cents per $100 of personal income to 40 cents. In addition, some analysts believe that the fact that federally funded food stamp benefits decline when AFDC

—Is the benefit provided in cash or in kind? Programs for the non-elderly poor seem to be weaker politically when benefits are provided in cash. The public may fear its tax dollars will go for alcohol, drugs, new cars, or extravagances rather than for food or medical treatment or other purposes deemed worthy of support. This point is related to the observation made earlier that programs providing certain types of services, such as health-related services for pregnant women and young children, tend to have greater political strength.

—Is the program an entitlement or a nonentitlement? There is a sharp divergence between how these programs fared in the 1980s. In this vein, I question Skocpol's citation of Head Start's failure to grow more quickly as an example of the weakness of targeted programs. A targeted nonentitlement program, Head Start has done considerably better in recent years than the typical nonentitlement program that is not targeted.

—Is the program perceived as effective? One reason the WIC was expanded and why Head Start is slated for major expansion in the next several years is that these programs are considered effective. Similarly, the belief that evaluations of welfare employment programs found these efforts effective contributed to the substantial funding increases they received in the Family Support Act of 1988. And evaluations giving high ratings to the Job Corps program helped insulate it from substantial reductions in the early 1980s when many other employment and training programs were being cut sharply.

In short, targeted programs tend to fare better in the political process when they are not viewed as a form of welfare (especially cash welfare), when they operate outside the welfare system, when they are viewed as providing benefits that have been earned or are otherwise linked to work, when the low-income constituency being served is broad (by virtue of including families with incomes of $10,000 to $20,000 or the elderly or both), when the program is an entitlement with federally prescribed and funded benefit levels, and when it is regarded as effective.

Universal Programs: The Problems of Budget Constraints

Some may argue that my discussion is beside the point because universal programs remain politically the strongest of all. This may be true, but it does not settle the question of what direction efforts to reduce poverty

benefits increase has influenced state decisions to allow AFDC benefits to fall sharply in real terms.

should take. Proposals to create new universal programs must face a major political obstacle: their large cost.

The nation is currently confronting budget deficits of more than $300 billion when the social security surplus is excluded from the calculations.[23] The Gramm-Rudman-Hollings law requires that the deficit be reduced to a prescribed level each year and that across-the-board spending cuts be instituted if these targets are not met. The combination of a large deficit and the strictures of Gramm-Rudman-Hollings makes it difficult to enact initiatives entailing large new expenditures. Such expenditures have to be accompanied by major reductions in other programs or significant tax increases or both.

The anticipated reductions in defense expenditures in the 1990s will not solve this problem. Some of the defense spending reductions are already reflected in the budget legislation enacted in 1990; those reductions cannot be used to finance new social programs. While significant further reductions in defense spending should be achievable, they too are likely to be used primarily to reduce the deficit. The budget legislation enacted in 1990 removed social security from the deficit calculations, while requiring that the deficit exclusive of social security be reduced to $83 billion by fiscal year 1995. Eventually, the Gramm-Rudman-Hollings law is likely to be extended beyond 1995 with a requirement that the federal budget be balanced sometime in the late 1990s. Achieving that goal will require another major round of revenue increases and program reductions, including further substantial cuts in defense.

Moreover, the budget legislation passed in 1990 contains another new element: a requirement that, through fiscal year 1995, any legislation creating or expanding entitlement benefits—as new universal programs generally would do—be offset through corresponding reductions in another entitlement or through tax increases. Under this new requirement a cut in defense spending could not be used to fund an expansion in an entitlement program unless Congress and the president agreed to override the new budget procedures. And it is highly unlikely that other entitlements would be cut enough to finance major new universal programs. In short, costly proposals for new universal social programs will probably have to be accompanied by tax increases. While some tax increases may be possible, there are likely to be political limits to how large they can be.

23. Deficits for both fiscal years 1991 and 1992 are projected to exceed $300 billion, excluding the social security trust fund, even after the deficit reduction measures enacted in the fall of 1990 are taken into account. The deficits for fiscal years 1993 through 1995 are projected to be lower.

The fate of the catastrophic health insurance legislation illustrates the difficulties of trying to enact new universal programs in the current fiscal climate. The legislation foundered because many members of Congress balked at the tax increases that were to finance it. (Some people who have advocated a new agenda of universal social programs dismiss this example, saying that the legislation should have been financed by a broad-based payroll-type tax on the general public, rather than a tax paid just by the elderly. But the tax on the elderly was proposed partly because financing the program through a general payroll tax increase was not considered politically viable.)[24]

Still another example is provided by the recommendations recently issued by the U.S. Bipartisan Commission on Comprehensive Health Care, known as the Pepper Commission, which issued a series of proposals to ensure universal access to basic health care and to long-term care. Yet while these proposals were supposed to help set the stage for an advance toward universal health care coverage, they are being accorded relatively little attention because a tax increase of $70 billion a year would be required to finance them.

Advocates of universal programs frequently contend that if a program will benefit the entire population, the public may accept a tax increase. To a degree this is probably true. But the amount of the tax increase the political system will accept will probably be limited for the foreseeable future. The 1990 deficit reduction law raised taxes $137 billion over five years, and taxes probably will have to be raised further in a few years because of continued deficit pressures. In addition, more revenues are likely to be needed to keep the medicare system solvent in future decades. New revenues may also be needed to help cover the costs of treating the increasing number of people with AIDS. And state taxes are likely to keep rising as state costs for health care, prisons, and the like continue to climb.

Thus new taxes to finance new universal programs would probably have to come on top of these other tax increases. In a nation with a historic aversion to the size of government and level of taxation found in Western Europe, the degree to which additional revenue can be raised for major new universal programs is likely to be limited for some time.

24. Another reason the catastrophic legislation was financed by a tax on the elderly was that some policymakers believed a tax on the general population would "crowd out" possibilities for other general tax increases to support future initiatives to assist the nonelderly. This is a further indication that there are political limits to the level of tax increases that can be passed for social program purposes.

Given the mounting pressures for reform in the health care system, new taxes might be raised to institute some form of universal health care coverage and possibly long-term care as well. These alone would require very large amounts of revenue. It is unlikely that other universal programs carrying substantial price tags will also be considered seriously during the 1990s. And by early in the next century the nation may be struggling mightily to find ways to raise the revenues to cover social security costs for the baby boom generation and cover other basic costs of government at the same time.

All these considerations, however, do not mean that certain universal policies without large costs, such as parental leave policies and stiff child support enforcement standards, cannot be mandated. And it should be politically feasible to make the child care tax credit already in the tax code into a "refundable" credit, so that low-income families incurring child care costs could benefit from it, just as middle- and upper-income families already do. Making the credit refundable would cost only $1.25 billion a year.[25]

Yet an attack on poverty that consists entirely of universal health coverage, parental leave policies, stiffened child support standards, and a refundable component to the child care tax credit would still leave most of the working poor with incomes below the poverty line. It would also do little to help those who have limited education and few skills and who face major barriers to employment, and it would barely affect many welfare families.

Establishing an "assured" child support assistance benefit, as Irwin Garfinkel, David Ellwood, and Skocpol have suggested, would represent an important policy innovation that could help many welfare families.[26] At present, however, only about one-fourth of those in the AFDC program have child support awards, and although that proportion should rise in coming years, it is likely that many will continue to lack such an award and hence be ineligible for assured payments.[27] It should also be

25. Currently this credit is not refundable, so that working families with incomes too low to owe income tax derive no benefit from it. As a result, it functions as a child care subsidy principally for middle- and upper-income parents. An Urban Institute study estimated that only 3 percent of all assistance provided through the credit goes to families in the bottom 30 percent of the income distribution. Barnes (1988), p. 4.

26. Ellwood (1988), chaps. 5, 7; Garfinkel and Uhr (1984); and Garfinkel (1985).

27. Skocpol envisions that *all* single-parent families, including those without awards, would receive the assured payments. This is not, however, how the child support assurance plan designed by Garfinkel would work. As he has noted, providing assured payments to single mothers who lack child support awards would likely prove politically unachievable.

noted that creation of an assured payment level may entail substantial cost, which could make it more difficult to enact.

The Need To Combine Universal and Targeted Approaches

Achieving a larger impact in reducing poverty is likely to require a mixture of universal and targeted approaches. Such a strategy would combine programs such as universal access to health care and assured child support with such carefully designed targeted approaches as further expansion of the earned income credit (particularly for large families), increased child care and housing assistance for low- and moderate-income working families, and increased funding for Head Start, WIC, childhood immunization, prenatal health care services, compensatory education for disadvantaged children, and other early-intervention programs that have good records and enjoy growing political support.

Such an antipoverty strategy should have certain broad goals. It should ensure that full-time work lifts family income above the poverty line (this will likely entail an increase in the minimum wage as well as an expanded EITC).[28] Excessive child care, health care, or housing costs should not then push such a family back into poverty. Policies should ensure that both parents contribute to the support of their children. Finally, early-intervention programs should reach all low-income children whose families wish to enroll them.

These programs and policies would need to be supplemented by an array of locally administered, highly intensive services for people facing serious employment barriers or other barriers to self-sufficiency. Although Skocpol seems to regard intensive service interventions, such as those described by Lisbeth Schorr in *Within Our Reach,* as distractions from a more universal agenda, some families and individuals may never get to the point where they can benefit from universal earned entitlements

---

He has also warned that attempting to provide assured payments to such mothers would make it considerably more difficult politically to secure approval of the assured payment concept. Asking taxpayers to agree to provide child support payments to mothers who provide too little information to track down an absent father and establish a child support award, or who do not know who the father is, is not likely to be politically viable. (Interview with Irwin Garfinkel, October 1989).

28. Restoring the minimum wage to its purchasing power of the 1960s and 1970s would help achieve these goals and likely have only a small impact on employment opportunities. See Shapiro (1988).

unless they receive intensive services that help them enter the mainstream economy.[29]

One illustration of the growing recognition of the need for such services is the current move to redesign the Job Training Partnership Act so that it focuses more employment and training services on disadvantaged youth and others with serious problems finding and holding jobs. Experience with state employment agencies and with current JTPA programs suggests that broad employment and training programs for the general population are likely to do little for those in the underclass or at risk of falling into it. Isabel Sawhill has recently argued, "if there is one lesson that we have learned from all the evaluations and research that has been conducted since the War on Poverty began, it is that [service] programs that provide limited benefits to many people, although politically popular, are not effective in responding to the problems of the most seriously disadvantaged." [30] She notes that one of the most effective programs for assisting disadvantaged youth, the Job Corps, is also one of the most highly targeted and points out that the current restructuring of JTPA stems from evidence that the program has provided insufficient services to the most disadvantaged segments of the population, in part because it has not been targeted enough.

The need for a mixed approach that combines both universal and targeted policies underscores another reason not to overemphasize universal strategies. With the funds available for social program interventions likely to remain limited, too heavy an emphasis on costly universal approaches could result in too few resources being directed to those at the bottom of the economic ladder. In assessing universal and targeted strategies to reduce poverty, Isabel Sawhill has sounded a cautionary note that should not be ignored:

> Consider what has happened since the early 1960s. Social insurance programs have expanded dramatically. Indeed, social security and medicare have been responsible for all of the increase in federal spending as a proportion of GNP since that time. Because of public resistance to paying higher overall taxes, this expansion has necessitated a lowering of income taxes to accommodate higher payroll taxes and has put tremendous downward pressure on discretionary [nonentitlement] programs, including programs for the poor. We shouldn't ignore this substitution effect in arguing for universal programs. Their trickle

29. Schorr (1988).
30. Sawhill (1989), p. 3.

down benefits have to be balanced against their costs in crowding out other efforts.[31]

31. Sawhill (1989), p. 3.

References

Barnes, Roberta Ott. 1988. "The Distributional Effects of Alternative Child Care Proposals." Paper prepared for the tenth annual meeting of the Association of Public Policy Analysis and Management. Washington: Urban Institute.

Bawden, D. Lee, and John L. Palmer. 1984. "Social Policy: Challenging the Welfare State." In *The Reagan Record: An Assessment of America's Changing Domestic Priorities,* edited by John L. Palmer and Isabel V. Sawhill. Cambridge, Mass: Ballinger.

Boehm, William T., Paul E. Nelson, and Kathryn A. Longen. 1980. *Progress Toward Eliminating Hunger in America.* Economics, Statistics, and Cooperatives Service, Department of Agriculture.

Congressional Budget Office. 1990. *The Economic and Budget Outlook: An Update.*

Ellwood, David T. 1988. *Poor Support: Poverty in the American Family.* Basic Books.

Garfinkel, Irwin. 1985. "Child Support Assurance: A New Tool for Achieving Social Security." University of Wisconsin.

Garfinkel, Irwin, and Elizabeth Uhr. 1984. "A New Approach to Child Support." *Public Interest* 74 (Spring), pp. 111–22.

Gold, Steven D. 1990. *The State Fiscal Agenda for the 1990s.* National Conference of State Legislatures.

House Committee on Ways and Means. 1990. *Background Material and Data on Programs within the Jurisdiction of the Committee on Ways and Means* (1990 Green Book).

Kotz, Nick. 1979. *Hunger in America: The Federal Response.* Field Foundation.

Leonard, Paul. 1989. "Changes in Low Income Discretionary Programs, FY81-FY89." Center on Budget and Policy Priorities.

Leonard, Paul A., Cushing N. Dolbeare, and Edward B. Lazere. 1989. *A Place to Call Home: The Crisis in Housing for the Poor.* Washington Center on Budget and Policy Priorities, Low Income Housing Information Service.

Moynihan, Daniel Patrick. 1986. *Family and Nation: The Godkin Lectures, Harvard University.* Harcourt, Brace, Jovanovich.

Palmer, John L., and Gregory B. Mills. 1982. "Budget Policy." In *The Reagan Experiment: An Examination of Economic and Social Policies under the Reagan Administration,* edited by John L. Palmer and Isabel V. Sawhill. Washington: Urban Institute.

Sawhill, Isabel V. 1989. "Comments on 'Targeting within Universalism: Politically Viable Policies to Combat Poverty in the U.S.' by Theda Skocpol." Unpublished paper.

Schorr, Lisbeth B., with Daniel Schorr. 1988. *Within Our Reach: Breaking the Cycle of Disadvantage.* Anchor Press.

Shapiro, Isaac. 1988. *The Minimum Wage and Job Loss.* Center on Budget and Policy Priorities.

Starr, Paul. 1986. "Health Care for the Poor: The Past Twenty Years." In *Fighting Poverty: What Works and What Doesn't,* edited by Sheldon H. Danziger and Daniel H. Weinberg. Harvard University Press.

Urban Institute. 1985. *The Effects of Legislative Changes in 1981 and 1982 on the Food Stamp Program,* vol. 1: *Final Report to Congress.* Washington: Urban Institute Press.

Wilson, William Julius. 1987. *The Truly Disadvantaged: The Inner City, the Underclass, and Public Policy.* University of Chicago Press.

Public Policy Research and
The Truly Disadvantaged

WILLIAM JULIUS WILSON

IN THE AFTERMATH of the controversy generated in 1965 by the Moynihan report on the black family, empirical research on inner-city poverty and other social dislocations ground to a halt. In the past few years, however, such research activity has revived as media reports and debates among academics have captured public interest in the growing problems of urban ghettos. Like the 1960s discussions of the causes and consequences of urban poverty that focused on the Moynihan report and on Oscar Lewis's work on the culture of poverty, much of the new discourse is contentious and acrimonious.[1] My book, *The Truly Disadvantaged*, has become a point of reference in this controversy and, as is too often true of controversies, a good deal of the discussion is based on inaccurate interpretations of the arguments set forth.

A worthy goal of any author is to write so as not to be misunderstood. But even the most carefully phrased statements on the underclass are unlikely to escape misinterpretation because, as Jennifer Hochschild has pointed out, the issues in this instance are "so complicated and politically sensitive that analysts have an apparently almost irresistible tendency to focus on that part of the problem that fits their own preconceptions and to deny or ignore those parts that violate their preconceptions."[2] Because the papers in this volume feature systematic empirical research and thoughtful formulations of concepts, however, my arguments tend to be carefully and accurately discussed. The few misinterpretations are probably caused by the lack of clarity with which my ideas were originally stated. Indeed, these misinterpretations could have been avoided if I had presented a more explicit statement of my theory, the hypotheses imbedded in the theory, and the conditions that must be present before they can be tested. Accordingly, to put the rest of my discussion here in proper

1. See Lewis (1959, 1961, 1966, 1968). For a comparative discussion of these two controversies, see Wilson (1988); and Rainwater and Yancey (1967).
2. Hochschild (1990), p. 2.

focus, I will first recapitulate the major arguments advanced in *The Truly Disadvantaged* and present the formal structure of the theoretical framework. I will then assess the empirical, conceptual, and policy arguments presented in the papers that directly or indirectly address the major hypotheses in the book.

A Summary of *The Truly Disadvantaged*

I argue in *The Truly Disadvantaged* that historical discrimination and a migration to large metropolises that kept the urban minority population relatively young created a problem of weak labor force attachment among urban blacks and, especially since 1970, made them particularly vulnerable to the industrial and geographic changes in the economy. The shift from goods-producing to service-producing industries, the increasing polarization of the labor market into low-wage and high-wage sectors, innovations in technology, the relocation of manufacturing industries out of central cities, and periodic recessions have forced up the rate of black joblessness (unemployment and nonparticipation in the labor market), despite the passage of antidiscrimination legislation and the creation of affirmative action programs. The rise in joblessness has in turn helped trigger an increase in the concentrations of poor people, a growing number of poor single-parent families, and an increase in welfare dependency. These problems have been especially evident in the ghetto neighborhoods of large cities, not only because the most impoverished minority populations live there but also because the neighborhoods have become less diversified in a way that has severely worsened the impact of the continuing economic changes.

Especially since 1970, inner-city neighborhoods have experienced an outmigration of working- and middle-class families previously confined to them by the restrictive covenants of higher-status city neighborhoods and suburbs. Combined with the increase in the number of poor caused by rising joblessness, this outmigration has sharply concentrated the poverty in inner-city neighborhoods. The number with poverty rates that exceed 40 percent—a threshold definition of "extreme poverty" neighborhoods—has risen precipitously. And the dwindling presence of middle- and working-class households has also removed an important social buffer that once deflected the full impact of the kind of prolonged high levels of joblessness in these neighborhoods that has stemmed from uneven economic growth and periodic recessions.

In earlier decades, not only were most of the adults in ghetto neighborhoods employed, but black working and middle classes brought stability. They invested economic and social resources in the neighborhoods, patronized the churches, stores, banks, and community organizations, sent their children to the local schools, reinforced societal norms and values, and made it meaningful for lower-class blacks in these segregated enclaves to envision the possibility of some upward mobility.

However, today the ghetto features a population, the underclass, whose primary predicament is joblessness reinforced by growing social isolation. Outmigration has decreased the contact between groups of different class and racial backgrounds and thereby concentrated the adverse effects of living in impoverished neighborhoods. These concentration effects, reflected, for example, in the residents' self-limiting social dispositions, are created by inadequate access to jobs and job networks, the lack of involvement in quality schools, the unavailability of suitable marriage partners, and the lack of exposure to informal mainstream social networks and conventional role models.

Accordingly, *The Truly Disadvantaged* argued that the factors associated with the recent increases in social dislocation in the ghetto are complex. They cannot be reduced to the easy explanations of a "culture of poverty" that have been advanced by those on the right, or of racism, posited by those on the left. Although the ghetto is a product of historical discrimination and although present-day discrimination has undoubtedly contributed to the deepening social and economic woes of its residents, to understand the sharp increase in these problems requires the specification of a complex web of other factors, including shifts in the American economy.

The Formal Structure of the Theoretical Framework

This summary of *The Truly Disadvantaged* does not make explicit the fact that social-structural, social-psychological, and cultural variables are integrated into my theoretical framework.[3] A more formal statement of this framework is that a structure of inequality has evolved which is linked to contemporary behavior in the inner city by a combination of constraints, opportunities, and social psychology.

The exogenous factors, representing the sources of the racial concentration of urban poverty, include racial discrimination, changes in the

3. In the ensuing discussion in this section, I benefited from the formal explication of *The Truly Disadvantaged* in Zelditch (1989).

economy that have relocated industries and restructured occupations, and political processes (antibias legislation and affirmative action programs) that have had the unanticipated consequence of widening class divisions among urban blacks. The endogenous determinants created by these exogenous factors include such demographic variables as urban migration, age structures, and the pool of marriageable men, and economic factors such as the distribution of employment and income. These variables are important for understanding the experiences of all low-income urban groups, not just the ghetto underclass.

The endogenous determinants further include social isolation, which is unique to the social environment of the underclass. Social isolation deprives residents of inner-city neighborhoods not only of resources and conventional role models, whose former presence buffered the effects of neighborhood joblessness, but also of the kind of cultural learning from mainstream social networks that facilitates social and economic advancement in modern industrial society. The lack of neighborhood material resources, the relative absence of conventional role models, and the circumscribed cultural learning produce outcomes, or concentration effects, that restrict social mobility. Some of these outcomes are structural (lack of labor force attachment and access to informal job networks), and some are social-psychological (negative social dispositions, limited aspirations, and casual work habits).

From the point of view of the accumulation of scientific knowledge, it is important to keep these theoretical issues in mind to establish clearly the empirical, conceptual, and theoretical contributions of the authors of the papers in furthering understanding of the underclass phenomenon.

The Economy and Weak Labor Force Attachment in the Inner City

In my attempt in *The Truly Disadvantaged* to examine empirically the problem of the growing concentration of poverty, I used census tracts as proxies for nonpoverty and inner-city areas. The latter was divided into poverty, high-poverty, and extreme poverty neighborhoods. Most of my analysis of concentrated poverty focused on areas of extreme poverty, that is, those in which at least 40 percent of the people are poor. More recent studies have followed this lead by defining ghettos as those areas with poverty rates of at least 40 percent. The ghetto poor are therefore identified as those among the poor in the inner city who reside in these neighborhoods of extreme poverty.[4]

The paper by Paul Jargowsky and Mary Jo Bane in this volume shows that the proportion of the poor who reside in ghetto neighborhoods varies dramatically by race. Whereas only 2 percent of the non-Hispanic white poor lived in ghettos in 1980, some 21 percent of black poor and 16 percent of Hispanic poor resided there. And almost a third of all metropolitan blacks lived in a ghetto in 1980. Sixty-five percent of the 2.4 million ghetto poor in the United States are black, 22 percent Hispanic, and 13 percent non-Hispanic and other races. Thus to speak of the ghetto poor in the United States is to refer primarily to blacks and Hispanics. This has both descriptive and theoretical significance.

What is not revealed in *The Truly Disadvantaged* and what is clearly spelled out by Jargowsky and Bane is that the increase of ghetto poverty occurred mainly in only two regions of the country: the Midwest and the Northeast. Moreover, ten cities accounted for three-fourths of the total rise of ghetto poverty during the 1970s. One-third of the increase was accounted for solely by New York City, and one-half by New York and Chicago together. By adding Philadelphia, Newark, and Detroit, two-thirds of the total increase is accounted for. The others in the top ten were Columbus, Ohio, Atlanta, Baltimore, Buffalo, and Paterson, New Jersey. Of the 195 standard metropolitan areas in 1970 that recorded some ghetto poverty, 88 experienced decreases in the number of ghetto poor by 1980. Those with the largest decreases were Texas cities with significant

4. See Wacquant and Wilson (1989) and Jargowsky and Bane (in this volume). In discussing the correspondence between ghetto neighborhoods and extreme poverty census tracts in Chicago, Wacquant and Wilson state, "Extreme-poverty neighborhoods comprise tracts with at least 40 percent of their residents in poverty in 1980. These tracts make up the historic heart of Chicago's black ghetto: over 82 percent of the respondents in this category inhabit the west and south sides of the city, in areas most of which have been all black for half a century and more, and an additional 13 percent live in immediately adjacent tracts. Thus when we counterpose extreme-poverty areas with low-poverty areas, we are in effect comparing ghetto neighborhoods with other black areas, most of which are moderately poor, that are not part of Chicago's traditional black belt" (p. 16). Jargowsky and Bane use the same rationale on a national level: "Visits to several cities confirmed that the 40 percent criterion came very close to identifying areas that looked like ghettos in terms of their housing conditions. Moreover, the areas selected by the 40 percent criterion corresponded rather closely with the neighborhoods that city officials and local Census Bureau officials considered ghettos."

Of course, not all the people who reside in ghettos are poor. In the ten largest American cities as of 1970, the number of Hispanic residents (poor and nonpoor) residing in ghetto areas tripled between 1970 and 1980; the number of blacks doubled.

declines in Hispanic ghetto poverty and southern cities with sharp drops in black ghetto poverty.

The focus of *The Truly Disadvantaged,* however, was on the increase in ghetto poverty. The questions are why did this increase occur and why was most of it confined to the large industrial metropolises of the Northeast and Midwest? Because these two regions experienced massive industrial restructuring and loss of blue-collar jobs. Cities of the frostbelt suffered overall employment decline because "growth in their predominantly information-processing industries could not numerically compensate for substantial losses in their more traditional industrial sectors, especially manufacturing."[5] Cities in the sunbelt experienced job growth in all major sectors of the economy (manufacturing, retail and wholesale, white-collar services, and blue-collar services) between 1970 and 1986.

In *The Truly Disadvantaged* I maintained that one result of these changes for many urban blacks has been a growing mismatch between the location of employment and residence in the inner city. Although studies based on data collected before 1970 did not show consistent or convincing effects on black employment as the result of this spatial mismatch, the employment of inner-city blacks relative to suburban ones has clearly deteriorated since then.[6] Recent research conducted mainly by urban and labor economists strongly shows that the decentralization of employment is continuing and that employment in manufacturing, most of which is already suburbanized, has decreased in central cities, particularly in the Northeast and Midwest. Blacks living in central cities have less access to employment, as measured by the ratio of jobs to people and the average travel time to and from work, than do central-city whites. Unlike most other groups of workers, less educated central-city blacks receive lower wages in the central city than less educated suburban blacks. And the decline in earnings of central-city blacks is positively associated with the extent of metropolitan job decentralization.[7]

But are the differences in employment between city and suburban blacks mainly the result of changes in the location of jobs? It is possible that in recent years the migration of blacks to the suburbs has become much more selective than in earlier years, so much so that the changes attributed to job location are really caused by this selective migration.[8] The pattern of black migration to the suburbs in the 1970s was similar to

---

5. Kasarda (1990a), p. 241.
6. Holzer (1990). For a study based on earlier data, see Ellwood (1986).
7. Holzer (1990).
8. Jencks and Mayer (1989b).

that of whites during the 1950s and 1960s in the sense that it was concentrated among the more educated and younger city residents.[9] However, in the 1970s this was even more true for blacks, creating a situation in which the education and income gaps between city and suburban blacks seemed to expand and that between city and suburban whites seemed to contract.[10] Accordingly, if one were to control for personal and family characteristics, how much of the employment gap between city and suburbs would remain?

This question was addressed in the study by James E. Rosenbaum and Susan J. Popkin in this volume of the Gautreaux program in Chicago. The design of the program permitted them to contrast systematically the employment experiences of a group of low-income blacks who had been assigned private apartments in the suburbs with the experiences of a control group with similar demographic characteristics and employment histories who had been assigned private apartments in the city. The authors' findings support the spatial mismatch hypothesis. After controlling for personal characteristics (including family background, family circumstances, human capital, motivation, and length of time since the respondent first moved to the Gautreaux program—all before the move—and education after moving), they found that those who moved to apartments in the suburbs were significantly more likely than those moving to apartments in the city to have a job after the move. When asked what makes it easier to obtain employment in the suburbs, nearly all the respondents mentioned the availability of jobs.

The occupational advancement of the more disadvantaged urban minority members has also been severely curtailed by industrial restructuring. John Kasarda's research demonstrates that "the bottom fell out in urban industrial demand for poorly educated blacks," particularly in the goods-producing industries, in northeastern and midwestern cities.[11] And data collected from the Chicago Urban Poverty and Family Life Survey show that efforts by out-of-school inner-city black men to obtain blue-collar jobs in the industries in which their fathers had been employed have been hampered by industrial restructuring. "The most common occupation reported by the cohort of respondents at ages 19 to 28 changed from operative and assembler jobs among the oldest cohorts to service jobs (waiters and janitors) among the youngest cohort."[12]

9. Frey (1985); and Grier and Grier (1988).
10. Holzer (1990).
11. Kasarda (1989), p. 35.
12. Testa and Krogh (1989).

Finally, a recent study shows that although black employment in New York City declined by 84,000 in durable and nondurable goods manufacturing—industries whose workers have lower levels of education—from 1970 to 1987, black employment increased by 104,000 in public administration and professional services—industries whose workers are more highly educated.[13] Thus if industrial restructuring has reduced opportunities for the least educated blacks, it may have improved opportunities for those more highly educated.

As I pointed out in *The Truly Disadvantaged,* manufacturing industries have been a major source of black employment in the twentieth century. Unfortunately, these industries are particularly sensitive to a slack economy, and blacks lost a considerable number of jobs during the recession-plagued decade of the 1970s.[14] A unique test of my argument that many of the employment problems among disadvantaged inner-city youths are the direct result of job losses in local labor markets was provided by Richard Freeman's paper. Examining the employment situation of disadvantaged black youths from 1983 to 1987 in metropolitan areas that had achieved the tightest labor markets by 1987, Freeman found that despite the social problems that beset these youths and "despite the 1980s twist in the American labor market against the less skilled, tight labor markets substantially improved the economic position of these workers." Although jobless rates remain high among disadvantaged minority youths, dramatic progress occurred during the economic recovery of the late 1980s in the metropolitan areas with the tightest labor markets.

If a tight labor market reduces joblessness among the disadvantaged, it also effectively reduces poverty, as the paper by Paul Osterman clearly shows. When Boston experienced full employment in the 1980s, not only was there a significant drop in poverty, but a high percentage of the poor had jobs. However, the strong economy did not significantly affect the prevalence of single-parent families. Was the period that Osterman observed (1980 to 1988) of sufficient length to allow for changes in family formation as a response to changes in the economy to emerge? Changes in employment and poverty are likely to appear much sooner following changes in the economy than changes in family formation because the latter not only represent a more indirect relationship to the economy but a more complex and subtle process of human experience as well.

The relationship between employment and marriage received more de-

13. Bailey (1989).
14. For a good discussion of this problem, see Levy (1987).

tailed attention in the paper by Robert Mare and Christopher Winship. They found only modest support for the hypothesis, emphasized in *The Truly Disadvantaged*, that associates the sharp rise in poor single-parent families with the declining employment status of young black men. "Changes in the employment of young black men," they concluded, "explain approximately 20 percent of the decline in their marriage rates since 1960." Their results are based on national surveys. But unlike *The Truly Disadvantaged*, their paper makes no effort to examine regional differences that may reflect the impact of changes in the industrial economies in the Northeast and Midwest.

The data that would be most relevant for understanding the relationship between employment and marriage among the underclass are those collected from inner cities. Since the publication of *The Truly Disadvantaged*, this relationship has been examined more closely with data from the inner-city neighborhoods of Chicago as a part of the Urban Poverty and Family Life Study. A recent paper by Mark Testa based on these data shows that black men in inner-city Chiago who have stable work are twice as likely to marry as black men who are jobless and are not in school or in the military.[15]

However, Testa's study also shows that the decline in marriage among inner-city blacks is not simply a function of the proportion of jobless men. Because the disparity in marriage rates between employed and jobless black men was smaller for older cohorts, it is reasonable to consider the effects of weaker social strictures against out-of-wedlock births. "In earlier years," he comments, "the social stigma of illegitimacy counterbalanced economic considerations in the decision to marry. As the norms of legitimacy weakened, marriage rates dropped precipitously among chronically jobless men as couples no longer felt obliged to legitimate the birth of a child for social reasons."[16]

In *The Truly Disadvantaged* I related the increasing jobless rate among black men to geographic, industrial, and other shifts in the economy. This hypothesis has drawn criticism because some observers believed that the focus on impersonal economic forces overlooked willful acts of employment discrimination against racial minorities.[17] Although empirical research on such discrimination is scarce, data from the Chicago Urban Poverty and Family Life Study's survey of employers, as reported in the paper by Joleen Kirschenman and Kathryn Neckerman, suggest that

15. Testa (1990).
16. Testa (1990), p. 22.
17. Bailey (1989); and Hochschild (1990).

inner-city blacks, particularly black men, do indeed face negative attitudes from employers. They report that many employers consider inner-city workers, especially young black men, to be uneducated, uncooperative, and unstable. Accordingly, employers may practice what economists call statistical discrimination, making judgments about an applicant's productivity, which are often too difficult or too expensive to measure, on the basis of his or her race, ethnic, or class background.[18] Although only a few employers explicitly expressed racist attitudes or a categorical loathing of blacks, many did in fact practice statistical discrimination by screening out black job applicants because of their social class, public school education, and inner-city residence. These factors also served as proxies for judgments about productivity.

As the research of Richard Freeman suggests, however, the practice of statistical discrimination will vary according to the tightness of the labor market. It therefore ought not be analyzed without reference to the overall state of the local or national economy. In a tight labor market, job vacancies are more prevalent, unemployment is of shorter duration, and wages are higher. The pool of potential workers expands because an increase in job opportunities not only lowers unemployment but also draws into the labor force those workers who respond to fading job prospects in slack markets by dropping out of the labor force altogether. Accordingly, the status of disadvantaged minorities improves in a tight labor market because unemployment is reduced, better jobs are available, and wages are higher. In contrast, in a slack labor market employers are—indeed, can afford to be—more selective in recruiting and in granting promotions. They inflate job prerequisites and the importance of experience. In such an economic climate, the level of employer discrimination rises and disadvantaged minorities suffer disproportionately.

Although basic economic transformations and changes in labor markets are important for understanding the life experiences of the urban minority poor, *The Truly Disadvantaged* also argued that the out-migration of higher-income residents from certain parts of the inner city resulted in a higher concentration of residents in ghetto neighborhoods. This contention has been controversial. Douglas Massey and Mitchell Eggers, for instance, have found that the increase of segregation among black social classes during the 1970s was not sufficient to account for the rise in concentrated urban black poverty. They argue that because of persisting segregation, higher-income blacks have been less able than the

18. See also Neckerman and Kirschenman (1990).

privileged of other groups to separate themselves from the poor.[19] Accordingly, an increase in the poverty rate of a highly segregated group will be automatically accompanied by an increase in the concentration of poverty. Reynolds Farley reaches the same conclusion in his paper in this volume: "Wilson's conclusion that poor blacks in Chicago lived in proportionally more impoverished neighborhoods in 1980 than in 1970 . . . is accurate . . . but the situation occurred because of overall increases in black poverty rather than because of higher levels of social class residential segregation or a new outmigration of prosperous blacks." In their paper in this volume, however, Paul Jargowsky and Mary Jo Bane turn down the argument that changes in poverty rates alone explain changes in ghetto poverty.

The conflicting findings and conclusions correspond with different measures of concentrated poverty. Massey and Eggers and Farley use an index of segregation to calculate the probability of intraclass contact among groups in metropolitan areas. Although this measure provides a unique description of the overall level of concentrated poverty in standard metropolitan statistical areas, as Jargowsky and Bane point out, it does not identify particular neighborhoods that are ghettos and others that are not. Focusing on Philadelphia, Cleveland, Milwaukee, and Memphis, they designate ghetto and nonghetto neighborhoods and report a significant geographic spreading of ghetto neighborhoods from 1970 to 1980. Areas that had become ghettos by 1980 had been mixed-income tracts in 1970, although they were contiguous to areas identified as ghettos. These results support the hypothesis that a major factor in the growth of ghetto poverty has been the exodus of the nonpoor from mixed income areas: "the poor were leaving as well, but the nonpoor left faster, leaving behind a group of people in 1980 that was poorer than in 1970."

These results also contradict Paul Peterson's argument in this volume that "very little, if any [of the increase in the number of poor people living in extremely poor neighborhoods] can be attributed to increasing class segregation within the black community." On the contrary, the data suggest that the increase of segregation among black social classes was one of several major factors that accounted for the growth of ghetto poverty. As Jargowsky and Bane point out, "In none [of the four cities] was the process a simple matter of the poor moving into ghetto areas or the nonpoor moving out. Nor can the situation in any city be described as one in

19. Massey and Eggers (1990), p. 1186.

which people basically stayed put but that changes in the poverty rate caused more areas to be pushed over the 40 percent line. Instead there was a general pattern of dispersion—probably part of a longer historical trend—interacting with changes in the poverty rate and continuing high levels of racial segregation." As the population spread out from areas of mixed income, Jargowsky and Bane go on to state, the next ring, mostly areas that were white and nonpoor, became the home of a "larger proportion of the black and poor population. The white nonpoor left these areas, which also lost population overall." [20] Thus the black middle-class out-migration was not followed by a significant rise of black interclass segregation in neighborhoods where the middle class relocated.

Unfortunately, the geographic spread of ghetto poverty cannot be captured in studies that focus on the concentration of poverty in SMSAs based on a segregation index. Although the studies by Farley and Massey and Eggers are important for understanding the significance of racial segregation in accounting for changes in the concentration of metropolitan poverty, they do not provide an appropriate test of the hypothesis that associates the increase of ghetto poverty with the out-migration of higher-income blacks from certain inner-city neighborhoods.

Social Environment and Labor Force Attachment in the Inner City

The exodus of higher-income blacks was not only a factor in the growth of ghetto poverty. It also deprived these neighborhoods of structural resources, such as social buffers to minimize the effects of growing joblessness, and cultural resources, such as conventional role models for neighborhood children, therefore further contributing to the economic marginality of the underclass.

In *The Truly Disadvantaged* I argued that the central problem of the underclass is joblessness reinforced by increasing social isolation in impoverished neighborhoods, as reflected, for example, in the residents' declining access to job information network systems. Martha Van Haitsma, in an important conceptual paper, has more sharply delineated the relationship between the social environment and experiences in the labor market by distinguishing those persons with weak attachment to the la-

---

20. For a comprehensive study that presents similar findings, see Coulton, Chow, and Pandey (1990).

bor force whose social context "tends to maintain or further weaken this attachment." [21] I would like to include this more explicit notion in my framework by equating the social context with the neighborhood.

Unlike the usage in the paper by Marta Tienda and Haya Stier in this volume, the term weak labor force attachment as used here does not imply a willingness or desire to work.[22] Rather, I view weak labor force attachment as a structural concept set in a theoretical framework that explains the vulnerability of certain groups to joblessness. In other words, the concept signifies the marginal position of some people in the labor force because of limited job opportunities or limited access to the informal job network systems. From a theoretical standpoint there are two major sources of weak labor force attachment: macrostructural processes in the larger society, particularly the economy, and the individual's social environment. The former has been discussed; let me now briefly focus on the latter.

To understand the unique position of the underclass, it is important to understand the association between attachment to the labor force and the neighborhood context. As Martha Van Haitsma points out, "environments with few opportunities for stable and legitimate employment and many opportunities for other types of income-generating activities, particularly those which are incompatible with regular employment," perpetuate weak labor force attachment.[23] Poor people who reside in neighborhoods that foster or support strong labor force attachment are in a much different social context than those with similar educations and occupational skills living in neighborhoods that promote or reinforce weak labor force attachment. Thus neighborhoods that have few legitimate employment opportunities, inadequate job information networks, and poor schools not only give rise to weak labor force attachment but also raise the likelihood that people will turn to illegal or deviant activities for income, thereby further weakening their attachment to the legitimate labor market. A jobless family in such a neighborhood is influenced by the behavior, beliefs, orientations, and social perceptions of other disadvantaged families disproportionately concentrated in the neighborhood. To capture this process I used the term "concentration effects," that is, the effects of living in an overwhelmingly impoverished environment.

Four papers in this volume address the hypothesis on concentration

21. Van Haitsma (1989), p. 28.
22. The concept of weak labor force attachment initially received systematic attention in the work of McLanahan and Garfinkel (1989).
23. Van Haitsma (1989), p. 29.

effects. Elijah Anderson's research in a ghetto neighborhood of Philadelphia provides ethnographic support by showing how a young woman's proximity to and degree of integration with certain neighborhood peer groups can significantly increase her chances of becoming pregnant. Jonathan Crane, relying on evidence from a unique data set (the neighborhood characteristics file from the 1970 Public Use Microdata Sample), provides quantitative support for the hypothesis by showing that neighborhood influence on teenage childbearing and dropping out among both blacks and whites was substantial in inner cities. Consistent with the arguments developed in *The Truly Disadvantaged,* Crane found that "neighborhood effects are much larger at the bottom of the neighborhood distribution than elsewhere." And Susan Mayer supports the hypothesis with data from the High School and Beyond Survey. She finds that teenagers attending schools of low socioeconomic status are more likely to give birth out of wedlock than those with the same socioeconomic background who attend schools of higher socioeconomic status.

In their paper on the political behavior of poor people, Jeffrey Berry, Kent Portney, and Ken Thomson present evidence that does not support the concentration-effects hypothesis. It is important to note, however, that the cities they selected for analysis included virtually no neighborhoods with a poverty level of 40 percent or more. Although their study used a poverty line below that of the official poverty line, the absence of extreme poverty or ghetto neighborhoods qualifies their conclusion that the concentration of poor blacks does not lead to distinctive patterns of political behavior.

It would also be interesting and important to replicate the study by Greg Duncan and Saul Hoffman in areas of extreme poverty. On the basis of national data from the Michigan Panel Study of Income Dynamics, they found that raising AFDC benefit levels increased slightly the chances that a teenager would have a child out of wedlock and would receive AFDC. Nonwelfare opportunities decreased the chances, and the effect was much stronger. The teenagers most likely to bear a child, they find, are those with the least to lose. This view is supported in Anderson's study: "Those who cannot go on to college, who lack an outlook, who fail to find a husband with whom they can pursue the dream and become upwardly mobile, appear to adapt to the situation of closed mobility they see before them." And as Crane's research demonstrates, this is far more likely to happen in an impoverished inner-city neighborhood than in one that is less poor. That is one of many reasons why the neighborhood environment is crucial to my definition of the underclass.

Social Theory and the Concept of the Underclass

In my formulation the concept of underclass derives its meaning from a theoretical framework that links structural, social-psychological, and cultural arguments. David Greenstone has thus misinterpreted the theoretical discussion in *The Truly Disadvantaged* when he argues that my analysis settles on one fundamental opposition: underclass behavior must be attributed either to responses to an economic predicament or to the cultural commitments to dysfunctional and irrational values. Simplistic either-or notions of culture and social structure impede the development of a broader theoretical context in which to examine questions recently raised by the ongoing debate on the underclass.

In early studies of the inner city, some observers argued that ghetto-specific behaviors were unique adaptations to the restricted opportunities of the disadvantaged in American society, not a different system of values.[24] Although they discussed the influence of culture—that is, the extent to which people follow their inclinations as they have been developed by learning from other members of the community—they did not argue that the influence takes on a life of its own or is autonomous in the ghetto. In other words, these authors demonstrated the possibility of seeing the importance of macrostructural constraints (that is, of avoiding the extreme assumption of a culture of poverty) while still recognizing the value of a more subtle cultural analysis of life in poverty. The question Ulf Hannerz raised twenty years ago remains an important research hypothesis today. Is there a fundamental difference between "a person who is alone in being exposed to certain macrostructural constraints" and a person "who is influenced both by these constraints and by the behavior of others who are affected by them"?[25]

What distinguishes members of the underclass from those of other economically disadvantaged groups is that their marginal economic position or weak attachment to the labor force is uniquely reinforced by the neighborhood or social milieu. For this reason Christopher Jencks's discussion in this volume of the concept of the underclass is not relevant. Although he has elegantly and impressively laid out the various ways that one can view the underclass, his typology has no underlying theoretical significance. He argues that what we now call the underclass bears a striking resemblance to what sociologists used to call the lower class. This is not

24. Clark (1965); Rainwater (1966, 1967); and Hannerz (1969).
25. Hannerz (1969), p. 184.

true for the formulation developed in *The Truly Disadvantaged* and further elaborated here. Indeed, I know of no previous studies that attempted to define lower class in terms of the dual problem of marginal economic position and social isolation in highly concentrated poverty areas, an important distinction that cannot be captured by using the standard designation "lower class." In America the problems this definition of the underclass connotes are more likely to be found in the inner-city ghettos.

Jencks argues that my definition of the underclass also turns out to mean a largely nonwhite population because I emphasize location. However, in my usage, the concept can be theoretically applied not only to all racial and ethnic groups, but also to different societies. In the United States the concept will more often refer to minorities because the white poor seldom live in extreme poverty or ghetto areas. However, there is nothing in the definition that restricts its application to nonwhites. Moreover, in other societies the combination of weak labor force attachment and social isolation may exist in certain urban environments without the same level of concentrated poverty inherent in American ghettos. For example, there is evidence that the long-term jobless in inner cities in the Netherlands have experienced sharply decreasing contact with conventional groups and institutions in the larger society despite levels of class and ethnic segregation far lower than those of American inner cities. This development has prompted some Dutch social scientists to discuss the formation of an underclass in the Netherlands in precisely the theoretical terms I outlined in *The Truly Disadvantaged*.[26]

Unless the concept of underclass is defined as a part of a theoretical framework, as I have done, its meaning will become hopelessly polluted and, as Herbert Gans has warned, will be used increasingly to discredit the urban minority poor.[27] Indeed, one of my concerns is that because of the atheoretical way that the concept is often defined by scholars and nonscholars alike, its use has become exceedingly controversial, so much so that the debate has often obscured the important theoretical and empirical issues discussed in this volume and outlined here.[28] The crucial question is whether a theoretically defined concept of underclass, which is by its very nature complex, will be overshadowed in the long run by nonsystematic, arbitrary, and atheoretical usages that often end up as

26. See, for example, Schuyt (1990); Kloosterman (1990); and Engbersen (1990). Also see Engbersen, Schuyt, and Timmer (1990).

27. Gans (1990).

28. See also Wilson (1990).

code words or ideological slogans, particularly in journalistic descriptions of inner-city behavior. If this proves true, research scholars ought to give serious consideration to dropping the term and carefully selecting another that also allows one to describe and highlight the important theoretical linkage between a disadvantaged group's position in the labor market and its social environment.

The Underclass and Public Policy

The growing concentration of poverty and social isolation of the inner cities has implications not only for the quality of life and patterns of social interaction in impoverished urban neighborhoods, but for the larger urban environment as well. None of these cities can escape the deleterious consequences of the social transformation of the inner city and the growth of an underclass.

The problem is not simply the fiscal burden created by the sharp deterioration of aggregate family income or the erosion of the municipal tax base caused by the growth in the number of "high-cost" citizens at the very time that large and increasing numbers of higher-income families have abandoned the cities. The deterioration of ghetto neighborhoods has also sapped the vitality of local businesses and other institutions, and it has led to fewer and shabbier movie theaters, bowling alleys, restaurants, public parks and playgrounds, and other recreational facilities. Residents of inner-city neighborhoods are therefore often compelled to seek leisure activity in other areas of the city, where they come into brief contact with citizens of different racial, ethnic, or class backgrounds. Sharp differences in cultural style and patterns of interaction that reflect the social isolation of neighborhood networks often lead to clashes. Both the white and minority classes have complained bitterly about how certain conveniently located areas of the central city have deteriorated following the influx of inner-city residents. The complaints have inevitably come to be directed at the underclass itself.

Meanwhile, racial tensions between poor blacks and working-class whites reflect an even more serious consequence of the social transformation of the inner city. Working-class whites, like inner-city minorities, have felt the full impact of the urban fiscal crisis in the United States. Unlike middle-class whites, they have been forced by financial exigencies to remain in the poorer parts of the cities and suffer the strains of crime, poorer services, and higher taxes. Unlike the more affluent whites who choose to remain in the wealthier sections of the cities, they cannot easily escape the problems of deteriorating public schools by sending their children to private schools, a problem made worse by the sharp decrease in the numbers of urban parochial schools. Thus, in recent years, the racial struggle for power and privilege in the cities has been essentially a struggle between the have-nots over access to and control of decent housing and decent neighborhoods.

Working-class whites are more likely than middle-class whites to express their hostility in blatantly racist terms and behavior, sometimes manifested in acts of violence such as the recent killing of a young black man in the white ethnic neighborhood of Bensonhurst in New York City, and they are less likely to distinguish between middle-class and disadvantaged minorities. Middle-class whites are more subtle in their expressions of hostility and are more likely to direct their racial antagonisms specifically toward poor minorities.

The increasing antagonism has been further aggravated by a conservative political atmosphere, particularly during the Reagan presidency, that has not only reinforced the dominant American belief system that poverty is a reflection of individual inadequacy but has discouraged efforts for new and stronger social programs to address the growing problems of urban inequality.

These changes in the racial and political climate in America have profound implications for the way we will address the problems of race and class in the inner cities. I am therefore reminded of the words of the late black economist, Vivian Henderson, who wrote, "The economic future of blacks in the United States is bound up with that of the rest of the nation. Policies, programs, and politics designed in the future to cope with the problems of the poor and victimized will also yield benefits to blacks. In contrast, any efforts to treat blacks separately from the rest of the nation are likely to lead to frustration, heightened racial animosities, and a waste of the country's resources and the precious resources of black people." [29]

I agree with Henderson. In the coming years the best political strategy for those committed to racial justice is to place more emphasis on race-neutral programs that would not only address the plight of the disadvantaged among minorities but would apply to all groups in America. After all, Americans across racial and class lines continue to be concerned about increased unemployment, decreased job security, deteriorating real wages, poorer public education, escalating medical and hospital costs,

29. Henderson (1975), p. 54.

the lack of good child care, and more crime and drug trafficking in their neighborhoods. Because these problems are more highly concentrated in the inner cities as a result of cumulative effects of decades of racial subjugation, programs that aggressively address them will disproportionately benefit the underclass.

The papers by Theda Skocpol and Robert Greenstein in this volume ought to be considered in this context. The issue is not simply the degree to which universal or targeted programs can sustain political support. The important question is whether costly programs perceived to be targeted to minorities can be generated and adequately supported in the present climate of budgetary constraint and racial antagonism. Although many social programs did indeed survive the Reagan budget cuts, they are hardly sufficient to address the manifold problems gripping the ghettos. We must generate new initiatives if we are indeed to move significant numbers of American citizens out of the underclass. Whether we follow Skocpol's program of targeting within universalism or Greenstein's argument that a mixture of universal and targeted approaches will likely be necessary to achieve a significant impact, the real challenge is to develop programs that not only meaningfully address the problems of the underclass but that draw broad support.

This was my concern when I wrote *The Truly Disadvantaged* and argued for improving the life chances of truly disadvantaged groups such as the ghetto underclass by emphasizing programs to which the more advantaged groups of all races and class backgrounds can positively relate. I now believe that this is best achieved not simply through a combination of targeted and universal initiatives, but through targeted and universal initiatives that are clearly race neutral.

References

Bailey, Thomas. 1989. "Black Employment Opportunities." In *Setting Municipal Priorities, 1990*, edited by Charles Brecher and Raymond D. Horton. New York University Press.

Bureau of the Census. 1988. "Characteristics of the Population below the Poverty Level," 1978–84; "Poverty in the U.S.," 1985–87; and "Money Income and Poverty Status in the U.S." (table 2). Department of Commerce.

Clark, Kenneth B. 1965. *Dark Ghetto: Dilemmas of Social Power.* Harper and Row.

Coulton, Claudia J., Julian Chow, and Shanta Pandey. 1990. *An Analysis of Poverty and Related Conditions in Cleveland Area Neighborhoods.* Cleveland: Center for Urban Poverty and Social Change, Case Western Reserve University.

Ellwood, David T. 1986. "The Spatial Mismatch Hypothesis: Are There Teenage

Jobs Missing in the Ghetto?" In *The Black Youth Employment Crisis,* edited by Richard B. Freeman and Harry J. Holzer. University of Chicago Press.

Engbersen, Godfried. 1990. "Modern Poverty in the Netherlands." Paper presented at the Leiden Workshop on Modern Poverty, Unemployment, and the Emergence of a Dutch Underclass, University of Leiden, Netherlands (August).

Engbersen, Godfried, Kees Schuyt, and Jaap Timmer. 1990. "Cultures of Unemployment: Long-Term Unemployment in Dutch Inner Cities." Working paper 4, Vakgroep Sociologie Rijksuniversiteit, Leiden, Netherlands.

Frey, William. 1985. "Mover Destination Selectivity and the Changing Suburbanization of Whites and Blacks." *Demography* 22 (May), pp. 223–43.

Gans, Herbert J. 1990. "Deconstructing the Underclass: The Term's Danger as a Planning Concept." *Journal of the American Planning Association* 56 (Summer), pp. 271–349.

Grier, Eunice S., and George Grier. 1988. "Minorities in Suburbia: A Mid-1980s Update." *Report prepared for the Urban Institute Symposium on Residential Mobility and Minority Incomes* (April).

Hamil, Pete. 1988. "Breaking the Silence." *Esquire,* March, pp. 91–113.

Hannerz, Ulf. 1969. *Soulside: Inquiries into Ghetto Culture and Community.* Columbia University Press.

Henderson, Vivian. 1975. "Race, Economics, and Public Policy," *Crisis* 82 (Fall), pp. 50–55.

Hochschild, Jennifer. 1990. "The Politics of the Estranged Poor." Princeton University (February).

Holzer, Harry J. 1990. "The Spatial Mismatch Hypothesis: What Has the Evidence Shown?" Paper presented at a conference on *The Truly Disadvantaged,* Northwestern University (October).

Jencks, Christopher, and Kathryn Edin. 1990. "The Real Welfare Problem." *American Prospect* (Spring), pp. 31–50.

Jencks, Christopher, and Susan E. Mayer. 1989a. "The Social Consequences of Growing Up in a Poor Neighborhood: A Review." Center for Urban Affairs and Policy Research working paper, Northwestern University.

———. 1989b. "Residential Segregation, Job Proximity, and Black Job Opportunities: The Empirical Status of the Spatial Mismatch Hypothesis." Center for Urban Affairs and Policy Research working paper, Northwestern University.

Kasarda, John D. 1989. "Urban Industrial Transition and the Underclass." *Annals of the American Academy of Political and Social Science* 501 (January), pp. 26–47.

———. 1990a. "Structural Factors Affecting the Location and Timing of Urban Underclass Growth." *Urban Geography* 11 (May–June), pp. 234–64.

———. 1990b. "City Jobs and Residents on a Collision Course: The Urban Underclass Dilemma." *Economic Development Quarterly* 4 (November).

Kloosterman, Robert C. 1990. "The Making of the Dutch Underclass? A Labour Market View." Paper presented at Workshop on Social Policy and the Underclass, University of Amsterdam, the Netherlands (August).

Levy, Frank. 1987. *Dollars and Dreams: The Changing American Income Distribution.* New York: Russell Sage Foundation.

Lewis, Oscar. 1959. *Five Families: Mexican Case Studies in the Culture of Poverty*. Basic Books.

———. 1961. *The Children of Sanchez: Autobiography of a Mexican Family*. Random House.

———. 1966. *La Vida: A Puerto Rican Family in the Culture of Poverty—San Juan and New York*. Random House.

———. 1968. "The Culture of Poverty." In *On Understanding Poverty: Perspectives from the Social Sciences*, edited by Daniel Patrick Moynihan. Basic Books.

Magnet, Myron. 1987. "America's Underclass: What to Do?" *Fortune*, May 11, pp. 130–34.

Massey, Douglas S., and Mitchell L. Eggers. 1990. "The Ecology of Inequality: Minorities and the Concentration of Poverty, 1970–1980." *American Journal of Sociology* 95 (March), pp. 1153–88.

McLanahan, Sara, and Irwin Garfinkel. 1989. "Single Mothers, The Underclass, and Social Policy." *Annals of the American Academy of Political and Social Science* 501 (January), pp. 92–104.

Moynihan, Daniel Patrick. 1965. *The Negro Family: The Case for National Action*. Department of Labor.

Murray, Charles. 1990. "Here's the Bad News on the Underclass." *Wall Street Journal*, March 8, p. A14.

Neckerman, Kathryn M., and Joleen Kirschenman. 1990. "Statistical Discrimination and Inner-City Workers: An Investigation of Employers' Hiring Decisions." Paper presented at the annual meeting of the American Sociological Association.

Osterman, Paul. 1990. "Welfare Participation in a Full Employment Economy: The Impact of Family Structure and Neighborhood." Massachusetts Institute of Technology.

Rainwater, Lee. 1966. "Crucible of Identity: The Negro Lower-Class Family." *Daedalus* 95 (Winter), pp. 176–216.

———. 1967. *Behind Ghetto Walls: Black Families in a Federal Slum*. Chicago: Aldine Press.

Rainwater, Lee, and William L. Yancey. 1967. *The Moynihan Report and the Politics of Controversy*. MIT Press.

Ricketts, Erol, and Ronald Mincy. 1986. *Growth of the Underclass 1970–1980*. Washington: Urban Institute.

Ricketts, Erol, and Isabel V. Sawhill. 1986. *Defining and Measuring the Underclass*. Washington: Urban Institute.

Ruggles, Patricia. 1990. "The Poverty Line—Too Low for the 1990s." *New York Times*, April 26, p. A31.

Schuyt, Kees. 1990. "The New Emerging Underclass in Europe: The Experience of Long-Term Unemployment in Dutch Inner Cities." Paper presented at the Leiden Workshop on Modern Poverty, Unemployment, and the Emergence of a Dutch Underclass, University of Leiden, Netherlands (August).

Testa, Mark. 1990. "Joblessness and Absent Fatherhood in the Inner City." Paper presented at the annual meeting of the American Sociological Association.

Testa, Mark, and Marilyn Krogh. 1989. "The Effect of Employment on Marriage among Black Males in Inner-City Chicago." University of Chicago.

Tienda, Marta. 1989. "Poor People and Poor Places: Deciphering Neighborhood Effects on Poverty Outcomes." Paper presented at the annual meeting of the American Sociological Association.

Van Haitsma, Martha. 1989. "A Contextual Definition of the Underclass." *Focus* 12 (Spring-Summer), pp. 27–31.

Wacquant, Loïc J. D., and William Julius Wilson. 1989. "Poverty, Joblessness and the Social Transformation of the Inner City." In *Welfare Policy for the 1990s,* edited by Phoebe H. Cottingham and David T. Ellwood. Harvard University Press.

Wilson, William Julius. 1987. *The Truly Disadvantaged: The Inner City, The Underclass, and Public Policy.* University of Chicago Press.

———. 1988. "The American Underclass: Inner-City Ghettos and the Norms of Citizenship." Godkin lecture, John F. Kennedy School of Government, Harvard University.

———. 1990. "Social Theory and Public-Agenda Research: The Challenge of Studying Inner-City Social Dislocations." Presidential address, annual meeting of the American Sociological Association.

Wilson, William Julius, Robert Aponte, Joleen Kirschenman, and Loïc J. D. Wacquant. 1988. "The Ghetto Underclass and the Changing Structure of American Poverty." In *Quiet Riots: Race and Poverty in the United States,* edited by Fred R. Harris and Roger W. Wilkins. Pantheon.

Zelditch, Morris, Jr. 1989. "Levels in the Logic of Macro-Historical Explanation." Paper presented at the annual meeting of the American Sociological Association.

Index